Lecture Notes in Computer Science

Vol. 142: Problems and Methodologies in Mathematical Software Production. Proceedings, 1980. Edited by P.C. Messina and A. Murli. VII, 271 pages. 1982.

Vol. 143: Operating Systems Engineering. Proceedings, 1980. Edited by M. Maekawa and L.A. Belady. VII, 465 pages. 1982.

Vol. 144: Computer Algebra. Proceedings, 1982. Edited by J. Calmet. XIV, 301 pages. 1982.

Vol. 145: Theoretical Computer Science. Proceedings, 1983. Edited by A.B. Cremers and H.P. Kriegel. X, 367 pages. 1982.

Vol. 146: Research and Development in Information Retrieval. Proceedings, 1982. Edited by G. Salton and H.-J. Schneider. IX, 311 pages. 1983.

Vol. 147: RIMS Symposia on Software Science and Engineering. Proceedings, 1982. Edited by E. Goto, I. Nakata, K. Furukawa, R. Nakajima, and A. Yonezawa. V. 232 pages. 1983.

Vol. 148: Logics of Programs and Their Applications. Proceedings, 1980. Edited by A. Salwicki. VI, 324 pages. 1983.

Vol. 149: Cryptography. Proceedings, 1982. Edited by T. Beth. VIII, 402 pages. 1983.

Vol. 150: Enduser Systems and Their Human Factors. Proceedings, 1983. Edited by A. Blaser and M. Zoeppritz. III, 138 pages. 1983.

Vol. 151: R. Piloty, M. Barbacci, D. Borrione, D. Dietmeyer, F. Hill, and P. Skelly, CONLAN Report. XII, 174 pages. 1983.

Vol. 152: Specification and Design of Software Systems. Proceedings, 1982. Edited by E. Knuth and E. J. Neuhold. V, 152 pages. 1983.

Vol. 153: Graph-Grammars and Their Application to Computer Science. Proceedings, 1982. Edited by H. Ehrig, M. Nagl, and G. Rozenberg. VII, 452 pages. 1983.

Vol. 154: Automata, Languages and Programming. Proceedings, 1983. Edited by J. Díaz. VIII, 734 pages. 1983.

Vol. 155: The Programming Language Ada. Reference Manual. Approved 17 February 1983. American National Standards Institute, Inc. ANSI/MIL-STD-1815A-1983. IX, 331 pages. 1983.

Vol. 156: M.H. Overmars, The Design of Dynamic Data Structures. VII, 181 pages. 1983.

Vol. 157: O. Østerby, Z. Zlatev, Direct Methods for Sparse Matrices. VIII, 127 pages. 1983.

Vol. 158: Foundations of Computation Theory. Proceedings, 1983. Edited by M. Karpinski, XI, 517 pages. 1983.

Vol. 159: CAAP'83. Proceedings, 1983. Edited by G. Ausiello and M. Protasi. VI, 416 pages. 1983.

Vol. 160: The IOTA Programming System. Edited by R. Nakajima and T. Yuasa. VII, 217 pages. 1983.

Vol. 161: DIANA, An Intermediate Language for Ada. Edited by G. Goos, W.A. Wulf, A. Evans, Jr. and K.J. Butler. VII, 201 pages. 1983.

Vol. 162: Computer Algebra. Proceedings, 1983. Edited by J.A. van Hulzen. XIII, 305 pages. 1983.

Vol. 163: VLSI Engineering. Proceedings. Edited by T.L. Kunii. VIII, 308 pages. 1984.

Vol. 164: Logics of Programs. Proceedings, 1983. Edited by E. Clarke and D. Kozen. VI, 528 pages. 1984.

Vol. 165: T.F. Coleman, Large Sparse Numerical Optimization. V, 105 pages. 1984.

Vol. 166: STACS 84. Symposium of Theoretical Aspects of Computer Science. Proceedings, 1984. Edited by M. Fontet and K. Mehlhorn. VI, 338 pages. 1984.

Vol. 167: International Symposium on Programming. Proceedings, 1984. Edited by C. Girault and M. Paul. VI, 262 pages. 1984.

Vol. 168: Methods and Tools for Computer Integrated Manufacturing. Edited by R. Dillmann and U. Rembold. XVI, 528 pages. 1984.

Vol. 169: Ch. Ronse, Feedback Shift Registers. II, 1-2, 145 pages. 1984.

Vol. 170: Seventh International Conference on Automated Deduction. Edited by R.E. Shostak. IV, 508 pages. 1984.

Vol. 171: Logic and Machines: Decision Problems and Complexity. Proceedings, 1983. Edited by E. Börger, G. Hasenjaeger and D. Rödding. VI, 456 pages. 1984.

Vol. 172: Automata, Languages and Programming. Proceedings, 1984. Edited by J. Paredaens. VIII, 527 pages. 1984.

Vol. 173: Semantics of Data Types. Proceedings, 1984. Edited by G. Kahn, D.B. MacQueen and G. Plotkin. VI, 391 pages. 1984.

Vol. 174: EUROSAM 84. Proceedings, 1984. Edited by J. Fitch. XI, 396 pages. 1984.

Vol. 175: A. Thayse, P-Functions and Boolean Matrix Factorization, VII, 248 pages. 1984.

Vol. 176: Mathematical Foundations of Computer Science 1984. Proceedings, 1984. Edited by M.P. Chytil and V. Koubek. XI, 581 pages. 1984.

Vol. 177: Programming Languages and Their Definition. Edited by C.B. Jones. XXXII, 254 pages. 1984.

Vol. 178: Readings on Cognitive Ergonomics – Mind and Computers. Proceedings, 1984. Edited by G.C. van der Veer, M.J. Tauber, T.R.G. Green and P. Gorny. VI, 269 pages. 1984.

Vol. 179: V. Pan, How to Multiply Matrices Faster. XI, 212 pages. 1984.

Vol. 180: Ada Software Tools Interfaces. Proceedings, 1983. Edited by P.J.L. Wallis. III, 164 pages. 1984.

Vol. 181: Foundations of Software Technology and Theoretical Computer Science. Proceedings, 1984. Edited by M. Joseph and R. Shyamasundar. VIII, 468 pages. 1984.

Vol. 182: STACS 85. 2nd Annual Symposium on Theoretical Aspects of Computer Science. Proceedings, 1985. Edited by K. Mehlhorn. VII, 374 pages. 1985.

Vol. 183: The Munich Project CIP. Volume I: The Wide Spectrum Language CIP-L. By the CIP Language Group. XI, 275 pages. 1985.

Vol. 184: Local Area Networks: An Advanced Course. Proceedings, 1983. Edited by D. Hutchison, J. Mariani and D. Shepherd. VIII, 497 pages. 1985.

Vol. 185: Mathematical Foundations of Software Development. Proceedings, 1985. Volume 1: Colloquium on Trees in Algebra and Programming (CAAP'85). Edited by H. Ehrig, C. Floyd, M. Nivat and J. Thatcher. XIV, 418 pages. 1985.

Vol. 186: Formal Methods and Software Development. Proceedings, 1985. Volume 2: Colloquium on Software Engineering (CSE). Edited by H. Ehrig, C. Floyd, M. Nivat and J. Thatcher. XIV, 455 pages. 1985.

Vol. 187: F.S. Chaghaghi, Time Series Package (TSPACK). III, 305 pages. 1985.

Vol. 188: Advances in Petri Nets 1984. Edited by G. Rozenberg with the cooperation of H. Genrich and G. Roucairol. VII, 467 pages. 1985.

Vol. 189: M.S. Sherman, Paragon. XI, 376 pages. 1985.

Vol. 190: M.W. Alford, J.P. Ansart, G. Hommel, L. Lamport, B. Liskov, G.P. Mullery and F.B. Schneider, Distributed Systems. Edited by M. Paul and H.J. Siegert. VI, 573 pages. 1985.

Vol. 191: H. Barringer, A Survey of Verification Techniques for Parallel Programs. VI, 115 pages. 1985.

Lecture Notes in Computer Science

Edited by G. Goos and J. Hartmanis

239

Mathematical Foundations of Programming Semantics

International Conference
Manhattan, Kansas, April 11–12, 1985
Proceedings

Edited by Austin Melton

Springer-Verlag

Editor

Austin Melton
Department of Computer Science, Kansas State University
Nichols Hall, Manhattan, Kansas 66506, USA

CR Subject Classifications (1985): D.31, F.3.2

ISBN 3-540-16816-8 Springer-Verlag Berlin Heidelberg New York
ISBN 0-387-16816-8 Springer-Verlag New York Berlin Heidelberg

Library of Congress Cataloging-in-Publication Data. Mathematical foundations of programming semantics. (Lecture notes in computer science; 239) 1. Programming languages (Electronic computers)–Semantics–Congresses. 2. Electronic digital computers–Programming–Congresses. I. Melton, Austin. II. Series. QA76.7.M38 1986 005.13'1 86-22054
ISBN 0-387-16816-8 (U.S.)

Printed in Germany

Printing and binding: Druckhaus Beltz, Hemsbach/Bergstr.
2145/3140-543210

FOREWORD

The purpose of the conference on the Mathematical Foundations of Programming Semantics was to bring together computer scientists and mathematicians so that (1) the computer scientists could become more familiar with relevant mathematical research, (2) the mathematicians could get a new perspective on their work by seeing it applied, and (3) both groups could become more aware of their common areas of research. It is, therefore, appropriate that these proceedings include papers about programming semantics, papers with mathematical results which are immediately applicable to semantics research, and papers with mathematical results which are potentially useful in semantics research.

This conference was made possible by financial support from the Computer Science Departments at Iowa State University, the University of Kansas, and the University of Nebraska; from the Computer Science Department and the Mathematics and Statistics Department at Wichita State University; and from the College of Arts and Sciences, the Graduate School, and the Computer Science Department at Kansas State University.

The keynote speaker was Dana S. Scott, Carnegie-Mellon University. The other invited speakers were Stephen D. Brookes, Carnegie-Mellon University; Carl A. Gunter, Carnegie-Mellon University; Horst Herrlich, University of Bremen, West Germany; George E. Strecker, Kansas State University; and Adrian Tang, University of Kansas.

The Conference and Program Committee consisted of Richard J. Greechie, Kansas State University; David A. Gustafson, Kansas State University; Tsutomu Kamimura, University of Kansas; Roy F. Keller, University of Nebraska; Austin Melton, co-chairperson, Kansas State University; Robert W. Neufeld, Wichita State University; Diana G. P. Palenz, Wichita State University; David A. Schmidt, Iowa State University; Elizabeth A. Unger, co-chairperson, Kansas State University; and Robert C. Wherritt, Wichita State University.

Thanks are due to the following persons in the Computer Science Department, Kansas State University: Virgil E. Wallentine, Head, for his support and advice, Robin Niederee and the entire secretarial staff for all their extra time and effort, and Rhonda Terry for her typing.

Austin Melton

CONTENTS

Standard, Storeless Semantics for ALGOL-Style Block Structure and Call-by-Name

S. Kamal Abdali
Computer Research Lab
Tektronix, Inc.
Beaverton, Oregon 97077

David S. Wise *
Computer Science Department
Indiana University
Bloomington, Indiana 47405

0. ABSTRACT

This paper presents a formulation for the standard semantics of block structure and ALGOL 60 style call-by-name. The main features of this formulation are the use of continuations and streams. Continuations are used in such a way that the semantics can be defined without requiring the idea of an explicit store. Thus the concepts of address or L- and R- values are not used, and simple continuations suffice for describing assignments, iterative control statements, compounds, blocks, and functions using call by value. (Side effects are still allowed via assignments to variables global to functions.) Call-by-name is handled by introducing the idea of multiple continuations. Input-output is treated by using streams. In conjunction with continuations, these allow the formulation of program "pipes" exactly like compound functions.

---

* Research supported (in part) by the National Science Foundation under Grant Number DCR84-05241.

1. Introduction

The purpose of denotational semantics, according to Milne and Strachey [8], is to provide an accurate standard by which designers and implementors of programming languages can judge their work. That standard must not be any more specific than is necessary, lest the definition of the language enforce too strong a constraint on its implementation; with new hardware and architectures becoming available one can easily foresee that an overly specific definition will preclude growth of software onto those new machines. "One singularly elegant sort of semantics, 'standard semantics,' is of special significance," because "it reduces to a minimum the amount of substantial information" that is manipulated; "whenever possible precedence should be given to standard semantics rather than store semantics." [8, pp.11–12] The semantics of a programming language should "be specified in the first instance by using standard semantics."

Following the spirit of that dictum, we here demonstrate how to avoid the ***store*** entirely in providing semantics for the archetype of languages that seem to require it. **ALGOL 60** was designed before development of the tools now familiar to denotational semanticists, but it was designed so carefully [9] that the need for such tools became obvious. By substantially solving the problem of specifying syntax precisely, its designers hastened the development of formal semantics [7].

It was designed, however, with the traditional store in mind. Thus, we believe, much of the early formal semantics also presumed the necessity of that structure. Here we show again [1], but more clearly, how the store might be avoided entirely without changing the (understood) meaning of **ALGOL**.

We are not the only ones doing this; Brookes attacks the same problem elsewhere in this volume [2]. His approach is beautiful, though abstract; ours is effective. To the extent that the lambda calculus is operational, one might say that ours is closer to an implementation; his is clean and elegant. We feel, however, that a simple implementation in the lambda calculus (and, except for the strange machinations of call-by-name, this is simple!) will be sufficiently abstract to generalize to almost any machine [5]. Indeed, we also believe that our semantics is 'fully abstract.'

Previous efforts to define most of the programming features in languages like **ALGOL 60** [e.g., 5, 8] pivot on store semantics, with the store as one domain that maps the so-called L-values (locations) to R-values (contents). This domain has been deemed necessary because even such fundamental features as program variables and assignments seemingly require the concept of an explicit memory. More complex features such as block storage, parameter passing mechanisms, sharing or aliasing of variables introduced by a same variable occurring in different actual parameter positions, etc., seem even more difficult to handle without introducing the store.

Abstractly, the trouble with a store is that the management of the L-values seems to preclude the semantics from being fully abstract in that it may not render the same meanings for the same expressions in different interpretation contexts. Intuitively, it raises problems with storage management: if memory overflow occurs, are we certain that memory was used densely at the penultimate instant? If the storage manager is not to be explicitly provided in the semantics, how are the designers and implementors of a language to understand its properties?

Such questions may be miscast. Like others, we feel that *failures* like these—due to resource exhaustion of time, heap, or stack—are different from *error* signals that might be necessary in the semantics of a programming language. The former restrictions, imposed by the operating system, may well vary from site to site, or with the hourly loading on a shared machine; their cure is as likely to be rescheduling as it is program termination. The latter, however, likely require uniform handling across all implementations and are, therefore, properly included in a formal semantics.

This paper presents an approach to standard, storeless semantics of **ALGOL 60** [9], the key ideas of which are a continuation-based scheme, already used for translating nearly all of **ALGOL 60** to the pure lambda calculus [1], and a clean treatment of input-output using streams [4]. These ideas are, respectively, ten and twenty years old; although he used them differently, streams were invented by Landin [7] to grapple with this very problem! But these ideas were previously used informally and with only intuitive justification. Both of these are newly cast into the rigorous domain theory necessary for denotational semantics. Instead of using a "store", *statically* accessible parameters are explicitly passed (as if a unit) around the system, to the (images of) statements and expressions.

This paper describes three semantic formulations. Section 2, following, introduces the domain equations and describes some salient features of this presentation. The first formulation, introduced in Section 3, covers assignments, blocks, control statements and I/O. The second formulation, in Section 4, provides for procedures with called-by-value parameters. Finally, in Section 5 the third formulation describes the manner in which multiple continuations are used to implement call-by-name. The resulting semantics is a toy language [5] with all the difficult facilities for ALGOL 60 call-by-name. Section 6 presents an example and conclusions.

2. Salient Features

We make heavy use of the concept of 'continuation' in order to implement the sequential nature of ALGOL implicitly through composition of functions. (There is no other way of enforcing a sequential order in an abstract language, like the lambda calculus, that admits alternative orders of evaluation.) Since continuations are likely to be alien to the reader, we have taken pains to force all to be essentially of two kinds: called either "continuation" or "program".

Figure 1 presents all the domains needed here, although not all are used immediately. Most important are **X**, which is the codomain of the significant semantic functions, and **K**, the domain of continuations that effect the sequentiality necessary in ALGOL.

The domain of continuations, **K**, is a bunch of functions, each of which maps a pending result (conceptually, the accumulator), environment (current bindings), and input file (its yet unread suffix) into the (yet ungenerated) suffix of the output file. Each may as well be perceived as a function that maps pending result and environment into a function from input files to output files. That last image is the familiar picture of a program, mapping input to output, so we may say that a continuation is merely a running program with the accumulator and current bindings abstracted away.

We do not distinguish between expressions and commands with regard to the nature of their semantics. Both commands and statements are mapped alike into functions, $\xi \in \mathbf{X}$, which at first thought seemed to map only from continuations to continuations. While one might easily overlook the importance of lexical level, one must notice that every phrase in the language resides at a lexical level which becomes essential information at the instant that the binding of a variable must be altered. Therefore, functions in **X** necessarily map from lexical levels, in **N**, as well, carrying the size of a suitable environment.

Any environment represents ***only*** those bindings that are accessible in the 'current' scope of the program. ALGOL, of course, is lexically scoped, so the number of bindings accessible at any point in the execution of a program is proportional to the lexical nesting level at that point in the program; it is independent of how much work 'has already been done' and of the number of pending (unfinished) function invocations. Unlike the number of L-values, therefore, this census of accessible bindings is fixed for any program, and it is likely to be relatively small (because programmers seem to write code structures wider than they are deep.)

The domain of environments, **R**, is structured here as a linear list; each environment is a pair composed of a reference to the first item on the list and a reference to the remainder of the list. The domain equation is isomorphic to that for linear lists. The linear structure is chosen because it is easy to extend (on block entry) and to attenuate on block exit. Indeed, many machines with hardware stacks have been built for ALGOLesque languages whose nested structure suggests this arrangement.

Each value to which an identifier might be bound is in **D**, the domain of denoted values. Denoted values are of three varieties, two of which involve functions and arguments. Since this presentation postpones the treatment of functions and procedures until later, for the moment we may perceive these $\delta \in \mathbf{D}$ as simple ground values. Then an environment is a list of such values read left-to-right as bound in the deepest-to-shallowest block.

The domain of streams, **S**, is defined similarly to that of environments, **R**. Streams are also linear lists of ground values. By structuring them as nested pairs, however, we achieve two conveniences for Input/Output semantics [4]. First, the head item on a file is readily accessible from a probe of the stream's left field. Second, the conventional behavior of advancing to the suffix of the file (obtained by removing that head character), is effected by passing its suffix, available from the right field, to a sequent function invocation. This behavior shows up in this semantics only at the interpretation of the expression **read**.

Similarly, 'output' can be effected by returning a pair as a result, whose left element is the ground value put out, and whose right element is a function invocation that is the 'remainder of the program-run,' which likely yields further output pairs. This shows up here only in the semantics for the command **output**.

Input/Output, then, is built on a model of a single input-stream and a single output-stream. Continuations and streams work together to provide a transparent, UNIX^{TM}-like piping of program composition along a single stream [10]. It is straightforward to extend the model to handle multiple I/O streams using functional combination [4], but not enough would be learned to justify the additional functionals necessary.

3. Semantics for a functionless language

Three features are to be observed in the semantic clauses of Figure 2. First is the use of streams, as discussed above for I/O. Second is the unique uniting of allocation and deallocation in the same clause for **begin-end** blocks. Last is the use of the object $\mathcal{A}m$ to effect assignment to the variable $\mathbf{I}_m$, whose binding appears m positions from the right (nested at Position $\nu - m$ in ρ of size ν).

The function that is the image of a program under this semantics deals only with the static environment (lexical scoping) of a program. This is much less confining than what results from premature concern with storage-allocation. A **begin-end** block is mapped as a unit onto a composition of entry, body, and exit functions, the first and the last being interdependent. Upon block entry the environment, ρ, is extended; upon block exit the additional binding is dropped. Thus, the allocation of a local variable is not allowed to become a problem independent of its deallocation [6]. The depth of the program tree, which is the maximum length of that (flattened) environment sequence, ρ, therefore, bounds the accessible storage needed to run the program.

Continuations are used to carry out the evaluation of an expression from the values of its constituents, as well as for propagating the effects of computation from statement to statement. Consequently there is no need for the usual (address-oriented) fetch and store functions. Fetch is provided in the portion of $\mathcal{E}$ dealing with I_m; from lexical level ν it finds position $\nu - m$ in ρ. Store into that same location is provided by $\xi = \mathcal{A}_m$, which reads similarly, but is written separately for reference below.

4. Introducing functions called-by-value

Now we introduce part of the domain of functions, **F**, the second component in **D**. Functions will initially be bound in declarations at block entry, but invocations occur both in ***application*** expressions and in ***call*** commands. Moreover, we also provide a ***result*** command to allow a block (function body) to render a value (for its invocations.) Each $\phi \in \mathbf{F}$ is a triple whose first component is boolean, and will be used (later) to distinguish functions with parameters called-by-name from those with a call-by-value protocol. For now all functions will have single parameters called-by-value, and so this flag will necessarily be **true**. Likewise, the third component of that triple will not be used yet.

Rather than repeating the entire semantics, we show in Figure 3 only the additions necessary to the semantics of the functionless case discussed just above. Introduction of functions and procedures with single arguments called-by-value affects most of the existing semantic clauses. Most importantly, $\mathcal{V}$ now has a non-trivial declaration.

Procedures with parameters called exclusively by value, with recursion, and/or with side-effects via assignments to non-locals do not introduce complexity beyond the domain equations. The images of user-defined functions are allowed as denoted values within the "block" that define them,, but the values on the stack now contain elements from **X**. Their manipulation of the stack, however, is exactly that of **E** or **D**, as already used in Section 3. They look up and store to explicit positions in the environment.

5. Call-by-name Arguments

We now discuss the semantics of call by name in the sense of ALGOL 60. We give the semantic equations in Figure 4, restricting, for simplicity, to procedures with a single argument. Although the semantics presented here provides only one argument called-by-name, we can provide several. Where we discuss a single binding below, however, all of the several simultaneously bound values must be treated. After describing the single argument case in detail, we shall complete the description of that treatment.

The idea for call-by-name semantics is that three continuations (thunks) are passed for each parameter called-by-name. The first, the "assignment program", is only invoked from $\mathcal{C}$ on an assignment to this parameter; it installs a new value as the binding in a calling environment for an identifier called-by-name. The second, the "evaluation program", is used to retrieve/compute values in the calling environment, and is only invoked from $\mathcal{E}$ as it discharges an identifier. In both instances the program provides for reconstruction of the (modified) called environment. The third restores the calling context upon final exit from the invocation, permanently abandoning the called environment; it is used in forming the exit continuation as a call-by-name function is invoked.

Now one can better understand the structure of the domain of functions, **F**. The boolean tags the parameter passing mechanism for the single argument; in the case of alternative argument structures, a domain of signatures for the alternatives would replace it. The program, ξ, is to be used later to restore the environment in which the function was defined (closed) before invoking its body. The continuation, κ, is defined according to the meaning ofthe function body, itself. The separation of ξ from κ is useful because ξ may need to be performed repeatedly—after every use of the argument called-by-name—but the body will only be invoked once for each invocation.

The argument, α is passed into the function as part of the "accumulator," in **E**. This convention allows us later to return a value (resulting from use of the "evaluation program") ***and*** a new α simultaneously. (When multiple arguments are called-by-name, the bindings of all in **A**must be so replaced when any one is used.)

From the preceding description one can anticipate the complications introduced by Call-by-Name: Invocation of such a function in $\mathcal{E}$ is complicated by the need to compute three continuations, and by redirecting the exit continuation through the third. The difference between the lexical level at which the function was declared (closed) and the lexical level at which the invocation takes place determines the amount of environment saving and restoration that must occur upon function entry/exit and upon each reference to its parameter. Closing such a function at its declaration in $\mathcal{V}$, therefore, includes the rudimentary structure of the argument triple based on the lexical level.

While the points on function closure and application are complicated, the semantics for interpreting a call-by-name parameter end up being quite direct. $\mathcal{C}$ or $\mathcal{E}$ need only invoke the appropriate piece of the bound triple. Thus, the complicated situation where one identifier called-by-need is bound to another sorts itself out quite nicely.

Upon a context switch for call-by-name, the variable sequence (stack) shrinks and then re-expands according to the declarations within the intervening blocks jumped by the closing of the function. This restoration is necessary to provide for side-effects to a non-local environment, particularly in the case where call-by-name identifiers are cascaded: bound to-one another in an arrangement wherein the use of one paramenter (called-by-name) causes multiple side effects in several others at different lexical levels.

It is really remarkable how much formalism is necessary to provide for this one "intuitive feature." As we set aside L-values, the introduction of call-by-name increases the bulk of semantic equations by 50% , approximating the burden it causes the implementor!

ALGOL 60's call-by-name is a particularly complex programming feature and was abandoned in its descendents. It is interesting to note, however, that the concept of closure in Scheme [11] and the newer Lisps resembles classic call-by-name. Moreover, the style of using continuations there resembles the method used in this paper to implement "store". But these vistiges do not include the difficulties of assignement to an identifier passed-by-name.

What about space limitations when arguments are called-by-name? The size of the lexical environment may always be bounded ***a priori*** according to the syntactic depth of the program. In the absence of call-by-name, we note that environments grow and shrink predictably according to static scoping rules. Call-by-value parameters require some environment saving and restoration via exit continuations, but only for simple bindings and only for the full duration of a function invocation. Thus, even storage within continuations can be anticipated before run-time, except for the effects of recursion.

The picture turns out little different for call-by-name (as long as upward functions are prohibited.) However, continuations and the storage necessary for state associated with them may be more expensive. A single argument called-by-name requires the meaning of our triple of continuations, but the three likely share the state information for restoring the calling environment. The allowed context switches may occur repeatedly, but only one context (at a time) need be remembered. In fact, though structured differently, the restoration information is exactly that kept for the exit continuation for call-by-name, though it is held in a manner to be used in any of the three ways. As before, recursion muddies the picture, but static binding still is a very good first bound on the space require for stacks and continuations.

This situation should be constrasted with that for a store, with L-values. There is no treatment here for bindings not either in the lexical environment or (implicitly) in a continuation. While this is a weaker space measure when recursive functions are considered, it is far simpler than those requiring explicit space release upon block exit and concerns about garbage collection and exhaustion of space [6]. While we do not give explicit semantics for space exhaustion, neither do standard machine-independent languages.

Finally, let us reconsider the effect of multiple arguments called-by-name. We have modified this semantics to run examples with n such arguments. All that is necessary is to augment each continuation in the triple to purge and later to restore all n bindings upon the use of any one. At first this seems like a great complication, but it isn't. The only change occurs in the meaning for $\mathcal{V}$ where each triple is established, and in the function application line of $\mathcal{E}$ where initial triples are provided. In fact, the third part of each triple (as described here) need only be provided as if it were the only argument, because function exit, provided by it, is parameter-independent.

6. Examples and Conclusions

The semantics described above has been verified by translating a number of programs and evaluating their $\mathcal{P}$-meanings applied to relevant inputs. A program has been written in Scheme to actually carry out this process automatically. Two sample programs used in the test are shown in Figure 5. Program P_1 illustrates both call by value and call by name used in one-argument procedures. The call by name part, though simple, involves the nontrivial operations of evaluating and altering the argument ***in the environment of the procedure call.*** This program consumes a single item from its input stream, and appends three items to its output stream. Thus, as a particular execution of this program, if $\mathcal{P}[\![P_1]\!]$is applied to the input stream represented by the tuple $\langle 3,1,4,1,5\rangle$, the result is the tuple $\langle 3,6,7,eof,\langle 1,4,1,5\rangle\rangle$.

Program P_2 provides a more interesting illustration of call by name. It highlights the use of global variables as called by name arguments whose evaluation and alteration requires crossing several block levels. It also shows nested procedure calls and rather complex side-effecting. We have used an straightforward syntactic convention for multi-argument procedures and functions in which ***all*** arguments are called alike, either by value or by name. The semantic equations for obtaining the $\mathcal{P}$-meaning of such programs are not given in Figure 4, but we have outlined the method of their translation in the previous section. This program does not read anything from its input, but writes two items on its output. As a particular execution of this program, if the expression $(\mathcal{P}[\![P_1]\!]\langle 3,1,4\rangle)$ representing the execution of the program with inputs cosisiting of 3, 1, and 4 is evaluated, the result is found to be the tuple $\langle 24,18,eof,\langle 3,1,4\rangle\rangle$.

We have not provided for recursive definitions here. While we know different ways to include it, none offer domain equations quite as elegant as appear here. The most tractable solution is to redefine the codomain of $\mathcal{V}$ to be reflexive—something other than **X**. That would suffice for recursive function definitions, but it would, for example, preclude initializing variables from input (using **read**). A complete solution confounds the domain definitions and, we feel, would detract from the Call-by-Name semantics which we want to highlight.

If an implementor would like to perceive a ***stack*** or ***display*** in this behavior, then she is likely to invent an efficient-on-current-hardware implementation of **ALGOL 60**, as correct as her extension of this semantics. But if she sees some other, efficient-on-future-hardware structure and faithfully uses it to extend this semantics, , then she will effect an implementation that is both correct and efficient on hardware yet unknown.

This last point is very important, because one of the virtues of formally describing languages like **ALGOL 60** is the ability to express meaning of existing programs on architectures unforeseen by the language designers. If one wanted to implement, say, **ALGOL 60** on a machine that had no easy way of providing L-values, would it be necessary to provide them? We have clearly answered that question in the negative, showing how an iterative, lexically scoped, but richly side-effecting language might be implemented on some pure Lambda-calculus machine. The implication is that applicative architectures will be able to run **ALGOL 60** programs, perhaps with little loss of efficiency (because they will only run into complicated code for the lesser-used pathologies of call-by-name.)

ALGOL 60 was not designed with the semantic rigor established by Denotational Semantics, but its definition set a very high standard in its day. Indeed, one can argue that the difficulties that arose in defining **ALGOL 60** led directly to the development of the denotational approach. That input/output and call-by-value is expressed so cleanly here is a testament to the relative simplicity of these features. That call-by-name (in the context of side effects) is so burdensome should not be surprising—its implications were not all that well understood even to the **ALGOL 60** committee.

REFERENCES

[1] S.K. Abdali, A lambda-calculus model of programming languages. ***J. Computer Languages*** **1** (1976), 287-301 + 303-320.

[2] S.D. Brookes. A fully abstract semantics and a proof system for an ALGOL-like language with sharing. (Included in this volume.)

[3] W.D. Clinger. ***Foundations of Actor Semantics***, Ph.D. dissertation, Artificial Intelligence Technical Report 633, Massachusetts Institute of Technology (1981), 86.

[4] D.P. Friedman and D.S. Wise. Applicative Programming for file systems. ***Proc. ACM Conf. on Language Design for Reliable Software, ACM SIGPLAN Notices*** **12**, 3 (March 1977), 41-55.

[5] M.J. Gordon. ***The Denotational Description of Programming Languages, An Introduction***, Springer, New York (1979).

[6] J.V. Halpern, A.R. Meyer, and B.A. Trakhtenbrot. The semantics of local storage, or what makes the free-list free. ***Conf. Rec. 11th ACM Symp. on Principles of Programming Languages***, ISBN 0-89791-125-3 (1983), 245-257.

[7] P.J. Landin. A correspondence between ALGOL 60 and Church's lambda notation, Part I. ***Comm. ACM*** **8**, 2 (February 1965), 89-101.

[8] R. Milne and C. Strachey. ***A theory of programming language semantics***, London, Chapman and Hall (1976).

[9] P. Naur (ed.) et al. Revised report on the algorithmic language ALGOL 60. ***Comm. ACM*** **6**, 1 (January 1963), 1-17.

[10] J.-C. Raoult and R. Sethi. Properties of a notation for combining functions. ***J. ACM*** **30**, 3 (July 1983), 595-611.

[11] G.L. Steele and G.J. Sussman. Scheme: an interpreter for extended lambda-calculus. Artificial Intelligence Lab Memo 349, Massachusetts Institute of Technology (December 1975).

Figure 1. Domain specifications

Syntactic Domains

I ∈ Ide	Identifiers
B ∈ Bas	Basic constants
O ∈ Opr	Operators
P ∈ Pro	Programs
E ∈ Exp	Expressions
C ∈ Com	Commands
V ∈ Val	Values declarable

Syntactic Clauses

I : Ide	::=	{ identifiers}	Identifiers
B : Bas	::=	**true** | **false** | 0 | 1 | −1 | 2 | −2 | ...	Basic Constants
O : Ope	::=	+ | − | × | ÷ | < | ≤ | = | > | ≥ | ...	Operators
P : Pro	::=	**program** C	Programs
E : Exp	::=	B | **true** | **false** | **read** | I |	Expressions
		if E_0 **then** E_1 **else** E_2 | $E_1 O E_2$ | $E_0 E_1$	
V : Val	::=	E |	Values declarable
		function I **value** C | **procedure** I **value** C	
		function I **name** C | **procedure** I **name** C	
C : Com	::=	I:= E | **output** E | (C_1; C_2) |	Commands
		if E_0 **then** C_1 **else** C_2 | **while** E **do** C |	
		begin var I:= E; C **end** | **call** $E_0 E_1$ | **result** E	

Semantic Domains

$\nu \in$	**N**	=	{**0**, **1**, **2**, **3**, ...}	integers
	B	=	{*TRUE*, *FALSE*}	booleans
	G	=	**N**+ {*eof*}	ground values
$\epsilon \in$	**E**	=	(**B**+ **G**+ **F**) ×**E**	expressed values (accumulator)
	D	=	**E**+ **A**	denoted values
$\sigma \in$	**S**	=	**G**×**S**	streams
$\kappa \in$	**K**	=	**E**→**R**→**S**→**S**	continuations
$\pi \in$	**P**	=	**K**→**K** = **K**→**E**→**R**→**S**→**S**	pure code
$\xi \in$	**X**	=	**N**→**P** = **N**→**K**→**E**→**R**→**S**→**S**	code
$\rho \in$	**R**	=	**D**×**R**	environments
$\phi \in$	**F**	=	**B**×**X**×**K**	functions
$\alpha \in$	**A**	=	**P**×**P**×**K**	arguments called by name

Semantic Functions

$\mathcal{P}$: Pro→**S**→**S**	meaning of program
$\mathcal{E}$: Exp→**X**	meaning of expression
$\mathcal{C}$: Com→**X**	meaning of command
$\mathcal{V}$: Val→**X**	meaning of decalarable values
$\mathcal{B}$: Bas→**E**	meaning of base values
$\mathcal{O}$: **G**×**G**→**G**	meaning of arithmetic opearators
$\mathcal{A}$: **N**→**X**	alteration to lexical position ν

Figure 2. Semantics for a functionless language

Semantic Clauses

$$\mathcal{P}[\![\texttt{program}\ \ \texttt{C}]\!] = \mathcal{C}[\![\texttt{C}]\!]0\ (\lambda\epsilon\rho\sigma.\ \langle eof,\sigma\rangle)\ \bot_{\mathbf{E}}\bot_{\mathbf{R}}$$

$$\begin{aligned}
\mathcal{E}[\![\texttt{B}]\!] &= \lambda\nu\kappa\epsilon.\kappa(\mathcal{B}[\![\texttt{B}]\!])\\
\mathcal{E}[\![\texttt{true}\ ]\!] &= \lambda\nu\kappa\epsilon.\kappa(\mathit{TRUE}\ \mathbf{in}\ \ \mathbf{E})\\
\mathcal{E}[\![\texttt{false}\ ]\!] &= \lambda\nu\kappa\epsilon.\kappa(\mathit{FALSE}\ \mathbf{in}\ \ \mathbf{E})\\
\mathcal{E}[\![\texttt{read}\ ]\!] &= \lambda\nu\kappa\epsilon\rho\sigma.\ \kappa(\sigma\downarrow 1\ \ \mathbf{in}\ \ \mathbf{E})\ \rho(\sigma\downarrow 2)
\end{aligned}$$

$$\begin{aligned}
\mathcal{E}[\![\texttt{I}_m]\!] = {} & \mathbf{fix}\ \ \lambda\xi.\ (\lambda\nu\kappa\epsilon_1\rho_1.\\
& (\nu{=}m \rightarrow \kappa(\rho_1\downarrow 1 \mid \mathbf{E})\rho_1,\\
& (\nu{>}m \rightarrow \xi(\nu{-}1)\ (\lambda\epsilon_2\rho_2.\ \kappa\epsilon_2\langle\rho_1\downarrow 1,\rho_2\rangle)\epsilon_1(\rho_1\downarrow 2),\\
& \qquad \bot_{\mathbf{S}\rightarrow\mathbf{S}}\ )))
\end{aligned}$$

$$\begin{aligned}
\mathcal{E}[\![\texttt{if}\ \ \texttt{E}_0\ \texttt{then}\ \ \texttt{E}_1\ \texttt{else}\ \ \texttt{E}_2]\!] = {} & \lambda\nu\kappa.\ \mathcal{E}[\![\texttt{E}_0]\!]\nu(\lambda\epsilon.\\
& (\epsilon|\mathbf{B} = \mathit{TRUE} \rightarrow \mathcal{E}[\![\texttt{E}_1]\!],\\
& (\epsilon|\mathbf{B} = \mathit{FALSE} \rightarrow \mathcal{E}[\![\texttt{E}_2]\!],\\
& \qquad\qquad \bot_{\mathbf{X}}))\nu\kappa\epsilon)
\end{aligned}$$

$$\begin{aligned}
\mathcal{E}[\![\texttt{E}_1\texttt{O}\ \texttt{E}_2]\!] = {} & \lambda\nu\kappa.\ \mathcal{E}[\![\texttt{E}_1]\!]\nu(\lambda\epsilon_1.\\
& \mathcal{E}[\![\texttt{E}_2]\!]\nu(\lambda\epsilon_2.\ \kappa((\mathcal{O}[\![\texttt{O}]\!](\epsilon_1|\mathbf{G})\ (\epsilon_2|\mathbf{G}))\ \ \mathbf{in}\ \ \mathbf{E}))\ \epsilon_1)
\end{aligned}$$

$$\mathcal{V} = \mathcal{E}$$

$$\mathcal{C}[\![\texttt{I}_m\texttt{:=}\ \texttt{E}]\!] = \lambda\nu\kappa.\ \mathcal{E}[\![\texttt{E}]\!]\nu(\mathcal{A}m\ \nu\kappa)$$

$$\mathcal{C}[\![\texttt{output}\ \ \texttt{E}]\!] = \lambda\nu\kappa.\ \mathcal{E}[\![\texttt{E}]\!]\nu(\lambda\epsilon\rho\sigma.\ \langle\epsilon|\mathbf{G},\ \kappa\epsilon\rho\sigma\rangle)$$

$$\begin{aligned}
\mathcal{C}[\![\texttt{if}\ \ \texttt{E}_0\ \texttt{then}\ \ \texttt{C}_1\ \texttt{else}\ \ \texttt{C}_2]\!] = {} & \lambda\nu\kappa.\ \mathcal{E}[\![\texttt{E}_0]\!]\nu(\lambda\epsilon.\\
& (\epsilon|\mathbf{B}{=}\ \mathit{TRUE} \rightarrow \mathcal{C}[\![\texttt{C}_1]\!],\\
& (\epsilon|\mathbf{B}{=}\ \mathit{FALSE} \rightarrow \mathcal{C}[\![\texttt{C}_2]\!],\\
& \qquad\qquad \bot_{\mathbf{X}}))\nu\kappa\epsilon)
\end{aligned}$$

$$\begin{aligned}
\mathcal{C}[\![\texttt{while}\ \ \texttt{E}\ \texttt{do}\ \ \texttt{C}]\!] = {} & \lambda\nu.\ (\ \mathbf{fix}\ \ \lambda\pi.\ (\lambda\kappa.\ \mathcal{E}[\![\texttt{E}]\!]\nu(\lambda\epsilon.\\
& (\epsilon|\mathbf{B}{=}\ \mathit{TRUE} \rightarrow \mathcal{C}[\![\texttt{C}]\!]\nu(\pi\kappa),\\
& (\epsilon|\mathbf{B}{=}\ \mathit{FALSE} \rightarrow \kappa,\\
& \qquad\qquad \bot_{\mathbf{K}}))\ \epsilon)))
\end{aligned}$$

$$\mathcal{C}[\![(\texttt{C}_1;\ \texttt{C}_2)\ ]\!] = \lambda\nu\kappa.\ \mathcal{C}[\![\texttt{C}_1]\!]\nu(\mathcal{C}[\![\texttt{C}_2]\!]\nu\kappa)$$

$$\begin{aligned}
\mathcal{C}[\![\texttt{begin}\ \ \texttt{var}\ \ \texttt{I:=}\ \texttt{E};\ \texttt{C}\ \texttt{end}\ ]\!] = {} & \lambda\nu\kappa.\ \mathcal{V}[\![\texttt{E}]\!]\nu(\lambda\epsilon_1\rho_1.\\
& \mathcal{C}[\![\texttt{C}]\!](\nu{+}1)\ (\lambda\epsilon_2\rho_2.\kappa\epsilon_2(\rho_2\downarrow 2))\ \epsilon_1\langle\epsilon_1\ \ \mathbf{in}\ \ \mathbf{D},\rho_1\rangle)
\end{aligned}$$

$$\begin{aligned}
\mathcal{A} = {} & \lambda m\ .\ (\ \mathbf{fix}\ \ \lambda\xi.\ (\lambda\nu\kappa\epsilon_1\rho_1\ .\\
& (\nu{=}m \rightarrow \kappa\epsilon_1\langle\epsilon_1\ \mathbf{in}\ \mathbf{D},\rho_1\downarrow 2\rangle\ ,\\
& (\nu{>}m \rightarrow \xi(\nu{-}\ 1)\ (\lambda\epsilon_2\rho_2\ .\ \kappa\epsilon_2\ \langle\rho_1\downarrow 1,\rho_2\rangle)\epsilon_1\ (\rho_1\downarrow 2),\\
& \qquad \bot_{\mathbf{S}\rightarrow\mathbf{S}}\ )))
\end{aligned}$$

Figure 3. Semantics for a language with call by value.

Syntactic Clauses.

I : Ide	::=	{ identifiers}	Identifiers
B : Bas	::=	**true** | **false** | 0 | 1 | −1 | 2 | −2 ...	Basic Constants
O : Ope	::=	+ | − | × | ÷ | < | ≤ | = | > | ≥ | ...	Operators
P : Pro	::=	**program** C	Programs
E : Exp	::=	B | **true** | **false** | **read** | I | **if** E_0 **then** E_1 **else** E_2 | E_1 O E_2 | E_0E_1	Expressions
V : Val	::=	E | **function** I **value** C | **procedure** I **value** C	Values declarable
C : Com	::=	I:= E | **output** E | **if** E_0 **then** C_1 **else** C_2 | **while** E **do** C | C_1; C_2 | **begin** **var** I:= E; C **end** | **call** E_0E_1 | **result** E	Commands

Semantic Clauses. (Additions to Fig. 2)

$$\mathcal{E}[\![E_0E_1]\!] = \lambda\nu_1\kappa_1.\ \mathcal{E}[\![E_0]\!]\nu_1(\lambda\epsilon_0.\ (\phi\downarrow 1 = TRUE \rightarrow \mathcal{E}[\![E_1]\!]\nu_1((\phi\downarrow 2)\ \nu_1\kappa_1)\epsilon_0,\ \bot_{S\rightarrow S}))$$

$$\mathcal{V}[\![\texttt{function}\ I\ \texttt{value}\ C]\!] = \lambda\nu_1\kappa_1\epsilon_1.\ \kappa_1\langle\ TRUE,\ \xi,\ \bot_{K}\rangle$$

where

$$\xi = \textbf{fix}\ \ \lambda\xi.\ (\lambda\nu_2\kappa_2\epsilon_2\rho_2.\ (\nu_2{=}\nu_1 \rightarrow \mathcal{C}[\![C]\!](\nu_1{+}1)(\lambda\epsilon_3\rho_3\ .\ \kappa_2\epsilon_3(\rho_3\downarrow 2)\epsilon_2\langle\epsilon_2,\rho_2\rangle),\ (\nu_2{>}\ \nu_1 \rightarrow \xi(\nu_2{-}1)\ (\lambda\epsilon_3\rho_3\ .\ \kappa_2\epsilon_3\langle\rho_2\downarrow 1,\rho_3\rangle)\epsilon_2(\rho_2\downarrow 2\ ),\ \bot_{S\rightarrow S})))$$

$$\mathcal{V}[\![\texttt{procedure}\ I\ \texttt{value}\ C]\!] = \mathcal{V}[\![\texttt{function}\ I\ \texttt{value}\ C]\!]$$

$$\mathcal{V}[\![E]\!] = \mathcal{E}[\![E]\!]$$

$$\mathcal{C}[\![\texttt{call}\ E_0E_1]\!] = \mathcal{E}[\![E_0E_1]\!]$$

$$\mathcal{C}[\![\texttt{result}\ E]\!] = \mathcal{E}[\![E]\!]$$

$$\mathcal{A} = \lambda m.\ (\ \textbf{fix}\ \ \lambda\xi.\ (\lambda\nu\kappa\epsilon_1\rho_1\ .\ (\nu{=}m \rightarrow\ (\ ((\rho_1\downarrow 1)\in\mathbf{E}\rightarrow\kappa\epsilon_1\langle\epsilon_1\ \textbf{in}\ \mathbf{D},\ \rho_1\downarrow 2\rangle\ ,\ \bot_{S\rightarrow S})),\ (\nu{>}m \rightarrow\xi(\nu-1)\ (\lambda\epsilon_2\rho_2\ .\ \kappa\epsilon_2\ \langle\rho_1\downarrow 1,\rho_2\rangle)\epsilon_1\ (\rho_1\downarrow 2),\ \bot_{S\rightarrow S}\ ))$$

Figure 4. Semantics for a language with call by name

Semantic Clauses

$$
\begin{aligned}
\mathcal{P}\llbracket \mathtt{program}\ \ \mathtt{C}\rrbracket &= \mathcal{C}\llbracket \mathtt{C}\rrbracket 0\ (\lambda\epsilon\rho\sigma.\ \langle eof,\sigma\rangle)\ \bot_{\mathbf{E}}\bot_{\mathbf{R}} \\[2ex]
\mathcal{E}\llbracket \mathtt{B}\rrbracket &= \lambda\nu\kappa\epsilon.\kappa(\mathcal{B}\llbracket \mathtt{B}\rrbracket) \\
\mathcal{E}\llbracket \mathtt{true}\ \rrbracket &= \lambda\nu\kappa\epsilon.\kappa(\mathit{TRUE}\ \ \mathbf{in}\ \ \mathbf{E}) \\
\mathcal{E}\llbracket \mathtt{false}\ \rrbracket &= \lambda\nu\kappa\epsilon.\kappa(\mathit{FALSE}\ \ \mathbf{in}\ \ \mathbf{E}) \\
\mathcal{E}\llbracket \mathtt{read}\ \rrbracket &= \lambda\nu\kappa\epsilon\rho\sigma.\ \kappa(\sigma{\downarrow}1\ \ \mathbf{in}\ \ \mathbf{E})\ \rho(\sigma{\downarrow}2) \\[2ex]
\mathcal{E}\llbracket \mathtt{I}_m\rrbracket &= \ \mathbf{fix}\ \ \lambda\xi.\ \ (\lambda\nu\kappa\epsilon_1\rho_1. \\
&\quad (\nu{=}m \rightarrow\ \ ((\rho_1{\downarrow}1)\in\mathbf{A}\rightarrow(\rho_1{\downarrow}1|\mathbf{A}{\downarrow}1)\ \nu\kappa\epsilon_1(\rho_1{\downarrow}2), \\
&\qquad\qquad\qquad \kappa(\rho_1{\downarrow}1\ |\ \mathbf{E})\ \rho_1), \\
&\quad (\nu{>}m \rightarrow\xi(\nu{-}1)\ (\lambda\epsilon_2\rho_2.\ \kappa\epsilon_2\langle\rho_1{\downarrow}1,\ \rho_2\rangle)\epsilon_1(\rho_1{\downarrow}2), \\
&\qquad\qquad \bot_{\mathbf{S}\rightarrow\mathbf{S}}))) \\
\mathcal{E}\llbracket \mathtt{if}\ \ \mathtt{E}_0\ \mathtt{then}\ \ \mathtt{E}_1\ \mathtt{else}\ \ \mathtt{E}_2\rrbracket &= \lambda\nu\kappa.\ \mathcal{E}\llbracket \mathtt{E}_0\rrbracket\nu(\lambda\epsilon. \\
&\quad (\epsilon|\mathbf{B} = \mathit{TRUE}\rightarrow\mathcal{E}\llbracket \mathtt{E}_1\rrbracket, \\
&\quad (\epsilon|\mathbf{B} = \mathit{FALSE}\rightarrow\mathcal{E}\llbracket \mathtt{E}_2\rrbracket, \\
&\qquad\qquad\qquad \bot_{\mathbf{X}}))\nu\kappa\epsilon) \\
\mathcal{E}\llbracket \mathtt{E}_1\mathtt{O}\ \mathtt{E}_2\rrbracket &= \lambda\nu\kappa.\ \mathcal{E}\llbracket \mathtt{E}_1\rrbracket\nu(\lambda\epsilon_1. \\
&\quad \mathcal{E}\llbracket \mathtt{E}_2\rrbracket\nu(\lambda\epsilon_2.\ \kappa((\mathcal{O}\llbracket \mathtt{O}\rrbracket(\epsilon_1|\mathbf{G})\ (\epsilon_2|\mathbf{G}))\ \ \mathbf{in}\ \ \mathbf{E}))\ \epsilon_1) \\[2ex]
\mathcal{E}\llbracket \mathtt{E}_0\mathtt{E}_1\rrbracket &= \lambda\nu_1\kappa_1.\ \mathcal{E}\llbracket \mathtt{E}_0\rrbracket\nu_1(\lambda\epsilon_0. \\
&\quad (\phi{\downarrow}1 = \mathit{TRUE}\rightarrow\mathcal{E}\llbracket \mathtt{E}_1\rrbracket\nu_1((\phi{\downarrow}2)\ \nu_1\kappa_1)\epsilon_0, \\
&\quad (\phi{\downarrow}1 = \mathit{FALSE}\rightarrow(\phi{\downarrow}2\ )\ \nu_1(\phi{\downarrow}3)\ (\langle\ \epsilon_0\ \mathbf{in}\ \ \mathbf{D},\alpha\rangle\ \ \mathbf{in}\ \ \mathbf{E})\ , \\
&\qquad\qquad\qquad \bot_{\mathbf{S}\rightarrow\mathbf{S}}\ ))) \\
&\mathbf{where} \\
&\qquad \phi = \epsilon_0|\ \mathbf{F} \\
&\mathbf{and} \\
&\qquad \alpha\ =\ \mathbf{fix}\ \ \lambda\alpha.\ \langle\ \lambda\kappa_2.\ \mathcal{E}\llbracket \mathtt{E}_1\rrbracket\nu_1(\lambda\epsilon_2.\ (\phi{\downarrow}2)\nu_1\kappa_2.\ \langle\epsilon_2,\ \alpha\rangle\ , \\
&\qquad\qquad \lambda\kappa_2.\ (\mathtt{E}_1{=}\mathtt{I}_m\rightarrow\mathcal{A}m,\ \bot_{\mathbf{X}})\ \nu_1(\lambda\epsilon_2. \\
&\qquad\qquad ((\phi{\downarrow}2)\nu_1\kappa_2(\langle\epsilon_2,\ \alpha\rangle\ \ \mathbf{in}\ \ \mathbf{E})\ ))\ , \\
&\qquad\qquad \kappa_1\rangle \\[2ex]
\mathcal{V}\llbracket \mathtt{function}\ \ \mathtt{I}\ \mathtt{value}\ \ \mathtt{C}\ \rrbracket &= \lambda\nu_1\kappa_1\epsilon_1.\ \kappa_1\langle\ \mathit{TRUE},\ \xi,\ \bot_{\mathbf{K}}\rangle \\
&\mathbf{where} \\
&\qquad \xi\ =\ \mathbf{fix}\ \ \lambda\xi.\ (\lambda\nu_2\kappa_2\epsilon_2\rho_2. \\
&\qquad\quad (\nu_2{=}\nu_1\ \rightarrow\ \mathcal{C}\llbracket \mathtt{C}\rrbracket(\nu_1{+}1)(\lambda\epsilon_3\rho_3\ .\ \kappa_2\epsilon_3(\rho_3\ {\downarrow}\ 2)\epsilon_2\langle\epsilon_2,\rho_2\rangle, \\
&\qquad\quad (\nu_2{>}\ \nu_1\ \rightarrow\xi(\nu_2{-}1)\ (\lambda\epsilon_3\rho_3\ .\ \kappa_2\epsilon_3\langle\rho_2\ {\downarrow}\ 1,\rho_3\rangle)\epsilon_2(\rho_2{\downarrow}2\ )\ , \\
&\qquad\qquad\qquad \bot_{\mathbf{S}\rightarrow\mathbf{S}}\ ))) \\
\mathcal{V}\llbracket \mathtt{procedure}\ \ \mathtt{I}\ \mathtt{value}\ \ \mathtt{C}\ \rrbracket &= \mathcal{V}\llbracket \mathtt{function}\ \ \mathtt{I}\ \mathtt{value}\ \ \mathtt{C}\ \rrbracket
\end{aligned}
$$

$$\mathcal{V}[\![\texttt{function I name C}]\!] = \lambda\nu_0\kappa_0\epsilon_0.\ \kappa_0\langle\ FALSE,\ \xi_{\mathrm{restore}}, \kappa_{\mathrm{start}}\rangle$$

where

$$\kappa_{\mathrm{start}} = \mathcal{C}[\![\mathrm{C}]\!](\ \nu_0+1)(\lambda\epsilon_1\rho_1.\ (\rho_1{\downarrow}1|\mathbf{A}{\downarrow}3)\epsilon_1(\rho_1{\downarrow}2)\ )$$

and

$$\begin{aligned}\xi_{\mathrm{restore}} = \ &\mathbf{fix}\ \ \lambda\xi.\ (\ \lambda\nu_1\kappa_1\epsilon_1\rho_1.\\ &(\nu_1{=}\nu_0 \to \kappa_1(\epsilon_1{\downarrow}1)\ \langle\epsilon_1\downarrow 2\ \mathbf{in}\ \mathbf{D},\rho_1\rangle,\\ &(\nu_1{>}\nu_0 \to \xi(\nu_1{-}1)\kappa_1(\langle\epsilon_1\downarrow 1,\alpha\rangle\ \ \mathbf{in}\ \ \mathbf{E})\ (\rho_1{\downarrow}2)\ ,\\ &\qquad \bot_{\mathbf{S}\to\mathbf{S}}\ )))\end{aligned}$$

where in turn

$$\begin{aligned}\alpha = \langle\ &\mathbf{fix}\ \ \lambda\pi_1\ .\ (\ \lambda\kappa_2\epsilon_2\rho_2.\ (\epsilon_1{\downarrow}2\ {\downarrow}1)\kappa_2\epsilon_2\langle\rho_1{\downarrow}1\ ,\ \rho_2\rangle),\\ &\mathbf{fix}\ \ \lambda\pi_2\ .\ (\ \lambda\kappa_2\epsilon_2\rho_2.\ (\epsilon_1{\downarrow}2\ {\downarrow}2)\ \kappa_2\epsilon_2\langle\rho_1{\downarrow}1\ ,\ \rho_2\rangle),\\ &\mathbf{fix}\ \ \lambda\kappa_3\ .\ (\ \lambda\epsilon_2\rho_2.\ (\epsilon_1{\downarrow}2\ {\downarrow}3)\ \epsilon_2\langle\rho_1{\downarrow}1\ ,\ \rho_2\rangle)\ \rangle\end{aligned}$$

$$\mathcal{V}[\![\texttt{procedure I name C}]\!] = \mathcal{V}[\![\texttt{function I name C}]\!]$$

$$\mathcal{V}[\![\mathrm{E}]\!] = \mathcal{E}[\![\mathrm{E}]\!]$$

$$\mathcal{C}[\![\mathrm{I}_m := \mathrm{E}]\!] = \lambda\nu\kappa.\ \mathcal{E}[\![\mathrm{E}]\!]\nu(\mathcal{A}m\nu\kappa)$$

$$\mathcal{C}[\![\texttt{output E}]\!] = \lambda\nu\kappa.\ \mathcal{E}[\![\mathrm{E}]\!]\nu(\lambda\epsilon\rho\sigma.\ \langle\epsilon|\ \mathbf{G},\ \kappa\epsilon\rho\sigma\rangle)$$

$$\begin{aligned}\mathcal{C}[\![\texttt{if } \mathrm{E}_0 \texttt{ then } \mathrm{C}_1 \texttt{ else } \mathrm{C}_2]\!] = \lambda\nu\kappa.\ &\mathcal{E}[\![\mathrm{E}_0]\!]\nu(\lambda\epsilon.\\ &(\epsilon|\mathbf{B}{=}\ TRUE \to \mathcal{C}[\![\mathrm{C}_1]\!],\\ &(\epsilon|\mathbf{B}{=}\ FALSE \to \mathcal{C}[\![\mathrm{C}_2]\!],\\ &\qquad \bot_{\mathbf{X}}))\nu\kappa\epsilon)\end{aligned}$$

$$\begin{aligned}\mathcal{C}[\![\texttt{while E do C}]\!] = \lambda\nu.\ (\ &\mathbf{fix}\ \ \lambda\pi.\ (\lambda\kappa.\ \mathcal{E}[\![\mathrm{E}]\!]\nu(\lambda\epsilon.\\ &(\epsilon|\mathbf{B}{=}\ TRUE \to \mathcal{C}[\![\mathrm{C}]\!]\nu(\pi\kappa),\\ &(\epsilon|\mathbf{B}{=}\ FALSE \to \kappa,\\ &\qquad \bot_{\mathbf{K}}))\ \epsilon)))\end{aligned}$$

$$\mathcal{C}[\![\mathrm{C}_1;\ \mathrm{C}_2]\!] = \lambda\nu\kappa.\ \mathcal{C}[\![\mathrm{C}_1]\!]\nu(\mathcal{C}[\![\mathrm{C}_2]\!]\nu\kappa)$$

$$\begin{aligned}\mathcal{C}[\![\texttt{begin var I= E; C end}]\!] = \lambda\nu\kappa.\ &\mathcal{V}[\![\mathrm{E}]\!]\nu(\lambda\epsilon_1\rho_1.\ \mathcal{C}[\![\mathrm{C}]\!](\nu{+}1)\ (\lambda\epsilon_2\rho_2\ .\\ &\kappa\epsilon_2(\rho_2\downarrow 2))\ \epsilon_1\langle\epsilon_1\ \ \mathbf{in}\ \ \mathbf{D},\rho_1\rangle)\end{aligned}$$

$$\mathcal{C}[\![\texttt{call } \mathrm{E}_0\mathrm{E}_1]\!] = \mathcal{E}[\![\mathrm{E}_0\mathrm{E}_1]\!]$$

$$\mathcal{C}[\![\texttt{result E}]\!] = \mathcal{E}[\![\mathrm{E}]\!]$$

$$\begin{aligned}\mathcal{A} = \lambda m.\ (\ &\mathbf{fix}\ \ \lambda\xi.\ \ (\lambda\nu\kappa\epsilon_1\rho_1\ .\\ &(\nu{=}m \to\quad ((\rho_1{\downarrow}1){\in}\mathbf{A}{\to}(\rho_1{\downarrow}1|\mathbf{A}{\downarrow}2)\nu\kappa\epsilon_1(\rho_1{\downarrow}2),\\ &\qquad\qquad ((\rho_1{\downarrow}1){\in}\mathbf{E}{\to}\kappa\epsilon_1\langle\epsilon_1\ \ \mathbf{in}\ \ \mathbf{D},\ \rho_1\downarrow 2\rangle\ ,\\ &\qquad\qquad\qquad \bot_{\mathbf{S}\to\mathbf{S}}\ )),\\ &(\nu{>}m \to \xi(\nu-\ 1)\ (\lambda\epsilon_2\rho_2\ .\ \kappa\epsilon_2\ \langle\rho_1\downarrow 1,\rho_2\rangle)\epsilon_1\ (\rho_1{\downarrow}2),\\ &\qquad \bot_{\mathbf{S}\to\mathbf{S}}\ ))\end{aligned}$$

Figure 5. Examples of programs using the call by name feature

```
P₁ ≡ program
        begin var dbl := function i value i := 2 × i;
          begin var inc := procedure i name i := i + 1;
            begin var x := read;
              ((((output x;
              x := dblx); output x);
              call inc x); output x)
            end
          end
        end

P₂ ≡ program
        begin var magic := function(n, i, a, b) name4
                    (i := 0; while i < n do ((i := i + 1; a := b); result 999));
          begin var prod := function(i, j, p, q) value4 result i × j;
            begin var p := 999;
              begin var q := 999;
                begin var dummy := 999;
                  begin var a := 1;
                    (((dummy := magic(4, p, a, a × p); output a); a := 0);
                    dummy := magic(2, p, dummy,
                          magic(3, q, a, (a + prod(p, q, dummy, dummy)))));
                    output a)
                  end
                end
              end
            end
          end
        end
```

Note that the second call to *magic* is effectively equivalent to the statements:

```
(p := 0;
while p < 2 do
  ((p := p + 1; q := 0);
  while q < 3 do
    (q := q + 1; a := a + p × q)))
```

CARTESIAN CLOSED CATEGORIES, QUASITOPOI AND TOPOLOGICAL UNIVERSES

Jiří Adámek,
Technical University
Faculty of Electrical Engineering
16627 Prague
Czechoslovakia

Horst Herrlich
Universität Bremen
Fachbereich Mathematik/Informatik
2800 Bremen
Fed. Rep. Germany

Abstract

For a concrete, topological category **K** over a suitable base category, the interrelationship of the concepts in the title is investigated. **K** is cartesian closed iff regular sinks are finitely productive. **K** is a quasitopos iff regular sinks are universal. For categories over **Set** with constant maps, the latter are precisely the topological universes. These can also be described as categories of sieves for Grothendieck topologies.

Introduction

We study concrete categories **K** over an arbitrary base-category **X**; we call **K** topological if it is finally (= initially) complete and small-fibred. Many convenient properties are lifted from **X** to topological categories over **X**, e.g., completeness, cocompleteness, factorization systems, etc. Others are in general not lifted, and we investigate conditions for their lifting: cartesian closedness, universality of colimits, quasitopos structure. For cartesian closedness, the problem has two levels: (a) when is **K** cartesian closed? (b) when is **K** concretely cartesian closed, i.e., with power-objects formed on the level of **X**? For suitable base categories **X**, we give necessary and sufficient conditions for both problems:

(1) A topological category is cartesian closed iff regular sinks are finitely productive.

(2) A topological category has concrete powers iff final sinks are finitely productive.

Analogously, we characterize topological categories, which are quasitopoi:

(3) A topological category is a quasitopos iff regular sinks are universal.

(4) A topological category is a quasitopos with concrete powers iff final sinks are universal.

Categories with the latter property are called universally topological. We give a constructure description:

(5) Universally topological categories are precisely the categories of γ-closed structured sieves for Grothendieck topologies γ.

For concrete categories **K** over **Set**, we study c-categories, i.e., those in which each constant function is a morphism, and topological universes, which are c-categories with universal final epi-sinks. Every concrete category over **Set** has a c-modification, and we obtain the following characterization:

(6) Topological universes are precisely the c-modifications of universally topological categories.

Consequently, topological universes are just the categories of γ-closed structured epi-sieves for Grothendieck topologies γ.

For terminology (such as concrete category, sink, factorization system, etc.) the reader may consult [1].

I. Cartesian Closed Topological Categories

Recall that a category is said to be cartesian closed if it has finite products, and for each object A the endofunctor $A \times -$ has a right adjoint. The values of the right adjoint are called power-objects and are denoted by [A,B]; the corresponding couniversal map is called evaluation and is denoted by

$$\text{eval}: A \times [A,B] \rightarrow B.$$

For example, **Set** is cartesian closed: [A,B] can be chosen as the set of all maps from A to B, and evaluation is the map defined by $\text{eval}(x,f) = f(x)$ for $x \in A$ and $f: A \rightarrow B$. Also the terminal category **T** is (trivially) cartesian closed.

If a topological category over **X** is cartesian closed, then **X** is cartesian closed (see [8]), and hence, we restrict our attention to cartesian closed base-categories. A crucial concept for the investigation of cartesian closedness is that of a regular sink.

I.1 Definition. [8] A sink $(A_i \xrightarrow{a_i} A)_{i \in I}$ is called regular if there exists a coproduct $\coprod_{j \in J} A_j$ ($J \subset I$ is a set) such that the canonical morphism $[a_j]: \coprod A_j \rightarrow A$ is a regular epimorphism. A category is said to have regular sink factorizations if it is cocomplete and for each sink $(A_i \xrightarrow{a_i} A)$ there exists a monomorphism $m: A' \rightarrow A$ and a regular sink $(A_i \xrightarrow{b_i} A')$ with $a_i = m \circ b_i$.

I.2 Examples.

(i) In **Set**, regular sinks are precisely the epi-sinks, i.e., sinks $(A_i \xrightarrow{a_i} A)$ such that $A = \bigcup a_i[A_i]$. **Set** has regular sink factorizations.

(ii) T has (trivial) regular factorizations.

(iii) Every topological category **K** over a base-category with regular sink factorizations has regular sink factorizations. Regular sinks in **K** are precisely the final sinks with regular underlying sinks.

Thus, regular sinks are just final epi-sinks in case **X** = **Set**, and they are the sinks $(A_i \to A)$ with $A = \operatorname{Sup} A_i$ in case **X** = **T**.

<u>I.3 Definition</u>. Regular sinks are <u>finitely productive</u> provided that for each regular sink $(A_i \xrightarrow{a_i} A)$ and each object B, the sink $(B\times A_i \xrightarrow{id_B \times a_i} B\times A)$ is regular.

<u>I.4 Remarks</u>.

(1) Regular sinks are finitely productive iff the product

$$\mathbf{A}\times\mathbf{B} = (A_i\times B_j \xrightarrow{a_i\times b_j} A\times B \mid A_i \xrightarrow{a_i} A \text{ in } \mathbf{A} \text{ and } B_j \xrightarrow{b_j} B \text{ in } \mathbf{B})$$

of regular sinks **A** and **B** is regular.

(2) The finite productivity of final sinks (or colimits or coproducts or regular epis) is defined by replacing "regular sinks" by "final sinks" (etc.) in the above definition.

(3) It is easy to see that colimits are finitely productive iff

(a) coproducts are finitely productive, i.e., we have canonical isomorphisms $\coprod_{i\in I} (B\times A_i) \cong B\times \coprod_{i\in I} A_i$,

and

(b) regular epimorphisms are finitely productive.

<u>I.5 Theorem</u>. [8] Let **X** be a cartesian closed category with regular sink factorizations. For each topological category **K** over **X**, the following conditions are equivalent:

(1) **K** is cartesian closed;

(2) For each K in **K** the functor K × - preserves colimits;

(3) Regular sinks are finitely productive in **K**;

(4) Coproducts and regular epimorphisms are finitely productive in **K**.

Proof. (1) → (2) → (4) Trivial.

(4) → (3) Let $(A_i \xrightarrow{a_i} A)_{i\in I}$ be a regular sink. We can assume that I is a set. Then the canonical morphism $[a_i]\colon \coprod A_i \to A$ is a regular epimorphism. For each object B, $id_B\times[a_i]$ is a regular epimorphism too. Since $\coprod (B\times A_i) \cong B\times\coprod A_i$, this is the canonical morphism for $(B\times A_i \xrightarrow{id\times a_i} B\times A)$.

(3) → (1) For each pair of objects K and L in **K** we will present the power-object [K,L] and the evaluation eval: K×[K,L] → L. Consider the evaluation in **X**:

$$\mathrm{eval}_o\colon\ |K|\times X_o \to |L|,\ \ X_o = [|K|,|L|],$$

and denote by **A** the structured sink of all $A_i \xrightarrow{a_i} X_o$ such that

$$\mathrm{eval}_o\circ(\mathrm{id}_K\times a_i)\colon\ K\times A_i \to L$$

is a morphism in **K**. The underlying sink of **A** has a regular factorization $(A_i \xrightarrow{a_i} X_o) = (A_i \xrightarrow{\hat{a}_i} X \xrightarrow{m} X_o)$. The final object of the structured sink $(A_i \xrightarrow{\hat{a}_i} X)$ will be denoted by [K,L], and we will prove that the map

$$\mathrm{eval} = \mathrm{eval}_o\circ(\mathrm{id}_K\times m)\colon\ K\times[K,L] \to L$$

has the required universal property.

(i) eval is a morphism in **K**, since the fact that $(A_i \xrightarrow{\hat{a}_i} [K,L])$ is a regular sink in **K** implies that $(K\times A_i \xrightarrow{\mathrm{id}\times\hat{a}_i} K\times[K,L])$ is regular, hence final, and for each i

$$\mathrm{eval}\circ(\mathrm{id}_K\times\hat{a}_i) = \mathrm{eval}_o\circ(\mathrm{id}_K\times a_i)\colon\ K\times A_i \to L$$

is a morphism in **K** by the definition of **A**.

(ii) For each morphism b: K×B → L in **K** there is a unique morphism a: $B \to X_o$ in **X** with $b = \mathrm{eval}_o\circ(\mathrm{id}_K\times a)$. This implies that $B \xrightarrow{a} X_o \in$ **A**. Hence we have a morphism â: B → [K,L] in **K** with a = m∘â. Consequently:

$$b = \mathrm{eval}_o\circ(\mathrm{id}_K\times m)\circ(\mathrm{id}_K\times\hat{a}) = \mathrm{eval}\circ(\mathrm{id}_K\times\hat{a}).$$

Uniqueness of â follows from the fact that m is a monomorphism.

I.6 Corollary. Cartesian closed topological categories over **T** are precisely the locales, i.e., complete lattices in which joins distribute over finite meets.

I.7 Examples of cartesian closed topological categories over **Set**.

(a) The category of (compact T_2)-generated topological spaces. Powers [K,L] have the underlying set hom(K,L) (of all continuous maps K → L) equipped with the (compact T_2)-generated modification of the compact-open topology.

(b) The category of sequential spaces, i.e., topological spaces in which closed subsets are precisely those closed under the formation of limits of sequences. Powers [K,L] have the underlying set hom(K,L), equipped with the structure of sequentially continuous convergence, i.e.,

$$(f_n) \to f \text{ in } [K,L]$$

iff

$$(f_n(x_n)) \to f(x) \text{ in } L \text{ for each } (x_n) \to x \text{ in } K.$$

(c) The category of convergence spaces. Powers [K,L] have the underlying set hom(K,L), equipped with the structure of continuous convergence, i.e.,

$$\mathbf{F} \to f \text{ in } [K,L]$$

iff

$$\text{eval}(\mathbf{F}\times\mathbf{G}) \to f(x) \text{ in } L \text{ for each } \mathbf{G} \to x \text{ in } K.$$

(d) The category of preordered sets, i.e., reflexive and transitive relations. Powers [K,L] have the underlying set hom(K,L), equipped with the pointwise preorder, i.e.,

$$f \leqslant g \text{ in } [K,L]$$

iff

$$f(x) \leqslant g(x) \text{ in } L \quad \text{for each } x \in K.$$

(e) The category **Rel** of binary relations (or directed graphs). Powers [K,L] have the underlying set of all (!) functions $|K| \to |L|$, equipped with the relation defined by

$$f \,\rho\, g \text{ in } [K,L]$$

iff

$$f(x) \,\rho\, g(y) \text{ in } L \qquad \text{for each } x \,\rho\, y \text{ in } K.$$

Observe that in the last example the underlying functor preserves the power-objects, whereas in the preceding ones, the power-objects are built on subsets of the corresponding power-objects in **Set**.

I.8 Definition. A cartesian closed topological category **K** is said to have

(a) concrete powers if for all objects K and L both $|[K,L]|=[|K|,|L|]$ and the evaluation maps in **K** and **X** coincide;

(b) subconcrete powers if for all objects K and L, $|[K,L]|$ is a subobject of $[|K|,|L|]$ and the evaluation in **K** is the restriction of the evaluation in **X**; more precisely, there is a monomorphism $m\colon |[K,L]| \to [|K|,|L|]$ such that the diagram

$$\begin{array}{ccc}
|K| \times [|K|,|L|] & \xrightarrow{\text{eval}_{\mathbf{X}}} & |L| \\
\uparrow{\scriptstyle \text{id}_{|K|}\times m} & & \uparrow{\scriptstyle \text{eval}_{\mathbf{K}}} \\
|K| \times |[K,L]| = |K \times [K,L]| & &
\end{array}$$

commutes.

I.9 Remark. If **K** has concrete powers, we call it concretely cartesian closed. This is the case iff for each K in **K**, the following functor square

$$\begin{array}{ccc} \mathbf{K} & \xrightarrow{[K,-]} & \mathbf{K} \\ {\scriptstyle |\,|}\downarrow & & \downarrow{\scriptstyle |\,|} \\ \mathbf{X} & \xrightarrow[{[|K|,-]}]{} & \mathbf{X} \end{array}$$

commutes. Analogously, subconcreteness of powers means that each $|\,| \circ [K,-]$ is a subfunctor of $[|K|,-] \circ |\,|$.

<u>I.10</u> <u>Proposition</u>. [8] Let **X** be a cartesian closed category with regular sink factorizations. Then each cartesian closed topological category over **X** has subconcrete powers.

This is actually proved in the proof of Theorem 1, where the corresponding monomorphism m: $|[K,L]| \to X_o = [|K|,|L|]$ is presented.

<u>I.11</u> <u>Theorem</u>. For each topological category **K** over a cartesian closed category **X**, the following conditions are equivalent:

(1) **K** is concretely cartesian closed;

(2) in **K** final sinks are finitely productive;

(3) **K** is cartesian closed, and each **K**-morphism with a discrete range has a discrete domain;

(4) **K** is cartesian closed, and in **K** each product $K \times D$ with a discrete factor D is discrete.

Proof. (1) $\longleftrightarrow$ (2) By the taught-lift theorem of Wyler [16], in each commuting square of functors

$$\begin{array}{ccc} \mathbf{K} & \xrightarrow{F} & \mathbf{K} \\ {\scriptstyle U}\downarrow & & \downarrow{\scriptstyle U} \\ \mathbf{X} & \xrightarrow[F_o]{} & \mathbf{X} \end{array}$$

(where U denotes the forgetful functor) in which F_o has a right adjoint G_o, the functor F preserves final sinks iff F has a right adjoint G with $U \circ G = G_o \circ U$. By applying this result to $F = K \times -$, $F_o = |K| \times -$ and $G_o = [|K|,-]$, we obtain the equivalence of (1) and (2).

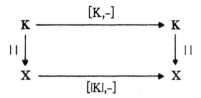

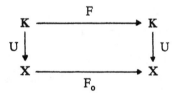

(2) → (4) Since (2) → (1), **K** is cartesian closed. A **K**-object D is discrete iff it is final for the empty sink, in which case each K×D is final for the empty sink, and hence, K×D is discrete.

(4) → (3) Let f: K → D be a **K**-morphism and let D be discrete. To prove that **K** is discrete, let g: |K| → |K'| be an arbitrary **X**-morphism. Since K×D is discrete,

$$g\circ\pi : K\times D \to K'$$

is a **K**-morphism, where π : K×D → K denotes the projection. Composing the **K**-morphism $(id_K,f) : K \to K\times D$ with $g\circ\pi$, we conclude that

$$g = g\circ\pi\circ(id_K,f) : K \to K'$$

is a **K**-morphism, and hence, K is discrete.

(3) → (1) For each pair of objects K and L, let eval: K×[K,L] → L be the evaluation in **K**. We prove that eval: |K|×|[K,L]| → |L| has the universal property in the base category **X**. Let X be an object of **X** and let f: |K|×X → |L| be an **X**-morphism. For the discrete object D with |D|=X we know that K×D is discrete (because the projection K×D → D is a **K**-morphism), and hence, f: K×D → L is a **K**-morphism. Consequently, there exists a unique **K**-morphism $\tilde{f}$: D → [K,L] with $f = eval\circ(id_K\times\tilde{f})$. Hence, $\tilde{f}$: X → |[K,L]| is the unique **X**-morphism with this property. Uniqueness follows from the fact that each **X**-morphism with domain X is a **K**-morphism with domain D. Therefore, |[K,L]| is the power-object of |K| and |L|.

<u>I.12</u> <u>Remarks.</u>

(i) No assumptions about factorization systems in **X** are needed for the preceding result (unlike Theorem I.5).

(ii) Let T_o denote a discrete **K**-object with underlying terminal **X**-object $|T_o|$. The condition in (4) that D discrete implies all K×D discrete is equivalent to the following:

(*) $K\times T_o$ is discrete for each **K**-object K.

In fact, if (*) is satisfied and if D is a discrete **K**-object, then $|D| = |T_o|\times|D|$ in **X** clearly implies $D = D\times T_o$ in **K**, and hence, all products

$$K\times D = K\times(D\times T_o) = (K\times D)\times T_o$$

are discrete.

<u>I.13</u> <u>Remark</u>. For cartesian closed topological categories over **Set**, it was shown in [8] that

(**) $$\hom(K,L) \subseteq |[K,L]| \subseteq [|K|,|L|]$$

in the sense of subconcrete powers.

In fact, since points in the underlying set of [K,L] correspond naturally to the morphisms $T_0 \to [K,L]$, we have

$$f \in |[K,L]|$$

for a function f: $|K| \to |L|$ iff

$$f \circ p\colon K \times T_0 \to L \text{ is a } \mathbf{K}\text{-morphism}$$

where p: $K \times T_0 \to K$ denotes the projection.

Categories for which the first inequality in (**) is always an equality are said to have <u>canonical function spaces</u>, see [2]. Thus, canonical function spaces are objects [K,L] with $|[K,L]| = \hom(K,L)$ and such that the canonical evaluation map has the universal property. In the Examples I.7 (a)-(d) above we presented categories with canonical function spaces, while **Rel** in (e) has concrete powers. In general, a cartesian closed topological category over **Set** need have neither concrete powers nor canonical function spaces, as can be seen in the following:

<u>I.14 Example</u>. Let **H** denote the category of triples $(X, \leqslant, \rho)$ where $\leqslant$ is a preorder and ρ is a binary relation. Morphisms are maps preserving both the preorder and the relation. **H** is a cartesian closed topological category over **Set**: the underlying set of [K,L] consists of precisely those functions f: $|K| \to |L|$ which preserve the preorder (hence, both inclusions in (**) can be proper). For such functions f and g we have in [K,L]

$$f \leqslant g \text{ iff } f(x) \leqslant g(x) \text{ in L for each } x \in |K|$$

and

$$f \,\rho\, g \text{ iff } f(x) \,\rho\, g(y) \text{ in L for each } x \,\rho\, y \text{ in K.}$$

<u>I.15 Definition</u> [8]. A c-category is a concrete category **K** over **Set** in which all constant functions $|K| \to |L|$ are **K**-morphisms $K \to L$.

<u>I.16 Proposition</u> [2,8]. A cartesian closed topological category over **Set** has canonical function spaces iff it is a c-category.

Proof. Let **K** have canonical function spaces. The projection $\pi\colon K \times L \to L$ factors as

$$\pi = \text{eval} \circ (\text{id} \times \tilde{\pi})$$

for a unique **K**-morphism $\tilde{\pi}\colon L \to [K,L]$. Since on the level of sets we have $\tilde{\pi}\colon |L| \to \hom(K,L)$ with

$$\pi(x,y) = y = \text{eval}(x, \tilde{\pi}(y)) \quad (x \in |K| \text{ and } y \in |L|),$$

we conclude that for each $y \in |L|$, $\tilde{\pi}(y)$ is the constant map with value y, and $\tilde{\pi}(y) \in \hom(K,L)$. Thus, **K** is a c-category.

The converse follows from I.13, since in each c-category T_0 is terminal.

II. Quasitopoi

Recall that a <u>topos</u> is a category **L** satisfying the following conditions:

(1) **L** has finite limits and colimits;

(2) **L** is cartesian closed;

(3) in **L** partial morphisms are representable, i.e., for each object A there exists a monomorphism $t_A : A \to A^*$ universal in the following sense: given a partial morphism into A (i.e., a pair consisting of a monomorphism m: $B \to C$ and a morphism f: $B \to A$), there exists a unique pullback

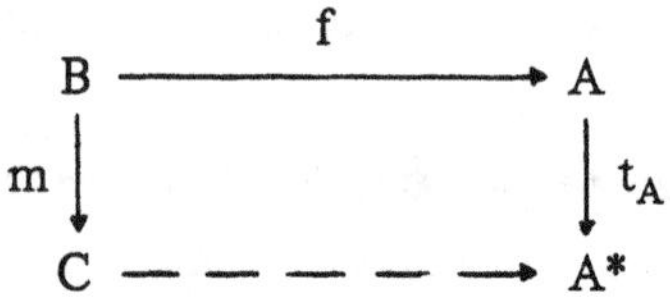

For example, **Set** is a topos: A* is a one-point extension of A; also **T** is (trivially) a topos.

The topos structure is never lifted from **X** to a non-trivial topological category over **X** simply because topoi are balanced categories. But a convenient weakening of the axiom (3), studied by Penon [14], gives an interesting concept for topological categories.

A <u>quasitopos</u> is a category **L** satisfying (1), (2) and the condition (3)* obtained from (3) by replacing "monomorphism" by "strong monomorphism". Recall that a monomorphism m is called strong if each commuting square

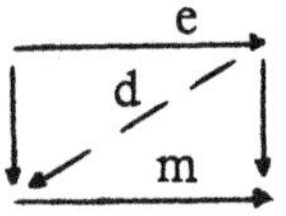

with e an epimorphism has a diagonal d. In **Set** every monomorphism is strong. In a topological category **K** over **X**, strong monomorphisms are just the initial morphisms with underlying morphism a strong monomorphism in **X**.

<u>II.1 Remark</u>. For each object L of a category **L**, we denote by **L**/L the comma-category of all morphisms with the codomain L. Penon proved in [14] that a category **L** is a quasitopos iff

(a) **L** has finite limits and colimits;

(b) **L**/L is cartesian closed for each L in **L**;

(c) <u>strong subobjects are representable</u>, i.e., there is a strong monomorphism t: T → Ω with T terminal such that for each strong monomorphism m: B → C there exists a unique pullback

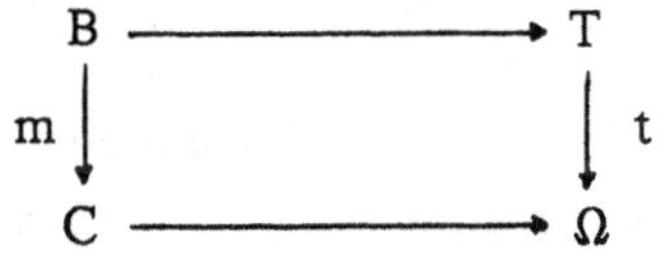

<u>II.2 Definition</u>. Regular sinks are <u>universal</u> provided for each regular sink $(A_i \xrightarrow{a_i} A)_{i \in I}$ and each morphism f: B → A there exists a regular sink $(B_j \xrightarrow{b_j} B)_{j \in J}$ such that each $f b_j$ factors through some $a_{i(j)}$:

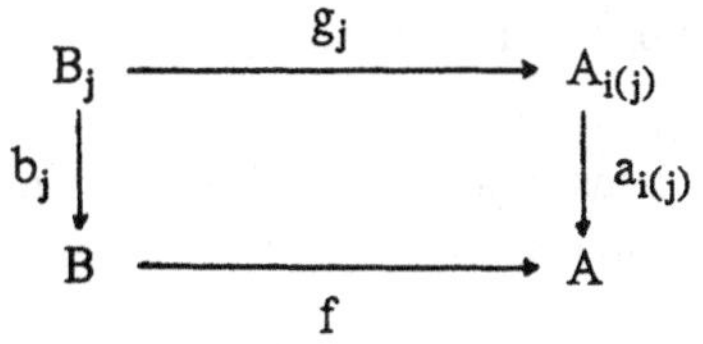

<u>II.3 Remarks.</u>

(i) As in I.4 we define universality of final sinks (and other types of sinks) by replacing in the above definition "regular sinks" by "final sinks" (etc.).

(ii) If **K** has pullbacks, then regular sinks are universal iff for each regular sink $(A_i \xrightarrow{a_i} A)_{i \in I}$ and each morphism f: B → A the sink $(B_i \xrightarrow{b_i} B)_{i \in I}$ obtained by pointwise pullbacks along f is regular.

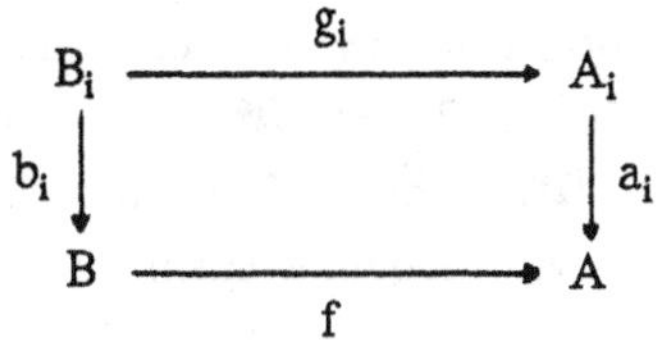

Similarly for universal final sinks, etc.

(iii) Universality of regular sinks implies their finite productivity. In fact, if f above is the projection $K \times A \rightarrow A$, then the resulting sink is $(K \times A_i \xrightarrow{id \times a_i} K \times A)$.

(iv) Colimits are universal iff both coproducts and regular epis are universal; this is analogous to I.4.

(v) By replacing in the above definition "morphism f" by "strong monomorphism f", we obtain the condition that <u>regular sinks are hereditary</u>. Analogously we obtain the heredity of final sinks and other types of sinks.

(vi) Regular sinks are universal iff they are both finitely productive and hereditary. This follows from the fact that each morphism $f: B \rightarrow A$ factors as $f = \pi \circ (id_B, f)$ where $\pi: B \times A \rightarrow A$ is the projection and $(id_B, f): B \rightarrow B \times A$ is a strong monomorphism (in fact, a section). Pullbacks along f are compsed of pullbacks along π followed by pullbacks along (id_B, f).
Analogously with other types of sinks:

universal = finitely productive and hereditary.

(vii) Colimits are hereditary iff

(a) coproducts are hereditary, i.e., if B is a strong subobject of $\coprod A_i$ then $B = \coprod (B \cap A_i)$;

(b) regular epimorphisms are hereditary.

<u>II.4 Theorem</u>. Let **X** be a quasitopos with regular sink factorizations. For each topological category **K** over **X**, the following conditions are equivalent:

(1) **K** is a quasitopos;

(2) in **K** regular sinks are universal;

(3) in **K** colimits are universal;

(4) in **K** coproducts and regular epimorphisms are both finitely productive and hereditary;

(5) **K** is cartesian closed and has hereditary colimits;

(6) **K**/K is cartesian closed for each K in **K**.

Proof. (1) $\longleftrightarrow$ (6) By II.1, it is sufficient to verify that strong monomorphisms are representable in any topological category **K**. Let $t: T \rightarrow \Omega$ be the representing strong monomorphism in **X**, and let $t: T^* \rightarrow \Omega^*$ be the corresponding **K**-morphism with indiscrete objects T^* and Ω^*. Then T^* is terminal in **K**, and t is a strong monomorphism. For each strong monomorphism $m: B \rightarrow C$ in **K** we have the unique pullback

$$\begin{array}{ccc} |B| & \longrightarrow & T \\ {\scriptstyle m}\downarrow & & \downarrow{\scriptstyle t} \\ |C| & \underset{m^*}{\longrightarrow} & \Omega \end{array}$$

in **X**.

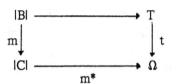

Indiscreteness of Ω^* and initiality of m immediately imply that

$$\begin{array}{ccc} B & \longrightarrow & T^* \\ {\scriptstyle m}\downarrow & & \downarrow{\scriptstyle t} \\ C & \underset{m^*}{\longrightarrow} & \Omega^* \end{array}$$

is the required unique pullback in **K**.

(2) $\longleftrightarrow$ (6) This is an immediate consequence of Theorem I.5 via the following simple observations. If **K** is topological over **X**, then **K**/K is topological over **X**/|K|. Regular sinks in **K**/K are precisely those sinks

$$\begin{array}{ccc} A_i & \xrightarrow{a_i} & A \\ & {\scriptstyle \alpha_i}\searrow \quad \swarrow{\scriptstyle \alpha} & \\ & K & \end{array}$$

for which the sink $(A_i \xrightarrow{a_i} A)_{i \in I}$ is regular in **K**. For each object (A,α) of **K**/K, the functor $(A,\alpha) \times - : \mathbf{K}/K \to \mathbf{K}/K$ is given by the formation of pullbacks along α in **K**.

The implications (2) $\to$ (5) $\to$ (4) $\to$ (3) are clear; (3) $\to$ (2) is proved analogously to (4) $\to$ (3) in I.5 above.

<u>II.5 Remark</u>. The equivalence of (1) and (6) does not require regular factorizations in **X**.

<u>II.6 Examples</u>.

(a) The category **Conv** of convergence spaces is a quasitopos.

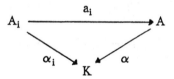

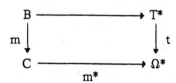

(b) The category of (compact T_2)-generated topological spaces fails to be a quasitopos although coproducts are universal and regular epimorphisms are finitely productive. Regular epimorphisms are not hereditary.
In fact, no non-trivial topological subcategory of the category of topological spaces is a quasitopos; see [7].

(c) The category **Mer** of merotopic spaces [12] fails to be a quasitopos although regular epimorphisms are universal and coproducts are hereditary. Coproducts are not finitely productive.

(d) A concretely cartesian closed topological category over **Set** need not be a quasitopos. For example, let **K** have objects (X,0) for all sets X and (X,1) for all non-empty sets X, and let f: (X,k) → (X',k') be a **K**-morphism iff f: X → X' is a map and $k \leqslant k'$. Then **K** is topological over **Set**. A sink $((X_i,k_i) \xrightarrow{f_i} (X,k))$ is final iff $k = \operatorname{Sup} k_i$. Hence, final sinks are productive, i.e., **K** is concretely cartesian closed over **Set**. Moreover regular epimorphisms in **K** are hereditary, but **K** does not have hereditary coproducts: if $a \neq b$, the coproduct of ({a},0) with ({b},1) is ({a,b},1); and its subobject ({a},1) is not the coproduct of the intersections ({a},0) and (∅,0).

(e) For complete lattices, considered as topological categories over **T** quasitopoi are precisely the locales, i.e., the cartesian closed ones. Any complete lattice which is not a locale is an example of a concrete category with universal regular epimorphisms and hereditary coproducts in which coproducts are not finitely productive.

(f) The quasi-category of quasi-topological spaces of Spannier is illegitimate, see [9], and hence not topological.

<u>II.7 Definition</u>. A topological category with universal final sinks is said to be <u>universally topological</u>.

<u>II.8 Theorem</u>. For each topological category **K** over a quasitopos, the following conditions are equivalent:

(1) **K** is universally topological;

(2) **K** is a quasitopos with concrete powers;

(3) **K** is a quasitopos and each **K**-morphism with a discrete range has a discrete domain;

(4) **K**/K is concretely cartesian closed over **X**/|K| for each K in **K**.

Proof. (1) → (2) See II.5 and I.11.

(2) → (3) See I.11.

(3) → (4) By I.11, it suffices to verify that in each K/K morphisms with discrete range have discrete domain. This follows from the fact that an object $A \xrightarrow{\alpha} K$ is discrete in K/K iff A is discrete in **K**.

(4) → (1) For each morphism f: K′ → K in **K**, the functor (K′,f)×− : **K**/K → **K**/K has a concrete right adjoint, and hence, it preserves final sinks in **K**/K by Wyler's taught lift theorem [16]. The functor (K′,f) ×− is given by the formation of pullbacks along f in **K**. Furthermore, final sinks in **K**/K are precisely those sinks

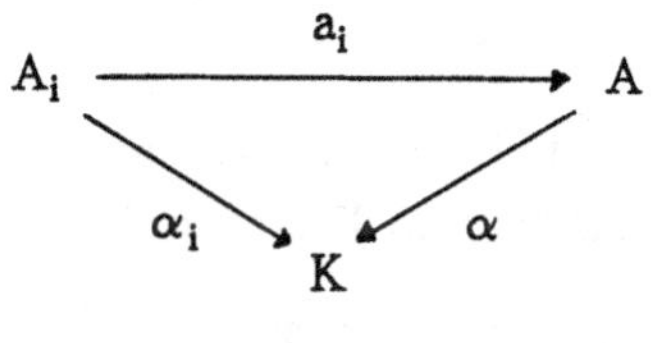

for which the sink $(A_i \xrightarrow{a_i} A)$ is final in **K**, and hence, pullbacks along any **K**-morphism f preserve final **K**-sinks.

II.9 Definition. [13] A topological universe is a topological c-category with universal final epi-sinks.

II.10 Remark. Since each epi-sink in **Set** is regular, topological universes are precisely those topological c-categories which are quasitopoi.

The category of convergence spaces is a topological universe.

II.11 Definition. [8] By the c−modification of a topological category **K** is meant the concrete subcategory $\mathbf{K}_c$ of **K**, consisting of those objects K for which all maps from a terminal **K**-object into K are **K**-morphisms.

II.12 Example. The c-modification of the category of relations is the category of reflexive relations.

II.13 Theorem. A concrete category over **Set** is a topological universe iff it is a c-modification of a universally topological category.

Proof.

(A) Let **K** be a topological universe. Denote by $\hat{\mathbf{K}}$ the category whose objects are all pairs (X,K) where X is a set and K is a **K**-object with $|K| \subset X$, and whose morphisms f: (X,K) → (X′,K′) are those maps f: X → X′ for which $f(|K|) \subset |K'|$

and the corresponding restriction $\hat{f}$ of f is a **K**-morphism $\hat{f}$: K → K′. $\hat{\mathbf{K}}$ is a concrete category over **Set**. A terminal object of $\hat{\mathbf{K}}$ is ({0},T), where T is terminal in **K** and |T| = {0}. Then $\mathbf{K} = \hat{\mathbf{K}}_c$, provided that each **K**-object K is identified with the $\hat{\mathbf{K}}$-object (| K |,K):

(a) If $(X,K) \in \hat{\mathbf{K}}_c$ then for each $x \in X$ we have a map f: {0} → X defined by f(0) = x. Since f: ({0},T) → (X,K) is a morphism, we conclude $x \in |K|$. Thus, (X,K) = (|K|,K) ∈ **K**.

(b) For each K ∈ **K** and each map f: {0} → K we know that f: T → K is a **K**-morphism, and hence, f: ({0},T) → (|K|,K) is a $\hat{\mathbf{K}}$-morphism. Thus, $(|K|,K) \in \hat{\mathbf{K}}_c$.

It remains to verify that $\hat{\mathbf{K}}$ is universally topological. Note that each $\hat{\mathbf{K}}$-object (X,K) is the coproduct of (|K|,K) and the discrete object (X-|K|,D) (where D denotes the initial **K**-object). For each $\hat{\mathbf{K}}$-structured sink $((X_i,K_i) \xrightarrow{f_i} X)_{i\in I}$ the final object is (X,K) where $|K| = \bigcup_{i\in I} f_i(|K_i|)$ and K is the final object in **K** of the **K**-structured sink of restricted maps $(K_i \xrightarrow{\hat{f}_i} |K|)_{i\in I}$. Thus, $\hat{\mathbf{K}}$ is topological (since fibres are obviously small in $\hat{\mathbf{K}}$). Let g: (X′,K′) → (X,K) be an arbitrary morphism, and let us form the pointwise pullbacks:

$$\begin{array}{ccc} (X'_i,K'_i) & \xrightarrow{\;g_i\;} & (X_i,K_i) \\ {\scriptstyle h_i}\downarrow & & \downarrow{\scriptstyle f_i} \\ (X',K') & \xrightarrow[\;g\;]{} & (X,K) \end{array}$$

Then the restricted morphisms $\hat{g}$: K′ → K and $\hat{f}_i$: K_i → K have the corresponding pullback

$$\begin{array}{ccc} K'_i & \xrightarrow{\;\hat{g}_i\;} & K_i \\ {\scriptstyle \hat{h}_i}\downarrow & & \downarrow{\scriptstyle \hat{f}_i} \\ K' & \xrightarrow[\;\hat{g}\;]{} & K \end{array}$$

in *K* (where $\hat{h}_i$ denotes the restriction of h_i, and $\hat{g}_i$ that of g_i). Since the sink $(K_i \xrightarrow{\hat{f}_i} K)$ is regular (because it is a final epi-sink) in **K**, by II.4 the sink $(K'_i \xrightarrow{\hat{h}_i} K')$ is also regular in **K**. Moreover $|K'| = \bigcup_{i\in I} f_i(|K'_i|)$ because for each $x \in |K'|$ we have $g(x) \in |K| = \bigcup f_i(|K_i|)$, and hence, there exists $i\in I$ and $y \in |K_i|$ with $g(x) = f_i(y)$.

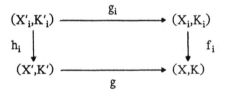

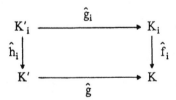

Since pullbacks are concrete in **K**, we conclude that there is $t \in |K'_i|$ with $\hat{h}_i(t)=x$ and $\hat{g}_i(t)=y$. Consequently, the sink $((X'_i,K'_i) \xrightarrow{h_i} (X',K'))$ is final in $\hat{\mathbf{K}}$.

(B) Let **K** be universally topological. Then $\mathbf{K}_c$ is topological because it is obviously closed under the formation of initial sources in **K**. Moreover, $\mathbf{K}_c$ is closed in **K** under the formation of final epi-sinks:

if $(K_i \xrightarrow{g_i} K)$ is a final epi-sink, then for each map f: $\{0\} \to |K|$ there exists $i \in I$ with $f(0) \in |K_i|$, and hence, there is a map f': $\{0\} \to |K_i|$ with $f=g_i \circ f'$. Since f': $T \to K_i$ is a morphism, so is f: $T \to K$. This proves that final epi-sinks are universal in $\mathbf{K}_c$ (since $\mathbf{K}_c$ is closed under pullbacks too). Since $\mathbf{K}_c$ is obviously a c-category, we conclude that $\mathbf{K}_c$ is a topological universe.

III. A Construction of Universally Topological Categories

The only examples of universally topological categories we have encountered so far were locales (over **T** and the category **Rel** of relations (over **Set**). We present now a variety of examples obtained by starting with an arbitrary concrete category and extending it to a universally topological one. It turns out that each universally topological category can be obtained in this way.

III.1 Definition. Let **K** be a category.

(1) A sink S in **K** is called a sieve provided the following implication holds:

$$(A \xrightarrow{f} B \in \text{Mor}\,\mathbf{K} \text{ and } B \xrightarrow{g} C \in S) \Rightarrow A \xrightarrow{gf} C \in S.$$

(2) For any object A the sieve consisting of all morphisms with codomain A is called the full sieve for A.

(3) A collection γ of sieves is called a Grothendieck topology for **K** provided it satisfies the following four conditions:

(T1) every full sieve belongs to γ;

(T2) γ is composition-closed, i.e., whenever $(A_i \xrightarrow{a_i} A)_{i\in I}$ belongs to γ and, for each $i\in I$, $(B_j \xrightarrow{b_j} A_i)_{j\in J_i}$ belongs to γ, then $(B_j \xrightarrow{a_i \circ b_j} A)_{i\in I, j\in J_i}$ belongs to γ;

(T3) γ is pullback-stable, i.e., whenever f: $A \to B$ is a morphism and S is a sieve with codomain B, which belongs to γ, then the sieve $f^{-1}S$, consisting of all morphisms $C \xrightarrow{g} A$ with $f \circ g \in S$, belongs to γ;

(T4) γ contains with any sieve any larger sieve.

(4) If **K** is a concrete category over **X** and γ is a Grothendieck topology for **K**, consisting of final sinks only, then $(\mathbf{K},\gamma)$ is called a concrete site over **X**.

III.2 Construction. For each concrete site $(\mathbf{K},\gamma)$ over $\mathbf{X}$ we construct a quasicategory over $\mathbf{X}$ (i.e., our construction is in general not legitimate; see below) as follows: a structured sink $A = (K_i \xrightarrow{f_i} X)_{i\in I}$ in $\mathbf{K}$ is said to be

(a) a structured sieve if for each $K \xrightarrow{f} X$ in A and each morphism $g\colon K' \to K$ in $\mathbf{K}$, $K' \xrightarrow{f\circ g} X$ is in A;

(b) γ–closed if for each $(K_i \xrightarrow{f_i} K)$ in γ and each $K \xrightarrow{g} X$ in $\mathbf{X}$, such that $K_i \xrightarrow{g\circ f_i} X$ is in A for all i, also $K \xrightarrow{g} X$ is in A. We denote by

$$\underline{\mathrm{Siev}}(\mathbf{K},\gamma)$$

the quasicategory of all γ-closed structured sieves. Morphisms from $A = (K_i \xrightarrow{f_i} X)_{i\in I}$ to $B = (L_j \xrightarrow{g_j} Y)_{j\in J}$ are those $\mathbf{X}$-morphisms $f\colon X \to Y$ for which $K_i \xrightarrow{f_i} X$ in A implies $K_i \xrightarrow{f\circ f_i} Y$ is in B. The forgetful functor of $\underline{\mathrm{Siev}}(\mathbf{K},\gamma)$ into $\mathbf{X}$ sends $(K_i \xrightarrow{f_i} X)$ to X. We consider $\mathbf{K}$ as a full subcategory of $\underline{\mathrm{Siev}}(\mathbf{K},\gamma)$ by identifying each object K with the full structured sieve

$$\tilde{K} = (L \xrightarrow{f} |K|)_{f\colon L \to K \text{ in } \mathbf{K}}.$$

Observe that for a γ-closed structured sieve $A = (K_i \xrightarrow{f_i} X)_{i\in I}$, a structured morphism $K \xrightarrow{f} X$ belongs to A iff $\tilde{K} \xrightarrow{f} A$ is a morphsim in $\underline{\mathrm{Siev}}(\mathbf{K},\gamma)$

III.3 Remark. There are two reasons why the construction above can be illegitimate:

(i) the objects can be proper classes in which case they are not elements of any class;

(ii) the conglomerate of all objects can be too large; for example, it can be in a bijective correspondence to the conglomerate of all subclasses of a proper class.

The latter obstacle is obviously the essential one. In case that the conglomerate of all objects is legitimate, i.e., in a bijective correspondence with some class $\mathbf{C}$, we can overcome (i) by using $\mathbf{C}$ as the class of objects of a category isomorphic (in an obvious way) to $\underline{\mathrm{Siev}}(\mathbf{K},\gamma)$. By an abuse of language, we call the latter category $\underline{\mathrm{Siev}}(\mathbf{K},\gamma)$ whenever the class of all γ-closed sieves is legitimate. In particular, this is the case whenever the quasicategory $\underline{\mathrm{Siev}}(\mathbf{K},\gamma)$ is small-fibred. We characterize such sites now.

Recall that a structured map $A \xrightarrow{a} X$ is a pair consisting of an object A in $\mathbf{K}$ and a morphism $a\colon |A| \to X$ in $\mathbf{X}$.

III.4 Definition.

Let $(\mathbf{K},\gamma)$ be a concrete site. For structured maps $A \xrightarrow{a} X$ and $A' \xrightarrow{a'} X$, we define

$$(A, a) \leqslant_{\gamma} (A',a')$$

provided that there exists a γ-sink $(B_i \xrightarrow{b_i} A)_{i\in I}$ and $\mathbf{K}$-morphisms $b'_i\colon B_i \to A'$ $(i\in I)$ with $a\circ b_i = a'\circ b'_i$ $(i\in I)$. Call (A,a) and (A',a') equivalent [in symbols: $(A,a) \equiv_{\gamma} (A',a')$] iff $(A,a) \leqslant_{\gamma} (A',a') \leqslant_{\gamma} (A,a)$.

We say that $(\mathbf{K},\gamma)$ is a structurally small site if for each X in $\mathbf{X}$ there exists a set of representatives of the equivalence $\equiv_{\gamma}$ on structured maps with range X.

III.5 Proposition. A concrete site $(\mathbf{K},\gamma)$ is structurally small if $\underline{\mathrm{Siev}}(\mathbf{K},\gamma)$ is a small-fibred (and hence a legitimate) category.

Proof.

(A) Let $\underline{\mathrm{Siev}}(\mathbf{K},\gamma)$ be small-fibred. For each structured map $A \xrightarrow{a} X$ consider the structured sink

$$\downarrow(A,a) = \{(A',a') \mid (A',a') \leqslant_{\gamma} (A,a)\}.$$

By the pullback-stability of γ, it is a structured sieve. By the composition-closedness of γ, it is γ-closed. Since

$$\downarrow(A_1,a_1) = \downarrow(A_2,a_2) \text{ iff } (A_1,a_1) \equiv_{\gamma} (A_2,a_2)$$

structural smallness of $(\mathbf{K},\gamma)$ follows immediately from fibre-smallness of $\underline{\mathrm{Siev}}(\mathbf{K},\gamma)$

(B) Let $(\mathbf{K},\gamma)$ be structurally small. For each X in $\mathbf{X}$ we have a set $(A_i \xrightarrow{a_i} X)_{i\in I}$ of representatives as in the above definition. Each γ-closed sieve $\mathbf{A}$ has the property that with any $(A,a)\in \mathbf{A}$ it contains all smaller elements, i.e.,

$$(A,a) \in \mathbf{A} \text{ implies } \downarrow(A,a) \subset \mathbf{A}.$$

Consequently, $\mathbf{A}$ is determined by the set $I(\mathbf{A}) = \{i\in I \mid (A_i,a_i)\in \mathbf{A}\}$ in the sense that for two γ-closed structured sieves on X,

$$I(\mathbf{A}_1) = I(\mathbf{A}_2) \text{ implies } \mathbf{A}_1 = \mathbf{A}_2.$$

Since the collection of all subsets of I is a set, $\underline{\mathrm{Siev}}(\mathbf{K},\gamma)$ is small-fibred.

III.6 Examples. Let γ_o be the (smallest) Grothendieck topology on $\mathbf{K}$, consisting of all full structured sieves. Then $(\mathbf{K},\gamma_o)$ is structurally small iff for each X in $\mathbf{X}$ the following equivalence has a set of representatives: $A \xrightarrow{a} X$ is equivalent to $B \xrightarrow{b} X$ iff there exist **K**-morphisms f: $A \to B$ with $a = b \circ f$, and g: $B \to A$ with $b = a \circ g$. In particular:

(a) (**Set**,γ_o) is structurally small over **Set**: $A \xrightarrow{a} X$ is equivalent to $B \xrightarrow{b} X$ iff $a(A) = b(B)$.

(b) As shown in [1], (**K**,γ_o) is not structurally small over **Set** for the categories **K** of metrizable spaces, relations and semigroups. In fact, <u>Siev</u>(**K**,γ_o) is not even legitimate for these categories.

(c) (**K**,γ_o) is structurally small over **T** iff **K** is small, i.e., a poset.

(d) More generally, for each Grothendieck topology γ on a small concrete category **K**, (**K**,γ) is structurally small.

<u>III.7 Theorem</u>. For a small-fibred concrete category **K** the following conditions are equivalent:

(1) **K** is universally topological;

(2) **K** $\cong$ <u>Siev</u>(**K**,γ) for some Grothendieck topology γ;

(3) **K** is concretely isomorphic to <u>Siev</u>(**L**,γ) for some structurally small site (**L**,γ).

Proof. (1) $\to$ (2) The collection γ of all final sinks in **K** is pullback-stable (since **K** is universally topological), and hence, γ is a Grothendieck topology. We are to prove that **K** $\cong$ <u>Siev</u>(**K**,γ), i.e., that each γ-closed structured sieve $\mathbf{A} = (A_i \xrightarrow{a_i} X)$ equals the full structured sieve $\tilde{K}$ of some **K**-object K. Let K be the final object in **K** of the structured sink **A**. Then the sink $\mathbf{A^*} = (A_i \xrightarrow{a_i} K)$ is in γ. The structured map $K \xrightarrow{id} X$ has the property that for each $A_i \xrightarrow{a_i} K$ in $\mathbf{A^*}$ we have $A_i \xrightarrow{id \circ a_i} X$ in **A**; since **A** is γ-closed, we conclude that $K \xrightarrow{id} X \in \mathbf{A}$. Then $\tilde{K} \subseteq \mathbf{A}$ because **A** is closed under composition, and hence $\tilde{K} = \mathbf{A}$.

(2) $\to$ (3) follows from III.5

(3) $\to$ (1) By III.5, <u>Siev</u>(**L**,γ) is small-fibred. It is sufficient to prove that it has universal final sinks. First, each structured sink $(A_i \xrightarrow{f_i} X)_{i \in I}$ in <u>Siev</u>(**L**,γ) has a final object: the sink **A** of all $A \xrightarrow{a} X$ for which there exists a γ-sink $(B_j \xrightarrow{b_j} A)_{j \in J}$ such that each $B_j \xrightarrow{a \circ b_j} X$ ($j \in J$) is equal to $B_j \xrightarrow{f_i \circ a'} X$ for some $i \in I$ and $B_j \xrightarrow{a'} |A_i|$ in $\mathbf{A}_i$. (It is easy to verify that **A** is a structured sieve, since γ is pullback-stable, and that **A** is γ-closed, since γ is composition-closed.)
To prove the universality, let **D** be a γ-closed structured sieve (with $|\mathbf{D}| = Y$); let $k: \mathbf{D} \to \mathbf{A}$ be a morphism in <u>Siev</u>(**L**,γ); and let S be the sink in <u>Siev</u>(**L**,γ), consisting of

those $g: B \to D$ for which $k \circ g$ factors through some f_i:

$$\begin{array}{ccc} B & \dashrightarrow & A_i \\ {\scriptstyle g}\downarrow & & \downarrow{\scriptstyle f_i} \\ D & \xrightarrow[k]{} & A \end{array}$$

To show that S is a final sink in Siev(L,γ), let $B \xrightarrow{d} |D|$ belong to D. Then $B \xrightarrow{kd} |A|$ belongs to A. Hence, by finality of $(A_i \xrightarrow{f_i} A)_{i \in I}$, there exists a γ-sink $(B_j \xrightarrow{b_j} B)_{j \in J}$ such that each kdb_j factors through some $f_{i(j)}$:

$$\begin{array}{ccccc} B_j & & \overset{g_j}{\dashrightarrow} & & A_{i(j)} \\ {\scriptstyle b_j}\downarrow & & & & \downarrow{\scriptstyle f_{i(j)}} \\ B & \xrightarrow[d]{} & D & \xrightarrow[k]{} & A \end{array}$$

By the definition of S, each db_j: $B_j \to D$ belongs to S. Hence, by the above description of final sinks in Siev(L,γ), S is final.

III.8 Examples.

(a) Let **L** be the concrete category over **Set** with single object L, $|L| = \{0,1\}$ and hom $(L,L) = \{id\}$, and let γ_o be the smallest Grothendieck topology on **L**. Then Siev(L,γ_o) is the category of relations.

(b) Let **L'** be the concrete category over **Set** with the single object L, $|L| = \{0,1\}$ and hom $(L,L) = \{id,f\}$ where f is the transposition, and let γ_o be the smallest Grothendieck topology on **L'**. Then Siev(L',γ_o) is the category of symmetric relations.

III.9 Corollary. Topological universes are precisely the concrete categories over **Set** concretely isomorphic to

$$\text{Siev}(L,\gamma)_c$$

for structurally small concrete sites (L,γ) over **Set**. The objects of Siev$(L,\gamma)_c$ are all γ-closed structured epi-sieves.

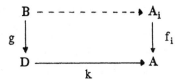

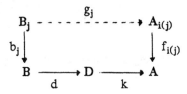

III.10 Examples.

(a) For L resp. L′ as in III.8, Siev$(L,\gamma_o)_c$ is the category of reflexive relations, and Siev$(L,\gamma_o)_c$ is the category of reflexive and symmetric relations.

(b) For **L** = **X** = **Set** and γ the topology generated by all finite sinks (i.e., a sieve S belongs to γ iff there exists a finite subset T of S such that every f$\in$S factors through some g$\in$T) Siev$(L,\gamma)_c$ is the category of bornological spaces [10].

(c) For the category **L** of finite sets, considered as a concrete category over **Set**, Siev$(L,\gamma_o)_c$ is the category of simplicial complexes.

III.11 Remark. Categorical investigations motivated by problems in analysis (duality theory and theory of manifolds) are concerned primarily with cartesian closed topological c-categories (see e.g. Frölicher [5] and Seip [15]) and with topological universes (see Binz [3], Hogbe-Nlend [10] and Nel [13]).

Similar constructions to that of Siev(K,γ) are considered by Dubuc [4], Nel [13] and Wyler [17].

References

[1] J. Adámek, H. Herrlich and G.E. Strecker, Least and largest initial completions, Comment. Math. Univ. Carolinae 20 (1979), 43-77.

[2] P. Antonine, Etude élémentaire des categories d'ensembles structurés, Bull. Soc. Math. Belgique 18 (1966), 142-164 and 387-414.

[3] E. Binz, Continuous convergence on C(X), Lect. Notes Mathem. 464, Springer-Verlag 1975.

[4] E. Dubuc, Concrete quasitopoi, Lect. Notes Mathem. 753 (1979), 239-254.

[5] A. Frölicher, Smooth structures, Lect. Notes Mathem. 962, Springer-Verlag 1982, 69-81.

[6] H. Herrlich, Categorical topology 1971-1981, Gen. Topol. Rel. Modern Analysis and Algebra V, Heldermann Verlag, Berlin 1982, 279-383.

[7] H. Herrlich, Are there convenient subcategories to Top?, Topol. Applications 15 (1983), 263-271.

[8] H. Herrlich, Universal topology, Categorical Topology Heldermann Verlag, Berlin 1984, 223-281.

[9] H. Herrlich and M. Rajagopalan, The quasicategory of quasispaces is illegitimate, Archiv. Math. 40 (1983), 364-366.

[10] M. Hogbe-Nlend, Bornologies and functional analyses, Mathematics Studies 29, North Holland 1977.

[11] P.T. Johnstone, Topos Theory, L.M.S. Mathematical Monographs 10, Academic Press 1977.

[12] M. Katetov, On continuity structures and spaces of mappings, Comment. Math. Univ. Carolinae 6 (1965), 257-278.

[13] L.D. Nel, Topological universes and smooth Gelfand-Naimark duality, to appear.

[14] J. Penon, Sur les quasi-topos, Cahier Topo. Geom. Diff. 18 (1977), 181-218.

[15] U. Seip, A convenient setting for smooth manifolds, J. Pure Appl. Algebra 21 (1981), 279-305.

[16] O. Wyler, Top categories and categorical topology, Gen. Topol. Applications 1 (1971), 17-28.

[17] O. Wyler, Are there topoi in topology?, Lect. Notes Mathem. 540 (1976), 699-719.

CONCRETE CATEGORIES AND INJECTIVITY

H. Bargenda, H. Herrlich, and G.E. Strecker

F.B. Mathematik
Universitat Bremen
2800 Bremen
Fed. Rep. Germany

and

Dept. of Mathematics
Kansas State University
Manhattan, Kansas 66506
U.S.A.

0. Abstract.

The paper consists of two parts. In the first part the concepts of injective objects, essential extensions, and injective hulls are illustrated by examples of known characterizations of these concepts in various familiar settings. In the second part the above notions are considered in quasicategories whose objects are concrete categories. It turns out that several types of 'completions' of concrete categories can be characterized as injective hulls.

1. Introduction.

The notion of injective objects, essential extensions, and injective hulls (or envelopes) has been studied in various settings for nearly half a century. Generally, injectives have been characterized as those objects satisfying a certain 'completeness' property and injective hulls as certain kinds of completions.

In this paper we first trace some of these developments, and then contrast them with recent results that give characterizations of the above concepts in several natural settings where the objects in question are concrete categories themselves. In particular, various types of 'completions' of concrete categories are characterized as particular injective hulls.

2. Injective Objects in Certain Concrete Categories

An object X in a category is called an <u>injective</u> object provided that for any object Y any morphism from Y to X can be extended to a morphism from any object Z in which Y is embedded.

The notion of injectivity and the first instance of a characterization of the injectives in some concrete category is due to Baer [2] who in 1940 proved that the injectives in the category of abelian groups are precisely the divisible groups. This result was extended in 1953 by Eckmann and Schopf [15] to a characterization of the injectives in categories of R-modules.

In 1956 Aronszajn and Panitchpakdi [1] proved that the injectives in the category of metric spaces and non-expansive mappings are exactly the hyperconvex spaces. Later, in 1969, Cohen [14] showed that for real (resp. complex) Banach spaces and linear maps with norm not exceeding 1, the injectives are just the spaces of real-valued (resp. complex-valued) maps on Boolean spaces, and that in the real case they are precisely the Banach spaces whose underlying metric spaces are hyperconvex (i.e., injectives in the category of metric spaces), but that for the complex case no injective (non-zero) Banach space has an injective underlying metric space.

In the order-theoretic realm, in 1948, Sikorski [26] showed that every complete Boolean algebra is injective in the category of Boolean algebras. This, together with the facts that every Boolean algebra can be embedded in a complete one (Sikorski [27]) and that every retract of a complete Boolean algebra is complete (Halmos [16]), shows that the injectives in this category are precisely the complete Boolean algebras. In 1967, Banaschewski and Bruns [5] characterized the injectives in the category of partially-ordered sets as the complete lattices. In the same year Balbes [7] (and independently in 1968 Banaschewski and Bruns [6]) showed that the injectives for distributive lattices are exactly the complete Boolean algebras. Then, in 1970, Balbes and Horn [8] proved that complete Boolean algebras are also precisely the injectives for the category of Heyting algebras. In the same year Bruns and Lakser [13] (and independently in 1971 Horn and Kimura [20]) characterized the injectives in the category of semilattices as the locales (i.e., the complete Heyting algebras).

Injectives in the categories of T_0-spaces, all topological spaces, and T_1-spaces have been characterized, respectively, by Banaschewski [4] in 1977, Wyler [28] in 1977, and Hoffmann [19] in 1981.

3. Essential Extensions and Injective Hulls

Objects that are not injective can often be embedded in injective ones. Among these embeddings there may happen to be a smallest one. A slightly stronger and more useful concept is the following. Its categorical formulation is due to Banaschewski and Bruns [5].

3.1 Definition.

1 An embedding $f:X \longrightarrow Y$ is called _essential_ provided that any morphism $g:Y \longrightarrow Z$ such that gf is an embedding is itself an embedding.

2 If $f:X \longrightarrow Y$ is an essential embedding and Y is an injective object, then (f,Y) is called an _injective hull_ of X.

Next we investigate certain properties of injective hulls. The results we give below are easily proved (and most are already contained in [3] or [24]. However, we provide proofs here to aid the reader in gaining familiarity with the concepts.

3.2 Proposition.

1. Injective hulls are _maximal essential extensions_, i.e., pairs (f,Y) with the property that f is an essential embedding and any embedding $g:Y \longrightarrow Z$ is an isomorphism if gf is an essential embedding.
2. Injective hulls are _minimal injective extensions_, i.e., pairs (f,Y) with the property that f is an embedding, Y is injective, and for any factorization
$$f = X \xrightarrow{g} Z \xrightarrow{h} Y$$
with g and h embeddings and Z injective, h must be an isomorphism.
3. If every object in a category has an injective hull, then the three concepts: injective hull, maximal essential extension, and minimal injective extension coincide in that category.

Proof.

1. If $f:X \longrightarrow Y$ is a injective hull, and if $g:Y \longrightarrow Z$ is an embedding such that gf is essential, then since Y is injective, $id_Y:Y \longrightarrow Y$ can be extended to $h:Z \longrightarrow Y$. But $hgf = f$ (an embedding), so that the essentialness of gf implies that h is an embedding. Since it is also a retraction, it must be an isomorphism, and hence, so must be g.

2. If $f:X \longrightarrow Y$ is a injective hull, and if

$$f = X \xrightarrow{g} Z \xrightarrow{h} Y$$

is a factorization with g and h embeddings and Z injective, then there exists a morphism p such that $ph = id_Z$. Since f is essential and $pf = phg = g$ (an embedding), it follows that p is an embedding (and a retraction), hence an isomorphism. Thus h is an isomorphism as well.

3. Parts 1. and 2. show that injective hulls always have the other properties.

Let $f:X \longrightarrow Y$ be a minimal injective extension. If $e:X \longrightarrow Z$ is an injective hull for X, then by the injectivity of Y there exists $h:Z \longrightarrow Y$ such that $he = f$. Since e is essential and f is an embedding, h must be an embedding, so by definition it must be an isomorphism. Thus f must be essential, i.e., (f,Y) is an injective hull.

Let $f:X \longrightarrow Y$ be a maximal essential extension. If $h:Y \longrightarrow Z$ is an injective hull for Y, then it is easily seen that hf is an essential embedding. Thus h must be an isomorphism, so that Y is injective. Hence (f,Y) is an injective hull.

3.3 Corollary.

Injective hulls are essentially unique in the sense that if (f,Y) and (f',Y') are each injective hulls of X, then there is an isomorphism $h:Y \longrightarrow Y'$ such that $f' = hf$.

Proof. By the injectivity of Y' there is $h:Y \longrightarrow Y'$ such that $f' = hf$. The essentialness of f implies that h is an embedding. Thus by either 1. or 2. of the Proposition, h must be an isomorphism.

In the categories mentioned in Section 2, except for **Top**, $\mathbf{Top_0}$, and $\mathbf{Top_1}$, every object has an injective hull. For metric spaces this was constructed by Isbell [21]. For T_0-spaces (resp. T_1-spaces) Banaschewski [4] (resp. Hoffmann [19]) showed that every object has a maximal essential extension, but these extensions usually fail to be injective hulls. Other conditions that guarantee that injective hulls coincide with maximal essential extensions and minimal injective extensions have been obtained by Porst [24].

4. The concept of Q-injectivity

If, in the definition of injective objects, embeddings are replaced by embeddings with additional properties, or even by an arbitrary class Q of morphisms, one arrives at the following more general and in certain respects more useful concepts.

4.1 Definition.

Given a class Q of morphisms in a category:

1. An object X is called a Q-<u>injective object</u> provided that for any morphism $g:Y \longrightarrow Z$ in Q and any morphism $f:Y \longrightarrow X$, there exists some morphism $h:Z \longrightarrow X$ such that $f = hg$.
2. A morphism $f:X \longrightarrow Y$ in Q is called Q-<u>essential</u> provided that any morphism $g:Y \longrightarrow Z$ is in Q whenever gf is in Q.
3. The pair (f,Y) is called the Q-<u>injective hull</u> of X provided that f is an essential morphism in Q and Y is Q-injective.

It should be noted that analogues of the results given in section 3. above hold in the more general context of Q-injective hulls.

It also can be shown that for every isomorphism-closed full reflective subcategory **A** of a category **B**, there exists a class Q of **B**-morphisms such that the **A**-objects are precisely the Q-injective objects and the **A**-reflections are precisely the Q-injective hulls. In particular,

1. in the category of metric spaces and uniformly continuous maps, complete metric spaces are precisely the Q-injective objects and completions are the Q-injective hulls, where Q consists of all dense (= epimorphic) embeddings.
2. in the category of T_0-spaces and continuous maps, sober spaces are precisely the Q-injective objects, and sobrifications (= sober reflections) are the Q-injective hulls, where Q consists of all b-dense (= epimorphic) embeddings. See Scott [25].

Conversely, a full subcategory consisting of all Q-injective objects need not be reflective. Examples in the category of topological spaces are:

1. the full subcategory of all compact spaces; compact spaces being exactly the Q-injective objects, where Q consists of all embeddings of discrete spaces into their corresponding Čech-Stone compactifications.
2. the full subcategory of pathwise connected spaces; pathwise connected spaces being exactly the Q-injective objects, where Q consists of the single embedding of the subspace of the closed unit interval, consisting of the two points 0 and 1, into the closed unit interval.

5. Certain Concrete Categories as Injective Objects

In section 2. we have seen that in various concrete categories the injective objects are frequently characterized as objects that have particular nice 'intrinsic' properties in their own right, and that these properties are often related to a natural notion of completeness in the categories in question. In this section we will look at concrete categories as objects themselves. Since they are usually large, they cannot be considered as objects in categories, but rather as objects in suitable quasicategories. Certain nice concrete categories can be characterized as injectives in these settings. As in the previous cases, injectivity usually describes a certain kind of completeness. We give characterizations of the essential embeddings as well. Injective hulls can usually be constructed in some higher universe. In order that they be injective hulls in the quasicategories considered, certain smallness conditions turn out to be both necessary and sufficient.

5.1 Definition.

1. A concrete category over a base category **X** is a pair (**A**,U) where **A** is a category and U:**A** ⟶**X** is a faithful amnestic functor.
2. A concrete functor F between concrete categories over **X** is a functor that commutes with the corresponding underlying functors.
3. A structured source in a concrete category (**A**,U) is a pair (X,S), where X is an **X**-object and S is a class of pairs (a,A) each consisting of an **A**-object A and an **X**-morphism a:X ⟶UA.
4. A source (B,S) in **A** is called U-initial iff for any **A**-object C, and and for any **X**-morphism h:UC ⟶UB the following equivalence holds:

   h:C ⟶B is an **A**-morphism if and only if
   for all (a,A) ε S, ah : C ⟶A is an **A**-morphism.
5. A concrete category is called topological (or initially-complete) provided that every structured source in (**A**,U) can be lifted to a initial source in **A**.
6. An extension of a concrete category over **X** is a full concrete embedding.
7. An extension E:**A** ⟶**B** is called initially-dense iff each **B**-object is the domain of the initial lift of some structured source in **A**. The dual notion is finally-dense.

5.2 Theorem. ([17], [12], [23])

If **X** is a category and **CAT(X)** is the quasicategory whose objects are the small-fibred concrete categories over **X** and whose morphisms are the concrete functors over **X**, then the following hold in **CAT(X)**:

1. an object is injective iff it is a topological category over **X**.
2. an extension is essential iff it is finally dense and initially dense.
3. injective hulls are the <u>topological</u> <u>hulls</u> (=small-fibred <u>MacNeille</u> <u>completions</u>).

For **X**=**1** these results immediately reduce to those of Banaschewski and Bruns [5] for partially-ordered sets.

The property of being a topological category is quite strong. Slightly more general, yet still very useful, is the notion of M-topological categories, defined below. The next result generalizes Theorem 5.2. (When M is the collection of all sources in **X** it coincides with Theorem 5.2.)

5.3 Definition.

1. If E is a class of morphisms and M is a collection of sources in a category **X**, then **X** is called an (E,M)-<u>category</u> provided that:
   a) every source in **X** has a factorization with first factor in E and second factor in M.
   b) **X** has the (unique) diagonal fill-in property with respect to morphisms in E and sources in M.
2. A concrete category (**A**,U) is called M-<u>topological</u> (or M-<u>initially-complete</u>) provided that every structured source in (**A**,U) that belongs to M can be lifted to a U-initial source in **A**.
3. An extension E:(**A**,U) $\longrightarrow$(**B**,V) is called M-<u>dense</u> iff for each **B**-object B there is a **B**-source $(b_i:B \longrightarrow EA_i)_I$ where each A_i is an **A**-object, and the source $(Vb_i:VB \longrightarrow UA_i)$ belongs to M.

5.4 Theorem. ([10])

If **X** is a (E,M)-category and **CAT(X)** is the quasicategory whose objects are the small-fibred concrete categories over **X** and whose morphisms are the concrete functors over **X**, and if Q is the collection of all M-dense extensions, then the following hold in **CAT(X)**:

1. an object is Q-injective iff it is an M-topological category over **X**.

2. an M-dense extension is Q-essential iff it is finally dense and initially dense.
3. Q-injective hulls are the <u>M-topological hulls</u>.

It is well known that topological categories have very nice completeness properties and that they lift nearly all of the convenient properties possessed by the base category. One exception to this rule is the fact that cartesian closedness of the base category (i.e., the existence of an appropriate exponential structure) need not be inherited by topological categories over it. However, we do have a complete analogue to the above theorem for an arbitrary cartesian closed base category **X**, and in this case cartesian closedness is inherited by the completion.

5.5 Definition.

1. A category **A** is called <u>cartesian closed</u> provided that it has finite products and for each **A**-object A, the endofunctor $A \times \_ : \mathbf{A} \longrightarrow \mathbf{A}$ has a right adjoint, usually denoted as exponentiation $(\_)^A : \mathbf{A} \longrightarrow \mathbf{A}$.
2. A concrete category $(\mathbf{A}, U)$ is called <u>concretely cartesian closed</u> provided that **A** is cartesian closed and U preserves the cartesian structure, i.e., it preserves finite products, exponentiation, and evaluation.
3. An extension $E:(\mathbf{A},U) \longrightarrow (\mathbf{B},V)$ is called <u>cartesian dense</u> if and only if $f:VB' \longrightarrow VB$ is a **B**-morphism provided that for any pair (P,Q) of **A**-objects and any **B**-morphism $g : P \times B \longrightarrow Q$, the composite $g(id_P \times f) : P \times B' \longrightarrow Q$ is a **B**-morphism.

5.6 Theorem. ([18])

If **X** is cartesian closed and $\mathbf{CAT}_p(\mathbf{X})$ is the quasicategory whose objects are the small fibred concrete categories over **X** with finite concrete products and whose morphisms are the concrete functors over **X** that preserve these products, then the following hold in $\mathbf{CAT}_p(\mathbf{X})$:

1. an object is injective iff it is a concretely cartesian closed topological category.
2. an extension is essential iff it is finally dense and cartesian dense.
3. injective hulls are the <u>concrete cartesian closed topological hulls</u>.

For X=**1** these results immediately reduce to the familiar ones for semilattices obtained by Bruns and Lakser [13] and Horn and Kimura [20].

We conclude with results of a more 'algebraic' nature.

5.7 Definition.

A concrete category (**A**,U) over a (regular epi, mono-source)-category **X** is called:

1. regular provided that U is right adjoint and creates (regular epi, mono-source)-factorizations.
2. varietal provided that it is regular and U reflects congruence relations.

5.8 Theorem. ([9], [11])

If **X** is a (regular epi, mono-source)-category with congruence relations and regular projectives and $\mathbf{CAT}_r(\mathbf{X})$ is the quasicategory whose objects are the regular concrete categories over **X** and whose morphisms are the concrete functors over **X**, and if Q is the collection of all (regular quotient)-dense extensions, then the following hold in $\mathbf{CAT}_r(\mathbf{X})$:

1. an object is Q-injective iff it is a varietal concrete category over **X**.
2. an extension is Q-essential iff it is (regular quotient)-dense.
3. injective hulls are the varietal hulls.

References:

[1] N. Aronszajn and P. Panitchpakdi, Extension of uniformly continuous transformations and hyperconvex metric spaces, Pacific J. Math. 6 (1956), 405-439.

[2] R. Baer, Abelian groups that are direct summands of every containing abelian group, Bull. Amer. Math. Soc. 46 (1940), 800-806.

[3] B. Banaschewski, Projective covers in categories of topological spaces and topological algebras, General Topology and Its Relations to Modern Analysis and Algebra (Proc. Kanpur Topological Conf. 1968), Academia Prague, 1971, 63-91.

[4] B. Banaschewski, Essential extensions of T_0-spaces, Gen. Top. Appl. 7 (1977), 233-246.

[5] B. Banaschewski and G. Brüns, Categorical characterization of the MacNeille completion, Arch. Math. 18 (1967), 369-377.

[6] B. Banaschewski and G. Bruns, Injective hulls in the category of distributive lattices, J. Reine Angew. 232 (1968), 102-109.

[7] R. Balbes, Projective and injective distributive lattices, Pacific J. Math. 21 (1967), 405-420.

[8] R. Balbes and A. Horn, Injective and projective Heyting algebras, Trans. Amer. Math Soc. 148 (1970), 549-559.

[9] H. Bargenda, Varietal and regular hulls as injective hulls of semi-regular functors, Preprint.

[10] H. Bargenda (**E**,**M**)-topological hulls as injective hulls, Preprint.

[11] H. Bargenda and G. Richter, Varietal hulls of functors, Quaestiones. Math. 4 (1980/81) 121-158.

[12] G.C.L. Brummer and R.-E. Hoffmann, An external characterization of topological functors, Proc. Internat. Conf. Categorical Topology (Mannheim 1975), Lecture Notes in Math., vol. 540, Springer-Verlag, Berlin and New York, 1976, 136-151.

[13] G. Bruns and H. Lakser, Injective hulls of semilattices, Canad. Math. Bull. 13 (1970), 115-118.

[14] H.B. Cohen, Injective envelopes of Banach spaces, Bull. Amer. Math. Soc. 70 (1969), 723-726.

[15] B. Eckmann and A. Schopf, Ueber injektive Moduln, Arch. d. Math. 9 (1953), 75-78.

[16] P. Halmos, Injective and projective Boolean algebras. Proc. Symposia on Pure Math. 2 (1961), 114-122.

[17] H. Herrlich, Initial Completions, Math. Z. 150 (1976), 101-110.

[18] H. Herrlich and G.E. Strecker, Cartesian closed topological hulls as injective hulls. Preprint.

[19] R.-E. Hoffmann, Essential extensions of T_1-spaces. Canad. Math. Bull. 24 (1981), 237-240.

[20] A. Horn and N. Kimura, The category of semilattices, Algebra Universalis 1 (1971), 26-38.

[21] J. Isbell, Six theorems about injective metric spaces, Comment. Math. Helv. 39 (1964), 65-76.

[22] J.-M. Maranda, Injective structures, Trans. Amer Math Soc. 110 (1964), 98-135.

[23] H.-E. Porst, Characterizations of Mac Neille completions and topological functors, Bull. Austral. Math. Soc. 18 (1978), 201-210.

[24] H.-E. Porst, Characterization of injective envelopes, Cahiers Top. Geom. Diff. 22 (1981), 399-406.

[25] D. Scott, Continuous lattices, Toposes, Algebraic Geometry and Logic, Lecture Notes in Math., vol. 274, Springer-Verlag, Berlin and New York, 1972, 97-136.

[26] R. Sikorski, A theorem on extension of homomorphisms, Ann. Soc. Pol. Math. 21 (1948), 332-335.

[27] R. Sikorski, Boolean Algebras, Springer Verlag, Berlin, 1960.

[28] O. Wyler, Injective spaces and essential extensions in TOP, Gen. Top. Appl. 7 (1977), 247-249.

Fixed points in process algebras with internal actions*

(Preliminary Note)

David B. Benson
Department of Computer Science
Washington State University
Pullman, WA 99164-1210

Jerzy Tiuryn
Instittue of Mathematics
University of Warsaw
00-901 Warsaw, PKIN 9p
Poland

Algebra of communicating processes with internal actions has been introduced in [1] by a set of axioms ACP_τ. It can be viewed as an algebraic (i.e. equational) reformulation of Milner's ideas in CCS [3]. In particular, ACP_τ contains the three Milner τ-laws (T1, T2, T3 in the table below.)

The language for this formalism consists of

the constants: $a \in A$, where A is the set of atoms, it includes two particular constants: δ (deadlock), τ (internal action).
binary operations: + (alternative compostion), $\cdot$ (sequential composition), $\|$ (parallel composition, or merge), $⌊\!⌊$ (left merge), $|$ (communication merge).
unary operations: ∂_H (encapsulation), τ_I (abstraction).

The axioms for ACP_τ are given in the table, taken from [1].

The present development of this theory enables one to study only finite processes. The presence of internal action τ causes serious difficulties in extending the algebraic calculus to infinite processes (cf. 4.3 in [1]). In particular it is not clear how to solve fixed point equations since there are already nontrivial fixed point equations with solutions being finite processes. We believe that the first step towards the extension to infinite processes should consist in a thorough analysis of fixed-points, existence of which is guaranteed by the axioms ACP_τ, i.e. in all models of ACP_τ. In this note, which is a preliminary report of on-going research, we provide this kind of analysis for semi-

*Research supported in part by NSF grant DCR-8402305.

ACP_τ

$x + y = y + x$	A1	$x\tau = x$	T1
$x + (y + z) = (x + y) + z$	A2	$\tau x + x = \tau x$	T2
$x + x = x$	A3	$a(\tau x + y) = a(\tau x + y) + ax$	T3
$(x + y)z = xz + yz$	A4		
$(xy)z = x(yz)$	A5		
$x + \delta = x$	A6		
$\delta x = \delta$	A7		
$a \mid b = b \mid a$	C1		
$(a \mid b) \mid c = a \mid (b \mid c)$	C2		
$\delta \mid a = \delta$	C3		
$x \parallel y = x \lfloor\!\lfloor y + y \lfloor\!\lfloor x + x \mid y$	CM1		
$a \lfloor\!\lfloor x = ax$	CM2	$\tau \lfloor\!\lfloor x = \tau x$	TM1
$(ax) \lfloor\!\lfloor y = a(x \parallel y)$	CM3	$(\tau x) \lfloor\!\lfloor y = \tau(x \parallel y)$	TM2
$(x + y) \lfloor\!\lfloor z = x \lfloor\!\lfloor z + y \lfloor\!\lfloor z$	CM4	$\tau \mid x = \delta$	TC1
$(ax) \mid b = (a \mid b)x$	CM5	$x \mid \tau = \delta$	TC2
$a \mid (bx) = (a \mid b)x$	CM6	$(\tau x) \mid y = x \mid y$	TC3
$(ax) \mid (by) = (a \mid b)(x \parallel y)$	CM7	$x \mid (\tau y) = x \mid y$	TC4
$(x + y) \mid z = x \mid z + y \mid z$	CM8		
$x \mid (y + z) = x \mid y + x \mid z$	CM9		
		$\partial_H(\tau) = \tau$	DT
		$\tau_I(\tau) = \tau$	TI1
$\partial_H(a) = a$ if $a \notin H$	D1	$\tau_I(a) = a$ if $a \notin I$	TI2
$\partial_H(a) = \delta$ if $a \in H$	D2	$\tau_I(a) = \tau$ if $a \in I$	TI3
$\partial_H(x + y) = \partial_H(x) + \partial_H(y)$	D3	$\tau_I(x + y) = \tau_I(x) + \tau_I(y)$	TI4
$\partial_H(xy) = \partial_H(x) \cdot \partial_H(y)$	D4	$\tau_I(xy) = \tau_I(x) \cdot \tau_I(y)$	TI5

linear polynomials (this notion is to be explained later). As a side product of our results we obtain a justification for Koomen's fair abstraction rule which was used in [2] for verification of the Alternating Bit Protocol (the latter is clearly an infinite process).

Let $A_\omega[x]$ denote the set of all terms having at most one variable x and built up from the constants, A, and the two operation symbols + and $\cdot$. Let $A_\omega \subseteq A_\omega[x]$ be the subset of all variable-free terms.

The set LS of <u>left simple terms</u> is defined as the least subset of $A^\omega[x]$ subject to the following conditions:

(1) $A_\omega \subseteq LS$,

(2) If $q \varepsilon A_\omega[x]$, then $xq \varepsilon LS$,

(3) If $p_1, p_2 \varepsilon LS$, then $p_1 + p_2 \varepsilon LS$ and $\tau p_1 \varepsilon LS$.

The following result justifies interest in LS.

<u>Proposition 1</u>

Let $p \varepsilon A_\omega[x]$. If $ACP_\tau \models \exists x(p(x)=x)$, then there exists $q \varepsilon LS$ such that $ACP_\tau \models p = q$.

In order to state the main results of this note we need two more notions. Let p be a left-simple term. The set RM_p of <u>right-multipliers</u> of p and the set C_p <u>constants</u> of p are defined inductively as follows.

- If p is of the form $c_1 \cdot c_2$ or a, for some $c_1, c_2 \varepsilon A_\omega$, $c_1 \neq \tau$, $a \varepsilon A$, then $RM_p = \emptyset$, $C_p = \{p\}$.
- If p is x, then $RM_p = \emptyset$, $C_p = \emptyset$.
- If p is of the form $x \cdot q$, for some $q \varepsilon A_\omega[x]$, then $RM_p = \{q\}$, $C_p = \emptyset$.
- $RM_{p_1+p_2} = RM_{p_1} \cup RM_{p_2}$, $C_{p_1+p_2} = C_{p_1} \cup C_{p_2}$.
- $RM_{\tau \cdot p} = RM_p$, $C_{\tau \cdot p} = C_p$.

Our next result provides a complete description of all fixed points of linear terms. This result also justifies the aforementioned Koomen's fair abstraction rule of [2].

<u>Theorem 1</u> Let $p \varepsilon LS$ be such that $RM_p \subseteq \{\tau\}$ (i.e. p is linear) and assume that p can be presented as $\tau p_1 + p_2$, such that x occurs in p_1. Then the following is a theorem of ACP_τ:

$$\forall x\ [x = p(x) \text{ iff } \exists y\colon x = \tau(\Sigma(c\colon c \varepsilon C_p) + y)]$$

Then Koomen's rule can be roughly explained as choosing the "simplest" solution of $x = p(x)$, i.e. the one with $y = \delta$.

If we start with δ and τ and close it under + and $\cdot$ then we end up (in every model of ACP_τ) in the set $T = \{\delta, \tau, \tau+\delta, \tau\delta, \tau + \tau\delta\}$. Call $p \in LS$ a semilinear term if $RM_p \subseteq T$. Our next result characterizes fixed points of all semilinear terms.

Theorem 2 Let p be semilinear. Then,

$$ACP_\tau \models p^6 = p^7,$$

i.e. $\forall x[x = p(x)$ iff $\exists y\ x = p^6(y))]$.

We strongly believe that the exponent in Theorem 2 is attained. We have written a computer program which incorporates laws A1-7, T1 and T2, all that are required here. The program demonstrates distinct powers p^i, $1 \le i \le 6$, for

$$p = \tau(a + x + x\delta + x(\tau + \tau\delta)) + \tau x$$

where a is an atom other than τ or δ. The example uses the following notation:

T for τ

d for δ

r for $(\tau + \tau\delta)$

Example

polynomial: T(x)+T(a+x+xd+xr)

iteration 1:

P1: T(x)+T(a+x+xd+xr)
RM1: T(ad+xd)+T(xd)
RM2: T(ar+xr+xd)+T(xr)

iteration 2:

P2: T(P1)+T(T(ar+xr+xd)+T(xr)+T(ad+xd)+T(xd)+T(x)
+T(a+x+xd+xr))
RM3: T(RM1)
RM4: T(T(ar+xr+xd)+T(xr)+T(ad+xd)+T(xd))+T(RM2)

iteration 3:

P3: T(P2)+T(T(T(ar+xr+xd)+T(xr)+T(ad+xd)+T(xd))
+T(RM2)+RM3+T(P1)+T(T(ar+xr+xd)+T(xr)+T(ad+xd)
+T(xd)+T(x)+T(a+x+xd+xr)))
RM5: T(T(T(ar+xr+xd)+T(xr)+T(ad+xd)+T(xd))+T(RM2)+RM3)
+T(RM4)

iteration 4:

P4: T(P3)+T(T(T(T(ar+xr+xd)+T(xr)+T(ad+xd)+T(xd))
+T(RM2)+RM3)+T(RM4)+T(P2)+T(T(T(ar+xr+xd)+T(xr)
+T(ad+xd)+T(xd))+T(RM2)+RM3+T(P1)+T(T(ar+xr+xd)
+T(xr)+T(ad+xd)+T(xd)+T(x)+T(a+x+xd+xr))))
RM6: T(RM5)

iteration 5:

P5: T(P4)+T(RM6+T(P3)+T(T(T(T(ar+xr+xd)+T(xr)+T(ad+xd)
+T(xd))+T(RM2)+RM3)+T(RM4)+T(P2)+T(T(T(ar+xr+xd)
+T(xr)+T(ad+xd)+T(xd))+T(RM2)+RM3+T(P1)
+T(T(ar+xr+xd)+T(xr)+T(ad+xd)+T(xd)+T(x)
+T(a+x+xd+xr)))))

iteration 6:

P6: T(P5)

iteration 7:

P6

For linear terms, in which $RM_p \subseteq \{\tau\}$, we can get a smaller exponent.

Theorem 3 Let p be linear. Then

$$ACP_\tau \models p^2 = p^3$$

References

[1] Bergstra, J.A. and J.W. Klop, "Algebra of communicating Processes," Research Report, Centrum voor Wiskunde en Informatica, Amsterdam, 1984.

[2] Bergstra, J.A. and J.W. Klop, "Verification of an alternating bit protocol by means of process algebra," Research Report, Centrum voor Wiskunde en Informatica, Amsterdam, 1984

[3] Milner, R., "A calculus for communicating systems," Springer-Verlag, LNCS 92, 1980.

A FULLY ABSTRACT SEMANTICS AND A PROOF SYSTEM FOR AN ALGOL-LIKE LANGUAGE WITH SHARING

Stephen D. Brookes
Computer Science Department
Carnegie-Mellon University
Pittsburgh
Pennsylvania 15213

0. Abstract.

In this paper we discuss the semantics of a simple block-structured programming language which allows *sharing* or *aliasing*. Sharing, which arises naturally in procedural languages which permit certain forms of parameter passing, has typically been regarded as problematical for the semantic treatment of a language. Difficulties have been encountered in both denotational and axiomatic treatments of sharing in the literature. Nevertheless, we find that it is possible to define a clean and elegant formal semantics for sharing. The key to our success is the choice of semantic model; we show that conventional approaches based on *locations* are less than satisfactory for the purposes of reasoning about partial correctness, and that in a well defined sense locations are unnecessary.

We begin by defining a denotational semantics for our programming language. The semantic model is not based on locations, but instead uses an abstract *sharing relation* on identifiers to represent the notion of aliasing, and uses an abstract state with a stack-like structure to capture the semantics of blocks and accurately model the scope rules. The semantics is shown to be *fully abstract* with respect to partial correctness properties, in contrast to conventional location-based models. This means that the semantics identifies terms if and only if they induce identical partial correctness behaviour in all program contexts. This property usually fails for location-based semantics because in such models it is possible to distinguish between terms on the basis of their effect on individual locations, which has no bearing on partial correctness.

We believe that axiomatic reasoning about program behaviour should be based directly on a semantic model specifically tailored for that purpose; full abstraction with respect to an appropriate behavioural notion is a formal criterion against which to judge the suitability of a semantics. The structure of a semantic model should be used directly to suggest the structure of an assertion language for expressing program properties. With this in mind, we build a Hoare-style (syntax-directed) proof system for partial correctness properties of our programming language, and we prove soundness and relative completeness of this system. The proof system is built up in a hierarchical manner which reflects the syntactic and semantic structure of the programming language. We first design a proof system for declarations, and then use it in building proof rules for commands. We claim that our proof rules are conceptually simpler to understand than other rules proposed in the literature for aliasing, without losing any expressive power. We show, for example, that it is possible to define a "generic" inference rule for blocks which is uniformly applicable to blocks headed by different forms of declaration. The important point here is that, unlike most of the proof systems for these constructs in the literature, we do not have to design a separate rule for blocks for each possible form of declaration. This results in greater flexibility and adaptability in our proof system. We demonstrate that some well known rules from the literature for blocks can be derived in our system.

1. Introduction.

To set the scene, here is a brief description of the current state of conventional denotational semantics as applied to imperative languages. Most of the published attempts at describing a semantics for block-structured languages have involved fairly complicated semantic structures intended to model the storage book-keeping which seems to be necessary when maintaining the proper sharing relationships. The reader is referred to [8,19,30] for example. Usually, following [17,31], a semantics for such a language treats as logically separate objects the *environment* and the *store*. The environment is most commonly thought of as a function from identifiers to *locations*; and the store specifies a *contents* function from locations to values, as well as an *area* function indicating the usage status of all locations. Conventionally, locations represent an abstraction of the notion of addresses in memory, and the store gives the current contents and usage status of these locations. The environment provides the association of identifiers with locations, so that the value of an expression or the effect of a command will depend in general on both the environment and the store. The splitting of "state" into the two components *environment* and *store* has been the standard method of treating aliasing; two identifiers which share are then bound in the environment to the same location.

Most commonly, the semantics of expressions is provided as a function from expressions to environments and stores and then to values; the domain of values typically contains (at least) integers and truth values. The semantics of a command, relative to an environment, is modelled as a *store transformation*. Within this type of semantic framework, treatments of many ALGOL-like languages have been given, notably [19,21,30]. The explicit separation of state into store and environment does indeed allow a proper treatment to be given of storage allocation and sharing. However, by mentioning locations explicitly in the semantics, these treatments inevitably allow too many semantic distinctions between program fragments. Using this type of semantics it is possible to distinguish between terms which have identical effects on the *values* of all program identifiers but differ in their effects on the store. For instance, the declaration

$$\mathbf{new}\ x = 0; \mathbf{new}\ y = 1$$

is conventionally described as binding x to the "first" available (*i.e.* unused) location and y to the "next" one, and this means that we are able to distinguish between the effects of this declaration and those of the permuted declaration in which the two bindings are performed in reverse order:

$$\textbf{new}\ y = 1; \textbf{new}\ x = 0.$$

Intuitively, the order of binding should have no effect on any subsequent evaluation, since the two declared identifiers get initialized to the same *values* in each case, and in each case there is the same effect on the sharing properties of identifiers: x and y do not share with any other identifiers. When we are merely concerned with the *partial correctness* properties of programs, we need to know only how the execution of a program will affect the *values* of identifiers; in other words, we need to know the *contents*, but not the *identity* of locations. Of course, we also need to know the sharing properties of identifiers, but even this need not mention locations explicitly. In such a setting, concerned solely with partial correctness, the structure of the store and the attendant details of storage allocation should be kept invisible. In this well defined sense, locations are indeed unnecessary in partial correctness semantics. Donahue [7] showed that locations were unnecessary in a semantic treatment of a language which did not permit aliasing, and we argue further that this is even true when aliasing is allowed.

At a suitably high level of abstraction, then, we do not want the storage mechanism or even the identities of individual locations to be accessible to the programmer. In other words, a reasonable partial correctness semantics should be ignorant of the particular choice of storage model on which it might be based. In this paper we will construct a semantics possessing these desirable properties. The semantic model is not location-based, but uses an abstract sharing relation on identifiers to represent aliasing, in a style somewhat reminiscent of the early work of Landin [17]. Our semantics also uses an abstract state with a stack-like structure to cope with block structure and to accurately model scope rules. Technically, our semantics will be *fully abstract* with respect to partial correctness behaviour. Full abstraction [20,25,26] guarantees that two terms of the language are semantically identical if and only if they are interchangeable in every program context. For us, this concept of full abstraction coincides with the equivalence induced by considering partial correctness behaviour. Location-based semantics typically fail to be fully abstract, because semantically distinct terms can nevertheless induce precisely the same partial correctness behaviour in all program contexts.

Of course, we might also want to be able to relate our *abstract* semantics to a more *concrete* implementation, perhaps intending to run our programs on a machine with a particular finite memory capacity and with a particular storage allocation algorithm. Although we do not give details here, it is possible to prove the correctness of a location-based implementation of our semantics.

Ever since Hoare's influential paper [14], which proposed an axiomatic basis for programming languages, many attempts have been made to extend Hoare's methods to more complicated languages. Hoare's paper gave an elegant syntax-directed proof system for an imperative language with (simple) assignment, sequential composition, conditionals, and loops, and introduced the notion of *partial correctness assertion* which has underlined the methods of axiomatic semantics. The appeal and influence of Hoare's work owes much to the syntax-directed nature of his logic and the simplicity of his assertion language.

Many authors have tried to extend Hoare's ideas to cover more complicated and powerful programming constructs, and a good survey is provided in [1]. Existing proof rules for aliasing seem to be fairly complicated in form [3,4], and many proof rules for blocks beg the question by explicitly assuming that there is no possibility of aliasing [15]. The complications are all the more evident in the case of proof rules for features such as array assignment and procedure calls (see [1,2] for example). We believe that many of the difficulties encountered when trying to find an adequate axiomatization for programming language constructs are caused not by any *inherent* complexity of the construct's semantics but by an inappropriate choice of semantic model or by an inappropriate choice of assertion language (but see Clarke [5] for examples of constructs which are inherently difficult to treat). This is particularly true for imperative languages in which storage allocation and the block discipline have persuaded semanticists that the correct level of abstraction should retain some of the details of the storage mechanism. This tends to result in axiom systems in which explicit reasoning about the identity of locations needs to be carried out, as in [13]. And it often happens that some proof rules which appear to be obviously sound are still difficult to prove correct. Apt [1] and de Bakker [2] discuss some notable examples, and Apt also makes the point that the choice of a semantics is a decisive factor for the complexity of soundness and completeness proofs. Almost every semantics used in the literature to support formal reasoning about partial correctness has been based on a location model. By choosing a more appropriate level of abstraction in our semantics we will find not only that it becomes easier to reason about the semantics of programs but that we can find a very simple and obviously sound Hoare-style proof system for the language. The semantics will guide us to a choice of assertion language and proof rules. Locations will not be needed as part of the assertion language, because they are not used in the semantics.

Although we only consider a very simple programming language with a small number of program constructs, we plan to extend our methods (with suitable modifications in the choice of semantic model) to much more powerful languages including various other features. We have more to say about these extensions in the conclusions of the paper. By focussing on a small number of features and their interactions we aim in this paper to clarify the central issues which arise in treatments of sharing, without having to keep extracting the crucial points from a larger setting.

Outline.

The outline of the paper is as follows. We begin by introducing the syntax of our programming language, together with a few relevant syntactic definitions. An informal description of the proposed semantics is given at this stage. Next we identify some general principles behind the semantic treatment of our language, and use them to decide on an appropriate semantic model. We then give a denotational semantics for the language and use it to deduce some useful properties.

Next we define a fairly natural notion of *program behaviour* which captures precisely our intention to concentrate purely on partial correctness properties. Intuitively, two programs should have the same behaviour if they always satisfy the same set of partial correctness assertions. In making these ideas precise, we define the behaviour of a command in a program context. We define a *behavioural equivalence* relation on terms from our language, which identifies two terms if and only if they yield the same behaviour in all program contexts. We then show that our *semantics* induces precisely this relation, so that we have indeed a fully abstract semantics with respect to this notion of behaviour.

We then develop a Hoare-style axiom system for our language, and prove its soundness with respect to our semantics. The proof system is also relatively complete in the usual sense [6]. We give some examples to illustrate the use of the system, and we demonstrate that some of the proof rules for blocks in the literature can be derived in our system.

In the final section of the paper we compare our work with that of other researchers, draw some conclusions and make some suggestions for future research.

2. The Programming Language.

As usual for an imperative language, we distinguish between the following syntactic categories:

$I \in \mathbf{Ide}$	identifiers,
$E \in \mathbf{Exp}$	expressions,
$\Delta \in \mathbf{Dec}$	declarations,
$\Gamma \in \mathbf{Com}$	commands,
$\Pi \in \mathbf{Prog}$	programs.

We assume that the syntax of identifiers and expressions is given; for concreteness, identifiers will be strings of lower-case italic letters. We assume also that it is possible syntactically to determine the identity of two identifiers; we write $I_0 = I_1$ when two identifiers are identical. The syntax of expressions will be ignored; some of our assumptions will become obvious in examples. For instance, an identifier is an expression, and so is a numeral.

We assume the usual notions of *free* and *bound* occurrences of identifiers in an expression, and we write free$[\![E]\!]$ for the set of identifiers which occur free in an expression E. An expression having no free identifier occurrences is said to be *closed*.

For the syntax of declarations and commands we specify:

$$\Delta ::= \textbf{null} \mid \textbf{new}\, I = E \mid \textbf{alias}\, I_0 = I_1 \mid \Delta_0; \Delta_1$$
$$\Gamma ::= \textbf{skip} \mid I{:=}E \mid \Gamma_0; \Gamma_1 \mid \textbf{begin}\, \Delta; \Gamma\, \textbf{end}.$$

Informally, we may explain the semantics of these constructs as follows.

Declarations. The purpose of a declaration is to introduce a new set of bindings:

- The **null** declaration has no effect.

- A *simple* declaration of the form

$$\textbf{new}\, I = E$$

introduces a new binding for I, with initial value the current (declaration time) value of the expression E. We refer to I as the *declared identifier*.

- A *sharing* declaration of the form

$$\textbf{alias}\, I_0 = I_1$$

introduces a new binding for I_0: the effect of the declaration is to make I_0 *share* with I_1, so that any assignment to I_0 within the scope of this declaration will also affect the value of I_1 (and conversely, an assignment to I_1 within this scope will also update I_0). The declaration also initializes the value of I_0 to the current value of I_1. We refer to I_0 as the declared identifier; note that I_1 is *not* declared here (unless $I_0 = I_1$).

- A *sequential composition* of declarations

$$\Delta_0; \Delta_1$$

accumulates effects from left to right; thus, the scope of Δ_0 in this setting will include Δ_1, but not vice versa. An identifier is declared by $\Delta_0; \Delta_1$ iff either it is declared by Δ_0 or it is declared by Δ_1. If a particular identifier is declared in both Δ_0 and Δ_1 then the latter declaration has precedence.

We adopt the usual notions of free and bound identifier occurrences in declarations, and our informal description above corresponds to the static scope rules familiar in ALGOL-like languages. We refer to

$$\text{dec}[\![\Delta]\!], \quad \text{free}[\![\Delta]\!],$$

as the set of declared (or bound) identifiers and the set of free identifiers of Δ. A declaration without any free identifier occurrences will be called *closed.* For example, the declaration

$$\Delta_0 : \quad \mathbf{new}\, x = 1; \mathbf{new}\, y = x + 1$$

is closed, and clearly its effect is to initialize the new copy of x to 1 and then y to 2. We have $\text{dec}[\![\Delta_0]\!] = \{x, y\}$ and $\text{free}[\![\Delta_0]\!] = \emptyset$. On the other hand, the declaration

$$\Delta_1 : \quad \mathbf{new}\, y = x + 1; \mathbf{new}\, x = 1$$

contains a free occurrence of x, and the value it gives to y will depend on the current (declaration-time) value of this free identifier. Here we have $\text{dec}[\![\Delta_1]\!] = \{x, y\}$ and $\text{free}[\![\Delta_1]\!] = \{x\}$.

Commands. The purpose of a command is to alter the values of identifiers by computing new values for them:

- The **skip** command has no effect.

- An *assignment* $I{:=}E$ updates the value of I to the current (execution-time) value of the expression E. This also has the effect of altering the values of all identifiers which share with I.

- Sequential composition of commands is denoted by $\Gamma_0; \Gamma_1$. The intention is first to perform Γ_0 and then to perform Γ_1, so that again effects accumulate from left to right.

- Finally, a *block*

$$\mathbf{begin}\ \Delta; \Gamma\ \mathbf{end}$$

allows the *block body* Γ to be executed within the scope of a declaration Δ. This means that the values computed within the block may be affected by the bindings introduced in the declaration; but the scope of the declaration does not extend outside the block, and these bindings are only used locally inside the block. Thus, the semantics of the block as a whole will not involve any changes in *bindings*, only changes in *values* as the result of assignments inside the block.

Examples.

1. The command $x{:=}x + 1; y{:=}y + 1$ first increases the value of all identifiers which share with x, and then increases the value of all identifiers which share with y; if x and y share, this of course will add 2 to the value of both x and y.

2. The block command

$$\begin{array}{l}\textbf{begin}\\ \quad \textbf{new}\ y = 0;\\ \quad x{:=}x + 1;\\ \quad y{:=}y + 1\\ \textbf{end}\end{array}$$

increments the value of identifiers which share with x; the assignment to the local identifier y has no effect outside of the block.

3. The block

$$\begin{array}{l}\textbf{begin}\\ \quad \textbf{alias}\ z = x;\\ \quad z{:=}z + 1;\\ \quad y{:=}y + 1\\ \textbf{end}\end{array}$$

has the same effect as the command in Example 1, because the local identifier z shares with the external identifier x. ∎

Again we use the usual syntactic notions of *free* and *bound* occurrences of identifiers in a command. We intend static scoping, as usual in an ALGOL-like language. In particular, for a block we specify

$$\text{free}[\![\textbf{begin}\ \Delta; \Gamma\ \textbf{end}]\!] = \text{free}[\![\Delta]\!] \cup (\text{free}[\![\Gamma]\!] - \text{dec}[\![\Delta]\!]).$$

Programs.

Now we give the syntax for a very simple form of program. A *program* has the following form:

$$\Pi ::= \textbf{begin}\ \Delta; \Gamma; \textbf{result}\ E\ \textbf{end},$$

where Δ is a closed declaration containing bindings for all of the free identifiers of Γ and E. In other words, a program contains no free identifier occurrences. This syntactic constraint is reasonable and is commonly imposed in practical programming languages; it will ensure that the effect of a program execution is uniquely determined. The semantics of a program will be represented by the value of the expression E after executing the declarations and command; in other words, we are interested in the *result* of executing a program. Since all of the free identifiers of E are bound in this context, we will see that there is no ambiguity about this value.

Of course, this is a particularly simple form of program; it has been chosen to correspond with a simple notion of partial correctness. The result expression can be regarded as a "post-condition" on the values of identifiers after executing a command. It should be clear how to extend the notion of program to allow (for example) sequential composition at the program level, or more than one result expression, possibly to be evaluated at different points during program execution (perhaps by adding an *output* command to the language).

3. Semantics.

Preliminaries.

We can define a semantics for our language as follows. The value of an expression may depend on the values of its free identifiers. An association of values with identifiers can be represented as a *valuation*, which is simply a function

$$\sigma : \mathbf{Ide} \rightarrow V,$$

where V is the set of expression values; for concreteness, we assume that V contains (at least) the integers and truth values, although the precise structure of this set is not crucial to our development. Remember that we are not committed to a particular expression language, except that we assume that expression evaluation does not cause side-effects.

The effect of a command will be to alter the values of some identifiers (and hence affect the values of expressions); this amounts to a change in the valuation function. Precisely which identifiers get altered will depend on the sharing relation, which should clearly be an *equivalence relation* ρ on the set of declared identifiers. The sharing relation can be modified by the execution of a declaration.

A sharing relation can be thought of as a function from identifiers to sets of identifiers:

$$\rho : \mathbf{Ide} \rightarrow \mathcal{P}(\mathbf{Ide}),$$

with its domain dom(ρ) consisting of all identifiers I such that $\rho(I) \neq \emptyset$. Thus, the conditions for ρ to be an equivalence relation on its domain are simply:

$$\begin{array}{ll} I \in \mathrm{dom}(\rho) \Rightarrow I \in \rho(I), & \text{(reflexivity)} \\ I_1 \in \rho(I_0) \Rightarrow I_0 \in \rho(I_1), & \text{(symmetry)} \\ I_1 \in \rho(I_0) \;\&\; I_2 \in \rho(I_1) \Rightarrow I_2 \in \rho(I_0). & \text{(transitivity)} \end{array}$$

But it must be the case that identifiers in the same sharing class have the same value. It is therefore more appropriate to think of a pair $\langle \rho, \sigma \rangle$ combining a sharing relation and a valuation, with the following *consistency* condition:

$$I_1 \in \rho(I_0) \Rightarrow \sigma(I_1) = \sigma(I_0). \qquad \text{(consistency)}$$

We will be particularly concerned with sharing relations in which there are only finitely many sharing classes, and in which all sharing classes are finite sets, since these correspond precisely to the situations which arise during program execution. These are simply the sharing relations with a finite domain, and we refer to them as *finitary* relations. We will refer to a combination $\langle \rho, \sigma \rangle$ of this type, satisfying these conditions, as a *frame*. We let R be the set of all finitary equivalence relations on **Ide** and Σ be the set of all valuations. We use F for the set of all frames, and let f range over F. For convenience, when we write f for a frame, it is implicit that ρ and σ are the components, and similarly f' has components ρ' and σ'; this convention also extends to subscripted terms f_i.

In order to cope properly with the block structure of our programming language, we will need to be able to distinguish the "local" frame used inside a block from the "global" frame in force outside of the block; this will allow us to treat properly a "hole in scope" created for a local identifier whose scope is delimited by the block but for which there is a corresponding global identifier. When we enter a block, a new frame should be created to represent the effect of the declaration which is executed at the head of the block; this new frame is in a sense an extension of the previous frame, and an assignment to an identifier inside the block will in general have an effect on the external frame as well as the local frame. When the block is exited, the original frame structure should be restored, although of course some alterations may have been made in the valuation. As is well known for statically scoped languages such as ours, the block discipline can be modelled or implemented with *stacks*. In our case, we can cope by introducing a special abstract form of stack, built up from frames of the type we have already introduced. We also need to maintain *links* between the successive levels of a stack, to keep track of the dependencies between identifiers at different levels; specifically, this will allow us to handle "holes in scope" properly. A link can be represented as function from identifiers to sets of identifiers satisfying some intuitive conditions. We introduce the notation

$$\tau \in T = \mathbf{Ide} \to \mathcal{P}(\mathbf{Ide}) \qquad \text{links},$$

and we use as stacks structures of the form

$$\langle \langle \rho_n, \sigma_n \rangle, \tau_n, \langle \rho_{n-1}, \sigma_{n-1} \rangle, \ldots, \tau_1, \langle \rho_0, \sigma_0 \rangle \rangle, \qquad (n \geq 0),$$

where each link τ_k is a relation on identifiers. The intention is that for an identifier I, the image set $\tau_k(I)$ should be the set of identifiers in the $(k-1)^{\text{th}}$ frame whose values (in that frame) are affected by an assignment to I in the kth frame. The τ functions thus make explicit the dependencies between identifiers declared at various block levels in a program. In addition to the consistency condition which we imposed on a single frame, we also require the following *link consistency* properties (for each k), which state essentially that each link is a partial 1–1 function between the sharing classes in the corresponding frames, and that the values of linked identifiers in different frames are the same:

$$\begin{aligned}
&\forall I' \in \rho_k(I).(\tau_k(I) = \tau_k(I')), && \text{(link consistency)}\\
&\tau_k(I) \cap \tau_k(I') \neq \emptyset \Rightarrow \rho_k(I) = \rho_k(I'),\\
&\forall I' \in \tau_k(I).(\tau_k(I) = \rho_{k-1}(I')),\\
&\forall I' \in \tau_k(I).(\sigma_k(I) = \sigma_{k-1}(I')).
\end{aligned}$$

In fact, a link will map all members of a sharing class in one frame either to the empty set, indicating that these identifiers do not correspond to any identifiers in the next frame, or to an entire sharing class of the next frame. The intuitions behind these constraints should be clear. Note that the sharing relation ρ provides a link between a frame $\langle\rho, \sigma\rangle$ and itself, the link consistency properties collapsing in this case to the frame consistency conditions described earlier. In addition, it is easy to see that whenever τ links f to f' and τ' links f' to f^*, then the composition $\tau' \circ \tau$ links f to f^*.

A stack in which all of these conditions is satisfied (so that all of its frames and links are consistent) will be called a *state*, and we will use S to stand for the set of states, with typical member s. We use analogues of the usual stack operations *push*, *unpush*, *pop*:

- push$(f, \tau)s$ produces a stack with a new top and a corresponding new top link;
- unpush(s) removes the top frame and its link, and returns the remaining stack;
- pop(s) produces the top frame (without its link).

Standard properties of these operations will be assumed; for instance,

$$\text{unpush}(\text{push}(f, \tau)(s)) = s.$$

We define some useful operations on frames and stacks. First, if we wish to alter the value of an identifier, we must also alter the values of the identifiers in its sharing class. Accordingly, we introduce the notation

$$\sigma + [X \mapsto v]$$

to denote the valuation which agrees with σ at all arguments except those in the set X, which it maps to the value v. Algebraic properties of this operation are fairly straightforward and will be used without proof.

In order to explain the semantics of a declaration, we need an operation which introduces a new sharing class while maintaining the conditions for an equivalence relation. We therefore introduce the notation

$$\rho + [X]$$

to denote the relation ρ' given by:

$$\begin{aligned}\rho'(x) &= X, && \text{if } x \in X,\\ &= \rho(x) - X && \text{otherwise.}\end{aligned}$$

It is easy to verify that if ρ is an equivalence relation then so is $\rho + [X]$.

It is also convenient to combine these two operations, giving a function

$$\text{alter} : \mathcal{P}(\mathbf{Ide}) \times V \to [F \to F]$$

which alters the sharing relation and updates the frame accordingly to maintain consistency. The definition is:

$$\text{alter}(X, v)\langle\rho, \sigma\rangle = \langle\rho + [X], \sigma + [X \mapsto v]\rangle.$$

It is straightforward to verify that if the frame $\langle\rho, \sigma\rangle$ is consistent then so is $\text{alter}(X, v)\langle\rho, \sigma\rangle$.

We may also extend the updating operations to a stack, in the obvious way, so that the required consistency conditions are maintained and so that updates are propagated through the links. If s is the stack

$$s = \langle\langle\rho_n, \sigma_n\rangle, \tau_n, \ldots, \tau_1, \langle\rho_0, \sigma_0\rangle\rangle,$$

then we define $\text{update}(I, v)s$ to be the stack arising from s by altering the valuations at all relevant levels, beginning at the top by setting the value of (the sharing class of) I to v, and then updating in a similar way the values at the next level of all identifiers linked to I; this operation applies at all levels of the stack which are accessible through the links from I. Thus,

$$\text{update}(I, v)(s) = \langle\langle\rho_n, \sigma'_n\rangle, \tau_n, \ldots, \tau_1, \langle\rho_0, \sigma'_0\rangle\rangle,$$

where for each i,

$$\sigma'_i = \sigma_i + [X_i \mapsto v],$$

with the sets X_i given by

$$\begin{aligned}X_n &= \rho_n(I),\\ X_{i-1} &= \tau_i(X_i) = \bigcup\{\, \tau_i(I') \mid I' \in X_i \,\}.\end{aligned}$$

Note that this stack updating operation does not affect the sharing relations or links of the stack, and that it preserves consistency in all frames.

A Denotational Semantics.

We are now ready to give the semantics. As usual for a denotational presentation, the definitions follow the syntax of the language; there is one semantic clause for each construct, the meaning of a compound term being built up from the meanings of its parts.

Identifiers. The meaning of identifiers is supplied explicitly by a frame, which gives the sharing class and the value of each identifier. In a frame $f = \langle \rho, \sigma \rangle$, the *sharing class* of I is $\rho(I)$; the *value* of I is $\sigma(I)$.

Expressions. As we remarked earlier, the semantics of expressions is taken for granted; it is assumed that expressions do not cause side-effects, so that the only important semantic feature of an expression is its *value*. We assume that all expressions, once supplied with values for their free identifiers, denote elements of a set V. The semantic function will be denoted

$$\mathcal{E} : \mathbf{Exp} \to [\Sigma \to V].$$

For any expression E and any valuation σ we refer to $\mathcal{E}[\![E]\!]\sigma$ as the value of E in σ. The only clause of importance at this point is the one for identifiers. We assume that the value of an identifier is supplied by the valuation:

$$\mathcal{E}[\![I]\!]\sigma = \sigma(I).$$

We also assume that the value denoted by an expression depends only on the values of its free identifiers. This is a standard property of statically scoped expression languages. To specify this property formally we need the notion of *agreement*. We say that two valuations σ and σ' agree on an identifier I if $\sigma(I) = \sigma'(I)$. This extends in the obvious elementwise way to agreement on a set of identifiers. Our development will depend on the following:

Assumption 1. If two valuations σ and σ' agree on all free identifiers of an expression E, then

$$\mathcal{E}[\![E]\!]\sigma = \mathcal{E}[\![E]\!]\sigma'. \quad \blacksquare$$

Corollary. If an expression E is closed its value is independent of the valuation. ∎

The only important property of the set V on which our results will depend is that every element of this set is indeed the value of some expression in **Exp**. Thus:

Assumption 2. For all $v \in V$, there exists a (closed) expression E_v with value v: for all σ,

$$\mathcal{E}[\![E_v]\!]\sigma = v. \quad \blacksquare$$

It would be straightforward to adapt our arguments to a particular expression language, provided the semantics satisfies the Assumptions above. By isolating the important semantic properties of expressions in this way, without being explicit about the syntax of expressions, we are able to prove some general results which are applicable to a wide variety of expression languages.

Declarations. A declaration produces a new frame, together with a linking function which shows the relationship between identifiers in the new (local) frame and the old (global) frame. We define a semantic function

$$\mathcal{D} : \mathbf{Dec} \rightarrow [F \rightarrow (F \times T)],$$

of corresponding type. If f is an initial frame, then $\mathcal{D}[\![\Delta]\!]f$ will define a new frame and a link. In fact, it is convenient to factor this semantic function into components by first defining

$$\mathcal{F} : \mathbf{Dec} \rightarrow [F \rightarrow F]$$

with the following semantic clauses:

$$\begin{aligned}
\mathcal{F}[\![\mathbf{null}]\!]f &= f \\
\mathcal{F}[\![\mathbf{new}\, I = E]\!]f &= \text{alter}(\{I\}, \mathcal{E}[\![E]\!]\sigma)f \\
\mathcal{F}[\![\mathbf{alias}\, I_0 = I_1]\!]f &= \text{alter}(\rho(I_1) \cup \{I_0\}, \mathcal{E}[\![I_1]\!]\sigma)f \\
\mathcal{F}[\![\Delta_0; \Delta_1]\!]f &= \mathcal{F}[\![\Delta_1]\!](\mathcal{F}[\![\Delta_0]\!]f).
\end{aligned}$$

This semantic function describes the effect of a sharing relation on frames, showing how the new frame is built up from the old one. The definition of the linking semantics is straightforward. We define the semantic function $\mathcal{T}$, of type

$$\mathcal{T} : \mathbf{Dec} \rightarrow [T \rightarrow T],$$

as follows:

$$\begin{aligned}
\mathcal{T}[\![\mathbf{null}]\!]\tau &= \tau \\
\mathcal{T}[\![\mathbf{new}\, I = E]\!]\tau &= \tau + [I \mapsto \emptyset] \\
\mathcal{T}[\![\mathbf{alias}\, I_0 = I_1]\!]\tau &= \tau + [I_0 \mapsto \tau(I_1)] \\
\mathcal{T}[\![\Delta_0; \Delta_1]\!]\tau &= \mathcal{T}[\![\Delta_1]\!](\mathcal{T}[\![\Delta_0]\!]\tau).
\end{aligned}$$

This function builds the link between the old and new frames. The relationship defining $\mathcal{D}$ in terms of these semantic functions is simply:

$$\mathcal{D}[\![\Delta]\!]f = \langle \mathcal{F}[\![\Delta]\!]f, \mathcal{T}[\![\Delta]\!]\rho \rangle.$$

Thus, the old sharing relation ρ is to be used in defining the link; it is clear from the definition that an identifier declared by an *alias* form of declaration links with the sharing class of the identifier on the right-hand side of the declaration, whereas a *new* declaration is strictly local in the sense that there is no link between the declared identifier and the old sharing relation. This is achieved by linking the identifier with the empty set.

The following properties of declarations are deducible from the above definitions: that all declarations preserve the consistency and the finitary nature of frames. This shows that our semantic functions are well defined. The proofs are simple structural inductions.

Lemma 1A. For all Δ and all finitary frames f, $\mathcal{F}[\![\Delta]\!]f$ is finitary. ∎

Lemma 1B. For all Δ and all consistent frames f, $\mathcal{F}[\![\Delta]\!]f$ is consistent. ∎

Lemma 1C. For all frames $f = \langle\rho, \sigma\rangle$, $\mathcal{T}[\![\Delta]\!]\rho$ is a link from $\mathcal{F}[\![\Delta]\!]f$ to f.

Proof. Show by structural induction on Δ that if τ links f to f' then $\mathcal{T}[\![\Delta]\!]\tau$ links $\mathcal{F}[\![\Delta]\!]f$ to f'. Since ρ links $\langle\rho, \sigma\rangle$ to itself trivially, the result then follows. ∎

Note that a declaration has a purely *declarative* semantic aspect, the effect it has on the sharing relation; and an updating or *imperative* aspect, the effect it has on the value of the bound identifiers. Indeed, it will be convenient later to be able to separate these two semantic aspects of declarations. We therefore introduce the functions

$$\mathcal{R} : \mathbf{Dec} \to [R \to R],$$
$$\mathcal{S} : \mathbf{Dec} \to [\Sigma \to \Sigma],$$

defined implicitly by

$$\mathcal{F}[\![\Delta]\!]\langle\rho, \sigma\rangle = \langle\mathcal{R}[\![\Delta]\!]\rho, \mathcal{S}[\![\Delta]\!]\sigma\rangle.$$

It is easy to verify from the definition of $\mathcal{F}$ that both $\mathcal{R}$ and $\mathcal{S}$ are well defined, in the sense that the declarative effect of a declaration depends only on the sharing component of the state, and the imperative effect of a declaration depends only on the valuation. In fact, these two semantic functions could have been defined in the denotational style.

Now that we have a formal definition of the semantics of declarations, we are able to prove some interesting and intuitive properties. These properties can be conveniently separated into two classes: *Invariance* and *Influence* Properties. Invariance concerns the set of identifiers which are unaffected by a declaration. Influence Properties indicate the set of identifiers whose values or sharing classes influence the results of a declaration.

Invariance Properties. It is easy to prove that a declaration can *only* alter the value of its *bound* identifiers. This is even true for a sharing declaration. This amounts to an Invariance Property of $\mathcal{S}$. In addition, the link between an identifier which is not redeclared in the new frame and the identifiers in the old frame is simply determined by the sharing relation, as we might expect. This can be formulated as an Invariance Property for $\mathcal{T}$. Finally, a declaration may alter the sharing classes of its declared identifiers and free identifiers. This corresponds to the third of our Invariance Properties, this time for $\mathcal{R}$. The following theorem states these properties precisely.

Theorem 1. For all Δ and all frames $\langle\rho, \sigma\rangle$,

$$I \not\subseteq \mathrm{dec}[\![\Delta]\!] \Rightarrow (\mathcal{S}[\![\Delta]\!]\sigma)(I) = \sigma(I),$$
$$I \not\subseteq \mathrm{dec}[\![\Delta]\!] \Rightarrow (\mathcal{T}[\![\Delta]\!]\rho)(I) = \rho(I),$$
$$I \not\subseteq \rho(\mathrm{free}[\![\Delta]\!] \cup \mathrm{dec}[\![\Delta]\!]) \Rightarrow (\mathcal{R}[\![\Delta]\!]\rho)(I) = \rho(I).$$

Influence Properties. We extend the notion of agreement to frames and links in the obvious way. For instance, two frames agree on an identifier if their sharing relations and their valuations agree on its sharing class and value. We will write $f(I) = \langle \rho(I), \sigma(I) \rangle$ and $\langle f, \tau \rangle(I) = \langle f(I), \tau(I) \rangle$. The effects of a declaration can be determined from the sharing classes and values of its free identifiers. We express this as an influence property. If two frames agree on the *free* identifiers of Δ then the bindings introduced by Δ in these frames will be identical. More precisely, the sharing classes, values and link classes of each declared identifier are the same in the two frames. The following theorem formalizes this property. Its proof depends on Assumption 1 for expressions.

Theorem 2. For all Δ, if f and f' agree on free$[\![\Delta]\!]$ then for all $I \in$ dec$[\![\Delta]\!]$,

$$(\mathcal{D}[\![\Delta]\!]f)(I) = (\mathcal{D}[\![\Delta]\!]f')(I). \quad \blacksquare$$

Corollary. The bindings introduced by a closed declaration do not depend on the frame. If Δ is closed, then for all f and f', and all identifiers $I \in$ dec$[\![\Delta]\!]$,

$$(\mathcal{D}[\![\Delta]\!]f)(I) = (\mathcal{D}[\![\Delta]\!]f')(I). \quad \blacksquare$$

In summary, then, we can see that every declaration affects the values of only a finite set of identifiers. Moreover, the values used in these bindings depend only on the free identifiers of the declaration (again, a finite set of identifiers). And any frame arising from an initial finitary and consistent frame by some combination of declarations is itself finitary and consistent.

Commands. We are interested only in the effect a command has on the values denoted by identifiers. This effect will depend on the sharing relation. This would suggest that we define the semantics of commands as a function $\mathcal{M}$ of type

$$\mathcal{M} : \mathbf{Com} \to [R \to [\Sigma \to \Sigma]].$$

However, during the execution of a command there may be block entrances and exits, which have the effect of locally modifying and restoring the local bindings of identifiers. This effect is modelled conveniently by an abstract stack. Of course, in general during an execution of a command the stack may contain more than one frame, the precise number being determined by the depth of the nested block structure of the command. In order to specify the effect of a command execution, we will therefore specify a semantic function

$$\mathcal{C} : \mathbf{Com} \to [S \to S],$$

which gives the effect of a command on an arbitrary stack. We will be able to verify that commands do not affect the sharing relations of a state, and we will be able to recover a semantic function $\mathcal{M}$ of the above type in a simple way. Given an initial state s, the result $\mathcal{C}[\![\Gamma]\!]s$ will be a state with the same sharing structure as the original one, giving the final values of all identifiers in each frame after execution of the command. In the special case when the stack has a single frame $\langle\rho, \sigma\rangle$, the result stack has a single frame $\langle\rho, \sigma'\rangle$ in which σ' reflects the changes made by assignments in Γ. This will enable us to give an implicit definition of $\mathcal{M}$.

Where convenient we will abuse notation and write $\mathcal{E}[\![E]\!]s$ for the value of E in the (valuation of the) top frame of s. A similar convention will be adopted for $\mathcal{D}$, so that we may write $\mathcal{D}[\![\Delta]\!]s$ instead of $\mathcal{D}[\![\Delta]\!](\mathrm{top}(s))$.

The semantic clauses are:

$$\begin{aligned}\mathcal{C}[\![\mathbf{skip}]\!]s &= s,\\ \mathcal{C}[\![I{:=}E]\!]s &= \mathrm{update}(I, \mathcal{E}[\![E]\!]s)s,\\ \mathcal{C}[\![\Gamma_0;\Gamma_1]\!]s &= \mathcal{C}[\![\Gamma_1]\!](\mathcal{C}[\![\Gamma_0]\!]s),\\ \mathcal{C}[\![\mathbf{begin}\ \Delta;\Gamma\ \mathbf{end}]\!]s &= \mathrm{unpush}(\mathcal{C}[\![\Gamma]\!](\mathrm{push}(\mathcal{D}[\![\Delta]\!]s)s)).\end{aligned}$$

Note that in the clause for a block, we specify that the block body Γ is to be executed in the scope of the declaration Δ by first pushing the new frame and link created by this declaration onto the stack. By unpushing at the end of the block body's execution, we ensure that the original bindings of the identifiers declared in Δ are restored on exiting the block; this is because the scope of the new bindings introduced in Δ does not extend outside the block, and the local meanings of the declared identifiers inside the block are unrelated to their meanings outside the block. This corresponds to the usual notion of static scope.

Examples.

1. $\mathcal{C}[\![\mathbf{begin}\ \Delta; \mathbf{skip}\ \mathbf{end}]\!]s = \mathrm{unpush}(\mathrm{push}(\mathcal{D}[\![\Delta]\!]s)(s)) = s.$

2. $\mathcal{C}[\![x{:=}x+1]\!]s = \mathrm{update}(x, \sigma(x)+1)(s)$, where $\langle\rho, \sigma\rangle = \mathrm{top}(s)$. In the top frame of this stack the values of all identifiers which share with x have been increased by 1, and the same is true of the identifiers which are linked to x in lower frames. ∎

It should be clear from the definitions that executing a command maintains consistency of the state, in the following sense.

Lemma 2A. For all Γ, and all consistent states s, the state $\mathcal{C}[\![\Gamma]\!]s$ is also consistent.

Proof. By structural induction on Γ, using Lemmas 1A, 1B and 1C. ∎

The following result establishes our claim that commands do not affect the sharing structure, by which we mean the local sharing relations in each frame of the state and the links between them.

Lemma 2B. For all Γ, and all consistent states s, the states s and $\mathcal{C}[\![\Gamma]\!]s$ have identical sharing structure.

Proof. By structural induction on Γ. ∎

As a consequence of this, we may indeed define a semantic function

$$\mathcal{M} : \mathbf{Com} \to [R \to [\Sigma \to \Sigma]],$$

with the implicit definition being simply:

$$\mathcal{C}[\![\Gamma]\!]\rho\sigma \;=\; \langle \rho, \mathcal{M}[\![\Gamma]\!]\rho\sigma \rangle.$$

It is possible to extract from the above implicit definition of $\mathcal{M}$ a denotational definition of the same function. This definition no longer refers explicitly to stacks.

Lemma 2C. The semantic function $\mathcal{M} : \mathbf{Com} \to [R \to [\Sigma \to \Sigma]]$ satisfies:

$$\begin{aligned}
\mathcal{M}[\![\mathbf{skip}]\!]\rho\sigma &= \sigma \\
\mathcal{M}[\![I{:=}E]\!]\rho\sigma &= \sigma + [\rho(I) \mapsto \mathcal{E}[\![E]\!]\sigma] \\
\mathcal{M}[\![\Gamma_0; \Gamma_1]\!]\rho\sigma &= \mathcal{M}[\![\Gamma_1]\!]\rho(\mathcal{M}[\![\Gamma_0]\!]\rho\sigma) \\
\mathcal{M}[\![\mathbf{begin}\ \Delta; \Gamma\ \mathbf{end}]\!]\rho\sigma &= \sigma + \sum_{I \in \mathbf{Ide}} [\tau(I) \mapsto \sigma'(I)], \\
\text{where } \sigma' &= \mathcal{M}[\![\Gamma]\!](\mathcal{R}[\![\Delta]\!]\rho)(\mathcal{S}[\![\Delta]\!]\sigma) \\
\text{and } \tau &= \mathcal{T}[\![\Delta]\!]\rho.
\end{aligned}$$

In the clause for a block we have used a generalization of the overwriting operation: the valuation on the right-hand side agrees with σ on all identifiers which are not linked through τ, and gives to an identifier $I' \in \tau(I)$ the value $\sigma'(I)$. This reflects the fact that the only way in which a command inside a block can affect identifiers outside of the block is through the links established on block entry. Of course, it is necessary to verify that the generalized overwriting operation makes sense here, but this is essentially the consistency property of Lemma 2A. It is enough to check that whenever $I' \in \tau(I_0) \cap \tau(I_1)$ we have $\sigma'(I_0) = \sigma'(I_1)$. ∎

Properties of $\mathcal{M}$ may be proved either by first establishing a corresponding property for $\mathcal{C}$, or by using the denotational definition directly. Conversely, the function $\mathcal{C}$ can be recovered from $\mathcal{M}$, simply by propagating effects through the links of a stack. We omit the details. From now on we will concentrate attention on the semantic function $\mathcal{M}$. Among the most interesting and useful results are the following properties, which state intuitively obvious facts about the effects of command execution. Again we separate these results into Invariance and Influence Properties. Firstly, invariance: a command can affect the values only of identifiers that share with its free identifiers.

Theorem 3. Let $\langle \rho, \sigma \rangle$ be a frame. Then for all commands Γ, if $I \not\in \rho(\text{free}[\![\Gamma]\!])$ then the valuations σ and $\mathcal{M}[\![\Gamma]\!]\rho\sigma$ agree on I.

Proof. By structural induction on Γ. ∎

Secondly, influence: the semantics of a command depends only on its free identifiers.

Theorem 4. If frames $\langle \rho, \sigma \rangle$ and $\langle \rho', \sigma' \rangle$ agree on free$[\![\Gamma]\!]$ then the valuations $\mathcal{M}[\![\Gamma]\!]\rho\sigma$ and $\mathcal{M}[\![\Gamma]\!]\rho'\sigma'$ agree on free$[\![\Gamma]\!]$.

Proof. By structural induction, using Theorems 1, 2 and 3. ∎

These two results, in summary, state that commands can affect and can be affected by the values of only finitely many identifiers. Next we state a useful and intuitive property of blocks. This shows that the effect of a block on an identifier that is not redeclared at the head of the block can be calculated entirely in the local frame.

Lemma 3. For all Δ, all Γ, and all frames $\langle \rho, \sigma \rangle$, the valuations

$$\mathcal{M}[\![\textbf{begin}\ \Delta; \Gamma\ \textbf{end}]\!]\rho\sigma \quad \text{and} \quad \mathcal{M}[\![\Gamma]\!](\mathcal{R}[\![\Delta]\!]\rho)(\mathcal{S}[\![\Delta]\!]\sigma)$$

agree on all identifiers $I \not\in \text{dec}[\![\Delta]\!]$.

Proof. By Lemma 2C and Theorem 1. ∎

Programs. For programs, we define the semantic function

$$\mathcal{P} : \textbf{Prog} \to V,$$

where V is the set of expression values. Recall that a program

$$\textbf{begin}\ \Delta; \Gamma; \textbf{result}\ E\ \textbf{end}$$

consists of a closed declaration, followed by a command and an expression, whose free identifiers are all bound by the head declaration. We want the value of this expression to be the result of executing the program. Since Δ is closed, it binds the free identifiers of Γ and E to sharing classes and values *independent* of the initial frame (Theorem 2). The execution of Γ affects only (a subset of) these identifiers (Theorem 3), and the values used in updates depend only on the initial values of these identifiers (Theorem 4), which are supplied by the declaration. Thus, the frame produced by executing the program body specifies values for the free identifiers of E which are again independent of the initial conditions. We may, therefore, define unambiguously the semantics of a program to be:

$$\mathcal{P}[\![\textbf{begin}\ \Delta; \Gamma; \textbf{result}\ E\ \textbf{end}]\!] = \mathcal{E}[\![E]\!](\mathcal{M}[\![\Gamma]\!](\mathcal{R}[\![\Delta]\!]\rho_0)(\mathcal{S}[\![\Delta]\!]\sigma_0)),$$

where $\langle\rho_0, \sigma_0\rangle$ is an initial frame (whose precise structure is irrelevant); for concreteness, we may take this initial frame to be one in which all the sharing relation is trivial and in which all identifiers have some dummy value.

For example, the program

$$\textbf{begin new } x = 0; \textbf{ new } y = x + 1; y{:=}y + 1; \textbf{ result } y \textbf{ end}$$

has result 2.

The initial frame is finitary and consistent. Using Lemmas 1A, 1B, 1C, 2A and 2B it is easy to show that all states arising during a program execution are finitary and consistent. By definition, this means that at all times during an execution there are only finitely many non-trivial sharing classes, each of which is itself finite. And the state is always consistent, so that at each level ρ is always an equivalence relation and σ always agrees on the value of each member of a sharing class; the links between the stack frames are always consistent with the valuations. From now on, we assume that all states are finitary and consistent. We have shown that no semantic details are lost by making this assumption, because the states occurring in any computation are guaranteed to have these properties.

4. Full Abstraction.

Now that we have defined a semantics for our language, we can use it to define the usual *semantic equivalence* relations. Two commands are semantically equivalent iff they denote the same value:

$$\Gamma_0 \equiv \Gamma_1 \quad \Leftrightarrow \quad \mathcal{M}[\![\Gamma_0]\!] = \mathcal{M}[\![\Gamma_1]\!].$$

Thus, two commands are identified by the semantics iff whenever executed from the same initial frame they produce the same final valuation: for all frames $\langle\rho, \sigma\rangle$, $\mathcal{M}[\![\Gamma_0]\!]\rho\sigma = \mathcal{M}[\![\Gamma_1]\!]\rho\sigma$.

Similarly, for the other syntactic categories we can define

$$E_0 \equiv E_1 \quad \Leftrightarrow \quad \mathcal{E}[\![E_0]\!] = \mathcal{E}[\![E_1]\!],$$
$$\Delta_0 \equiv \Delta_1 \quad \Leftrightarrow \quad \mathcal{D}[\![\Delta_0]\!] = \mathcal{D}[\![\Delta_1]\!].$$

Two expressions are equivalent iff they always evaluate to the same value: for all valuations σ, $\mathcal{E}[\![E_0]\!]\sigma = \mathcal{E}[\![E_1]\!]\sigma$. And two declarations are equivalent iff they always introduce the same bindings: for all frames f, $\mathcal{D}[\![\Delta_0]\!]f = \mathcal{D}[\![\Delta_1]\!]f$. Semantic equivalence of identifiers is trivial, coinciding with syntactic identity, so we do not bother to introduce a new notation for it.

Finally, for programs we define

$$\Pi_0 \equiv \Pi_1 \quad \Leftrightarrow \quad \mathcal{P}[\![\Pi_0]\!] = \mathcal{P}[\![\Pi_1]\!].$$

Two programs are equivalent iff their results are the same.

Clearly, each of these relations is an equivalence relation. We would like to be sure that our semantics identifies pairs of terms if and only if they are interchangeable, without affecting the semantics, in all program contexts. In other words, we would like semantic equivalence to coincide with *behavioural equivalence*.

There is, for each syntactic category, a set of *program contexts* suitable for filling by members of that category. For instance, the following are program contexts of type *expression*:

$$\textbf{begin new } x = [\,\cdot\,];\ x{:=}\,1;\ \textbf{result } 42\ \textbf{end},$$
$$\textbf{begin new } x = 0;\ \textbf{new } y = x+1;\ y{:=}[\,\cdot\,];\ \textbf{result } y\ \textbf{end}$$
$$\textbf{begin new } x = 0;\ \textbf{new } y = x+1;\ y{:=}y+1;\ \textbf{result } [\,\cdot\,]\ \textbf{end}.$$

It is possible, but not particularly illuminating, to define rigorously a syntax for program contexts of these types. We omit the details. We will use the notation $\Pi[\,\cdot\,]$ for a program context, with the type being inferrable from the usage. We also use the notation $\Pi[t]$ for the result of filling the hole of a context with a term t of the appropriate type. It should be understood that we will only consider this substitution to be defined when the result is indeed a syntactically correct program.

Since we have defined our semantics in the denotational style, we know that semantic equivalence implies behavioural equivalence. In other words, for all Δ_i, all E_i, and all Γ_i,

$$\begin{aligned}
\Delta_0 \equiv \Delta_1 &\quad\Rightarrow\quad \forall \Pi[\,\cdot\,].(\Pi[\Delta_0] \equiv \Pi[\Delta_1]),\\
E_0 \equiv E_1 &\quad\Rightarrow\quad \forall \Pi[\,\cdot\,].(\Pi[E_0] \equiv \Pi[E_1]),\\
\Gamma_0 \equiv \Gamma_1 &\quad\Rightarrow\quad \forall \Pi[\,\cdot\,].(\Pi[\Gamma_0] \equiv \Pi[\Gamma_1]).
\end{aligned}$$

The converse relations, however, are not so obvious. Does behavioural equivalence guarantee semantic equivalence? It is precisely here that problems arise with location-based semantics. If the semantics includes explicit mention of the locations used by a command, then the two commands

$$\textbf{begin new } x = 0;\ \textbf{skip end}, \qquad \textbf{skip}$$

will fail to be semantically equivalent, unless the semantics provides explicitly for the releasing of locally claimed storage on exiting a block. Yet they induce the same behaviour in all program contexts, since neither of them alters the value of any identifier. Similarly, a location-based semantics will fail to identify the two declarations

$$\textbf{new } x = 0;\ \textbf{new } y = 1,$$
$$\textbf{new } y = 1;\ \textbf{new } x = 0,$$

which obviously have the same behaviour in all contexts; this will even be true in the case of a deallocating semantics.

Our semantics does identify these pairs of terms. In fact, our semantics is *fully abstract*: it identifies terms *if and only if* they produce identical results in all program contexts. Thus, semantic equivalence coincides with behavioural equivalence.

The full abstraction result depends on a simple *expressivity* property of the expression language **Exp** (*Assumption 2*). For convenience, we restate this assumption here.

Assumption 2. For every $v \in V$ there exists a closed expression $E_v \in \mathbf{Exp}$ such that for all valuations σ, $\mathcal{E}[\![E_v]\!]\sigma = v$. ∎

Provided the expression language **Exp** satisfies this (very reasonable) condition, we can always define a program which, given a finite piece of information about a state, produces a state consistent with this information during a computation. If two terms have a different semantics in some state, then we can build a program context in which the two terms would induce different behaviours. The important property of terms is that they only depend on and affect the values of *finitely many* identifiers. This was established by Theorems 1, 2, 3, and 4.

Lemma 5. For any finitary frame f and any finite set of identifiers A, there is a declaration Δ_f^A such that for all f'

$$\mathcal{F}[\![\Delta_f^A]\!]f' \text{ and } f \text{ agree on } A.$$

Proof. Let $f(A) = \{\, f(I) \mid I \in A \,\}$ be the set of sharing classes and values determined by A and f. We use an induction on the size of this set.

• If $f(A) = \emptyset$ there is nothing to prove, since this can only happen if A is empty, and all pairs of frames agree trivially on the empty set; in this case, we put $\Delta_f^{\emptyset} = \mathbf{null}$.

• For the inductive step, where $f(A)$ is non-empty, we have $f(A) = \{\, f(I) \,\} \cup f(B)$, for some $I \in A$, where $f(B)$ has smaller size. Let $f(I) = \langle X, v \rangle$. Let the distinct elements of X be $I_1, \ldots, I_k$; the set is finite because f is finitary. By our hypothesis on the expression language, there is a (closed) expression E_v having value v. Define the declaration Δ_f^I to be:

$$\mathbf{new}\, I = E_v;\, \mathbf{alias}\, I_1 = I; \ldots; \mathbf{alias}\, I_k = I.$$

Clearly, this declaration places the identifiers $I_1, \ldots, I_k$ into a new sharing class initialized to the value v. Thus, for all f', the frames f and $\mathcal{F}[\![\Delta_f^I]\!]f'$ will agree on I. By the inductive hypothesis, there is a declaration Δ_f^B which produces agreement on B. We may put

$$\Delta_f^A = \Delta_f^I; \Delta_f^B.$$

Actually, the order does not matter, and $\Delta_f^B; \Delta_f^I$ would have the same effect. ∎

A similar result for commands may be stated and proved in an analogous manner.

Lemma 6. For any finitary frame $f = \langle \rho, \sigma \rangle$, and any finite set A of identifiers, there is a command Γ_f^A such that for all σ' consistent with ρ

$$\mathcal{M}[\![\Gamma_f^A]\!]\rho\sigma' \text{ and } \sigma \text{ agree on } A.$$

These results may be used to prove the full abstraction theorem:

Theorem 5. The semantic functions $\mathcal{E}$, $\mathcal{D}$, and $\mathcal{M}$ are fully abstract.

Proof.

- For $\mathcal{E}$, by assumption.

- For $\mathcal{D}$, we wish to show that for all declarations Δ_0 and Δ_1,

$$\forall \Pi[\cdot].(\Pi[\Delta_0] \equiv \Pi[\Delta_1]) \quad \Rightarrow \mathcal{D}[\![\Delta_0]\!] = \mathcal{D}[\![\Delta_1]\!].$$

Suppose that $\mathcal{D}[\![\Delta_0]\!] \neq \mathcal{D}[\![\Delta_1]\!]$. We will construct a program context to distinguish between these two declarations. We know by Theorems 1 and 2 that if two declarations Δ_0 and Δ_1 have different semantics then there is a finitary frame f and an identifier I such that

$$(\mathcal{D}[\![\Delta_0]\!]f)(I) \neq (\mathcal{D}[\![\Delta_1]\!]f)(I).$$

Let $\mathcal{D}[\![\Delta_i]\!]f = \langle\langle \rho_i, \sigma_i \rangle, \tau_i \rangle$, for $i = 0, 1$, and let $f_i = \langle \rho_i, \sigma_i \rangle$ stand for the two frames. We know that either the *values* $\sigma_i(I)$ differ, or the (local) *sharing classes* $\rho_i(I)$ differ, or else the *links* $\tau_i(I)$ differ. There are thus three cases to consider.

Firstly, if the value of I is different in f_0 and f_1, let $A = \text{free}[\![\Delta_0]\!] \cup \text{free}[\![\Delta_1]\!]$. Using Lemma 5, we can find a declaration Δ_f^A as above. Then the program context

$$\textbf{begin } \Delta_f^A; [\cdot]; \textbf{skip}; \textbf{result } I \textbf{ end}$$

will distinguish between Δ_0 and Δ_1.

Secondly, if the sharing class of I is different in f_0 and f_1, we can choose an identifier I' which shares with I in only one of the frames f_0, f_1. And we can choose an expression E' to have a different value from the value of I in f_0 and f_1. Let

$$A = \text{free}[\![\Delta_0]\!] \cup \text{free}[\![\Delta_1]\!] \cup \text{free}[\![I' := E']\!].$$

By Lemma 5 there is a declaration Δ_f^A as above. The program context

$$\textbf{begin } \Delta_f^A; [\cdot]; I' := E'; \textbf{result } I \textbf{ end}$$

will distinguish between Δ_0 and Δ_1.

Finally, if the link differs, there must be an identifier (say, I') linked to I in only one of the two cases. With an appropriate choice of A, the context

$$\textbf{begin } \Delta_f^A; \textbf{ begin } [\cdot]; I{:=}I+1 \textbf{ end}; \textbf{ result } I' \textbf{ end}$$

will distinguish between Δ_0 and Δ_1.

- For $\mathcal{M}$ a similar argument can be based on Lemmas 5 and 6. ∎

5. Axiomatic Semantics.

In this section we show how we can use the structure of the semantics to suggest assertion languages for expressing semantic properties of the terms of our programming language, and then build an axiomatic proof system for the language. The choice of assertion languages and the proof rules are suggested directly by the semantics, and this means that soundness and relative completeness of the proof system are easy to establish. Moreover, the fact that we have defined separate semantic functions for declarations and commands allows us to separate the axiomatic treatment into two parts: an axiomatization of the purely declarative part of our programming language, and an axiomatization of the imperative part of the language. Since the semantic descriptions were *denotational*, i.e. syntax-directed, we will be able to build syntax-directed (Hoare-style) proof systems.

In this programming language, declarations have effects on both the sharing relation (a *declarative* effect) and on the association of identifiers to values (an *imperative* effect), because of the initializations that take place when a declaration is performed. Commands have an effect only on the values of identifiers, and do not alter the sharing relation (except locally, during block execution). At all times during the execution of a program the sharing classes are all finite, and all but finitely many of them are trivial. Moreover, the constitution of each sharing class is syntactically determined: the set of declarations in whose scope a command is executing determines the sharing classes precisely. There is a reasonably obvious notion of when a declaration Δ specifies that the set X of identifiers is a sharing class. We may formalize this notion precisely. Once we have axiomatized the declarative semantics, we will then be able to construct a Hoare-style proof system for the imperative effects of commands and declarations.

Declarative Proof System.

The purely *declarative* effect of a declaration is to alter the structure of the sharing relation, in the manner described by the semantic function $\mathcal{R}$. Our approach is to choose a simple language of *assertions* about sharing classes. Specifically, an assertion will be a finite set X of identifiers, or more generally a finite conjunction (written as a list) of a disjoint collection of such sets. The intention is that an assertion

$$X_1, \ldots, X_n$$

lists *all* of the non-trivial sharing classes. Since we know that sharing relations have a finite domain, it is certainly possible to find a finite description of a sharing relation as such a list. There is a simple "propositional" calculus of assertions, which we will largely take for granted. In particular, we use juxtaposition for conjunction and we write

$$X_1, \ldots, X_n \Rightarrow Y_1, \ldots, Y_m$$

when the Y_j list is simply a re-ordering of the X_i list with the possible inclusion of some extra trivial (empty) classes. The interpretation of such an assertion is clear: the two lists describe precisely the same sharing relation; in this sense, "implication" is trivial for our class of assertions.

We will use X, Y, and Z to stand for finite sets of identifiers (*sharing classes*) and ϕ, ψ, for conjunctions of these (*sharing assertions*). It is convenient to introduce the notation

$$\phi(I) = Y$$

to mean that the sharing class of I, specified by ϕ, is Y. Thus, for instance, if ϕ is $\langle X_1, \ldots, X_n \rangle$ and I belongs to X_i, then $\phi(I) = X_i$; if I is not included in any of the listed classes, then $\phi(I) = \emptyset$. We also introduce the notation $\phi - I$ for the result of removing I from every sharing class in the list ϕ. And we use $\phi \backslash I$ for the result of deleting the sharing class $\phi(I)$ from the list ϕ.

We now design a Hoare-style, syntax-directed proof system for declarations. The assertion

$$\langle \phi \rangle \Delta \langle \psi \rangle$$

is interpreted as saying that if ϕ describes the sharing relation before executing the declaration Δ then ψ will describe the sharing relation afterwards. We use angled brackets instead of conventional set brackets merely to indicate that we are axiomatizing the properties of a different syntactic category from the usual one (commands).

We give one axiom or rule for each syntactic form of declaration.

- An empty declaration, which we represent by **null**, does not alter any sharing classes:

$$\langle \phi \rangle \mathbf{null} \langle \phi \rangle \tag{A1}$$

- A simple declaration produces a new sharing class containing a single identifier; it removes the newly declared identifier from its old sharing class, and all other sharing classes remain unchanged:

$$\langle \phi \rangle \mathbf{new}\ I = E\langle \{ I \}, \phi - I \rangle \tag{A2}$$

• A sharing declaration has slightly more complicated properties. Specifically, the declared identifier is to be inserted in the sharing class of the identifier on the right-hand side of the declaration, while being removed from its old sharing class. Thus, we specify the axiom:

$$\langle \phi \rangle \mathbf{alias}\ I_0 = I_1 \langle \phi(I_1) \cup \{ I_0 \}, (\phi \backslash I_1) - I_0 \rangle \tag{A3}$$

• Finally, consider a sequential composition. Since the second declaration is executed within the scope of the first, the effects should accumulate from left to right. The desired rule to capture this is analogous to the usual rule for sequential composition of commands:

$$\frac{\langle \phi \rangle \Delta_0 \langle \phi' \rangle \quad \langle \phi' \rangle \Delta_1 \langle \psi \rangle}{\langle \phi \rangle \Delta_0; \Delta_1 \langle \psi \rangle} \tag{A4}$$

• The following rule allows us to "strengthen" pre-conditions and "weaken" post-conditions:

$$\frac{\phi \Rightarrow \phi' \qquad \langle \phi' \rangle \Delta \langle \psi' \rangle \qquad \psi' \Rightarrow \psi}{\langle \phi \rangle \Delta \langle \psi \rangle} \tag{A5}$$

For an example, let $\langle\,\rangle$ denote the assertion which states that there are no non-trivial sharing classes. Then we have

$$\begin{aligned}
&\langle\,\rangle \mathbf{new}\ x = 0 \langle \{ x \} \rangle \\
&\langle \{ x \} \rangle \mathbf{alias}\ y = x \langle \{ x, y \} \rangle \\
&\langle \{ x, y \} \rangle \mathbf{alias}\ z = w \langle \{ x, y \}, \{ z, w \} \rangle \\
&\langle \{ x \} \rangle \mathbf{alias}\ y = x; \mathbf{alias}\ z = y \langle \{ x, y, z \} \rangle.
\end{aligned}$$

It should be clear that these axioms correspond very closely with the semantic function $\mathcal{R}$. Indeed, it is easy to formalize the validity notion for our assertions: let us write

$$\rho \models \phi$$

to denote that the sharing relation ρ satisfies assertion ϕ. Formally, this is defined in a manner corresponding to the informal interpretation given earlier: ϕ lists all of the non-trivial sharing classes, so that

$$\rho \models (X_1, \ldots, X_n) \iff \forall i.(I \in X_i \iff \rho(I) = X_i) \\ \& \quad \forall I \notin \bigcup_{i=1}^{n} X_i.\,(\rho(I) = \emptyset).$$

Similarly, we define validity of an assertion $\langle\phi\rangle\Delta\langle\psi\rangle$:

$$\models \langle\phi\rangle\Delta\langle\psi\rangle \iff \forall\rho.(\rho \models \phi \text{ implies } \mathcal{R}[\![\Delta]\!]\rho \models \psi).$$

This proof system is sound and complete.

Theorem 6. (Soundness) For all Δ and all ϕ, ψ,

$$\vdash \langle\phi\rangle\Delta\langle\psi\rangle \text{ implies } \models \langle\phi\rangle\Delta\langle\psi\rangle.$$

Theorem 7. (Completeness) For all Δ and all ϕ, ψ,

$$\models \langle\phi\rangle\Delta\langle\psi\rangle \text{ implies } \vdash \langle\phi\rangle\Delta\langle\psi\rangle.$$

Note that none of the assertions gives any information about the *values* denoted by any of the sharing classes. We will see that this will not cause a problem; on the contrary, it is a distinct advantage when we come to formulate proof rules for commands. Essentially, we are separating entirely the purely binding effect of a declaration from the initialization effect it causes. The latter is more properly regarded as a command-like feature, and we will build it into the proof system for commands.

Imperative Proof System.

For commands, we use assertions of a more conventional style. Pre- and post-conditions are drawn from a simple logical language; examples of conditions are

$$x = 3, \qquad x = y \,\&\, y \neq z.$$

We use P and Q to range over conditions. Each condition represents a predicate on the (valuation part of) state. In conventional Hoare logics for simple sequential languages without sharing, assertions of the form $\{P\}\Gamma\{Q\}$ are used and interpreted as follows: whenever Γ is executed from an initial state satisfying P then (if the computation terminates) the final state will satisfy Q. For languages without sharing this is of course natural, since the effect of a command does not depend on any notion of sharing. However, our semantics for commands involved the sharing relation explicitly. We are led to a natural generalization of these Hoare assertions, incorporating a condition or assumption on the sharing relation. The assertion

$$\phi \vdash \{P\}\Gamma\{Q\}$$

states that whenever the command Γ is executed, with ϕ specifying the sharing classes, from an initial valuation satisfying P, then (provided the computation terminates) the final valuation will satisfy Q. Note that the structure of our generalized assertion matches the type of the semantic function $\mathcal{M}$.

For declarations, we observed that the (local) imperative effect of a declaration, described by the semantic function $\mathcal{S}$, was uniquely determined by the valuation, and does not depend on the sharing relation. This suggests that we use assertions of the form

$$\{P\}\Delta\{Q\},$$

with the interpretation that when the declaration Δ is executed from an initial valuation satisfying P, the resulting valuation satisfies Q.

We propose the following axioms and rules of inference for the imperative part of our language. As usual, we give a clause for each command construct. However, in addition, we propose rules of inference for the imperative aspects of declarations. This will enable us to give a simple proof rule for blocks. Our prior axiomatization of declarative semantics will be used.

- A **skip** command has no effect, regardless of the sharing relation:

$$\phi \vdash \{P\}\mathbf{skip}\{P\} \tag{B1}$$

- An assignment affects the values of all identifiers in the sharing class of the target identifier, and is thus akin to a simultaneous assignment to a set of distinct identifiers. We use the notation $[E\backslash Y]P$ for the simultaneous syntactic replacement in P of all free occurrences of identifiers in Y by the expression E. This is a generalization of the single substitution operation $[E\backslash I]P$, and coincides with the latter when Y is a singleton set. The desired axiom is:

$$\frac{\phi(I) = Y}{\phi \vdash \{[E\backslash Y]P\}I{:=}E\{P\}} \tag{B2}$$

The soundness of this rule relies on a standard property of syntactic substitution. The statement of this property for our expression language is that for all valuations σ and all $Y \subseteq \mathbf{Ide}$ we have

$$\mathcal{E}[\![[E\backslash Y]E']\!]\sigma = \mathcal{E}[\![E']\!](\sigma + [Y \mapsto \mathcal{E}[\![E]\!]\sigma]).$$

• The rule for sequential composition is again simple. The two commands are to be executed with the same sharing relation, their effects accumulating from left to right.

$$\frac{\phi \vdash \{P\}\Gamma_1\{Q\} \qquad \phi \vdash \{Q\}\Gamma_2\{R\}}{\phi \vdash \{P\}\Gamma_1;\Gamma_2\{R\}} \tag{B3}$$

• For a block beginning with a declaration we have to take into account both the declarative and imperative aspects of the declaration, which may affect the execution of the block body. The following rule takes all of these factors into account. Note that the premisses of the rule involve assertions about both the imperative and declarative effect of the declaration at the head of the block. It is here more than anywhere that the separate axiomatization of declarative semantics is helpful. The rule is sound provided none of the bound identifiers in Δ occurs free in P or R:

$$\frac{\{P\}\Delta\{Q\} \qquad \langle\phi\rangle\Delta\langle\psi\rangle \qquad \psi \vdash \{Q\}\Gamma\{R\}}{\phi \vdash \{P\}\mathbf{begin}\ \Delta;\Gamma\ \mathbf{end}\{R\}} \tag{B4}$$

The need for the syntactic constraints was mentioned earlier in the statement of Lemma 3, which guarantees the soundness of this rule.

For the imperative effects of declarations, we provide the following rules.

• A null declaration has no effect:

$$\{P\}\mathbf{null}\{P\} \tag{B5}$$

• A simple declaration has an effect similar to that of an assignment, and it updates the value of the declared identifier:

$$\{[E\backslash I]P\}\mathbf{new}\ I = E\{P\} \tag{B6}$$

• For a sharing declaration, the initializing effect is similar:

$$\{[I'\backslash I]P\}\mathbf{alias}\ I = I'\{P\} \tag{B7}$$

• Sequential composition of declarations behaves simply:

$$\frac{\{P\}\Delta_0\{Q\} \qquad \{Q\}\Delta_1\{R\}}{\{P\}\Delta_0;\Delta_1\{R\}} \tag{B8}$$

So far we do not have any rule corresponding to "change of bound variable." The block rule (B4) above only allows us to use pre- and post-conditions which do not involve the bound identifiers of the block. This is as it should be, since these identifiers are redeclared on entry to the block; the meanings of these identifiers inside the block are unrelated to their meaning outside the block (except through the link). We can suppress the need to reason explicitly about the links by changing bound identifiers to avoid hole-in-scope problems. We need, therefore, to be able to deduce an arbitrary partial correctness formula for a block if we can first prove a version in which we have renamed some of the bound identifiers. The following is an adaptation to our setting of standard rules from the literature (see [1,2] for example). Let $\langle y\backslash x\rangle\Delta$ denote the result of replacing all *bound* occurrences of x in Δ by y; let $[y\backslash x]\Gamma$ denote the result of replacing all *free* occurrences of x in Γ by y, with appropriate name changes to avoid clashes. The rule is:

$$\frac{\phi \vdash \{P\}\textbf{begin } \langle y\backslash x\rangle\Delta;\ [y\backslash x]\Gamma \textbf{ end}\{Q\}}{\phi \vdash \{P\}\textbf{begin } \Delta;\Gamma \textbf{ end}\{Q\}} \tag{B9}$$

provided x is declared in Δ, y does not occur free in Γ or Δ, and y does not occur bound in Δ. The soundness of this rule, and the need for these syntactic constraints, are easily established.

In addition to the above syntactically motivated rules, the utility and necessity of the following rule should be self-evident. It allows us to use the consistency property of states to conclude from an assertion about a single identifier I a corresponding assertion about all identifiers in its sharing class. Let us use the notation

$$P_I^X = \bigwedge_{I' \in X} [I'\backslash I]P$$

when X is a finite set of identifiers. For example, we have

$$(x = z + 1)_x^{\{x,y\}} = (x = z + 1 \,\&\, y = z + 1).$$

The rule we propose is simply:

$$\frac{\phi(I) = Y}{\phi \vdash (P \Rightarrow P_I^Y)} \tag{B10}$$

Finally, we include versions of the rule of consequence. Note that it is necessary to include the sharing assertion explicitly in the rule of consequence for commands.

$$\frac{\phi \vdash (P \Rightarrow P') \quad \phi \vdash \{P'\}\Gamma\{Q'\} \quad \phi \vdash (Q' \Rightarrow Q)}{\phi \vdash \{P\}\Gamma\{Q\}} \tag{B11}$$

$$\frac{(P \Rightarrow P') \quad \{P'\}\Delta\{Q'\} \quad (Q' \Rightarrow Q)}{\{P\}\Delta\{Q\}} \tag{B12}$$

Comparison with other proof rules.

Clearly, many of our proof rules and axioms have essentially the same form as well known rules in the literature. Indeed, in the absence of (non-trivial) sharing, our axioms and rules for commands collapse down to standard rules, as we would expect. In particular, the assignment rule collapses to Hoare's original axiom [14]:

$$\{\, [E\backslash I]P\,\} I{:=}E \{\, P\,\},$$

and our rule for sequential composition of commands collapses to Hoare's rule. The main differences are evident in the treatment of aliasing relationships. By axiomatizing the properties of declarations, we were able to build a rule for assignment which incorporates explicit reasoning about sharing and generalizes Hoare's assignment rule in the obvious simple manner, replacing a single substitution by a multiple simultaneous substitution. A similar rule for a multiple assignment statement appears in [9,10], although aliasing was not considered there.

A further benefit of our prior axiomatization of the effect of declarations on the sharing relation is that we are able to design simple proof rules for blocks. Our rule (B4) for blocks can be said to be more truly syntax-directed than is usual in the literature, because the rule as given here is in a "generic" form applicable to more than one form of declaration. The structure of the rule does not depend on the precise form of declaration with which the block begins. The following specialized rules are derivable. These are special cases of our general rules in which we have chosen a specific form for the declaration at the head of a block. They are related to rules in the literature, especially those of [1,2,3,4], although direct comparison is somewhat hampered by the differences in syntax. In these references, in particular, *new* declarations do not also initialize the value of the declared identifier to the value of an expression. Aliasing is not treated in [1,2], so that the block rule stated there is interpreted in a sharing-free setting.

A rule for a block beginning with a *new* declaration can be obtained from rules (A2), (B4) and (B9), together with rule (B6). Firstly, note that if I does not occur free in E and P, then the following will be provable as a special case of (B6) after an application of the rule of consequence:

$$\{P\}\mathbf{new}\, I = E\{P \ \&\ I = E\}.$$

Therefore, if I does not occur free in P, E, or R, we can use rules (B4) and (A2) to derive the rule:

$$\frac{\phi - I, \{I\} \vdash \{P \ \&\ I = E\}\Gamma\{R\}}{\phi \vdash \{P\}\mathbf{begin\ new}\, I = E; \Gamma\{R\}} \qquad \text{(D1)}$$

If we also make use of the change of bound variables rule to ensure the necessary constraints, we obtain the following derived rule. If I' is a fresh identifier which does not occur free in Γ, E, P, or R, then

$$\frac{\phi - I', \{I'\} \vdash \{P \;\&\; I' = E\}[I'\backslash I]\Gamma\{R\}}{\phi \vdash \{P\}\textbf{begin new}\, I = E; \Gamma\, \textbf{end}\{R\}}. \qquad \text{(D2)}$$

In this form, the rule is a generalization of the Variable Declaration Rule (Rule 16) of [1], with suitable modification to allow for the initialization effect of a declaration and for the sharing assumption.

A similar rule for a block headed by a sharing declaration is also obtainable:

$$\frac{\langle\phi\rangle\textbf{alias}\, I_0 = I_1\langle\psi\rangle \quad \psi \vdash \{P \;\&\; I_0 = I_1\}\Gamma\{R\}}{\phi \vdash \{P\}\textbf{begin alias}\, I_0 = I_1; \Gamma\, \textbf{end}\{R\}}, \qquad \text{(D3)}$$

provided I_0 does not occur free in P, Q, Γ. Again, a version incorporating a change of bound variable can also be formulated, and an explicit representation for ψ can be derived from rule (A3).

An important point to note here is that these block rules from the literature turn up as *derived* rules and not primitive rules in our system. This suggests, as we claimed earlier, that our formulation of the proof system is more truly syntax-directed. We would be able to add new forms of declaration to the language, and to add new axioms and rules for these extra constructs, without modifying the structure of the proof rule for blocks (provided, of course, that the additional constructs can be semantically modelled inside our current framework); we would not have to introduce a separate proof rule for blocks beginning with each different form of declaration, although of course specialized versions of the block rule would be derivable. It is this adaptability of our proof system that we regard as an important asset.

In the language under consideration in this paper, declarations have both imperative and declarative aspects, and we were able to focus on these aspects independently. If the programming language only allowed purely declarative declarations which do not have any non-trivial initializing effect (for example an uninitialized declaration **new** x), we would not need any assertions of the form $\{P\}\Delta\{Q\}$; our proof system could then be adapted to this setting in an obvious way. Conversely, if we add declarations whose declarative effect depends on the valuation as well as on the sharing relation, the imperative assertions for declarations would need to be made more complicated. This would be the case, for instance, if we allowed array declarations, so that one could then declare **alias** $x = a[y]$. The declaration-time value of y would then determine the sharing class of x. One solution here would be to use assertions of the form $\phi \vdash \{P\}\Delta\langle\psi\rangle$, or some alternative sugared form; in any case, the assertion would need some subterm to represent an assumption about the initial valuation. The point is that we believe that our general methods will be applicable in a wider setting than the one considered in this paper, provided we are ready to adopt the use of assertions whose structure more closely follows the semantic structure of the programming language under examination.

Examples.

Example 1. Consider the following command, which we will denote Γ:

$$\begin{array}{l}\textbf{begin}\\ \quad \textbf{new}\, t = x;\\ \quad x{:=}y;\\ \quad y{:=}t\\ \textbf{end}.\end{array}$$

We claim that this command exchanges the value of x and y, regardless of the sharing relation. We can prove an instance of this very easily. Let ϕ be a sharing assertion with $\phi(x) = X$ and $\phi(y) = Y$. We will prove the assertion

$$\langle\phi\rangle \vdash \{x = 0 \ \& \ y = 1\}\Gamma\{x = 1 \ \& \ y = 0\}.$$

The proof is simple. Firstly, we have

$$\phi \vdash \{x = 0 \ \& \ y = 1\}\textbf{new}\, t = x\{x = 0 \ \& \ y = 1 \ \& \ t = 0\}$$

by (B6) and (B12). We also have, by (A2),

$$\langle\phi\rangle\textbf{new}\, t = x\langle\psi\rangle,$$

where $\psi(x) = X - \{t\}, \psi(y) = Y - \{t\}, \psi(t) = \{t\}$. This shows that t does not share with x or y inside the block. Then we have

$$\psi \vdash \{x = 0 \ \& \ y = 1 \ \& \ t = 0\}x{:=}y\{x = 1 \ \& \ y = 1 \ \& \ t = 0\},$$

by the assignment rule (B2). Similarly,

$$\psi \vdash \{x = 1 \ \& \ y = 1 \ \& \ t = 0\}y{:=}t\{x = 1 \ \& \ y = 0 \ \& \ t = 0\}.$$

Applying rule (B3) for sequential composition, we get

$$\{x = 0 \ \& \ y = 1 \ \& \ t = 0\}x{:=}y; y{:=}t\{x = 1 \ \& \ y = 0 \ \& \ t = 0\}.$$

The result follows by the block rule (B4) and the rule of consequence (B12).

Example 2. To illustrate reasoning about sharing, consider the command

$$\textbf{begin alias}\ z = x;\ \textbf{alias}\ y = z;\ y{:=}x + 1\ \textbf{end}.$$

This should have the effect of increasing the value of all identifiers which share with x. We prove this as follows. Let ϕ be a sharing assertion and let $X = \phi(x)$. Let w be an identifier which does not belong to X, so that w does not share with x. The rules for *alias* and sequential composition of declarations give

$$\vdash \langle\phi\rangle \textbf{alias } z = x; \textbf{alias } y = z\langle\psi\rangle,$$

where $\psi(x) = X \cup \{y, z\}$. From this, the assignment rule and the consistency rule gives

$$\langle\psi\rangle \vdash \{x = w\} z := x + 1 \{x = y = z = w + 1\},$$

since $w \not\in X$. From this, using the rule of consequence, and the block rule, we get

$$\langle\phi\rangle \vdash \{x = w\} \textbf{begin alias } z = x; \textbf{alias } y = x; y := z + 1 \textbf{ end} \{x = w + 1\}.$$

That completes the proof.

Soundness and Completeness.

We claim that our imperative proof system is sound and relatively complete. We have already established this for the purely declarative proof system, which is used in building up the imperative system. Now we have to tackle the proof rules for imperative semantics of declarations and commands. We have already given a satisfaction relation $\models$ for sharing relations and assertions. We also need a satisfaction relation for valuations and conditions. Since we have not been specific about the condition language, we will assume here that we are given a satisfaction relation $\sigma \models P$, which behaves correctly with repsect to the usual logical connectives and with respect to syntactic substitution. By this we mean that for all conditions P, all $Y \subseteq \textbf{Ide}$ and all $E \in \textbf{Exp}$ we have

$$\sigma \models [E \backslash Y]P \quad \Leftrightarrow \quad (\sigma + [Y \mapsto \mathcal{E}[\![E]\!]\sigma]) \models P.$$

These are standard assumptions which are usually made tacitly in axiomatic treatments.

We say that an assertion

$$\phi \vdash \{P\}\Gamma\{Q\}$$

is satisfied in a frame f, written

$$f \models (\phi \vdash \{P\}\Gamma\{Q\}),$$

if when the initial valuation σ of f satisfies P and the sharing relation ρ of f satisfies ϕ, then the final valuation $\mathcal{M}[\![\Gamma]\!]\rho\sigma$ satisfies Q:

$$\rho \models \phi \ \& \ \sigma \models P \quad \text{implies} \quad \mathcal{M}[\![\Gamma]\!]\rho\sigma \models Q.$$

Similarly, a valuation σ satisfies an assertion $\{P\}\Delta\{Q\}$ if the analogous relationship holds:

$$\sigma \models P \quad \text{implies} \quad \mathcal{S}[\![\Delta]\!]\sigma \models Q.$$

An assertion is *valid*, denoted

$$\models (\phi \vdash \{P\}\Gamma\{Q\})$$

if it is satisfied in all frames. For declarations we require that the assertion be satisfied in all valuations.

We need to show that all valid assertions are provable, and every provable assertion is valid. As usual, following Cook [6], we are assuming that we can use any true (valid) assertion of the form $\phi \vdash P$ or P as an assumption in a proof. Let **Th** be the set of valid conditions of this form:

$$(\phi \vdash P) \in \mathbf{Th} \quad \Leftrightarrow \quad \models (\phi \vdash P),$$
$$P \in \mathbf{Th} \quad \Leftrightarrow \quad \models P.$$

We want to prove that all valid assertions are provable *relative to* **Th**, the standard notion of *relative completeness*.

The proofs of soundness are straightforward. We prove that each axiom is valid, and that each inference rule preserves validity. It follows that every proof preserves validity, and that every provable assertion is valid.

Theorem 8.(Soundness) For all Δ and all P and Q,

$$\mathbf{Th} \vdash \{P\}\Delta\{Q\} \quad \text{implies} \quad \models \{P\}\Delta\{Q\} \quad \blacksquare$$

Theorem 9.(Soundness) For all Γ and all ϕ, P and Q,

$$\mathbf{Th} \vdash (\phi \vdash \{P\}\Gamma\{Q\}) \quad \text{implies} \quad \models (\phi \vdash \{P\}\Gamma\{Q\}) \quad \blacksquare$$

For example, the soundness of the block rule (B4) follows from Lemma 3. The soundness of the rules for sequential composition of declarations and commands follows directly from the semantic definitions. The consistency rule (B10) is sound because it can be proved by structural induction that the semantic definitions preserve consistency of the valuation with respect to the sharing relation.

We already know that the declarative system is complete. For the imperative system, we can show that "weakest pre-conditions" can be expressed for each syntactic construct in our assertion language. In other words, our assertion language is *expressive*. Essentially, we define weakest pre-conditions with respect to a sharing relation.

Theorem 10.(Completeness) For all Δ and all P and Q,

$$\models \{P\}\Delta\{Q\} \quad \text{implies} \quad \mathbf{Th} \vdash \{P\}\Delta\{Q\} \quad \blacksquare$$

Theorem 11.(Completeness) For all Γ and for all ϕ, P and Q,

$$\models (\phi \vdash \{P\}\Gamma\{Q\}) \quad \text{implies} \quad \mathbf{Th} \vdash (\phi \vdash \{P\}\Gamma\{Q\}) \quad \blacksquare$$

6. Conclusions.

The work reported in this paper is an attempt to design a clean and mathematically tractable semantics for a programming language, a semantics which is specifically intended to serve as a basis for reasoning about a particular type of program behaviour: in this case partial correctness. We considered a simple programming language with block structure and a form of aliasing, so that we were able to concentrate on the problems inherent in these features alone. The underlying semantic model with respect to which we proved soundness and completeness was location-free, and we proved its suitability as the basis for formal reasoning about partial correctness by demonstrating that the semantics was fully abstract with respect to a related notion of program behaviour. We further demonstrate this suitability by using the semantics directly in the design of an assertion language and proof system for reasoning about partial correctness of programs. The semantics may be used to prove the soundness and relative completeness of this proof system, and as a consequence of the choice of semantic model these proofs may be formulated rather cleanly. We were also able to derive some well known proof rules from the literature.

One description of our semantics ($\mathcal{C}$) involved an abstract notion of stacks, which provided a clean and elegant way to cope with the scope rules and block structure of our language. It is well known that block structured languages with static scope rules can be implemented with stacks, and several semantic treatments have been suggested which incorporate such techniques, notably by Landin [17], Jones [16], Olderog [22,23] and Langmaack [18]. Landin used an abstract machine with a "sharing component" which explicitly described the sharing relationships among program variables, and gave operational semantics to a variety of programming languages. Jones also tried to use sharing relations and consistent valuations, in an operational semantic framework. Langmaack and Olderog give axiomatic treatments of aliasing which involve a notion of sharing classes, specifically to deal with sharing among actual parameters in procedure calls. They did not give a separate denotational description of sharing classes and their manipulation during program execution, and their notion of stacks seems to involve locations rather more explicitly. We feel that our treatment is somewhat cleaner, and gains in simplicity and clarity by explicitly focussing on the need to describe separately the denotational semantics of declarations; nevertheless, we should also admit that some of the extra clarity is obtained because we are working with a less complicated programming language.

Although it may be argued that stacks have an operational flavour, we would counter by pointing out that the same is true of location-based models, in which storage allocation needs to be modelled. It is at least arguable that the use of stacks is a fairly natural way of explaining the effects of block entry and exit, and that in our semantics we have made no operational commitment with regard to "implementation": although the semantics uses abstract stacks to describe the effect of commands, this will not force us to implement the language on a stack machine. Indeed, we were also able to describe the partial correctness semantics $\mathcal{M}$ of commands in a stack-independent manner (Lemma 2C). Despite our decision to abstract away from the notion of location, it is possible to relate our semantics to a more concrete location-based model for the language, although we do not discuss this in detail here.

An approach to the semantics of block-structured languages based on category theory has been developed by Oles and Reynolds [24], and there appear to be connections between their abstract store models and our sharing class model. These connections need to be examined more closely; roughly speaking, our frames and links can be regarded as the objects and arrows of a category which seems to be related to the category of *store shapes* introduced by Oles and Reynolds. Further influences of the work of Reynolds are visible in some of our semantic results which were used in the full abstraction proof. Our theorems 1–4 can be thought of as a rigorous analysis of the relevant notions of *interference* for our programming language [27,28,29,32], since they state precisely the conditions under which a declaration or command can affect or be affected by the value of identifiers.

We believe that many existing programming language features still lack elegant and tractable formal description, and that their axiomatization has been attempted somewhat prematurely, with insufficient attention to semantic issues. Full abstraction gives a criterion for judging the suitability of a semantics for supporting formal reasoning about prrogram behaviour. The construction of fully abstract semantics for many programming languages, even with respect to such well known behavioural criteria as partial correctness, has not yet been adequately investigated (notable exceptions being [20,25;26]). The use of semantics directly in the design and construction of assertion languages for reasoning about program properties should be advocated more extensively. Our work in this paper is a small step in this direction.

In principle, it should be possible to use a semantics directly to build axiom systems for each syntactic category of a programming language, and combine them to get a Hoare-style proof system for the whole language, as we did here for our simple language. An advantage of this approach is that the hierarchical structure of a proof system built in this way will reflect the syntactic structure of the programming language: in the example language considered here, for instance, the declarative system is a subsystem used inside the imperative system, and this corresponds to the fact that declarations can appear as syntactic components of commands. Of course, for more complicated languages, we may need different choices of assertion language; and the axioms and rules may not be as clean as the ones we were able to use here. However, we are confident that the adoption of a more widely based notion of Hoare system, with more attention on the semantic foundations, will lead to significant improvements in the axiomatic treatment of many programming language constructs.

An important suggestion illustrated by our results and technique is that Hoare-style proof systems should be designed not only for imperative languages—as was the case in Hoare's original paper—but that it is advantageous to extend Hoare's principle to syntactic categories other than commands. We designed a Hoare-style proof system for declarations, and found that this helped in the construction of a proof system for commands. Our decision to separate the different semantic aspects of the programming language and to build a hierarchical proof system whose structure reflects the syntactic and semantic structure of the language has been influenced by some of the ideas in Reynolds' *specification logic*, although Reynolds points out in [28] that in its present state specification logic does not seem to support reasoning about call-by-reference (which is analogous to our form of alias declaration).

Our methods suggest, we feel, a general basis for constructing Hoare-like semantics for even more complicated languages involving sharing, such as languages including array declarations and array assignments. Our approach here would probably lead to proof rules involving explicit reasoning about the sharing classes of array expressions, unlike the rules of [2], which used a generalization of syntactic substitution to cope with array assignments. It should also be possible to treat more complex forms of sharing, such as the hierarchical sharing structures required to deal with ALGOL 68 *ref* declarations and pointers. It is certainly easy to include conditional commands and loops in our language, without changing the structure of the semantic model. We merely adapt Hoare's proof rules for conditionals and loops [14] to this setting, by including sharing assertions. We feel sure that our methods are applicable (with some modifications, of course, in the choice of semantic model and assertion language) to procedural languages involving various parameter mechanisms and even allowing the use of recursion. Some results relevant to this have been discussed by Reynolds [27,28].

Langmaack [18] and Olderog [22,23] also give axiomatic treatments of aliasing which involve a notion of sharing classes, specifically to deal with sharing among actual parameters in procedure calls. They did not give a separate axiomatic and denotational description of sharing classes and their manipulation during program execution, and their notion of stacks seems to involve locations rather more explicitly. We feel that our treatment is somewhat cleaner, and gains in simplicity and clarity by explicitly focussing on the need to axiomatize separately the semantics of declarations and commands; nevertheless, we should also admit that some of the extra clarity is obtained because we are working with a less complicated programming language.

Other related work includes the proof system of [11] and the semantic treatments of [12,13], based on a rather intricate notion of "store-models"; in contrast to the approach used there, our underlying semantic model is arguably cleaner and we have proved full abstraction. We also feel that our proof rules are more natural, although again some of this "benefit" arises because we have a simpler programming language, and it remains to be seen what happens when we extend our methods to a language with procedures of higher type.

As we stated earlier, we intended in this paper to focus on a small number of programming language features and to concentrate exclusively on the problems caused by aliasing. The programming language consequently omitted many features which would be required in any more realistic setting. We believe that our methods can be adapted to cover some more complicated languages. With minor modifications we can add loops and conditionals; the only essential difference is that we then need to justify the use of recursive definitions in the semantic description of loops. This is straightforward if we impose a natural partial ordering on the relevant semantic structure and follow the standard lines of the Scott-Strachey approach. We can still obtain a full abstraction result for the enlarged language and its semantics. Similarly, although this paper ignored the possibility of run-time errors such as an attempt to evaluate or assign to an undeclared or uninitialized identifier, it is easy to modify the syntax and semantics of the language in order to cope with these problems.

Adding procedures with various forms of parameter passing is a much more interesting and difficult problem. We expect to be able to incorporate these features into our setting too, provided we give a careful treatment of scoping which correctly handles free identifiers in procedure bodies. Since procedure calls in statically scoped languages can be implemented by a form of copy rule, replacing a procedure call by a block containing a declaration which binds formal parameters to actual parameters, we hope that it is convincing that our treatment may be extended as indicated: we do provide already a treatment for blocks and two forms of declaration which correspond to well known forms of parameter passing. Of course, recursive procedures and procedures which take procedures as parameters are of even more interest. A semantic model for a programming language with these features may be based on an abstract stack which incorporates procedure bindings in addition to sharing relations. It does not seem to be possible to extract a "stack-free" semantics for such a language. It should be possible to prove the correctness of a more concrete stack-based implementation of procedures, using an abstract semantics as the basis. These problems will be the subject of future work.

Acknowledgements. The author is grateful to Robert Cartwright, Joe Halpern, Albert Meyer, and Boris Trakhtenbrot for helpful comments and criticism, and to Allen Stoughton for pointing out an error in an earlier definition of $\mathcal{M}$. Suggestions by Paola Giannini, Ulrik Jørring, Brad White, and Bill Roscoe led to improvements in the presentation and development of the material.

7. References.

(LNCS refers to the Springer Verlag Lecture Notes in Computer Science series.)

[1] Apt, K. R., Ten Years of Hoare's Logic: A survey–Part 1, ACM TOPLAS, Vol. 3 pp 431-483 (1981).

[2] de Bakker, J. W., *Mathematical Theory of Program Correctness*, Prentice-Hall 1980.

[3] Cartwright, R., and Oppen, D., The Logic of Aliasing, Acta Informatica 15, pp 365-384 (1981).

[4] Cartwright, R., and Oppen, D., Unrestricted Procedure Calls in Hoare's Logic, Proc. 5th ACM Symposium on Principles of Programming Languages, ACM New York.

[5] Clarke, E. M., Programming language constructs for which it is impossible to obtain good Hoare axioms, JACM 26 pp 129-147 (1979).

[6] Cook, S., Soundness and completeness of an axiom system for program verification, SIAM J. Comput. 7, pp 70-90 (1978).

[7] Donahue, James, Locations Considered Unnecessary, Acta Informatica 8, pp 221–242 (1977).

[8] Gordon, M., *The Denotational Description of Programming Languages*, Springer Verlag 1978.

[9] Gries, D., The Multiple Assignment Statement, IEEE Trans. Software Engrg, SE-4, pp 89-93 (1978).

[10] Gries, D., and Levin, G., Assignment and procedure call proof rules, ACM TOPLAS 2, pp 564-579 (1980).

[11] Halpern, J., A Good Hoare Axiom System for an Algol-like language, Proc. POPL 1984.

[12] Halpern, J., Meyer, A., and Trakhtenbrot, B., The Semantics of Local Storage, or What Makes the Free-list Free?, Proc. POPL 1984.

[13] Halpern, J., Meyer, A., and Trakhtenbrot, B., From Denotational to Operational and Axiomatic Semantics for ALGOL-like languages: An Overview, Proc. 1983 Workshop on Logics of Programs, Springer Verlag LNCS 164 (1984).

[14] Hoare, C. A. R., An Axiomatic Basis for Computer Programming, CACM 12, pp 576-580 (1969).

[15] Hoare, C. A. R., Procedures and parameters: An axiomatic approach, in: *Symposium on Semantics of Algorithmic Languages*, Springer Verlag LNCS 188 (1971).

[16] Jones, C. B., Yet Another Proof of the Correctness of Block Implementation, IBM Laboratory, Vienna (August 1970).

[17] Landin, P. J., A Correspondence between Algol 60 and Church's lambda notation, CACM 8, 89-101 and 158-165 (1965).

[18] Langmaack, H.,On Termination Problems for Finitely Interpreted ALGOL-like Programs, Acta Informatica 18, pp 79-108 (1972).

[19] Milne, R., and Strachey, C., *A Theory of Programming Language Semantics*, Chapman and Hall 1976.

[20] Milner, R., Fully Abstract Models of Typed λ-calculi, Theoretical Computer Science (1977).

[21] Mosses, P. D., The Mathematical Semantics of ALGOL 60, Technical Monograph PRG-12, Oxford University Computing Laboratory, Programming Research Group (1974).

[22] Olderog, E-R., Correctness of Programs with Pascal-like Procedures without Global Variables, Theoretical Computer Science 30 (1984) 49-90.

[23] Olderog, E-R., Sound and Complete Hoare-like Calculi Based on Copy Rules, Acta Informatica 16, pp 161-197 (1981).

[24] Oles, F. J., A Category-theoretic Approach to the Semantics of ALGOL-like Languages, Ph. D. thesis, Syracuse University (August 1982).

[25] Plotkin, G. D., LCF Considered as a Programming Language, Theoretical Computer Science 5, pp 223-255 (1977).

[26] Plotkin, G. D., and Hennessy, M. C. B., Full Abstraction for a Simple Parallel Programming Language, Proc. MFCS 1979, Springer LNCS 74, pp 108-120 (1979).

[27] Reynolds, J., *The Craft of Programming*, Prentice-Hall 1981.

[28] Reynolds, J., Idealized Algol and its specification logic, Technical Report 1-81, Dept. of Computer and Information Science, Syracuse University (July 1981).

[29] Reynolds, J., Syntactic control of interference, Proceedings of the 5th ACM Symposium on Principles of Programming Languages, ACM New York, pp 39-46 (1978).

[30] Stoy, J. E., *Denotational Semantics*, MIT Press 1977.

[31] Strachey, C., Towards a formal semantics, in: Formal Language Description Languages for Computer Programming, ed. T. B. Steel, Jr., North-Holland, Amsterdam (1966).

[32] Tennent, R. D., Semantics of interference control, Theoretical Computer Science 27 (1983) 293-310.

COMPARING CATEGORIES OF DOMAINS

by

Carl A. Gunter[1]
Department of Computer Science
Carnegie-Mellon University
Pittsburgh, Pennsylvania 15213

Abstract. We discuss some of the reasons for the proliferation of categories of domains suggested for the mathematical foundations of the Scott-Strachey theory of programming semantics. Five general conditions are presented which such a category should satisfy and they are used to motivate a number of examples. An attempt is made to survey some of the methods whereby these examples may be compared and their relationships expressed. We also ask a few mathematical questions about the examples.

1. Introduction.

A great variety of mathematical structures have been proposed for use as semantic domains for programming languages. We focus on one line of investigation which uses certain classes of partially ordered sets and aims to give a semantics which is denotational in nature. This approach was introduced by Dana Scott and Chris Strachey in the late sixties ([24], [30]) and it remains an area of active research today. The original category used by Scott and Strachey had complete lattices as objects and monotone functions that preserve least upper bounds of directed collections as arrows. But in the decade and a half since their work a host of other closely related categories have been investigated. Discussing the reasons that these alternatives have been suggested and the relationships between the different categories is the goal of the current document. A secondary objective is to ask a few mathematical questions about the categories. Most of the questions mentioned are not motivated by any particular problem in programming semantics. It is hoped, however, that they will evoke the curiosity of the reader as they have that of the author.

The paper is divided into four sections and an appendix. Section two discusses some of the conditions from programming semantics which motivate the choice of a category of domains. A collection of five such conditions are enumerated and we discuss how these conditions are satisfied to one degree or another by specific categories. Section three discusses what might be called "distinguishing conditions" on categories. The most important of these is Smyth's Theorem and we state some of its generalizations. The fourth section introduces the categories of "continuous

---

[1]This research was sponsored by the Defense Advanced Research Projects Agency (DOD), ARPA Order No. 3597, monitored by the Air Force Avionics Laboratory under Contract F33615-84-K-1520. The views and conclusions contained in this document are those of the author and should not be interpreted as representing the official policies, either expressed or implied, of the Defense Advanced Research Projects Agency or the US Government.

domains" which are a current area of investigation. Proofs of most of the theorems stated below can be found scattered throughout the literature (see, in particular, [4], [17] and [29]). A few short proofs that do not require much background have been included in an appendix. A result whose proof may be found there is marked with an asterisk (*).

The reader is assumed to be familiar with the following concepts from category theory: category, functor, object, arrow, product and coproduct, terminal and initial objects, equivalence and isomorphism between categories, inverse limit, and continuous functor. Definitions may be found in any of the standard references on category theory ([1], [5], [13]).

2. In search of the perfect category of domains.

Basic definitions and notation. A *poset* is a set with a binary relation $\sqsubseteq$ which is reflexive, antisymmetric and transitive. If D is a poset, a subset $M \subseteq D$ is *directed* if every finite subset of M has a bound in M. A poset D is *directed complete* if every directed $M \subseteq D$ has a least upper bound $\bigsqcup M$ in D. A function $f : D \to E$ is *Scott continuous* if it is monotone and $f(\bigsqcup M) = \bigsqcup f(M)$ for each directed $M \subseteq D$. The term "continuous" comes form the fact that it is possible to define a topology on a dcpo which makes these directed lub preserving maps exactly the continuous functions. If D is a dcpo then a subset $\mathcal{O} \subseteq D$ is said to be *Scott open* if

1. If $x \in \mathcal{O}$ and $x \sqsubseteq y$ then $y \in \mathcal{O}$.
2. If M is directed and $\bigsqcup M \in \mathcal{O}$ then $M \cap \mathcal{O} \neq \emptyset$.

These open sets form a T_0 topology on D called the *Scott topology.*

We denote by **DCPO** the category of directed complete posets and continuous functions. All of the domains that we consider below will be dcpo's. We therefore adopt the following convention: unless otherwise stated, every category **C** is assumed to be a full subcategory of **DCPO**. Here are a few examples:

- Let S be any set. Order S discretely, *i.e.* $x \sqsubseteq y$ iff $x = y$. These discretely ordered posets are all dcpo's. If S and T are discretely ordered posets then *any* function $f : S \to T$ is continuous.
- Any finite poset is a dcpo.
- If α is an ordinal then $\alpha + 1$ is a dcpo.
- If S is a set then the powerset of S, ordered by set inclusion, is a dcpo.
- The extended reals (*i.e.* the reals under the usual ordering with a largest and smallest element added) form a dcpo.

DCPO is a rather "large" category. Indeed, the discretely ordered posets mentioned above form a full subcategory **Set** $\subseteq$ **DCPO** which is isomorphic to the category of sets. There are, however, familiar partially ordered sets which are *not* dcpo's. For example, the rational numbers do not form a dcpo for two reasons. First, there would need to be a top (greatest) element to act as a least upper bound for the whole set of rationals (since any linear order is directed). But the second and less trivial reason is that the irrationals are "missing". In short, the rationals are simply not dense enough to be a dcpo.

The class of dcpo's having a bottom (least) element is of considerable importance in domain theory. If a domain D has a least element then it is usually denoted by the symbol $\perp_D$ (bottom) and the subscript is dropped when there is no likelihood of confusion. A domain with a least element is said to be *pointed*. If $\mathbf{C} \subseteq \mathbf{DCPO}$ then $\mathbf{C}_\perp$ is defined to be the full subcategory of **DCPO** which has as objects those dcpo's in **C** which have a least element.

Operations on dcpo's. In giving the semantics of a programming language it is necessary to utilize a number of operators on dcpo's to build up the desired data types from given primitive data types (such as integers or booleans). Here are some of the operators commonly used:

- Product: $D \times E$,
- Function space: $[D \to E]$,
- Disjoint sum: $D + E$,
- Separated sum: $D \oplus E$,
- Lift: $D_\perp$.

The product and function space are ordered coordinatewise and *only* continuous functions are included in $[D \to E]$. To get the disjoint sum of domains D and E, one "colors" D and E so their elements cannot be confused and then takes the union of the two (colored) posets. This is different from the separated sum which is used in most of the literature on denotational semantics. It is defined by $D \oplus E = (D + E)_\perp$ where $F_\perp$ is the result of adjoining a new bottom element to a domain F. All of the operators listed above except $+$ are closed on $\mathbf{DCPO}_\perp$. The first three operators ($\times$, $\to$, and $+$) are also closed on **Set**. There is another commonly used flavor of sum which is called the *coalesced sum*. If $D_\perp$ and $E_\perp$ are pointed dcpo's, then their coalesced sum is $D \oplus E$. Note that the coalesced sum only makes sense on pointed domains. Between the disjoint, separated and coalesced sums, the disjoint sum is certainly the most elegant and natural mathematically. In **DCPO**, it is the *categorical coproduct* and consequently has several nice relationships with the operators $\times$ and $\to$. For example, the following isomophism holds for all domains D, E, F: $D \times (E + F) \cong (D \times E) + (D \times F)$. Moreover, $+$ and $\to$ are related by the following isomorphism: $[(D + E) \to F] \cong [D \to F] \times [E \to F]$.

Cartesian closure. There is an important categorical condition which has arisen as being particularly significant for domain theory. This is the notion of a *cartesian closed category*. In mathematics, cartesian closed categories are somewhat rare. No doubt the best known example is the category of sets and functions. For sets there is an isomorphism

$$\text{curry} : [(D \times E) \to F] \cong [D \to [E \to F]]$$

defined as follows. If $f : D \times E \to F$ and $(x, y) \in D \times E$, then $\text{curry}(f)(x)(y) = f(x, y)$. It is well outside the scope of the current document to discuss all of the reasons that ccc's are important for programming semantics. Besides, there is a wealth of literature available on the subject ([9], [10], [20]). Most of it is concerned with the connection between ccc's and models of typed and untyped λ-calculus. For our purposes, a (full) subcategory $\mathbf{C} \subseteq \mathbf{DCPO}$ is cartesian closed iff it is closed under the product ($\times$) and function space ($\to$) operations. The objects of $\mathbf{C}$ should also include the one point domain 1. This is a specialization of the actual definition which one finds in category theory books. We now offer up the first of our conditions on a category of domains:

> **CONDITION 1:** The category must be closed under the desired operators. (Particularly product and function space operators: cartesian closure is a good technical condition.)

And we have the following:

Theorem 1: DCPO *is a cartesian closed category.* **Set** *and* $\mathbf{DCPO}_\perp$ *are also cartesian closed.*
□

In fact, **DCPO** and **Set** are endowed with the additional nicity of being closed under the disjoint sum operation +. Moreover, the empty poset 0 is an identity for + which is initial in the **DCPO**. A cartesian closed category which has a coproduct and initial object is said to be *bicartesian closed.*

Equational specification. Much of the essence of the denotational semantics of programming languages involves the equational specification of meanings for language constructs. For example, one might write something like to following equation to specify the meaning of a while loop:

$$[\![\textbf{while } B \textbf{ do } C]\!]\sigma = \begin{cases} \sigma & \text{if } [\![B]\!]\sigma = \text{false;} \\ [\![\textbf{while } B \textbf{ do } C]\!]([\![C]\!]\sigma) & \text{if } [\![B]\!]\sigma = \text{true.} \end{cases}$$

were σ is a machine state. One needs a proper theory of what sort of domains are used in interpreting the various operators in the above equation in order to get good general conditions for when such an equation has a *canonical* solution. When the data types involved are dcpo's and the functions are continuous, the following theorem is the key fact:

Theorem 2: *Suppose D is a dcpo and $f : D \to D$ is continuous. If $x \sqsubseteq f(x)$ for some $x \in D$ then there is a least $y \in D$ such that $x \sqsubseteq y$ and $y = f(y)$. In particular, if D has a $\perp$ then f has a least fixed point.* □

The proof of the theorem is not difficult. If $x \sqsubseteq f(x)$ then the directed completeness of D allows us to find a point $y = \bigsqcup f^i(x)$. But f is continuous, so $f(y) = f(\bigsqcup f^i(x)) = \bigsqcup f^{i+1}(x) = y$.

It is, moreover, possible to specify *data types* using equations (or, to be a bit more precise, isomorphisms) Here are a few examples:

- Simple binary tree: $T \cong T \oplus T$.
- S-expressions: $T \cong At \oplus (T \times T)$.
- λ-calculus: $D \cong At \oplus [D \to D]$.
- Finitely branching trees T and forests F of finitely branching trees:

$$T \cong At \times F$$
$$F \cong 1 \oplus (T \times F).$$

A great deal of thought has been given to the issue of specifying data types in this way. Papers such as [11], [29] and [32] seek to find a general categorical framework within which one may find canonical solutions to such equations. Typically this involves considering categories with some order structure on their hom sets and finding a fixed point of a continuous functor F by locating an initial object in a category defined from F and $\mathbf{C}$. We now sketch the way this treatment applies to **DCPO** (which is, in any event, a primary motiviating example in these categorical treatments.) The following notion is central to the success of the approach:

Definition: Let D and E be dcpo's. A continuous function $f : E \to D$ is a *retraction* if there is a continuous $g : D \to E$ such that $f \circ g = \mathrm{id}_D$. If g satisfies the further condition that $g \circ f \sqsubseteq \mathrm{id}_E$ then f is called a *projection* and g an *embedding*. □

Remark: if a dcpo D is pointed then the (unique) function $!_D : D \to 1$ is a projection. If $\mathbf{C} \subseteq \mathbf{DCPO}$, let $\mathbf{C}^P$ be the category having the same objects as $\mathbf{C}$ and having projections as arrows. The remark amounts to saying that the domain 1 is terminal in the category $\mathbf{DCPO}_\perp^P$. The significance of this fact comes from the following fixed point existence theorem:

Theorem 3: *Suppose $\mathbf{C} \subseteq \mathbf{DCPO}$ and $\mathbf{C}^P$ has limits for countable inverse systems. If $F : \mathbf{C}^P \to \mathbf{C}^P$ is a continuous functor and there is a domain $I \in \mathbf{C}$ and a projection $p : F(I) \to I$, then there is a dcpo $D \in \mathbf{C}$ such that $D \cong F(D)$.* □

Because of its importance, let us look at a brief sketch of the proof of this theorem. If $p : F(I) \to I$ then because F is a functor there is a projection $F(p) : F^2(I) \to F(I)$. Continuing in this way, one builds an inverse system:

$$I \xleftarrow{p} F(I) \xleftarrow{F(p)} F^2(I) \xleftarrow{F^2(p)} \cdots$$

Now, let $D = \varprojlim F^i(I)$ be the limit of this system. Then by continuity we compute: $F(D) = F(\varprojlim F^i(I)) \cong \varprojlim F^{i+1}(I) \cong D$. Note the similarity between this proof and the proof of Theorem 2.

Suppose that $\mathbf{C}_\perp$ is a category of pointed domains with $1 \in \mathbf{C}$ and suppose $\mathbf{C}_\perp^P$ has limits for countable inverse systems. If $F : \mathbf{C}_\perp^P \to \mathbf{C}_\perp^P$ is continuous, then it has a fixed point because the domain 1 can serve as the object I in the theorem. Of course, this situation is highly analogous to the one which arose when we set down conditions in Theorem 2 for the existence of a fixed point of a continuous *function*. The object I is like the point x such that $x \sqsubseteq f(x)$. A category of pointed dcpo's is therefore like a domain with a least element. This analogy between continuous functions on a domain and continuous functors on a category of domains is often helpful.

It is a well-known fact from the domain theory literature that all of the operators on dcpo's that we have mentioned so far can be made into continuous functors on $\mathbf{DCPO}^P$ by a proper choice of action on morphisms. The most interesting example is the function space operator $\rightarrow$. If $p_D : D \rightarrow D'$, and $p_E : E \rightarrow E'$ are projections then we define a projection

$$[p_D \rightarrow p_E] : [D \rightarrow E] \rightarrow [D' \rightarrow E']$$

by letting $[p_D \rightarrow p_E](f) = p_E \circ f \circ q_D$ where q_D is the embedding that corresponds to p_D. Proof that this defines a continuous functor can be found in [4] or [29].

The situation with fixed points can be a bit problematic, however. Theorem 3 can be used to show that a fixed point *exists* but it does not insure that the solution constucted will be non-trivial. For example, the operator $F(X) = [X \rightarrow X]$ is closed on pointed dcpo's so it has a fixed point. But the result that one gets from using $I = 1$ is just the one element domain itself! The solution to this problem is to start with a non-trivial domain I. If I is *pointed* then it is possible to find a projection $p : [I \rightarrow I] \rightarrow I$ so there are also plenty of solutions for $X \cong [X \rightarrow X]$. This also works for getting non-trivial solutions to other equations like $X \cong X \times X$. One can show that for any pointed dcpo I, there is a projection $p : I \times I \rightarrow I$ so non-trivial solutions to this equation are also abundant.

Actually, the functor $\times$ is continuous on dcpo's with *arbitrary* continuous functions as arrows. A fact similar to that expressed by Theorem 3 can be proved and used to find still more fixed points for the $X \times X$ operator using continuous functions $f : I \times I \rightarrow I$. This is not true for the function space operator, however. The functor $\rightarrow$ on $\mathbf{DCPO}$ is contravariant in its second argument and therefore is not continuous. In fact this is one of the primary reasons for using *projections* as arrows. As noted above, with projections as arrows, it is possible to get an action of $\rightarrow$ on arrows making it a continuous functor. Note, however, that no discrete set other than 1 can be projected onto its function space. Moreover, no finite poset (other than 1) has this property. In short, there can be a problem in deciding of a given equation whether Theorem 3 will help. For example, the equation $X \cong X + X$ has many solutions since any infinite discrete set X will work. However, the equation $X \cong 1 + [X \rightarrow X]$ has *no* solution. (To prove this count the number of disjoint components in X and $1 + [X \rightarrow X]$.) The equation $X \cong [X \rightarrow 0]$ also has no solution. The following question is suggested: *Is there a procedure for effectively deciding whether an operator built up from constants and the operators* $+, \times, \rightarrow$ *has a fixed point in* **DCPO***?*

We summarize the need for solutions to recursive equations as our second condition:

CONDITION 2: There should be (canonical) solutions for recursive equations.

The condition is to be taken as expressing a *generally desirable* property. It is not really necessary that *all* equations have fixed points but there should be good conditions for when an equation does have a solution. We offer the claim that **DCPO** (or at least $\mathbf{DCPO}_\perp$) meets the condition quite nicely.

Since the hypothesis in Theorem 3 requires the existence of *countable* inverse limits (*i.e.* limits for countable inverse systems), we adopt the convention that all inverse limits that we mention below are limits of countable systems. We might have adopted a similar convention for dcpo's, requiring only that *countable* directed collections have a least upper bound. This would not interfere with Theorem 2 because the proof uses only the existence of the least upper bound of an ω-chain. In much of the literature this weaker condition of *chain completeness* is used instead of arbitrary directed completeness. For the purposes of this paper, it makes no difference which notion is used.

Computability. One of the most natural conditions for a category of semantic domains for compter programming languages to satisfy is that there be a good notion of computability. In particular, it should be possible to say what it means for a domain to be *effectively given* and what it means for a function between effectively given domains to be *computable*. A definition of a *computable element* would, one expects, have the following property: a *function* $f : D \to E$ between effectively given domains D and E is computable iff the *element* $f \in [D \to E]$ is computable. One should also have a satisfactory notion of *computable data type constructor* or, more precisely, *computable functor*. One hopes that the constructors we have mentioned so far turn out to be computable and that important arrows associated with those operators turn out to be computable.

To do this, it appears that **DCPO** is *not* the right category. For a proper notion of computability, a domain needs to have some kind of basis of "finite" or "one-step computable" elements which can be used to approximate the *infinite* elements of the domain. Stated vaguely we ask that the following be satisfied:

CONDITION 3: There should be a flexible and intuitive theory of computability through finitary approximation.

The details of how to derive this theory of computability are beyond the scope of this paper. It has been the object of intense study over the last decade. The topic is discussed for particular categories in [19], [21], [25], and [33]. The issue of getting effective presentations for domains that are specified as fixed points is the central topic of [7], [8], and [34]. McCarty [14] studies the use of intuitionistic set theory for getting a theory of computability. All of these approaches deal in some degree with subcategories of **DCPO** for which the objects have a basis. Several of the studies use the following notion:

Definition: Let D be a dcpo. An element $x \in D$ is said to be *finite* if whenever $M \subseteq D$ is directed and $x \sqsubseteq \bigsqcup M$, then $x \sqsubseteq y$ for some $y \in M$. Let D^0 denote the set of finite elements of D. Then D is said to be *algebraic* if for every $x \in D$, $M = D^0 \cap \downarrow x$ is directed and $x = \bigsqcup M$. If D^0 is countable, then D is said to be ω-algebraic. □

The above-mentioned literature shows how to define a quite satisfactory notion of computability for ω-algebraic dcpo's and continuous functions between them. Such a treatment depends crucially upon the countability of the basis for the domain. We therefore adopt the following convention: all algebraic dcpo's will be assumed to have a countable basis. Accordingly, henceforth, **Set** is the category of *countable* discretely ordered posets. We define **Alg** to be the category of (ω-)algebraic dcpo's.

Computability and Condition 1. Unfortunately, **Alg** is *not* cartesian closed and therefore does not satisfy our closure condition. The problem is that there are algebraic dcpo's D such that $[D \to D]$ fails to be algebraic (see [27]). It is therefore necessary to look for cartesian closed subcategories of **Alg**. Fortunately, there are quite a few of these. We need a few terms:

Definition: A poset $A \neq \emptyset$ is *bounded complete* if every finite bounded $u \subseteq A$, has a least upper bound. A is *coherent* if every finite $u \subseteq A$ which is pair-wise bounded has a least upper bound. □

We use the following notation:

- **AlgLat** = algebraic lattices,
- **CohAlg** = coherent algebraic dcpo's,
- **BCAlg** = bounded complete algebraic dcpo's.

The main fact is this:

Theorem 4: AlgLat, CohAlg, BCAlg *are cartesian closed and have the corresponding categories with projections as arrows have inverse limits.* □

Simplicity. Certainly one would like to work with a category which is easy to describe and understand. Proving the basic properties (such as cartesian closure and existence of desirable arrows) should also be straight-forward. Part of the reason that the three categories in the theorem above are the ones most commonly used in programming semantics today is the degree to which they satisfy the following:

> **CONDITION 4:** The category should be natural to motivate and simple to describe.

Of course, what one considers "natural" or "simple" is a matter of taste and domain theory has been criticized for failing to do more toward satisfying Condition 4. Scott ([19], [21], [22], [23]) has made an effort to correct this (perceived) problem with his original treatment [18]. This has been followed up by other researchers (for example, [2], [4] and [33]) and some progress has been made but the final word has probably not yet been written.

Basic Data Types. The reader may be curious about why *three* cartesian closed subcategories of **Alg** have been considered. The algebraic lattices were given a rather thorough treatment by Scott [19] but some domain theorists complained that the existence of a top element in the domains was unnatural and inconvenient. For example, the infinite discrete set N must have a bottom element and top element added to it to get a lattice. The resulting domain $N_\perp^\top$ is then used as the natural numbers data type. The intuition is that the bottom element is the value of a divergent computation. Plotkin [16] urged the use of the category of coherent algebraic dcpo's as an alternative and gave a treatment for this class which is analogous to Scott's treatment of the algebraic lattices. For example, the natural number data type can be taken as $N_\perp$ rather than $N_\perp^\top$ because the former is coherent (although not a lattice). Subsequently, Scott ([21], [22], [23]) has urged the use of the bounded complete algebraics on the grounds that the troublesome top element is avoided and **BCAlg** is larger and simpler than **CohAlg**. We summarize (part of) this issue in the following:

> **CONDITION 5:** The category must possess the desired basic data types (or facsimiles thereof).

3. Profinite domains and Smyth's Theorem.

One problem with the categories **AlgLat, CohAlg, BCAlg** is that there are operators such as + and the convex powerdomain ([15], [26] [28]) which are not closed on these classes. A noteworthy category which *is* closed under these operators is the category of *profinite* domains. These are defined as follows:

Definition: A dcpo is (ω-)*profinite* if it is isomorphic to a countable inverse limit (in $\mathbf{DCPO}^P$) of finite posets. □

One drawback to this definition is that it does not define the profinites *intrinsically*. In other words, to tell whether a domain is profinite requires that one locate an inverse system of finite sets. It would be better to find a condition on a domain D which shows that D is profinite without reference to other posets. Such an intrinsic characterization is provided by the following:

Theorem 5: *Let D be a dcpo and let M be the set of continuous functions $p : D \to D$ such that $p = p \circ p \sqsubseteq \mathrm{id}_D$ and $im(p)$ is finite. Then D is profinite if M is countable, directed and $\bigsqcup M = \mathrm{id}_D$.* □

Several other intrinsic characterizations of profinite domains are possible ([15], [4]). The point is that the profinites are not far from satisfying Condition 4. The category **P** of profinite domains is also quite large:

Theorem 6: $\mathbf{AlgLat} \subseteq \mathbf{CohAlg} \subseteq \mathbf{BCAlg} \subseteq \mathbf{P}_\perp \subseteq \mathbf{P} \subseteq \mathbf{Alg}$ *and none of these inclusions is reversible.* □

Indeed, there are many domains which are profinite but not bounded complete. For example, *all* finite posets are in $\mathbf{P}$. However, no infinite discrete set is profinite. $\mathbf{P}$ also has limits for proving the existence of fixed points:

Theorem 7: $\mathbf{P}^P$ *and* $\mathbf{P}_\perp^P$ *have limits for inverse systems.* □

Gunter [4] has shown that it is possible to enumerate those operators built up from constants and $+, \times, \rightarrow$ which have fixed points. However, it is not known whether this fixed point existence property is decidable.

The primary reason for interest in the profinites is the following fact:

Theorem 8: *Suppose* $F : \mathbf{DCPO}^P \rightarrow \mathbf{DCPO}^P$ *is a continuous functor. If* $F(A)$ *is finite whenever* A *is finite then* $F(D)$ *is profinite whenever* D *is profinite.* □

This says that $\mathbf{P}$ has rather robust closure properties. There is an obvious generalization of the theorem to multiary functors, so the theorem may be applied to show, for example, that $\mathbf{P}$ is bicartesian closed. The subcategory $\mathbf{P}_\perp$ of pointed profinite domains is also a pleasing one. On can prove closure results for it by using the following observation. Suppose $F : \mathbf{DCPO}^P \rightarrow \mathbf{DCPO}^P$ is a continuous functor. For finite posets A, if $F(A)$ has a $\perp$ whenever A does then $F(D)$ has a $\perp$ whenever D does. In particular, $\mathbf{P}_\perp$ is cartesian closed (but not bicartesian closed).

Other bicartesian closed categories. The following observation of Scott shows the existence of quite a few bicartesian closed categories of domains:

Theorem* 9: *Suppose* $\mathbf{C} \subseteq \mathbf{DCPO}_\perp$ *is cartesian closed. If* $\mathbf{C}'$ *is the category whose objects include* 0 *and all dcpo's of the form*

$$D_1 + \cdots + D_n$$

where $D_1, \ldots, D_n$ *are in* $\mathbf{C}$, *then* $\mathbf{C}'$ *is bicartesian closed. Moreover, if* $\mathbf{C} \subseteq \mathbf{Alg}_\perp$ *then* $\mathbf{C}' \subseteq \mathbf{P}$. □

However, as was noted in the previous section, none of these categories has solutions for equations like $X \cong 1 + [X \rightarrow X]$. *Is there an interesting bicartesian closed category on which operations built up from* $\times, \rightarrow, +$ *etc. all have fixed points?* One stab at answering the question is to consider non-trivial complete Heyting algebras. These are bicartesian closed categories for which the fixed point theorem applies. Unfortunately, the negation operator, $\neg X = [X \rightarrow 0]$, is not continuous and does not have a fixed point in any such algebra. Perhaps the question is expressed a bit too strongly. There are, after all, quite a few strange looking operators that one can build using 0.

Smyth's Theorem. The intuition that the profinites form a "large" subcategory of $\mathbf{Alg}$ is confirmed by a theorem of Smyth [27]. Smyth proved the following conjecture of Plotkin:

Theorem 10: (Smyth) *If D and $[D \to D]$ are pointed and algebraic then D is profinite.* □

This is especially significant in light of Condition 1 because it yields the following:

Corollary 11: (Smyth) *If $\mathbf{C} \subseteq \mathbf{Alg}_\perp$ is cartesian closed then $\mathbf{C} \subseteq \mathbf{P}_\perp$.* □

Warning: Smyth's Theorem may *fail* if the domain D is not countably based. The theorem also leaves open several related questions. It is, for example, not difficult to show that one of the hypotheses may be weakened slightly:

Theorem* 12: *If D is a pointed dcpo and $[D \to D]$ is algebraic then D is profinite.* □

With some care, the proof of Smyth's Theorem can be modified [4] to extend the result to algebraic dcpo's which are not pointed:

Theorem 13: *If D and $[D \to D]$ are algebraic then D is profinite.* □

However, the author does not know an answer to the following question: *If D is a dcpo and $[D \to D]$ is algebraic then is D profinite?*

Strongly algebraic domains and partial functions. Another approach to finding a good category of domains involves not only restricting the *objects* but also working with a different kind of *arrow*. We make the following definition and observation:

Definition: A dcpo D is *strongly algebraic* if $D_\perp$ is profinite. Let **SA** be the category of strongly algebraic domains. □

Theorem 14: *$\mathbf{P} \subseteq \mathbf{SA} \subseteq \mathbf{Alg}$ and none of the inclusions is reversible.* □

In fact, **SA** has quite a lot of objects that **P** does not have. In particular, $\mathbf{Set} \subseteq \mathbf{SA}$. However, it follows from Theorem 13 that **SA** is not closed under function spaces. But this flaw may be partially remedied by changing the arrows on the category to allow *partiality.*

Definition: Let D and E be dcpo's. A partial function $\phi : D \rightharpoonup E$ is continuous iff it is defined on an open subset of D and preserves directed lub's. If $\psi : D \rightharpoonup E$ then say $\phi \sqsubseteq \psi$ iff for every $x \in D$, $\phi(x)\downarrow$ implies $\psi(x)\downarrow$ and $\phi(x) \sqsubseteq \psi(x)$. Let $[D \rightharpoonup E]$ be the poset of continuous partial functions from D to E. □

For any category **C** of dcpo's, let $\mathbf{C}^\partial$ be the category having the same objects as **C** and continuous partial functions as arrows. Note that: $\mathbf{Set}^\partial \subseteq \mathbf{SA}^\partial$. We have the following:

Theorem 15: *If D and E are dcpo's then $[D \rightharpoonup E]$ is a dcpo and if D and E are strongly algebraic then $[D \rightharpoonup E]$ is strongly algebraic.* □

While $\mathbf{SA}^\partial$ still fails to be cartesian closed, it does have nice categorical properties closely resembling cartesian closure (In [12], for example, such categories are called *partial cartesian closed.*) It is easy to show that $D + E$ and $D \times E$ are strongly algebraic whenever D and E are. Although $+$ is still a categorical coproduct even with the new partial functions $\times$ is *not* a categorical product on $\mathbf{SA}^\partial$. Actually, there *is* a product on $\mathbf{SA}^\partial$ given by the operator

$A \times\times B = A + (A \times B) + B$ but $\times\times$ is less important than $\times$. We now show that $\mathbf{SA}^\partial$ satisfies Condition 2 quite nicely.

Definition: A continuous partial function $\phi : E \rightharpoonup D$ is a *projection* if there is a continuous partial function $\psi : D \rightharpoonup E$ such that $\phi \circ \psi = \text{id}$ and $\psi \circ \phi \sqsubseteq \text{id}$. □

Let $\mathbf{C}^{\partial P}$ have the obvious meaning. Then we have the following:

Theorem 16: *If $\mathbf{C}^{\partial P}$ has inverse limits and $F : \mathbf{C}^{\partial P} \to \mathbf{C}^{\partial P}$ is continuous then there is a D such that $D \cong F(D)$.* □

Now, except for $\to$, all of the operators so far defined (including the partial funtion space) can be made into continuous functors on $\mathbf{DCPO}^{\partial P}$ and $\mathbf{SA}^{\partial P}$. Moreover, both of these categories have inverse limits. Since the empty set 0 is a terminal object in both categories, we can find fixed points for *all* of the operators (except those involving the total function space). So the sacrifice of cartesian closure offers a nice return on fixed point existence for data type specification. Moreover, when the meaning of a program construct is being specified via a fixed point equation, this is typically done by getting a fixed point for a total function $\gamma : [D \rightharpoonup D] \to [D \rightharpoonup D]$. But for every D, the space $[D \rightharpoonup D]$ of continuous partial functions has a least element—namely the totally undefined function. Thus, γ has a canonical fixed point. So Condition 2 is taken well in hand by $\mathbf{SA}^\partial$

$\mathbf{SA}^\partial$ has one more pleasing feature. Namely, it satisfies a "Smyth-like" theorem with respect to the algebraics:

Theorem 17: *If D is algebraic and $[D \rightharpoonup D]$ is algebraic then D is a strongly algebraic.* □

Proof of the theorem is quite easily obtained by making a few (quite minor) additions to the standard proof of Theorem 10. The trick is to use the notion of a *strict function* between pointed domains. A continuous function $f : D_\perp \to E_\perp$ is *strict* if $f(\perp) = \perp$. It is not hard to show that $\mathbf{Alg}^\partial$ is isomorphic to the category $\mathbf{Alg}_\perp^{strict}$ of pointed algebraic dcpo's with strict functions and it is easy to see how to carry out Smyth's argument in this latter category. But this is really not a very efficient method of proof. The following question is motivated: *Is there are proof of Theorem 17 from Smyth's Theorem?*

There is also a nice topological link between the profinite domains and the strongly algebraic domains:

Theorem 18: *A strongly algebraic domain D is profinite iff the Scott topology on D is compact.* □

A definability result for $\mathbf{BCAlg}$. If one thinks of Smyth's theorem as saying that $\mathbf{P}_\perp$ is the largest subcategory of $\mathbf{Alg}$ having an interesting property P then one can ask of some of the other categories we have discussed whether they may likewise be distinguished by an picking an appropriate property P. There is a notion from logic which does this for **BCAlg**. We make the following:

Definition: Let us say that a class $\mathcal{K}$ of algebraic dcpo's is *definable* if there is a first order theory T in the language of posets such that

1. T extends the theory of posets, and
2. for any algebraic cpo D, $D \in \mathcal{K}$ iff D^0 is countable and $D^0 \models T$. □

Let us show that **BCAlg** is definable. For each $n > 1$, let $\mathrm{UB}_n(\mathbf{u}, \mathbf{v}_1, \ldots, \mathbf{v}_n)$ be the formula $\mathbf{v}_1 \preceq \mathbf{u} \wedge \ldots \wedge \mathbf{v}_n \preceq \mathbf{u}$ where $\preceq$ is a binary relation symbol. Now, consider the theory T generated by the universal closure of the following axiom scheme:

$$(\exists \mathbf{u}.\ \mathrm{UB}_n(\mathbf{u}, \mathbf{v}_1, \ldots, \mathbf{v}_n)) \rightarrow \exists \mathbf{u}.\ \mathrm{UB}_n(\mathbf{u}, \mathbf{v}_1, \ldots, \mathbf{v}_n) \wedge (\forall \mathbf{w}.\ \mathrm{UB}_n(\mathbf{u}, \mathbf{v}_1, \ldots, \mathbf{v}_n) \rightarrow \mathbf{u} \preceq \mathbf{w})$$

together with the axioms which assert that $\preceq$ is reflexive, anti-symmetric and transitive. The models of T are exactly the bounded complete posets. One can show that an ω-algebraic dcpo is bounded complete iff its basis is countable and bounded complete. It follows therefore that **BCAlg** is definable. One may use the Compactness Theorem for first order logic, together with Theorem 13 to show that, in fact, the following holds:

Theorem* 19: *The bounded complete algebraic dcpo's are the largest cartesian closed definable category.* □

4. Continuous dcpo's.

There is a Condition 5 problem with all of the categories mentioned so far if one wishes to have the *real number data type*. The problem is that the extended reals are *not* algebraic! The main difficulty in dealing with this is to get a more general class of dcpo's which satisfy Condition 3. To accomplish this we use the following:

Definition: Let D be a dcpo. For $x, y \in D$, $y \ll x$ if for every directed subset $M \subseteq D$, $\bigsqcup M \sqsupseteq x$ implies $z \sqsupseteq y$ for some $z \in M$. D is (ω-)*continuous* if there is a countable set $B \subseteq D$ called a *basis* for D such that for each $x \in D$, the set $\hat{x} = \{y \in B \mid y \ll x\}$ is directed and $x = \bigsqcup \hat{x}$. □

The idea of a continuous *lattice* is due to Scott [18] and they have been studied in quite a lot of detail [3]. Continuous dcpo's have received less attention because they are less tractable and because most of the continuous dcpo's that come up in mathematics are lattices. But as far as domain theory goes, the more general notion is useful. The main point is this: it is possible to define a quite satisfactory notion of computability for (ω-)continuous dcpo's and continuous functions between them. See [32] for a nice exposition. Moreover, this theory generalizes the computability theory for algebraic dcpo's. For the rest of this section we assume that all of the continuous dcpo's are countably based. There is a close relationship between algebraic and continuous dcpo'given by the following:

ALGEBRAIC	*CONTINUOUS*
Alg	Continuous dcpo's
P	**RP**
$\mathbf{P}_\perp$	$\mathbf{RP}_\perp$
BCAlg	Bounded complete continuous dcpo's
CohAlg	Coherent continuous dcpo's
AlgLat	Continuous Lattices

Table 1: Categories of retracts.

Theorem 20: *A dcpo D is continuous if and only if there is a algebraic dcpo E and retraction $r : E \to D$.* □

Like the algebraics, the continuous dcpo's fail to form a ccc. It is easy to find cartesian closed subcategories, however, because of the following:

Theorem 21: *If* **C** *is cartesian closed then the category* **RC** *of retracts of objects of* **C** *is also cartesian closed. Moreover, the category* **PC** *of projects of objects of* **C** *is cartesian closed.* □

Table 1 lists some of what this tells us. The column on the right lists the category that one gets from the corresponding category on its left through taking retracts. Except for the continuous dcpo's, all of the categories listed in the "continuous" column are ccc's. Note how simply the classes of retracts of objects in **BCAlg, CohAlg,** and **AlgLat** can be described. Relatively little is known about this retracts correspondence in general beyond facts that come out of the proof of Theorem 21. For example: *If* $\mathbf{C}^P$ *has inverse limits, does* $\mathbf{RC}^P$ *also have inverse limits? What about* $\mathbf{PC}^P$*? When does* $\mathbf{RC} = \mathbf{PC}$*?*

Properties of **RP.** Some things are known about the specific categories mentioned in Table 1. It is well-known that the last three categories in the "continuous" column have inverse limits and that the retracts and projects categories are the same. Gunter [4] has shown that it is possible to find fixed points for a large class of operators on **RP**, but these results fall shy of showing that $\mathbf{RP}^P$ has inverse limits. It has long been an unsolved problem to characterize the retracts of profinites *intrinsically*. The following partial solution is due to Gordon Plotkin and Achim Jung:

Theorem* 22: *Let D be a dcpo. The following are equivalent:*

1. *D is a retract of a profinite domain.*
2. *D is a project of a profinite domain.*
3. *There is an ω-sequence of continuous functions $f_i : D \to D$ such that for each $i, j \in \omega$,*
   (a) *$i \leq j$ implies $f_i \sqsubseteq f_j$,*
   (b) *$im(f_i)$ is finite,*

(c) $\bigsqcup_{i \in \omega} f_i = \mathrm{id}_D$. □

The theorem has two interesting consequences:

Theorem* 23: $\mathbf{P} = \mathbf{Alg} \cap \mathbf{RP}$. □

Theorem 24: *Suppose $D \in \mathbf{RP}$. Then D is profinite if and only if the Scott topology on D has a basis of compact open sets.* □

Another intrinsic characterization which concentrates more on the basis of the domain was derived independently by Kamimura and Tang [6].

We end by mentioning two more unanswered questions about **RP**. Scott [18] showed a correspondence between the continuous lattices and the T_0-injectives. A similar result characterizes the bounded complete continuous dcpo's as corresponding to a natural class of topological spaces. It seems reasonable to ask: *is there some way of characterizing the retracts of profinites topologically?* A second question is whether there is a "Smyth-like" theorem for **RP**. This is Tang's Conjecture: *If $[D \to D]$ is continuous then D is a retract of a profinite domain.*

Appendix.

Proofs of Theorems in Section 3.

Proof of Theorem 9: We need the following isomorphisms:

1. $D \times (E + F) \cong (D \times E) + (D \times F)$,
2. $[(D + E) \to F] \cong [D \to F] \times [E \to F]$.

These hold for any D, E, F. If, moreover, D has a least element then we also have the following:

3. $[D \to (E + F)] \cong [D \to E] + [D \to F]$.

Proofs of 1 and 2 are left for the reader. To see 3, suppose $f : D \to (E + F)$ is continuous. If $f(\perp) \in E$ then $im(f) \subseteq E$, for if $x \in D$ then $\perp \sqsubseteq x$ so $f(\perp) \sqsubseteq f(x)$. Similarly, $f(\perp) \in F$ implies $im(f) \subseteq F$. Now, if $f(\perp) \in E$ then define $\hat{f} : D \to E$ to be the corestriction of f to E. This makes sense because $im(f) \subseteq E$. Also, $\hat{f}$ is obviously continuous. If, on the other hand, $f(\perp) \in F$ then take $\hat{f} : D \to F$ to be the corestriction of f to F. It is not hard to see that the correspondence $f \mapsto \hat{f}$ is an isomorphism between $[D \to (E + F)]$ and $[D \to E] + [D \to F]$.

It follows immediately from Isomorphism 1 that $\mathbf{C}'$ is closed under products. To see that it is also closed under ther function space operation, suppose S and T are in $\mathbf{C}'$. To save ourselves some subscripts, let's just assume that $S = D + E$ and $T = F + G$ where D, E, F, G are in $\mathbf{C}$ (the calculations go through equally well if S or T has any finite number of such disjoint components). We compute as follows:

$$
\begin{aligned}
[(D + E) \to (F + G)] &\cong [D \to (F + G)] \times [E \to (F + G)] && \text{by Iso 2} \\
&\cong ([D \to F] + [D \to G]) \times ([E \to F] + [E \to G]) && \text{by Iso 3}
\end{aligned}
$$

since D and E have least elements. After using Isomorphism 1 to pull the +'s to the outside of the expression the result has the form of an object in $\mathbf{C}'$. Finally, if $\mathbf{C} \subseteq \mathbf{Alg}_\perp$ then $\mathbf{C}' \subseteq \mathbf{Alg}$ so by Theorem 13, $\mathbf{C}' \subseteq \mathbf{P}$. □

Proof of Theorem 12: We may obtain the Theorem as a corollary of Smyth's Theorem together with the following:

Lemma 25: *If D is a pointed dcpo and $[D \to D]$ is algebraic, then D is algebraic.*

Proof. Suppose $f : D \to D$ is finite (as an element of $[D \to D]$). We claim that $f(\perp)$ is finite. Suppose $a_0 \sqsubseteq a_1 \sqsubseteq \cdots$ is a chain in D with $f(\perp) = \bigsqcup_n a_n$. For each n, define $f_n : D \to D$ by

$$f_n(x) = \begin{cases} f(x) & \text{if } x \neq \perp; \\ a_n & \text{if } x = \perp. \end{cases}$$

These functions are all continuous and $\bigsqcup_n f_n = f$ so $f = f_n$ for some n. Hence $f(\perp) = f_n(\perp) = a_n$ and $f(\perp)$ must therefore be finite. Now, suppose $d \in D$ and let $f(x) = d$ be the constant function determined by d. Since $[D \to D]$ is ω-algebraic, there are finite functions $f_0 \sqsubseteq f_1 \sqsubseteq \cdots$ such that $f = \bigsqcup_n f_n$. Hence $\bigsqcup_n f_n(\perp) = f(\perp) = d$. But $f_n(\perp)$ is finite for each n so D must be algebraic. □

Proof of Theorem 19: Let A be a poset and suppose $u \subseteq A$. An upper bound x for u is said to be *minimal* if whenever $y \sqsubseteq z$ for every $y \in u$ and $z \sqsubseteq x$ then $x = z$. Let

$$\mathrm{MUB}_A(u) = \{x \mid x \text{ is a minimal upper bound for } u \text{ in } A\}.$$

We will need the following fact about profinite domains (see [4] or [15]): if D is profinite and $u \subseteq D^0$ is bounded then $\mathrm{MUB}_{D^0}(u)$ is *finite and non-empty*. Let us call this "property (*)".

We work in a language with a single binary relation symbol $\preceq$ Let T be a first order theory extending the theory of posets. Suppose, moreover, that if A is a model of T then $A \times A$ is a model of T and that every model of T has property (*). Let A be a model of T in which the interpretation of $\preceq$ is not bounded complete. Then there is a finite (possibly empty) set $u \subseteq A$ such that $\mathrm{MUB}(u)$ has at least two elements. Suppose u has n elements. For each integer $m \geq 2$ we show that there is a model of T satisfying the first order axiom

$$\phi_m \equiv \exists \mathbf{v}_1 \cdots \exists \mathbf{v}_m. \bigwedge_{i \neq j} \mathbf{v}_i \neq \mathbf{v}_j \wedge \mathbf{v}_i \in \mathrm{MUB}(\{\mathbf{c}_1, \ldots, \mathbf{c}_n\})$$

for constants $\mathbf{c}_1, \ldots, \mathbf{c}_n$ not contained in $\mathcal{L}$. Note that A is a model of ϕ_2 if $\mathbf{c}_1, \ldots, \mathbf{c}_n$ are interpreted by the elements of u. So suppose we know that $T \cup \{\phi_m\}$ has a model B in which $\mathbf{c}_1, \ldots, \mathbf{c}_n$ are interpreted by $X_1, \ldots, X_n$. We claim that $B \times B$ is a model of $T \cup \{\phi_{m+1}\}$ when $\mathbf{c}_1, \ldots, \mathbf{c}_n$ are interpreted by $(X_1, X_1), \ldots, (X_n, X_n)$. To see this, let $v = \{X_1, \ldots, X_n\}$ and $w = \{(X_1, X_1), \ldots, (X_n, X_n)\}$. Then

$$\mathrm{MUB}(w) = \mathrm{MUB}(v) \times \mathrm{MUB}(v).$$

But there are m^2 elements in $\mathrm{MUB}(v) \times \mathrm{MUB}(v)$. Since $m^2 > m+1$ for $m > 1$ we are done. Now, for each m, $\phi_{m+1} \rightarrow \phi_m$ so we may deduce that any finite subset of $T \cup \{\phi_m \mid m \geq 2\}$ has a model. Hence, by the Compactness Theorem, there is a model C of $T \cup \{\phi_m \mid m \geq 2\}$. But if C interprets $\mathbf{c}_1, \ldots, \mathbf{c}_n$ by $Y_1, \ldots, Y_n$ respectively then C cannot have property $(*)$ because $\mathrm{MUB}(\{Y_1, \ldots, Y_n\})$ must be infinite. But this contradicts our assumption that models of T satisfy $(*)$. We conclude that all of the models of T must be bounded complete.

We are therefore able to conclude that the bounded complete dcpo's are the largest definable subcategory of the profinites which is closed under products. But by Theorem 13, any cartesian closed category subcategory of the algebraics must be a subcategory of the profinites. The desired conslusion therefore follows. □

Proofs of Theorems in Section 3.

Proof of Theorem 22: Since a projection is a retraction we certainly have (2) $\Rightarrow$ (1). We show that (3) $\Rightarrow$ (2) and (1) $\Rightarrow$ (3).

(1) $\Rightarrow$ (3). Suppose E is ω-profinite and there are continuous functions $r : E \rightarrow D$ and $r' : D \rightarrow E$ such that $r \circ r' = \mathrm{id}_D$. Since E is ω-profinite, there is a sequence $\langle p_i \rangle_{i \in \omega}$ of continuous idempotents on E such that $im(p_i)$ is finite for each i, $p_i \sqsubseteq p_j$ whenever $i \leq j$ and $\bigsqcup_i p_i = \mathrm{id}_E$. For each $i \in \omega$, define a continuous function $f_i = r \circ p_i \circ r' : D \rightarrow D$. If $i \leq j$ then $f_i = r \circ p_i \circ r' = r \circ p_j \circ r' = f_j$. Moreover, $\bigsqcup_i f_i = \bigsqcup_i r \circ p_i \circ r' = r \circ (\bigsqcup_i p_i) \circ r' = r \circ r' = \mathrm{id}_D$. Finally, $im(f_i)$ is finite for each i because $im(p_i)$ is. Thus the sequence $\langle f_i \rangle_{i \in \omega}$ satisfies (a), (b) and (c).

(3) $\Rightarrow$ (2). Suppose D is a dcpo and $\langle f_i \rangle_{i \in \omega}$ is a sequence of functions satisfying conditions (a), (b) and (c). Let E be the set of *monotone* sequences $x : \omega \rightarrow D$ such that for each $i \in \omega$, $x_i \in F_i = \bigcup_{j \leq i} im(f_j)$ and

$$f_i(\bigsqcup_{j \in \omega} x_j) \sqsubseteq x_i. \qquad (*)$$

Order E coordinatewise, *i.e.* $x \sqsubseteq y$ if and only if $x_i \sqsubseteq y_i$ for each i. We claim that E is profinite. To see that E is a dcpo, suppose $M \subseteq E$ is directed. We show that the least upper bound x of M in $\prod_{i \in \omega} F_i$ is in E. Now, x is certainly monotone; to prove that x satisfies condition $(*)$, we calculate

$$\begin{aligned} f_i(\bigsqcup_{j \in \omega} x_j) &= f_i(\bigsqcup_{j \in \omega} \sqcup\{y_j \mid y \in M\}) \\ &= f(\sqcup\{\bigsqcup_{j \in \omega} y_j \mid y \in M\}) \\ &= \sqcup\{f_i(\bigsqcup_{j \in \omega} y_j) \mid y \in M\} \\ &\sqsubseteq \sqcup\{y_i \mid y \in M\} && \text{by } (*) \text{ for } y \in M \\ &= x_i. \end{aligned}$$

To see that E is profinite, define for each $n \in \omega$ a function $p_n : E \to E$ by letting $p_n(x) = y$ where

$$y_i = \begin{cases} x_i & \text{if } i \leq n; \\ x_n & \text{otherwise.} \end{cases}$$

The following conditions are satisfied for each n:

- p_n is continuous,
- $p_n = p_n \circ p_n \sqsubseteq \mathrm{id}_D$,
- $im(p_n)$ is finite, and
- $p_n \sqsubseteq p_m$ for $n \leq m$.

Since we also have $\bigsqcup_{n \in \omega} p_n = \mathrm{id}_D$, it follows that E is profinite. To complete the proof, define $p : E \to D$ by $p : x \mapsto \bigsqcup_{j \in \omega} x_j$ and $q : D \to E$ by $q : x \mapsto \langle f_i(x) \rangle_{i \in \omega}$. It is easy to check that p and q are continuous. If $x \in D$ then $(p \circ q)(x) = \bigsqcup_{i \in \omega} f_i(x) = x$. If $x \in E$ then $(q \circ p)(x) = q(\bigsqcup_{j \in \omega} x_j) = \langle f_i(\bigsqcup_{j \in \omega} x_j) \rangle_{i \in \omega} \sqsubseteq \langle x_i \rangle_{i \in \omega}$. Hence D is the continuous projection of a countably based profinite domain. □

Proof of Theorem 23: If a domain is profinite then it is algebraic and it is a retract of itself, so to prove the theorem we must show that a retract of a profinite domain which is algebraic is profinite. The proof uses the characterizations of **P** and **RP** given by Theorems 5 and 22(3) respectively.

Suppose $f : D \to D$ is a continuous function with a finite image such that $f(x) \sqsubseteq x$ for each x. Then for any n and any x, $f^{n+1}(x) \sqsubseteq f^n(x)$. Since f has a finite image it follows that for some m, $f^{m+1}(x) = f^m(x)$. So define $f_\infty : D \to D$ by setting $f_\infty(x) = f^m(x)$ where $f^{m+1}(x) = f^m(x)$. This function is monotone, for if $x \sqsubseteq y$, $f^m(x) = f_\infty(x)$ and $f^n(y) = f_\infty(y)$ then for any $l \geq m, n$ we have $f_\infty(x) = f^l(x) \sqsubseteq f^l(y) = f_\infty(y)$. Since the image of f_∞ is finite, it follows that f_∞ is continuous. Moreover, if $x \in D$ and $f^{n+1}(x) = f^n(x)$ then $f_\infty^2(x) = f^{2n}(x) = f^n(x) = f_\infty(x)$ so f_∞ is idempotent. The set $M_\infty = \{f_\infty \mid f \in M\}$ is directed so there is a continuous function $g = \bigsqcup M_\infty$. We claim that g is the identity map on D. To see this, suppose $e \in D^0$. Now $e = (\bigsqcup M)(e)$ so $e \sqsubseteq f(e)$ for some $f \in M$. Hence $f(e) = e$. But this means $f^n(e) = e$ for all n so apparently $f_\infty(e) = e$. Thus $g(e) = e$ and since D is algebraic we conclude that g is the identity function. □

Acknowledgements.

I would like to thank the following people for suggestions and encouragement: Achim Jung, Gordon Plotkin, Pino Rosolini, Dana Scott, Rick Statman, Adrian Tang.

REFERENCES

[1] Arbib, M. and Manes, E. G., **Structures and Functors: the Categorical Imperative.** Academic Press, 1975, 185 pp.

[2] Coppo, M., Dezani, M. and Longo, G., *Applicative information systems.* In: **Trees in Algebra and Programming,** L'Aquila, edited by G. Ausiello and M. Protasi. **Lecture Notes in Computer Science,** vol. 159, Springer-Verlag, 1983, pp. 35–64.

[3] Gierz, G., Hofmann, K. H., Keimel, K., Lawson, J. D., Mislove, M. and Scott, D. S., **A Compendium of Continuous Lattices.** Springer-Verlag, 1981, 371 pp.

[4] Gunter, C., **Profinite Solutions for Recursive Domain Equations.** Doctoral Dissertation, University of Wisconsin, Madison, 1985, 181 pp.

[5] Herrlich, H. and Strecker, G., **Category Theory.** Allyn and Bacon Inc., 1973, 400 pp.

[6] Kamimura, T. and Tang, A., *Finitely continuous posets.* To appear in **Theoretical Computer Science,** 1985.

[7] Kanda, A., *Fully effective solutions of recursive domain equations.* In: **MFCS 79,** edited by J. Bečvař. **Lecture Notes in Computer Science,** vol. 74, Springer-Verlag, 1979.

[8] Kanda, A., **Effective Solutions of Recursive Domain Equations.** Doctoral Dissertation, Warwick University, 1980.

[9] Koymans, C. P. J., *Models of the lambda calculus.* **Information and Control,** vol. 52, 1982, pp. 306–332.

[10] Lambek J., *From lambda-calculus to cartesian closed categories.* In: **To H. B. Curry: Essays on Combinatory Logic, Lambda Calculus and Formalism,** edited by J. P. Seldin and R. Hindley. Academic Press, 1980, pp. 375–402.

[11] Lehmann, D. J., and Smyth M. B., *Algebraic specification of data types: a synthetic approach.* **Mathematical Systems Theory,** vol. 14, 1981, pp. 97–139.

[12] Longo, G. and Moggi, E., *Cartesian closed categories of enumerations for effective type structures (parts I and II).* In: **Semantics of Data Types,** Sophia-Antipolis, edited by G. Kahn and G. D. Plotkin. **Lecture Notes in Computer Science,** vol. 173, Springer-Verlag, 1984, pp. 235–256.

[13] MacLane, S., **Categories for the Working Mathematician.** Springer-Verlag, 1971, 262 pp.

[14] McCarty, D., **Realizability and Recursive Mathematics.** Doctoral Dissertation, Merton College, Oxford, 1984, 281 pp.

[15] Plotkin, G. D., *A powerdomain construction.* **SIAM Journal of Computing,** vol. 5, 1976, pp. 452–487.

[16] Plotkin, G. D., *The category of complete partial orders: a tool for making meanings.* In: **Proceedings of the Summer School on foundations of Artificial Intelligence and Computer Science,** Instituto di Scienze dell'Informazione, University di Pisa, 1978.

[17] Plotkin, G. D., *T^{ω} as a universal domain.* **Journal of Computer System Sciences,** vol. 17, 1978, pp. 209–236.

[18] Scott, D. S., *Continuous lattices.* In: **Toposes, Algebraic Geometry and Logic,** edited by F. W. Lawvere. **Lecture Notes in Mathematics,** vol. 274, Springer-Verlag, 1972, pp. 97–136.

[19] Scott, D. S., *Data types as lattices.* **SIAM Journal of Computing,** vol. 5, 1976, pp. 522–587.

[20] Scott, D. S., *Relating theories of the λ-calculus.* In: **To H. B. Curry: Essays on Combinatory Logic, Lambda Calculus and Formalism,** edited by J. P. Seldin and R. Hindley. Academic Press, 1980, pp. 403–450.

[21] Scott, D. S., *Lectures on a mathematical theory of computation.* Technical Report, no. PRG-19, Oxford University Computing Laboratory, 1981, 148 pp.

[22] Scott, D. S., *Some ordered sets in computer science.* In: **Ordered Sets,** Banff, Canada, edited by I. Rival. D. Reidel Publishing Company, 1981, pp. 677–718.

[23] Scott, D. S., *Domains for denotational semantics.* In: **ICALP 82,** Aarhus, Denmark, edited by M. Nielsen and E. M. Schmidt. **Lecture Notes in Computer Science,** vol. 140, Springer-Verlag, 1982, pp. 577–613.

[24] Scott, D. S., and Strachey, C., *Toward a mathematical semantics for computer languages.* Technical Report, no. PRG-6, Oxford University Computing Laboratory, 1971.

[25] Smyth, M. B., *Effectively given domains.* **Theoretical Computer Science** vol. 5, 1977, pp. 257–274.

[26] Smyth, M. B., *Powerdomains.* **Journal of Computer System Sciences,** vol. 16, 1978, pp. 23–36.

[27] Smyth, M. B., *The largest cartesian closed category of domains.* **Theoretical Computer Science,** vol. 27, 1983, pp 109–119.

[28] Smyth, M. B., *Powerdomains and predicate transformers: a topological view.* In: **ICALP 83,** edited by J. Diaz. **Lecture Notes in Computer Science,** vol. 154, Springer-Verlag, 1983, pp. 662–676.

[29] Smyth, M. B. and Plotkin, G. D., *The category-theoretic solution of recursive domain equations.* **SIAM Journal of Computing,** vol. 11, 1982, pp. 761–783.

[30] Stoy, J. E., **Denotational Semantics: The Scott-Strachey Approach to Programming Language Theory.** M.I.T. Press, 1977, 414 pp.

[31] Wand, M., *Fixed point constructions in order-enriched categories.* **Theoretical Computer Scence**, vol. 26, 1983, pp. 131–147.

[32] Weihrauch, K. and Deil, T., *Berechenbarkeit auf cpo's.* Technical Report no. 63, RWTH, Aachen, 1980, 101 pp.

[33] Winskel, G. and Larsen, K., *Using information systems to solve recursive domain equations effectively.* In: **Semantics of Data Types**, Sophia-Antipolis, edited by G. Kahn and G. D. Plotkin. **Lecture Notes in Computer Science**, vol. 173, Springer-Verlag, 1984, pp. 109–130.

Galois Connections

Horst Herrlich
Fachbereich Mathememeatik
und Informatik
Universität Bremen
2800 Bremen
Fed. Red. Germany

Miroslav Hušek
Matematicky Ustav
Karlovy University
Sokolovska 83
18600-Praha 8 Karlin
CSSR

Introduction

About 1830 E. Galois discovered and investigated a connection, for a given field extension $K \to L$, between the collection of all subfields of L containing K and the collection of all automorphisms of L leaving K pointwise fixed. The formal properties of this connection remain valid in more abstract settings. In 1940 G. Birkhoff [1] associated with any relation a connection, which he called a polarity. Generalizing this concept, O. Ore [8] introduced in 1944 Galois connexions between partially ordered sets. These, as well as the polarities, have a contravariant form. Its covariant version was introduced in 1953 by J. Schmidt [11] under the name Galois connections of mixed type. Categorists observed that these connections are nothing else but adjoint situations between partially ordered sets, considered in the standard way as categories (see S. Mac Lane [7]). Unfortunately most properties of Galois connections, in fact all of the interesting ones, are no longer valid in the realm of adjoint situations. Hence, for Galois connections, adjoint functors form an inappropriate level of generality. The aim of this note is to provide suitable levels of generality.

We start by recalling the classical descriptions of Galois connections by G. Birkhoff and O. Ore in their covariant forms.

§1 Galois connections of the first kind (polarities)

1.1 Definition (G. Birkhoff [1]): Let $\rho = (X,R,Y)$ be a relation between the sets X and Y. Denote by A resp. B the powersets of X resp. Y, ordered by inverse inclusion resp. by inclusion. Define maps $G\colon A \to B$ and $F\colon B \to A$ by $G(a) = \{y \in Y \mid \forall x \in a \ x\rho y\}$ and $F(b) = \{x \in X \mid \forall y \in b \ x\rho y\}$. Then (F,G) is called a Galois connection of the first kind.

1.2 Proposition (G. Birkhoff [1]): Let (F,G) be a Galois connection of the first kind. Then with the above notation and with $A^* = FB$ and $B^* = GA$ the following hold:

(0) $G\colon A \to B$ and $F\colon B \to A$ are monotone maps

(1) $Fb \leqslant a \Leftrightarrow b \leqslant Ga$ for $a \in A$ and $b \in B$

(2) $FGa \leqslant a$ and $b \leqslant GFb$ for $a \in A$ and $b \in B$

(3) $G(\bigcup a_i) = \bigcap G(a_i)$ and $F(\bigcup b_i) = \bigcap F(b_i)$

(4) $GFG = G$ and $FGF = F$

(5) $(GF)^2 = GF$ and $(FG)^2 = FG$

(6) $A^* = FGA = \{a \in A \mid FGa = a\}$ and
$B^* = GFB = \{b \in B \mid GFb = b\}$

(7) G and F restrict to order-isomorphisms $G^*: A^* \to B^*$ and $F^*: B^* \to A^*$, inverse to each other.

§2 Galois connections of the second kind

2.1 Definition (O. Ore [8], J. Schmidt [11]): Let $G: A \to B$ and $F: B \to A$ be monotone functions between partially ordered classes. Then (F,G) is called a Galois connection of the second kind provided the following equivalence holds:

$$Fb \leqslant a \Longleftrightarrow b \leqslant Ga.$$

2.2 Proposition (O. Ore [8], J. Schmidt [11]): Let $G: A \to B$ and $F: B \to A$ be monotone functions between partially ordered classes. Then the following conditions (1) and (2) are equivalent and imply the remaining ones, where $A^* = FB$ and $B^* = GA$:

(1) (F,G) is a Galois connection of the second kind

(2) $FGa \leqslant a$ and $b \leqslant GFb$ for $a \in A$ and $b \in B$

(3) G preserves meets and F preserves joins

(4) $GFG = G$ and $FGF = F$

(5) $(GF)^2 = GF$ and $(FG)^2 = FG$

(6) $A^* = FGA = \{a \in A \mid FGa = a\}$ and $B^* = GFB = \{b \in B \mid GFb = b\}$

(7) G and F restrict to order isomorphisms $G^*: A^* \to B^*$ and $F^*: B^* \to A^*$, inverse to each other.

2.3 Proposition (G. Pickert [9]): If $G: A \to B$ is a function from a complete lattice A to a partially ordered class B, then the following conditions are equivalent:

(1) G preserves meets

(2) there exists a (unique) map $F: B \to A$ such that (F,G) is a Galois connection of the second kind.

2.4 Proposition (O. Ore [8]): For Galois connections (F,G) of the second kind the following conditions are equivalent:

(1) G is injective

(2) F is surjective.

2.5 Proposition (O. Ore [8], C. J. Everett [3], J. Schmidt [11]): Let X and Y be sets; let A resp. B be the powersets of X resp. Y, ordered by inverse inclusion resp. by inclusion, and let $G: A \to B$ and $F: B \to A$ be functions. Then the following are equivalent:

(1) (F,G) is a Galois connection of the first kind

(2) (F,G) is a Galois connection of the second kind.

2.6 Remark: Since, up to order isomorphisms, powersets (ordered by inclusion or by inverse inclusion) are precisely the atomic complete Boolean algebras, Galois connections of the first kind are essentially Galois connections of the second kind between atomic complete Boolean algebras.

§3 Galois connections of the third kind

Let $\mathbf{X}$ be a category. Concrete categories over $\mathbf{X}$ are pairs $(\mathbf{A},U)$ consisting of a category $\mathbf{A}$ and a forgetful (= underlying = faithful and amnestic) functor $U: \mathbf{A} \to \mathbf{X}$ (where U is called amnestic iff any $\mathbf{A}$-isomorphism f is an $\mathbf{A}$-identity provided Uf is an $\mathbf{X}$-identity). By abuse of language we will not distinguish notationally between $(\mathbf{A},U)$ and $\mathbf{A}$ as well as between $\mathbf{A}$-morphisms f and their underlying $\mathbf{X}$-morphisms Uf. In particular, instead of saying that for $\mathbf{A}$-objects A and B and for an $\mathbf{X}$-morphism $f: UA \to UB$ "there exists a (necessarily unique) $\mathbf{A}$-morphism $g: A \to B$ with $Ug = f$" we will just say that "$f: A \to B$ is an $\mathbf{A}$-morphism" etc. If U is not specified notationally, the underlying $\mathbf{X}$-object of an $\mathbf{A}$-object A is sometimes denoted by $|A|$. A concrete functor $G: (\mathbf{A},U) \to (\mathbf{B},V)$ between concrete categories over $\mathbf{X}$ is a functor $G: \mathbf{A} \to \mathbf{B}$ which commutes with the forgetful functors, i.e., satisfies the equation $VG = U$. Concrete functors G are completely determined by their behaviour on objects. In particular with our above notational convention we have $G(A \xrightarrow{f} B) = GA \xrightarrow{f} GB$. On each concrete category $(\mathbf{A},U)$ there exists a natural order relation on the class of $\mathbf{A}$-objects, defined by:

$$A \leqslant B \Longleftrightarrow (UA = UB \text{ and } id_{UA}: A \to B \in \mathrm{Mor}\,\mathbf{A}).$$

For any pair of concrete categories $(\mathbf{A},U)$ and $(\mathbf{B},V)$ over $\mathbf{X}$ there exists a natural order relation on the class of all concrete functors from $(\mathbf{A},U)$ to $(\mathbf{B},V)$, defined by:

$$F \leqslant G \Longleftrightarrow \forall A \in \mathrm{Ob}\,\mathbf{A} \;\; FA \leqslant GA.$$

3.1 Definition: Let $G: \mathbf{A} \to \mathbf{B}$ and $F: \mathbf{B} \to \mathbf{A}$ be concrete functors between concrete categories $\mathbf{A}$ and $\mathbf{B}$ over $\mathbf{X}$. Then (F,G) is called a Galois connection of the third kind (over $\mathbf{X}$) provided the following equivalence holds

$$FB \xrightarrow{f} A \in \mathrm{Mor}\,\mathbf{A} \Longleftrightarrow B \xrightarrow{f} GA \in \mathrm{Mor}\,\mathbf{B}$$

for $A \in \mathrm{Ob}\,\mathbf{A}$, $B \in \mathrm{Ob}\,\mathbf{B}$ and $f \in \mathrm{Mor}\,\mathbf{X}$.

3.2 Remark: If partially ordered classes are interpreted in the standard way as concrete categories over a category $\mathbf{T}$ having precisely one morphism, then Galois connections of the second kind are just Galois connections of the third kind over $\mathbf{T}$.

3.3 Proposition:

(1) If (F,G) is a Galois connection of the third kind over $\mathbf{X}$, then (G^{op},F^{op}) is a Galois connection of the third kind over $\mathbf{X}^{op}$.

(2) If (F,G) and $(\bar{F},\bar{G})$ are Galois connections of the third kind over $\mathbf{X}$ and F and $\bar{G}$ have the same domain, then $(F\circ\bar{F}, \bar{G}\circ G)$ is a Galois connection of the third kind over $\mathbf{X}$.

(3) If H is a concrete isomorphism, then (H^{-1},H) is a Galois connection of the third kind.

Hence, there is a duality theory for Galois connections and Galois connections compose. In 3.10 we will show that Galois connections of the third kind can be decomposed into particularly simple ones.

3.4 Theorem: Let $G: \mathbf{A} \to \mathbf{B}$ and $F: \mathbf{B} \to \mathbf{A}$ be concrete functors over $\mathbf{X}$. Then the following conditions (1) - (4) are equivalent and imply the remaining ones, where $\mathbf{A}^*$ (resp. $\mathbf{B}^*$) is the full subcategory of $\mathbf{A}$ (resp. $\mathbf{B}$), whose objects are of the form FB with $B \in \mathrm{Ob}\,\mathbf{B}$ (resp. GA with $A \in \mathrm{Ob}\,\mathbf{A}$):

(1) (F,G) is a Galois connection of the third kind

(2) $FG \leqslant id_{\mathbf{A}}$ and $id_{\mathbf{B}} \leqslant GF$

(3) F is a left-adjoint of G and the G-universal maps are carried by X-identities $id_{|B|}: B \to GFB$

(4) G is a right adjoint of F and the F-couniversal maps are carried by X-identities $id_{|A|}: FGA \to A$

(5) G preserves initial sources and F preserves final sinks

(6) $GFG = G$ and $FGF = F$

(7) $(GF)^2 = GF$ and $(FG)^2 = FG$

(8) $A \in \mathrm{Ob}\,\mathbf{A}^* \iff \exists\, A' \in \mathbf{A}\ \ A = FGA' \iff A = FGA$
$B \in \mathrm{Ob}\,\mathbf{B}^* \iff \exists\, B' \in \mathbf{B}\ \ B = GFB' \iff B = GFB$

(9) G and F restrict to concrete isomorphisms $G^*: \mathbf{A}^* \to \mathbf{B}^*$ and $F^*: \mathbf{B}^* \to \mathbf{A}^*$, inverse to each other.

Proof: (1) ⇒ (2) By (1) $FGA \leqslant A \iff GA \leqslant GA$ and $B \leqslant GFB \iff FB \leqslant FB$. Hence (2).

(2) ⇒ (1) $FB \xrightarrow{f} A \in \mathrm{Mor}\,\mathbf{A} \Rightarrow GFB \xrightarrow{f} GA \in \mathrm{Mor}\,\mathbf{B} \Rightarrow$
$B \xrightarrow{id_{|B|}} GFA \xrightarrow{f} GA \in \mathrm{Mor}\,\mathbf{B} \Rightarrow B \xrightarrow{f} GA \in \mathrm{Mor}\,\mathbf{B} \Rightarrow$
$FB \xrightarrow{f} FGA \in \mathrm{Mor}\,\mathbf{A} \Rightarrow FB \xrightarrow{f} FGA \xrightarrow{id_{|B|}} A \in \mathrm{Mor}\,\mathbf{A} \Rightarrow FB \xrightarrow{f} A \in \mathrm{Mor}\,\mathbf{A}$. Hence (1).

(3) ⇔ (1) ⇔ (4) These are just reformulations.

(1) ⇒ (5) Let $(A \xrightarrow{f_i} A_i)_{i\in I}$ be an initial source in $\mathbf{A}$ and let $B \xrightarrow{g} GA$ be an $\mathbf{X}$-morphism with $B \xrightarrow{g} GA \xrightarrow{f_i} GA_i \in \mathrm{Mor}\,\mathbf{B}$ for each $i \in I$. Then $FB \xrightarrow{f_i \cdot g} A_i \in \mathrm{Mor}\,\mathbf{A}$ for each $i \in I$. Hence by initiality $FB \xrightarrow{g} A \in \mathrm{Mor}\,\mathbf{A}$. Thus $B \xrightarrow{g} GA \in \mathrm{Mor}\,\mathbf{B}$. Consequently $(GA \xrightarrow{f_i} GA_i)_{i\in I}$ is an initial source in $\mathbf{B}$. That F preserves final sinks follows by duality.

(2) ⇒ (6) Composing the first inequality of (2) with G on the left yields $GFG \leqslant G$. Composing the second inequality of (2) with G on the right yields $G \leqslant GFG$. Hence $GFG = G$. By duality $FGF = F$.

(6) ⇒ (7) ∧ (8) ∧ (9) Trivial.

3.5 Proposition:

(1) If (F,G) and (F′,G) are Galois connections of the third kind, then F = F′.

(2) If (F,G) and (F,G′) are Galois connections of the third kind, then G = G′.

Proof: (1) resp. (2) follow via amnesticity immediately from (3) resp. (4) of the above theorem.

For the next result compare O. Wyler [12], Theorem 6.3 and G.C.L. Brümmer [2], Theorem 2.6.

3.6 Theorem: If $G: \mathbf{A} \to \mathbf{B}$ is a concrete functor over $\mathbf{X}$ and $\mathbf{A}$ is initially complete, then the following conditions are equivalent:

(1) There exists some F such that (F,G) is a Galois connection of the third kind

(2) G has a concrete left adjoint

(3) G preserves initial sources.

Proof: (1) ⇒ (2) follows immediately from Theorem 3.4.
(2) ⇒ (3). Let F be a concrete left adjoint of G with G-universal maps $\eta_B: B \to GFB$ and F-couniversal maps $\epsilon_A: FGA \to A$. Then $\epsilon_{FB} \cdot F\eta_B = id_{FB}$ for each $\mathbf{B}$-object B. Hence each $F\eta_B$ is a section in $\mathbf{A}$. Since F is concrete, each η_B is a section in $\mathbf{X}$. To show that $\eta_B: B \to GFB$ is an epimorphism in $\mathbf{X}$ as well, let $GFB \overset{r}{\underset{s}{\rightrightarrows}} X$ be a pair of $\mathbf{X}$-morphisms with $r \cdot \eta_B = s \cdot \eta_B$. Let A be the indiscrete $\mathbf{A}$-object with $|A| = X$. Then $FB \overset{r}{\underset{s}{\rightrightarrows}} A$ is a pair of $\mathbf{A}$-morphisms with $Gr \cdot \eta_B = Gs \cdot \eta_B$. Since η_B is a G-universal map, this implies r = s. Hence each η_B is an $\mathbf{X}$-isomorphism. To show that this implies (3), let $(A \xrightarrow{f_i} A_i)_{i \in I}$ be an initial source in $\mathbf{A}$ and let $B \xrightarrow{g} GA$ be an $\mathbf{X}$-morphism with $B \xrightarrow{g} GA \xrightarrow{f_i} GA_i \in \mathrm{Mor}\,\mathbf{B}$ for each $i \in I$. In $\mathbf{X}$ consider the commutative diagram:

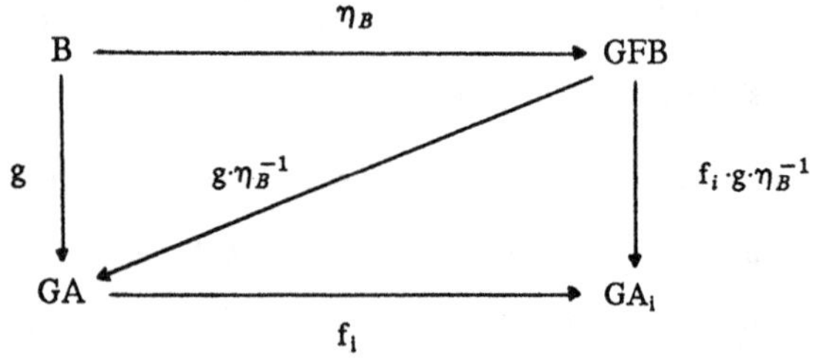

By the universal property of η_B and the fact that all $B \xrightarrow{g} GA \xrightarrow{f_i} GA_i$ are $\mathbf{B}$-morphisms, we conclude that all $FB \xrightarrow{f_i \cdot g \cdot \eta_B^{-1}} A_i$ are $\mathbf{A}$-morphisms. Hence, by initiality, $FB \xrightarrow{g \cdot \eta_B^{-1}} A$ is an $\mathbf{A}$-morphism. Consequently,

$$B \xrightarrow{g} GA = B \xrightarrow{\eta_B} GFB \xrightarrow{g \cdot \eta_B^{-1}} GA$$

is, as composite of $\mathbf{B}$-morphisms, a $\mathbf{B}$-morphism itself. Hence $(GA \xrightarrow{f_i} GA_i)_{i \in I}$ is an initial source in **B**.

(3) ⇒ (1) For each **B**-object B consider the initial lift in **A** $(A \xrightarrow{f_i} A_i)$ of the **A**-structured source $(|B| \xrightarrow{f_i} A_i)$, which consists of all **B**-morphisms of the form $B \xrightarrow{f_i} GA_i$. By (3), $(GA \xrightarrow{f_i} GA_i)$ is an initial source in **B**. This immediately implies that $B \xrightarrow{id_{|B|}} GA$ is a **B**-morphism; hence a G-universal map for **B**. Via Theorem 3.4 (3) this implies (1).

3.7 Remarks: (1) Conditions (1) and (2) of the above theorem are equivalent under rather mild constraints (e.g. if **A** has indiscrete objects, or if **B** has discrete objects, or if G is full). But they are not equivalent in general, as the following example demonstrates:

Let **X** be the full subcategory of **Set** with the single object $\mathbb{N}$. Let **B** be a concrete category over **X** with countably many objects $B_n, n \in \mathbb{N}$, and with morphisms $f: B_n \to B_m$ those monotone maps $f: \mathbb{N} \to \mathbb{N}$ which satisfy

(a) $f(n) \leqslant m$ and

(b) $f(n+p) = m+p$ for each $p \geqslant 1$.

Let **A** be the object-full subcategory of **B** with those **B**-morphisms $f: B_n \to B_m$ which satisfy

(c) $f(n) = m$.

Let $G: \mathbf{A} \to \mathbf{B}$ be the canonical embedding and let $F: \mathbf{B} \to \mathbf{A}$ be the concrete functor, defined by $FB_n = B_{n+1}$. Then F is a concrete left adjoint for G with G-universal maps $\eta_n: B_n \to GFB_n$, defined by

$$\eta_n(k) = \begin{cases} k, & \text{if } k \leqslant n \\ k+1, & \text{if } k > n \end{cases}$$

and F-couniversal maps $\epsilon_n: FGB_n \to B_n$, defined by

$$\epsilon_n(k) = \begin{cases} k, & \text{if } k \leqslant n \\ k-1, & \text{if } k > n \end{cases}$$

Since some of these maps (in fact all of them) are non-**X**-isomorphisms, the functor G has no concrete left adjoint with **X**-isomorphic G-universal maps. Hence there exists no F′ such that (F′,G) is a Galois connection of the third kind.

(2) Also it may be worth noting that when $F: \mathbf{B} \to \mathbf{A}$ is a concrete left adjoint for a concrete functor $G: \mathbf{A} \to \mathbf{B}$ with **X**-isomorphic G-universal maps, then (F,G) need not be a Galois connection of the third kind. This is shown by the following example:

Let **X** be a category, consisting of a single object X and two morphisms id_X and s with $s^2 = id_X$. Let **A** be the concrete category over **X**, consisting of two objects A_0 and A_1 and the following morphisms:

$$\hom_{\mathbf{A}}(A_i,A_j) = \begin{cases} id_X, & \text{if } i=j \\ s, & \text{if } i\neq j \end{cases}$$

Then there exist precisely two concrete isomorphisms $\mathbf{A} \to \mathbf{A}$, namely G, defined by $GA_i = A_i$, and F, defined by $FA_i = A_{1-i}$. As can be seen easily, G and F are naturally equivalent; both are concrete left adjoints of G; (G,G) is a Galois connection of the third kind; but (F,G) is not.

3.8 Remark: A full subcategory **A** of a concrete category **B** is called a reflective (resp. coreflective) modification of **B** iff the embedding functor G: $\mathbf{A} \to \mathbf{B}$ has a concrete left (resp. right) adjoint F with the G-universal (resp. F-couniversal) maps being carried by **X**-identities. In view of 3.4 this is the case iff there exists a concrete functor F: $\mathbf{B} \to \mathbf{A}$ such that (F,G) (resp. (G,F)) is a Galois connection of the third kind. Next we characterize these particular Galois connections and then we demonstrate that every Galois connection of the third kind can be decomposed up to a concrete isomorphism into these particularly simple ones.

3.9 Proposition: For Galois connections (F,G) of the third kind the following conditions are equivalent:

(1) G is a full embeddng

(2) G is full

(3) G is injective on objects

(4) F is surjective on objects

(5) $FG = id_{\mathbf{A}}$

Proof: (1) ⇒ (2) Trivial.

(2) ⇒ (3) If $GA = GA'$, then $A \leqslant A'$ and $A' \leqslant A$ by fullness of G; hence $A = A'$ by amnesticity.

(3) ⇒ (4) For any **A**-object A we have $GFGA = GA$; hence $F(GA) = A$ by (3).

(4) ⇒ (5) For any **A**-object A there exists, by (4), a **B**-object B with $FB = A$. Hence $FGA = FGFB = FB = A$.

(5) ⇒ (1) Obviously G is injective, i.e., an embedding. To show fullness let $GA \xrightarrow{f} GA'$ be a **B**-morphism. Then $FGA \xrightarrow{f} FGA' = A \xrightarrow{f} A'$ is an **A**-morphism.

3.10 Theorem: Let G: $\mathbf{A} \to \mathbf{B}$ and F: $\mathbf{B} \to \mathbf{A}$ be concrete functors, let $\mathbf{A}^*$ (resp. $\mathbf{B}^*$) be the full subcategory of **A** (resp. **B**) whose objects are of the form FB with $B \in \mathrm{Ob}\,\mathbf{B}$ (resp. GA with $A \in \mathrm{Ob}\,\mathbf{A}$), and let $E_{\mathbf{A}}: \mathbf{A}^* \to \mathbf{A}$ (resp. $E_{\mathbf{B}}: \mathbf{B}^* \to \mathbf{B}$) be the corresponding embedding. Then the following conditions are equivalent:

(1) (F,G) is a Galois connection of the third kind

(2) $\mathbf{A}^*$ is a coreflective modification of **A** with coreflector C, $\mathbf{B}^*$ is a reflective modification of **B** with reflector R, and there exists a concrete isomorphism H: $\mathbf{A}^* \to \mathbf{B}^*$ with $G = E_{\mathbf{B}} \cdot H \cdot C$ and $F = E_{\mathbf{A}} \cdot H^{-1} \cdot R$.

Moreover, if (1) and (2) hold, then

(a) $F \cdot G = E_{\mathbf{A}} \cdot C$

(b) $G \cdot F = E_B \cdot R$.

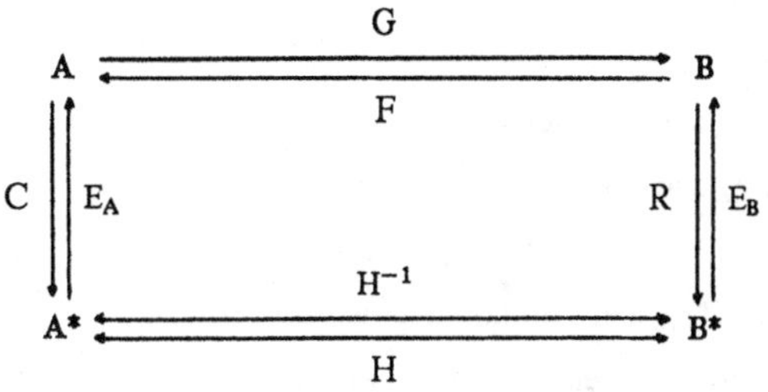

Proof: (1) ⇒ (2) Let $H: \mathbf{A}^* \to \mathbf{B}^*$ (resp. $C: \mathbf{A} \to \mathbf{A}^*$, resp. $R: \mathbf{B} \to \mathbf{B}^*$) be the restriction of G (resp. FG, resp. GF). By 3.4 H is a concrete isomorphism with inverse $H^{-1}: \mathbf{B}^* \to \mathbf{A}^*$ being the restriction of F. For $A \in \mathrm{Ob}\,\mathbf{A}$ and $A^* = FB \in \mathrm{Ob}\,\mathbf{A}^*$ we have $E_A CA = FGA \leqslant A$ and $CE_A A^* = CE_A FB = FGFB = FB = A^*$. Hence $\mathbf{A}^*$ is a coreflective modification of $\mathbf{A}$ with coreflector C. By duality $\mathbf{B}^*$ is a reflective modification of $\mathbf{B}$ with reflector R. Further $E_B HCA = E_B GFGA = GA$; hence $E_B HC = G$. By duality $E_A H^{-1} R = F$. Moreover (a) and (b) follow immediately from the above definitions.

(2) ⇒ (1) Let A be an $\mathbf{A}$-object. Then
$FGA = E_A H^{-1} R E_B HCA = E_A H^{-1}\, \mathrm{id}_{\mathbf{B}^*}\, HCA = E_A CA \leqslant A$. Dually $B \leqslant GFB$ for any $\mathbf{B}$-object B. Hence (1) holds.

By means of the above result Galois connections of the third kind are perfectly understood if (and only if) we understand reflective and coreflective modifications. For the following result compare G.C.L. Brümmer [2], Propositions 4.1 and 4.2.

3.11 Proposition: Let $T: \mathbf{A} \to \mathbf{A}$ be a concrete endofunctor, let $\mathbf{A}^*$ be the full subcategory of $\mathbf{A}$ whose objects are of the form TA, and let $E: \mathbf{A}^* \to \mathbf{A}$ be the corresponding embedding. Then the following conditions are equivalent:

(1) There exists a Galois connection (F,G) with $T = FG$

(2) $\mathbf{A}^*$ is a coreflective modification of $\mathbf{A}$ whose coreflector C satifies $T = E \cdot C$

(3) $T^2 = T$ and $T \leqslant \mathrm{id}_{\mathbf{A}}$

Proof: (1) ⇒ (3) by 3.4.

(3) ⇒ (2) Let $C: \mathbf{A} \to \mathbf{A}^*$ be the restriction of T. For $A \in \mathrm{Ob}\,\mathbf{A}$ we have $ECA = TA \leqslant A$. For $A^* = TB \in \mathrm{Ob}\,\mathbf{A}^*$ we have $CEA^* = TTB = TB = A$. Hence (2).

(2) ⇒ (1) Trivial.

§4 Galois connections of the fourth kind

Galois connections can be abstracted further, losing some results but retaining others. There is a more rigid and a more flexible version. We develop the former one in detail. Recall the following:

4.1 Lemma: If (η,ϵ): $F \dashv G$: $(\mathbf{A},\mathbf{B})$ is an adjoint situation, then the following hold:

4.1 Lemma: If (η,ϵ): $F \dashv G$: $(\mathbf{A},\mathbf{B})$ is an adjoint situation, then the following hold:

(1) $\epsilon_{FB} \circ F\eta_B = id_{FB}$

(2) $G\epsilon_A \circ \eta_{GA} = id_{GA}$

(3) G is full iff all ϵ_A's are sections

(4) F is full iff all η_B's are retractions

(5) G is faithful iff all ϵ_A's are epimorphisms

(6) F is faithful iff all η_B's are monomorphisms

(7) G is equivalent to a full embedding iff all ϵ_A's are isomorphisms

(8) F is eqivalent to a full embedding iff all η_B's are isomorphisms

(9) (ϵ,η): $G^{op} \dashv F^{op}$: $(\mathbf{B}^{op},\mathbf{A}^{op})$ is an adjoint situation

(10) if $(\bar{\eta},\bar{\epsilon})$: $\bar{F} \dashv \bar{G}$: $(\mathbf{B},\mathbf{C})$ is an adjoint situation, then $(\bar{G}\eta\bar{F} \circ \bar{\eta},\ \epsilon \circ F\bar{\epsilon}G)^*$ $F \circ \bar{F} \dashv \bar{G} \circ G$: $(\mathbf{A},\mathbf{C})$ is an adjoint situation.

4.2 Definition: (F,G) is called a Galois connection of the fourth kind iff there exists an adjoint situation (η,ϵ): $F \dashv G$: $(\mathbf{A},\mathbf{B})$ with all η_{GA}'s and all ϵ_{FB}'s being identities.

4.3 Proposition: If (F,G) is a Galois connection of the fourth kind, then so is (G^{op},F^{op})

Proof: 4.1(9).

4.4 Remark: Adjoint situations can be composed (see 4.1(10)). As opposed to Galois connections of the third kind, Galois connections of the fourth kind are not closed under composition. In fact, as we will see below, every adjoint situation can be expressed as the composite of two Galois connections of the fourth kind. Nevertheless we will obtain a structure theorem for Galois connections of the fourth kind, resembling the corresponding result for Galois connections of the third kind.

4.5 Theorem: Let $\mathbf{A} \underset{F}{\overset{G}{\rightleftarrows}} \mathbf{B}$ be functors such that (F,G) is a Galois connection of the fourth kind and let $\mathbf{A}^*$ (resp. $\mathbf{B}^*$) be the full subcategory of $\mathbf{A}$ (resp. $\mathbf{B}$) whose objects are of the form GB (resp. FA). Then the following hold:

(1) GFG = G and FGF = F

(2) $(GF)^2 = GF$ and $(FG)^2 = FG$

(3) $A \in \mathrm{Ob}\,\mathbf{A}^* \iff \exists A' \in \mathrm{Ob}\,\mathbf{A}\ \ A = FGA' \iff A = FGA$

$B \in \mathrm{Ob}\,\mathbf{B}^* \iff \exists B' \in \mathrm{Ob}\,\mathbf{B}\ \ B = GFB' \iff B = GFB$

(4) G and F restrict to isomorphisms G^*: $\mathbf{A}^* \to \mathbf{B}^*$ and F^*: $\mathbf{B}^* \to \mathbf{A}^*$, inverse to each other

(5) FG and GF restrict to functors C: $\mathbf{A} \to \mathbf{A}^*$ and R: $\mathbf{B} \to \mathbf{B}^*$. If E_A: $\mathbf{A}^* \to \mathbf{A}$ and E_B: $\mathbf{B}^* \to \mathbf{B}$ are the embeddings, then the outer and the inner rectangle of the following diagram commute

and (E_A, C), (F^*, G^*) and (R, E_B) are Galois connections of the fourth kind.

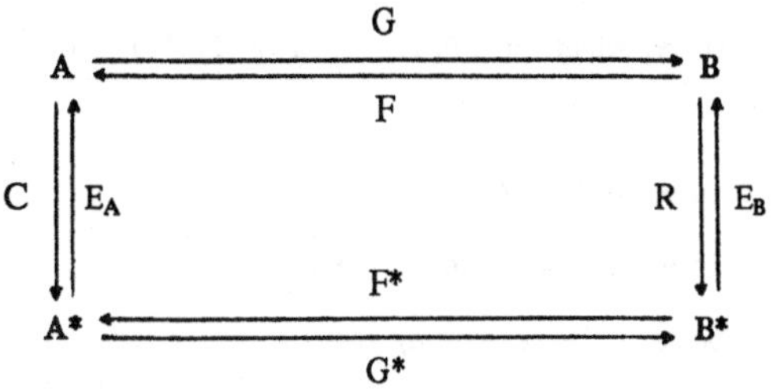

Proof: as before.

4.6 Proposition: For adjoint situations $(\eta, \epsilon)\colon F \dashv G(\mathbf{A},\mathbf{B})$ the following conditions are equivalent:

(1) all ϵ_A's are identities

(2) all ϵ_{FB}'s are identities and $F \circ G = id_{\mathbf{A}}$

(3) all ϵ_{FB}'s are identities and F is surjective on objects

(4) all η_{GA}'s are identities and G is a full embedding

(5) all η_{GA}'s are identities and G is injective on objects.

Proof: (1) $\Rightarrow$ (2) $\Rightarrow$ (3) $\Rightarrow$ (1) and (4) $\Rightarrow$ (5) hold trivially.

(1) $\Rightarrow$ (4) By 4.1 all η_{GA}'s are identities and G is full and faithful. Since (1) implies $F \circ G = id_A$, G is injective on objects, hence a full embedding.

(5) $\Rightarrow$ (1) For each **A**-object A we have GA = GFGA. Since G is injective on objects, this implies A = FGA. Hence $\epsilon_A = \epsilon_{FGA} = \epsilon_{FGA} \circ F\eta_{GA} = id_{FGA}$ by 4.1.

4.7 Corollary: For Galois connections (F,G) of the fourth kind the following conditions are equivalent:

(1) G is a full embedding

(2) G is injective on objects

(3) F is surjective on objects

(4) $F \circ G = id_{\mathbf{A}}$.

4.8 Remark: Let **A** be a subcategory of a category **B** with embedding G: $\mathbf{A} \to \mathbf{B}$. Then **A** is full and reflective (resp. coreflective) in **B** iff there exists a necessarily unique functor F such that (F,G) (resp. (G,F)) is a Galois connection of the fourth kind. This justifies the following convenient terminology.

4.9 Definition: A Galois connection (F,G) of the fourth kind is called a full reflection (resp. a full coreflection) iff G (resp. F) is a full embedding.

4.10 Theorem: Equivalent are:

(1) (F,G) is a Galois connection of the fourth kind

(2) there exist a full coreflection (F_1,G_1) and a full reflection (F_2,G_2) with $(F,G) = (F_1 \circ F_2, G_2 \circ G_1)$.

Proof: (1) ⇒ (2) follows immediately from 4.5(5).

(2) ⇒ (1) follows immediately from 4.6 and 4.1(10).

In marked contrast to the above is the following result:

4.11 Theorem: For each adjoint situation (η,ϵ): $F \dashv G$: $(\mathbf{A},\mathbf{B})$ there exist a full reflection (F_1,G_1) and a full coreflection (F_2,G_2) with $(F,G) = (F_1 \circ F_2, G_2 \circ G_1)$.

Proof: Define a category **C** in the following way (cf.[4]): take the disjoint union of **A** and **B**; add for any **A**-object A and for any **B**-object B morphism sets

$$\hom_{\mathbf{C}}(B,A) = \hom_{\mathbf{A}}(FB,A) \text{ and } \hom_{\mathbf{C}}(A,B) = \emptyset;$$

make the morphism sets disjoint; and define composition in the obvious way. Then the embedding $G_1\colon \mathbf{A} \to \mathbf{C}$ has a left adjoint $F_1\colon \mathbf{C} \to \mathbf{A}$ with $F_1|\mathbf{A} = id_{\mathbf{A}}$, $F_1|\mathbf{B} = F$ and $F_1(B \xrightarrow{f} A) = FB \xrightarrow{f} A$; and the embedding $F_2\colon \mathbf{B} \to \mathbf{C}$ has a right adjoint $G_2\colon \mathbf{C} \to \mathbf{B}$ with $G_2|\mathbf{A} = G$, $G_2|\mathbf{B} = id_{\mathbf{B}}$ and $G_2(B \xrightarrow{f} A) = B \xrightarrow{\eta_B} GFB \xrightarrow{Gf} GA$.
It follows easily that (F_1,G_1) is a full reflection, (F_2,G_2) is a full coreflection and $(F,G) = (F_1 \circ F_2, G_2 \circ G_1)$.

4.12 Remark: If in the definition of Galois connections of the fourth kind, the requirement that all η_{GA}'s and all ϵ_{FB}'s are identities is replaced by the condition that all η_{GA}'s and all ϵ_{FB}'s are isomorphisms, we obtain a less rigid concept. This has some advantages and some disadvantages. A disadvantage is that most results become more complicated, e.g., GFG is only equivalent to G, and (F,G) is only equivalent to the composition of what becomes a full coreflection and a full reflection in this context. An advantage is that in view of the following result the requirements can be reduced to half:

4.13 Proposition: (D. Pumplün [10]): For adjoint situations (η,ϵ): $F \dashv G$: $(\mathbf{A},\mathbf{B})$ the following conditions are equivalent:

(1) $GF\eta = \eta GF$

(2) $FG\epsilon = \epsilon FG$

(3) ηG is an isotransformation (i.e. a natural equivalence)

(4) ηG is an epitransformation

(5) $F\eta$ is an isotransformation

(6) $F\eta$ is a epitransformation

(7) $G\epsilon$ is an isotransformation

(8) $G\epsilon$ is a monotransformation

(9) ϵF is an isotransformation

(10) ϵF is a monotransformation

(11) $G\epsilon F$ is an iostransformation

(12) $F\eta G$ is an isotransformation.

Proof: Recall the equalities (a) $\epsilon F \circ F\eta =$ identity and (b) $G\epsilon \circ \eta G =$ identitiy.

(1) ⇒ (5) By (1) and (b) we get

$G(F\eta \circ \epsilon F) \circ \eta GF = GF\eta \circ G\epsilon F \circ \eta GF = GF\eta \circ (G\epsilon \circ \eta G)F = GF\eta = \eta GF$, which implies $F\eta \circ \epsilon F =$ identity. Hence (5) follows from (a).

(2) ⇒ (3) follows similarly.

(5) ⇔ (6) ⇔ (9) ⇔ (10) follows from (a).

(3) ⇔ (4) ⇔ (7) ⇔ (8) follows from (b).

(3) ⇒ (12), (5) ⇒ (12), (7) ⇒ (11) and (9) ⇒ (11) are trivial.

(11) ⇒ (1) In view of (a) and (b), (11) implies $GF\eta =$ identitiy $= \eta GF$.

(12) ⇒ (2) In view of (a) and (b), (12) implies $\epsilon FG =$ identity $= FG\epsilon$.

4.14 Remark. Using transfinite methods the last proposition can be considerably strengthened: if for any **B**-object B (or any **A**-object A) there is some "combination" of (finite or transfinite) powers of F,G,η of ϵ, which is an isomorphism on B, then all the conditions of 4.13 hold.

For further results on Galois adjunctions, i.e., adjoint situations satisfying the equivalent conditions of 4.13, see D. Pumplün [10]. Cf. also J.R. Isbell [5].

References

[1] G. Birkhoff, Lattice Theory. Amer. Math. Soc. Collog. Publ. 25 (1940).

[2] G.C.L. Brümmer, Topological functors and structure functors. Springer Lecture Notes Math. 540 (1976) 109-135.

[3] C.J. Everett, Closure operators and Galois theory in lattices. Trans. Amer. Math. Soc. 55 (1944) 514-525.

[4] H. Herrlich, Factorizations of morphisms f: B → FA. Math. Z. 114 (1970) 180-186.

[5] J.R. Isbell, Top and its adjoint relatives. Gen. Topology and its Relations to Modern Analysis and Algebra (Prague 1971), 143-154.

[6] A. Melton and G.E. Strecker, Structures supporting Galois connections. Preprint.

[7] S. Mac Lane, Categories for the Working Mathematician. Springer-Verlag 1971.

[8] O. Ore, Galois connexions. Trans. Amer. Math. Soc. 55 (1944) 493-513.

[9] G. Pickert, Bemerkungen über Galois-Verbindungen. Archiv Math. 3 (1952) 285-289.

[10] D. Pumplün, Kategorien Vorlesungsskript Univ. Münster 1972.

[11] J. Schmidt, Beiträge zur Filtertheorie II. Math. Nachr. 10 (1953) 197-232.

[12] O. Wyler, On the categories of general topology and topological algebra. Archiv Math. 22 (1971) 7-17.

RETRACTS OF SFP OBJECTS*

Tsutomu Kamimura and Adrian Tang
Department of Computer Science
University of Kansas
Lawrence, Kansas 66045

0. Introduction

Domains play a central role in denotational semantics of programming languages. They are certain mathematical structures used to describe meanings of programs. There are various notions of domains studied in literature, ranging from continuous lattices [9], coherent cpo's [8], bounded complete cpo's [11,12], to SFP objects [7]. All these notions introduce domains as continuous posets (partially ordered sets) with some completeness property. "Continuous" means that the posets have a countable basis so that every element can be approximated using the basis elements. Completeness property defines a way to combine a consistent set of information.

One of the fundamental concepts in the study of domains is domain construction. It is common practice in high-level programming languages to define structured data types from primitive data types. This necessitates a systematic way of constructing new domains from old domains modeling some given primitive types. For this reason, various domain constructions such as disjoint sum (+), cartesian product (x), and exponentiation (→) were introduced, and methods of solving domain equations have been established [11,15].

Advance of programming languages introduces various new mechanisms such as nondeterminism, concurrency, coroutines and probablistic constructs such as random assignment, thereby calling for new domain constructs to accommodate these mechanisms. In this direction, Plotkin [7] introduced SFP objects and a powerdomain construct for bounded nondeterminism, and it has been shown that mechanisms such as parallelism and coroutines can be adequately handled in Plotkin's framework. More recently, Smyth [14] showed that the category of SFP objects is indeed the largest cartesian closed category of algebraic domains, i.e. domains with a basis of compact elements. It is widely accepted that most of the domains used in denotational semantics are algebraic. A notable exception, however, is Scott's domain for the reals [10]. As

*This work was supported by National Science Foundation Grant DCR-8415919

SFP objects are all algebraic, they do not cover the reals or some of the nonalgebraic domains that may arise in the semantics of programs with probablistic behavior [1,5,6]. To include these nonalgebraic domains as well as SFP objects, we study retracts of SFP objects (or RSFP in short) in this paper. The category of RSFP objects and continuous maps is also cartesian closed and contains nonalgebraic domains such as the reals. It is conceivable that RSFP objects form the largest cartesian closed category of continuous posets.

To obtain a better understanding of RSFP objects, we present in this paper two different characterizations of RSFP objects. Our first characterization has an operational flavor where we will show how every RSFP object can be obtained as the limit of a finitely continuous sequence of finite posets. Consequently, domain constructions such as $+$, $\times$, $\rightarrow$ and P (powerdomain constructions) can be carried out at the level of finite posets. Our operational formulation also provides us with a very intuitive notion of effectively given domains where one can formulate the notion of computable elements and computable maps. We will show that the effectively given RSFP objects can be given by computable retracts of the recursive SFP objects up to isomorphism. Because of our operational characterization, RSFP objects will also be called finitely continuous posets in this paper. It is our belief that finitely continuous posets provide the most general notion of domains for denotational semantics of programming languages.

In our second characterization, we give an extensional view of finitely continuous posets. An extensional characterization of SFP objects can be given in terms of the basis of compact elements. Indeed Plotkin [7] gave necessary and sufficient conditions on the compact basis for an algebraic domain to be SFP. Such a characterization for SFP objects is possible because every algebraic domain has the smallest basis, namely, the compact basis. A nonalgebraic domain, however, does not have the smallest basis, and for this reason, it is difficult to find a characterization of a finitely continuous poset in terms of a given basis. In this paper we provide a characterization of finitely continuous posets in terms of a basis and a base of Scott topology on the domain. This characterization also leads us to a second notion of effectively given domains which will be shown to be equivalent to our first notion.

1. SFP Objects

All posets in this paper contain the bottom element $\perp$. A chain-complete poset D is called a cpo. D is a ccpo (continuous cpo) if it has a countable basis $E \subseteq D$ in the following sense: for every $x \in D$, the set $\{e \in E | e \ll x\}$ is directed and has x as the least upper bound (the way below relation $\ll$ was introduced by Scott in [9]). E is a compact basis if $e \ll e$ for every $e \in E$. A cpo D is algebraic if it has a compact basis.

We will give two characterizations of SFP objects, one for each of the views mentioned in the introduction. The operational description is provided by Plotkin's definition [7] where he used a projective sequence. A projective sequence of finite posets E_i's ($i \in \omega$) is one where each E_i is a subposet of E_{i+1} and furthermore, E_i is a projection of E_{i+1}, i.e. for every $x \in E_{i+1}$, $P_{i+1}(x)$ defined as $\sqcup\{y \in E_i | y \sqsubseteq x\}$ exists in E_i. Let E be the poset given by the union of all the E_i's. The limit of the projective sequence $\lim E_i$ is defined as the algebraic completion of E, thus $\lim E_i$ is an algebraic cpo with E as its compact basis. Equivalently, $\lim E_i$ can be identified with the cpo whose underlying elements are infinite sequences $\langle x_i \rangle_{i \in \omega}$ satisfying $x_i \in E_i$ and $x_i = p_{i+1}(x_{i+1})$ (for every $i \in \omega$) and the partial ordering is simply pointwise ordering. It is well known that each poset E_i is a projection of the completion $\lim E_i$; thus for every $x \in D$, $\pi_i(x) = \sqcup\{y \in E_i | y \sqsubseteq x\}$ (the ith-projection of x) is well defined. Now Plotkin's SFP objects are exactly those algebraic cpo's obtained as completions of projective sequences of finite posets. Note that such a definition is operational because it shows us how to construct a domain from a sequence of finite posets. The advantage of such a formulation is that domain constructions such as +, x, $\rightarrow$ and P can be carried out at the level of finite posets.

The extensional characterization of SFP objects, unlike the operational description, is given at the level of the domain. Let D be an algebraic cpo with the compact basis E. The following characterization gives us necessary and sufficient conditions on E for D to be SFP.

Proposition 1

D is SFP iff there exists an enumeration $\{e_i\}_{i \in \omega}$ of E (where $e_0 = \perp$) and a monotonic operation $*: F\omega \rightarrow F\omega$ (where $F\omega$ consists of all the finite subsets of ω) such that $I \cup \{0\} \subseteq I^*$ for every $I \in F\omega$ and

<u>Finite Continuity Axiom</u>: for every $x \in D$ and $I \in F\omega$, the set $\{e_t | t \in I^*$ and $e_t \sqsubseteq x\}$ is directed with x^I as the largest element and $x = \bigsqcup_{I \in F\omega} x^I$

Proof:

($\Rightarrow$) Suppose that $D = \lim E_i$ for some projective sequence of E_i's and that $\{e_i\}_{i \in \omega}$ is some enumeration of $E = \bigcup_n E_n$ without repetitions (with $e_0 = \perp$). Given $I \in F\omega$, let $k \in \omega$ be the smallest integer satisfying $I \subseteq \{t | e_t \in E_k\}$. Now define I^* to be the finite set $\{t | e_t \in E_k\}$ for such k. Clearly $I \cup \{0\} \subseteq I^*$ and $I \subseteq J$ implies $I^* \subseteq J^*$. For every $x \in D$ and $I \in F\omega$, the set $\{e_t | t \in I^*$ and $e_t \sqsubseteq x\}$ is directed with the largest element x^I given by $\pi_k(x)$ (k as defined above). Since $x = \bigsqcup_k \pi_k(x)$, the Finite Continuity Axiom is satisfied.

($\Leftarrow$) Let $h: \omega \to \omega$ be a function such that $D_{h(t)} \in F\omega$ denotes the set $\{0,1,..,t\}$ or the first t natural numbers. For each $t \in \omega$, define the poset E_t to be $\{e_i | i \in D^*_{h(t)}\}$ with the induced ordering from D. Given $x \in E_{t+1}$, $p_{t+1}(x) = \bigsqcup\{y \in E_t | y \sqsubseteq x\} = \bigsqcup\{e_i | i \in D^*_{h(t)}$ and $e_i \sqsubseteq x\}$ exists by the Finite Continuity Axiom. Hence E_t's form a projective sequence and D, being the algebraic completion of E which is the union of all the E_t's, must be SFP. □

Note that the Finite Continuity Axiom is so called because it says that every $x \in D$ can be given by the lub of a directed set of x^I's where x^I is essentially the best approximation of x among all the names given in the non-empty finite set I^*. In Section 3, we will combine the enumeration $\{e_i\}_{i \in \omega}$ with the * operator satisfying the Finite Continuity Axiom to formulate the notion of a finitely continuous presentation.

2. Finitely Continuous Sequences

In this section, we introduce finitely continuous sequences as a generalization of projective sequences. Then we define limits of finitely continuous sequences which turn out to give all the RSFP objects, thus providing an operational description of RSFP objects.

First we introduce <-posets (pronounced as way below posets). $\langle D,r \rangle$ is a <u><-poset</u> if D is a finite poset (with $\perp$) and $r: D \to D$ is a monotonic function satisfying $r \circ r \sqsubseteq r$. A <-poset can also be described by some transitive binary relation on D. To see this, let us define a binary relation < on D as follows:

$$x < y \quad \text{iff} \quad x \sqsubseteq r(y)$$

Then $<$ is transitive and furthermore it has the following properties:

(i) $\perp < x$ for every $x \in D$;
(ii) $a \sqsubseteq x < y \sqsubseteq b$ implies $a < b$; and
(iii) for every $x \in D$, the set $\{y \in D \mid y < x\}$ is $(\sqsubseteq)$-bounded.

Conversely, any transitive relation $<$ on D satisfying the above three properties will define a monotonic function $r: D \to D$ satisfying $r \circ r \sqsubseteq r$ and $x < y$ iff $x \sqsubseteq r(y)$. For define $r: D \to D$ as follows:

$$r(x) = \bigsqcup \{y \in D \mid y < x\}$$

Note that the lub of $\{y \in D \mid y < x\}$ exists because of property (iii). Monotonicity of r is guaranteed by property (ii). Finally transitivity of $<$ implies $r \circ r \sqsubseteq r$. Thus there is a 1-1 correspondence between monotonic functions $r: D \to D$ satisfying $r \circ r \sqsubseteq r$ and transitive binary relations $<$ on D satisfying the above three properties. These posets are called way below posets because Scott's way below relation $<<$ on a cpo satisfy all those properties.

Note that every finite poset D can be identified as the $<$-poset $\langle D, id \rangle$ where $id: D \to D$ is the identity function. Treating $<$-posets as algebras, we can define operations on them corresponding to $+$, x, $\to$ and P as used in domain constructions.

A <u>finitely continuous sequence</u> of $<$-posets $\langle E_n, r_n \rangle$'s is one where the E_n's form a projective sequence and furthermore, $r_n \sqsubseteq r^2_{n+1}$ for every $n \in \omega$. It follows from $r_n \sqsubseteq r^2_{n+1}$ and the assumption $r^2_n \sqsubseteq r_n$ that $r_n \sqsubseteq r_{n+1}$ for every $n \in \omega$. Every projective sequence of poset E_n's defines a finitely continuous sequence of $\langle E_n, id \rangle$'s in a trivial manner. The following proposition shows that every retraction map on a SFP object defines a finitely continuous sequence which somehow characterizes the retraction.

<u>Proposition 2</u>

Suppose that r is a retraction map on an SFP object D. Then there is a finitely continuous sequence of $<$-posets $\langle E_n, r_n \rangle$'s such that $\bigcup_n E_n$ is the compact basis of D, and furthermore, $r = \bigsqcup_n r_n \circ \pi_n$.

Proof:
Suppose that D is given by $\lim A_n$ for some projective sequence of finite posets A_n's.

Claim: $r = \bigsqcup_n \{s \in [A_n \to A_n] \mid s^2 \sqsubseteq s \text{ and } s \sqsubseteq r\}$ where the set $\{s \in [A_n \to A_n] \mid s^2 \sqsubseteq s,\ s \sqsubseteq r \text{ and } n \in \omega\}$ is directed.

Proof: Given $n\in\omega$, define $s_n\in[A_n\to A_n]$ as follows:

$s_n(x)=\pi_n\circ r(x)$ for $x\in A_n$. Note that $s_n^2\sqsubseteq s_n$ and $r=\bigsqcup_n s_n$. Furthermore, any $s\in[A_n\to A_n]$ satisfying $s\sqsubseteq r$ must be bounded by s_n. Hence the set $\{s\in[A_n\to A_n]\mid s^2\sqsubseteq s,\ s\sqsubseteq r$ and $n\in\omega\}$ is directed and has r as the lub.

We will define the required finitely continuous sequence of <-posets $\langle E_n,r_n\rangle$'s by induction. For the basis step, simply let $E_0=\{\bot\}$ and r_0 be th trivial function on E_0. Suppose that the <-poset $\langle E_n,r_n\rangle$ has been defined satisfying $E_n\subseteq\bigcup_i A_i$ and $r_n\sqsubseteq r$. For each $x\in E_n$,

$$r_n(x)\sqsubseteq r(x)=\bigsqcup_m\{s(x)\mid s\in[A_m\to A_m],\ s^2\sqsubseteq s\ \&\ s\sqsubseteq r\}$$
$$=\bigsqcup_m\{s^2(x)\mid s\in[A_m\to A_m],\ s^2\sqsubseteq s\ \&\ s\sqsubseteq r\}$$
$$(\text{since } r^2=r)$$

Hence $r_n(x)\sqsubseteq s^2(x)$ for some $m\in\omega$ & $s\in[A_m\to A_m]$ satisfying $s^2\sqsubseteq s$ and $s\sqsubseteq r$. Since E_n is a finite poset, we can find some $m\geq n+1$ and some $s\in[A_m\to A_m]$ such that $s^2\sqsubseteq s$, $s\sqsubseteq r$ and:

(i) $E_n\subseteq A_m$;

(ii) $r_n(x)\sqsubseteq s^2(x)$ for every $x\in E_n$; and

(iii) for every $x\in E_n$, $\bigsqcup\{y\in E_n\mid y\sqsubseteq r(x)\}\sqsubseteq s(x)$.

Now define $\langle E_{n+1},r_{n+1}\rangle$ to be $\langle A_m,s\rangle$ where m and $s\in[A_m\to A_m]$ satisfy the above conditions. Obviously $\langle E_n,r_n\rangle$'s form a finitely continuous sequence. The assumption $m\geq n+1$ guarantees $\bigcup_n E_n=\bigcup_i A_i$ (=compact basis). Finally condition (iii) above ensures $r=\bigsqcup_n r_n\circ\pi_n$. □

Given a finitely continuous sequence of <-posets $\langle E_n,r_n\rangle$'s, define the poset E to be the union of all the E_n's. We can turn E into an R-structure [13] $\langle E,<\rangle$ by defining a binary relation < on E as follows:

$$x<y \quad\text{iff}\quad x\sqsubseteq r_n(y) \text{ for some } n\in\omega$$

The following properties of an R-structure can be verified:

(i) < is transitive; and

(ii) s, t<x implies s, t<u and u<x for some $u\in E$.

In view of the fact that $\langle E,<\rangle$ is an R-structure, we can define a ccpo from $\langle E,<\rangle$ by taking Smyth's completion [13]. Using the fact that E is obtained from a finitely continuous sequence, we can define the completion of E in a much more straightforward manner. First we note that $\lim E_n$ is SFP. Next define a continuous map $\bar{r}$: $\lim E_n\to\lim E_n$ as follows

$$\bar{r}(x)=\bigsqcup_n r_n\circ\pi_n(x)$$

Proposition 3

The above map $\bar{r}: \lim E_n \to \lim E_n$ is a retraction.

Proof:

$$\begin{aligned}\bar{r}\circ\bar{r}(x) &= \bar{r}(\bigsqcup_n r_n\circ\pi_n(x)) \\ &= \bigsqcup_m \bigsqcup_n r_m\circ\pi_m\circ r_n\circ\pi_n(x) \\ &= \bigsqcup_k r_k\circ r_k\circ\pi_k(x) \\ &= \bigsqcup_k r_k\circ\pi_k(x) \\ &\quad (\text{since } r_k^2 \sqsubseteq r_k \text{ and } r_k \sqsubseteq r_{k+1}^2) \\ &= \bar{r}(x)\end{aligned}$$

From Proposition 3, we can define the completion $\lim \langle E_n, r_n\rangle$ of the given finitely continuous sequence to be the retract $\bar{r}(\lim E_n)$ of the SFP object $\lim E_n$. Hence $\lim \langle E_n, r_n\rangle$ is an RSFP object. Note that when all the r_n's are identity maps, then $\lim \langle E_n, r_n\rangle = \lim \langle E_n, id\rangle = \lim E_n$, hence our notion of completion here is consistent with the notion of completion of a projective sequence. In the following theorem, we show that RSFP objects can be characterized as completions of finitely continuous sequences.

Theorem 1

RSFP objects are given by completions of finitely continuous sequences up to isomorphism.

Proof:

It suffices to show that given a SFP object D and a retraction $r: D \to D$, the retract $r(D)$ is isomorphic to the completion of some finitely continuous sequence. Proposition 2 shows that r defines a finitely continuous sequence of $\langle E_n, r_n\rangle$'s where $D = \lim E_n$ and $r = \bigsqcup_n r_n\circ\pi_n$. However $\bar{r}$ is also defined to be $\bigsqcup_n r_n\circ\pi_n$. Hence $r(D) = \bar{r}(D) = \bar{r}(\lim E_n)$ and the theorem.

□

Because of Theorem 1, RSFP objects will be called FC posets (=finitely continuous posets) for the rest of the paper.

Suppose that D,D' are FC posets defined as completions of finitely continuous sequences. From the given sequences, one can define finitely continuous sequences whose completions will give us D+D', D×D', [D→D'] and P[D]. The importance of this observation is that Scott's domain constructions can be carried out at the level of <-posets which are finite structures.

Our operational view of FC posets suggests the following effective notions. A recursive finitely continuous sequence of <-posets $\langle E_n, r_n \rangle$'s is one where there is an enumeration of E_n's in which $\sqsubseteq$ and r_n are both recursive. Given a recursive finitely continuous sequence of $\langle E_n, r_n \rangle$'s, the completion $\lim \langle E_n, r_n \rangle$ is said to be effectively given and the SFP object $\lim E_n$ is said to be recursive. (Note that recursive SFP objects are the same as completions of recursive projective sequences.) Proposition 3 says that $\lim \langle E_n, r_n \rangle$ is a retract of $\lim E_n$ via the retraction map $\bar{r}$ ($= \bigsqcup_n r_n \circ \pi_n$). One might then ask whether there is certain effective property of this retraction map $\bar{r}$. For this purpose, we need to formulate the notion of a computable map on a recursive SFP object $\lim E_n$. Given a recursive projective sequence of E_n's, we can define an enumeration of all the functions in $[E_n \to E_n]$ $(n \in \omega)$ in which pointwise ordering (between functions) is recursive. Functions in $[E_n \to E_n]$ are called finite or step functions and their domains can be extended to $\lim E_n$ in a straightforward manner using the projection map π_n. It is well known [9] that these step functions form a basis of the entire function space $[\lim E_n \to \lim E_n]$. A continuous function $f \in [\lim E_n \to \lim E_n]$ is said to be computable if we can effectively enumerate all the step functions that are $\sqsubseteq f$. The following proposition says that the above retraction map $\bar{r}$ is computable.

Proposition 4

Given a recursive finitely continuous sequence of <-posets $\langle E_n, r_n \rangle$'s, the retraction map $\bar{r} = \bigsqcup_n r_n \circ \pi_n$ on the recursive SFP object $\lim E_n$ is computable.

Proof:
Let the variable s range over all the step functions. Then:

$$s(\in [E_m \to E_m]) \sqsubseteq \bar{r} \quad \text{iff} \quad s \sqsubseteq \bigsqcup_n r_n \circ \pi_n$$
$$\text{iff for some } n \geq m,\ s(x) \sqsubseteq r_n \circ \pi_n(x)$$
$$\text{for all } x \in E_m$$

Since E_m is a finite poset and $s(x) \sqsubseteq r_n \circ \pi_n(x)$ is recursive in n, x and s, we conclude that the predicate $s \sqsubseteq \bar{r}$ is recursively enumerable in s. □

By Proposition 4, the completion $\lim \langle E_n, r_n \rangle$ is a computable retract of the recursive SFP object $\lim E_n$. In the following theorem, we show that every computable retract of a recursive SFP object is isomorphic to the completion of some recursive finitely continuous sequence. Consequently, effectively given domains (defined earlier as completions of recursive finitely continuous sequences) can be characterized as computable retracts of recursive SFP objects.

Theorem 2

Effectively given domains are given by computable retracts of recursive SFP objects.

Proof:

It suffices to show that given a recursive SFP object D and a computable retraction map r on D, the computable retract r(D) is isomorphic to the completion of some recursive finitely continuous sequence of <-posets. Proposition 2 says that r defines some finitely continuous sequence of <-posets $\langle E_n, r_n \rangle$'s such that $r = \bigsqcup_n r_n \circ \pi_n$ and $D = \lim E_n$. Let us re-examine our construction of $\langle E_n, r_n \rangle$'s. Since r is a computable map and $\sqsubseteq$ is recursive, the set $\{s \mid s \in [A_m \to A_m],\ m \in \omega,\ s^2 \sqsubseteq s \text{ and } s \sqsubseteq r\}$ of step functions must have some effective enumeration, say $\{s_k\}_{k \in \omega}$. In defining r_{n+1} in our inductive step, we need to choose some s_k and an $m \geq n+1$ satisfying:

(i) $E_n \subseteq A_m$;

(ii) $r_n(x) \sqsubseteq s_k^2(x)$ for every $x \in E_n$; and

(iii) for every $x \in E_n$, $\bigsqcup\{y \in E_n \mid y \sqsubseteq r(x)\} \sqsubseteq s_k(x)$.

We note that all of the above conditions except (iii) are decidable. The intent of (iii) is to ensure $r = \bigsqcup_n r_n \circ \pi_n$. However we can still ensure $r = \bigsqcup_n r_n \circ \pi_n$ by changing (iii) to the following (iii)' which is decidable:

(iii)' $s_i \sqsubseteq s_k$ for all $i \leq n$ such that $s_i \in [E_n \to E_n]$

Since an s_k satisfying (i), (ii) & (iii)' can be chosen effectively, we conclude that by defining r_{n+1} to be any such s_k, we obtain a recursive finitely continuous sequence of <-posets $\langle E_n, r_n \rangle$'s. □

3. Finitely Continuous Presentations

Proposition 1 gave an extensional characterization of SFP objects in terms of the compact basis. Since each compact element e_i determines a Scott open set $U_i = \uparrow e_i = \{x \mid e_i \sqsubseteq x\}$, the Finite Continuity Axiom in Proposition 1 can be restated as follows: for every $x \in D$ and $I \in F\omega$, the set $\{e_t \mid t \in I^* \text{ and } x \in U_t\}$ is directed with x^I as the largest element and $x = \bigsqcup_{I \in F\omega} x^I$. Thus the Finite Continuity Axiom says that we can compute a given x in D using properties of x which are Scott open sets.

In a domain D which may not be algebraic, $\uparrow e_i$ of a given basis element e_i may not be Scott open. For this reason, it is nontrivial to find a characterization of FC posets in terms of a given basis. Indeed, a non-algebraic ccpo may have many incomparable bases. Nonetheless, we can provide a characterization of FC posets in terms of finitely continuous presentations or FC presentations in short. Given a ccpo D, a <u>FC presentation</u> is a 4-tuple $\langle D, E=\{e_i\}_{i\in\omega}, U=\{U_i\}_{i\in\omega}, *\rangle$ where E is a basis of D (with $e_0=\bot$), U is a base of Scott topology on D satisfying the following:

(i) <u>Structual Axiom</u>

$e_i \sqsubseteq x$ for every $x\in U_i$; and

(ii) <u>Finite Continuity Axiom</u>

$*:F\omega\to F\omega$ is a monotonic operator such that $I\cup\{0\}\subseteq I^*$ for every $I\in F\omega$, and for every $x\in D$ and $I\in F\omega$, the set $\{e_t \mid t\in I^* \text{ and } x\in U_t\}$ is directed with x^I as the largest element and $x=\bigsqcup_{I\in F\omega} x^I$.

For further motivations and technical details, we refer the reader to [4]. In terms of presentations, Proposition 1 can be restated as follows: an algebraic domain D with a compact basis E is SFP iff there exists an enumeration $\{e_i\}_{i\in\omega}$ of E and an operator $*:F\omega\to F\omega$ such that $\langle D, \{e_i\}_{i\in\omega}, \{\uparrow e_i\}_{i\in\omega}, *\rangle$ forms a FC presentation. Thus every SFP object has a FC presentation where the basis open sets are actually determined by the basis elements. The following proposition shows that every FC poset has a FC presentation.

<u>Proposition 4</u>

Every FC poset has a FC presentation.

Proof:

Suppose that D is a SFP object with a FC presentation $\langle D, E=\{e_i\}_{i\in\omega}, U=\{U_i\}_{i\in\omega}, *\rangle$ and that $r:D\to D$ is a retraction. We want to show that $\langle r(D), \{r(e_i)\}_{i\in\omega}, \{U_i\cap r(D)\}_{i\in\omega}, *\rangle$ is a FC presentation for $r(D)$. Clearly $\{r(e_i)\}_{i\in\omega}$ and $\{U_i\cap r(D)\}_{i\in\omega}$ form a basis and a base respectively. The Structural Axiom is obvious since for every $r(x)\in U_i\cap r(D)$, $e_i\sqsubseteq r(x)$ (because $\langle D,E,U\rangle$ is a FC presentation of D) and thus $r(e_i)\sqsubseteq r\circ r(x)=r(x)$. To verify the Finite Continuity Axiom, we need to show that for every $r(x)\in r(D)$ and $I\in F\omega$, the set $B_{r(x),I}=\{r(e_t) \mid t\in I^* \text{ and } r(x)\in U_t\cap r(D)\}$ is directed with $r(r(x)^I)$ as the largest element and $r(x)=\bigsqcup_{I\in F\omega} r(r(x)^I)$. Since $\langle D,E,U\rangle$ is a FC presentation, the set $A_{r(x),I}=\{e_t \mid t\in I^*$ and

$r(x) \in U_t \cap r(D)\}$ is directed with $r(x)^I$ as the largest element and $r(x) = \bigsqcup_{I \in F\omega} r(x)^I$. Note that $B_{r(x),I} = r(A_{r(x),I})$, hence directedness of $B_{r(x),I}$ follows from directedness of $A_{r(x),I}$ and the largest element in $B_{r(x),I}$ is $r(r(x)^I)$. Since $r(x) = \bigsqcup_{I \in \omega} r(x)^I$, we derive $r(x) = r(r(x)) = r(\bigsqcup_{I \in \omega} r(x)^I) = \bigsqcup_{I \in \omega} r(r(x)^I)$, hence the Finite Continuity Axiom.

□

Conversely, suppose that a cpo D has a FC presentation $\langle D,\ E = \{e_i\}_{i \in \omega},\ U = \{U_i\}_{i \in \omega},\ * \rangle$, we can show that D must be a FC poset. To do this, we need to construct a SFP object first and then show that D is a retract of it. For $I \in F\omega$, let Cons(I) mean that the set $\{e_t \mid t \in I\}$ is directed; i.e., it has a maximal element. For every $n \in \omega$, let the poset A_n be $\{I \in \{0,1,..,n-1\}^* \mid \text{Cons}(I) \text{ true}\}$ partially ordered by subset inclusion. Clearly A_n is a subposet of A_{n+1}. The required SFP object A_∞ is defined as follows: the elements A_∞ are infinite sequences $\langle I_n \rangle_{n \in \omega}$ with $I_n \in A_n$ and $I_n \sqsubseteq I_{n+1}$ for every $n \in \omega$, and the ordering is simply pointwise ordering. The compact elements in A_∞ are "finite" sequences; i.e., those $\langle I_n \rangle_{n \in \omega}$'s where for some $k \in \omega$, $I_m = I_k$ for all $m \geq k$. It can be easily demonstrated that finite sequences of length k form a projection of finite sequences of length k+1, hence A_∞ is SFP. We claim that the given cpo D is a retraction of A_∞ in the following theorem.

<u>Theorem 3</u>

FC posets are given by cpo's which have a FC presentation.

Proof:

It suffices to show that if a cpo D has a FC presentation $\langle D,\ E = \{e_i\}_{i \in \omega},\ U = \{U_i\}_{i \in \omega},\ * \rangle$, then D is a retract of the SFP object A_∞. We define $\phi : A_\infty \to D$ and $\psi : D \to A_\infty$ as follows:

$$\phi(\langle I_n \rangle_{n \in \omega}) = \bigsqcup_n e_{I_n}$$

(where e_{I_n} stands for the maximal element in the consistent set $\{e_t \mid t \in I_n\}$)

$$\psi(x) = \langle \{t \in \{0,..,n-1\}^* \mid x \in U_t\} \rangle_{n \in \omega}$$

Note that Finite Continuity Axiom implies $\text{Cons}(\{t \in \{0,..,n-1\}^* \mid x \in U_t\})$ for every $n \in \omega$ and thus ψ is well-defined. Given $x \in D$,

$$\phi\circ\psi(x) = \phi(\langle \{t \in \{0,..n-1\}^* | x\in U_t\}\rangle_{n\in\omega})$$
$$= \bigsqcup_n x^{\{0,..,n-1\}}$$

(where we recall that $x^{\{0,..,n-1\}}$ is the largest element in the directed set $\{e_t | t\in\{0,..n-1\}^*$ and $x\in U_t\}$.)

$$= x \qquad \text{(by Finite Continuity Axiom)}$$

showing that $\psi\circ\phi:A_\infty\to A_\infty$ is a retraction. Hence D is a FC poset. □

We next want to characterize effectively given domains using effectively given FC presentations. A 5-tuple $\langle D, E=\{e_i\}_{i\in\omega}, U=\{U_i\}_{i\in\omega}, *, \text{Comp}\rangle$ is an effectively given FC presentation if $\langle D,E,U,*\rangle$ is a FC presentation, $*:F\omega\to F\omega$ is recursive and Comp is a recursive predicate on $F\omega$ satisfying the following:

(i) Comp ($\{i\}$) holds for every $i\in\omega$;

(ii) for $x\in D$ and $I\in F\omega$, Comp($\{t\in I^* | x\in U_t\}$) holds;

(iii) for $I\in F\omega$, Comp(I) implies Cons(I); and

(iv) the predicate "Comp(I)$\Rightarrow e_I\in U_j$" is recursively enumerable in I and j where e_I is the maximal element in the consistent set $\{e_t | t\in I\}$.

First we give some examples of effectively given FC presentations. Suppose that D is a recursive SFP object; i.e., D is given by the completion of some recursive projective sequence of E_n's. Since $\sqsubseteq$ among the compact elements is recursive, we can assume without loss of generality that there is no repetition of names in the given enumeration; i.e., $e_i = e_j$ implies i=j. For every $I\in F\omega$, define $I^*\in F\omega$ to be the set of all the names in the smallest E_t containing the set $\{e_i | i\in I\}$, and Comp(I) to be the same as Cons(I). Obviously * is computable and Comp is a recursive predicate. Therefore, $\langle D, E=\{e_i\}_{i\in\omega}, \{\uparrow e_i\}_{i\in\omega}, *, \text{Comp}\rangle$ is an effectively given FC presentation for D. Next we show that every computable retract of a recursive SFP object also has an effectively given FC presentation.

Proposition 5

Every computable retract of a recursive SFP object has an effectively given FC presentation.

Proof:

Suppose that $\langle D, E=\{e_i\}_{i\in\omega}, U=\{U_i\}_{i\in\omega}, *, \text{Comp}\rangle$ is an effectively given FC presentation of a recursive SFP object D and that $r:D\to D$ is a computable retraction map. We noted in Proposition 4 that $\langle r(D), \{r(e_i)\}_{i\in\omega}, \{U_i\cap r(D)\}_{i\in\omega}, *\rangle$ is a FC presentation of $r(D)$. We claim that $\langle r(D), \{r(e_i)\}_{i\in\omega}, \{U_i\cap r(D)\}_{i\in\omega}, *, \text{Comp}\rangle$ is an effectively given FC presentation of $r(D)$. It suffices to verify conditions (ii), (iii) and (iv) of a Comp predicate.

(ii): note that $\text{Comp}(\{t\in I^* \mid r(x)\in U_t\cap r(D)\})$ iff $\text{Comp}(\{t\in I^* \mid r(x)\in U_t\})$ which always holds.

(iii): $\text{Comp}(I) \Rightarrow \{e_t \mid t\in I\}$ is directed
$\Rightarrow \{r(e_t) \mid t\in I\}$ is directed

(iv): "$\text{Comp}(I) \Rightarrow r(e_I)\in U_j$" iff $\neg\text{Comp}(I) \vee r(e_I)\in U_j$
iff $\neg\text{Comp}(I) \vee (\exists t\in I^*)(r(e_t)\in U_j)$

which is clearly recursively enumerable in I and j because r is a computable map and * is a recursive operator.

□

To conclude this section, we prove the converse of Proposition 5.

<u>Theorem 4</u>

Effectively given domains are given by those cpo's which have an effectively given FC presentation.

Proof:

It suffices to show that if D has an effectively given FC presentation $\langle D, E=\{e_i\}_{i\in\omega}, U=\{U_i\}_{i\in\omega}, *, \text{Comp}\rangle$, then D is a computable retract of some recursive SFP object.

The proof here is analogous to our proof of Theorem 3 except that we want to replace the predicate Cons by the decidable predicate Comp. More precisely, for every $n\in\omega$, define the poset A_n to be $\{I\in\{0,..,n-1\}^* \mid \text{Comp}(I) \text{ true}\}$ partially ordered by set inclusion. Since Comp is decidable, the SFP object A_∞ (as defined for the proof of Theorem 3) is recursive. We claim that D is a computable retract of this recursive SFP object A_∞. Again we define $\phi:A_\infty\to D$ and $\psi:D\to A_\infty$ as follows:

$$\phi(\langle I_n\rangle_{n\in\omega}) = \bigsqcup_n e_{I_n}$$

and $$\psi(x) = \langle \{t\in\{0,..n-1\}^* \mid x\in U_t\}\rangle_{n\in\omega}$$

Since $\text{Comp}(\{t\in\{0,..,n-1\}^* \mid x\in U_t\})$ holds for every n and x, the map ψ is defined. As in the proof of Theorem 3, it can be shown that $\psi\circ\phi:A_\infty\to A_\infty$

is a retraction map. To show that $\psi \circ \phi$ is computable, it suffices to verify that the predicate "$J \subseteq \{t \in \{0,..,n-1\}^* | e_I \in U_t\}$" is recursively enumerable in n,I and J with $I,J \in F\omega$ satisfying Comp. First we note that there is an effective enumeration of all the J's in $F\omega$ satisfying Comp since Comp is decidable. Also the set $\{t \in \{0,..,n-1\}^* | e_I \in U_t\}$ is recursively enumerable in n and I - this is assumed in the notion of an effectively given FC presentation. Thus, the predicate "$J \subseteq \{t \in \{0,..,n-1\}^* | e_I \in U_t\}$" is recursively enumerable in n, I and J.

References

[1] Esorig, D. F. Probablistic Powerdomain, manuscript, 1983.

[2] Kamimura, T. and Tang, A. "Algebraic Relations and Presentations," Theoretical Computer Science 27, 1983, pp. 39-60.

[3] Kamimura, T. and Tang, A. "Effectively Given Spaces," Theoretical Computer Science 29, 1984, pp. 155-166.

[4] Kamimura, T. and Tang, A. Finitely Continuous Posets, University of Kansas, TR-84-1, February, 1984.

[5] Kozen, D. "Semantics of Probablistic Programs," 20th IEEE Symposium on Foundations of Computer Sciences 1979, pp. 101-114.

[6] Main, G. M. "Semiring Module Powerdomains," University of Colorado, CU-CS-286-84, December 1984.

[7] Plotkin, G. D. "A Powerdomain Construction," SIAM J. Computing, Vol. 5, No. 3, 1976, pp. 452-587.

[8] Plotkin, G. D. "T^ω as a Universal Domain," Journal of Computer System Sciences, Vol. 17 (1978), pp. 209-236.

[9] Scott, D. "Continuous Lattices," Lecture Notes in Mathematics 274 (1970), pp. 97-136.

[10] Scott, D. "Lattice Theory, Data Types and Semantics," Formal Semantics of Programming Languages (edited by R. Rustin), 1972, pp. 65-106.

[11] Scott, D. Lecture on a Mathematical Theory of Computation, Oxford University Computing Laboratory, Techn. Monograph PRG-19, 1981.

[12] Scott, D. "Domains for Denotational Semantics," Proc. of 9th ICALP, 1982.

[13] Smyth, M. B. "Effectively Given Domains," Theoretical Computer Science, Vol. 5, 1977, pp. 257-274.

[14] Smyth, M. B. "The Largest Cartesian Closed Category of Domains," Theoretical Computer Science 27, 1983, pp. 109-119.

[15] Smyth, M. B. and Plotkin, G. D. "Categorical Solutions of Reflexive Domain Equations," Proceedings of FOCS, 1977.

CONTINUOUS CATEGORIES

Jürgen Koslowski
Department of Mathematics
Kansas State University
Manhattan
Kansas 66506-7082

0 ABSTRACT

Our aim is to translate the order-theoretic notion of a continuous poset into a category theory setting. The generalisation is based on "way-below morphisms", which replace the well-known way-below relation. The emphasis of this note is on motivation; hence, most proofs are omitted. The ideas presented here are special cases of a more general construction which will appear in [K]. However, it seems useful to extract the aspects interesting to an audience mainly oriented towards computer science.

After comparing the familiar order-theoretic notions of finiteness and algebraicity with well-known categorical concepts, we show that way-below morphisms arise as a very natural generalization of the way-below relation for posets. (The "wavy arrows" of Johnstone and Joyal [JJ] present a different generalisation.) Next, following the order-theoretic ideas of Erné [EO], we try to eliminate the cocompleteness requirements on the categories. This essentially amounts to defining categorical analogues of Dedekind cuts.

There are basically two ways of generalizing the notion of an ideal from lattices to partially ordered sets. Either one can consider order ideals (which are just directed lower sets) or ideals in the sense of Frink [F] (which are lower sets containing the Dedekind cuts generated by each of their finite subsets). These lead to different generalizations of the concepts of algebraicity and continuity for posets, originally defined for complete lattices.

In order to translate these order-theoretical notions into categorical terms, we recall that the principal ideals are supremum-dense in the complete lattice of lower sets and how different kinds of lower sets can be characterized in terms of principal ideals. The lower sets of a poset $(X,\leq)$ via characteristic functions can be interpreted as monotone functions from $(X,\leq)^{op}$ into the two-element chain 2. If one considers posets as categories "over 2" (in the sense of V-categories), it seems natural to study the contravariant *SET*-valued functors for an ordinary category X instead. Then, in particular, representable functors will correspond to principal ideals.

Johnstone and Joyal [JJ] in their approach to continuous categories have used a categorical version of order ideals, namely directed colimits of representable functors, to play the rôle of ideals. Frink ideals on the other hand should correspond to directed colimits of the categorical analogues of Dedekind cuts. We will investigate the latter approach.

1 THE STANDARD NOTIONS

In this section we require $(X,\leq)$ to be a poset in which suprema of directed sets exist, and X to be a category which has colimits for all directed small diagrams, i.e., diagrams whose domain is a directed set. (This is equivalent to having colimits for all cofiltered small diagrams, cf. [AN].)

The following two definitions arise from translating equivalent characterizations of finiteness for sets into different settings.

1.00 DEFINITION

$a \in X$ is called <u>finite</u> or <u>compact</u> with respect to $\leq$, if for every directed subset D of X with supremum c, $a \leq c$ implies $a \leq d$ for some $d \in D$.

1.01 DEFINITION

An X-object A is called <u>finitely presentable</u>, if for every X-morphism $A \xrightarrow{g} C$ into the colimit (m,C) of a directed small diagram $I \xrightarrow{D} X$ there exists an X-morphism $A \xrightarrow{h} ID$ for some I-object I with $g=h.Im$, i.e., the following diagram commutes:

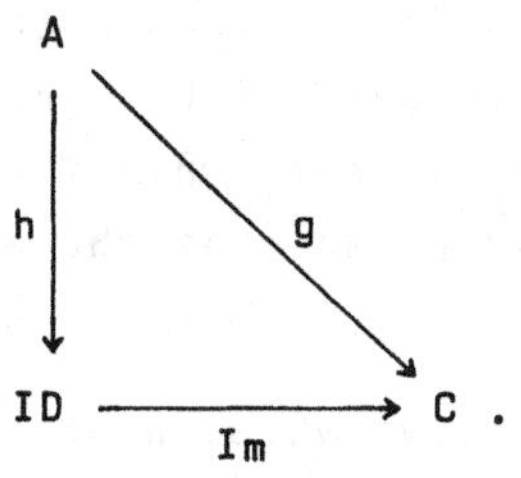

It turns out that A is finitely presentable iff the functor $(A,-)\underline{X}$ preserves colimits of directed small diagrams.

Of particular interest are those posets (resp. categories) which are determined by their finite elements (resp. finitely presentable objects).

1.02 DEFINITION

$(X,\leq)$ is called

(0) an <u>algebraic</u> <u>lattice</u>, if $(X,\leq)$ is a complete lattice and the finite elements of X form a supremum-dense subset;

(1) an <u>ω-algebraic</u> <u>lattice</u>, if $(X,\leq)$ is an algebraic lattice and the set of finite elements is countable;

(2) an <u>algebraic</u> <u>poset</u>, if the finite elements form a supremum-dense subset and for every b X the set $\{ a \leq b : a \text{ finite} \}$ is directed;

(3) an <u>ω-algebraic</u> <u>poset</u>, if $(X,\leq)$ is an algebraic poset and the set of finite elements is countable.

The following categorical notion is due to Gabriel and Ulmer [GU, Definition 7.1]. Based on [GU, Satz 7.4] we present a formulation, which makes the analogy with the order-theoretic notions above very explicite. Again we have a size restriction, resembling ω-algebraic lattices.

1.03 DEFINITION

X is called <u>locally</u> <u>finitely</u> <u>presentable</u>, if X is cocomplete, and has a set $G \subseteq X\text{-Ob}$ of generators, which detects isomorphisms.

Examples of locally finitely presentable categories include all categories of classical universal algebra, e.g., the categories of groups, rings, lattices, etc., where only finitary operations are involved. It comes as no surprise that the subobject-lattices in these categories are algebraic.

Next we consider a relative version of finiteness.

1.04 DEFINITION

$(a,b) \in X \times X$ satisfies the <u>way-below</u> <u>relation</u>, denoted $a \ll b$, if for every directed subset D of X with supremum c, $b \leq c$ implies $a \leq d$ for some $d \in D$.

Notice in particular that $a \ll b$ implies $a \leq b$, and $a \ll a$ is equivalent to a being finite. This motivates us to extend the definition of finite presentability from the objects of a category to its morphisms.

1.05 DEFINITION

$A \xrightarrow{f} B$ is called a <u>way-below</u> <u>morphism</u>, if for every $\mathcal{X}$-morphism $B \xrightarrow{g} C$ into the colimit (m,C) of a directed small diagram $\mathcal{I} \xrightarrow{D} \mathcal{X}$, there exists an $\mathcal{X}$-morphism $A \xrightarrow{h} ID$ for some $\mathcal{I}$-object I with $f.g=h.Im$, i.e., the following diagram commutes:

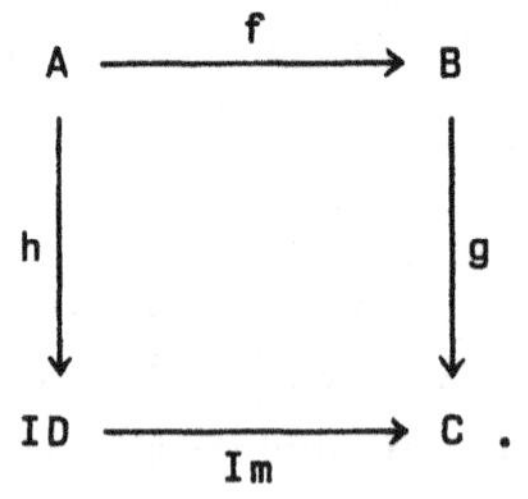

One could now reformulate 1.02 for this relative version of finiteness, but we restrict ourselves to the poset case.

1.06 **DEFINITION**

$(X,\leq)$ is called

(0) a <u>continuous poset</u>, if the set $\{a \in X : a \ll b\}$ is directed for every $b \in X$ and has supremum b ;

(1) an <u>ω-continuous poset</u>, if $(X,\leq)$ has a countable <u>base</u>, i.e., a countable subset G of X, such that the set $\{a \in G : a \ll b\}$ is directed for every $b \in X$ and has supremum b .

Continuous posets (and lattices) can be characterized in a different fashion without using the way-below relation. The supremum function from the poset of order ideals (=directed lower sets, ordered by inclusion) of $(X,\leq)$ into $(X,\leq)$ has a left adjoint iff $(X,\leq)$ is a continuous poset. A categorical generalization of this idea can be found in [JJ].

Before we return to this discussion in section 3, we want to pursue the way-below concept in order to define continuous categories. Moreover, we want to avoid any cocompleteness requirements on our categories.

2 WAY-BELOW MORPHISMS IN ARBITRARY CATEGORIES

In general the collection of order ideals of a poset is not closed under finite intersections. Furthermore, continuous posets defined in terms of order ideals (cf. 1.6) have two other drawbacks. The normal completion by cuts of a continuous poset need not be a continuous lattice, and if the normal completion of a poset with directed suprema is a continuous lattice, the poset itself need not be continuous.

These shortcomings prompted Erné [E0], [E1] to consider Frink ideals instead of order ideals, and he was thereby able to solve all three of the problems outlined above. We extend this approach to the categorical setting.

Let $(X,\leq)$ be an arbitrary poset.

2.00 DEFINITION

$a \in X$ is called a <u>lower bound</u> of $I \subseteq X$, if $a \leq i$ holds for each $i \in I$. I_+ denotes the set of all lower bounds of I.

DUAL NOTION: I^+ denotes the set of all <u>upper bounds</u> of I.

2.01 DEFINITION

$(a,b) \in X \times X$ satisfies the <u>way-below relation</u>, $a \ll b$, if for each directed subset D of X, $b \in D^+{}_+$ implies $a \leq d$ for some $d \in D$.

(Our definition of the way-below relation differs from the one used by Erné in [EO] to preserve the connection with finiteness.)

For a given element $b \in X$ the set $\{a \in X : a \ll b\}$ need not be directed (it could be empty), but it still is a Frink ideal.

2.02 DEFINITION

$G \subseteq X$ is called a <u>Dedekind cut</u> (resp. <u>Frink ideal</u>), if $I^+{}_+ \subseteq G$ holds for every subset (resp. every finite subset) I of G.

DUAL NOTIONS: <u>Dedekind cocut</u>, <u>Frink filter</u>.

2.03 REMARKS

(0) It is well known that $^+{}_+$ is a closure operator on the powerset of X, i.e., it is idempotent, extensive, and monotone. Hence a Dedekind cut $G \subseteq X$, which in particular satisfies $G^+{}_+ = G$, uniquely determines a Dedekind cocut, namely G^+, and vice versa; i.e., the concept of Dedekind cuts in posets is self-dual.

(1) Notice that the Dedekind cuts generated by particular subsets of G (namely all subsets or all finite subsets) are used to test G for being of a special type (Dedekind cut or Frink ideal).

(2) Principal ideals are Dedekind cuts, and Dedekind cuts are Frink ideals. Moreover, order ideals are Frink ideals, but the converse can fail to be true.

(3) The empty set is a Dedekind cut iff $(X,\leq)$ has no least element.

(4) Up to isomorphism the collection of Frink ideals, ordered by inclusion, forms the smallest algebraic lattice containing X as the set of finite elements.

(5) Every lower set is the union of principal ideals, and every Dedekind cut is the intersection of principal ideals. Moreover, each Frink ideal is the directed union of Dedekind cuts. In particular, order ideals are directed unions of principal ideals.

(6) If $(X,\leq)$ is cocomplete, and if G is a Dedekind cut, then for every subset I of G the supremum of I is in G . In particular, G contains its own supremum, i.e., G is a principal ideal. Viewed as a monotone map from $(X,\leq)^{op}$ into 2 , G preserves limits.

(7) If $(X,\leq)$ is a sup-semilattice, i.e., finitely cocomplete, and if G is a Frink ideal, then for every finite subset I of G the supremum of I is in G . In particular, G is directed. Viewed as a monotone map from $(X,\leq)^{op}$ into 2 , G preserves finite limits.

In an arbitrary category $\mathcal{X}$ we use cones instead of lower bounds.

2.04 DEFINITION

For a functor $\mathcal{I} \xrightarrow{F} \mathcal{X}$ a <u>natural</u> <u>F-source</u> or <u>F-cone</u> is a pair (A,a) consisting of an $\mathcal{X}$-object A and a natural transformation a from the constant functor $\mathcal{I} \longrightarrow \mathcal{X}$ with value A to F . The category F_+ of F-cones has as morphisms from (A,a) to (B,b) those $\mathcal{X}$-morphisms $A \xrightarrow{f} B$ which satisfy $Ia = f.Ib$ for every $\mathcal{I}$-object I . F_0 denotes the faithful functor from F_+ into $\mathcal{X}$, which maps $(A,a) \xrightarrow{f} (B,b)$ to $A \xrightarrow{f} C$.

DUAL NOTIONS: <u>natural</u> <u>F-sink</u> or <u>F-cocone</u>; $F^+ \xrightarrow{F^0} \mathcal{X}$.

In particular, for every $\mathcal{I}$-object I there is an important canonical F^0-cone $I\dot{F}$ with $a(I\dot{F}) = Ia$ for each F-cocone (a,A) . Moreover, the F-image of an I-morphism $I \xrightarrow{k} J$ is an $F^0{}_+$-morphism from $I\dot{F}$ to $J\dot{F}$, since for each F-cocone (a,A) by the naturality of a we have

$$kF.a(J\dot{F}) = kF.Ja = Ia = a(I\dot{F}) .$$

$\dot{F}$ denotes the resulting functor from $\mathcal{I}$ to $F^0{}_+$.

2.05 DEFINITION

$A \xrightarrow{f} B$ is called a <u>way-below</u> <u>morphism</u>, if for every directed diagram $I \xrightarrow{D} X$ and each D^o-cone (B,b) the D^o-cone $(A,f.b)$ factors through $I\dot{D}$ for some I-object I .

Notice that we do not require D to be small anymore since this definition does not depend on the cocompleteness of X .

Now for an X-object B we need a categorical entity to play the rôle the Frink ideal $\{a \in X : a \ll b\}$ plays for $b \in X$. If f is a way-below morphism, so is $e.f.g$, whenever e and g are X-morphisms composable with f . Thus for each X-object B we get a subfunctor $\hat{B}$ of the representable functor $(-,B)\underline{X}$, which maps A to the subset of $(A,B)\underline{X}$ consisting of all way-below morphisms from A to B . In whatever way one defines the categorical notion of Frink ideal, this functor should certainly be one.

We denote the Yoneda embedding of X into $[X^{op},SET]$ by X_y .

2.06 DEFINITION

$X^{op} \xrightarrow{G} SET$ is called a <u>Dedekind</u> <u>functor</u>, if there exists some diagram $W \xrightarrow{H} X$ such that G is the domain of a limit-cone for HX_y . $X_{\langle D\rangle}$ denotes the full subcategory of $[X^{op},SET]$, whose objects are all Dedekind functors.

Notice that $X_{\langle D\rangle}$ might be a proper quasi-category, i.e., some hom-classes need not be sets. Nevertheless, $X_{\langle D\rangle}$ has all small limits.

In order to keep the presentation simple, we require that $X_{\langle D\rangle}$ also be finitely cocomplete, which in general need not be the case. This actually is a smallness condition on X making an assertion, for every X-object B , about the class of X-morphisms with domain B . The following definition in a modified form could be made for any category X . In fact, it is a particular case of a more general categorical concept of ideal, which will be presented in full detail in [K].

2.07 DEFINITION

$\mathcal{X}^{op} \xrightarrow{G} SET$ is called a <u>Frink functor</u>, if for every finite diagram $J \xrightarrow{F} \mathcal{X}$ each $F\mathcal{X}_y$-cocone with codomain G uniquely factors through the colimit of $F\mathcal{X}_y$ in $\mathcal{X}_{\langle D\rangle}$. $\mathcal{X}_{\langle F\rangle}$ denotes the full subcategory of $[\mathcal{X}^{op}, SET]$, whose objects are the Frink functors.

For posets this reduces to the usual definition of a Frink ideal. Since the representable functors from $(X,\leq)^{op}$ into SET take only the empty set and certain singletons as values, i.e., up to natural isomorphism they factor through the canonical embedding of 2 into SET, Dedekind functors for $(X,\leq)$ reduce similarly. Therefore on posets Dedekind functors are just the characteristic functions of Dedekind cuts. The uniqueness condition makes it easy to see that a Frink functor $(X,\leq)^{op} \xrightarrow{G} SET$ (up to isomorphism) also has to factor through 2, i.e., it is just the characteristic function of a Frink ideal.

Since the Yoneda embedding of $\mathcal{X}$ into $\mathcal{X}_{\langle D\rangle}$ preserves limits <u>and</u> colimits, the very definition of Frink functor implies:

2.08 PROPOSITION

Every Frink functor preserves finite limits. $\square$

The converse implication that a finite limit preserving functor from $\mathcal{X}^{op}$ into SET is a Frink ideal only holds for finitely cocomplete $\mathcal{X}$. Frink ideals therefore are more than just finite limit preserving functors; they even preserve finite limits which do not exist.

The following result justifies our definition of Frink functor.

2.09 PROPOSITION

For every $\mathcal{X}$-object B the functor $\mathcal{X}^{op} \xrightarrow{\hat{B}} SET$, which maps an $\mathcal{X}$-object A to the set of way-below morphisms from A to B, is a Frink functor.

PROOF:

Let $\mathcal{J} \xrightarrow{F} \mathcal{X}$ be a finite diagram, $(u,\hat{B})$ an $F\mathcal{X}_y$-cocone, and (m,H) a colimit of $F\mathcal{X}_y$ in $\mathcal{X}_{<D>}$. It is easy to see that up to natural isomorphism H maps an $\mathcal{X}$-object A to the set of F^o-cones with domain A, and the projection $(A,JF)\underline{X} \xrightarrow{AJm} AH$ maps an $\mathcal{X}$-morphism $A \xrightarrow{f} JF$ to the pullback of the F^o-cocone $J\dot{F}$ along f, whenever J is a $\mathcal{J}$-object.

Clearly the $F\mathcal{X}_y$-cocone $(u,\hat{B})$ uniquely corresponds to an F-cocone $(\tilde{u},B)$ such that $JF \xrightarrow{J\tilde{u}} B$ is a way-below morphism for each $\mathcal{J}$-object J. We claim that for any F^o-cone (A,a) the morphism $A \xrightarrow{\tilde{u}a} B$ is a way-below morphism as well.

Consider a directed diagram $\mathcal{I} \xrightarrow{D} \mathcal{X}$ and a D^o-cone (B,b). Since $\mathcal{I}$ is directed, $\mathcal{J}$ is finite, and $J\tilde{u}$ is a way-below morphism for every $\mathcal{J}$-object J, there exists an $\mathcal{I}$-object I and an F-cocone (k,ID), such that the D^o-cone $(JF,J\tilde{u}.b)$ factors through $I\dot{D}$ via Jk for every $\mathcal{J}$-object J. Therefore the D^o-cone $(A,\tilde{u}a.b)$ factors through $I\dot{D}$ via $A \xrightarrow{ka} ID$, and the claim is proved.

Thus we have defined a function $AH \xrightarrow{Ap} A\hat{B}$ for every $\mathcal{X}$-object A, and one can easyly show that p is a natural transformation with $Jm.p = Ju$ for every $\mathcal{J}$-object J.

To show that p is unique we observe that the composition of p with the subfunctor inclusion $\hat{B} \xrightarrow{i} B\mathcal{X}_y$ is the unique $\mathcal{X}_{<D>}$-morphism from H into $B\mathcal{X}_y$ induced by the universal property of the colimit (m,H), i is a monomorphism, and $\mathcal{X}_{<D>}$ is a full subcategory of $[\mathcal{X}^{op},\mathcal{SET}]$. □

The analogy with the order-theoretic results can be taken even further.

2.10 **PROPOSITION**

$\mathcal{X}^{op} \xrightarrow{G} \mathcal{SET}$ is a Frink functor iff G is the colimit of a directed diagram of Dedekind functors. □

The "only if" part of the last proposition requires $\mathcal{X}_{<D>}$ to be finitely cocomplete; the "if" part is true in general.

3 CONTINUOUS CATEGORIES

Let us recall the definition of the comma category X/B for a category X and an X-object B. Its objects are the X-morphisms with codomain B, and a morphism from $A \xrightarrow{f} B$ to $A' \xrightarrow{f'} B$ is an X-morphism $A \xrightarrow{h} A'$ with $f = h.f'$. Let $X"B$ denote the "domain functor" from X/B into X, which maps $f \xrightarrow{h} f'$ to $A \xrightarrow{h} A'$. In a poset $(X,\leq)$ this functor corresponds to the inclusion of the principal ideal generated by $b \in X$ into X. The representable functor $X^{op} \xrightarrow{BX_y} SET$ plays the same rôle for the comma category X/B as the characteristic function plays for a principal ideal.

As b is the supremum of its principal ideal for each $b \in X$, so $X"B$ has a colimit with codomain B for every X-object B.

The question now arises, whether these comma categories can be made "thinner", i.e., can be replaced by full subcategories in some functorial way without affecting the colimits. Any such choice will be called <u>conservative</u>, and we will refer to the objects in the chosen subcategories as <u>approximations</u>, since they carry all the information about the respective colimits.

In the theory of computation the objective is to make conservative choices, in which the subcategories are "nice" in some sense. In the case of posets the standard approach to "niceness" requires the subcategories (here: lower sets) to be directed; that is, given any two distinct approximations, one can find a better one. Accordingly, in the categorical setting these subcategories should be cofiltered, i.e., every finite diagram should be the base of a cocone.

It is easy to see that for any X-object B there is an order-preserving isomorphism between the collections of full subcategories of X/B and of pointwise subfunctors of $BX_y = (-,B)\underline{X}$. "Nice subcategory" thus translates into "well-behaved subfunctor". Usually the subfunctors are required to be directed (or cofiltered) colimits of representable functors. If on the other hand we require them to be Frink functors, for the resulting subcategories this means that every finite diagram of approximations, which does not have the desired colimit, can be extended.

We now return to the discussion at the end of section 1. Suppose we have specified certain "niceness" properties which the categories of approximations are supposed to have. Thus we obtain a certain full subcategory $X_{\langle nice \rangle}$ of $[X^{op},SET]$ consisting of the corresponding well-behaved functors. We assume that the representable functors belong to $X_{\langle nice \rangle}$.

If we now require the Yoneda embedding X_y of X into $X_{\langle nice \rangle}$ to have a left adjoint S, this means that for every well-behaved functor $X^{op} \xrightarrow{G} SET$ the functor $X_y/G \xrightarrow{X_y"G} X$ has a colimit with codomain GS, cf. [M, Theorem X.2]. X_y/G hereby denotes a more general type of comma category whose objects are natural transformations $AX_y \xrightarrow{a} G$, and whose morphisms from $AX_y \xrightarrow{a} G$ to $BX_y \xrightarrow{b} G$ are X-morphisms $A \xrightarrow{f} B$ which satisfy $a = fX_y.b$. $X_y"G$ is the corresponding "domain functor". In the poset case this means that all lower sets of a certain type have a supremum.

After spending some effort in section 2 on the elimination of any cocompleteness requirements, it seems inappropriate to introduce them again in the definition of continuous categories. However, our previous discussion indicates what the correct definition should be.

3.00 **DEFINITION**

(0) By a <u>pointwise subfunctor</u> of $X \xrightarrow{X_y} X_{\langle nice \rangle}$ we mean a pair (W,i), where i is a natural transformation from $X \xrightarrow{W} X_{\langle nice \rangle}$ to X_y, such that ABi is an injection from ABW to $ABX_y = (A,B)\underline{X}$, for all X-objects A and B.

(1) We call a pointwise subfunctor (W,i) <u>conservative</u>, if the corresponding choice of subcategories of the comma categories X/B, $B \in X$-Ob, is conservative.

3.01 **DEFINITION**

X is called <u>continuous</u> (with rerspect to the chosen "niceness" properties), if the naturally ordered collection of conservative pointwise subfunctors of X_y has a smallest element.

In the language of posets this definition says that $(X,\leq)$ is continuous, if there exists a smallest choice of "nice" lower sets bW with supremum b, $b \in X$. Such a choice automatically is functorial.

If we require "nice" functors to be Frink functors, the following question arises for a continuous category $\mathcal{X}$: Is the way-below functor $\mathcal{X} \xrightarrow{\mathcal{X}_w} \mathcal{X}_{\langle F \rangle}$, which maps an $\mathcal{X}$-object B to $\hat{B}$, the smallest conservative pointwise subfunctor of $\mathcal{X}_y$? Erné has shown [E0, Example 3.1] that even for posets this need not be true. He constructs a poset with a finite element a_0 , whose principal ideal properly contains a Frink ideal with supremum a_0 .

REFERENCES

[AN] H. Andréka, I. Németi, Direct limits and filtered colimits are strongly equivalent in all categories. Universal Algebra and Applications, Banach Center Pub. 9, Polish Scientific Publishers, Warsaw, 1982, 75-88.

[E0] M. Erné, Completion-invariant extension of the concept of continuous lattices. Continuous Lattices, Proceedings, Bremen 1979, Lecture Notes in Math. **871**, Springer Verlag, Berlin - Heidelberg - New York, 1981, 45-60.

[E1] M. Erné, Scott convergence and Scott topology in partially ordered sets, II. Continuous Lattices, Proceedings, Bremen 1979, Lecture Notes in Math. **871**, Springer Verlag, Berlin - Heidelberg - New York, 1981, 61-96.

[E2] M. Erné, Einführung in die Ordnungstheorie. Bibliographisches Institut, Mannheim - Wien - Zürich, 1982.

[F] O. Frink, Ideals in partially ordered sets. Amer. Math. Monthly **61** (1954), 223-234.

[GH] G. Gierz, K. H. Hofmann et al., A Compendium of Continuous Lattices. Springer Verlag, Berlin - Heidelberg - New York, 1980.

[GU] P. Gabriel, F. Ulmer, Lokal präsentierbare Kategorien. Lecture Notes in Math. **221**, Springer Verlag, Berlin - Heidelberg - New York, 1971.

[HS] H. Herrlich, G. E. Strecker, Category Theory, 2nd ed.. Heldermann Verlag, Berlin, 1979.

[JJ] P. T. Johnstone, A. Joyal, Continuous categories and exponentiable toposes. Journal of Pure and Applied Algebra **25** (1982), 255-296.

[K] J. Koslowski, Hypercontinuous functors. Thesis, in preparation.

[M] S. MacLane, Categories for the Working Mathematician. Graduate Texts in Math. 5, Springer Verlag, Berlin - Heidelberg - New York, 1971.

[Ma] G. Markowsky, A motivation and generalization of Scott's notion of a continuous lattice. Continuous Lattices, Proceedings, Bremen 1979, Lecture Notes in Math. **871**, Springer Verlag, Berlin - Heidelberg - New York, 1981, 298-307.

[T] W. Tholen, Completions of categories and shape theory. Proc. Fifth Prague Topol. Symp., 1981, Heldermann Verlag, Berlin, 1982, 593-607.

FREE CONSTRUCTIONS OF POWERDOMAINS*

Michael G. Main
Department of Computer Science
University of Colorado
Boulder, CO 80309 USA
Phone: 303-492-7579

ABSTRACT

A *powerdomain* is a CPO together with extra algebraic structure for handling nondeterministic values. In the first powerdomains, the algebraic structure was a continuous binary operation **or**, which met certain axioms. Plotkin [9] and Smyth [14] showed how such a structure could be added to certain kinds of CPOs in a free or universal manner. This paper extends the work of Plotkin and Smyth by giving free constructions of powerdomains for a more adaptable algebraic structure: semiring modules. Prior to the constructions, three detailed examples are given, showing how the semiring module structure can capture information about nondeterministic behavior. By putting the available information in an algebraic framework, the algebraic properties can supplement the usual order-theoretic properties in program proofs.

1. MOTIVATION

About ten years ago, researchers began studying the idea of a CPO for nondeterministic values. The idea was this: take a CPO C, and embed it in another CPO which has additional algebraic structure for handling nondeterminism. Such a structure is called a nondeterministic-CPO or *powerdomain*. So, what we are looking for is a powerdomain, $P(C)$, together with a strict+ continuous function $\eta: C \rightarrow P(C)$, which embeds C in the powerdomain. In order to make the construction as general as

*This research has been supported in part by National Science Foundation grant DCR-8402341.

+A *strict* function is one which preserves the least element; some powerdomain constructions consider embeddings which are continuous, but not necessarily strict. In general, the mathematics is more straight-forward if we restrict ourselves to strict embeddings. For a case where non-strict functions raise difficulties, see exercise 101 in chapter 8 of Plotkin's postgraduate notes [10].

possible, the embedding function η should be *universal*. That is: if Q is any powerdomain and $g:C \rightarrow Q$ is any strict continuous function, then there is a unique strict continuous function $\hat{g}:P(C) \rightarrow Q$ which preserves the algebraic structure and makes the following diagram commute:

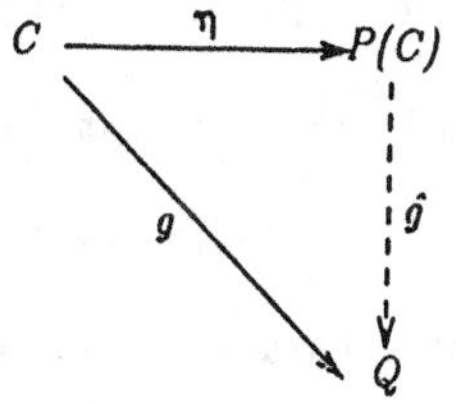

Thus, any way of making C into a powerdomain can be obtained from $P(C)$ and η by a unique morphism. $P(C)$ is called the *free* powerdomain generated by C, with insertion η.

Generally, the existence of the universal $P(C)$ and η can be obtained from categorical considerations, but it is not always clear how to characterize the construction in a convenient set-theoretic manner that is appropriate for semantic studies. Plotkin's original powerdomain [9] is a constructive characterization of $P(C)$ for the case where C is an ω-algebraic CPO, and the algebraic structure of the powerdomain is an associative binary operator **or**, which is commutative, idempotent and continuous with respect to the partial order. (An element x **or** y in such a powerdomain is a nondeterministic choice between x and y.) Several alternative powerdomains [10,14] are modifications of Plotkin's construction, obtained by imposing additional axioms on the algebraic structure. The additional axioms are designed to capture various aspects of nondeterminism.

Different aspects of nondeterminism can also be studied by imposing further algebraic structure on the powerdomain. The structure used in this paper is a *semiring module* (a generalization of a ring module, or vector space). Section 2 gives three detailed examples of the use of semiring modules in this capacity. The examples use different underlying semirings to capture different information about nondeterminism. By putting the available information in an algebraic framework, the algebraic properties can supplement the usual order-theoretic properties in program proofs.

Each of the three examples is aided by the fact that the utilized powerdomain is a free powerdomain generated by a flat CPO. Following the examples are the major results of this paper, giving constructive characterization of free powerdomains generated by certain sorts of CPOs. The Smyth powerdomain and its dual (sometimes called the Hoare powerdomain) are special cases of these constructions.

Terminology and notation: Throughout the paper, function compositions and applications are written in diagram order (which is more convenient for the denotational semantics). Thus $f \circ g$ is the function f followed by g. The application of f to x is written $(x)f$ or xf. A CPO is a partially ordered set (the order denoted $\sqsubseteq$) with a least element (usually $\perp$) and least upper bounds of all countably infinite non-decreasing chains (called ω-chains). The least upper-bound of a chain $x_0 \sqsubseteq x_1 \sqsubseteq \cdots$ is denoted $\bigsqcup x_i$. A function $f{:}C \to D$ between two CPOs is *strict* if it preserves the least element, and *continuous* if it is monotonic and preserves the least upper-bound of any ω-chain.

2. THREE EXAMPLES

This section gives denotational semantics for three sorts of **while**-programs with different kinds of nondeterminism. In each case, there is a fixed but arbitrary set D of "deterministic states" for the computations. The elements of D might be environments (*i.e.*, assignments of values to program variables) or some other notion of "state", but the exact formulation of D is unimportant. Also common to the three different sorts of programs is a collection Γ of "deterministic state transformations", and a collection Ω of "state predicates". For each $c \in \Gamma$, the interpretation of c is a total function $c_I{:}D \to D$; for each $p \in \Omega$, the interpretation of p is a subset $p_I \subseteq D$.

2.1 Ephemeral Nondeterminism

Sometimes when a device is started-up there is a short period of time when its behavior is unstable, but eventually it settles down to a deterministic sequence of actions. Similar behavior may occur in a distributed network of processors when a restart signal is propagating the network. This temporarily unstable behavior is called *ephemeral nondeterminism*. It can be modeled in a programming language by adding a programming construct $s \bigcirc t$, where s and t are arbitrary statements. With a finite number of exceptions, the behavior of $s \bigcirc t$ is exactly like that of s. However, finitely often, $s \bigcirc t$ may behave like t. Thus, if $s \bigcirc t$ is executed an infinite number of times, then t may be chosen only finitely often. (If $s \bigcirc t$ is executed only a finite number of times, then it is exactly like the usual nondeterministic choice between s and t.) The statement s is called the *stable choice,* while t is the *unstable choice*. Note that $s \bigcirc (t \bigcirc u)$ has the same meaning as $(s \bigcirc t) \bigcirc u$; both must eventually settle down to s.

In the usual nondeterministic semantics, it is sufficient to keep track of what possible results a nondeterministic program can produce. In ephemeral nondeterminism, more information can be recorded. For each possible result x, we can record the minimal number of unstable choices which can produce x. If x is not possible at all, then this number is infinity. Formally, a "nondeterministic state" is a function $\alpha: D_\perp \to \overline{\mathbb{N}}$, where $D_\perp$ is $D \cup \{\perp\}$, and $\overline{\mathbb{N}}$ is the set of natural numbers together with an infinity element. The value of α at $\perp$ is the minimal number of unstable choices which may result in a non-terminating computation, while for each $x \in D$, $(x)\alpha$ is the minimal number of unstable choices which may result in x.

Not all functions $\alpha: D_\perp \to \overline{\mathbb{N}}$ are nondeterministic states. We require α to meet these two criteria:

$$\text{For all } n < (\perp)\alpha\text{: } \{x \in D \mid (x)\alpha = n\} \text{ is finite.}$$

$$\text{For all } n > (\perp)\alpha\text{: } \{x \in D \mid (x)\alpha = n\} \text{ is empty.}$$

A theoretical justification of this choice of functions will be given by a free construction of section 3. Intuitively, the first requirement means that if non-termination is impossible with n unstable choices, then the number of possible actions with n unstable choices is finite (similar to Dijkstra's requirement [2, chapter 9]). The second requirement means that the resulting denotational semantics will only be appropriate for determining what a program "must" do; thus if non-termination is possible with n unstable choices, then it does not matter what other things the program might do with n or more unstable choices (similar to the Smyth or "must" powerdomain [1,7,10,15]).

In this subsection, let M be the collection of all functions $\alpha: D_\perp \to \overline{\mathbb{N}}$ which meet the above two conditions. M is a CPO with pointwise ordering: $\alpha \sqsubseteq \beta$ iff for all $x \in D_\perp$, $(x)\alpha \le (x)\beta$. With respect to this CPO order, there are two useful continuous operations on M:

Pointwise Minimum:

For α and β in M, α **or** β is the pointwise minimum, *i.e.*, $(x)(\alpha \textbf{ or } \beta)$ is the minimum of $(x)\alpha$ and $(x)\beta$. This is the result of a program which can produce either α or β. The function **impossible**:$M \to M$ which maps every element to ∞, is the identity for this operation.

Addition of a Constant:

For $\alpha \in M$ and $n \in \overline{\mathbf{N}}$, $n\alpha$ is the function which results from ***adding n*** at each point, *i.e.*, $(x)(n\alpha)$ is $n + (x)\alpha$. Note that $0\alpha = \alpha$.

The semantics of **while**-programs can be given by assigning a strict continuous function $[\![f]\!]:M \to M$ to each **while**-program f. Each $[\![f]\!]$ will preserve the two operations on M. That is:

$$\text{For all } \alpha,\beta \in M\text{: } (\alpha \text{ or } \beta)[\![f]\!] = \alpha[\![f]\!] \text{ or } \beta[\![f]\!].$$

$$\text{For all } \alpha \in M \text{ and } n \in \overline{\mathbf{N}}\text{: } (n\alpha)[\![f]\!] = n((\alpha)[\![f]\!]).$$

A strict continuous function on M which meets these two properties is a ***morphism***. Certain universal properties are of aid in specifying such morphisms on M. Specifically, we will use these three properties (which are guaranteed by the free construction of section 3):

- For each $x \in D$, there is a distinct element $\eta_x \in M$ such that η_x applied to x is 0, and η_x is ∞ elsewhere. These elements are called the ***base elements***. Usually we will write just $x \in M$ instead of $\eta_x \in M$. In this way, D is a subset of M.

- The subset $D \subseteq M$ "generates" M in the usual way. Specifically, every function $g:D \to M$ has a unique extension to a morphism $\hat{g}:M \to M$ with $(x)\hat{g} = (x)g$ for every $x \in D$. Thus, any morphism is completely specified by giving its value on the base elements, and these values can be arbitrary.

- The collection of morphisms from M to itself is a CPO, with pointwise ordering. Hence, every continuous functional on this collection has a least fixed-point, calculated by the usual Kleene formula. Note that the least morphism does not map every element to "bottom" in M. Rather, it is the extension of the function which maps every base element to "bottom" in M.

Using these three properties, here is an inductive definition of **while**-programs and their semantics:

SYNTAX	SEMANTICS
1. Simple commands: Each command $c \in \Gamma$ is a program.	1. $[\![c]\!]: M \to M$ is defined by giving its values on base elements. Namely, for each $x \in D$: $(x)[\![c]\!] = (x)c_I$.
2. Compositon: If f and g are programs, then so is $f;g$.	2. $[\![f;g]\!]$ is the composition $[\![f]\!] \circ [\![g]\!]$.
3. Conditional: If f and g are programs, and $p \in \Omega$ is a state predicate, then **if** p **then** f **else** g **fi** is a program.	3. Let $p_{true}: M \to M$ and $p_{false}: M \to M$ be the unique morphisms such that for all $x \in D$: $(x)p_{true}$ = if $x \in p_I$ then x else impossible $(x)p_{false}$ = if $x \in p_I$ then impossible else x Then $[\![$**if** p **then** f **else** g **fi**$]\!]$ is $(p_{true} \circ [\![f]\!])$ **or** $(p_{false} \circ [\![g]\!])$. Here, the operation **or** is extended pointwise to morphisms.
4. Iteration: If f is a program, and $p \in \Omega$ is a state predicate, then **while** p **do** f **od** is a program.	4. Let p_{true} and p_{false} be as in the last statement. Then $[\![$**while** p **do** f **od**$]\!]$ is the least morphism h such that $h = p_{true} \circ [\![f]\!] \circ h$ **or** p_{false}. The existence of this solution follows from the free construction M in the section 3.
5. Ephemeral nondeterminism: If f and g are programs, then so is $(f \bigcirc g)$.	5. $[\![(f \bigcirc g)]\!]$ is $[\![f]\!]$ **or** $1[\![g]\!]$. Here, $1[\![g]\!]$ is the morphism whose value at α is $1(\alpha [\![g]\!])$.

Here is an example of the sort of result obtainable with the ephemeral semantics: An element $\alpha \in M$ is called *total* provided that $(\bot)\alpha = \infty$. A **while**-program f is total if $[\![f]\!]$ preserves total elements. Intuitively, these are the programs which cannot loop. A relationship between totality, iteration and ephemeral nondeterminism is given in the following:

Theorem: *Let $p \in \Omega$ be any state predicate, and let g and h be total programs. The program*

$$\textbf{while } p \textbf{ do } (g \bigcirc h) \textbf{ od}$$

is total iff $\bigsqcup\{(p_{true} \circ g)^i \mid i = 0,1,\cdots\}$ *is* **impossible**. *($\bigsqcup$ indicates the pointwise least upper bound of morphisms).*

Proof: The necessity of the condition is straight-forward. To see that it is sufficient, we will use the following notation:

$$f : M \to M \text{ is } [\![\textbf{while } p \textbf{ do } (g \bigcirc h) \textbf{ od}]\!].$$

$$\text{For any } \alpha \in M,\ [\alpha] \text{ is its value at } \bot.$$

$$\beta \text{ is a total element of } M \text{ such that } [\beta f] \text{ is minimal.}$$

We must show that $[\beta f] = \infty$. First note that the fixed-point property of f gives the equality: $[\beta f] = minimum\{[\beta(p_{true} \circ [\![g]\!] \circ f)],\ 1 + [\beta(p_{true} \circ [\![h]\!] \circ f)],\ [\beta p_{false}]\}$. But, $[\beta p_{false}] = \infty$, since p_{false} preserves total elements; so $[\beta f]$ is

$$minimum\ \{[\beta(p_{true} \circ [\![g]\!] \circ f)]\ ,\ 1 + [\beta(p_{true} \circ [\![h]\!] \circ f)]\}.$$

This further reduces to $[\beta f] = [\beta(p_{true} \circ [\![g]\!] \circ f)]$, since $1 + [\beta(p_{true} \circ [\![h]\!]) \circ f)]$ is either infinite, or else it is strictly greater than $[\beta f]$ (since we choose β to make $[\beta f]$ minimal). From this last equality we get $[\beta f] = [\beta((p_{true} \circ [\![g]\!])^i \circ f)]$, for any i, hence:

$$[\beta f] = \lim_{i=0}^{\infty} [\beta((p_{true} \circ [\![g]\!])^i \circ f)] \geq \lim_{i=0}^{\infty} minimum\{(x)(\beta((p_{true} \circ [\![g]\!])^i) \mid x \in D\} = \infty.$$

The inequality $\geq$ follows from the fact that a morphism cannot lower the value of $[\alpha]$ below $minimum\{(x)\alpha \mid x \in D\}$ (otherwise it does not preserve addition of a scalar). Thus, $[\beta f] = \infty$, as required. $\square$

2.2 Discrete Probabilistic Nondeterminism

Discrete probabilistic programs are formed by allowing probabilistic choices to be made in the conditional and iterative statements of ordinary **while**-programs. The programs are similar to those used by Dexter Kozen [4], although continuous probability distributions are not allowed.

For this sort of nondeterminism, a nondeterministic state is a function $\alpha{:}D\to\overline{\mathbf{R}}_+$, from the deterministic states D to the non-negative real numbers $\overline{\mathbf{R}}_+$ (which includes ∞). The meaning of $(x)\alpha$ is the probability that the deterministic state x will occur*. The domain, D, does not need to include a "bottom" element because of a "conservation of mass" principle that programs will have.

As in the previous example, we restrict ourselves to certain sorts of functions from D to $\overline{\mathbf{R}}_+$. In this subsection, M consists of those $\alpha{:}D\to\overline{\mathbf{R}}_+$ such that $\{x\in D\,|\,(x)\alpha\neq 0\}$ is countable. M is a CPO with the order $\alpha\sqsubseteq\beta$ iff for all $x\in D$: $(x)\alpha\leq(x)\beta$. M is closed under these continuous operations:

Pointwise Addition:

For α and β in M, α **or** β is the pointwise sum, *i.e.*, $(x)(\alpha \textbf{ or } \beta)$ is $(x)\alpha+(x)\beta$. The function **impossible**:$M\to M$ which maps every element to 0, is the identity for this operation.

Scalar Multiplication:

For $\alpha\in M$ and $r\in\overline{\mathbf{R}}_+$, $r\alpha$ is the function which results from pointwise multiplication of α by r, *i.e.*, $(x)(r\alpha)$ is $r((x)\alpha)$.

Strict continuous functions from M to itself are morphisms if they preserve these two operations. The three universal properties of M in the previous example also hold here. The only change is that the base element η_x associated with an element $x\in D$ is the function which maps x to 1, and all other elements to 0. Thus, $D\subseteq M$ is a

*The codomain might be restricted to the interval [0..1], but using all of $\overline{\mathbf{R}}_+$ makes the algebra more straightforward.

generating subset of M, as before. These base elements are the deterministic elements of M -- those which have a fixed value (with probability 1).

The syntax and semantics of discrete probabilistic programs have much in common with the ephemeral nondeterministic programs. For each program f we give a denotation $[\![f]\!]$ which is a morphism on M:

SYNTAX	SEMANTICS
1. Simple commands, Composition, Conditional and *Iteration* are unchanged from the last example.	1. The denotation for a simple command, composition, conditional or iterative statement is unchanged from the last example.
2. Probabilistic conditional: Let Δ be a collection of function symbols (disjoint from Ω), such that each $p \in \Delta$ has an associated function $p_I: D \to [0..1]$. If f and g are programs, and $p \in \Delta$, then if p then f else g fi is a program.	2. Let $p_{true}: M \to M$ and $p_{false}: M \to M$ be the unique morphisms such that for all $x \in D$: $(x)p_{true} = (xp_I)x$ $(x)p_{false} = (1 - xp_I)x$ Thus, $(x)p_{true}$ and $(x)p_{false}$ are always scalar multiples of x. Then $[\![$if p then f else g fi$]\!]$ is $(p_{true} \circ [\![f]\!])$ or $(p_{false} \circ [\![g]\!])$. Here, the operation or is extended pointwise to morphisms.
3. Probabilistic iteration: Let p and f be as above. Then while p do f od is a program.	3. Let p_{true} and p_{false} be as in the last statement. Then $[\![$while p do f od$]\!]$ is the least morphism h such that $h = p_{true} \circ [\![f]\!] \circ h$ or p_{false}.

The denotations of probabilistic programs cannot create new "mass" in this sense: For any $\alpha \in M$, define (α)**MASS** to be the infinite sum $\sum_{x \in D} (x)\alpha$. Then for any program f

and $\alpha \in M$, the inequality $(\alpha)\mathbf{MASS} \geq (\alpha f)\mathbf{MASS}$ holds. A decrease in mass can occur in a **while** loop, since non-terminating branches have no mass. This suggests that a total element is one with $(\alpha)\mathbf{MASS}=1$; a total program has a denotation which preserves total elements.

As a concrete application of this idea, consider programs with one program variable x, which ranges over the positive natural numbers. Thus, the set of deterministic states consists of the positive natural numbers $\mathbf{P} = \{1,2,3,...\}$. The following result is from a motivating example of an earlier paper [6]:

Theorem: *Let $p \in \Delta$ be any function symbol such that $(x)p_I > 0$ for all $x \in \mathbf{P}$, and let $q: \mathbf{P} \to [0..1)$ be defined by $(x)q = 1-(x)p_I$. Then the program*

$$\mathbf{while}\ p\ \mathbf{do}\ x := x + 1\ \mathbf{od}$$

is total iff the series $q(1) + q(2) + \cdots$ diverges. □

Therefore, this program will terminate (with probability 1):

$$\mathbf{while}\ 1 - \frac{1}{x+1}\ \mathbf{do}\ x := x + 1\ \mathbf{od}$$

On the other hand, this program has a non-zero probability of non-termination:

$$\mathbf{while}\ 1 - \frac{1}{x^2+1}\ \mathbf{do}\ x := x + 1\ \mathbf{od}$$

2.3 Oracle Nondeterminism

In this example, we consider the behavior of a nondeterministic program to be completely determined by a set of circumstances which may be beyond our control (or even beyond our ability to observe them directly). Presumably, an omniscient oracle could tell us in advance what such a program will do, but our access to such an oracle might be only partial, so any reasoning about programs will be dependent on the unknown circumstances that hold during its execution. Note that such a program need not have repeatable behavior, since the circumstances of one execution may differ from those of another.

To formalize this, let U be a set of "possible universes". Intuitively, each universe is a complete specification of all the circumstances which may effect a program. A non-deterministic state is a function α which assigns to each deterministic state $x \in D$ a *set* $(x)\alpha$ of *possible universes*. These are the universes in which state x may occur. As in the last example, we only allow functions such that $\{x \in D \mid (x)\alpha \neq \emptyset\}$ is countable. In this subsection, M is the set of all these countably-nonempty functions. Once again, M is a CPO with the order $\alpha \sqsubseteq \beta$ iff for all $x \in D$: $(x)\alpha \subseteq (x)\beta$. The two continuous operations on M are:

Pointwise Union:

For α and β in M, α **or** β is the pointwise union, *i.e.*, $(x)(\alpha$ **or** $\beta)$ is $(x)\alpha \cup (x)\beta$. The function **impossible**:$M \to M$ which maps every element to $\emptyset$, is the identity for this operation.

Scalar Intersection:

For $\alpha \in M$ and any subset $r \subseteq U$ of universes, $r\alpha$ is the function which results from pointwise intersection of α with r, *i.e.*, $(x)(r\alpha)$ is $r \cap ((x)\alpha)$.

Strict continuous functions from M to itself are morphisms if they preserve these two operations. The three universal properties in the previous examples also hold here; the base element η_x associated with an element $x \in D$ is the function which maps x to U, and all other elements to $\emptyset$. As expected, $D \subseteq M$ is a generating subset of M.

Here are the syntax and semantics of the oracle programs, with much stolen from the existing examples:

SYNTAX	SEMANTICS
1. Simple commands, Composition, Conditional and *Iteration* are unchanged from the other examples.	1. The denotation for a simple command, composition, conditional or iterative statement is unchanged from the previous examples.
2. Oracle conditional: Let Δ be a collection of function symbols (disjoint from Ω), such that each $p \in \Delta$ has an associated function $p_I : D \to 2^U$ -- where 2^U is the powerset of U. If f and g are programs, and $p \in \Delta$, then if p then f else g fi is a program.	2. Let $p_{true} : M \to M$ and $p_{false} : M \to M$ be the unique morphisms such that for all $x \in D$: $(x)p_{true} = (xp_I)x$ $(x)p_{false} = (U - xp_I)x$ Thus, $(x)p_{true}$ and $(x)p_{false}$ are always scalar intersections of x. Then $[\![$if p then f else g fi$]\!]$ is $(p_{true} \circ [\![f]\!])$ or $(p_{false} \circ [\![g]\!])$. Note that this is identical to the probabilistic conditional, with U taking the role of 1. Similarly, oracle iteration has the same semantics as probabilistic iteration.
3. Oracle iteration: Let p and f be as above. Then while p do f od is a program.	3. Let p_{true} and p_{false} be as in the last statement. Then $[\![$while p do f od$]\!]$ is the least morphism h such that $h = p_{true} \circ [\![f]\!] \circ h$ or p_{false}.

As in the probabilistic example, we can define the "mass" of an element $\alpha \in M$ as $(\alpha)\mathbf{MASS} = \bigcup_{x \in D} (x)\alpha$. An element is *total* if $(\alpha)\mathbf{MASS} = U$, and a program is total if it preserves total elements.

We can make this example more concrete by choosing a set of universes. Let U be all "fair" infinite sequences over the characters $\{a,b\}$. (Choose your favorite definition of "fair", such as [5,8,11] -- it doesn't really matter.) Let the deterministic states, D, be $\mathbf{P} \times S$, where $\mathbf{P}$ is the set of positive natural numbers, and S is the "state set" for the programs of interest. A special element $nextchoice \in \Gamma$ is defined so that $(n,s)nextchoice_I = (n+1,s)$. A "fair" choice between actions f and g is the program:

if A **then** f **else** g **fi**; $nextchoice$,

where the interpretation A_I of A takes (n,s) to those universes which have "a" as the nth element in the sequence.* The usual results about fair nondeterminism can be proved in this setting.

3. FREE CONSTRUCTIONS

The three examples of section 2 have a common underlying structure. In each case, there is a fixed semiring of scalars -- $\overline{\mathbf{N}}$, $\overline{\mathbf{R}}_+$ or 2^U, and nondeterministic states are functions whose codomain is this semiring. In fact, these semirings are CPO-semirings, as defined in Table 1.

Table 1: CPO-semirings

A *CPO-semiring* is a CPO with two continuous binary operations, usually called addition (+) and multiplication (*). The addition forms a commutative monoid, with an identity called the *zero* (0). The multiplication is a monoid, with an identity called the *unit* (1). Also, these three axioms must be met for all elements x,y,z:

$$x*0 = 0 = 0*x$$

$$x*(y+z) = (x*y)+(x*z)$$

$$(x+y)*z = (x*z)+(y*z)$$

In writing expressions, multiplication has priority over addition, so that $x+y*z$ is $x+(y*z)$.

Three examples of CPO-semirings used in the last section are given below:

Semiring	*Addition*	*Multiplication*	*Order*
Natural numbers plus infinity	MINIMUM	Usual addition of numbers	$\leq$
Positive reals plus infinity	Usual addition	Usual multiplication	$\leq$
Powerset of the universes	Union	Intersection	Subset

*This assumes that atomic programs other than *nextchoice* do not effect the P component of D.

Table 2: CPO-modules

Let K be a fixed CPO-semiring. A CPO-module over K is a CPO M, together with two continuous operations:

Addition: a binary operation (written $+$) on M, forming a commutative monoid. The unit is called the *zero (0)*.

Scalar multiplication: an operation from $K \times M$ to M (the image of (r,x) being written rx). Scalar multiplication meets these axioms for all $x,y \in M$ and $r,s \in K$:

$$(r + s)x = (rx) + (sx)$$

$$r(x + y) + (rx) + (ry)$$

$$(r * s)x = r(sx)$$

$$0x = 0 \quad \text{and} \quad 1x = x$$

K is called the semiring of *scalars;* in expressions, scalar multiplication has precedence over addition, so that $rx + y = (rx) + y$. Note that the symbols $+$ and 0 are each used in two different ways: the addition and zero for K and also for M.

If M and N are two CPO-modules over K, then a strict continuous function $f{:}M \to N$ is called a *morphism* provided that it preserves the module operations. That is, for all $x,y \in M$ and $r \in K$: $(x + y)f = (x)f + (y)f$, and $(rx)f = r(xf)$.

For each of the examples in section 2, M is a CPO-module; the addition is the operation **or**, and the zero is the element called **impossible**.

In each of the examples, the set of nondeterministic states (M) is a module over the given semiring. The denotations of programs are morphisms on M. Table 2 gives the formal definitions of morphisms and semiring modules. The claim made by section 2 is that this algebraic structure can capture information about nondeterminism in many cases. The purpose of this section is to show how to add a module structure to a fixed CPO in a free manner. The exact problem is this: Let K be a CPO-semiring, and let C be a CPO. Then the *free CPO-module* generated by C (with respect to K) is a CPO-module $P(C)$ together with a strict continuous function $\eta{:}C \to P(C)$. The function η (called the *insertion*) must be universal in this way: if Q is any other CPO-module (over K), and $g{:}C \to Q$ is a strict continuous function, then there is a unique morphism $\hat{g}:P(C)\to Q$ such that $g = \eta\circ\hat{g}$, as in this triangle:

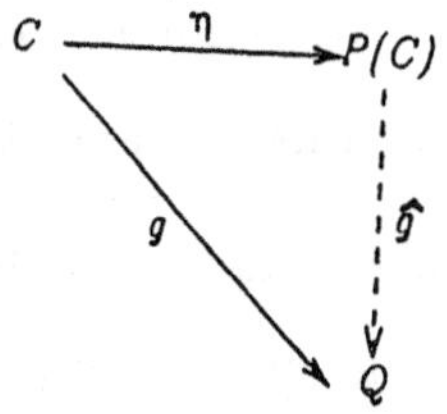

Using categorical techniques, it is not difficult to prove the existence of $P(C)$ and η meeting these requirements. But, the goal here is a convenient constructive description of $P(C)$, such as the definitions of the three modules in the examples. (In fact, it will turn out that these three modules are free CPO-modules generated by the flat CPO $D_\perp$.) In order to obtain such convenient constructions, some generality must be sacrificed -- both in restrictions on the semiring K and in restrictions on the generating CPO C. Three different cases of such restrictions are handled in the next two subsections. Each of the cases is a generalization of one of the examples in section 2. The CPO-notions in table 3 are used in these subsections.

Table 3: Some CPO notions

Flat CPOs: If D is any set, then the *flat* CPO over D (denoted $D_\perp$) consists of the elements $D\cup\{\perp\}$. The relation $x \sqsubseteq y$ holds iff $x = y$ or $x = \perp$.

Isolated elements: An element r in a CPO D is *isolated* provided that whenever $s_0 \sqsubseteq s_1 \sqsubseteq \cdots$ is a chain with $r \sqsubseteq \bigsqcup s_i$, then there exists an i such that $r \sqsubseteq s_i$.

Algebraic and ω-algebraic CPOs: A CPO is algebraic iff every element is the limit of a chain of isolated elements. If, in addition, there are but a countable number of isolated elements, then the CPO is ω-algebraic.

3.1 Generalization of the Smyth Powerdomain

Throughout this subsection, K is a CPO-semiring such that the least element is the unit (1) and the CPO-structure on K is algebraic. Note that the CPO $\overline{\mathbb{N}}$ in section 2.1 meets this requirement, with all elements (except ∞) being isolated.

The result of this section is a construction of the free CPO-module, $P(D_\perp)$, generated by a flat CPO $D_\perp$ (with respect to K). The elements of $P(D_\perp)$ are certain functions from $D_\perp$ to K. Specifically, we take those functions α such that:

(SMYTH 1): For all isolated s in K: $s \sqsubseteq (\perp)\alpha$ implies $\{x \in D \mid s \not\sqsubseteq (x)\alpha\}$ is finite.

(SMYTH 2): For all $x \in D$: $(x)\alpha \sqsubseteq (\perp)\alpha$.

(A moment's consideration verifies that these are the same two conditions that were imposed on the elements of M in section 2.1, although there they could be stated more simply because of the specific structure of $\overline{\mathbb{N}}$). Demonstrating that $P(D_\perp)$ is a CPO is easy:

Lemma: *$P(D_\perp)$ is a CPO under pointwise order and pointwise least upper-bound.*

Proof: Obviously the pointwise order is a partial order with a least element. We need only show that $P(D_\perp)$ is closed under least upper-bound of ω-chains. Toward this end, let

$\beta_0 \sqsubseteq \beta_1 \sqsubseteq \cdots$ be an ω-chain in $P(D_\perp)$, and let β be the pointwise least upper-bound of this chain. Condition SMYTH-2 holds for β, since it holds for each β_i. As for condition SMYTH-1, let s be an isolated element of K with $s \sqsubseteq (\perp)\beta = \bigsqcup(\perp)\beta_i$. Since s is isolated, there exists a j such that $s \sqsubseteq (\perp)\beta_j$. At this point, $\{x \in D \mid s \not\sqsubseteq (x)\beta_j\}$ is finite (since SMYTH-1 holds for β_j). Also, for any $x \in D$: $(x)\beta_j \sqsubseteq (x)\beta$, hence $s \not\sqsubseteq (x)\beta$ implies $s \not\sqsubseteq (x)\beta_j$ -- or equivalently:

$$\{x \in D \mid s \not\sqsubseteq (x)\beta\} \subseteq \{x \in D \mid s \not\sqsubseteq (x)\beta_j\}.$$

This implies that $\{x \in D \mid s \not\sqsubseteq (x)\beta\}$ is also finite, which is exactly what's needed for SMYTH-1. □

The module operations on $P(D_\perp)$ are also pointwise -- for example, $(x)(\alpha+\beta) = (x)\alpha+(x)\beta$. The axioms of a CPO-module are easily met -- provided that $P(D_\perp)$ is closed under pointwise addition and scalar multiplication. The proofs of these closures (omitted here) depend on the fact that $P(D_\perp)$ is in fact an algebraic CPO; the isolated elements are those α such that $(x)\alpha$ is an isolated element of K for every $x \in D_\perp$.

The insertion function $\eta:D_\perp \to P(D_\perp)$ takes each element $x \in D$ to the function $\eta_x:D_\perp \to K$ which is 1 at x and 0 elsewhere. (The insertion takes $\perp \in D_\perp$ to the least element of $P(D_\perp)$, as it must, in order to be strict. This element has a value 1 at every point.)

Here's the promised result of this section:

Theorem: *$P(D_\perp)$ is the free CPO-module generated by $D_\perp$ with insertion $\eta:D_\perp \to P(D_\perp)$.*

Proof outline: Let Q be another CPO-module (over K) and let $g:D_\perp \to Q$ be a strict function. We must demonstrate a unique morphism $\hat{g}:P(D_\perp) \to Q$ such that $g = \eta \circ \hat{g}$. To define $\hat{g}$, recall that the isolated elements of $P(D_\perp)$ are those α such that $(x)\alpha$ is an isolated element of K for every $x \in D_\perp$. For such an element, the set $\{x \in X | (x)\alpha \neq (\perp)\alpha\}$ must be finite (by conditions SMYTH-1 and SMYTH-2, plus the fact that $(\perp)\alpha$ is isolated). Thus, in this case we can define $(\alpha)\hat{g}$ to be

$$(\perp\alpha)\perp_Q \ + \sum_{(x)\alpha \neq (\perp)\alpha} (x\alpha)(xg),$$

where $\perp_Q$ is the least element of Q. For a non-isolated element β, choose any ω-chain of isolated elements $\beta_0 \sqsubseteq \beta_1 \sqsubseteq \cdots$ with $\beta = \bigsqcup \beta_i$, and define $(\beta)\hat{g} = \bigsqcup((\beta_i)\hat{g})$. Properties of algebraic CPOs show that this is a well-defined morphism, and $g = \eta \circ \hat{g}$. Finally, the fact that every isolated element of $P(D_\perp)$ can be formed by applying the module operations to elements of the form η_x guarantees that $\hat{g}$ is unique. □

It's already been pointed out that this case generalizes the example in section 2.1. It also generalizes the "Smyth powerdomain" of a flat CPO [10], which has been used for "must" semantics. Specifically, by choosing the semiring K to consist of only {0,1}, with $1 \sqsubseteq 0$, the free CPO-module generated by a CPO C is exactly the Smyth powerdomain over C.*

3.2 Generaralization of the Hoare Powerdomain

Throughout this section, K is a CPO-semiring and C is a CPO such that:

- Zero (0) is the least element of K, and
- Either C is ω-algebraic and $1+1=1$ in K, or $C = D_\perp$ is flat.

In the case that C is ω-algebraic, we let $D \subset C$ be the set of isolated elements of C -- excepting $\perp$ (which is exactly what D is when $C = D_\perp$ too). The CPOs $\overline{\mathbf{R}}_+$ and 2^U in section 2 both have zero as the least element, and 2^U has $1+1=1$.

The result of this section is a construction of the free CPO-module, $P(C)$, generated by C (with respect to K). The elements of $P(C)$ are certain functions from the subset D to K. Specifically, we take those functions α such that:

$$\text{(HOARE 1): } \{x \in D \mid (x)\alpha \neq 0\} \text{ is countable.}$$

$$\text{(HOARE 2): For all } x,y \in D\text{: } x \sqsubseteq y \text{ implies } (y)\alpha \sqsubseteq (x)\alpha.$$

(When $C = D_\perp$, then the second condition is trivial; when C is ω-algebraic, then the first condition is trivial. Nevertheless, there are enough commonalities between these two cases that it makes sense to present them together.)

The module operations, order and least upper-bounds on $P(C)$ are all pointwise. It is easy to verify that the two properties are conserved under these pointwise operations, so $P(C)$ is closed under the needed operations. The module axioms are also easily verified.

The insertion function $\eta: C \to P(C)$ needs to associate a function $\eta_x: D \to K$ with each $x \in C$. For any $y \in D$ and $x \in C$, the value of $(y)\eta_x$ is defined as:

$$(y)\eta_x = \text{ if } y \sqsubseteq x \text{ then } 1 \text{ else } 0.$$

The function η is strict (mapping $\perp$ to the always zero function) and it is continuous.

* This correspondence, as well as the next correspondence with the "Hoare powerdomain" was pointed out by Gordon Plotkin.

Here is the main result, showing that η is the universal insertion into $P(C)$:

Theorem: *$P(C)$ is the free CPO-module generated by C with insertion $\eta: C \to P(C)$.*

Proof outline: Let Q be another CPO-module (over K) and let $g: C \to Q$ be a strict continuous function. We must demonstrate a unique morphism $\hat{g}: P(C) \to Q$ such that $g = \eta \circ \hat{g}$. Let α be any element of $P(C)$ -- we define $(\alpha)\hat{g}$ as follows: First, recall that the set $\{x \in D \mid (x)\alpha \neq 0\}$ is countable. So, we can make a list (possibly countably infinite) of these elements: $x_1, x_2, \cdots$. This list defines a corresponding list $(x_1)g, (x_2)g, \cdots$ in Q. Moreover, this is a chain:

$$(x_1)g \sqsubseteq (x_1)g + (x_2)g \sqsubseteq (x_1)g + (x_2)g + (x_3)g \sqsubseteq \cdots$$

(The fact that this is a chain follows from zero being the least element of K which implies that the zero in Q is also its least element). The value of $(\alpha)\hat{g}$ is defined to be the least upper bound of this chain. Standard algebraic properties show that this is a well-defined morphism, and $g = \eta \circ \hat{g}$. Finally, the fact that every element of $P(C)$ can be formed by applying the module operations and least upper-bounds to elements of the form η_x guarantees that $\hat{g}$ is unique. □

This construction generalizes the examples in section 2.2 and 2.3. The CPO-semiring 2^U in section 2.3 also has $1+1=1$, so that example extends to any ω-algebraic CPO C. This section also generalizes the "Hoare powerdomain" of an ω-algebraic CPO [10], which has been used for "may" semantics. Specifically, by choosing the semiring K to consist of only {0,1}, with $0 \sqsubseteq 1$, the free CPO-module generated by a CPO C is exactly the Hoare powerdomain over C.

3.3 The General Case

The Smyth and Hoare generalizations are convenient set-theoretic characterizations of free CPO-modules, for specific sorts of generating CPOs and underlying semirings. Although it is easy to show that free CPO-modules always exist (for any generating CPO and underlying semiring), no simple set-theoretic characterization of these modules is known. However, a characterization in terms of the Plotkin powerdomain and a previously used tensor product construction is known. Specifically, the free CPO-module generated by a CPO C with respect to an underlying semiring K can be written as $K \otimes PLOTKIN(C)$, where PLOTKIN(C) is the usual Plotkin power-domain [10], and $\otimes$ is the tensor product used by Hennessy and Plotkin [3,12,13]. Complete details are given in a more theoretically inclined paper [6].

4. SUMMARY

The three introductory examples of this paper illustrate how knowledge about the workings of a nondeterministic program can be captured in a denotational semantics. The additional knowledge can be used in proofs of program correctness and termination. All three examples have a common underlying structure of a free CPO-module. The importance of the free CPO-modules is in two properties:

- Any morphism whose domain is a free CPO-module is completely determined by its image on the base elements. Conversely, any strict continuous function on the base elements gives rise to a unique morphism. This property was used frequently in the definitions of the denotations in section 2.
- The collection of all morphisms from a free CPO-module to itself is also a CPO. (In general this is not true for CPO-modules; but in the free case, it follows as a direct consequence of the previous property.) This property guarantees the existence of least solutions to continuous equations such as those used in section 2 for the denotations of **while**-constructs.

The constructions in section 3 give a convenient set-theoretic characterization of free CPO-modules for some special cases motivated by the examples.

ACKNOWLEDGEMENTS: The use of semiring modules to capture different facets of nondeterminism was developed jointly with David Benson at Washington State University. While we were visiting Edinburgh University, Gordon Plotkin suggested how the algebraic structure could be augmented by order-theoretic semantics.

References

(1) S. Abramsky. Experiments, powerdomains and fully abstract models for applicative multiprogramming, in: *Foundations of Computation Theory*, LNCS 158, (Springer-Verlag, 1983), 1-13.

(2) E.W. Dijkstra. *A Discipline of Programming*, (Prentice-Hall, 1976).

(3) M.C.B. Hennessy and G.D. Plotkin. Full abstraction for a simple parallel programming language, in: *Mathematical Foundations of Computer Science 79*, LNCS 74, (Springer-Verlag, 1979), 108-120.

(4) D. Kozen. Semantics of probabilistic programs, *Journal of Computer and System Sciences* 22 (1981), 328-350.

(5) D. Lehmann, A. Pnueli and J. Stavi. Impartiality, justice and fairness: the ethics of concurrent computation, in: *Automata, Languages and Programming, 8th Colloquium*, LNCS 115, (Springer-Verlag, 1981), 264-277.

(6) M.G. Main, Semiring Module Powerdomains, Technical Report Number CU-CS-286-84, Department of Computer Science, University of Colorado at Boulder, Boulder, CO 80309 (1984).

(7) R. de Nicola and M.C.B. Hennessy. Testing equivalences for processes, in: *Automata, Languages and Programming, 10th Colloquium*, LNCS 154, (Springer-Verlag, 1983), 548-560.

(8) D. Park. On the semantics of fair parallelism, in: *Abstract Software Specifications* LNCS 86 (Springer-Verlag, 1980), 504-526.

(9) G.D. Plotkin. A powerdomain construction, *SIAM J. Computing* 5 (1976), 452-487.

(10) G.D. Plotkin. *Computer Science Postgraduate Course Notes*, University of Edinburgh, 1980-81.

(11) A. Pnueli. On the extremely fair treatment of probabilistic algorithms, in: *Proceedings of the 15th Annual ACM Symposium on Theory of Computing*, (1983), 278-290.

(12) A. Poigne. Using least fixed points to characterize formal computations of nondeterminate equations, in: *Formalizations of Programming Concepts* (J. Diaz and I. Ramos, Eds.), LNCS 107, (Springer-Verlag, 1981), 447-459.

(13) A. Poigne. On effective computations of nondeterministic schemes, in: *5th International Symposium on Programming*, LNCS 137, (Springer-Verlag, 1982), 323-336.

(14) M. Smyth. Powerdomains, *Journal of Computer and System Sciences* 16 (1978), 23-36.

(15) G. Winskel. Synchronisation trees, in: *Automata, Languages and Programming, 10th Colloquium*, LNCS 154, (Springer-Verlag, 1983), 696-711.

ADDITIVE DOMAINS

Ernest G. Manes
Department of Mathematics and Statistics
University of Massachusetts
Amherst
Massachusetts 01003

Domains occurring naturally in program semantics usually carry an "additive" structure as well. This paper provides an axiomatic theory. Proofs will not be given here, for the most part. They are either routine or easily adapted from similar results in partially-additive semantics (1,2,10,11,12,15).

In a "control category" $\underline{\underline{C}}$, the set $\underline{\underline{C}}(X,Y)$ of morphisms from X to Y is an additive domain (though X, Y need not be). In such a category, all iterative flowcharts and all recursive specifications whose atomic pieces are interpreted in the category have denotational semantics as a morphism. It can be shown that Boolean tests and guard morphisms exist explicitly so that, for example, the Hoare iteration rule (8) and standard properties of the weakest precondition operator (4) may be established. This means that some aspects of "assertion semantics" are independent of choice of programming language and do not require a concept of program "state". This paper provides basic definitions and facts about the control category.

Extensions of the theory to data types, already begun in e.g. (9,3,11), will not be further developed here. The basic idea, however, is that a data type --be it presented by equational specification (5), as a functorial fixed point (9) or by some other means-- is at least bound to be a diagram in some category of "primitive" data types. Since any diagram category (13) over a control category is again a control category, aspects of control which should apply mutatis mutandis to all data types will do so.

1. Semantics of Recursion

$\underline{\underline{1}}$ f ::= K(f) = if P then (if P then f else a) else a

with f, a in the set $\underline{\underline{Pfn}}(X,Y)$ of partial functions from X to Y and P a test on X simplifies to

$\underline{\underline{2}}$ f ::= L(f) = if P then f else a

In (1), Michael Arbib and I introduced a calculus to formalize such simplifications. The idea is to explicitly represent the effect of each computation path. Thus if P

The research reported in this paper was supported in part by National Science Foundation grant MCS-8205168.

is represented as the guard function $p(x) = x$ with domain those x which pass the test P, and the complement p' is defined similarly, we have 1 in the form

3 $f ::= K(f) = (fp + ap')p + ap'$

where for any family (f_i) in Pfn(X,Y) their sum (written + in the finite case) is defined if and only if f_i, f_j have disjoint domains for distinct i, j and is then

4 $(\sum f_i)(x) = f_j(x)$ for the unique j (if any) with $f_j(x)$ defined

Disjointness is required for summability to respect the idea that for deterministic programs computation paths are unique. The desired simplification process is then based on the identities $p^2 = p$, $p'p = 0 = pp'$ and the laying bare of the three computation paths fp^2, $ap'p$ and ap':

$$K(f) = (fp + ap')p + ap' = fp^2 + ap'p + ap' = fp + ap' = L(f)$$

The notation of an additive domain is introduced to provide simultaneously an axiomatic form of the sum of 4 and an approximation ordering.

5 Definition An additive domain is a non-empty set X equipped with a "sum" operation $\sum$ defined on some, not necessarily all, countable families in X (we say (x_i) is summable if $\sum x_i \in X$ is defined) subject to axioms 6-9:

6 Unary sum axiom A one-element family is summable and its unique member is the sum.

7 Partition-associativity axiom If I, J are countable sets and if $(I_j : j \in I)$ partitions I (any number of I_j may be empty) then for any family $(x_i : i \in I)$,

$$\sum(\sum(x_i : i \in I_j) : j \in J) = \sum(x_i : i \in I)$$

in the strong sense that if one side is defined than so is the other and then they are equal.

Related partially-defined infinite sums occur elsewhere in mathematics. See (15) for a survey.

It follows from 6, 7 that any subfamily of a summable family is summable and that the empty sum provides an additive zero 0 which may be added or deleted countably often with impunity. Further, isomorphic families have the same sum so that a standard index set may be used to describe $\sum$ if desired.

8 Sum-ordering axiom The relation $x \leq y$ if $y = x + h$ for some h, necessarily

reflexive and transitive, is also antisymmetric.

Clearly 0 is the least element and we shall use 0 instead of the bottom symbol.

9 Limit axiom A countable family all of whose finite subfamilies are summable is itself summable. Further, if for some x each finite subsum is $\leq x$ then the sum of the entire family is $\leq x$.

10 Definition An additive map $f : (X, \sum) \longrightarrow (Y, \sum)$ (we will denote all sums with $\sum$ if no confusion results) of additive domains is a total function $f : X \to Y$ such that whenever (x_i) is summable then so is (fx_i) and $\sum fx_i = f(\sum x_i)$. This gives rise to the category Add-Dom of additive domains and additive maps.

11 Theorem If $(X, \sum)$ is an additive domain, $(X, \leq)$ is a domain. Each additive map is continuous and strict.
Proof idea: If $x_{n+1} = x_n + h_n$ is an ascending chain, $x_0 + \sum(h_n : n \geq 0)$ exists by the limit axiom and provides $\mathrm{Sup}(x_n)$. This construction makes the continuity of additive maps clear.

12 Observation Add-Dom has products and inverse limits. This is useful for simultaneous recursions and building new examples including reflexive domains (discussed below following 16). The usual product and coordinatewise sum work and yield the coordinatewise ordering for the domain structure.

13 Example The flat domain obtained as the disjoint union $Y + \{0\}$ is that induced by the additive structure for which $\sum y_i$ is defined if and only if the set $\{i : y_i \neq 0\}$ has at most one element. For any set X, the X-fold product of this domain produces the additive domain Pfn(X,Y) whose sum operator is that of 4 and whose domain structure is the usual extension ordering for partial functions.

14 Example Let $(D, \leq)$ be a poset with least element 0. A subset of D is consistent if each of its finite subsets has an upper bound. Assume that every consistent countable subset of D has a supremum. Then $(D, \leq)$ is a domain which arises from the additive domain whose sum operation is supremum for countable consistent families. The extension ordering on Pfn(X,Y) induces a sum in this way which is more often defined than that of 4 which serves to show that different additive domains can coincide as domains. The complete lattice Rel(X,Y) of relations from X to Y becomes an additive domain with this construction.

15 Theorem Any sum of continuous maps is continuous, that is, if f_i is a family of continuous maps between the additive domains X, Y such that $f_i x$ is summable in Y

for each x in X then $f = \sum f_i$ is continuous.

Proof idea: If x_n is an ascending chain with supremum x let $f_n(x) = f_n(x_0) + \sum_i h_{n,i}$. Then $f(x) = f(x_0) + \sum_i h_i = \mathrm{Sup}(fx_n)$ if $h_i = \sum_n h_{n,i}$.

16 Corollary If D is an additive domain then the continuous function space $[D \rightarrow D]$ is again an additive domain.

In fact, if D_0 is an additive domain then the adjoint pair $D_0 \rightleftarrows [D_0 \rightarrow D_0]$ (constant maps and evaluation at 0) are additive. It follows from this and 12 that the D_∞-construction of (14) produces a reflexive additive domain with an additive isomorphism $D_\infty \cong [D_\infty \rightarrow D_\infty]$.

We conjecture that, in general, domain fixed point equations of interest in computer science are additive in a natural way.

One of the pleasant aspects of the theory of domains is that a separately continuous map on a product of domains is necessarily jointly continuous. Additive maps do not behave so nicely so that the "power-series" needed as functionals for recursive specification require certain technical complications in the development of their theory. In the long run, both approaches yield least-fixed-point semantics and interact in useful ways.

17 Definition If $(X, \sum)$ is an additive domain, a power-series on $(X, \sum)$ is a family $(H_m : m = 0, 1, 2, \ldots)$ of m-additive maps $H_m : X^m \longrightarrow X$ (i.e. maps additive in each variable separately, 0-additive meaning constant) such that for all $k \geqslant 0$ the sum $\sum(H_m(-) : m = 0,\ldots,k)$ exists no matter how the arguments for the various H_m are filled in. The induced power-series map is then $H : X \longrightarrow X$ given by $H(x) = \sum(H_m(x,\ldots,x) : m = 0, 1, 2, \ldots)$.

We remark that different power-series may give rise to the same map.

The thesis is that for an additive domain such as Pfn(X,Y), for a least-fixed-point recursive specification $f ::= K(f)$, K is not only continuous but is a power-series map. (Building on 15, it is easy to see that every power-series map is continuous). Thus the "patterns-of-call" are the elements of X arising as follows:

18 H_0 is a pattern-of-call (the "exit")

if $m > 0$ and $x_1,\ldots,x_m$ are patterns-of-call so too is $H_m(x_1,\ldots,x_m)$.

Further examples and motivation for power-series maps are given in (2) where the definition is weaker than in 17 because we did not adequately allow for the problems that arise in using power series to give a formal semantics. Consider, for example, the problem of proving that if p then f else g is a power-series map if p, f, g are (p can be used as a test by choosing a "true" value). This is trivial in the continuous case since if-then-else is separately and hence jointly continous considered, say, $\underline{Pfn}(X,X) \times \underline{Pfn}(X,Y) \times \underline{Pfn}(X,Y) \longrightarrow \underline{Pfn}(X,Y)$. But this map is neither 3-additive nor additive. Rather, it is 2-additive when the second two factors are grouped together. Despite such subtleties, suitable proofs can be given. At this time we know of no serious example of a continuous recursive specification that is not expressible with power series. A theorem asserting that a "reasonable" continuous map is a power-series map would be useful!

19 **Theorem** If (H_m) is a power-series on an additive domain, the sum of all patterns-of-call in 18 exists and coincides with the least fixed point of H.

We mention the following proof rule as an exaple of interaction between order-theoretic and additive ideas:

20 **Partial correctness tree induction rule** If (H_m) is a power-series on an additive domain and if H has least fixed point x then to prove $x \leqslant y$ it is necessary and sufficient to prove that whenever $m \geqslant 0$, $x_1,\ldots,x_m \leqslant y$ then also $H_m(x_1,\ldots,x_m) \leqslant y$.

2. Control Categories

1 **Definition** A <u>control category</u> is a category $\underline{C}$ additionally structured (but see 8 below) so that for each two objects X, Y the set $\underline{C}(X,Y)$ of $\underline{C}$-morphisms from X to Y is an additive domain, subject to axioms 2, 3, 6, 7, 10.

2 **Axiom** For all $f : X \longrightarrow Y$, $g : Z \longrightarrow W$ the composition functions

$$\underline{C}(Y,Z) \xrightarrow{\;-\cdot f\;} \underline{C}(X,Z) \qquad\qquad \underline{C}(Y,Z) \xrightarrow{\;g\cdot -\;} \underline{C}(Y,W)$$

are additive.

3 **Axiom** Every countable family $(X_i : i \in I)$ of $\underline{C}$-objects has a coproduct $in_j : X_j \longrightarrow \coprod X_i$. Copowers are denoted $I\cdot X$.

It follows from 2, 3 that $\underline{C}$ has zero morphisms and that we may then define <u>quasi-projections</u> $\pi_k : \coprod X_i \longrightarrow X_k$ by

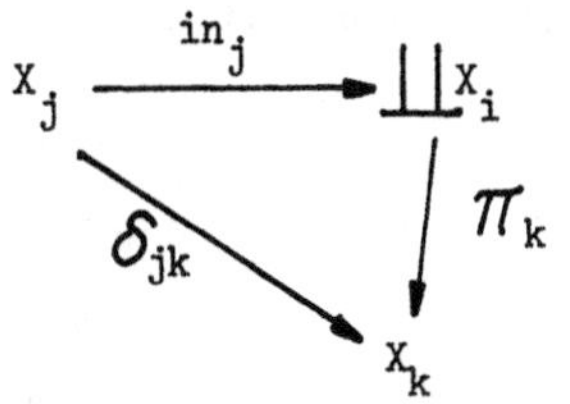

$$\delta_{jk} = \begin{cases} id_{X_k} & \text{if } j = k \\ 0 & \text{if } j \neq k \end{cases}$$

and say a countable family $f_i : X \longrightarrow Y$ is <u>compatible</u> if there exists f with

5

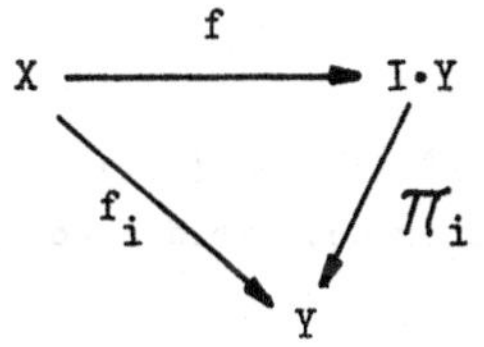

for all i

In the category $\underline{\underline{\underline{Pfn}}}$ of sets and partial functions, coproducts are disjoint unions and a family is compatible if and only if its domains are pairwise disjoint. In the category $\underline{\underline{\underline{Rel}}}$ of sets and relations, coproducts are disjoint unions once again but here all countable families are compatible. In general, we require

6 **Axiom** Every compatible family is summable.

The next axiom expresses the idea that since computation paths are disjoint (in the deterministic case) merged output lines can be separated.

7 **Axiom** If $f_i : X \longrightarrow Y$ is summable, so is $in_i\, f_i : X \longrightarrow I\cdot Y$.

(The axiom holds in nondeterministic cases because more families are summable, although the interpretation is not the same).

8 **Theorem** A family $f_i : X \longrightarrow Y$ is summable if and only if it is compatible. In that case the $f : X \longrightarrow I\cdot Y$ of 5 is unique and $\sum f_i = s f$ if $s : I\cdot Y \longrightarrow Y$ is defined by $s\, in_i = id_Y$. Thus a category cannot be structured as a control category in more than one way.

9 **Definition** Say that $f : X \longrightarrow Y$ is <u>total</u> if for all $t : T \longrightarrow X$, if $ft = 0$ then $t = 0$.

In $\underline{\underline{\underline{Pfn}}}$ these are the usual total functions. In $\underline{\underline{\underline{Rel}}}$ these are those relations $f : X \longrightarrow Y$ with $f(x)$ nonempty for all x.

The final axiom on a control category guarantees that every morphism has a kernel and a domain:

10 **Axiom** For each morphism $f : X \longrightarrow Y$ there exists a coproduct

$$K(f) \xrightarrow{\ i\ } X \xleftarrow{\ j\ } D(f)$$

such that $fi = 0$ and fj is total.

It is shown in (10) that $i : K(f) \longrightarrow X$ is the kernel of f whereas D(f) is the largest summand of X restricted to which f is total. It follows that such (K(f),i,D(f),j) is unique up to isomorphism and we call it the kernel-domain decomposition of f. D(f) is called the domain of f.

11 **Example** **Pfn** is a control category in the expected way, following 1.13. By the uniqueness result in 8, the more-often-defined sum of 1.14 does not yield a control category; indeed, axiom 7 fails here.

12 **Example** **Rel** is a control category. The additive domain structure is given in 1.14. For kernel-domain decompositions, K(f) is the subset on which f is empty and D(f) is the complement of K(f). Our approach to nondeterministic semantics, then, would be to choose a control category whose morphisms are nondeterministic in the desired way. For another possibility, consider

13 **Example** Let M be any monoid (a likely choice being a meet semilattice) of "reliability values". The unit e of M represents "totally reliable". Define a category $\mathbf{C}$ whose objects are all sets but with $\mathbf{C}(X,Y) = \mathbf{Pfn}(X, M \times Y)$. If $f : X \longrightarrow Y$ in $\mathbf{C}$ with $f(x) = (a,y)$ we say "$f(x) = y$ with reliability a". To define composition, given $g : Y \longrightarrow Z$ then $(gf)(x) = (ba,z)$ is z with reliability ba providing that $f(x) = (a,y)$ and $g(y) = (b,z)$. This is a category with identities $id_X(x) = (e,x)$. Coproducts are disjoint unions and $\mathbf{C}$ is a control category with the obvious kernel-domain decompositions.

14 **Example** **Add-Dom**(X,Y) is an additive domain (the analogue of 1.15 holds). **Add-Dom** satisfies axiom 2 and has coproducts (the disjoint union with 0's identified) but is not a control category as axiom 6 fails.

15 **Example** Using (1,Theorem 5.3) it can be shown that the category of partial morphisms of a Grothendieck topos (7) is a control category. Any diagram category over the category of sets and total functions is a Grothendieck topos.

16 **Theorem** (12) In a control category, the set

$$\mathrm{Guard}(X) = \Big\{p \in \mathbf{C}(X,X) : \text{there exists (necessarily unique) } p' \in \mathbf{C}(X,X) \text{ with } p+p' = id_X,\ pp' = 0 = p'p\Big\}$$

is order-isomorphic to the poset center of the unit interval $[0, id_X]$ of $\mathbf{C}(X,X)$

and so is a Boolean algebra. The Boolean operations are

$$p \wedge q = pq$$

$$p \vee q = pq + p'q + p'q = p + p'q$$

(sums which necessarily exist) and with p' as complement. Furthermore, each element of Guard(X) commutes with every element of the unit interval.

17 Lemma As in additive categories (6, 13) $A \xrightarrow{i} X \xleftarrow{j} B$ is a coproduct in a control category if and only if it extends to a <u>direct</u> <u>sum</u> <u>system</u>

18 $$A \underset{\eta}{\overset{i}{\rightleftarrows}} X \underset{\pi}{\overset{j}{\leftrightarrows}} B$$

with $\eta i = id_A$, $\pi j = id_B$, $\pi i = 0$, $\eta j = 0$ and $i\eta + j\pi$ defined and $= id_X$.

19 Theorem (10) The poset Summ(X) of direct summands of X (with the usual subobject ordering) is order-isomorphic to Guard(X) via (using the notation of 17) $A \mapsto i\eta$, with inverse $p \mapsto D(p)$. Hence Summ(X) is a Boolean algebra in any control category. Intersections in Summ(X) are constructed as pullbacks which necessarily exist as appropriate kernels.

For $f : X \longrightarrow Y$, the guard morphism corresponding to D(f) will be written as $\overleftarrow{f} \in$ Guard(X).

20 Observation In striking contrast to additive categories, in any control category we have

$$K(\sum f_i) = \bigcap K(f_i)$$

$$D(\sum f_i) = \bigcup D(f_i)$$

in the sense that if (f_i) is summable then the right-hand sides necessarily exist. This follows easily from partition-associativity which guarantees in any additive domain that

21 if $\sum g_i = 0$ then each $g_i = 0$

This is so because whenever $g + h = 0$, $g = g + (h+g) + (h+g) + \ldots = (g+h) + (g+h) + \ldots = 0$.

22 Theorem If $P_i \in$ Summ(X) with corresponding guards p_i then X is the coproduct of the P_i if and only if (p_i) is a <u>partition</u> in the sense that $p_i p_j = 0$ when $i \neq j$ and $\sum p_i$ exists and is id_X.

The category structure gives rise to an alternate natural partial order:

23 Definition For a control category $\underline{\underline{C}}$, the *extension ordering* on $\underline{\underline{C}}(X,Y)$ is

$$f \subseteq g \quad \text{if} \quad f = gp \text{ for some } p \in \mathrm{Guard}(X)$$

If $f \subseteq g$ then $f \leqslant g$ (as $g = g(p+p') = gp + gp' = f + h$ for $h = gp'$) from which it follows that $\subseteq$ is a partial order which coincides with $\leqslant$ on Guard(X). In general, $\subseteq$ is coarser than $\leqslant$ but the precise relationship between them is given by

24 Theorem In a control category, the following three statements are equivalent for $f, g : X \longrightarrow Y$.

(i) $f \subseteq g$

(ii) $g = g\overleftarrow{f}$

(iii) There exists h with $g = f + h$, $h\overleftarrow{f} = 0$.

3. Assertion Semantics

We work in a control category $\underline{\underline{C}}$.

1 Notation We often use capital letters P, Q, R, ... for summands and corresponding lower case letters p, q, r, ... for the corresponding guards of 2.19.

2 Definitions "Pascal control structures" exist in a control category. For $f : X \longrightarrow Y$, $g : Y \longrightarrow Z$, f;g is just $gf : X \longrightarrow Z$. For $f, g : X \longrightarrow Y$, $P \in \mathrm{Summ}(X)$,

$$\text{if P then f else g} \quad = \quad fp + gp'$$

and for $f : X \longrightarrow X$, $P \in \mathrm{Summ}(X)$

$$\text{while P do f} \quad = \quad \sum p'(fp)^n$$

This sum can be proved to exist from the axioms on a control category.

3 Definition For $f : X \longrightarrow Y$, $P \in \mathrm{Summ}(X)$, $Q \in \mathrm{Summ}(Y)$ define $\{P\}\ f\ \{Q\}$ to mean that there exists (necessarily unique) f_0 with

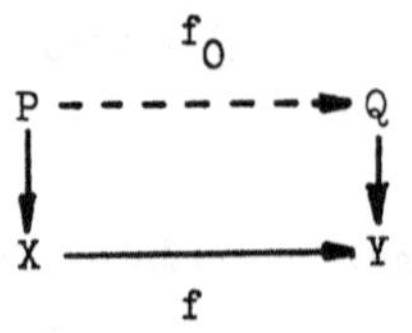

In $\underline{\underline{Pfn}}$, this asserts "if f(x) is defined with $x \in P$ then $f(x) \in Q$". In $\underline{\underline{Rel}}$, the assertion is "if $x \in P$ then $f(x) \subset Q$".

4 Lemma $\{P\}\ f\ \{Q\}$ if and only if $q'fp = 0$.

5 Conditional Rule

$$\frac{\{P \cap Q\}\ f\ \{R\}, \quad \{P \cap Q'\}\ g\ \{R\}}{\{Q\}\ \text{if } P \text{ then } f \text{ else } g\ \{R\}}$$

Proof: We have $r'(fp+gp')q = r'fpq + r'gp'q = 0 + 0 = 0$.

6 Iteration Rule

$$\frac{\{P \cap Q\}\ f\ \{Q\}}{\{Q\}\ \text{while } P \text{ do } f\ \{P' \cap Q\}}$$

7 Definition The weakest liberal precondition operator wlp is defined by

$$\mathrm{wlp}(f,Q) = K(q'f) \in \mathrm{Summ}(X)$$

for $f : X \to Y$, $Q \in \mathrm{Summ}(Y)$. It is easily shown that this arises as the pullback

$$\begin{array}{ccc} \mathrm{wlp}(f,Q) & \longrightarrow & Q \\ \downarrow & & \downarrow \\ X & \xrightarrow[f]{} & Y \end{array}$$

Thus, in Pfn, $\mathrm{wlp}(f,Q) = \{x \in X : f(x) \text{ is defined and is in } Q\}$. Here, and generally,

8 $P \leq \mathrm{wlp}(f,Q) \Leftrightarrow \{P\}\ f\ \{Q\}$

9 Properties of wlp For $f, f_i : X \to Y$, $f : Y \to Z$,

(i) $\mathrm{wlp}(f,Y) = X$.

(ii) $\mathrm{wlp}(f,-)$ preserves intersections (all finite intersections exist).

(iii) $\mathrm{wlp}(f,\mathrm{wlp}(g,R)) = \mathrm{wlp}(gf,R)$.

(iv) If $f : X \to Y$ is a summand of Y, $\mathrm{wlp}(f,Q) = X \cap Q$ in Summ(Y).

(v) $\mathrm{wlp}(\sum f_i, Q) = \bigcap \mathrm{wlp}(f_i,Q)$ if (f_i) is summable.

(vi) If $f : X \to X$ then if $f \leq id_X$, $\{Q\}\ f\ \{Q\}$ for every summand Q and if $f \in \mathrm{Guard}(X)$ the corresponding f_0 of 3 is in Guard (Q).

The properties in 9 can be used to establish

10 Theorem The function $(q_i) \mapsto \coprod q_i$ establishes a Boolean algebra isomorphism

$$\prod \mathrm{Guard}(X_i) \longrightarrow \mathrm{Guard}(\coprod X_i)$$

In turn, **10** is used to show

11 **Example** The network category $\mathbf{C}^{\#}$ of the control category $\mathbf{C}$ has as objects all tuples $(X_1,\ldots,X_m)$ $(m \geq 0)$ of $\mathbf{C}$-objects and, as morphisms,

$$\mathbf{C}^{\#}((X_1,\ldots,X_m),(Y_1,\ldots,Y_n)) = \mathbf{C}(X_1+\ldots+X_m,Y_1+\ldots+Y_n)$$

(such a morphism representing a "network" with m inputs and n outputs). Composition, identities and additive domain structure are at the level $\mathbf{C}$. It follows from **10** that if K, D give the kernel-domain decomposition of $f : X_1+\ldots+X_m \longrightarrow Y_1+\ldots+Y_n$ in $\mathbf{C}$ then $(K_1,\ldots,K_m)$, $(D_1,\ldots,D_m)$ provides the needed kernel-domain decomposition in $\mathbf{C}^{\#}$ for $K_i = X_i \bigcap K$, $D_i = X_i \bigcap D$. Thus $\mathbf{C}^{\#}$ is a control category.

A definition of the weakest precondition operator suggested by **8** is

12 **Definition** For $f : X \longrightarrow Y$, $Q \in \mathrm{Summ}(Y)$, $wp(f,Q) = D(f) \bigcap wlp(f,Q)$.

13 **Properties of wp** For $f : X \longrightarrow Y$,

(i) $wp(f,Y) = D(f)$

(ii) $wp(f,0) = 0$ (where the zero object 0 arises as K(f) for any total f and provides a least element of Summ(Z) for every Z).

(iii) wp(f,-) preserves intersections.

We conclude with

14 **Theorem** In a control category, the following are equivalent.

(i) For all $f : X \longrightarrow Y$, $g : Y \longrightarrow Z$, $R \in \mathrm{Summ}(Z)$, $wp(f,wp(g,R)) = wp(gf,R)$.

(ii) For all $f : X \longrightarrow Y$, D(f) has the following universal property:

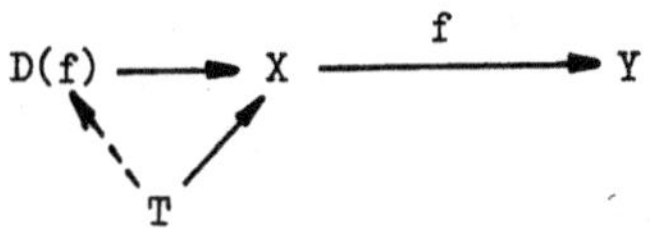

For all t with ft total there exists unique u as shown.

(iii) Total maps pull back binary coproducts.

(iv) The category is isomorphic to the partial morphism category of its subcategory of total morphisms.

This theorem shows how categories play a useful role in program semantics both in providing a precise framework to pose a question (in this case, the nature of the composition rule for weakest precondition) and in answering the question. The theorem clarifies why the composition rule holds in **Pfn** but not in **Rel**.

REFERENCES

1. M. A. Arbib and E. G. Manes, Partially-additive categories and the semantics of flow diagrams, J. Algebra 62, 1980, 203-227.

2. M. A. Arbib and E. G. Manes, The pattern-of-calls expansion is the canonical fixpoint for recursive definitions, J. Assoc. Comput. Mach. 29, 1982, 557-602.

3. M. A. Arbib and E. G. Manes, Parametrized data types do not need highly constrained parameters, Information and Control 52, 1982, 139-158.

4. E. W. Dijkstra, A Discipline of Programming, Prentice-Hall, 1976.

5. H. Ehrig and B. Mahr, Fundamentals of Algebraic Specification 1, Springer-Verlag, 1985.

6. P. Freyd, Abelian Categories, Harper and Row, 1964.

7. R. Goldblatt, Topoi: The Categorial Analysis of Logic, North-Holland, 1979.

8. C. A. R. Hoare, An axiomatic basis for computer programming, Comm. Assoc. Comput. Mach. 12, 1969, 576-580, 583.

9. D. J. Lehmann and M. B. Smyth, Algebraic specification of data types: a synthetic approach, Math. Systems Theory 14, 1981, 97-139.

10. E. G. Manes, Partially-additive proof rules, Theoretical Computer Science, to appear.

11. E. G. Manes and M. A. Arbib, Algebraic Approaches to Program Semantics, Springer-Verlag, to appear.

12. E. G. Manes and D. B. Benson, The inverse semigroup of a sum-ordered semiring, Semigroup Forum 31, 1985, 129-152.

13. B. Mitchell, Theory of Categories, Academic Press, 1965.

14. D. S. Scott, Continuous lattices, Lecture Notes in Mathematics 274, Springer-Verlag, 1972, 97-136.

15. M. E. Steenstrup, Sum-ordered partial semirings, Ph. D. dissertation, Computer and Information Science Department, University of Massachusetts, Amherst, MA 01003, USA, February 1985; available as COINS Technical Report #85-01.

A TOPOLOGICAL FRAMEWORK FOR CPOS LACKING BOTTOM ELEMENTS

Austin C. Melton
Computer Science Department
Kansas State University
Manhattan, KS 66506

David A. Schmidt
Computer Science Department
Iowa State University
Ames, IA 50011

The Scott topology has proved to be a useful tool in the analysis of traditional semantic domains (that is, consistently complete algebraic cpos with bottom elements). It has been used to justify the definition of partial order continuous functions because it is the case that a function is partial order continuous iff it is Scott topologically continuous. Further, the usual product, sum, and function domain constructions produce domains whose Scott topologies are the traditional product, disjoint union, and weak topologies, respectively.

The definition of a semantic domain is sometimes weakened to include cpos without bottom elements [Rey, Sch]. For example, the set of natural numbers $\mathbb{N}$ (discretely ordered: $n \sqsubseteq m$ iff $n = m$) is the preferred domain for defining the numbers manipulated by a hand held calculator, and the set $\mathbb{N} \rightarrow \mathbb{N}$ (also discretely ordered) is the natural domain for a unary calculator operation. However, when a bottom element is not present, the choice of the Scott topology as the canonical one is not as strongly justified. In some cases the Scott topology includes so many sets that being Scott open is not distinctive. For example, the Scott topology on $\mathbb{N} \rightarrow \mathbb{N}$ is finer than the weak topology; it is in fact discrete, i.e., every function by itself forms an open set. Thus, a primary insight gained by introducing topological concepts— that open sets are detectable properties and elements are bundles of properties— is of no value.

Roughly speaking, a topology on a cpo can be useful for programming language semantics if it is T_0 and if topological continuity implies partial order continuity. This class of topologies is called the *order consistent topologies* [Gie, pp. 108-109]. It is noteworthy that the Scott topology on a domain is the finest order consistent topology on that domain.

We are particularly interested in studying the order consistent topologies in terms of their topological subbases. Therefore we introduce an equivalent definition of order consistency in terms of subbases. The alternative definition is useful in the study of cpos lacking bottom. We define a calculus for building cpos without bottom elements and their topologies, and we prove that the product, sum, and function space cpos constructed using the calculus have topologies that are exactly the product, disjoint union, and weak topologies, respectively, on the domains. Further, when a domain is built from components that are consistently complete algebraic cpos with bottom elements, then the domain's topology coincides with the Scott topology, suggesting that the calculus is a suitable generalization of the traditional one used for domain building.

1. Fundamental definitions

1.1 Definition: *A complete partial order (cpo) is a partially ordered set such that every directed subset has a least upper bound. A pointed cpo is a cpo with a least element, $\bot$ (read "bottom").*

1.2 Definition: *For cpos A and B, a function $f{:}A\to B$ is partial order continuous iff for all directed $D\subseteq A$, $f(\bigsqcup D)=\bigsqcup_{d:D}f(d)$.*

1.3 Definition: *For cpo A, a set $U\subseteq A$ is Scott open iff*
i) for all $a{:}U$ and $b{:}A$, $a\sqsubseteq b$ implies $b{:}U$;
ii) for all directed $D\subseteq A$, $\bigsqcup D{:}U$ implies that there exists a $d{:}D$ such that $d{:}U$.

The Scott open sets of A form a topology on A. Further, it is well known that a function $f{:}A\to B$ is partial order continuous iff it is topologically continuous with respect to the Scott topologies on A and B [Gie]. This fact is significant, for it confirms our intuitions that our definition of partial order continuity is the proper one and that the collection $A\to B$ of partial order continuous maps from A to B is the "right" collection to be studied.

Another criterion for judging the suitability of the space $A\to B$ is the quality of the topology placed on $A\to B$. We desire that the function space possess the weakest topology such that function application be continuous for each $a{:}A$. (That is, the function space should have the *weak* or *Tychonoff topology* [Wil].) The Scott topology for $A\to B$ coincides with the weak topology when A is a consistently complete algebraic cpo and B is a consistently complete algebraic pointed cpo, but the coincidence does *not* hold when B lacks bottom.

As noted in the introduction, the Scott topology on $\mathbf{N}\to\mathbf{N}$, the collection of continuous functions from $\mathbf{N}$ to $\mathbf{N}$, is finer than the weak topology. In this case the Scott topology makes too fine of a distinction between the elements. One approach which would give a coarser topology on $\mathbf{N}\to\mathbf{N}$ is to treat $\mathbf{N}\to\mathbf{N}$ as a subspace of $\mathbf{N}_\bot\to\mathbf{N}_\bot$ ($\mathbf{N}_\bot$ is the pointed cpo built from $\mathbf{N}$ by adding a $\bot$ element) and use the subspace topology [Kam]. However, rather than pursue a domain building calculus which depends on subspaces, we refine the function space and its topology so that the weak topology naturally results.

2. The topological framework

We wish to restrict the number of open sets in the topology of a cpo. We want the topology to be T_0 and we want every open set to be Scott open. Further, any function that is topologically continuous must also be partial order continuous. As is shown below, a topology that satisifes these constraints is order consistent.

2.1 Definition: *For a cpo A, a topology* $\tau(A) \subseteq \mathbb{P}(A)$ *is an order consistent topology (OC-topology) iff*
i) for all $a{:}A$, $closure\{a\} = \downarrow a$
ii) for all directed sets $D \subseteq A$, $a = \bigsqcup D$ *implies* $a = lim\ D$
where $\downarrow a = \{ b{:}A \mid b \sqsubseteq a \}$, *and lim D is the topological limit of D.*

The topological limit of a directed set D, i.e., $lim\ D$, need not represent a unique element in A. In fact, it is straightforward to show that for each OC-topology on A if $a = \bigsqcup D$ for a directed set D, then $\downarrow a = lim\ D$. Thus, $\bigsqcup D = \bigsqcup lim\ D = a$.

A cpo A may have more than one OC-topology defined on it, that is, the OC-topologies defined on a cpo A form a collection of topologies. Each topology in this collection could be helpful in studying programming language semantics; in fact, we want this collection to contain all the topologies which would seem to be useful for programming language semantics. It is thus appropriate that, as the next proposition shows, the Scott topology is in this collection. However, as we hope to demonstrate in this paper, there exist situations in which the Scott topology may not be the best topology for programming language semantics.

2.2 Proposition: *For cpos A and B,*
i) each OC-topology on A is T_0;
ii) the coarsest OC-topology on A is generated by $\{ A - \downarrow a \mid a{:}A \}$;
iii) the finest OC-topology on A is the Scott topology;
iv) for OC-topologies $\tau(A)$ *and* $\tau(B)$, *if* $f{:}A \to B$ *is topologically continuous, then it is partial order continuous.*
Further, ii) is equivalent to: for every $a{:}A$, *the set* $A - \downarrow a$ *is in each OC-topology on A.*

Proof: (i) and (ii) follow from Definition 2.1(i). For (iii), we need to show that each open set in an OC-topology is Scott open and that the Scott topology is an OC-topology. Let U be an open set in an OC-topology on A. Let $a{:}U$ and $b{:}A$ with $a \sqsubseteq b$. If not $(b{:}U)$, then $closure\{b\} \cap U = \emptyset$. However, $a{:}closure\{b\} = \downarrow b$. Therefore, $b{:}U$. Thus, since Definition 2.1(ii) implies Definition 1.3(ii), then U is Scott open. It is well known that for each $a{:}A$, $\downarrow a$ is a closed set in the Scott topology. Since Scott open sets are "up-closed" (1.3(i)), $closure\{a\} = \downarrow a$. Since 1.3(ii) and the up-closedness of Scott open sets imply 2.1(ii) (the up-closedness gives the tail of 2.1(ii)), then the Scott topology on A is an OC-topology.

For (iv), let $\tau(A)$ and $\tau(B)$ be topologies on A and B, respectively, and let $f{:}A \to B$ be continuous with respect to $\tau(A)$ and $\tau(B)$. First we claim that f is monotone. Let $a \sqsubseteq b$ in A. $\downarrow f(b)$ is a closed set in B, and therefore, $f^{-1}(\downarrow f(b))$ is closed in A. Since $b{:}f^{-1}(\downarrow f(b))$, then $closure\{b\} \subseteq f^{-1}(\downarrow f(b))$; and thus, since $closure\{b\} = \downarrow b$, then $a{:}f^{-1}(\downarrow f(b))$. It follows that $f(a) : \downarrow f(b)$. Therefore, $f(a) \sqsubseteq f(b)$, and f is monotone. Now suppose that D is a directed subset of A and that $a = \bigsqcup D$. By Definition 2.1(ii), $a = lim\ D$. Since f is topologically continuous, $f(a) = lim\ f(D)$. Thus, $f(a) : \downarrow(\bigsqcup f(D))$; but is $f(a) = \bigsqcup f(D)$? Yes, $f(a) = \bigsqcup f(D)$ because f is monotone. Therefore, f is partial order continuous.

A characteristic of an OC-topology $\tau(A)$ on a cpo A is that for all $a,b{:}A$, $a \sqsubseteq b$ iff for all $U{:}\tau(A)$, $a{:}U$ implies $b{:}U$. Hence, the topological structure is consistent with the partial ordering. For this reason we can work with the open sets directly. We think of an open set as a "detectable property," and we want to represent the collection of detectable properties in a simple yet elegant manner. Thus, we work with pairs (A, T_A), where A is a set, and $\mathrm{T}_A \subseteq \mathbf{P}(A)$ is a collection of detectable properties and is a subbase for a topology on A.

When an $a{:}A$ belongs to some $P{:}\mathrm{T}_A$, we write Pa. Similarly, we write $\mathrm{P}a$ when $\mathrm{P} \subseteq \mathrm{T}_A$ and, for all $P{:}\mathrm{P}$, Pa. For $a_1,a_2{:}A$ we write $a_1 \sqsubseteq a_2$ iff, for all $P{:}\mathrm{T}$, Pa_1 implies Pa_2. (Clearly $\sqsubseteq$ is a preorder.) We use $s(a)$ to name the set $\{ P{:}\mathrm{T}_A \mid Pa \}$ for $a{:}A$, and let $\mathbf{S}_A$ denote the set $\{ s(a) \mid a{:}A \}$.

2.3 Proposition: *For the pair* (A, T_A), $(A, \sqsubseteq)$ *is a cpo and* T_A *is the subbase of an OC-topology iff*
i) for all $a, a'{:}A$, $s(a) = s(a')$ *implies* $a = a'$.
ii) for all directed $D \subseteq \mathbf{S}_A$, $\bigcup D {:} \mathbf{S}_A$.

Proof: Only if: For (i), the result follows from Proposition 2.2(i). For (ii), let $D \subseteq \mathbf{S}_A$ be directed. Each $d{:}D$ represents an element $d'{:}A$, and all the elements form a directed set D' in A. Further, $\bigcup D$ represents an element in A, and that element is clearly $\bigsqcup D'$.
If: Properties (i) and (ii) imply that $(A, \sqsubseteq)$ is a cpo; in particular, for a directed $D \subseteq A$, $\bigcup \{ s(d) \mid d{:}D \} = s(\bigsqcup D)$. To show Definition 2.1(i), for any closed set C such that $a{:}C$, we have $not(a{:}A-C)$; hence, $b \sqsubseteq a$ implies $not(b{:}A-C)$ as well; hence, $\downarrow a \subseteq C$. Thus, $\downarrow a \subseteq \bigcap \{ C \mid a{:}C$ *and* C *closed* $\}$. Now $\downarrow a$ is closed because its complement is open: for b such that $b \not\sqsubseteq a$, there exists some U such that $b{:}U$ and $not(a{:}U)$. Hence $a{:}A-U$ and $\downarrow a{:}A-U$ as well. Since $U \subseteq A - \downarrow a$, $A - \downarrow a = \bigcup \{ U \mid b{:}U, b \not\sqsubseteq a, \textit{and } not(a{:}U) \}$, which is open. Finally, 2.1(ii) follows from the earlier observation that $\bigcup \{ s(d) \mid d{:}D \} = s(\bigsqcup D)$. Note that the domain $(\mathbf{S}_A, \subseteq)$ is order-isomorphic to $(A, \sqsubseteq)$, which shows that the elements of A are "bundles of properties." Further, a limit point in A contains exactly the information contained in the directed sets that approximate it— least upper bound ($\bigsqcup$) corresponds to union ($\bigcup$).

We call (A, T_A) a *domain inducing pair* when T_A is the subbase of an OC-topology on $(A, \sqsubseteq)$. We denote by $top(\mathrm{T}_A)$ the topology generated by T_A.

The following fact is the statement in our terminology that a set U is open if about each point in U there is a basic open set that is contained in U.

2.4 Fact: *A set* $U \subseteq A$ *is in* $top(\mathrm{T}_A)$ *iff for every* $a{:}U$, *there exists a finite* $\mathrm{Q} \subseteq \mathrm{T}_A$ *such that*
i) $\mathrm{Q}a$;
ii) for all $a'{:}A$, $\mathrm{Q}a'$ *implies* $a'{:}U$.

The following fact is a pointwise definition of topological continuity with respect to OC-topologies. (Note that it deals with subbasic open sets in the codomain and basic open sets in the domain.)

2.5 Fact: *For top*(T_A) *and top*(T_B), *a function* $f{:}A \to B$ *is continuous iff for each* $a{:}A$, *when* $P{:}T_B$ *and* $P(fa)$ *holds, then there exists a finite* $Q \subseteq T_A$ *such that*
i) Qa;
ii) for all $a'{:}A$, Qa' *implies* $P(fa')$.

There exist functions $f{:}A \to B$ and domain inducing pairs (A, T_A) and (B, T_B) such that f is partial order continuous but not topologically continuous with respect to *top*(T_A) and *top*(T_B). We will produce an important example in the next section.

Proposition 2.3 shows that we obtain precisely the OC-topologies from the domain inducing pairs. However, we are still faced with the problem of deciding which OC-topology (or which domain induced topology) should be chosen for programming language semantics. One criterion for making this decision is presented in the next section.

3. A domain building calculus

To provide useful topologies for cpos lacking bottom elements, we define a domain calculus consisting of
i) primitive domains D (that is, sets with the discrete partial ordering);
ii) cartesian products $A \times B$;
iii) disjoint unions $A+B$;
iv) function spaces $A \to B$;
v) lifted spaces $A_\perp$ (that is, A augmented by a new, least element, $\perp$);

accompanied by the usual construction and destruction operations. The domain constructions are defined using domain inducing pairs in the following two propositions.

3.1 Proposition: *For a set* D, *the pair* $(D, \{\{d\} \mid d{:}D\})$ *induces a primitive domain.*

Proof: Trivial.

Once an OC-topology has been fixed for a set A, then we use the expression *OC-open set* to refer to a set in the fixed OC-topology. Likewise, once OC-topologies have been fixed for sets A and B, a function which is continuous with respect to the fixed OC-topologies on A and B is called an *OC-continuous function from A to B.*

3.2 Proposition: *For domain inducing pairs* (A, T_A) *and* (B, T_B),
i) the pair $(A \times B, \{\{(a,b) \mid Pa\} \mid P{:}T_A\} \cup \{\{(a,b) \mid Pb\} \mid P{:}T_B\})$, *where* $A \times B$ *is the cartesian product of A and B, induces a product domain where* $c \sqsubseteq_{A\times B} c'$ *iff* $c_1 \sqsubseteq_A c'_1$ *and* $c_2 \sqsubseteq_B c'_2$.
ii) the pair $(A+B, \{\{(\text{"left"}, a) \mid Pa\} \mid P{:}T_A\} \cup \{\{(\text{"right"}, b) \mid Pb\} \mid P{:}T_B\})$, *where* $A+B$ *is the disjoint union of A and B, induces a domain where* $c \sqsubseteq_{A+B} c'$ *iff* $c_1 = c'_1$ *and* $c_2 \sqsubseteq c'_2$.
iii) the pair $(A \to B, \{\{f \mid P(fa)\} \mid P{:}T_B, a{:}A\})$, *where* $A \to B$ *is the collection of continuous functions from* $(A, top(T_A))$ *to* $(B, top(T_B))$ *induces a domain where* $f \sqsubseteq_{A\to B} g$ *iff for all* $a{:}A$, $fa \sqsubseteq_B ga$.

iv) *the pair* $(A_\perp, \{\{(\text{"up"}, a) \mid Pa\} \mid P{:}\mathrm{T}_A\} \cup \{A_\perp\})$, *where* $A_\perp$ *is the set* $\{(\text{"up"}, a) \mid a{:}A\} \cup \{(\text{"down"}, \perp)\}$, *induces a domain where* $c \sqsubseteq_{A_\perp} c'$ *iff* $c_1 = \text{"down"}$ *or* $c_1 = c'_1$ *and* $c_2 \sqsubseteq_A c'_2$.

Proof: The proofs are tedious but entirely straightforward. We do the proof for case iii), the function space: The claim that $f \sqsubseteq_{A\to B} g$ iff $f \sqsubseteq_B ga$, for all $a{:}A$, follows directly from the definition of the property sets $\{f \mid P(fa)\}$, $P{:}\mathrm{T}_B$, $a{:}A$.

(2.3(i)): for $f, g{:}A\to B$, let $s(f) = s(g)$. Hence, for $a_0{:}A$, $s(fa_0) = s(ga_0)$, implying $fa_0 = ga_0$. By extensionality, $f = g$.

(2.3(ii)): let $D \subseteq \mathbf{S}_A$ be directed. Now D represents a directed set of functions $d^* \subseteq A \to B$. First, a straightforward proof shows that the function $h = (\lambda a. \bigsqcup\{da \mid d{:}D^*\})$ is OC-continuous. Further, h is the least upper bound of D^* in $A \to B$, implying that $\bigcup D \subseteq s(h)$. To show the other inclusion, let Ph hold; this is exactly $P_0(ha_0)$, for some $P_0{:}\mathrm{T}_B$, $a_0{:}A$. This implies that $P_0(\bigsqcup\{da_0 \mid d{:}D^*\})$ holds, which means that $P_0(d_0a_0)$ holds for some $d_0{:}D^*$. Hence $P(d_0)$ holds. Now we show that the domains built using the calculus have the desired topologies:

3.3 Proposition: *A primitive domain induced from* $(D, \{\{d\} \mid d{:}D\})$ *has the discrete topology.*

Proof: Trivial.

3.4 Proposition: *The domain induced from* $(A\times B, \mathrm{T}_{A\times B})$ *has the product topology, that is, the basic open sets are* $\{(a,b) \mid a{:}U, U \text{ open}\subseteq A, b{:}V, V \text{ open}\subseteq B\}$. *Further, the associated operations* $fst{:}A\times B \to A$ *and* $snd{:}A\times B\to B$ *are OC-continuous, as is* $\langle f,g\rangle{:}C\to A\times B$ *when* $f{:}C\to A$ *and* $g{:}C\to B$ *are.*

Proof: Follows from the definition of $\mathrm{T}_{A\times B}$ in a straightforward fashion.

3.5 Proposition: *The domain induced from* $(A+B, \mathrm{T}_{A+B})$ *has the disjoint union topology, that is, a basis for the open sets of* $A+B$ *are the open sets of* A *disjointly unioned with the open sets of* B. *Further, the associated operations* $inA{:}A\to A+B$ *and* $inB{:}B\to A+B$ *are OC-continuous, as is* $[f,g]{:}A+B\to C$ *when* $f{:}A\to C$ *and* $g{:}B\to C$ *are.*

Proof: Follows from the definition of T_{A+B} in a straightforward fashion.

3.6 Theorem: *The domain induced from* $(A\to B, \mathrm{T}_{A\to B})$ *has the weak topology, that is, the topology whose subbasis is* $\{\{f \mid fa{:}U\} \mid a{:}A, U \text{ open}\subseteq B\}$. *Further, the associated operation* $apply{:}(A\to B)\times A\to B$ *is OC-continuous, as is* $curry\, f{:}A\to (B\to C)$ *when* $f{:}(A\times B)\to C$ *is.*

Proof: It is easy to show that function application is OC-continuous, so the weak topology is contained in the OC-topology. To show that each OC-open set is open in the weak topology, we show that every OC-open set is a union of weak basic open ones. For an OC-open set $V \subseteq A\to B$, $V = \bigcup_{f:V} (\bigcap_{P:\mathrm{Q}_f} P)$ where for each f, Q_f corresponds to the Q in Fact 2.4. (That is, V is a union of basic OC-open sets.) By the definition of $\mathrm{T}_{A\to B}$, each P must have the form $\{f_0 \mid P_0(f_0a)\}$ for $P_0{:}\mathrm{T}_B$, $a_0{:}A$. Since P_0 is subbasic open in B, $P = \{f \mid fa_0{:}P_0\}$, and $P_0 \text{ open}\subseteq B$. Thus, the subbasic open set P is exactly a subbasic open set in the weak topology.

Next, considering the associated operations with the domain, it is easy to show that *apply* is OC-continuous. For *curry f*, assume that $f:(A \times B) \rightarrow C$ is OC-continuous. If $P(curry\, f(a))$ holds, then P must have structure $\{ f \mid P'(fa_0) \}$, implying $P'((curry\, f)\, a_0\, b)$ holds. Thus $P'(f(a,b))$, leading to the result.

3.7 Proposition: *The domain induced from* $(A_\perp, T_{A_\perp})$ *has A's topology plus the set* $A_\perp$. *The associated operation up:*$A \rightarrow A_\perp$ *is OC-continuous, as is strict* $f:A_\perp \rightarrow B_\perp$ *when* $f:A \rightarrow B_\perp$ *is.*

Proof: Trivial.

If domain A with associated topology τ can be obtained by using our domain building calculus, then τ is called a DC-topology. Elements of a DC-topology are called DC-open sets, and functions which are continuous with respect to DC-topologies are called DC-continuous functions. Clearly, each DC-topology is also an OC-topology. An important corollary of the above series of results is that the lambda-calculus function notation used for defining operations on domain elements always describes DC-continuous functions [Plo, Sch]. Thus, a useful model theory for denotational semantics has been derived.

Aside from these technical results, the domain constructions are useful for building the proper versions of total function spaces. Many unnatural total functions are excluded because they are not DC-continuous. For example, let the cpo $(\mathbb{N}, \sqsubseteq)$ be induced from the pair $(\mathbb{N}, \{\{n\} \mid n:\mathbb{N}\})$; then $(\mathbb{N} \rightarrow \mathbb{N}, \sqsubseteq)$ is the cpo induced from the pair $(\mathbb{N} \rightarrow \mathbb{N}, \{\{f \mid f(m) = n\} \mid m,n:\mathbb{N}\})$. Both cpos have the discrete partial ordering. The function $w: (\mathbb{N} \rightarrow \mathbb{N}) \rightarrow \mathbb{N}$, defined as

$$w(f) = \begin{cases} 1 \text{ if } f \text{ is the identity function on } \mathbb{N} \\ 0 \text{ otherwise} \end{cases}$$

is partially order continous but is not DC-continuous. Consider the property $P_0:T_{\mathbb{N}}$, $P_0 = \{1\}$, and the argument $id:\mathbb{N} \rightarrow \mathbb{N}$, the identity function on $\mathbb{N}$. For w to be DC-continuous, it must satisfy Fact 2.5, that is, there must exist a finite $Q_0 \subseteq T_{\mathbb{N}\mathbb{N}}$ such that for all $g: \mathbb{N} \rightarrow \mathbb{N}$, $Q_0(g)$ implies $P_0(w(g))$. But id is the only element in $\mathbb{N} \rightarrow \mathbb{N}$ whose image under w satisfies P_0, implying that Q_0 must represent the set $\{id\}$. Since this set is not open in the topology on $\mathbb{N} \rightarrow \mathbb{N}$, Q_0 does not exist. In fact, the cardinality of the domain of DC-continuous functions in $(\mathbb{N} \rightarrow \mathbb{N}) \rightarrow \mathbb{N}$ is the continuum. (The proof is too messy to be shown here.)

The DC-open sets restrict the kinds of total functions that appear in the higher order function spaces in the same way that the partial functions restrict them in pointed cpos. The open sets carry the structure of the domain, which is critical for flat domains such as $\mathbb{N} \rightarrow \mathbb{N}$, $(\mathbb{N} \rightarrow \mathbb{N}) \rightarrow \mathbb{N}$, etc., which lack structure in the elements themselves.

We can also show that our calculus of domain constructions produces the Scott topology whenever a "traditional" pointed cpo is built. We do this by showing that a topological base of such a domain is exactly the set of principal filters of the compact elements in the domain.

3.8 Definition: *An element a:A is compact iff for all directed* $D \subseteq A$, $a \sqsubseteq \bigsqcup D$ *implies there exists some d:D such that* $a \sqsubseteq d$.

3.9 Proposition: *If $e{:}D$ is compact, then the set $\uparrow e = \{d{:}D \mid e \sqsubseteq d\}$ is characterized by a finite set of properties Q_e when the cpo D is built using the following calculus:*
(i) the primitive domain construction, as defined in Proposition 3.1;
(ii) product $A \times B$, as defined in Proposition 3.2(i);
(iii) sum $A+B$, as defined in 3.2(ii);
(iv) lifted space $A_\perp$, as defined in 3.2(iv);
(v) function space $A \to B$, with B being a pointed cpo, as defined in 3.2(iii).

Proof: (i) Choose $Q_e = \{\{d\}\}$.
(ii) For compact $(a,b){:}A \times B$, use $Q_{(a,b)} = \{\{(a',b') \mid P(a')\} \mid P{:}Q_a\} \cup \{\{(a',b') \mid P(b')\} \mid P{:}Q_b\}$;
(iii) For compact $(\text{"left"},a)$, use $Q_{(left,a)} = \{\{(\text{"left"},a') \mid P(a')\} \mid P{:}Q_a\}$; $Q_{(right,b)}$ is defined similarly.
(iv) For $\perp$, choose $\{\}$; for compact $(\text{"up"},a)$, choose $\{\{(\text{"up"},a') \mid Pa'\} \mid P{:}Q_a\}$;
(v) First consider the compact step function

$$step_{ab} = \lambda x. \begin{cases} b & \text{if } a \sqsubseteq x \\ \perp & \text{otherwise} \end{cases}$$

for compact elements $a{:}A$ and $b{:}B$. Now, $step_{ab}$ is DC-continuous by Fact 2.5, for if $P(\perp)$ holds, for some $P{:}T_B$, use $\{\}$ for $Q \subseteq T_A$; if Pb holds, use $Q = Q_a$. Define $Q_{step_{ab}} = \{\{f \mid P(fa)\} \mid P{:}Q_b\}$. (Note that $y{:}\uparrow b$ iff $Q_b y$.) We claim that for all f, $f{:}Q_{step_{ab}}$ iff $f{:}\uparrow step_{ab}$. The "if" part is easy. For the "only if" part, assume that $P{:}Q_b$, $P(fa)$ holds for all $P{:}Q_b$. Then $fa{:}\uparrow b$, implying that $b \sqsubseteq fa$. So is $step_{ab} \sqsubseteq f$? Consider these cases: first, for y such that $a \sqsubseteq y$, $step_{ab}y = b \sqsubseteq fa \sqsubseteq fy$; second, for y such that $a \not\sqsubseteq y$, $step_{ab}y = \perp \sqsubseteq fy$. So the claim holds. The proof of (v) follows since all compact members of $A \to B$ are finite least upper bounds of the step functions. A "traditional" semantic domain is a consistently complete algebraic cpo:

3.10 Definition: *A cpo is algebraic iff for all $a{:}A$, $a = \bigsqcup\{e \mid e$ is compact and $e \sqsubseteq a\}$.*

3.11 Definition: *A cpo A is consistently complete iff for all $a,b{:}A$, if an upper bound of a and b exists in A, so does $a \sqcup b$.*

3.12 Proposition: *A cpo built using the calculus in Proposition 3.9 is consistently complete algebraic, and the set of principal filters of its compact elements is a topological base.*

Proof: Since the partial orders on the domains are the usual ones, the proofs of algebraicity and consistent completeness are the usual ones [Plo]. Let U be open and $a{:}U$. By algebraicity, there exists a compact $e_a \sqsubseteq a$ in U, implying $\uparrow e_a \subseteq U$; by Proposition 3.9, $\uparrow e_a$ is basic open, implying $U = \bigcup_{a:U} \uparrow e_a$.

3.13 Corollary: *The DC-topologies associated with the domains in Proposition 3.9 are the Scott topologies.*

Proof: The Scott topology of a consistently complete algebraic cpo has as its base the set of principal filters of its compact elements [Gie].

4. Conclusion

The characterization of a domain and its OC-topologies in Proposition 2.3 bears resemblance to the neighborhood systems and information systems defined by Scott [Sco1, Sco2]. In the latter two methods, a semantic domain is specified by listing the "properties" relevant to it and the ways in which the properties can be consistently combined. The elements of a domain are generated as "closures" of consistent property sets. The generated domain is a consistently complete algebraic pointed cpo, and the consistent property sets name the (sub)basic open sets of the Scott topology for the domain. Constructions also exist for building property sets for product, sum, and function domains. These constructions parallel the ones in Proposition 3.2, for their definitions build the topological bases for the product, disjoint union, and weak topologies.

But the OC-axiomatization does not require us to induce the elements of a cpo from a set of properties. This is for two reasons:

(i) The method is intended to be a framework for judging the suitability of topologies for an existing domain, regardless of how the domain is built.

(ii) The neighborhood and information system constructions work nicely for generating algebraic pointed cpos, but do not easily generalize for building cpos lacking bottom. In any case, the existing notion of algebraicity for cpos without bottom has questionable value. All of $\mathbb{N}$, $\mathbb{N}\to\mathbb{N}$, $(\mathbb{N}\to\mathbb{N})\to\mathbb{N}$, $((\mathbb{N}\to\mathbb{N})\to\mathbb{N})\to\mathbb{N}$, $\cdots$ are algebraic because all of their elements are compact. No longer does the term "compact" correspond with "contains a finite amount of information." A suitable notion of algebraicity in a category for cpos like $\mathbb{N}$ and its higher order descendants is a topic for future study.

Acknowledgement: Michael Mislove pointed out that the conditions in Proposition 2.3 described the order consistent topologies.

5. References

[Gie] Gierz, G., et. al. *A Compendium of Continuous Lattices*, Springer-Verlag, Berlin, 1980.

[Kam] Kamimura, T., and Tang, A. *Total objects of domains*, *Theoretical Computer Science* 1984.

[Plo] Plotkin, G. *The category of complete partial orders*, Postgraduate lecture notes, Computer Science Dept., Edinburgh University, Scotland, 1982.

[Rey] Reynolds, J. *Semantics of the domain of flow diagrams*, *Journal of the ACM* 24-3(1977) 484-503.

[Sch] Schmidt, D. *Denotational Semantics*, Allyn and Bacon, Boston, in press.

[Sco1] Scott, D. *Lectures on a mathematical theory of computation*, Report PRG-19, Programming Research Group, Oxford University, 1980.

[Sco2] Scott, D. *Domains for denotational semantics*, Proc. Ninth ICALP, Lecture Notes in Computer Science 140, Springer-Verlag, 1982, pp.577-613.

[Wil] Willard, S. *General Topology*, Addison-Wesley, Boston, 1968.

DETECTING LOCAL FINITE BREADTH IN CONTINUOUS LATTICES AND SEMILATTICES

Michael Mislove
Department of Mathematics
Tulane University
New Orleans, LA 70118

Introduction.

In this paper we survey several notions concerning the breadth of a (semi)lattice and we describe some of the results which have been obtained utilizing these notions. We then raise some questions about the possible applications of these and other results to the structure of domains which are used to model the denotational semantics of programming languages.

Lattices and semilattices of finite breadth. We begin with the classical definition of finite breadth in a semilattice or lattice.

Definition. Let L be an inf semilattice and let n be a positive integer. We say L has breadth $\leq n$ if each finite subset $F \subset L$ has a subset $A \subset F$ with $\inf A = \inf F$ and $|A| \leq n$. We say L has breadth n if L has breadth $\leq n$, but L does not have breadth $\leq n-1$. □

For example, the unit interval $I = [0,1]$ with the usual min operation has breadth 1, the square I^2 with the product order has breadth 2, and, in general, the lattice I^n has breadth n. If we let $2 = \{0,1\}$ in the usual order, then 2^n also has breadth n for each n. On the other hand, if $\mathbb{N}$ denotes the natural numbers, then $2^{\mathbb{N}}$ has infinite breadth. But we do not have to "jump" to $2^{\mathbb{N}}$ to find a lattice with infinite breadth. Indeed, consider the lattice obtained by "stacking" the lattices 2^n on top of each other; more precisely, let L be the lattice obtained by starting with the lattice 2 and then adjoining the lattice 2^2 to 2, identifying the identity of 2 with the zero of 2^2, and then adjoining 2^3 so that the identity of 2^2 is identified with the zero of 2^3, and so on. Then add an identity to the resulting union as the top point. A diagram of this lattice is given below.

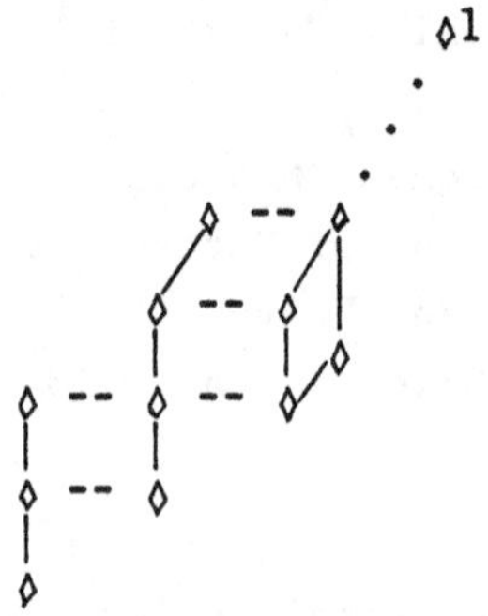

Figure 1: The lattice $L = 2 \cup 2^2 \cup \ldots \cup 2^n \cup \ldots \cup \{1\}$

It should be clear that the lattice L of Figure 1 does not contain a copy of $2^{\mathbb{N}}$, but, on the other hand, L does not have finite breadth. We are interested in how to detect lattices such as L which do not have finite breadth, but which nonetheless contain no copy of $2^{\mathbb{N}}$. We define a <u>finite</u> subset A of the lattice L to be <u>meet irredundant</u> if $\inf A < \inf X$ for every proper subset $X \subset A$, and we say the infinite subset A is meet irredundant if each of its finite subsets is meet irredundant. As we shall see, the following notion is central to characterizing lattices of infinite breadth which do not contain a copy of $2^{\mathbb{N}}$.

<u>Definition</u> [GLS]. If L is a lattice and $x \in L$, define the $\wedge$-<u>breadth of</u> L at x by

$$\wedge\text{-br}(x) = \sup\{|A| \mid A \text{ is meet irredundant and } \inf A = x\}.$$

We say that L has <u>locally finite</u> ($\wedge$-)<u>breadth</u> if $\wedge\text{-br}(x)$ is finite for all $x \in L$. □

If L has finite breadth, then the breadth of L is the largest value of $\wedge\text{-br}(x)$ for $x \in L$. Note that the lattice L of Figure 1 has locally finite breadth, but L has infinite breadth.

We now describe several results which give equivalent conditions for a lattice or semilattice to contain a copy of $2^{\mathbb{N}}$. We begin with the most algebraic of these results, one which applies to completely distributive algebraic lattices.

Let L be a complete lattice. The subset $D \subset L$ is <u>directed</u> if for all $d, d' \in D$, there is some $d'' \in D$ with $d, d' \leq d''$. The element $k \in L$ is <u>compact</u> if, whenever $k \leq \sup D$ for a directed subset D of L, then there is some $d \in D$ with $k \leq d$. We denote by $K(L)$ the set of compact elements of L. A lattice L is <u>algebraic</u> if $x = \sup(\downarrow x \cap K(L))$ for all $x \in L$. We say that L is <u>completely distributive</u> if L satisfies the most general of distributivity laws:

$$\inf_{i \in I} \sup_{j \in J} a_{i,j} = \sup_{f \in F} \inf_{j \in J} a_{j,f(j)},$$

where $F = I^J$ is the family of all functions from J to I. Completely distributive algebraic lattices are easy to find. Namely, let P be any poset and consider the lattice $I(P)$ of all lower sets of P, i.e.,

$$I(P) = \{A \subset P \mid A = \downarrow A\}.$$

Then $I(P)$ is a complete ring of sets, which means $I(P)$ is closed in 2^P under all intersections and all unions (we allow $A = \emptyset$ as a lower set). The finitely generated lower sets are easily seen to be the compact elements in $I(P)$, so $I(P)$ is a completely distributive algebraic lattice in the usual containment order. Conversely, any completely distributive algebraic lattice L is $I(P)$ for some set P (see [M1] for details).

Notice that the elements $\downarrow x$, $x \in P$ play a special role in $I(P)$. Each lower set is the union of such elements, and these elements are complete $\cup$-prime; i.e., if $\downarrow x \subset \cup\underline{A}$ for some subset $\underline{A} \subset I(P)$, then there is some $A \in \underline{A}$ with $x \in A$, and so $\downarrow x \subset A$ for this lower set A. The elements $\downarrow x$, $x \in P$, hold the key to whether $I(P)$ has a copy of $2^{\mathbb{N}}$ or not, as the following shows:

<u>Theorem 1</u> [LMP]. Let P be a poset, and let $I(P)$ denote the lattice of lower sets of P. The following are then equivalent:

1) $I(P)$ contains copy of the lattice $2^{\mathbb{N}}$.
2) P has an infinite antichain. □

By an infinite antichain, we mean an infinite subset $X \subset P$ such that $x, y \in X$ implies $x \nleq y$ and $y \nleq x$. That $I(P)$ contains a copy of $2^{\mathbb{N}}$ means there is a monomorphism $f : 2^{\mathbb{N}} \to L$ preserving all infima and all suprema. Regarding $2^{\mathbb{N}}$ as the lattice of subsets of $\mathbb{N}$, this means f must preserve all unions and all intersections. This is not as restrictive as it initially appears: it happens that $I(P)$ contains a copy of $2^{\mathbb{N}}$ in this sense if and only if there is a monomorphism $f : 2^{\mathbb{N}} \to L$ preserving all infima (or, dually, all suprema). Theorem 1 was used to establish results about the structure of the ordered set P in terms of the lattice $I(P)$ [LMP]. The idea is to determine conditions on the poset P which have implications for the structure of $I(P)$, and vice versa.

Theorem 1 says that $I(P)$ has no copy of $2^{\mathbb{N}}$ precisely when P has no infinite antichains. We translate this condition into one concerning $I(P)$ alone. First, recall that an <u>order ideal</u> of the poset P is a directed lower set of P. The family $Id(P)$ denotes the set of order ideals of P. Note that $\downarrow x$ is an order ideal of P for each $x \in P$, and so each lower set of P is the union of those order ideals which it contains. Order ideals can be characterized intrinsically as the $\cup$-primes of $I(P)$. That is, if $I \in Id(P)$ and $A_1, \ldots, A_n \in I(P)$ with $I \subset A_1 \cup \ldots \cup A_n$, then $I \subset A_i$ for some index i: indeed, if $I \not\subset A_i$ for each i, then we could find elements $x_i \in I \setminus A_i$ for each i. Since I is directed there is some $x \in I$ with $x_i \leq x$ for each i, and so $x \notin A_i$ for all i, contradicting $I \subset \cup A_i$. The following result characterizes when $I(P)$ contains no copy of $2^{\mathbb{N}}$:

<u>Theorem 2</u> [LMP]. For the lattice $I(P)$, the following are equivalent:

1) $I(P)$ contains no copy of $2^{\mathbb{N}}$.
2) Each lower set $A \in I(P)$ is the union of finitely many order ideals of P. □

Actually, Theorem 2 generalizes to a much larger class of lattices than those of the form $I(P)$ for some poset P. The class of distributive continuous lattices can be described as follows. If L is a complete lattice and $x, y \in L$, then we write $x \ll y$ (and say x is <u>way below</u> y) if for every directed set $D \subset L$, $y \leq \sup D$ implies $x \leq d$ for some $d \in D$. The lattice L is a <u>continuous lattice</u> if $y = \sup\{x \in L \mid x \ll y\}$ for every $y \in L$. Since $k \ll y$ whenever $k \leq y$ if k is a compact element of L, continuous lattices generalize the notion of algebraic lattices.

Recall that a lattice L is <u>distributive</u> if it satisfies the laws

$$x\wedge(y\vee z) = (x\wedge y)\vee(x\wedge z) \quad \text{and} \quad x\vee(y\wedge z) = (x\vee y)\wedge(x\vee z)$$

for all x, y, and $z \in L$. The element $p \in L$ is <u>prime</u> if $p \neq 1$ and $a\wedge b \leq p$ implies $a \leq p$ or $b \leq p$ for all $a, b \in L$. We denote by $\operatorname{Spec} L$ the set of primes of L. Finally, the lattice L is <u>primally generated</u> if each element of L is the infimum of those primes above it; i.e., $x = \inf\{p \in \operatorname{Spec} L \mid x \leq p\}$ for all $x \in L$. The spectral theory for continuous lattices says that each distributive continuous lattice L is primally generated, and, in fact, that the lattice L is isomorphic to the lattice of open subsets of the space $\operatorname{Spec} L$ endowed with the hull-kernel topology (cf. [C], Chapter V for details). It is easy to detect when such a lattice L has breadth n or locally finite breadth.

<u>Theorem 3</u> [M1]. Let L be a distributive continuous lattice. Then,

1) L has breadth $\leq n$ if and only if each element $x \in L$ can be written as the infimum of at most n primes from L.
2) L has locally finite breadth if and only if each element is the infimum of finitely many primes. □

For example, each element of $I = [0,1]$ is prime, and I has breadth 1; similarly, the primes of I^2 are those elements with at least one coordinate 1, and each element is the infimum of at most two of these. In general, the primes of I^n are those elements with all coordinates 1 except one, and each element is the infimum of at most n of these elements. Notice that the lattice L from Figure 1 has the property that each element is the infimum of finitely many primes from L: indeed, the primes of L are those elements which are prime in one of the copies of 2^n. This example illustrates the following result, which is the promised generalization of Theorem 2.

<u>Theorem 4</u> [M2]. For a distributive continuous lattice L, the following are equivalent:

1) L has no copy of $2^{\mathbb{N}}$.
2) Each element of L is the infimum of finitely many primes of L.
3) L has locally finite breadth. □

In this context containing a copy of $2^{\mathbb{N}}$ means that there is a continuous lattice copy of $2^{\mathbb{N}}$ in L; i.e., there is a monomorphism $f : 2^{\mathbb{N}} \to L$ preserving all infs and all directed sups. Theorem 4 proved useful in studying the fine structure of distributive continuous lattices. Briefly, a non-degenerate chain C in the lattice L is <u>order dense</u> if for any $x, y \in C$ with $x < y$, there is some $z \in C$ with $x < z < y$. For example, the set of rationals in $[0,1]$ is order dense, as is $[0,1]$ itself. Since each continuous lattice is a compact Hausdorff space in the Lawson topology, if such a lattice contains an order dense chain C, then there is a copy of the usual Cantor set in the topological closure of C. It is natural to ask whether a continuous lattice containing a copy of the Cantor set (topologically, but not necessarily as a chain) must contain an order dense chain. In [M2] it is shown that the answer is yes provided the lattice L is distributive, and an example is given of a non-distributive continuous lattice which contains a copy of the Cantor set but has no order dense chains.

The results we have presented so far have limited application, the most general result applying to the class of distributive continuous lattices. We now indicate a more general result which applies well beyond the class of continuous lattices. A locally compact (inf-)semilattice is a locally compact Hausdorff space S which is also an (inf-)semilattice and for which the map $(x,y) \mapsto x \wedge y : S \times S \to S$ is continuous. For example, any continuous lattice endowed with the Lawson topology satisfies this property since any continuous lattice is a compact semilattice in the Lawson topology. Since a locally compact semilattice may not have a largest element, it is too restrictive to consider whether S has a copy of $2^{\mathbb{N}}$; it is more appropriate to consider the question of when S contains a copy of $2^{\mathbb{N}} \backslash \{1\}$. To generalize the Theorems mentioned thus far, we must first find conditions which do not depend on the prime elements of a lattice since a locally compact semilattice may have no primes at all. The relevant property comprises the following definition:

Definition. A locally compact semilattice S has compactly finite breadth if each compact subset $X \subset S$ has a finite subset $F \subset X$ with $\inf F = \inf X$. □

A locally compact semilattice is a Lawson semilattice if each point has a neighborhood basis of subsemilattices. The Fundamental Theorem for Compact Semilattices ([C], Theorem VI-3.1) asserts that the compact Lawson semilattices with identity are exactly the continuous lattices endowed with the Lawson topology. The following result characterizes when locally compact Lawson semilattices have a copy of $2^{\mathbb{N}} \backslash \{1\}$.

Theorem 5 [LM2]. For the locally compact Lawson semilattice S, the following are equivalent:

1) S contains no copy of $2^{\mathbb{N}} \backslash \{1\}$.
2) S has compactly finite breadth. □

By a copy of $2^{\mathbb{N}} \backslash \{1\}$, we mean a monomorphism $f : 2^{\mathbb{N}} \backslash \{1\} \to S$ which is a continuous homomorphism of locally compact semilattices. Actually, more can be said here. It was recently shown in [LM1] that a locally compact non-Lawson semilattice must always contain a copy of $2^{\mathbb{N}}$, and so a locally compact semilattice must be a Lawson semilattice if it has a compactly finite breadth. Note that one particular consequence of Theorem 5 is that a continuous lattice has no copy of $2^{\mathbb{N}}$ precisely when it has compactly finite breadth (in the Lawson topology). These results were of use in the harmonic analysis of such semilattices. If M(S) denotes the Banach algebra of all finite regular Borel measures on the locally compact semilattice S, then Theorem 5 was used to characterize how the complex homomorphisms of M(S) arise. Namely, each Borel homomorphism $h : S \to 2$ gives rise to a complex homomorphism via $h(\mu) = \int h(x)\, d\mu(x)$. In [LM2] it is shown that the locally compact semilattices of compactly finite breadth are exactly those locally compact Lawson semilattices with the property that every complex homomorphism of $M(S)$ arises in this fashion. It was already known that $M(2^{\mathbb{N}})$ has complex homomorphisms which do not arise in this fashion; it follows that the semilattices of compactly finite breadth are exactly the locally compact semilattices S such that all of the complex homomorphisms of $M(S)$ are given in this fashion.

Applications to domain theory. The remainder of this paper is devoted to considering applications of the results quoted above to domain theory. To begin, recall that an information system is a triple $\underline{A}$ = (A, Con, |-) consisting of a set A of tokens, a family Con of finite subsets of A, and a relation |- from Con to A (see, e.g., [LW] for details here). The elements of $\underline{A}$, denoted $|\underline{A}|$ is the family of all consistent, deductively closed subsets of A. This family is a consistently complete algebraic complete partial order, or what is also commonly called a domain. In fact, $|\underline{A}|$ is closed in 2^A under all non-empty intersections and all increasing unions. Hence $|\underline{A}|$ is an algebraic semilattice whose compact elements are the sets X^- (where $^-$ denotes deductive closure) for $X \in$ Con. Thus $|\underline{A}|$ is almost a complete ring of sets, and if $|\underline{A}|^*$ denotes $|\underline{A}|$ with an isolated identity adjoined, then $|\underline{A}|^*$ is an algebraic lattice. Theorems 1 and 2 indicate exactly when a complete ring of sets can contain a copy of $2^{\mathbb{N}}$, and we wonder what this could mean for $|\underline{A}|$. That is

Question 1: What does it mean for the information system A that $|\underline{A}|$ has no copy of $2^{\mathbb{N}}$?

Now there certainly are information systems with no copy of $2^{\mathbb{N}}$, but an important class of domains for this question are those domains D which satisfy equations such as $D \simeq [D \to D]$. The following result of Plotkin shows these must all contain a copy of $2^{\mathbb{N}}$.

Lemma. Let D be a domain which satisfies $D \simeq [D \to D]$. Then there is a sequence $\{a_i\} \subset K(D)$ with $\bot = a_0 < a_1 < a_2 < \dots$.

Proof. Since D satisfies $D \simeq [D \to D]$, D cannot be finite, and so the identity map $I : D \to D$ has infinite range. For each $a \in D$, let $f_a : D \to D$ denote the map defined by $f_a(x) = a$ if $a \ll x$, and $f_a(x) = \bot$ otherwise. Note that $a \in K(D)$ implies that $f_a \in [D \to D]$, and since D is algebraic, it follows readily that $I = \sup\{f_a \mid a \in K(D)\}$. Now I cannot be the sup of finitely many maps of the form f_a, for then I would have finite range, which it does not. Thus there is an x with $K(\downarrow x)$ infinite, and this implies there is a chain $\bot = a_0 < a_1 < \ldots$. □

<u>Proposition</u> (Plotkin). If D is a domain which satisfies $D \simeq [D \to D]$, then there is a map $f : 2^{\mathbb{N}} \to D$ preserving all sups and all filtered infs.

<u>Proof</u>. According to the Lemma above, there is a sequence $\{a_i\} \subset K(D)$ with $\bot = a_0 < a_1 < \ldots$. Let $f : 2^{\mathbb{N}} \to D$ by $f(X) = \sup\{f_x \mid x \in X\}$, where we regard $2^{\mathbb{N}}$ as the set of subsets of $\mathbb{N}$ under containment. Then f preserves all sups (unions) and all filtered infs (downward intersections), as is easily verified. □

Of course, this is not the same question we posed above. Namely, the map f provided in the Proposition does not preserve directed sups and all infs, as one might expect. However, we can guarantee the existence of a map which does preserve these operations. Namely, the map f guaranteed by the Proposition is an isomorphism of $2^{\mathbb{N}}$ onto its image in D, and the family $C = \{f(\mathbb{N}\backslash\{n\}) \mid n \in \mathbb{N}\} \cup \{f(\mathbb{N})\}$ is a compact subset of D. Now, if $n \in \mathbb{N}$ and if $A \subset \mathbb{N}$ with $n \notin A$, then $\inf\{f(\mathbb{N}\backslash\{m\}) \mid m \in A\} \not\leq f(\mathbb{N}\backslash\{n\})$ if the inf is taken in $f(2^{\mathbb{N}})$, and so this must also hold in D, since infs taken in the larger domain D can only be larger than those taken in the subset $f(2^{\mathbb{N}})$. The map $g : 2^{\mathbb{N}} \to D$ defined by $g(X) = \inf\{f(\mathbb{N}\backslash\{x\}) \mid x \in X\}$ then preserves all infs and all directed sups.

Knowing that any domain D satisfying $D \simeq [D \to D]$ must contain a copy of $2^{\mathbb{N}}$ has no obvious importance for domain theory. Probably a more important result would be provided by answering the following question also raised by Plotkin:

<u>Question 2</u>: Must every domain D with $D \simeq [D \to D]$ contain a copy of the universal domain T^{ω}?

Theorems 1-4 above concern the primes of a distributive lattice. Unfortunately, a domain may not have any primes at all. The elements which are most closely related to them are so-called "ideal elements" of the set of elements $|\underline{A}|$, namely those which are not compact. An interesting question regarding these elements was pointed out to us by Samson Abramsky:

<u>Question 3</u>: Do the ideal elements of a domain D determine the domain? In particular, can one describe a domain in terms of its ideal elements?

Answering this question would involve generalizing the spectral theory for continuous lattices. But even for the algebraic case, it would be interesting to know how the ideals elements of a domain determine the domain.

Actually, it is not reasonable to believe that Theorems 1-4 should apply to information systems in general since the set of elements of such a system isn't usually distributive. But $|\underline{A}|$ is an algebraic semilattice, and so Theorem 5 does apply. This is not so pleasing since it involves a topological result, rather than a purely algebraic one. One possible way around this problem may be the following. Recall that an element x of a lattice L is <u>irreducible</u> if $x = a \wedge b$ implies $x = a$ or $x = b$; i.e., x is irreducible if x is prime in $\uparrow x$. While an irreducible element may be compact if the domain in question is algebraic, by and large they are ideal elements of the domain. In any event, any continuous lattice is order generated by its set of irreducible elements. As a generalization of Theorem 2, we believe the following result is true:

<u>Question 4</u>: Is it true that a locally compact semilattice of compactly finite breadth has the property that every every element is the infimum of finitely many irreducible elements?

In a sense, Plotkin's Proposition above is more in the spirit of domain theory than the questions we are raising, since our questions amount to "turning things upside down". That is, domains are usually regarded as being built up from below (much the way algebraic lattices are built up from their compact elements), and since the ideal elements of a domain lie at the top of the domain, the questions we raise concern how the domain is built from the "top down". In terms of computation, this may not be a fruitful way of looking at things, since the whole idea of the theory is to build up large pieces of information in terms of their smaller parts.

References

[G] Gierz, G., et al., A Compendium of Continuous Lattices, Springer-Verlag, Berlin, New York, Heidelberg (1980), 371pp.

[GLS] Gierz, G., J. D. Lawson, and A. R. Stralka, Intrinsic topologies on semilattices of finite breadth, Semigroup Forum 31 (1985), 1-18.

[LM1] Lawson, J. and M. Mislove, Semilattices which must contain a copy of $2^{\mathbb{N}}$, Semigroup Forum, to appear.

[LMP] Lawson, J., M. Mislove, and H. Priestley, Infinite antichains in ordered sets, submitted.

[LM2] Liukkonen, J. and M. Mislove, Measure algebras of semilattices, in: Lecture Notes in Math. 998, (1983), 202-214.

[LW] Larsen, K. and G. Winskel, Using information systems to solve recursive domain equations effectively, preprint.

[M1] Mislove, M., When are order scattered and topologically scattered the same?, Annals of Discrete Mathematics 23, (1984), 61-80.

[M2] Mislove, M., Order scattered distributive continuous lattices are topologically scattered, Houston Journal of Math., to appear.

[P] Plotkin, G., T^{ω} as a universal domain, JCSS 17 (1978), 209-236.

ON THE VARIETY CONCEPT FOR ω-CONTINUOUS ALGEBRAS. APPLICATION OF A GENERAL APPROACH

Ana Pasztor
Department of Mathematics
Carnegie-Mellon University
Pittsburgh
Pennsylvania 15213

0. First Introduction. The Problem.

Since Dana Scott's Mathematical Theory of Computation [33], the amount of work done on ordered structures, in particular on continuous algebras, has grown so considerably that any attempt to give a survey of it here would surely go beyond the scope of this paper. However, the reader interested in the above mentioned work is kindly referred to Andreka-Nemeti's excellent surveys [10].

In the study of classes of ordered structures like complete posets and continuous algebras, a special interest has been taken in those classes which are definable by a set of axioms (e.g., inequations, identities or quasi-identities in Bloom [14], Lehmann [22], Guessarian [19], Meseguer [26] and [27], Nelson [28], Adamek-Nelson-Reiterman [2], etc.).

The reason for this interest is the fact that the axioms provide an effective formal specification of classes of models (called semantic domains or interpretations) of programming languages and also of abstract data types viewed as the initial objects of such classes (cf. ADJ [6]).

A main concern in the study of axiomatizable classes of ordered structures is to prove Birkhoff-type theorems which say that a given class $\mathcal{C}$ is axiomatizable by axioms of a given form (e.g., inequalities) iff it has certain well defined algebraic closure properties (e.g., closure under "homomorphic images", "subalgebras" and products). Another concern is to assure that the axioms guarantee the existence of the above mentioned initial objects.

Given the fact that unlike the case for standard universal algebras, in the categories of ordered structures (like certain complete posets or continuous algebras) the concepts of homomorphic image and subalgebra are not unique, various concepts of varieties and quasi-varieties are floating around in the literature (e.g., the algebraic variety concept of Meseguer [26], the semi-variety concept of Lehmann [22], the variety concept of Bloom [14], of Nelson [28], or that of Adamek-Nelson-Reiterman [2], etc.

It is exactly this kind of situation at which H. Andreka, I. Nemeti and I. Sain aimed a whole series of papers starting with Andreka-Nemeti [8] (see also Andreka-Nemeti [9] and Nemeti-Sain [29]). Their main idea is this: Given a category $\mathcal{C}$, a universal formula is represented by a cone of the category $\mathcal{C}$. Restrictions on the shape of a cone represent several types of universal formulas. Validity of a universal formula is represented by injectivity w.r.t. a cone. For example, if $\mathcal{C}$ is the similarity class of relational structures with two binary relation symbols ρ and σ, then the cone K below corresponds to the formula $\forall x \forall y(\rho(x,y) \rightarrow \sigma(y,x) \vee x = y)$, and it is satisfied in A (i.e., A is injective w.r.t. the cone: $A \in \mathrm{Inj}K$) if for any homomorphism $f : D \rightarrow A$ there is a homomorphism $f_1 : D_1 \rightarrow A$ or $f_2 : D_2 \rightarrow A$ such that $e_1 \cdot f_1 = f$ or $e_2 \cdot f_2 = f$, respectively.

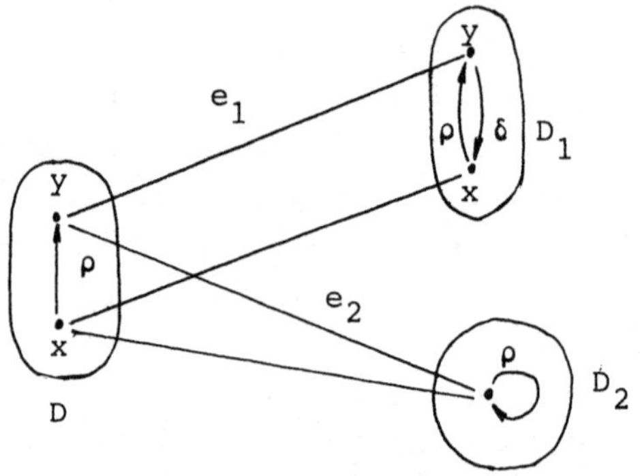

Their main result is an abstract axiomatizability theorem which has three parameters H, S and F, where H stands for "concept of homomorphic image", S stands for "concept of subalgebra", and F stands for a "concept of product". Any choice of the parameters H, S, F defines a class K_{HSF} of cones of the category $\mathcal{C}$ in a precisely defined way. The Birkhoff-type main theorem then says that if certain conditions are satisfied, then $\mathrm{Inj}\, K_{HSF}\mathfrak{G} = HSF\, \mathfrak{G}$ for any class $\mathfrak{G}$ of objects of $\mathcal{C}$, i.e., the HSF-closure of $\mathfrak{G}$ is exactly the class of all models of the K_{HSF}-theory of $\mathfrak{G}$.

In view of this result I have now this one question: Why reinvent the wheel?

For some reason, unknown to me, the results of Andreka-Nemeti-Sain have not been applied at all so far in the literature concerned with the generalization of universal algebraic axiomatizability results to ordered structures.

In the present paper I will try to show why and how we should apply their results. Concentrating on one special kind of axiomatizable class, the varieties, I will first try to motivate Andreka-Nemeti's [8] definition of a generalized variety (in Part 1). Parts 2 and 3 form a selfcontained unit aimed at a <u>simple</u> formulation of those <u>basic</u> results and proofs concerning the generalized varieties, which usually are reproved by authors again and again for their favorite category, and which can and should be applied (almost mechanically) to ordered structures (e.g., existence of free objects, the "Read-from" Theorem and the generalized Birkhoff theorem).

Proposition 2 of Part 3 is new in that it gives a direct translation of morphisms into implications and injectivity into validity, hopefully causing the "aha-effect", which might be missed when reading Andreka-Nemeti [8]. Part 4 finally gives an interesting and new application of the previous results to ω-continuous algebras.

By letting S be the full sub-algebra concept, and H the strong homomorphic image concept and by applying the results of Part 3, we obtain the following new result: a given class of ω-continuous Σ-algebras (Σ being possibly <u>infinitary</u>) is closed under H, S and $\mathbb{P}$ (i.e., products) exactly if it is axiomatizable by implications of the form $\bigwedge_{i\in I} x_i \leq y_i \to \tau_1 \leq \tau_2$, where I is a set, all the x_i's and y_i's are pairwise distinct and τ_1 and τ_2 are Σ'-terms, where Σ' is obtained from Σ by adding one ω-ary operation symbol $\bigsqcup$ (for l.u.b.'s of ω-chains) and a constant symbol $\perp$ (for bottom). Similar new results are obtained for other choices of H and S.

Concluding, let me emphasize that <u>any</u> axiomatizability result (other than those concerning varieties) of Andreka-Nemeti-Sain can and should also be applied to ordered structures. Their papers mentioned above also contain the <u>finitarization</u> results surely missed in the present paper and provide a <u>calculus</u> for the language, which is in fact indispensable in a Birkhoff-type theorem.

1. <u>Second Introduction. On the why and how of generalizing the concept of variety</u>.

One of the first papers to generalize the concepts of variety (= equational class) and of quasivariety (= quasiequational class) to arbitrary categories, is Banaschewski-Herrlich [13]. In the following I will first quote some of its motivations, definitions, and results. Then I will show some examples in which Birkhoff-type theorems hold but which do not follow from the quoted results. Finally I will present Andreka-Nemeti's [8] method and results for proving general Birkhoff-type theorems.

If F is a free algebra in the category Alg_Σ of all algebras of a given type Σ (and their homomorphisms) then a pair (P,C) of subsets of $F^2 = F \times F$ can be viewed as representing an <u>implicational</u>

condition in the sense that an algebra $A \in \mathrm{Alg}_\Sigma$ may be said to satisfy the implication (P,C) iff, for any homomorphism $h : F \to A$, $P \subseteq \theta(h)$ implies $C \subseteq \theta(h)$ where $\theta(h)$ is the kernel congruence of h, i.e., $\{(s,t) \mid h(s) = h(t)\}$. The individual pairs $(s,t) \in P$ could then be considered as the equations whose conjunction is represented by P, and the same goes for C; thus P is seen as the premise, and C as the conclusion, each describing conjunctions of (an arbitrary number of) equations, in an implicational condition.

Given F and (P,C) as above, let θ and Λ be the congruences on F generated by P and $P \cup C$, respectively, and $\mu : F/\theta \to F/\Lambda$ the natural homomorphism which maps each θ-block to the Λ-block containing it. Basic facts about the factorization of homomorphisms then imply that the following two conditions are equivalent for any algebra $A \in \mathrm{Alg}_\Sigma$:

(IMP) For all $h : F \to A$, if $P \subseteq \theta(h)$ then $C \subseteq \theta(h)$

(INJ) For all $f : F/\theta \to A$, there exists a $g : F/\Lambda \to A$ such that $f = g\mu$.

The latter condition is familiar. It is usually expressed by saying A is injective with respect to μ, just as injectivity with respect to a whole class of maps in a category means injectivity with respect to each member of the class. Noting further that the above homomorphism μ, being a quotient map, is a regular epimorphism in the category Alg_Σ, we are led to the following

Definition 1: A subcategory $\mathcal{G}$ of a category $\mathcal{C}$ will be called implicational (in $\mathcal{C}$) iff there exists a class H of regular epimorphisms in $\mathcal{C}$ such that the objects of $\mathcal{G}$ are exactly the H-injective objects of $\mathcal{C}$

In the following, Inj(H) will be the class of all H-injective objects of $\mathcal{C}$ for a given H.

Remark: Notice that implications are now morphisms and validity is injectivity.

Equational classes of algebras are particular implicational classes which can be described in terms of the above condition (IMP) by taking P to be empty. In the corresponding condition (INJ), this makes the congruence θ trivial, and since the free algebras in any Alg_Σ are the regular-projectives (i.e., the projectives w.r.t. the regular epis), a subcategory $\mathcal{G}$ of a category $\mathcal{C}$ is called equational if it is INJ(H) for some class H of regular epis each of which has a regular-projective domain.

The counterparts of Birkhoff's theorems about quasivarieties and varieties of algebras now read as follows:

Proposition 1: Let $\mathcal{C}$ be a regular cowellpowered category which has products and (regular epi, mono)-factorizations. Then any subcategory $\mathfrak{a}$ of $\mathcal{C}$ is implicational in $\mathcal{C}$ iff it is hereditary (i.e., $A \in \mathfrak{a}$ whenever $f : A \to B$ is a mono and $B \in \mathfrak{a}$) and productive (i.e., any product of factors in $\mathfrak{a}$ is also in $\mathfrak{a}$).

Proposition 2: Any equational subcategory $\mathfrak{a}$ of a category $\mathcal{C}$ satisfying the conditions of Proposition 1 is hereditary, productive and regular-cohereditary (i.e., $A \in \mathfrak{a}$ whenever $f : B \to A$ is a regular epi and $B \in \mathfrak{a}$).

At this point it seems that while implicational subcategories are generalizations of quasivarieties, i.e., classes of algebras defined by implications of the form $\bigwedge_{i \in I} t_i = t_i' \to s = s'$ ($\{(t_i, t_i'), (s,s') : i \in I\} \subseteq F^2$ for some free algebra), and equational classes generalize varieties, i.e., classes of algebra defined by equations of the form $s = s'$ ($(s,s') \in F^2$ for some free algebra F), the generalization of quasiprimitive classes of algebras are hereditary and productive classes and the generalization of primitive classes of algebras are hereditary, productive and regular-cohereditary classes.

The first question which comes to one's mind at this point is this: Are equational classes always defined by equations?

Let's take now $\mathcal{C}_1$ to be the full subcategory of those algebras of some type Σ the elements of which might be colored by red, i.e., let's endow the algebras with one unary relation R.

Let $\mathfrak{a}_1$ be the class (i.e., the full subcategory) defined by the implication $Rx \wedge Ry \to x = y$. The class $\mathfrak{a}_1$ cannot be defined by equations (since it is not closed under homomorphic images - see Mal'cev [23]) and yet, it is equational: $\mathfrak{a}_1 = \mathrm{Inj}(H)$ where H consists of the regular epi $F_1 \xrightarrow{\eta_\theta} F_1/\theta$, F_1 being the free algebra generated by $\{x,y\}$ with $x,y \in R^{F_1}$ and θ being the congruence relation generated by $x = y$. One can check that F_1 is regular-projective. This shows that the generalized notion of equation does not translate to identities (in the sense of Mal'cev [23]), but is just a class of certain morphisms. Satisfaction is injectivity. In the same way implications might not translate into quasi-identities (in the sense of Mal'cev [23]). Even more, there are categories in which implications translate to existential formulas.

There is a second question which comes to one's mind at this point: Does the fact that $\mathfrak{a} \subset \mathcal{C}$ is defined by implications, say of the form $\bigwedge_{i \in I} \alpha_i \to \alpha$, α_i and α being atomic formulas in the language of $\mathcal{C}$, imply that $\mathcal{A}$ is hereditary and productive in $\mathcal{C}$?

Take again the category $\mathcal{C}_1$ of algebras of some type consisting now of only one binary operation +, the elements of which might be red. Let $\mathcal{A}_2$ this time be defined by $R(x+y)$. Surely $\mathcal{A}_2$ is not hereditary. (Just erase the color from an algebra in $\mathcal{A}_2$. One obtains a subalgebra of it which is no more in $\mathcal{A}_2$.) Also, $\mathcal{A}_2$ is not equational and not even implicational: $\mathcal{A}_2 = \mathrm{Inj}(H)$, where $H = \{F_2 \xrightarrow{id} F_2'\}$, F_2 being the free algebra generated by $\{x,y\}$ and F_2' being F_2 except that $x+y$ is red; but $\mathcal{A}_2 \neq \mathrm{Inj}(H)$ for a class H of regular epis. (One can check that F_2 is surjective-projective.) This latter kind of situation led Banaschewski-Herrlich [13] to the following definitions:

Given an (E,M)-category $\mathcal{C}$, a subcategory $\mathcal{A}$ is, (i) E-implicational (or an E-quasivariety), or (ii) E-equational (or an E-variety) if $\mathcal{A} = \mathrm{Inj}(H)$ where, respectively, (i) $H \subseteq E$, or (ii) $H \subseteq E$ and each map in H has E-projective domain.

Analogously, $\mathcal{A}$ is M-hereditary if $A \in \mathcal{A}$ whenever $f: A \to B \in M$ and $B \in \mathcal{A}$ and $\mathcal{A}$ is E-cohereditary if $B \in \mathcal{A}$ whenever $f: A \to B \in E$ and $A \in \mathcal{A}$. By these we obtain the concepts of M-quasiprimitive (for M-hereditary and productive class) and E-primitive (for E-cohereditary, M-hereditary and productive class).

Propositions 1 and 2 still hold if we replace regular epi by E and mono by M.

By the new notations and $\mathcal{C}_1$ being a $\langle H_{sur}, S_s\rangle$-category, $\mathcal{A}_2$ is an H_{sur}-variety, where H_{sur} is the class of surjective homomorphisms and S_s the class of strong monos ($f: A \to B \in S_s$ iff f mono and $f(a) \in R$ implies $a \in R$).

$\mathcal{C}_1$ being a $\langle H_{reg}, S_w\rangle$-category, $\mathcal{A}_1$ is an H_{reg}-variety, where H_{reg} is the class of regular epis and S_w the class of monos.

Now let $\mathcal{A}_3 \subseteq \mathcal{C}_1$ be the class defined by $Rx \wedge Ry \to R(x+y)$. $\mathcal{A}_3$ is S_s-hereditary, H_{reg}-cohereditary and productive, but it is not primitive in the above sense, because $\mathcal{C}_1$ is not a (H_{reg}, S_s)-category. $\mathcal{C}_1$ is a (H_{reg}, S_w) and a (H_{sur}, S_s)-category but $\mathcal{A}_3$ is neither S_w-hereditary nor H_{sur}-cohereditary. Also note that $\mathcal{A}_3$ is a quasivariety since $\mathcal{A}_3 = \mathrm{Inj}(H)$ with $H = \{F_1 \xrightarrow{id} F_1'\}$, where F_1' is F_1 except with $x+y$ being red.

We know that F_1 is H_{reg}-projective and we notice that id is surjective and that $\mathcal{C}_1$ is a (H_{sur}, S_s)-category.

Of course, it would be nonsense to accept $\mathcal{A}_1$ (defined by $Rx \wedge Ry \to x = y$) to be a variety and not to accept $\mathcal{A}_3$ (defined by $Rx \wedge Ry \to R(x+y)$) to be a variety.

The chaos indicated above is worsened by the fact that there are E-implicational and E-equational classes, which are not definable by implications, but, e.g., only by existential formulas. A (happy) end to this chaos was set by Andreka-Nemeti [8] by defining a class $\mathcal{G} \subseteq \mathcal{C}$ to be an <u>HS-variety</u>, if $\mathcal{G} = \mathrm{Inj}(E)$ for a class $E \subseteq \mathcal{H}$ of morphisms such that (i) $\langle \mathcal{H}, S\rangle$ is a factorization system in $\mathcal{C}$, and (ii) the domains of the morphisms in E are H-projective. Notice that H and S are now <u>independent parameters</u>, while earlier we had $H = \mathcal{H} = E$ and $S = M$!

Analogously, $\mathcal{G} \subseteq \mathcal{C}$ is HS-primitive (in $\mathcal{C}$) if $\mathcal{G} = H\,S\,\mathbb{P}\,\mathcal{G}$, i.e., if $\mathcal{G}$ is H-cohereditary, S-hereditary and productive.

One of the main results of Andreka-Nemeti [8] (see also [9] and Nemeti-Sain [29]) is the following fact, which we call the

<u>MAIN AN-THEOREM</u>:

Let $\mathcal{C}$ be a category, let $\mathcal{H}, S \subseteq \mathrm{Mor}\,\mathcal{C}$, suppose that $\mathcal{C}$ is $\mathcal{H}$-cowell-powered, has products, has enough H-projectives and also suppose that $\langle \mathcal{H}, S\rangle$ is a factorization system in $\mathcal{C}$ and that for each commutative diagram  , $h \in H$ holds. Then the HS-varities are exactly the HS-primitive classes in $\mathcal{C}$. In other words $\mathcal{G} = \mathrm{Inj}(E)$ for some $E \subseteq \mathcal{H}$, the elements of which have H-projective domain, iff $\mathcal{G} = H\,S\,\mathbb{P}\,\mathcal{G}$.

<u>Remarks</u>:

1. Generalized identities are the morphisms in $\mathcal{H}$ whose domain is H-projective.
2. Validity is injectivity.
3. Let $H = \mathrm{Is}$ the class of all isomorphisms of $\mathcal{C}$. Then every object of $\mathcal{C}$ is H-projective, so identities are exactly the elements of $\mathcal{H}$. Then $\mathcal{G} = \mathrm{Inj}(E)$ for some $E \subseteq \mathcal{H}$ iff $\mathcal{G} = S\,\mathbb{P}\,\mathcal{G}$.

By this <u>S-quasivarieties</u> are just IsS-varieties (as, in fact, it is the case with algebras).
4. H. Andreka, I. Nemeti and I. Sain have generalized and characterized by closure properties many other notions of axiomatizability - see [8], [9], [11], [29], [30], and [32].

2. Free extensions, the generalized variety concept, the "Read-from" Theorem and the proof of the Main AN-Theorem.

$\mathcal{C}$ will denote a category, Mor $\mathcal{C}$ its class of morphisms and $|\mathcal{C}|$ its class of objects. I will write composition of morphisms as

If $A \in |\mathcal{C}|$ and $e : B \to C \in$ Mor $\mathcal{C}$, we say A is injective w.r.t. e (and write $A \in$ Inj e) if for each $f : B \to A$ there is a $g : C \to A$ such that

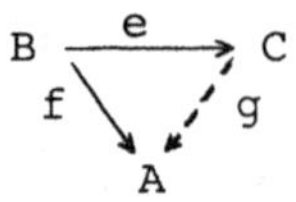

commutes.

Remark 1: The above definition can be read as "A satisfies the identity e ($A \models e$) if for each evaluation f of the variables of e, A satisfies e with f ($A \models e[f]$), i.e., there is a g such that $e \cdot g = f$".

If $E \subseteq$ Mor $\mathcal{C}$, Inj E denotes the class of all objects which are injective w.r.t. each $e \in E$.
Let $\mathcal{G} \subseteq |\mathcal{C}|$.

$\mathbb{P}\,\mathcal{G} := \{ \prod_{i \in I} A_i \mid A_i \in \mathcal{G}$, I is a set $\}$ is the class of all direct products of objects in $\mathcal{G}$.

For any $M \subseteq$ Mor $\mathcal{C}$

$\underset{\rightarrow}{M}\,\mathcal{G} := \{A \mid A \in |\mathcal{C}|$ and $(\exists f : A \to B) B \in \mathcal{G}$ and $f \in M\}$ is the class of all M-subobjects of objects in $\mathcal{G}$.

$\underset{\leftarrow}{M}\,\mathcal{G} := \{A \mid A \in |\mathcal{C}|$ and $(\exists f : B \to A) B \in \mathcal{G}$ and $f \in M\}$ is the class of all M-images of objects in $\mathcal{G}$.

Let $H \subseteq$ Mor $\mathcal{C}$ and $A \in |\mathcal{C}|$. We call A H-projective (and write $A \in$ Pj(H)) if for each diagram

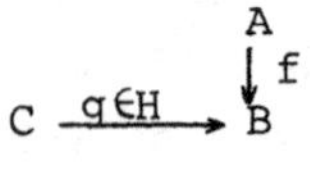

there is an $h : A \to C$ such that $h \cdot g = f$.

Example: Let $\mathcal{C}$ = POS - the category of posets. Then the surjective-projective objects are the discretely ordered sets, while the extremal (or strong) epi-projectives are those posets in which every element is comparable with at most one other element.

$\mathcal{C}$ has enough H-projectives if $|\mathcal{C}| \subseteq \underset{\leftarrow}{H}\,$Pj(H).

Let $\mathcal{H} \subseteq$ Mor $\mathcal{C}$. $\mathcal{C}$ is $\mathcal{H}$-cowellpowered if the class of $\mathcal{H}$-images of any $A \in |\mathcal{C}|$ is (up to isomorphism) a set, i.e., if for any $A \in |\mathcal{C}|$ there is a set $\mathcal{G} \subseteq \underset{\leftarrow}{\mathcal{H}}\{A\}$ such that $\underset{\leftarrow}{Is}\,\mathcal{G} \supseteq \underset{\leftarrow}{\mathcal{H}}\{A\}$.

Is is the class of all isomorphisms of $\mathbb{C}$.

Let $\mathfrak{M}, S \subseteq \mathrm{Mor}\ \mathbb{C}$. The pair $\langle \mathfrak{M}, S\rangle$ is a factorization system in $\mathbb{C}$ if

(i) each $f \in \mathrm{Mor}\ \mathbb{C}$ can be written as $e \cdot s$ with $e \in \mathfrak{M}$, $s \in S$.

(ii) $\mathfrak{M} \cap S \supseteq \mathrm{Is}$

(iii) To each commutative diagram 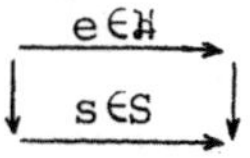

there is a unique "diagonal fill-in" 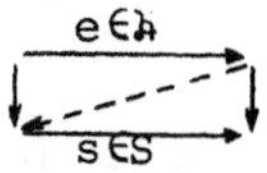

such that both the upper and the lower triangles are commutative.

Given a factorization system $\langle \mathfrak{M}, S\rangle$ in $\mathbb{C}$, a class $H \subseteq \mathrm{Mor}\ \mathbb{C}$ and a class $\mathfrak{A} \subseteq |\mathbb{C}|$,

$E_{HS}(\mathfrak{A}) := \{e : A \to B \mid e \in \mathfrak{M},\ \mathfrak{A} \subseteq \mathrm{Inj}\ e \text{ and } A \in \mathrm{Pj}(H)\}$.

In other words $E_{HS}(\mathfrak{A})$ is the class of all HS-identities true in $\mathfrak{A}$.

Remark 2: In their papers H. Andreka, I. Nemeti and I. Sain have proved Birkhoff-type theorems for a large variety of identity concepts like $H\mathbb{P}$-, $S\mathbb{P}\,\mathrm{Up}$ - etc. identities, where the ones defined above are called $HS\mathbb{P}$-identities - cf. Nemeti-Sain [29].

Let $\mathfrak{M} \subseteq \mathrm{Mor}\ \mathbb{C}$, $A \in |\mathbb{C}|$ and $\mathfrak{A} \subseteq |\mathbb{C}|$.

The $\mathfrak{A}$-free $\mathfrak{M}$-extension of A, denoted by $fr_A^{\mathfrak{M}}\mathfrak{A} : A \to Fr_A^{\mathfrak{M}}\mathfrak{A}$, is a morphism $f : A \to B$ such that

(i) $f \in \mathfrak{M}$ and $\mathfrak{A} \subseteq \mathrm{Inj}\ f$

(ii) for every $g : A \to C \in \mathfrak{M}$, if $\mathfrak{A} \subseteq \mathrm{Inj}\ g$, then there is a unique $h : C \to B$ such that $g \cdot h = f$

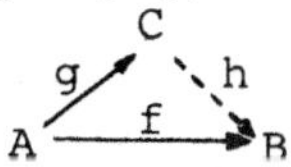

Remarks 3: (1) The above definition says that if $\langle \mathfrak{M}, S\rangle$ is a factorization system in $\mathbb{C}$, then $fr_A^{\mathfrak{M}}\mathfrak{A}$ is the "largest IsS-identity true in $\mathfrak{A}$ with the elements of A as variables.

(2) Whenever $e : A \to B$ is in $\mathfrak{M}$, $\mathfrak{A} \subseteq \mathrm{Inj}\ e$ iff e is a consequence of $fr_A^{\mathfrak{M}}\mathfrak{A}$, i.e., $C \in \mathrm{Inj}\ fr_A^{\mathfrak{M}}\mathfrak{A}$ implies $C \in \mathrm{Inj}\ e$ for every $C \in |\mathbb{C}|$.

Proof: (a) Let $\mathfrak{A} \subseteq \mathrm{Inj}\ e$ and suppose $fr_A^{\mathfrak{M}}\mathfrak{A}$ is true in some $C \in |\mathbb{C}|$, i.e., $C \in \mathrm{Inj}\ fr_A^{\mathfrak{M}}\mathfrak{A}$. We want to prove that e is also true in C, i.e., $C \in \mathrm{Inj}\ e$. Let therefore $f : A \to C$ (be an evaluation map). By the definition of $fr_A^{\mathfrak{M}}\mathfrak{A}$ there is an $\hat{f} : Fr_A^{\mathfrak{M}}\mathfrak{A} \to C$ such that $fr_A^{\mathfrak{M}}\mathfrak{A} \cdot \hat{f} = f$. But there is also an $h : B \to Fr_A^{\mathfrak{M}}\mathfrak{A}$ such that $e \cdot h = fr_A^{\mathfrak{M}}\mathfrak{A}$ by the definition of $fr_A^{\mathfrak{M}}\mathfrak{A}$.

So $e\cdot(h\cdot\hat{f}) = fr_A^{\mathcal{H}}\cdot\hat{f} = f$, i.e., $C \in \mathrm{Inj}\ e$.

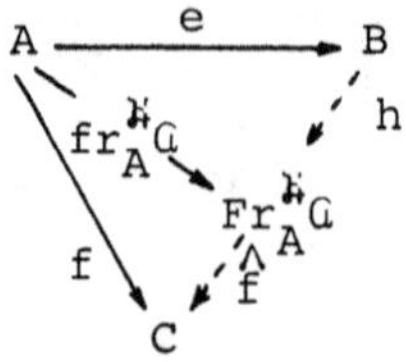

(b) Suppose e is a consequence of $fr_A^{\mathcal{H}}\mathcal{G}$. Since $\mathcal{G} \subseteq \mathrm{Inj}\ fr_A^{\mathcal{H}}\mathcal{G}$, also $\mathcal{G} \subseteq \mathrm{Inj}\ e$. ■

(3) If $A \in Pj(H)$ then $Fr_A^{\mathcal{H}}\mathcal{G}$ plays the role of a free object.

<u>Example</u>: In the category of all algebras of a given type the surjective-projectives are exactly the word algebras. So their $\mathcal{G}$-free surjective-extensions are exactly the $\mathcal{G}$-free algebras.

(4) If $Fr_A^{\mathcal{H}}\mathcal{G} \in \mathcal{G}$, then $fr_A^{\mathcal{H}}\mathcal{G}$ is the so called $\mathcal{H}$-reflection or $\mathcal{H}$-replica of A in $\mathcal{G}$ (cf. Herrlich-Strecker [20] and Mal'cev [23]).

Considering Remark 1 let us now write <u>$A \models e$</u> if $A \in \mathrm{Inj}\ e$ and write <u>$A \models e[f]$</u> if $e : B \to C$ (is an identity), $f : B \to A$ (is an evaluation) and there is a $g : C \to A$ such that $e\cdot g = f$.

<u>Proposition 1</u> ("Read-from" Theorem): Let $\mathcal{G} \subseteq |\mathcal{C}|$ and $e : A \to B \in \mathcal{H} \subseteq \mathrm{Mor}\ \mathcal{C}$. Then

$$\mathcal{G} \models e \quad \text{iff} \quad Fr_A^{\mathcal{H}}\mathcal{G} \models e[fr_A^{\mathcal{H}}\mathcal{G}].$$

<u>Proof</u>: (a) Let $\mathcal{G} \models e$, i.e., $\mathcal{G} \subseteq \mathrm{Inj}\ e$. Then by the definition of $fr_A^{\mathcal{H}}\mathcal{G}$ there is an $f : B \to Fr_A^{\mathcal{H}}\mathcal{G}$ such that $e\cdot f = fr_A^{\mathcal{H}}\mathcal{G}$. So $Fr_A^{\mathcal{H}}\mathcal{G} \models e[fr_A^{\mathcal{H}}\mathcal{G}]$.

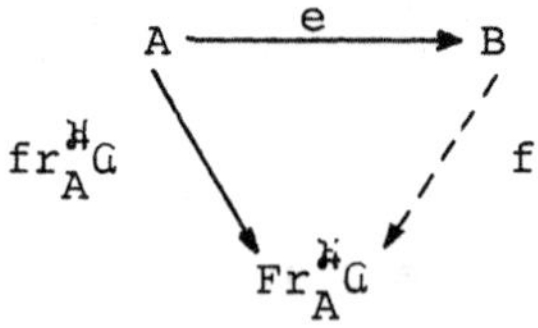

(b) Suppose $Fr_A^{\mathcal{H}}\mathcal{G} \models e[fr_A^{\mathcal{H}}\mathcal{G}]$. Then there is an $f : B \to Fr_A^{\mathcal{H}}\mathcal{G}$ with $e\cdot f = fr_A^{\mathcal{H}}\mathcal{G}$. Let $g : A \to C$ be an evaluation with $C \in \mathcal{G}$. Then there is a $\hat{g} : Fr_A^{\mathcal{H}}\mathcal{G} \to C$ with $fr_A^{\mathcal{H}}\mathcal{G}\cdot\hat{g} = g$ and so $e\cdot(f\cdot\hat{g}) = fr_A^{\mathcal{H}}\mathcal{G}\cdot\hat{g} = g$, hence $\mathcal{G} \models e$. ■

<u>Remark 4</u>: In order to know whether an identity with domain (or "variables in") A is true in $\mathcal{G}$ it is enough to check whether it is true in $Fr_A^{\mathcal{H}}\mathcal{G}$ with the evaluation $fr_A^{\mathcal{H}}\mathcal{G}$.

Proposition 2 (Existence of $fr_A^{\mathfrak{H}}\mathfrak{A}$): Let $\langle \mathfrak{H}, S \rangle$ be a factorization system in $\mathcal{C}$, let $A \in |\mathcal{C}|$, $\mathfrak{A} \subseteq |\mathcal{C}|$ and suppose that $\mathcal{C}$ is $\mathfrak{H}$-cowellpowered and that it has products.

Then $fr_A^{\mathfrak{H}}\mathfrak{A}$ exists and $Fr_A^{\mathfrak{H}}\mathfrak{A} \in S\,\mathbb{P}\,\mathfrak{A}$. (Henceforth we will write $S\mathfrak{A}$ for $\underset{\rightarrow}{S}\mathfrak{A}$ and $H\mathfrak{A}$ for $\underset{\leftarrow}{H}\mathfrak{A}$ for any $\mathfrak{A} \subseteq |\mathcal{C}|$).

Proof: Let $M := \{f \mid f \in \text{Mor}\,\mathcal{C}$ and $f : A \to B$ for some $B \in \mathfrak{A}\}$. Each $f \in M$ has a unique factorization $h_f \cdot s_f$ with $h_f : A \to A_f \in \mathfrak{H}$ and $s_f : A_f \to B_f \in S$. Let $\mathfrak{F} := \{h_f : f \in M\}$. Since $\mathfrak{F} \subseteq \mathfrak{H}$ and $\mathcal{C}$ is $\mathfrak{H}$-cowellpowered, there is a set $\mathfrak{F}' \subseteq \mathfrak{F}$ such that $\mathfrak{F}'$ is the set of all isomorphism classes of $\mathfrak{F}$. Let $P := \prod_{h_f \in \mathfrak{F}'} A_f$. By the definition of products there is a unique $g : A \to P$ such that $g \cdot \pi_h = h$ for each $h \in \mathfrak{F}'$, π_h denoting the hth projection. Now g also has a unique factorization $e \cdot s$ with $e : A \to F \in \mathfrak{H}$ and $s : F \to P \in S$.

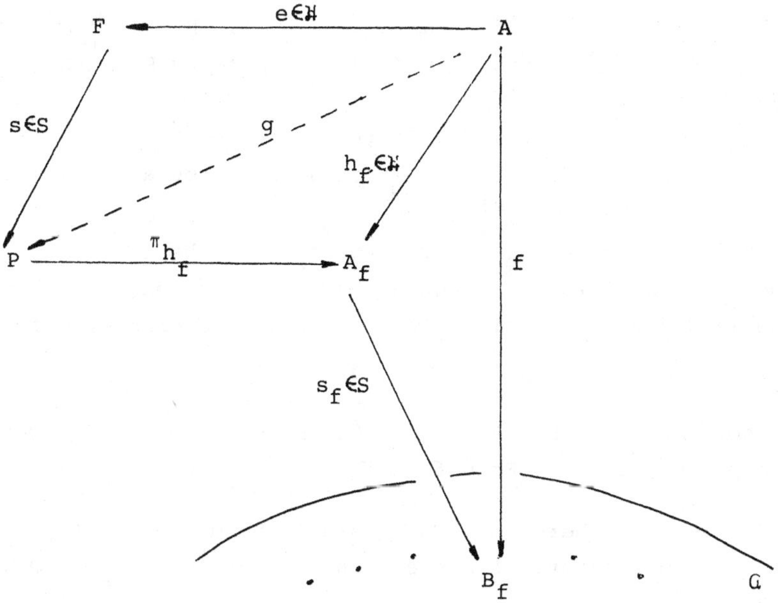

<u>Claim</u>: $e = \mathrm{fr}_A^{\mathcal{H}}\mathcal{G}$.

<u>Proof of the Claim</u>: First we prove $\mathcal{G} \subseteq \mathrm{Inj}\ e$. Let $f : A \to B \in \mathrm{Mor}\ \mathcal{C}$ with $B \in \mathcal{G}$. Then $f \in M$ and so $f = h_f \cdot s_f$ with $s_f \in S$ and $h_f \in \mathfrak{F}'$. (Note that we identify isomorphic morphisms.) Let $\hat{f} = s \cdot \pi_{h_f} \cdot s_f$. Then $e \cdot \hat{f} = e \cdot s \cdot \pi_{h_f} \cdot s_f = g \cdot \pi_{h_f} \cdot s_f = h_f \cdot s_f = f$. So $\mathcal{G} \subseteq \mathrm{Inj}\ e$.

Now let $e' : A \to A' \in \mathcal{H}$ such that $\mathcal{G} \subseteq \mathrm{Inj}\ e'$. Then for each $f \in M$ there is an f' such that $e' \cdot f' = f$.

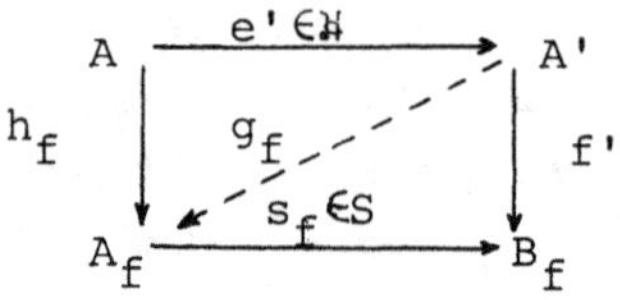

Since $\langle \mathcal{H}, S \rangle$ is a factorization system, for each $f \in M$ there is a unique g_f with $e' \cdot g_f = h_f$ and $g_f \cdot s_f = f'$. But $\langle \pi_{h_f} : h_f \in \mathfrak{F}' \rangle$ being a natural source, there is a unique $p : A' \to P$ with $p \cdot \pi_{h_f} = g_f$ for each $h_f \in \mathfrak{F}'$.

The diagram

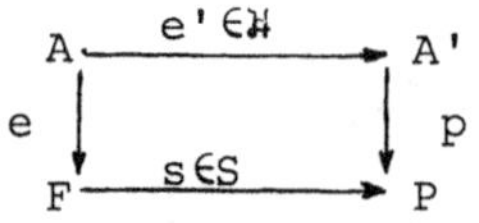

being commutative ($e' \cdot p \cdot \pi_{h_f} = e' \cdot g_f = h_f = g \cdot \pi_f = e \cdot s \cdot \pi_{h_f}$ for each $h_f \in \mathfrak{F}'$, hence $e' \cdot p = e \cdot s$) and $\langle \mathcal{H}, S \rangle$ being a factorization system, there is a unique $q : A' \to F$ with $e' \cdot q = e$ (and $q \cdot s = p$). This fulfills the second condition for e to be $\mathrm{fr}_A^{\mathcal{H}}\mathcal{G}$.

■ Claim

By construction $F \in S\,\mathbb{P}\,S\,\mathcal{G}$. But $\mathbb{P}\,S\,\mathcal{G} \subseteq S\,\mathbb{P}\,\mathcal{G}$ and $S\,S\,\mathcal{G} \subseteq S\,\mathcal{G}$ (easy to prove), so $F = \mathrm{Fr}_A^{\mathcal{H}}\mathcal{G} \in S\,\mathbb{P}\,\mathcal{G}$. ■

<u>Remark 5</u>: We prove here only the basic theorems about $\mathrm{fr}_A^{\mathcal{H}}\mathcal{G}$. However, it is easy to prove further properties, say $\mathrm{fr}_A^{\mathcal{H}}\mathcal{G} = \mathrm{fr}_A^{\mathcal{H}}\,H\,S\,\mathbb{P}\,\mathcal{G}$ for $A \in \mathrm{Pj}(H)$.

<u>Proposition 3</u> (generalized Birkhoff Theorem): Let $\mathcal{C}$, $\mathcal{H}$ and S satisfy the conditions of Proposition 2. Also let $H \subseteq \mathrm{Mor}\ \mathcal{C}$ and suppose that $\mathcal{C}$ has enough H-projectives and that for each commutative diagram

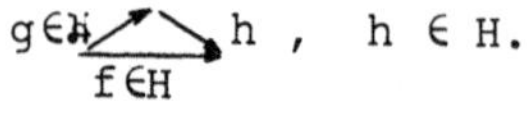

, $h \in H$.

Then for any $\mathcal{G} \subseteq |\mathcal{C}|$

(a) $\mathrm{Inj}\{\mathrm{fr}_A^{\mathcal{H}}\mathcal{G} \mid A \in \mathrm{Pj}(H)\} = H\,S\,\mathbb{P}\,\mathcal{G}$.

(b) $H\{\mathrm{Fr}_A^{\mathcal{H}}\mathcal{G} \mid A \in \mathrm{Pj}(H)\} = H\,S\,\mathbb{P}\,\mathcal{G}$.

<u>Remarks 6:</u>

1. By Remarks 3/(2) we know that for every $A \in Pj(H)$ $\mathrm{fr}_A^{\mathfrak{H}}\mathfrak{G}$ implies all other HS-identities true in $\mathfrak{G}$ with domain A.
2. Point (b) of Proposition 3 corresponds to the universal algebraic fact that a variety consists of the homomorphic images of its free algebras.
3. If in (a) we set $H = Is$, we obtain Mal'cev's [24] result (p. 28) about replete classes.

<u>Proof of Proposition 3:</u>

(a) First let $B \in \mathrm{Inj}\{\mathrm{fr}_A^{\mathfrak{H}}\mathfrak{G} \mid A \in Pj(H)\}$. Since $\mathfrak{C}$ has enough H-projectives, there is a $B' \in Pj(H)$ and $f : B' \to B \in H$. Then there is an $\hat{f} : \mathrm{Fr}_{B'}^{\mathfrak{H}}\mathfrak{G} \to B$ such that $\mathrm{fr}_{B'}^{\mathfrak{H}}\mathfrak{G} \cdot \hat{f} = f$. But then $\hat{f} \in H$ and since $\mathrm{Fr}_{B'}^{\mathfrak{H}}\mathfrak{G} \in S\,\mathbb{P}\,\mathfrak{G}$, this proves $B \in H\,S\,\mathbb{P}\mathfrak{G}$.

Now let $A \in H\,S\,\mathbb{P}\mathfrak{G}$. Let $B \in Pj(H)$ be arbitrary. We show that $A \in \mathrm{Inj}\ \mathrm{fr}_B^{\mathfrak{H}}\mathfrak{G}$. Therefore let $f : B \to A$. Since $A \in H\,S\,\mathbb{P}\,\mathfrak{G}$ we have the following figure:

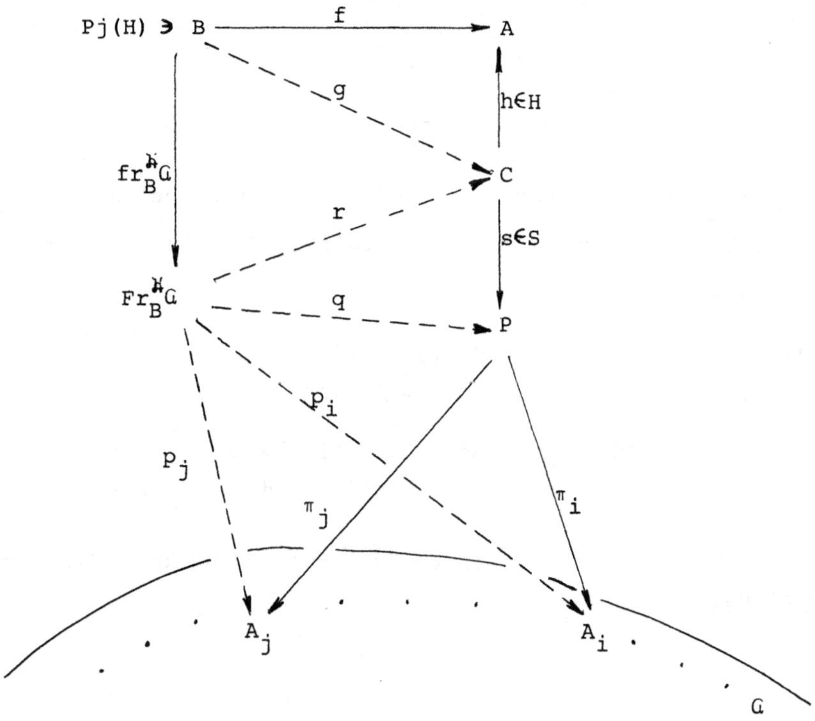

Since $B \in Pj(H)$ there is a $g : B \to C$ such that $g \cdot h = f$. Since $g \cdot s \cdot \pi_i : B \to A_i \in \mathcal{A}$, for each $i \in I$ there is a unique $p_i : Fr_B^{\mathcal{H}}\mathcal{A} \to A_i$ such that $g \cdot s \cdot \pi_i = fr_B^{\mathcal{H}}\mathcal{A} \cdot p_i$. But $\langle \pi_i : i \in I \rangle$ is a natural source, so there is a unique $q : Fr_B^{\mathcal{H}}\mathcal{A} \to P$ such that $q \cdot \pi_i = p_i$ for each $i \in I$.

Since the diagram 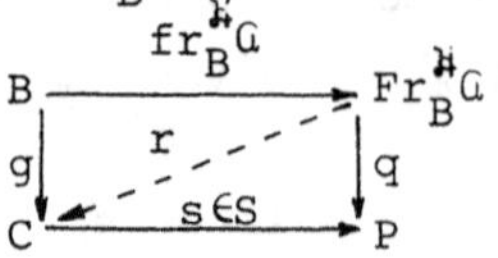 commutes (for each $i \in I$

$fr_B^{\mathcal{H}}\mathcal{A} \cdot q \cdot \pi_i = fr_B^{\mathcal{H}}\mathcal{A} \cdot p_i = g \cdot s \cdot \pi_i$) and $\langle \mathcal{H}, S \rangle$ is a factorization system, there is a unique $r : Fr_B^{\mathcal{H}}\mathcal{A} \to C$ such that $fr_B^{\mathcal{H}}\mathcal{A} \cdot r = g$ and $r \cdot s = q$.

Since $fr_B^{\mathcal{H}}\mathcal{A} \cdot (r \cdot h) = g \cdot h = f$, this proves $A \in \text{Inj } fr_B^{\mathcal{H}}\mathcal{A}$.

(b) Since $\{Fr_A^{\mathcal{H}} \mid A \in Pj(H)\} \subseteq S\,\mathbb{P}\,\mathcal{A}$ by Proposition 2, $H\{Fr_A^{\mathcal{H}}\mathcal{A} \mid A \in Pj(H)\} \subseteq H\,S\,\mathbb{P}\mathcal{A}$. Now let $B \in H\,S\,\mathbb{P}\,\mathcal{A}$. By (a) $B \in \text{Inj}\{fr_A^{\mathcal{H}}\mathcal{A} \mid A \in Pj(H)\}$. There is $A \in Pj(H)$ and $f : A \to B \in H$. By Proposition 2 $fr_A^{\mathcal{H}}\mathcal{A}$ exists, so $B \in \text{Inj } fr_A^{\mathcal{H}}\mathcal{A}$. Therefore there is a $\hat{f} : Fr_A^{\mathcal{H}}\mathcal{A} \to B$ with $fr_A^{\mathcal{H}}\mathcal{A} \cdot \hat{f} = f$. Since $f \in H$, we obtain $\hat{f} \in H$. So $B \in H\{Fr_A^{\mathcal{H}}\mathcal{A}\}$.

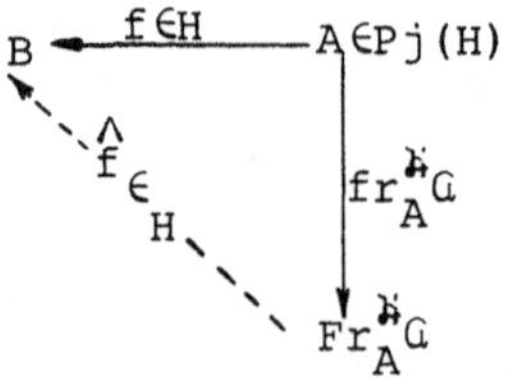

■

<u>Corollary 4</u> (The Main AN-Theorem - see second Introduction):

Let the conditions of Proposition 3 be fulfilled. Then for any $\mathcal{A} \subseteq |\mathcal{C}|$

$$\text{Inj } E_{HS}(\mathcal{A}) = H\,S\,\mathbb{P}\,\mathcal{A}.$$

<u>Proof</u>: (1) $\{fr_A^{\mathcal{H}}\mathcal{A} \mid A \in Pj(H)\} \subseteq E_{HS}(\mathcal{A})$, so

$\text{Inj } E_{HS}(\mathcal{A}) \subseteq \text{Inj}\{fr_A^{\mathcal{H}}\mathcal{A} \mid A \in Pj(H)\} = H\,S\,\mathbb{P}\,\mathcal{A}$.

(2) Let $B \in H\,S\,\mathbb{P}\,\mathcal{A}$. Then $B \in \text{Inj}\{fr_A^{\mathcal{H}}\mathcal{A} \mid A \in Pj(H)\}$. But then $B \in \text{Inj } e$ for each $e \in E_{HS}(\mathcal{A})$ by Remarks 3/(2). ■

<u>Remark 7</u>: For $H = Is$ we obtain the generalized Birkhoff Theorem about <u>quasivarieties</u>.

3. Implementation of the category theoretical results of part 2 by abstract model theoretical means.

The aim of the generalization of the variety concept to arbitrary abstract categories $\mathbb{C}$ was to provide a purely mechanical method for stating Birkhoff-type theorems in any concretely given category. As they are now, the results are too abstract for (a mechanical) application. We need a more concrete concept of language with the appropriate notions of formula and validity. In this section we pursue Andreka-Nemeti's [8] translation of the HS-identities into implications of the language, and of injectivity into validity. The final abstract model theoretical results can then be applied almost mechanically to the language of our favorite category ($\perp \mathrm{Alg}_\Sigma(\omega)$ in this case).

3.1. The language.

A language is a triple $\mathcal{L} = \langle L, M, \models \rangle$ such that $\models \subseteq M \times L$ and $\models$ satisfies the axioms A1 - A5 below. L is the class of all formulas of $\mathcal{L}$, M is the class of its models and $\models$ is the validity relation.

(A1). $M = |\mathbb{C}|$ for some (fixed) category $\mathbb{C}$. $\mathcal{S}$ denotes here the category of sets with an additional object $V := \mathrm{Ord}$ - the class of all ordinals. The morphisms of $\mathcal{S}$ are the maps between the objects. Given is also a faithful functor $U : \mathbb{C} \to \mathcal{S}$. (We think of $U(A)$ for $A \in |\mathbb{C}|$ as the "underlying set" of A.) For $A \in |\mathbb{C}|$ we write A' for $U(A)$ and f' for $U(f)$.

Remark 1: If $\mathbb{C}$, the aim of our applications, were a category of many sorted structures, we would have to change "set" into "family of sets" and "map" into "family of maps". The translation would be easy throughout this section.

(A2). For each $A \in |\mathbb{C}|$ and ("evaluation map") $k : V \to A'$, the statement $A \models \varphi[k]$ (read: k satisfies φ in A or A satisfies φ with k) is defined (i.e., makes sense) for each $\varphi \in L$, and it is either true or false.

(A3). For each $\varphi \in L$ and $A \in |\mathbb{C}|$, $A \models \varphi$ iff for all $k : V \to A'$, $A \models \varphi[k]$ is true.

(A4). The language contains the connectives $\wedge$, $\vee$ and $\to$, i.e.,
(a) if $\varphi, \psi \in L$ then $(\varphi \to \psi) \in L$ and for every $A \in |\mathbb{C}|$ and $k : V \to A'$, $A \models (\varphi \to \psi)[k]$ iff $A \models \psi[k]$ or $A \not\models \varphi[k]$.
(b) If $\{\varphi_i : i \in I\} \subseteq L$ is a set, then $\left(\bigwedge_{i\in I} \varphi_i\right)$, $\left(\bigvee_{i\in I} \varphi_i\right) \in L$ and for each $A \in |\mathbb{C}|$ and $k : V \to A$, $A \models \left(\bigwedge_{i\in I} \varphi_i\right)[k]$ iff $A \models \varphi_i[k]$ for each $i \in I$ and $A \models \left(\bigvee_{i\in I} \varphi_i\right)[k]$ iff $A \models \varphi_i[k]$ for some $i \in I$.

Given $\varphi \in L$ and $R \subseteq V$ we say that R <u>contains the class of all free variables of φ</u> ($R \supseteq \mathrm{Var}\,\varphi$) if for each $A \in |\mathcal{C}|$ and $k_1, k_2 : V \to A'$, if $k_1 \upharpoonright R = k_2 \upharpoonright R$ then $A \models \varphi[k_1]$ iff $A \models \varphi[k_2]$.

(A5). For each $R \subseteq V$, if R is a set, then $\{\varphi \in L \mid \mathrm{Var}\,\varphi \subseteq R\}$ is again a set (up to elementary equivalence).

The validity relation $\models$ defines a Galois correspondence between L and M:

For a $T \subseteq L$ <u>Md T</u>$:= \{A \in |\mathcal{C}| : A \models \varphi$ for every $\varphi \in T\}$. For any fixed $E \subseteq L$ and $\mathcal{A} \subseteq |\mathcal{C}|$, <u>E(𝒜)</u>$:= \{\varphi \in E \mid \mathcal{A} \models \varphi\}$, where $\mathcal{A} \models \varphi$ means $A \models \varphi$ for every $A \in \mathcal{A}$. <u>$A \models T$</u> means $A \models \varphi$ for every $\varphi \in T$, and <u>$T \models \varphi$</u> means φ is a consequence of T, i.e., for every $A \in M$, $A \models T$ implies $A \models \varphi$.

3.2. <u>The primitive formulas</u>.

When translating the HS-identities into formulas of our language $\mathcal{L}$, the primitive formulas become the <u>atoms</u> of those formulas.

Primitive formulas will be defined to be all formulas satisfying the primitive conditions PR1 - PR5($\mathcal{H}$) below. Given $F \subseteq L$ and $\mathcal{H}, S \subseteq \mathrm{Mor}\,\mathcal{C}$, <u>F satisfies the primitive conditions w.r.t. $\mathcal{H}$ and S</u> if

PR1: All morphisms preserve the formulas in F, i.e., for each $p \in F$, $f : A \to B \in \mathrm{Mor}\,\mathcal{C}$ and $k : V \to A'$, if $A \models p[k]$ then $B \models p[k \cdot f']$.

PR2: The formulas in F determine the morphisms, i.e., given $R \subseteq V$ and $V \begin{array}{l} \xrightarrow{k} A' \\ \xrightarrow[\ell]{} B' \end{array}$ such that $k \upharpoonright R$ is bijective and for each $p \in F$ with $\mathrm{Var}\,p \subseteq R$ $A \models p[k]$ implies $B \models p[\ell]$, then <u>there is a morphism $f : A \to B$</u> such that $(k \cdot f') \upharpoonright R = \ell \upharpoonright R$.

PR3(S): The morphisms in S reflect the formulas in F, i.e., for any $f : A \to B \in S$, any $p \in F$ and $k : V \to A'$, if $B \models p[k \cdot f']$, then $A \models p[k]$.

PR4: Direct products preserve the formulas in F, i.e., for any direct product $\prod_{i \in I} A_i$, if $k : V \to \left(\prod_{i \in I} A_i\right)'$, $p \in F$ and for each $i \in I$ $A_i \models p[k \cdot \pi_i']$, then $\prod_{i \in I} A_i \models p[k]$.

PR5($\mathcal{H}$): F is large enough to make the $\mathcal{H}$-homomorphism Theorem hold, i.e., given $A \begin{array}{l} \xrightarrow{f \in \mathcal{H}} B \\ \xrightarrow[g]{} C \end{array}$ and $k : V \to A'$ and $R \subseteq V$ such that $k \upharpoonright R$ is bijective and if for each $p \in F$ with $\mathrm{Var}\,p \subseteq R$ $B \models p[k \cdot f']$ implies $C \models p[k \cdot g']$, then there is an $h : B \to C$ with $f \cdot h = g$.

3.3. The F-diagram of an object.

Let $A \in |\mathcal{C}|$ and for each $a \in A'$ let $x_a \in V$ such that for each two $a \neq b$ in A, $x_a \neq x_b$. Let $k : V \to A'$ be such that for each $a \in A$ $k(x_a) = a$. Let $V_A := \{x_a \mid a \in A\}$. Suppose F is a set. The F-diagram of A is

$$\Delta^F_{A,k} := \wedge\{p \in F \mid A \models p[k] \text{ and } \operatorname{Var} p \subseteq V_A\}.$$

Lemma 1:

Let $F \subseteq L$ be a set satisfying PR1 and PR2. Then for any map $f : A' \to B'$ $B \models \Delta^F_{A,k}[k\cdot f]$ iff there is a $g : A \to B \in \operatorname{Mor} \mathcal{C}$ with $g' = f$.

Remark 2: Notice that the above lemma just restates in the generalized setting the universal algebraic fact that a map preserves the atomic diagram of an algebra iff it is a homomorphism.

Proof of Lemma 1:

(1) Suppose that there is a $g : A \to B \in \operatorname{Mor} \mathcal{C}$ with $g' = f$. Then $B \models \Delta^k_{A,F}[k\cdot f]$ by PR1.

(2) Suppose $B \models \Delta^k_{A,F}[k\cdot f]$. We have the following situation:

$V_A \subseteq V$ and $V \begin{array}{l} \xrightarrow{\ k\ } A' \\ \xrightarrow{\ k\cdot f\ } B' \end{array}$ and $k \restriction V_A$ is bijective by the definition of V_A and for each $p \in F$ with $\operatorname{Var} p \subseteq V_A$ $A \models p[k]$ implies $B \models p[k\cdot f]$. Then by PR2 there is a $g : A \to B \in \operatorname{Mor} \mathcal{C}$ such that $(k\cdot g') \restriction V_A = (k\cdot f) \restriction V_A$. But k being surjective this implies $g' = f$. ∎

3.4. The Implementation.

Now we are ready to represent S-identities, i.e., the morphisms of $\mathcal{E}$, and injectivity in our language.

Proposition 2: (The morphisms of $\mathcal{E}$ are implications and injectivity is validity).

Let $\mathcal{E}, S \subseteq \operatorname{Mor} \mathcal{C}$, suppose that $\mathcal{C}$ has products, is $\mathcal{E}$-cowellpowered and that $\langle \mathcal{E}, S\rangle$ is a factorization system in $\mathcal{C}$. Further let $F \subseteq L$ be a set satisfying the primitive conditions w.r.t. $\mathcal{E}$ and S. Then

(i) to each $e : A \to B \in \mathcal{E}$ there is a set $I = \{(\Delta^F_{A,k} \to p) \mid p \in F' \subseteq F$ and $\operatorname{Var} p \subseteq V_A\}$ of implications such that for any $C \in |\mathcal{C}|$

$$C \models (\wedge I) \text{ iff } C \in \operatorname{Inj} e, \text{ and}$$

(ii) to each implication $i = (\Delta^F_{A,k} \to p)$ with $A \in |\mathcal{C}|$ and $p \in F$ such that $\operatorname{Var} p \subseteq V_A$, there is an $e : A \to B \in \mathcal{E}$ such that for any $C \in |\mathfrak{C}|$

$C \models i$ iff $C \in \mathrm{Inj}\ e$.

Proof:

(i) Let $e : A \to B \in \aleph$. We define

$I := \{(\Delta^F_{A,k} \to p) \mid p \in F,\ \mathrm{Var}\ p \subseteq V_A,\ B \models p[k\cdot e']\}$.

We want to prove $C \models (\wedge I)$ iff $C \in \mathrm{Inj}\ e$ for every $C \in |\mathfrak{C}|$.

(ia) Suppose $C \models (\wedge I)$ and let $f : A \to C$:

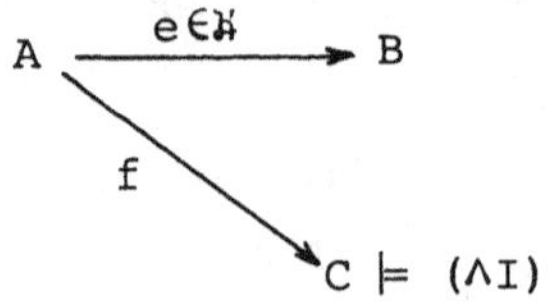

Since $C \models (\wedge I)[k\cdot f']$ and by Lemma 1 also $C \models \Delta^F_{A,k}[k\cdot f']$, $C \models p[k\cdot f']$ holds for every $p \in F$ such that $\mathrm{Var}\ p \subseteq V_A$ and $B \models p[k\cdot e']$. Applying now PR5($\aleph$) we obtain that there is a $g : B \to C$ such that $f = e\cdot g$.

(ib) Let $C \in \mathrm{Inj}\ e$ and suppose that $C \models \Delta^F_{A,k}[\ell]$ for an $\ell : V \to C'$. Let $f : A' \to C'$ be defined by $f(a) := \ell(x_a)$ for each $a \in A'$. Then f is a map and $\ell = k\cdot f$ and $C \models \Delta^F_{A,k}[k\cdot f]$. By Lemma 1 there is a $g : A \to C$ with $g' = f$.

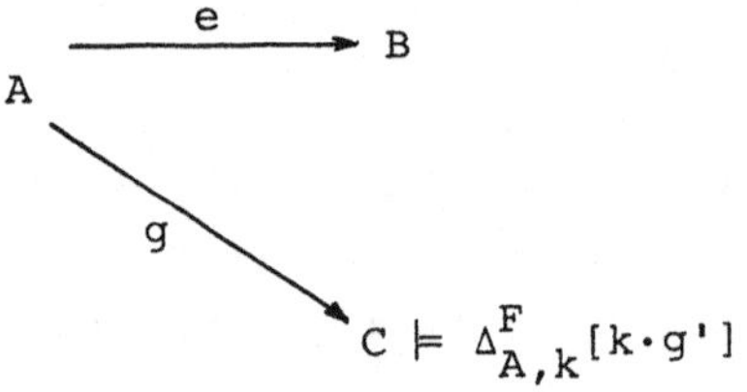

Since $C \in \mathrm{Inj}\ e$, there is an $h : B \to C$ with $e\cdot h = g$. Let $p \in F$ such that $\mathrm{Var}\ p \subseteq V_A$ and $B \models p[k\cdot e']$. By PR1 then $C \models p[k\cdot e'\cdot h']$, but $k\cdot e'\cdot h' = k\cdot g' = \ell$, so $C \models p[\ell]$. This proves $C \models (\wedge I)\,[\ell]$ for any $\ell : V \to C'$.

(ii) Let $i = (\Delta^F_{A,k} \to p)$ for some $A \in |\mathfrak{C}|$ and $p \in F$ with $\mathrm{Var}\ p \subseteq V_A$. Let $\mathfrak{G} := \{B \in |\mathfrak{C}| \mid B \models i\}$. Let $e := \mathrm{fr}^{\aleph}_A \mathfrak{G}$. By Proposition 2 of part 2, $\mathrm{fr}^{\aleph}_A \mathfrak{G}$ exists. We have to prove $C \models i$ iff $C \in \mathrm{Inj}\ e$ for each $C \in |\mathfrak{C}|$

(iia) If $C \models i$ then $C \in \mathfrak{G}$ and then $C \in \mathrm{Inj}\ \mathrm{fr}^{\aleph}_A \mathfrak{G}$.

(iib) Let $C \in \mathrm{Inj}\ e$. The proof is very similar to (ib). Suppose $\ell : V \to C'$ and $C \models \Delta^F_{A,k}[\ell]$. Define $f : A \to C$ by $f(a) = \ell(x_a)$ for each $a \in A'$. Then $\ell = k\cdot f$ and by Lemma 1 there is a $g : A \to C$ with $g' = f$. Then $C \in \mathrm{Inj}\ e$ implies the existence of an $h : \mathrm{Fr}^{\aleph}_A \mathfrak{G} \to C$ such that $e\cdot h = g$. Now we will prove $\underline{\mathrm{Fr}^{\aleph}_A \mathfrak{G} \models p[k\cdot e']}$. $\mathrm{Fr}^{\aleph}_A \mathfrak{G} \in \mathbb{S}\,\mathbb{P}\,\mathfrak{G}$ implies the following situation:

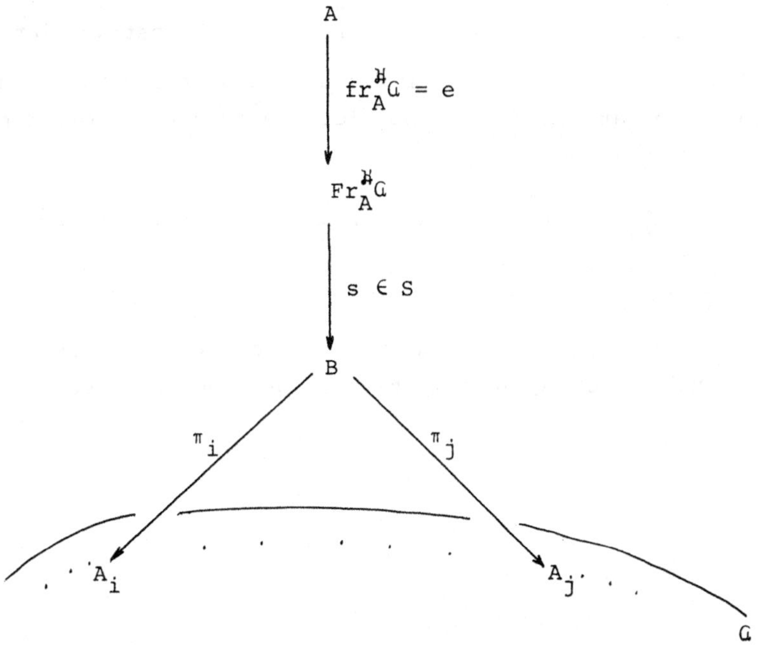

By Lemma 1 for each $i \in I$ $A_i \models \Delta^F_{A,k}[k\cdot(fr_A^{\aleph}\mathcal{G}\cdot s\cdot\pi_i)']$. But for each $i \in I$ $A_i \models i$, so for each $i \in I$ $A_i \models p[k\cdot fr_A^{\aleph}\mathcal{G}\cdot s\cdot\pi_i)']$. By PR3(S) and PR4 then $Fr_A^{\aleph}\mathcal{G} \models p[k\cdot e']$. By PR1 then $C \models p[k\cdot e'\cdot h']$, i.e., $C \models p[\ell]$. This proves $C \models i[\ell]$ for any $\ell : V \to A'$. ■

<u>Remarks 3</u>:

1. Notice that the above proposition just generalizes the universal algebraic fact that there is a one-to-one correspondence between the satisfaction of implication $P \to C$ ($P, C \subseteq F^2$ for some free algebra F) and the injectivity w.r.t surjective (= $\aleph$) homomorphisms — cf. condition (IMP) and (INJ) of part 1.
2. Notice that part (iib) of the above proof also proves the following

<u>Proposition 3</u>: ("Read-from" Theorem — cf. Adamek-Nelson-Reiterman [2])

Under the conditions of Proposition 2 for any $\mathcal{G} \subseteq |\mathcal{C}|$, $A \in |\mathcal{C}|$ and $p \in F$ with $\mathrm{Var}\, p \subseteq V_A$,

$$\mathcal{G} \models (\Delta^F_{A,k} \to p) \text{ iff } Fr_A^{\aleph}\mathcal{G} \models [k\cdot(fr_A^{\aleph}\mathcal{G})'].$$

Corollary 4: (generalized Birkhoff Theorem for our abstract language $\mathcal{L}$)

Let $H, \mathcal{K}, S \subseteq \text{Mor}\ \mathbb{C}$ and $F \subseteq L$ be such that the conditions of Proposition 2 are satisfied. Further let the conditions of Proposition 3 of part 2 also be satisfied.

Define $I_{HS} := \{(\Delta^F_{A,k} \to p) \mid A \in Pj(H),\ p \in F$ and $\text{Var}\ p \subseteq V_A\}$.
Then $\underline{\text{Md}\ I_{HS}(\mathbb{G}) = HS\,\mathbb{P}\,\mathbb{G}}$ for any $\mathbb{G} \subseteq |\mathbb{C}|$.

Now, given any concrete category $\mathbb{C}$, in order to obtain the generalized Birkhoff Theorem, we only have to provide the needed "ingredients".

4. Application to ω-continuous algebras.

4.1. The category:

Henceforth $\mathcal{C} = \bot\,\mathrm{Alg}_\Sigma(\omega)$ for some arbitrary but fixed signature Σ.

A signature (or type) Σ is a set of operation symbols. Also given is a map $r : \Sigma \to \mathrm{Ord}$, which to each $\sigma \in \Sigma$ assigns an ordinal $r(\sigma)$, its arity. The objects of $\bot\,\mathrm{Alg}_\Sigma(\omega)$ are ω-continuous Σ-algebras. To define the ω-continuous algebras we need some more definitions.

A poset A is ω-complete if

(i) it has a least element $\bot_A$

(ii) every countable chain (ω-chain) $(a_n)_{n\in\omega}$ in A has a l.u.b. $\sup_{\leq_A}(a_n)_{n\in\omega}$ in A.

Given two ω-complete posets A and B, a map $f : A \to B$ is ω-continuous of

(i) $f(\bot_A) = \bot_B$ and

(ii) f preserves l.u.b.s of ω-chains, i.e., if $(a_n)_{n\in\omega}$ is an ω-chain in A, then $\sup_{\leq_B}(f(a_n))_{n\in\omega}$ exists and equals $f(\sup_{\leq_A}(a_n)_{n\in\omega})$.

Remark 1: ω-continuous maps are monotone: let $(a_n)_{n\in\omega}$ above be of length 2.

An algebra of type Σ (a Σ-algebra) A is an ω-continuous Σ-algebra if it is endowed with a partial order w.r.t. which it forms an ω-complete poset and all operations are ω-continuous.

The morphisms of $\bot\,\mathrm{Alg}_\Sigma(\omega)$ are the ω-continuous, $\bot$-preserving homomorphisms.

4.2. A choice of subalgebra concept and of a language.

There are many classes of monos in $\bot\,\mathrm{Alg}_\Sigma(\omega)$, each of which gives rise to another notion of subalgebra: the class of all monos, the class of extremal monos, the class of full monos, the class of those monos which are extremal in $\bot\,\mathrm{POS}(\omega)$ — the category of ω-complete posets, etc.

Although each of them has a factorization pair $\aleph$, we will choose S to be the class of the full monos. An $f : A \to B \in \mathrm{Mor}\,\bot\,\mathrm{Alg}_\Sigma(\omega)$ is a full mono if $f(a) \leq_B f(b)$ iff $a \leq_A b$ for all $a,b \in A$. Thus, given an ω-continuous Σ-algebra A, its full subalgebras are the subalgebras B which are closed under formation of l.u.b.s of ω-chains in A, endowed with $\leq_A \cap B^2$.

Remark 2: While there exists no structural characterization of the extremal monos in $\perp \mathrm{Alg}_\Sigma(\omega)$, those monos which are extremal in $\perp \mathrm{POS}(\omega)$ seem to require primitive formulas which are purely second order.

Let $A \in |\perp \mathrm{Alg}_\Sigma(\omega)|$ and $X \subseteq A$. The dense closure of X in A, $\mathrm{cl}_A(X)$, is the least full subalgebra of A containing X. An ω-continuous homomorphism $f : A \to B$ is dense if $\mathrm{cl}_B(f(A)) = B$.

Notice that dense ω-continuous homomorphisms are epis.

Let $\mathcal{H}$ be the class of all dense ω-continuous homomorphisms.

Proposition 1: $\langle \mathcal{H}, S\rangle$ is a factorization system in $\perp \mathrm{Alg}_\Sigma(\omega)$.

Proof: By Pasztor [31], $\perp \mathrm{Alg}_\Sigma(\omega)$ is a full (reflective) subcategory of $\mathrm{Palg}_{\Sigma'}$, the category of all partial Σ'-algebras, where $\Sigma' = \Sigma \dot\cup \{\sqcup, +, \perp\}$ with $r(\sqcup) = \omega$, $r(+) = 2$, $r(\perp) = 0$. It is easy to see that $\mathcal{H}$ is the class of all epis of $\mathrm{Palg}_{\Sigma'}$ which are in $\perp \mathrm{Alg}_\Sigma(\omega)$ and similarly, S is the class of all strong monos which belong to $\perp \mathrm{Alg}_\Sigma(\omega)$. Since in $\mathrm{Palg}_{\Sigma'}$ $\langle$Epi, Strong mono$\rangle$ is a factorization system, $\langle \mathcal{H}, S\rangle$ is a factorization system in $\perp \mathrm{Alg}_\Sigma(\omega)$. ■

For any signature Σ let $\Sigma' := \Sigma \dot\cup \{\sqcup, \perp\}$ with $r(\sqcup) = \omega$ and $r(\perp) = 0$.

$T_{\Sigma,\omega}$ denotes the class of all ("classical") terms of signature Σ' with variables in V.

Remarks 3: (1) Recall that $V = \mathrm{Ord}$, i.e., V is a class. Therefore $T_{\Sigma,\omega}$ is a class, rather than a set.

(2) If we wanted to apply the results to $\perp \mathrm{Alg}_\Sigma(Z)$ for an arbitrary subset system Z, rather than to $\perp \mathrm{Alg}_\Sigma(\omega)$, we would have to define $T_{\Sigma,\omega}$ in a manner analogous to Definition 3.2 of Adamek-Nelson-Reiterman [2], unless Z was bounded. Of course, we would apply all l.u.b.s and all operations in each step — see Remarks 5/(3).

Let $A \in |\perp \mathrm{Alg}_\Sigma(\omega)|$ and let $k : V \to A$ be an evaluation map. For any $\tau \in T_{\Sigma,\omega}$ we define $\tau^A[k]$ recursively. (cf. Adamek-Nelson-Reiterman [2] 3.4):

(i) if $\tau = x \in V$, then $\tau^A[k] := k(x)$.

(ii) Suppose $\tau = \sigma(\tau_i : i \in r(\sigma))$ for some $\sigma \in \Sigma$ and that for each $i \in r(\sigma)$ $\tau_i^A[k]$ is given.

(ii_i) If $\sigma = \perp$, then $\tau_i^A[k] = \perp_A$.

(ii_ii) If $\sigma \in \Sigma$, then

$$\tau^A[k] = \begin{cases} \sigma^A(\tau_i^A[k] : i \in r(\sigma)) & \text{if for all } i \in r(\sigma) \\ & \tau_i^A[k] \text{ is defined} \\ \text{undefined} & \text{else} \end{cases}$$

(ii_{iii}) If $\sigma = \sqcup$, then

$$\tau^A[k] = \begin{cases} \sup_{\leq_A}(\tau_i^A[k])_{i\in\omega} & \text{if } (\tau_i^A[k])_{i\in\omega} \text{ is an } \omega\text{-chain in } A \\ \text{undefined} & \text{else} \end{cases}$$

$\underline{A_{\Sigma,\omega}}$ is the class of all atomic formulas of the language $L_{\Sigma,\omega}$ to be defined.

A formula is <u>atomic</u> if it is of the form $\tau_1 = \tau_2$ or $\tau_1 \leq \tau_2$, where $\tau_1, \tau_2 \in T_{\Sigma,\omega}$.

Given $A \in |\bot\, Alg_\Sigma(\omega)|$ and $k: V \to A$, $\underline{A \models (\tau_1 \overset{(\leq)}{=} \tau_2)[k]}$ if both $\tau_1^A[k]$ and $\tau_2^A[k]$ are defined and $\tau_1^A[k] \overset{(\leq_A)}{=} \tau_2^A[k]$.

<u>Remark 4</u>: For every $\tau_1, \tau_2 \in T_{\Sigma,\omega}$, $(\tau_1 \leq \tau_2) \models\!\!\dashv (\tau = \tau)$, where $\tau = \sqcup(\tau^i)_{i\in\omega}$ and $\tau^1 = \tau_1$ and $\tau^j = \tau_2$ for every $j > 1$.

The class $F_{\Sigma,\omega}$ of all <u>formulas</u> of $L_{\Sigma,\omega}$ is now defined to be the smallest class satisfying.

(i) $A_{\Sigma,\omega} \subseteq F_{\Sigma,\omega}$

(ii) If $\phi \subseteq F_{\Sigma,\omega}$ is a <u>set</u>, then $(\wedge\phi), (\vee\phi) \in F_{\Sigma,\omega}$

(iii) If $\varphi, \psi \in F_{\Sigma,\omega}$, then $(\varphi \to \psi)$ and $\exists x\varphi \in F_{\Sigma,\omega}$ for all $x \in V$.

Given a formula φ and a map $k: V \to A$ for $A \in |\bot\, Alg_\Sigma(\omega)|$, $A \models \varphi[k]$ is defined in the usual way from the satisfaction of the atomic formulas occurring in φ. Notice that the axioms A1 - A5 determine these definitions anyhow. The same holds for the definition of $A \models \varphi$: by A3 $A \models \varphi$ iff $A \models \varphi[k]$ for every $k: V \to A$.

Notice that $Var\,\varphi \subseteq R \subseteq V$ iff R contains the <u>set</u> of all free variables of φ. Axiom A5 is obviously satisfied, given the fact that both Σ and the arities are sets.

4.3. <u>The primitive formulas</u>.

<u>Proposition 2</u>: $A_{\Sigma,\omega}$ satisfies the primitive conditions w.r.t. S and $\aleph$.

<u>Proof</u>: In view of Remark 4 it is enough to prove that $P := \{\tau_1 = \tau_2 \mid \tau_1, \tau_2 \in T_{\Sigma,\omega}\}$ satisfies the primitive conditions w.r.t. S and $\aleph$.

<u>(PR1)</u>: Let $f: A \to B \in Mor\ \bot Alg_\Sigma(\omega)$, $\tau_1 = \tau_2 \in P$ and $k: V \to A$ be given and suppose $A \models (\tau_1 = \tau_2)[k]$. Then $\tau_1^A[k] = \tau_2^A[k]$ and so $f(\tau_1^A[k]) = f(\tau_2^A[k])$. But f being an ω-continuous $\bot$-preserving homomorphism $\underline{f(\tau^A[k]) = \tau^B[k\cdot f]}$ for any $\tau \in T_{\Sigma,\omega}$, which is easily proved

by induction on τ. This proves $\tau_1^B[k\cdot f] = \tau_2^B[k\cdot f]$, i.e., $B \models (\tau_1 = \tau_2)[k\cdot f]$.

(PR 2): Let $R \subseteq V$ and let

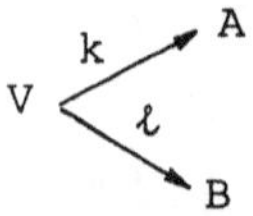

be such that $k \restriction R$ is bijective. Suppose that $A \models (\tau_1 = \tau_2)[k]$ implies $B \models (\tau_1 = \tau_2)[\ell]$ for all $(\tau_1 = \tau_2) \in P$ whose variables are in R. Let $f := (k \restriction R)^{-1}\cdot \ell$.

Claim 1: f is a $\perp$-preserving homomorphism.

Proof: Let $a = \perp_A$ in A. Then $A \models (x_a = \perp)[k]$, where $x_a := (k \restriction R)^{-1}(a)$. Then $B \models (x_a = \perp)[\ell]$, i.e., $\ell(x_a) = \perp_B$, but $\ell(x_a) = f(a) = f(\perp_A)$. So $f(\perp_A) = \perp_B$.

The proof for f to be a homomorphism is similar: let $\sigma \in \Sigma$ and $a = \sigma^A(\underline{a})$ in A. Let $x_a := (k \restriction R)^{-1}(a)$ and $x_{\underline{a}(i)} := (k \restriction R)^{-1}(\underline{a}(i))$ for every $i \in r(\sigma)$. Then $A \models (x_a = \sigma(x_{\underline{a}(i)} : i \in r(\sigma)))[k]$, so $B \models (x_a = \sigma(x_{\underline{a}(i)} : i \in r(\sigma)))[\ell]$, i.e., $f(a) = \ell(x_a) = \sigma^B(\ell(x_{\underline{a}(i)}) : i \in r(\sigma)) = \sigma^B(f\circ\underline{a})$. ■ Claim 1

Claim 2: f is ω-continuous.

Proof: Let $a = \sup_{\leq_A}(a_n)_{n\in\omega}$ in A and let again $x_a := (k \restriction R)^{-1}(a)$ and $x_{a_n} := (k \restriction R)^{-1}(a_n)$ for each $n \in \omega$. Then $A \models (x_a = \bigsqcup(x_{a_n})_{n\in\omega})[k]$, so $B \models (x_a = \bigsqcup(x_{a_n})_{n\in\omega})[\ell]$, therefore $f(a) = \ell(x_a) = \sup_{\leq_B}(\ell(x_{a_n}))_{n\in\omega} = \sup_{\leq_B}(f(a_n))_{n\in\omega}$, which was to be proved. ■ Claim 2

(PR 3(S)): Let $f: A \to B \in S$, $k: V \to A$ and suppose $B \models (\tau_1 = \tau_2)[k\cdot f]$ for some $\tau_1 = \tau_2 \in P$. Then $\tau_1^B[k\cdot f] = \tau_2^B[k\cdot f]$.

Lemma 3: For any $\tau \in T_{\Sigma,\omega}$ if $\tau^B[k\cdot f]$ is defined, then $\tau^A[k]$ is also defined and $\tau^B[k\cdot f] = f(\tau^A[k])$.

Proof: By induction on τ. If $\tau = x \in V$, then the statement is trivial.

Suppose $\tau = \sigma(\tau_i : i < r(\sigma))$ for some $\sigma \in \Sigma'$ and all τ_i's satisfy the lemma. Suppose $\tau^B[k\cdot f]$ is defined. Then

(i) if $\sigma = \perp$, then $\tau^B[k\cdot f] = \perp_B = f(\perp_A) = f(\tau^A[k])$.

(ii) if $\sigma \in \Sigma$, then $\tau^B[k\cdot f] = \sigma^B(\tau_i^B[k\cdot f] : i \in r(\sigma)) = \sigma^B(f(\tau_i^A[k]) : i \in r(\sigma)) = f(\sigma^A(\tau_i^A[k] : i \in r(\sigma))) = f(\tau^A[k])$ by the fact that all $\tau_i^B[k\cdot f]$'s are defined, by the induction hypothesis and by f being a homomorphism, respectively.

(iii) if $\sigma = \sqcup$, then $\tau^B[k\cdot f] = \sup_{\leq_B}(\tau_i^B[k\cdot f])_{i\in\omega}$, where $(\tau_i^B[k\cdot f])_{i\in\omega}$ is an ω-chain in B. By the induction hypothesis $\tau_i^B[k\cdot f] = f(\tau_i^A[k])$ for every $i \in \omega$, so f being full $(\tau_i^A[k])_{i\in\omega}$ is an ω-chain in A. Therefore $\sup_{\leq_A}(\tau_i^A[k])_{i\in\omega} = \tau^A[k]$ must exist in A and since f is ω-continuous, $f(\sup_{\leq_A}(\tau_i^A[k])_{i\in\omega}) = f(\tau^A[k]) = \sup_{\leq_B}(f(\tau_i^A[k]))_{i\in\omega} = \tau^B[k\cdot f]$. ■

Lemma 3

By Lemma 3 $\tau_1^B[k\cdot f] = \tau_2^B[k\cdot f]$ implies $f(\tau_1^A[k]) = f(\tau_2^A[k])$, which implies $\tau_1^A[k] = \tau_2^A[k]$ since f is mono. So $A \models (\tau_1 = \tau_2)[k]$, which was to be proved.

(PR 4): Let $\langle A_i \rangle_{i\in I}$ be a family of ω-continuous Σ-algebras, let $k : V \to \prod_{i\in I} A_i =: A$ and suppose that $A_i \models (\tau_1 = \tau_2)[k\cdot\pi_i]$ for each $i \in I$.

Proof: By induction on τ. If $\tau = x \in V$ the statement is obvious, since $k(x) = (\pi_i(k(x)) : i \in I)$.

Let $\tau = \sigma(\tau_i : i \in r(\sigma))$ and suppose that all τ_i's satisfy the lemma. Then

(i) for $\sigma = \perp$, $\tau^A[k] = \perp_A = (\perp_{A_i} : i \in I) = (\tau^{A_i}[k\cdot\pi_i] : i \in I)$.

(ii) for $\sigma \in \Sigma$, $\tau^A[k]$ is defined iff $\sigma^A(\tau_i^A[k] : i \in r(\sigma))$ is defined iff (by induction hypothesis) $\sigma^{A_j}(\tau_i^{A_j}[k\cdot\pi_j] : i \in r(\sigma))$ is defined for every $j \in I$ iff $\tau^{A_j}[k\cdot\pi_j]$ is defined for every $j \in I$, and then $\tau^A[k] = (\tau^{A_j}[k\cdot\pi_j] : j \in I)$.

(iii) for $\sigma = \sqcup$ $\tau^A[k]$ is defined iff $\sup_{\leq_A}(\tau_i^A[k])_{i\in\omega}$ is defined iff $(\tau_i^A[k])_{i\in\omega}$ is an ω-chain in A iff $(\tau_i^{A_j}[k\cdot\pi_j])_{i\in\omega}$ is an ω-chain in A_j $(j \in I)$ (by the induction hypothesis and by the definition of $\leq_A$) iff $\sup_{\leq_{A_j}}(\tau_i^{A_j}[k\cdot\pi_j])_{i\in\omega}$ exists in A_j $(j \in I)$ iff $\tau^{A_j}[k\cdot\pi_j]$ exists in A_j $(j \in I)$, and then $\tau^A[k] = (\tau^{A_j}[k\cdot\pi_j] : j \in I)$ by the definition of $\sqcup^A$. ■

Lemma 4

By Lemma 4 $A_i \models (\tau_1 = \tau_2)[k\cdot\pi_i]$ $(i \in I)$ implies that $\tau_1^A[k]$ and $\tau_2^A[k]$ are defined and that $\pi_i(\tau_1^A[k]) = \pi_i(\tau_2^A[k])$ for every $i \in I$. The source $\langle \pi_i : i \in I \rangle$ being monic, $\tau_1^A[k] = \tau_2^A[k]$, so $A \models (\tau_1 = \tau_2)[k]$.

(PR 5(ℵ)): Let $k \subseteq V$ and $A \xrightarrow{f \in \aleph} B$, $A \xrightarrow{g} C$ be given and suppose that $k : V \to A$ is such that $k \restriction R$ is bijective. Also suppose that $B \models (\tau_1 = \tau_2)[k \cdot f]$ implies $C \models (\tau_1 = \tau_2)[k \cdot g]$ for all $\tau_1 = \tau_2 \in P$ whose variables are in R. We need to prove the existence of an $h : B \to C$ such that $f \cdot h = g$.

Lemma 5: Let $k : V \to A \xrightarrow{f \in \aleph} B$ such that k is surjective. Then

$$B = \{\tau^B[k \cdot f] \mid \tau \in T_{\Sigma,\omega},\ \tau^B[k \cdot f] \text{ defined}\} (=: B').$$

Proof: By the definition of $\aleph$, B is its own least full subalgebra containing $f(A)$. We will prove that B' is a full subalgebra of B containing $f(A)$.

(1) $f(A) \subseteq B'$: let $f(a) \in f(A)$ and $\tau := x_a \in k^{-1}(a)$. Then $f(a) = \tau^B[k \cdot f] \in B'$.

(2) B' is a full subalgebra of B: let $\sigma \in \Sigma$ and $(\tau_i^B[k \cdot f] : i \in r(\sigma)) \in {}^{r(\sigma)}B'$. Then $\sigma^B(\tau_i^B[k \cdot f] : i \in r(\sigma)$ is defined and is equal to $(\sigma(\tau_i : i \in r(\sigma)))^B[k \cdot f] \in B'$. Let $(\tau_i^B[k \cdot f])_{i \in \omega} \in {}^{\omega}B$ be an ω-chain in B. Then $\sup(\tau_i^B[k \cdot f])_{i \in \omega}$ exists and is equal to $(\bigsqcup!(\tau_i)_{i \in \omega})^B[k \cdot f] \in B'$. $\leq_B$

∎

By these we proved $B = B'$. Lemma 5

Now let $h : B \to C$ be defined by $h(\tau^B[k \cdot f]) := \tau^C[k \cdot g]$ for all $\tau \in T_{\Sigma,\omega}$ for which $\tau^B[k \cdot f]$ is defined.

(1) h is a map: suppose $\tau_1^B[k \cdot f] = \tau_2^B[k \cdot f]$ in B; then $B \models (\tau_1 = \tau_2)[k \cdot f]$ and so $C \models (\tau_1 = \tau_2)[k \cdot g]$, i.e., $h(\tau_1^B[k \cdot f]) = \tau_1^C[k \cdot g] = \tau_2^C[k \cdot g] = h(\tau_2^B[k \cdot f])$. (Notice that this includes the case $\tau_1 = \tau_2$, too.)

(2) h is a $\perp$-preserving ω-continuous homomorphism: $h(\perp_B) = h(\perp^B[k \cdot f]) = \perp^C[k \cdot g] = \perp_C$. For any $\sigma \in \Sigma$, if $(\tau_i^B[k \cdot f] : i \in r(\sigma)) \in {}^{r(\sigma)}B$ then $h(\sigma^B(\tau_i^B[k \cdot f] : i \in r(\sigma))) = \sigma^C(\tau_i^C[k \cdot g] : i \in r(\sigma))) = \sigma^C(h(\tau_i^B[k \cdot f]) : i \in r(\sigma))$. Let $(\tau_i^B[k \cdot f])_{i \in \omega}$ be an ω-chain in B. Then $h(\sup_{\leq_B}(\tau_i^B[k \cdot f])_{i \in \omega}) = (\bigsqcup(\tau_i)_{i \in \omega})^C[k \cdot g] = \sup_{\leq_C}(\tau_i^C[k \cdot g])_{i \in \omega} = \sup_{\leq_C}(h(\tau_i^B[k \cdot f]))_{i \in \omega}$.

Also $f \cdot h = g$ holds, since for any $a \in A$, $h(f(a)) = h(x_a^B[k \cdot f]) = x_a^C[k \cdot g] = g(k(x_a)) = g(a)$, where $x_a \in k^{-1}(a)$. This proves PR 5(ℵ).

∎

Proposition 2

Remarks 5:

1. It might seem to the reader that the choice of the language, or more precisely the choice of $T_{\Sigma,\omega}$ is quite ad hoc. But, roughly speaking, $T_{\Sigma,\omega}$ consists of those expressions whose existence is reflected by morphisms in S. Also, the primitive formulas are formulas which are reflected by the morphisms of S. The reason for having been able to prove Proposition 2 for P is that monotonicity is implied by ω-continuity. (For this cf. Adamek-Nelson-Reiterman [2] 0.3 and 3.7.)
2. If we wanted to apply the results of the previous parts to $\perp Alg_{\Sigma}(Z)$ for an arbitrary subset system Z, we would have to define S according to Adamek-Nelson-Reiterman [2] 2.2.
3. Notice that it is in fact PR 5($\mathcal{H}$) which tells us which kind of terms we have to use for the primitive formulas. (Recall that $\langle \mathcal{H}, S\rangle$ is a factorization system, in fact S is exactly the class of those morphisms which reflect the morphisms of $\mathcal{H}$ considered as identities.)

Recalling Lemma 5, it says that for every $f : A \to B \in \mathcal{H}$, $B = \{\tau^B[k\cdot f] \mid \tau \in T_{\Sigma,\omega}, \tau^B[k\cdot f] \text{ defined}\}$. In fact we can do better.

Let $B_1 := f(A)$ and for every $n \in \omega$ let $B_{n+1} := \{\sup\limits_{\leq_B}(a_n)_{n\in\omega} :$ $(a_n)_{n\in\omega}$ is an ω-chain in $B_n\}$. It is easy to see that for every $n \in \omega$ B_n is a subalgebra of B, i.e., B_n is closed under the operations.

Let $B_\omega := \bigcup\limits_{n\in\omega} B_n$. One can easily check, that for <u>finitary</u> Σ B_ω <u>is</u> again a subalgebra of B (cf. Adamek-Nelson-Reiterman [2], Definition 3.2) while for <u>infinitary</u> Σ <u>not</u>. This leads to

<u>Lemma 6</u>: Let $f : A \to B \in \mathcal{H}$. Define $B_1 := f(A)$; for each $i \in \text{Ord}$

(i) if i is a successor ordinal then

(i_i) $B_i = \{\sup\limits_{\leq_B}(a_n)_{n\in\omega} \mid (a_n)_{n\in\omega}$ is an ω-chain in $B_{i-1}\}$ if $i-1$ is a successor ordinal, too, and

(i_{ii}) $B_i = B_{i-1} \cup \{\sigma^B(a_j : j \in r(\sigma)) \mid \sigma \in \Sigma$ and $(a_j : j \in r(\sigma)) \in {}^{r(\sigma)}B_{i-1}\}$, else

(ii) if i is a limit ordinal, then $B_i = \bigcup\limits_{j<i} B_j$. Then $B = \bigcup\limits_{i\in\sigma(\Sigma,\omega)} B_i$, where $\sigma(\Sigma,\omega) = \max\{\omega_1, \text{ordinal dimension of } \Sigma\}$. ∎

As a consequence we can define $T_1 := T_\Sigma(V)$ the class of all ("classical") terms of type Σ with variables in V. For $i > 1$

(i) $T_i = \{\bigsqcup(a_n)_{n\in\omega} \mid (a_n)_{n\in\omega} \in {}^{\omega}T_{i-1}\}$ if $i-1$ is also a successor ordinal

(i_{ii}) $T_i = T_{i-1} \cup \{\sigma(a_j : j \in r(\sigma)) \mid \sigma \in \Sigma$ and $(a_j : j \in r(\sigma)) \in {}^{r(\sigma)}T_{i-1}\}$, else

(ii) for i being a limit ordinal, $T_i = \bigcup\limits_{j<i} T_j$.

Let $T^S_{\Sigma,\omega} := \bigcup_{i \in \sigma(\Sigma,\omega)} T_i$.

Now it is easy to check that the class $\{\tau_1 = \tau_2 \mid \tau_1, \tau_2 \in T^S_{\Sigma,\omega}\}$ satisfies the primitive conditions w.r.t. S and $\mathcal{H}$. (Obviously, the definition of satisfaction remains unchanged.)

4. If we choose S to be the class of all monos (and hence $\mathcal{H}$ to be the class of all strong epis), then the class $\{\tau_1 = \tau_2 \mid \tau_1$ and τ_2 are "classical" terms of type Σ (rather than Σ')$\}$ satisfies the primitive conditions w.r.t. these $\mathcal{H}$ and S.

We need one more result concerning $\mathcal{H}$.

Proposition 7: $\perp\mathrm{Alg}_\Sigma(\omega)$ is $\mathcal{H}$-cowellpowered.

Proof: By Pasztor [31] $\perp\mathrm{Alg}_\Sigma(\omega)$ is a variety of $\mathrm{Palg}_{\Sigma'}$ (see the proof of Proposition 1), and $\mathcal{H}$ is the class of those morphisms which are epis in $\mathrm{Palg}_{\Sigma'}$. But $\mathrm{Palg}_{\Sigma'}$ is cowellpowered, which proves the statement. ∎

4.4. The choice of H. The H-projectives.

Recalling the results of Parts 2 and 3, we can see that having fixed S and the primitive formulas implies having fixed the possible conclusions of the HS-identities, namely formulas $\tau_1 \leq \tau_2$ for $\tau_1, \tau_2 \in T_{\Sigma,\omega}$. (Note that $(\tau_1 = \tau_2) \models\!\dashv (\tau_1 \leq \tau_2 \wedge \tau_2 \leq \tau_1)$.)

The premises of the HS-identities are the atomic diagrams of H-projectives, so they depend on the choice of H.

Again, we have more than one possibility to choose H: the class of all surjective morphisms, the class of all strong and surjective morphisms, the class of all isomorphisms, etc. Surjective morphisms and isomorphisms are the two extremes: the surjective-projectives are exactly the free ω-continuous Σ-algebras over "flatly" ordered sets, so nothing nontrivial is true about them, which means that the HS-identities in this case have empty premises (cf., e.g., the variety concept of Adamek-Nelson-Reiterman [2]); on the other hand the isomorphism-projectives are all ω-continuous Σ-algebras, so they lead to (H)S-identities whose premises are of the form $\bigwedge_{i \in I} \tau_i \leq \tau'_i$ for $\tau_i, \tau'_i \in T_{\Sigma,\omega} (i \in I)$ (cf. the quasivariety concept of Adamek-Nelson-Reiterman [2]).

For the present application I choose H to be the class of all strong surjections. An $f: A \to B \in \mathrm{Mor}\ \perp\mathrm{Alg}_\Sigma(\omega)$ is a strong surjection if for any $a, b \in B$ $a \leq_B b$ implies $a' \leq_A b'$ for some $a' \in f^{-1}(a)$ and $b' \in f^{-1}(b)$.

Contradicting Adamek-Nelson-Reiterman's [2] Remark 0.2, this H gives rise to a more general concept of HSP-class than the merely surjective morphisms. Besides, it has the "classical" property, that for any ω-continuous Σ-algebra A, any of its H-images is uniquely determined by a congruence relation on A.

Lemma 8: Let $f : A \to B \in H$ factorize as $g \cdot h$. Then $h \in H$.

Proof: Easy exercise. ∎

Proposition 9 (the strong surjective-projectives):

The H-projective ω-continuous Σ-algebras are exactly the free ω-continuous Σ-algebras over posets X with the following property (*): for every $x \in X$ there is at most one $y \neq x$ such that $x \leq y$ or $y \leq x$, unless $x = \bot$ or $y = \bot$.

Proof: (1) Let $A \in Pj(H)$.

Lemma 10: To each $A \in |\bot\, Alg_{\Sigma}(\omega)|$ there is a poset Y with property (*), such that A is the H-image of $Fr_{\Sigma,\omega}(Y)$ - the free ω-continuous Σ-algebra over Y.

Proof: For every $a \in A$ let $A_a := \{a_{(b,c)} : (a=b \text{ or } a=c) \text{ and } b \leq_A c\}$. Let $Y := \bigcup_{a \in A} A_a$.

Define $\leq_Y := Id \cup \{(x,y) \mid x = a_{(a,b)} \text{ and } y = b_{(a,b)} \text{ for some } a,b \in A\} \cup \{(\bot_{(\bot,\bot)}, x \mid x \in Y\}$.

It is easy to see, that for every $a_{(b,c)} \in Y$ there is at most one $d_{(e,f)}$ (namely $c_{(a,c)}$ if $a = b$ and $b_{(b,a)}$ if $c = a$) such that $a_{(b,c)} \leq d_{(e,f)}$ or $d_{(e,f)} \leq a_{(b,c)}$, unless one of them is $\bot_{(\bot,\bot)}$. So Y has property (*). Let $f : Y \to A$ be defined by $f(a_{(b,c)}) = a$ for every $a \in A$. Obviously f is an ω-continuous and $\bot$-preserving surjective map and its unique extension $\hat{f} : Fr_{\Sigma,\omega}(Y) \to A \in H$. (See Nelson [28] or Adamek-Nelson-Reiterman [2] 3.3 for the construction of $Fr_{\Sigma,\omega}(Y)$.) ∎ Lemma 10

The above $\hat{f} : Fr_{\Sigma,\omega}(Y) \to A$ being in H and since $A \in Pj(H)$, there is a $g : A \to Fr_{\Sigma,\omega}(Y)$ with $g \cdot \hat{f} = 1_A$. Notice that g is a section. Let $X := \{a \in A \mid a \neq \sigma^A(\underline{a}) \text{ for any } \sigma \in \Sigma \text{ and } \underline{a} \in {}^{r(\sigma)}A\}$.

Certainly, $g(X) \subseteq Y$, because otherwise there is an $x \in X$ such such that $g(x) = \sigma^{Fr_{\Sigma,\omega}(Y)}(\underline{a})$ for some (unique) $\sigma \in \Sigma$ and $\underline{a} \in {}^{r(\sigma)}Fr_{\Sigma,\omega}(Y)$. But then $x = \hat{f}(g(x)) = \sigma^A(\hat{f} \circ \underline{a}) \notin X$. Also $\bot_A \in X$ since otherwise $\bot_A = \sigma^A(\underline{a})$ for some $\sigma \in \Sigma$ and $\underline{a} \in {}^{r(\sigma)}A$, and then $\bot_{Fr_{\Sigma,\omega}(Y)} = \sigma^{Fr_{\Sigma,\omega}(Y)}(g \circ \underline{a})$ which is not possible.

Claim: X generates A, i.e., A is the least full subalgebra of A containing X.

Proof: Recall from Nelson [28] that for every $y \in Fr_{\Sigma,\omega}(Y)$, either (i) $y = \tau^{Fr_{\Sigma,\omega}(Y)}[k]$ for a unique Σ-term τ and (up to variables not occurring in τ) unique $k : V \to Y$, or (ii) $y = \sup_{\leq Fr_{\Sigma,\omega}(Y)} (y|i)_{i \in \omega}$ (where $y|i$ is the restriction of y to all sequences (in m^*) of length $\leq i$), and for every $i \in \omega$ $y|i = \tau_i^{Fr_{\Sigma,\omega}(Y)}[k_i]$ for some unique Σ-term τ_i and (up to variables not occurring in τ_i) unique $k_i : V \to Y$. Let $y = g(a)$ for some $a \in A$. In case (i) we claim that $\hat{f}(k(x)) \in X$ for every x occurring in τ: Suppose $\hat{f}(k(x)) \notin X$ for some x occurring in τ. Then $k(x) \notin g(X)$ and $\hat{f}(k(x)) = \sigma^A(\underline{a})$ for some $\sigma \in \Sigma$ and $\underline{a} \in {}^{r(\sigma)}A$. Then $a = \hat{f}(g(a)) = \tau^A[k \cdot \hat{f}] = \tau_1^A[k_1]$, where $\tau_1 = \tau[x|\sigma(\underline{v})]$, i.e., τ_1 is obtained from τ by substituting every occurrence of x by $\sigma(\underline{v})$, (let $\underline{v}(i)$ $(i \in r(\sigma))$ not occur in τ) and for any $v \in V$

$$k_1(v) = \begin{cases} \hat{f}(k(v)) & \text{if } v \neq x \\ \underline{a}(i) & \text{if } v = \underline{v}(i) \end{cases}$$

Then $g(a) = \tau_1^{Fr_{\Sigma,\omega}(Y)}[k_1 \cdot g]$, which is not possible, since $\tau_1 \neq \tau$ (and k and $k_1 \cdot g$ are different on variables occurring in τ_1).

In case (ii) we also claim that $\hat{f}(k_i(x)) \in X$ for all $i \in \omega$ and all x occurring in τ_i: Suppose $\hat{f}(k_i(x)) \notin X$ for some $i \in \omega$ and some x occurring in τ_i. Then $k_i(x) \notin g(X)$. Let $u \in m^*$ be that sequence for which $(g(a)|i)(u) = k_i(x) (\notin g(X))$. Since $\bot_{Fr_{\Sigma,\omega}(Y)} \in g(X)$, this implies that $g(a)(u) \in Y(\setminus\{\bot_{Fr_{\Sigma,\omega}(Y)}\})$, since otherwise $g(a)(u) \in \Sigma$ and so $k_i(x) \not\leq g(a)(u)$. Since $\hat{f}(k_i(x)) \notin X$, $\hat{f}(k_i(x)) = \sigma^A(\underline{a})$ for some $\sigma \in \Sigma$ and $\underline{a} \in {}^{r(\sigma)}A$, and so $\hat{f}(g(a)|i) = \gamma^A[\ell]$, where $\gamma = \tau_i[x|\sigma(\underline{v})]$ ($(\underline{v})(i)$ does not occur in τ_i for any $i \in r(\sigma)$) and for every $v \in V$

$$\ell(v) = \begin{cases} \hat{f}(k_i(v)) & \text{if } v \neq x \\ \underline{a}(j) & \text{if } v = \underline{v}(j). \end{cases}$$

Then $a = \hat{f}(g(a)) = \sup_{\leq_A} (\alpha_j^A[m_j])_{j \in \omega}$, where for each $i \in \omega$

$$\alpha_j = \begin{cases} \tau_j & \text{if } j \neq 1 \\ \gamma & \text{else} \end{cases} \quad \text{and} \quad m_j = \begin{cases} k_j \cdot \hat{f} & \text{if } j \neq 1 \\ \ell. & \text{else.} \end{cases}$$

Then $g(a) = \sup_{\leq_{Fr_{\Sigma,\omega}(Y)}} (\alpha^{Fr_{\Sigma,\omega}(Y)}[m_j \cdot g])_{j\in\omega}$, which implies $g(a)(u) = \sigma \notin Y$ (since $(\gamma^{Fr_{\Sigma,\omega}(Y)}[\ell \cdot g])(u) = \sigma$). This obviously is a contradiction.

By these we have proved that either (i) $g(a) = \tau^{Fr_{\Sigma,\omega}(Y)}[k]$ for some Σ-term τ and $k : V \to Y$ such that $\hat{f}(k(x)) \in X$ for every x occurring in τ and then $a = \tau^A[k \cdot \hat{f}]$ and $k \cdot \hat{f} : V \to X$, or (ii) $g(a) = \sup_{\leq_{Fr_{\Sigma,\omega}(Y)}} (\tau_i^{Fr_{\Sigma,\omega}(Y)}[k_i])_{i\in\omega}$ for some Σ-terms τ_i and $k_i : V \to Y$ such that for all i and x occurring in τ_i $\hat{f}(k_i(x)) \in X$ and then $a = \sup_{\leq_A}(\tau_i^A[k_i \cdot \hat{f}])_{i\in\omega}$ and $k_i \cdot \hat{f} : V \to X$ for all $i \in \omega$. This then proves that X generates A. ■

Claim

Now g being a section, we can conclude that $A \cong Fr_{\Sigma,\omega} g(X)$.

(2). Let $A = Fr_{\Sigma,\omega}(X)$ for some X having property (*). Suppose we are given

$$\begin{array}{ccc} & & A \\ & & \downarrow f \\ C & \xrightarrow{g \in H} & B \end{array}$$

We define $h : X \to C$ as follows: $h(\bot_A) = \bot_C$ and for each $a \in X$ $(a \neq \bot_A)$ (i) $h \in g^{-1}(f(a))$ and (ii) if $b \neq \bot_A$ and $a \leq_A b$ of $b \leq_A a$, then $h(a) \leq_C h(b)$ or $h(b) \leq_C h(a)$, respectively.

Since for every $a \in X$ $(a \neq \bot_A)$ there is at most one such b and $g \in H$, such a map h exists. Then there is a unique $\hat{h} : A \to C$ with $\hat{h} \upharpoonright X = h$. Since $(\hat{h} \cdot g) \upharpoonright X = f \upharpoonright X$, $\hat{h} \cdot g = f$. This proves $A \in Pj(H)$. ■

Proposition 9

<u>Proposition 11</u>: $\bot Alg_\Sigma(\omega)$ has enough H-projectives.

<u>Proof</u>: By Lemma 10 and Proposition 9. ■

Let $A = Fr_{\Sigma,\omega}X \in Pj(H)$ and denote by Δ_A its atomic diagram. Suppose that $\leq_X = Id \,\dot{\cup}\, \{(x_i, y_i) : i \in I\} \,\dot{\cup}\, \{(\bot, x) : x \in X\}$. Let $\Delta_X := \wedge\{x_i \leq y_i : i \in I\}$. By Proposition 9 all x_i's and y_i's are pairwise distinct. Let $p \in A_{\Sigma,\omega}$. Then it is easy to see that any implication $\Delta_A \to p$ is equivalent to $\Delta_X \to p'$, where p' is obtained from p by replacing every variable $x_a \in V_A$ for which $a \notin X$ by a term τ with variables only in X for which $A \models (x_a = \tau)[k]$.

Summing up, we have obtained the following result:

Proposition 12 (A Birkhoff-type theorem for HS-varieties):

Any class $\mathfrak{A}$ of ω-continuous Σ-algebras is closed w.r.t. H-images, S-subobjects and products iff it is axiomatizable by implications of the form $\bigwedge_{i\in I} x_i \leq y_i \rightarrow \tau_1 \leq \tau_2$, where I is a set, all x_i's and y_i's are pairwise distinct and $\tau_1, \tau_2 \in T_{\Sigma,\omega}$.

4.5. Two examples.

1. Let Σ consist of two binary operations $+$ and $\cdot$. Let $\mathfrak{A}$ be defined by the following axioms:

$$x \cdot y \leq y$$
$$x \cdot y \leq x$$
$$y \leq x + y$$
$$x \leq x + y$$
$$(x+y) + z = x + (y+z)$$
$$(x \cdot y) \cdot z = x \cdot (y \cdot z)$$
$$x \leq y \rightarrow x \cdot y = x$$
$$x \leq y \rightarrow x + y = y.$$

Then $\mathfrak{A}$ is the class of those ω-continuous Σ-algebras A which are lattices w.r.t. $\leq_A$ and in which $+^A$ is the l.u.b. operation and $\cdot^A$ the g.l.b. operation.

2. Let Σ consist of one binary operation $\cdot$. Let $\mathfrak{A}$ be defined by $x \leq y \rightarrow \bigsqcup(x^n)_{n\in\omega} = \bigsqcup(y^n)_{n\in\omega}$. Notice that for every $A \in \mathfrak{A}$ and $a \in A$, $(a, a^2, a^3, \ldots)$ is an ω-chain and for $a \leq b$ $\sup_{\leq_A}(a^n)_{n\in\omega} = \sup_{\leq_A}(b^n)_{n\in\omega}$.

References

[1] J. Adamek, E. Nelson, J. Reiterman: "Tree Construction of Free Continuous Algebras", J. Comp. Syst. Sciences 24 (1982), 114-146.

[2] J. Adamek, E. Nelson, J. Reiterman: "The Birkhoff Variety Theorem for Continuous Algebras", Preprint, 1984.

[3] ADJ (= J.A. Goguen, J.W. Thatcher, E.G. Wagner, and J.B. Wright), "Some fundamentals of order-algebraic semantics", in Proc. Symp. Math. Found. of Comp. Sci., Gdansk, Poland, Sept. 1976, Springer-Verlag Lecture Notes in Computer Science (1976), 153-168.

[4] ADJ, "Initial algebra semantics and continuous theories", J. Assoc. Comput. Mach. 24 (1977), 68-95.

[5] ADJ, "Free Continuous Theories", IBM Res. Repart 6909, Yorktown Heights (1977).

[6] ADJ, "An initial algebra approach to the specification, correctness and implementation of abstract data types", Current Trends in Programming Methodology 3, Data Structuring, R.T. Yeh, ed., Prentice Hall (1977).

7] H. Andreka, P. Burmeister, I. Nemeti, "Quasivarieties of partial algebras - a unifying approach towards a two-valued model theory for partial algebras", to appear in Studia Sci. Math. Hungar.

8] H. Andreka, I. Nemeti, "Generalization of variety and quasivariety concept to partial algebras through category theory", preprint Math. Inst. Hungar. Acad. Sci. (1976), and Dissertationes Mathem. (Rozprawy Math.) 204, PWN-Polish Scientific Publishers, Warsaw (1982), 1-56.

9] H. Andreka, I. Nemeti, "A general axiomatizability theorem formulated in terms of cone-injective subcategories", Universal Algebra (Proc. Coll. Esthergom 77), Colloq. Math. Soc. J. Bolyai 29 (1981), 13-35.

0] H. Andreka, I. Nemeti:"Applications of universal algebra, model theory, and categories in computer science". (Survey and bibliography.) Parts I - III, Part I in CL & CL 13 (1979), 152-282. Part II in CL & CL 14 (1980), 7-20. Part III("Some universal algebraic and model theoretic results in computer science") in: Fundamentals of Computation Theory (Szeged 1981) Springer-Verlag, Lecture Notes in Computer Science 117 (1981), 16-23.

1] H. Andreka, I. Nemeti:"Injectivity in categories to represent all first order formulas". Demonstratio Mathematicae 12 (1979), 717-732.

2] H. Andreka, I. Nemeti:"Los lemma holds in every category". Studia Sci. Math. Hungar. 13 (1978), 361-376.

3] B. Banaschewski, H. Herrlich:"Subcategories defined by implications", Houston J. Math. 2 (1976), 149-171.

14] S.L. Bloom, "Varieties of ordered algebras", J. Comp. & Systems Sci. 13 (1976), 200-212.

15] P. Burmeister, "Partial algebras - survey of a unifying approach towards a two-valued model theory for partial algebras", Algebra Universalis 15 (1982), 306-358.

16] B. Courcelle, M. Nivat:"Algebraic families of interpretations", 17th IEEE Symp. FOCS (1976), 137-146.

17] J.H. Gallier, "n-Rational Algebras. Part I: Basic Properties and Free Algebras; Part II: Varieties and Logic of Inequalities", to appear in SIAM On Computing.

18] I. Guessarian,"Algebraic Semantics", Springer-Verlag, Lecture Notes in Computer Science 99 (1981).

19] I. Guessarian, "Survey on classes of interpretations and some of their applications", Laboratoire informatique theorique et programmation - Report 82-46, October, 1982.

20] H. Herrlich, G.E. Strecker,"Category Theory", Allyn and Bacon, Inc., Boston (1973).

21] B.H. Hien, I. Sain:"Elementary classes in the injective subcategories approach to abstract model theory". Preprint, Math. Inst. Hungar. Acad. Sci. 15 (1982).

[22] D. Lehmann, "On the algebra of order", J. Comp. Systems Sci. 21/1 (1980), 1-23.

[23] A.I. Mal'cev:"Algebraic Systems", Springer Verlag (1973).

[24] A.I. Mal'cev:"The Metamathematics of Algebraic Systems", North Holland (1971).

[25] J. Meseguer, "On order-complete universal algebra and enriched functorial semantics", Springer-Verlag, Lecture Notes in Computer Science 56 (1977), 294-301.

[26] J. Meseguer, "A Birkhoff-like theorem for algebraic classes of interpretations of program schemes", Springer-Verlag, Lecture Notes in Computer Science 107 (1981), 152-168.

[27] J. Meseguer:"Varieties of chain-complete algebras". J. Pure Appl. Algebra 19 (1980), 347-383.

[28] E. Nelson, "Free Z-continuous algebras", Springer-Verlag, Lecture Notes in Mathematics 871 (1981), 315-334.

[29] I. Nemeti, I. Sain, "Cone-implicational subcategories and some Birkhoff-type theorems", Universal Algebra (Proc. Coll. Esztergom 1977), Colloq. Math. Soc, J. Bolyai 29, North-Holland (1981), 535-578.

[30] I. Nemeti:"On notions of factorization systems and their applications to cone-injective subcategories". Periodica Math. Hungar. 13/3 (1982), 229-235.

[31] A. Pasztor, "Chain-continuous algebras - a variety of partial algebras", in Fundamenta Informatica vi/3-4 (1983), 275-288.

[32] I. Sain, B.H. Hien,"In which categories are first order axiomatizable hulls characterizable by ultra products". Cahiers Top. Geom. Diff. xxiv-2 (1983), 215-222.

[33] D. Scott, "Outline of a math. theory of computation", in Proc. 4th Ann. Princeton Conf. on Inf. Sci. & Systems (1969), 169-176.

ON DENOTATIONAL SEMANTICS

OF DATA BASES

Naphtali Rishe

Department of Computer Science
University of California
Santa Barbara, Ca 93106

ABSTRACT

A method of denotational formalization of data bases, of data base management systems, and of related structures is proposed, aiming to improve their understanding, specification and rigorous investigation. The method provides a uniform treatment of different information layers: from instantaneous data bases (the first layer), via schemata and integrity rules, to classes of data base models. It unifies in one mathematical notion the apparently different notions of the semantics of stored data, semantics of data base processes, conceptual semantics of data bases, integrity semantics of data bases and denotational semantics of languages. The unification is based on hierarchies of domains of continuous mappings between different representations of information (from "less semantic" representations into "more semantic" ones).

1. A Hierarchy of Information Levels

In this study of data bases the term ***information*** means somehow closed or complete knowledge — with respect to certain criteria that are informally described in this section. This term may be used in plural, *e.g.* "two instantaneous data bases may represent two informations."

In order to treat data base semantics, we have to distinguish between at least three levels of information related to a data base system. (These levels should not be confused with ANSI-SPARC layers — internal, conceptual, and external — which are in fact orthogonal to the classification described in this section.) The following is a preliminary discussion, not aiming yet to define formal semantics. Neither information representations nor their semantics are studied in this section.

It is customary to classify data base information according to levels of its descriptivity. Usually, three levels are distinguished. These three levels are:

1) *Inf*^{1}—the information represented by an instantaneous data base (one *Inf*^{1} object is the information represented by a whole instantaneous data base, *e.g.* a collection of tables).

2) *Inf*^{2}—the information about the common properties of *Inf*^{1} information which can be represented at any instant of time by a given data base (provided the properties and the purpose of the data base are kept constant). A part of an *Inf*^{2} information is represented by the schema of a data base.

   An *Inf*^{2} information can contain or impose certain laws on a data base, some of them are of the following types:

   - *integrity laws*—specifying principally what are the valid states of this data base;
   - *inference laws*—specifying how from information entered to the data base other information can be deduced (by the DBMS or elsewhere);
   - *laws of operations*—specifying what operations (including atomic, complex, queries, updates or whole processes, sessions, etc.) are permissible on the data base and what are their results depending on the states of the data base. A law of operations may be a consequence of the aforementioned laws.

   These laws and other parts of an *Inf*^{2} information can be accumulated in a data base schema, *exit routines*, basic application programs, etc.

3) *Inf*^{3}—the information describing all possible *Inf*^{2} informations which a data base can posses under a given DBMS. An *Inf*^{3} information can be considered as accumulated (at least partly) in the code of a DBMS.

   More important parts of an *Inf*^{3} are syntax and meaning of data base languages, including data manipulation languages (programming), a data definition language in which schemata and some laws are defined, a query language, etc.

Inf^2 level requires further discussion. A part of an *Inf*^{2} information can be represented by a schema of the data base according to a certain data base model, *e.g.* the Relational Model.

Example 1.1.

The following is a relational schema of a data base recording meetings between pairs of participants (having *Id*entification numbers, first names and surnames):

(*MEETINGS(Id1, Id2, Time*: integers), *PEOPLE(Id*: integer; *F-name, S-name*: strings))

Another part can be represented by an additional "semantic schema" (as it is called by some authors.)

Example 1.2.

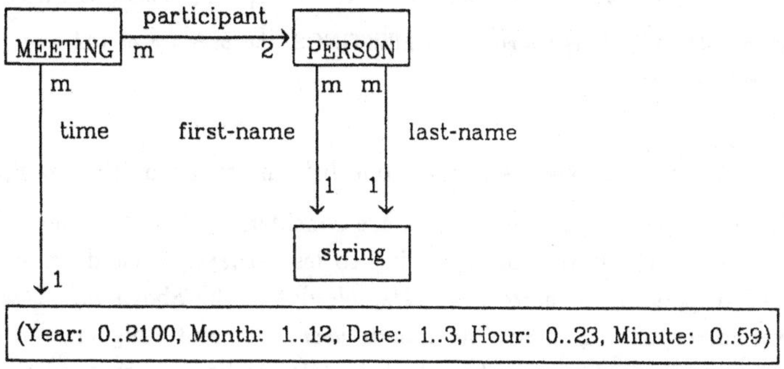

The part of information which is represented by a "semantic" schema is syntactically formalized in some data base systems. In other systems this is "just" known to the community of users of the data base.

Example 1.3.

An integrity law for the sample data base consists of two parts:

a) the part in responsibility of the DBMS, which should reject all the data base updates violating any of these constraints:

- *F-name* and *S-name* of PEOPLE depend functionally on *Id*;
- the integers and the strings obey implementational restrictions (width of fields, etc.);
- the instantaneous data base matches the schema.

b) though it is desirable to have the DBMS responsible for most of the constraints, the following constraints, which form a part of the integrity law, are left in most systems to a user's responsibility and are implemented by *exit routines*, by preprocessing, or by outside manual sorting of the input.

- every participant's *Id* in MEETINGS must be in PEOPLE;
- the representations of time are legal according to the pattern "yymmddhhmm";
- the projection of MEETINGS to the columns (*Id1, Id2*) is irreflexive.

Example 1.4.

An inference law for the sample database, which (the law) is not supported by an unsophisticated DBMS, but is supported by application software or is just understood by the user, can be represented by the following statement:

"if A met B at t then B met A at t too".

Example 1.5.

The following part of an update law would usually be in the responsibility of application software:

a) when (*id1*, *id2*, *t*) is deleted from MEETINGS, (*id2*, *id1*, *t*) must be deleted too;

b) when (*id1*, *id2*, *t*) is inserted into MEETINGS, the presence of *id1* and *id2* in PEOPLE must be verified.

The five examples given above are parts of one Inf^2 information of the sample data base.

For some purpose, more than three levels are considered. *E.g.*, the above Inf^1 level can be subdivided into two: the lower corresponding to less *general/stable* data in the data base and the higher corresponding to more *general/stable* data; the above Inf^2 level can be split into a lower level corresponding to *subschemata* or *user-views* and a higher level corresponding to schemata; the above Inf^3 level can be split into a lower level corresponding to versions of DBMS, an intermediate level corresponding to principal DBMS, and a higher level corresponding to principal models (such as hierarchic, network, relational, binary, etc.).

The user of the proposed approach shall identify all the levels and sublevels of interest and renumber them consecutively receiving a total of n levels. For many applications n=3. For the sake of generalization, in the following sections I assume that n levels must be considered.

For any k from 1 to $n-1$, any Inf^{k+1} *information* describes a whole range of Inf^k "*informations*". At the highest level n considered, only one specific *information* is of interest. Otherwise, the user should have identified a higher level of information (n+1), the only *information* of which is the list of all relevant *informations* of the Inf^n level.

2. Existing Meanings of the Term "DB Semantics" and Approaches to Its Formalization

The term "data base semantics" is widely used with different meanings. Among them: operational or denotational semantics of data base operations, logical constraints, information implication rules and user-world orientation of data base models.

Several meanings of the term "data base semantics" and approaches to its formalization are surveyed in the following:

[Earley-72] defines the semantics of a data structure as the "abstract properties it has with respect to access, possible change of structure, relationship between data items, etc."

Most authors, *e.g.* [Schmid-75], regard data base semantics as a system of constraints on information that can be stored in the data base.

[Cadiou-76] adds to this a collection of time-invariant properties of a data base.

[Weber-76] defines data semantics as a description of the information types, which should be represented in a data base for a certain purpose.

According to [Falkenberg-78], "the semantics of an application-specific universe of discourse is determined by the set of elementary facts and by the set of associated semantic rules. These semantic rules include type definitions, rules governing cardinalities, rules governing dependencies between sets, etc., and can be used for consistency checks or for deduction purposes."

Some aspects of data base semantics were formalized, at least partially,

- in [Weber-76], who defined a formal (non-semantical) model of constraints and assigned to it semantics in the Operational style;
- in [Biller-76], who defined denotational semantics of data base schemata, mapping them to sets of world states, and of a data base manipulation language, mapping its programs to pairs of world states;
- in [Bjorner-80], who defined mappings from data base operations and abstract states of the data base to its new states and output;
- in [Neuhold and Olnhoff -81], who mapped the commands of a relational data manipulation language to transitions between virtual states of external and conceptual data base and to transitions between physical states of an internal data base in ANSI-SPARC three-layer data base architecture;
- in [Zaniolo-84] and [Vassiliou-79], who formalized some aspects of null-values in relational data bases;
- in [Clifford and Warren - 83], who formalized the time scale in data bases.

Recently, standardization was attempted as to the formal semantics of data base operations for the relational (table-oriented) data base model: [Brodie and Schmidt-82], [Date-82], [Hardgrave-82].

In the proposed approach an attempt is made, *inter alia*, to unify the existing meanings of "data base semantics". DB semantics is viewed as transformations of some representations of information systems (inter alia instantaneous data bases, schemata, data base management systems, data base models) into other representations thereof which are chosen (for a given user in a given environment) to be more comprehensive, more self-explanatory, more explicit, and less dependent on implementation or on linguistical or representational conventions than the former representations.

In most cases an information system of a given high level in a hierarchy of information systems will be thus mapped to a mathematical object which explicitly shows:

- how such semantics is assigned to all relevant information systems of the lower levels;

- which of these systems are not integral (detectably erroneous by the manipulating software with respect to integrity constraints, or undetectably erroneous);
- how these lower-level systems are made more explicit (due to inference rules, etc.);
- and what is the denotational semantics of manipulation languages and processes applicable to representations of information systems of the lower level.

3. Some Objectives of Defining Formal Semantics of Data Bases and DBMS

The design of the proposed approach was guided by the objectives of defining formal denotational data base semantics which are discussed in this section:

1) To provide meaningful formal description of

   - DBMS and its DDL, DML, and QUERY languages;
   - the *schema* and the administrating software complex (including exit routines, etc.) of a data base;
   - the *subschema/user-view* and the software complex of an application;
   - instantaneous data bases;
   - etc. for other levels of data base information.

   a) Such an exact specification is needed by users when certain properties are only vaguely described in manuals.

   b) It is desirable for the implementor to get an exact specification of the properties that his software should possess. After the software is programmed, its correctness with respect to the specification can be proved by the methods of programming language semantics. This is true both for the programming of a DBMS and for programming in other levels: application, exit routines, etc.

   General Examples

   1. Such a description of a DBMS should specify *inter alia* the following:

      a) what are the supportable *instantaneous data bases* and what are their limitations with respect to the widths of the fields, number of relations, etc.;

      b) what are the supportable schemata;

      c) for every supportable schema what instantaneous data bases may exist under the schema;

      d) what application software is permitted;

e) what are the syntactically correct programs in the *Data Manipulation Language* (this DML is interpreted by the DBMS);

f) for every given schema, DML program and ***instantaneous data base***, will the program terminate, and if so what changes will it produce in the data base; what happens if several DML programs are run in parallel by several users;

g) as above for the *Data Definition Language* with respect to alterations in schemata;

h) as above for query languages, etc.

2. Such a description of an ***instantaneous data base*** can imply some properties of an ***instantaneous universe of discourse***, i.e. the relevant part of the real world at a given instant of time.

2) To study properties of constructions in different data base levels, and to have a formal basis to prove claims about these properties.

Example 3.1.

For the sample data base of the previous section we may wish to prove that there will never be one *Id* in two rows of the PEOPLE table. To prove this we need to know the semantics of the schema, *etc.* (an Inf^2) *or* the semantics of the DBMS (an Inf^3).

Example 3.2.

For the inference and integrity laws of examples of the previous section we may wish to prove that they are implementable by application software or that it does not matter what is done first: a deduction by the inference law and *then* a verification of the integrity, *or vice versa.*

3) To achieve a degree of automatization in constructing (or programming, generating, etc.) of

- an instantaneous data base (or a part thereof), when the meaning of the information which should be represented in it is given;
- a data base schema, a subschema and (maybe as a utopia) data base administrating and application software, according to a specification of the needed properties;
- (maybe as a utopia) DBMS, according to requirements from it;
- etc.

It is a long way to go from the proposals of this work to the realization of automatization, but the aim is to exploit existing and future techniques of automatic generation of programs and data structures starting from denotational specifications of these constructions or from their formalized properties which are equivalent to their full or non-full (non-deterministic) specifications.

4) To provide a means for verification of certain constructions (such as schemata, syntactic specifications or integrity laws, system parameters, etc.) against the needed properties of the behavior of a data base. Unlike par. (2) above, here we start with denotational descriptions and produce a syntactic construction which is proved then to be correct.

Example 3.3.

Given a set of the possible histories of meetings between persons of a given potential population, and

given a formal definition of what should happen if a new person or a new meeting is reported of if wrong data (loaded earlier by mistake) is corrected, and (maybe) should the meeting or the person's data be reflected in the data base,

a schema can be produced, with its denotational semantics found and proved to match or to be equal to the definition of the needs or to imply that definition.

This can also be used to prove the equivalence of constructions with respect to certain criteria of their behavior or reflection of the real world. Such a proof is needed *e.g.* if the construction is technically refined or if representations need be translated from one model, *e.g. relational*, to another, *e.g. network*.

Example 3.4.

The relational schema
MEETINGS [*Id1, Id2, Time*: integers;
F-name-1, S-name-1, F-name-2, S-name-2: strings]
plus the integrity constraint:
F-name-1 and *S-name-1* functionally depend on *Id1*
F-name-2 and *S-name-2* functionally depend on *Id2*
is equivalent to the schema
(*MEETINGS(Id1, Id2, Time*: integers), *PEOPLE(Id*: integer;
F-name, S-name: strings))
plus the integrity constraint:
F-name and *S-name* functionally depend on *Id*
provided the DBMS permits "*unknown*" values in fields.

Example 3.5.

The schemata + the constraints of the previous example are equivalent to the following network schema:

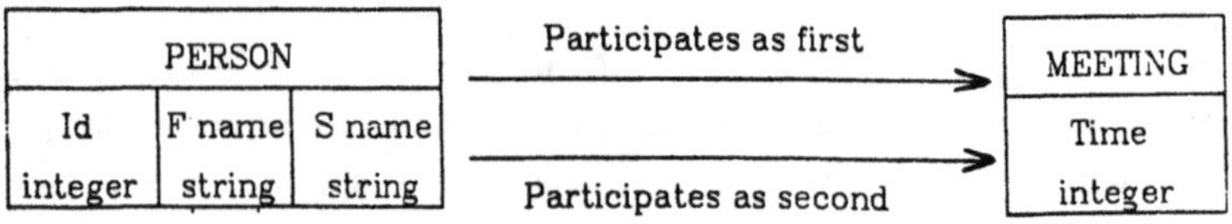

And are not equivalent to the following network schema (whose application world is closer to the reality):

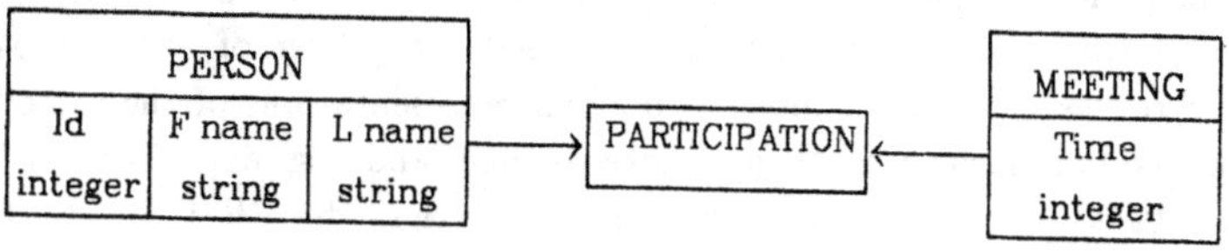

5) To study desired properties of the design of DDL, DML, and other related languages. This is parallel to one of the most important present-day objectives of the study of formal semantics of programming languages. Desired properties of Query languages include most of those of programming languages ("generality", "purity", "independency on representational or implementational aspects", etc.) as well as *approximation of end-user's concepts and his reasoning.*

6) When desired properties of data base behavior cannot be satisfied (implemented) by any construction (or software), to find the constructions (or software) which *approximately* (as must be defined) satisfy the properties. Among these, a best selection (with respect to certain criteria) can be chosen.

Example 3.6.

A relational DBMS is needed to support tables containing real numbers in range (0..1). This is not implementable. An approximation would be a DBMS supporting rational numbers up to a fixed number of digits.

Example 3.7.

The relevant world to be represented in a data base is too large. At some stage a part of the information has been loaded. The *instantaneous data base* at this stage can already be used for queries, etc., though it is only an approximation of the needed one.

Example 3.8.

An integrity law needs to be imposed on the data base, but its holding for some *instantaneous data bases* cannot be algorithmically checked. An implementable approximation thereof can be a law distinguishing between *integrity, non-integrity,* and *undefined-integrity*. This means that an implementation may loop infinitely when treating instantaneous data bases whose *integrity* is undefined.

4. Representations of Information and Data Semantics

More semantic and *less semantic* representations of information are distinguished here comparatively and subjectively according to the needs of a user of the approach and his comprehension of representations. Among two given representations of the same information usually the more comprehensive of them—more explicit and less dependent on higher-level information—will be considered by him as more semantic than the other.

Data semantics functions are defined in this section. They map subjectively "*less semantic*" representations to "*more semantic*" ones; identify erroneous representations (i.e. non-integral) which ought to be revealed by managing software; isolate erroneous representations revealing which the managing software would loop. The functions are defined to possess properties which are essential for their implementability either in a computer or by mental or manual procedures.

4.1. Domains of representations

Let us consider now ***representations*** of ***informations*** of some Inf^k level ($0<k<n$). Any one Inf^k information can be represented in different ways: implicit, explicit, computer-oriented, end-user-oriented, db-specialist-oriented, denoted by known terms, mathematically abstracted, ***denotatively semanticized***, etc. Comprehending and interpreting any representation usually necessitates knowledge of an Inf^{k+1} information. When two representations of the same information are considered by a solver of a problem (a user of this approach), from the point of view of his purposes and his exploitation and perception of them, one of them can be more comprehensive, clear and usable (subjectively for the user), and its perception can be less dependent on a deep knowledge of the Inf^{k+1}, than that of the other. In this case we would call the former representation [*more*] ***semantic***, and the latter ***less semantic***. The proposed distinction between ***less*** and ***more semantic*** representation is comparative and not absolute. A chain of representations, from a ***non-semantic*** to a ***very semantic*** can be considered.

Example 4.1.*1*.

A certain Inf^2 can be represented by a schema. This representation is *less semantic* relatively to the *more semantic* representation as a set of all the possible states of the given data base. Yet, the latter representation is less semantic than a complete description of possible behavior of this data base. (One can learn of this behavior from a representation of the Inf^2 and the known Inf^3.)

Example 4.1.*2*.

The Inf^3 information accumulated in the software of a certain DBMS, can be represented by the string 'System-R Version 1 Release 1 ', which is perceivable with the use of the Inf^4, which, *inter alia*, relates all identifications of DBMS-s to their full descriptions. Another, *more semantic*, representation of the same

Inf^3 is a user manual for this DBMS (for the perception of which the user "less needs to consult" the Inf^4). Actually, the latter representation can be inadequate for many purposes of semantization. A better representation will be discussed later.

When a collection of Inf^k *informations* is of interest, for every one of which there is a *more semantic* representation and a *less semantic* representation, two domains[1] can be considered, one containing (*inter alia*) the *less semantic* representations, and the other—the *more semantic* representations. Let us denote these domains $\langle \mathit{Synt\ Inf}^k \rangle$ and $\langle \mathit{Sem\ Inf}^k \rangle$ respectively.

4.2. Data semantics functions

Let x be a given Inf^{k+1} information, and let there be two given domains of representations of Inf^k informations, one of them chosen to contain the less-semantic representations and the other — the more-semantic ones, called $\langle \mathit{Synt\ Inf}^k \rangle$ and $\langle \mathit{Sem\ Inf}^k \rangle$ respectively. From x one can learn, *inter alia*, the following:

a) what $\mathit{Synt\ Inf}^k$-s (i.e. elements of $\langle \mathit{Synt\ Inf}^k \rangle$) represent Inf^k permissible according to x;

b) what $\mathit{Sem\ Inf}^k$-s represent Inf^k informations permissible (alternatively, implementable by a $\mathit{Synt\ Inf}^k$ or representable by a $\mathit{Synt\ Inf}^k$) according to x;

c) what is the correspondence between the valid elements of $\langle \mathit{Synt\ Inf}^k \rangle$ and the valid elements of $\langle \mathit{Sem\ Inf}^k \rangle$.

This knowledge is expressed in a *data semantics function*[2] which maps every $\mathit{Synt\ Inf}^k$ representation into its data semantics, i.e. the corresponding $\mathit{Sem\ Inf}^k$ representation, if the latter exists.

This function can be just a ***partial function*** from $\langle \mathit{Synt\ Inf}^k \rangle$ to $\langle \mathit{Sem\ Inf}^k \rangle$. However, we shall revise the form of these functions and the definition of domains in order to

- eliminate meaningless functions, i.e. functions which cannot potentially be data semantic functions;
- provide means for achievement of the aforementioned purpose of approximations;
- be compatible with methods of mathematical semantics of programming languages and provide means of specification and verification of software related to a data

[1] for the meanwhile, a domain is just a mathematical set, but later we shall require equipping the set with some orders.

[2] The term *data semantics* is used in order to distinguish this from the later discussed semantics of operations.

base system (*e.g.* DBMS or applications);

- simplify treatment of invalid representations;
- distinguish between different kinds of invalidity of a syntactic representation: the detectable by the DBMS and the non-detectable;
- be able to use known results on least fixed points,
- be able to treat errors, loops, routines, etc. in DML, DDL, *exit* procedures, etc.

We now assume that any considered domain is a set with a *complete partial order*[3] relating *less defined* to *better* defined elements, having the minimum element called $\perp$, or *undefined*, and having a special element called *meaningless*, or *ERROR*. Any simple set that needs to be considered is convertible to a domain satisfying the above by adding to it two special elements: $\perp$ and *ERROR*, and the *flat order*[4].

A data semantics function which was defined as partial can be extended so that those *less semantic* representations which were not mapped to *more semantic* ones will now be mapped to one of the special elements:

- *ERROR*, meaning usually that the *less semantic* representation was illegal and the managing process can detect its illegality,
- or $\perp$, meaning usually that the managing process would loop infinitely trying to check the validity of the invalid *less semantic* representation.

Every *semantic function* of interest should propagate $\perp$ and *ERROR*.

Example 4.2.1.

Consider a chain of three domains: a *non-semantic*, an *intermediate*, and a *semantic* domain, and two functions between them: f_1 and f_2 such that $f \equiv (f_1 \circ f_2)$ is a *semantic function* from the *non-semantic* to the *very semantic* domain.

If $f_1(a) \equiv \perp$ or $f_1(a) \equiv ERROR$ then a is *illegal*. Thus $f(a)$ must be respectively $\perp$ or *ERROR*. Thus $f_2(\perp) \equiv \perp$ and $f_2(ERROR) \equiv ERROR$. Thus f_2 propagates $\perp$ and *ERROR*.

A generalization of propagating $\perp$ is being *monotonic*. f is monotonic if whenever x is less defined than or equal to y, $f(x)$ is less defined than or equal to $f(y)$.

Every semantic function of interest must be *continuous* because otherwise it cannot be "implemented" by computer software or by an outside process of reasoning. This *continuity* property will be exploited later, *inter alia* for finding *least fixed points* of equations and for reasoning about *computability*.

---

[3] a *partial order* is called *complete* if for every subset of its domain there is an infimum, and for every increasing sequence in the domain has a supremum.

[4] The flat order over a domain D with minimum $\perp$ is $\{(x, y) \in D^2 \mid x \equiv \perp \vee x \equiv y\}$.

Unlike the above example, many domains of interest on the Inf^1 level are *flat* and for them "continuity" of a function is equivalent to its being *monotonic*. Even though, the proposed later domains for higher levels, *e.g.* Inf^2, are constructed using domains of functions over lower domains (with *pointwise* order between the functions), and they are no longer *flat*.

A reason for requesting non-flat order already on Inf^1 level can be user's need to investigate data bases from the point of view of *open-world* assumption as explained in the following.

The owner of a data base can assume either that the world is "closed" or that it is "open".

According to *closed-world* assumption every legal instantaneous data base must reflect all of the information existing in a given instant of time in the relevant (for this data base) part of the world.

According to the *open-world* assumption an instantaneous data base represents just a fraction of the relevant instantaneous information, the fraction that has been loaded into the data base: more of the relevant information possibly could have been loaded but has not been. Thus assertions that cannot be proved "true" according to the instantaneous data base can still be "true" in the reality of that time. So some instantaneous data bases can be better approximations of the reality than the other.

According to *closed-world* assumption different instantaneous data bases are not comparable. For them one would define a *flat order*.

If the user exploits the *open-world* assumption then I suggest enriching the order with the following relationships: i_1 is less defined or equal than i_2 if every simple fact reflected in i_1 is reflected also in i_2. To insure *completeness* of the order, the set of all possible simple representable facts is restricted to be finite ("finite-universe assumption").

Example 4.2.2.

Consider the sample relational data base of meetings. An instantaneous data base $(meetings-table_1, people-table_1)$ is less defined or equal than $(meetings-table_2, people-table_2)$ if the first tables are respectively included in the second ones. It is assumed that there is a given finite population and a finite time-scale. If "*unknown*" is permitted as a value in fields, then the order is enriched even more.

More generally, a data base can be *partially–open*. In this case the schema should define what types of information (relations and categories in the binary model) are *open*, and what are *closed*. An instantaneous data base would consist then of two parts: $idb = (idb_{open}, idb_{closed})$, and the order would be:

idb1 is less defined or equal to *idb2* iff $idb1_{closed} = idb2_{closed} \wedge idb1_{open} \subseteq idb2_{open}$.

We now define the domain containing all the possible *Data Semantics Functions* (corresponding to different Inf^{k+1}-s) from <*Synt* Inf^k> to <*Sem* Inf^k> as the domain of all the *continuous* functions between these domains[5]:

<Data Semantics Functions (from <Synt Inf^k*> <Sem* Inf^k*>)>*
= [*<Synt* Inf^k*>* → *<Sem* Inf^k*>*]

If an Inf^{k+1} information inf_1^{k+1} yields a data semantic function which maps a representation $s \in$ *<Synt* Inf^k*>* into $\perp$ or *ERROR*, then s is assumed to be illegal according to inf_1^{k+1}. The difference between the illegal representations is in the ability of the system to detect the invalidity. Usually *ERROR* would denote a detectable invalidity, while $\perp$—the one which would cause the detecting software to loop infinitely.

5. Semantics of Data Base Operations

Defined here *semantics of operations* resembles Bjorner's data base semantics ([Bjorner-80]) but in my approach it is only *auxiliary semantics of operations* (a minor part of data base semantics), and the principal semantization is in *data semantics.*

Operations on Inf^1 are queries, updates, etc. Operations on Inf^2 are *e.g.* data definition (DDL) programs, in which schemata and laws are defined and updated.

An Inf^k level operations' semantics is defined as a function which maps every Inf^k operation together with its external input to the corresponding *continuous* transformation from old states to new states and output. (These states are *less-semantic* representations of Inf^k level information.)

Let *<Operations on* Inf^k*>* be a *syntactic* domain of operations that are of interest and can be candidates to be executed (unless forbidden) on the k-th level in a data base system. If there are no executable operations on this level that are of interest, or if there are no executable operations at all on this level (for the DBMS level and higher), then the domain is empty. Operations can be primitive, complex, they can be whole programs, terminal sessions, parallel processes, etc. *E.g.*, for the instantaneous data base level, the syntactic domain can be equal to a data manipulation language (DML), and for the db/schema level it can be equal to a DDL.

We regard external input to an operation as an integral part of it. *E.g.*, the *query schema* like "get a name of a man from the terminal and fetch the times of his meetings from the data base" stands for the set of operations each of which is a pair composed of this

---

[5] This domain of functions has the point-wise *C.P.O.*, meaning that one semantics function is *less defined* than another or *approximates* it. $\text{POINT-WISE-ORDER}_{order} \equiv$
$\{(f_1, f_2) \in (dom(order) \rightarrow dom(order)) \mid \forall x \in dom(order): f_1(x) \; order \; f_2(x)\}$

scheme and the name of a man.

Let <*Output*^{k}> be a domain of external outputs from the operations of <*Operations on Inf*^{k}>. In many cases this can be the domain of strings over some alphabet, plus the error elements. For a given *Inf*$^{k+1}$ it is known for every *operation* ∈<*Operations on Inf*^{k}>, whether it is legal, and if so, how it would change the k-th level of the data base and what external output it would produce depending on the previous status of the data base. Thus, from the given information of (k+1)-th level, we can extract an *operations semantics function*:

[<*Operations on Inf*^{k}> →
  [<*Representations of Inf*^{k}> →
    <*Representations of Inf*^{k}> × <*Output*^{k}>]]

We have to choose which domain, <*Representations of Inf*^{k}>, is suitable for the above transformation. It could be the domain of the *more semantic* representations or the domain of the *less semantic* representations. As we have *data semantic functions* from the latter domain to the former, the latter domain is preferred as the domain of the representations, mappings between which are established by operations. *E.g.*, we would semanticize DDL programs as transformations on schemata (*syntax*), and not as transformations on such semantic representations as data base behavior. Thus, the domain of *operations semantics functions* is the following:

<*Inf*^{k} *Operations Semantics Function*> =
  [<*Operations on Inf*^{k}> →
    [<*Synt Inf*^{k}> →
      <*Synt Inf*^{k}> × <*Output*^{k}>]]

6. Principal Semantic Domains

The idea of *data semantics functions* has been presented in Section 4. This idea can be used to establish relationships between any pair of domains, one of which is *more semantic* for a particular user's purposes. The goal of this section is to elaborate such semantic domains that they would suit the purposes of most users of this approach to data base semantics.

Assume that for every relevant information level k the following conventional domains are given: a less-semantic domain of *Inf*^{k} informations' representations, <*SYNT Inf*^{k}>, a less-semantic domain of data base operations (activities) on this level (<*Operations on Inf*^{k}>), and a domain of all their possible outputs, <*Output*^{k}>.

Example 6.1.

$<SYNT\ Inf^1>$ is the domain of all possible relational instantaneous data bases, i.e. collections of tables.

$<SYNT\ Inf^2>$ is the domain of all possible combinations of relational schemata, integrity laws, inference laws, exit routines, etc.

$<SYNT\ Inf^3>$ is the domain of all possible relational data base management systems.

$<Operations\ on\ Inf^1>$ is a union of data manipulation languages, query languages, etc.

$<Operations\ on\ Inf^2>$ is a union of data definition languages.

$<Output^k>$ for every k is a domain of all possible texts and dot-matrices which can be displayed on a terminal.

6.1. Semantic domains for non-first levels

Postponing the definition of a principal $<SEM\ Inf^1>$, the principal semantic domains for all other levels are defined in this subsection.

The definition is recursive. Assume that $<SEM\ Inf^k>$ has been defined.

Let inf_1^{k+1} be an information of Inf^{k+1}-th level. A semantic representation for inf_1^{k+1} must be explicit, comprehensive, simple, and its perception should not necessitate knowledge of information from higher levels of information.

inf_1^{k+1} induces a *data semantics function* on Inf^k level and *semantics-of-operations function* on Inf^k level. Thus, these two things, and nothing else, should be extractable from the most semantic representation of inf_1^{k+1}. Thus we define a principal semantic representation of inf_1^{k+1} as a pair: a data semantics function on Inf^k and an operations-semantics function.

Thus:

$$<SEM\ Inf^{k+1}> =$$

$$(<Inf^k\ Data\ Semantics> \times <Inf^k\ Operations\ Semantics>) =$$

$$[<SYNT\ Inf^k> \rightarrow <SEM\ Inf^k>] \times$$
$$[<Operations\ on\ Inf^k> \rightarrow$$
$$[<SYNT\ Inf^k> \rightarrow <SYNT\ Inf^k> \times <Output^k>]]$$

Example 6.1.1.

$$
\begin{aligned}
&<SEM\ Inf^3> = \\
&[<SYNT\ Inf^2> \rightarrow ([<SYNT\ Inf^1> \rightarrow <SEM\ Inf^1>] \times \\
&\qquad [<Operations\ on\ Inf^1> \rightarrow \\
&\qquad [<SYNT\ Inf^1> \rightarrow (<SYNT\ Inf^1> \times \\
&\qquad\qquad <Output^1>)]])] \times \\
&\times[<Operations\ on\ Inf^2> \rightarrow \\
&[<SYNT\ Inf^2> \rightarrow <SYNT\ Inf^2> \times <Output^2>] \overset{e.g.}{=}
\end{aligned}
$$

$$
\begin{aligned}
&\text{for } \overset{example}{=}\ [DATA-DESCRIPTIONS \rightarrow \\
&\quad ([INSTANTANEOUS-DATA-BASES \rightarrow \\
&\qquad INFERRED-INSTANTANEOUS-DATA-BASES] \times \\
&\quad [DATA-MANIPULATION-LANGUAGE \cup QUERY-LANGUAGE \rightarrow \\
&\qquad [INSTANTANEOUS-DATA-BASES \rightarrow \\
&\qquad\quad INSTANTANEOUS-DATA-BASES \times \\
&\qquad\quad OUTPUT-TEXTS]])] \times \\
&\times[DATA-DEFINITION-LANGUAGE \rightarrow \\
&\quad [DATA-DESCRIPTIONS \rightarrow \\
&\qquad DATA-DESCRIPTIONS \times \\
&\qquad OUTPUT-TEXTS]]
\end{aligned}
$$

Remark.

The principal domain $<SEM\ Inf^{k+1}>$ is defined above as a Cartesian product. The representations belonging to this domain are only 97% comprehensive, i.e. bearing all their meaning in themselves. This is because in order to perceive them we use, *inter alia*, the following high-level knowledge:

- The first component of every pair is a data semantics function on Inf^k;
- for every less-semantic representation in $<SYNT-Inf^k>$, this data semantics function provides semantics as a structure belonging to the principal semantic domain for Inf^k, $<SEM\ Inf^k>$;
- the representations mapped to $\perp$ or *ERROR* are illegal; those mapped to *ERROR* can be detected by the software systems; those mapped to $\perp$ will cause the software system to loop infinitely when trying to detect the invalidity.
- The second component of every pair is a semantics-of-operations function on Inf^k;
- this function assigns every less-semantic representation of an operation on Inf^k with the semantics of that operation, i.e. a function which for every less-semantic representation of Inf^k gives a pair:
  - the first component thereof is the new less-semantic representation on Inf^k level produced by performing the operation on the former representation;
  - the second component thereof is an external output, printed or displayed;
- external inputs of operations, *e.g.* query parameters and standard input files of DML programs, are considered syntactic parts of operations themselves.

In order to increase the comprehensiveness of $<SEM\ Inf^{k+1}>$ by covering more of the foregoing high-level information, the definition of $<SEM\ Inf^{k+1}>$ can be refined using ***abstract syntax notation*** :

$<SEM\ Inf^{k+1}>$: :

Inf^{k}*−Data−Semantics*:
  ([$<SYNT\ Inf^{k}> \rightarrow <SEM\ Inf^{k}>$]),
 Inf^{k} *−Semantics−of−Operations*:
  ([$<$*Operations on* $Inf^{k}> \rightarrow$
   [*Old−representation*:$<SYNT\ Inf^{k}> \rightarrow$
     Operation−Outcome:
      (*New−representation*: $<SYNT\ Inf^{k}>$,
      External−output: $<Output^{k}>$)]])

6.2. Semantic domains for level Inf^1

The choice of $<SEM\ Inf^1>$ depends on the requirements of the problem. Usually, a $SEM\ Inf^1$ would be a more user-oriented representation of an instantaneous data base than a $SYNT\ Inf^1$. Here are some possibilities:

1) According to ANSI-SPARC proposal of data base systems architecture three types of Inf^1 information representations should be considered: ***internal*** (organized according to ***internal schemata***, convenient to the implementation and logically supportable by a DBMS), ***conceptual*** (organized according to a ***conceptual schema*** and being a comprehensive logical description independent of user-views and of the implementation aspects), and ***external*** (organized according to ***external schemata*** and convenient to users). It is very important to define and treat formally mappings between these representations. For this purpose, one representation (***e.g. internal***) can be defined as a $SYNT\ Inf^1$ and another (***e.g. conceptual***) can be defined as a $SEM\ Inf^1$.

2) When, for any other reason, one logical structure of data is represented by another, ***e.g. binary*** by ***relational***, the latter can be considered a $SYNT\ Inf^1$, and the former a $SEM\ Inf^1$. ***Inter alia***, this can be when a DML of one model is used with a data base of another model via a translator, or when the design of a data base was in the Binary model, but due to environmental reasons it has been implemented in a more data-dependent model.

3) $<SEM\ Inf^1>$ can be equal to $<SYNT\ Inf^1>$ and every considered Inf^1 semantic function can be a ***semi-identity*** function, i.e. mapping every $SYNT\ Inf^1$ to itself or to $\perp$ or to *ERROR*. This is when the only considered aspect of the Inf^2 is what Inf^1-s (or their representations) are permitted by data integrity laws.

4) $<SEM\ Inf^1>$ can be formally equal to $<SYNT\ Inf^1>$, yet some ***data semantics*** functions which are not ***semi-identity*** functions can be considered. ***Inter alia***, they can represent

inference transformations with respect to knowledge in Inf^2 of *inference laws.*

Example 6.2.1.

Let $<SEM\ Inf^1> = <SYNT\ Inf^1> = X \times X \cup \{\perp, ERROR\}$. Let inf^2 be one information of Inf^2 level. Let inf_1^2 imply that every information of Inf^1 is a transitive relation. Thus, inf_1^2 induces a data semantic function which maps every relation to its transitive closure. *E.g.*,

$$\{(x_1, x_2), (x_2, x_3)\} \in <SYNT\ Inf^1>$$

is mapped to

$$\{(x_1, x_2), (x_2, x_3), (x_1, x_3)\} \in <SEM\ Inf^1>$$

The latter representation is more comprehensive than the former. In order to perceive it less knowledge of inf_1^2 is needed.

Now let inf_2^2 be another information of Inf^2 level. Let inf_2^2 imply that every information of Inf^1 level is an irreflexive symmetric relation. Then the induced ***data semantics function*** maps $\{(x_1, x_2), (x_2, x_3)\}$ into $\{(x_1, x_2), (x_2, x_3), (x_2, x_1), (x_3, x_2)\}$, but $\{(x_1, x_1), (x_2, x_3)\}$ is mapped into *ERROR.*

7. APPENDIX: Some Applications

Using the proposed approach, the following subjects have been studied in [Rishe-85]:

a) Data base integrity and inference laws expressible by assertions. They have been modeled, and their semantics has been defined as the behavior of data bases. Determinism and implementability of these laws have been investigated and several results have been proven demonstrating the power of the approach. Among the results is the following theorem: "Intersection-closed assertional inference laws are deterministic."

b) A version of the Conceptual Binary data base model has been developed and formally semanticized. This version has been based on data semantics, on data base integrity and inference laws and on their expressibility in data base schemata.

Categories and binary relations are treated in it uniformly according to their properties defined in schemata. These properties are treated as meta-relations and meta-categories, and are defined together with their meta-properties in a DBMS description, which is regarded as a meta-schema.

c) A data base model has been defined, having data manipulation and data definition non-procedural languages of maximal power: they can define every Turing-implementable query, update, integrity-law, inference-law.

This to covers the *relational*, *network* and *hierarchic* models which are shown in [Rishe-84] to be particular cases of the binary model.

7.1. Semantics of Assertional Inference and Integrity Laws in Data Bases

Data base inference laws are often expressed as assertions.

Example 7.1.1.

In a binary schema, the assertion "*STUDENT is a* **subcatregory** *of PERSON*" is an inference rule, a part of the inference law of the data base. If a fact "*x is a STUDENT*" has been stored in the data base, the system can infer: "*x is a PERSON*"

Unlike this, the assertion "*the categories PERSON* and *DEPARTMENT are disjoint*" is an integrity constraint, a part of an integrity law.

Such inference laws can be expressed syntacticly as programs yielding a Boolean value, or in a language equivalent to a predicate calculus, or in a schema of a data base.

Any of these representations can be converted into a slightly more semantic representation, which is a Boolean function over the domain *IDB* of all possible instantaneous data bases.

Yet, a more semantic representation of such an inference law is a transformation on *IDB*, i.e. a function: $[IDB \rightarrow IDB \cup \{ERROR, \perp\}]$. Taking into account also an integrity law, for every instantaneous data base this function should give a new inferred instantaneous data base, if possible.

The inferred instantaneous data base must satisfy the following conditions:

(1) It contains all the information represented in the original data base.

(2) It contains all the inferred information, i.e. satisfies the assertion of the inference law.

(3) It contains no extraneous information, i.e no proper subset of the inferred instantaneous data base satisfies (1)&(2).

(4) It satisfies the assertion of the integrity law.

The above definition is not deterministic. All the possible transformations corresponding to a given pair of assertional integrity and inference laws are formally defined in [Rishe-85]. Using an implementation-dependent enumeration of instantaneous data bases, one of the transformations is identified as a standard one. A function mapping every pair of laws into a standard transformation is constructively defined in [Rishe-85] using *lambda-calculus* and is shown to be computable, i.e. implementable by a DBMS.

The determinism of inference laws is studied. An inference law is strictly-deterministic if for every two transformations corresponding to it, t_1 and t_2, and for every instantaneous data base *idb*, $t_1(idb) \in \{t_2(idb), \perp, ERROR\}$.

Theorem. An assertional inference law is strictly-deterministic if and only if it is *intersection-closed* (i.e. for every two instantaneous data bases satisfying the assertion of the law, their intersection satisfies the assertion too.)

7.2. Formalization of a simplified binary model defined by a metaschema

The following simplified binary model is formalized.

An instantaneous data base is a set of elementary facts. An elementary fact is either a binary fact: a relationship between two objects, or a unary fact: a statement that an object belongs to a category. The objects are either uninterpreted abstract objects or values.

The *less semantic representation* of an instantaneous data base is a set of basic elementary facts, i.e facts which have been reported by users via updates of the data base. The *more semantic* representation is an error-state (*ERROR or* $\perp$), or a set of all elementary facts: basic facts and facts which can be inferred from them.

The operations on instantaneous data bases are update transactions. A less-semantic representation of an update transaction is a pair of sets of elementary facts: a set of facts to be deleted from the data base and a set of facts to be inserted after the deletion.)[7]

The least semantic representation considered of a data base description is a collection of meta-facts comprising the schema of a data base. These meta-facts define all the categories and the relations of the data base and their integrity properties (domains and ranges of relations, disjointness of categories, etc.) and inference properties (symmetry and transitivity of relations, the meta-relation *subcategory* between categories etc.)

This representation can be formally considered an instantaneous data base in itself and described by a *meta–schema*.

Example 7.2.1.

" *Jack is a student*" and "*Jack is a person*" are two facts.

[7] This representation is actually more semantic than a representation by a program. The reason to consider sets of facts rather than breaking a transaction into steps is the possibility of dissatisfaction of data base integrity when only a part of a transaction has been done.

" *STUDENT is a CATEGORY*" and "*STUDENT is a subcategory of PERSON*" are two meta-facts.

" *SUBCATEGORY is a transitive meta-relation between categories*" is a couple of meta-meta-facts.

The operations on data base descriptions are updates analogous to the update transactions of instantaneous data bases. Their semantics is deduced from the meta-schema.

The full formalization of the model is provided by finding the semantic object corresponding to the meta-schema. This semantic object is a principal semantic representation of Inf^3, composed of an Inf^2 data-semantics function and an Inf^2 semantics-of-operations function.

Its *data−semantics* component maps every schema to the behavior of a database.

The mapping is decomposed into three mappings as shown in

(i) A valid schema, which is a collection of consistent meta-facts, is mapped into a collection of all inferable meta-facts.

(ii) A collection of all inferable meta-facts is mapped into a pair of predicates over the domain semantic representations of instantaneous data bases: an integrity law, and an assertional inference law, specifying what semantic representations contain all the inferable facts.

(iii) The above pair is mapped into a principal semantic representation of Inf^2.

The four domains of Inf^2 representations considered in the above constitute a chain from a less-semantic domain to the principal semantic domain.

The semantics of the meta-schema is defined in [Rishe-85] constructively, using lambda-calculus, and it is proved there that the semantics is computable, and thus implementable by a DBMS.

7.3. Complete Semantics of a DBMS of an Absolutely Complete Power

[Rishe-85] proposed a non-procedural data-independent language model for data bases, in which *all* partial *Turing-computable* queries are specifiable. (As opposed to limited expressiveness of of "Codd-complete" languages, e.g. the relational calculus, and even of languages based on Horn-clauses, e.g. Prolog.) Every query is formulated in the language as a predicate calculus assertion expressing the desired relationship between the state of the data base, the information needed to be displayed, and auxiliary concepts. Interpretation of a query is a partial Turing-computable non-deterministic transformation which for any input state of the data base gives a minimal output to satisfy the assertion.

The language model proposed in [Rishe-85] yields query languages of complete computability power and also languages which are intended to restrict the use of undesirable or meaningless operations on objects. One of the important cases differentiates between abstract objects, representing real-world entities, and concrete values. A more general case is parametrized by a family of permitted operations on the domain of objects and its subdomains. The languages are able to express every data base query reasonable within the restrictions parametrizing the languages.

The queries are syntaxed there as assertions, whose assertional semantic functions can produce *true*, *false*, or $\perp$ when applied to an instantaneous data base. The transformational semantics of queries, mapping instantaneous data bases to outputs or $\perp$, was defined there as follows.

$IDB \equiv INSTANTANEOUS\text{-}DATA\text{-}BASES$[8]

ASSERTION:

$[THE\text{-}LANGUAGE \rightarrow [IDB \rightarrow BOOLEAN_{\perp}]]$[9]

semantics-of-queries:

$[THE\text{-}LANGUAGE \rightarrow [IDB \rightarrow OUTPUT_{\perp}]]$

$$\textbf{\textit{semantics-of-queries}}(\underset{THE\text{-}LANGUAGE}{query \in}, \underset{INSTANTANEOUS\text{-}DATA\text{-}BASES}{idb \in}) =$$

let $\phi = ASSERTION(query)$ **in**

$$\text{choose}_{\perp}\left(\left\{ (result, temp) \;\middle|\; \begin{array}{c} \phi(idb \dot{\cup} result \dot{\cup} temp) \wedge {}^{)10} \\ \forall vdb. \\ \textbf{if } idb \subseteq vdb \subset (idb \dot{\cup} result \dot{\cup} temp) \\ \textbf{then } \phi(vdb) \equiv false \end{array} \right\}\right)_{\substack{project1 \\ (\text{take only } result \text{ component})}}$$

Semantics of queries was shown to be computable (equivalent to a partial recursive function), although this is not obvious from the above specification.

Here I shall use the language model proposed in [Rishe-85] to define a complete semantics of a data base management systems, covering ***all*** *Turing-computable* queries, integrity laws, inference laws, and update transactions (in

---

[8] For the relational model (having a denumerable domain D of objects),

$$IDB \equiv \text{POWERSET}(NAMES-OF-RELATIONS \times D^{*}) \underset{D}{\cap}$$

Using the binary model, $D \cup D \times D$ is sufficient instead of D^{*}.

[9] $X_{\perp}$ is $X \cup \{\perp\}$; $\perp$ means *undefined*.

[10] $\dot{\cup}$ is a decomposable union: for $\alpha,\beta,\gamma,\delta \in IDB$, $\delta = (\alpha \dot{\cup} \beta \dot{\cup} \gamma)$ **iff** $(\alpha,\beta,\gamma) = \text{split}(\delta)$

the presence of integrity and inference laws).

semantics-of-operations:

$[DATA\text{-}SEMANTIC\text{-}FUNCTIONS \rightarrow [IDB \rightarrow IDB_{\perp} \times OUTPUT_{\perp}]]$

DATA-SEMANTIC-FUNCTIONS=

$[IDB \rightarrow IDB_{\perp,ERROR}]$

semantics-of-laws:

$[THE\text{-}LANGUAGE \times THE\text{-}LANGUAGE \rightarrow DATA\text{-}SEMANTIC\text{-}FUNCTIONS]$

$$\textbf{semantics-of-laws}\big((\underset{\in THE\text{-}LANGUAGE}{integrity}, \underset{\in THE\text{-}LANGUAGE}{inference}), \underset{\in INSTANTANEOUS\text{-}DATA\text{-}BASES}{idb}\big)=$$

let $\phi = ASSERTION(integrity)$, $\psi = ASSERTION(inference)$ **in**

let $inferred = idb \cup$

$$\text{choose}_{\perp}\left(\left\{(extension, temp) \;\middle|\; \begin{array}{c} \psi(idb \dot{\cup} extension \dot{\cup} temp) \wedge \\ \forall vdb. \\ \textbf{if } idb \subseteq vdb \subset (idb \dot{\cup} extension \dot{\cup} temp) \\ \textbf{then } \psi(vdb) \equiv false \end{array}\right\}\right)_{\text{project1}}$$

in(**if** $\phi(inferred)$ **then** $inferred$ **else** $ERROR$)

$$\textbf{semantics-of-operations}\big(\underset{\substack{\in DATA\text{-}SEMANTIC\text{-}FUNCTIONS \\ \text{(semantics of integrity and inference laws)}}}{datasem}, \underset{\in THE\text{-}LANGUAGE}{operation}, \underset{\in INSTANTANEOUS\text{-}DATA\text{-}BASES}{idb}\big)=$$

let $(display, delete, insert) =$

split($query\text{-}semantics(operation, datasem(idb))$) **in**

if $datasem((idb - delete) \cup insert) \underset{\perp}{=} ERROR$ [11]

then $(idb, ERROR)$

else $((idb - delete) \cup insert), display)$

The following definitions complete the full specification of a DBMS semantics.

The only type of data-definition operations in this language model is replacing and old pair of syntacticly-specified integrity and inference laws with a new pair of laws.

---

[11] $\underset{\perp}{=}$ is equality which can be undefined: $(x \underset{\perp}{=} \perp) \equiv \perp$

Thus : $DATA\text{-}DEFINITION\text{-}OPERATIONS = THE\text{-}LANGUAGE \times THE\text{-}LANGUAGE$

$$\boldsymbol{semantics\text{-}of\text{-}data\text{-}definition\text{-}operations}_{(new\text{-}integrity,\ new\text{-}inference)}(old\text{-}integrity,\ old\text{-}inference) = ((new\text{-}integrity, new\text{-}inference), \underset{(\text{no output})}{\varnothing})$$

$\boldsymbol{semantics\text{-}of\text{-}the\text{-}DBMS} \in$

$$[DATA{-}DESCRIPTIONS \rightarrow ([IDB \rightarrow INFERRED{-}INSTANTANEOUS{-}DATA{-}BASES] \times [DATA{-}OPERATIONS \rightarrow [INSTANTANEOUS{-}DATA{-}BASES \rightarrow INSTANTANEOUS{-}DATA{-}BASES \times OUTPUT]])] \times$$

$$\times[DATA{-}DEFINITION{-}OPERATIONS \rightarrow [DATA{-}DESCRIPTIONS \rightarrow DATA{-}DESCRIPTIONS \times OUTPUT]]$$

$\boldsymbol{semantics\text{-}of\text{-}the\text{-}DBMS} =$

$$(\lambda(integrity, inference) \in THE\text{-}LANGUAGE \times THE\text{-}LANGUAGE.\ (semantics\text{-}of\text{-}laws_{(integrity, inference)}, semantics\text{-}of\text{-}operations_{(integrity, inference)}), semantics\text{-}of\text{-}data\text{-}definition\text{-}operations)$$

References

H. Biller, W. Glathaar, and E. Neuhold, "On the Semantics of Data Bases: The Semantics of Data Manipulation Languages," *Modelling in Data Base Management Systems, IFIP Working Conference on Modelling in DBMS's*, 1976.

M. Brodie and J. Schmidt, "Final Report of the Relational Database Task Group," *ANSI-X3-SPARC-DBTG, ACM SIGMOD RECORD*, vol. 12, no. 4, 1982.

J. M. Cadiou, "On Semantic Issues in the Relational Model of Data," *Mathematical Foundations of Computer Science, Proc. of 5th Symposium*, Springer-Verlag, 1976.

J. Clifford and D. S. Warren, "Formal Semantics for Time in Database System," *ACM Transaction on Database System*, vol. 18, 1983.

C. J. Date, "A Formal Definition of the Relational Model," *ACM SIGMOD RECORD*, vol. 13, no. 1, 1982.

Jay Earley, "On the Semantics of Data Structures," *Data Base Systems, COURANT Computer Science Symposium 6*, 1972.

E. D. Falkenberg, "Data Models: The Next Five Years," *INFOTECH Report: Data Base Technology*, vol. 1, 1978.

W. T. Hardgrave, "Ambiguity in processing Boolean Queries on TDMS Tree Structures: A Study for Four Different Philosophies," *IEEE Transactions on Software Engineering*, pp. 357-372, July 1980.

E. J. Neuhold and Th. Olnhoff, "Building Data Base Management Systems Through Formal Specification," *Springer LNCS #107*, 1981.

N. Rishe. [84] *Algorithms for Design of Relational, Network and Hierarchic Schemata from Conceptual Binary Schemata.* Tech. Rep. TRCS84-15, University of California, Santa Barbara, 1984.

N. Rishe. "Postconditional Semantics of Data Base Queries". Proceedings of the Conference on Mathematical Foundations of Programming Semantics (Manhattan, Kansas, April 1985).

N. Rishe. [85b] *Semantics of Universal Languages and Informations Structures in Data Bases.* Technical report TRCS85-010, Computer Science Department, University of California, Santa Barbara, 1985.

H. Schmid and S. Swenson, "On the Semantics of the Relational Data Model," *ACM-SIGMOD International Conf. on Management of Data*, San Jose, 1975.

J. Stoy, "The Scott-Strachey Approach to Programming Language Theory," *Denotational Semantics*, 1977.

Y. Vassiliou, "Null values in database management: A denotational semantics approach," *Proc. of: ACM-SIGMOD international conference on Management of data*, pp. 162-169, Boston, May 30 - June 1 , 1979.

H. Weber, "A Semantic Model of Integrity Constraints on a Relational Data Base," in *Modeling in Data Base Management Systems, IFIP Working Conference on Modeling in DBMS's*, ed. G. M. Nijssen, pp. 162-169, Boston, May 30 - June 1 , 1976.

C. Zaniolo, "Database Relations with Null Values," *Journal of Computer and System Sciences*, vol. 28, pp. 142-166, 1984.

POSTCONDITIONAL SEMANTICS OF DATA BASE QUERIES

Naphtali Rishe

Department of Computer Science
University of California
Santa Barbara, CA 93106

A data-independent fully non-procedural language model for binary and relational data bases is designed, in which *all* partial Turing-computable queries are specifiable. A large class of the queries is expressible in a natural and user-friendly way. Every query is formulated in the language as an applied first-order predicate calculus assertion expressing the desired relationship between the state of the data base, the information needed to be displayed, and auxiliary concepts. Interpretation of a query is a partial Turing-computable non-deterministic transformation which for any input state of the data base gives a minimal output to satisfy the assertion.

This general model is implementable effectively but not efficiently. It is intended to serve in investigation, generation and extraction of sublanguages which are user friendly and efficiently implementable.

The proposed general language has sublanguages which are intended to restrict use of undesirable or meaningless operations on objects. One of the important cases differentiates between abstract objects, representing real-world entities, and concrete values. A more general case is parametrized by a family of permitted operations on the domain of objects and its subdomains. The sublanguages are able to express every data base transformation reasonable within the restrictions parametrizing the sublanguages.

1. MOTIVATION

An instantaneous data base is a finite structure of facts (elementary propositions) which is regarded as describing a state of an application world. A data base schema describes time-independent properties of an application world and is a generator for a set, usually infinite, of instantaneous data bases for that application world. A data base model is a generator for an infinite set of structures every one of which can be regarded as an instantaneous data base for *a* state of *an* application world. (The model should be rich enough to provide a representation for every possible state of every reasonable application world.)

Data base models are supplied with general user languages. Some of them are called query languages. A query is a specification of information which a user wants to extract or deduce from an instantaneous data base without knowing its exact extent. A query is interpreted as a partial function from instantaneous data bases to some data structures.

Other data base languages are called update (transaction) languages. An update transaction expresses a transition between states of an application world plus a query. It is interpreted as a partial function from instantaneous data bases to instantaneous data bases plus data structures containing information to be displayed. (Unlike interpretation of queries, interpretation of updates usually also depends on some laws fixed for an application. These laws are known as integrity and inference laws, as discussed later.) These functions are not total when the implementing software may loop infinitely in some cases.

It is usually desired that data base user languages possess the following properties:

(1) They should be powerful enough to provide expressions for all "reasonable" requirements of users for any "reasonable" application world. A "reasonable query" must be physical-data-independent, at least in the following senses of [Bancilhon-78]:

- Its output may not depend on the actual ordering of data in the physical data base. This is avoided by regarding a query as a transformation on an abstracted model of data bases, *e.g.* the relational data base model as defined in [Codd-70] (where an instantaneous data base is a collection of named n-ary *mathematical relations* over domains of values) or a binary data model — [Abrial-74] (where an instantaneous data base is a collection of named unary and binary relations).

- Its output may not depend on the physical representation of abstract objects in a data base (In the binary model some objects are uninterpreted, representing real-world entities, and some are concrete values. There is no such clear distinction in the relational model since all the objects are logically represented there by values supplied by the user.) This principle may be extended by defining several types of objects:

  (i) the uninterpreted objects (the only meaningful mathematical operation on them is the binary function "=" yielding a Boolean value),

(ii) fully-interpreted objects (e.g. integers, on which every partial recursive function may be meaningful), and

(iii) semi-interpreted objects, on which a collection of meaningful functions may be defined (e.g. the comparators >, <, etc. on names of people).

Any of these types may be empty for a particular application. The first two types are special cases of types of semi-interpreted objects. So all the types can be collapsed into one by defining one set of meaningful functions from tuples of objects to objects or error elements.

(2) They should allow convenient expression of at least "frequent" requirements.

(3) They should be implementable by software.

There is no consensus on the extent of "reasonable" requirements of a query language's expressive power beyond the minimal data-independency. Unlike the language proposed herein, other proposals for query languages did not provide the possibility to express all meaningful queries and used a narrow interpretation of "reasonable requirements". These requirements are sometimes restricted to those expressible by Codd's Relational Algebra (or by Relational Calculus), and thus languages whose expressivity is equivalent to Relational Calculus are called Codd-complete (*cf.* [Codd-72]). [Aho and Ullman - 79] showed that quite reasonable queries, such as those involving transitive closure are unexpressible in Codd's Algebra and proposed to extend the Algebra by a fix-point operator. A more powerful class of languages, using Horn clauses, is advocated in [Gallaire-78] and [Gallaire-81]. A representative of this class is Prolog (*cf.* [Li-84]). Incomplete expressibility of Horn clauses was shown in [Chandra and Harel - 82]. [Chandra and Harel - 80] propose a much richer language model which supports all computable data-independent queries excluding those necessitating generation of new uninterpreted objects (e.g by an update transaction) and still keeping some restrictions on computations that necessitates interpretation of values. (Their language has a powerful capability of calculation of values, including aggregative calculations, e.g. counting, but does not allow all meaningful computations.) Unfortunately, their language is highly-procedural, unnatural and inconvenient to use. The exclusion of value-computations is argued by most authors by the desirability of enforcing the separation between data extraction (specified by a query) and data computation (specified by a program). Such separation may not always be justified, especially when one wishes to use queries for updates or for specification of inference laws.

An objective of this work is to define a query language which possesses the following properties:

(1) It is **absolutely complete**, i.e. every *computable* transformation is expressible in it. (A computable transformation is a partial recursive function of numbers effectively representing *sets* of tuples of objects.)

(2) It is user-friendly:

- The user states not how to extract the information, but what properties the extracted information should possess.
- No query needs to regard types of information which are irrelevant to it.
- Queries are independent of representation and of computer-oriented decisions.
- The users are enabled to exploit indeterminism.
- Both the binary-oriented and the table-oriented user are provided with appropriate syntax.
- The user can easily specify calculations on values when needed. Arbitrary aggregative calculations (such as summation, counting etc.) are also expressible.
- The language is provided with "syntactic sugar" to make it more "friendly" to the end-user. (More "sugar" is still desired.)
- The same syntax can be used to specify update transactions and integrity and inference laws.

(3) The language is implementable. Yet, heuristic techniques need to be designed to implement efficiently some important subsets of the language. Otherwise the language will serve principally as a model for generation of efficiently-implementable *sub*languages and for comparison of different languages.

(4) For any definition of data-independency expressed by a set of meaningful operations on objects, there is a restricted syntax of the language, which generates all and only the data-independent queries and transformations.

2. THE PROPOSED LANGUAGE

The proposed language is a set of formulas, called queries, which are interpreted as partial transformations over the set *IDB* of instantaneous relational data bases. In the considered data base model *IDB*, an instantaneous relational data base is a finite family of named finite relations over a fixed denumerable set *D*, called the domain of objects. (*D* can be further subdivided into domains of concrete mathematical values and domains of abstract objects.) When a instantaneous data base is transformed to another one (by a query or by an update), the former data base is called "the input" and the latter "the result".

The **semantics of a query** is defined in two steps: **First**, the formula is assigned with an **assertional interpretation** which is a partial predicate over *IDB*. **Then**, a **transformation** is derived from it. It transforms any input data base into a *result* such that there exists a data base, called a **virtual data base**, which:

- consists of three distinguishable parts: the input, the *result* and temporary data;
- **satisfies the assertion;**
- is **minimal for this input:** every other data base included in it and having the same input part contradicts the assertion;
- is (**non-deterministically**) chosen if other "minimal" data bases exist.

The result can be undefined if all the (virtual) data bases, in which the input is embedded, contradict the assertion, or if for every satisfying the assertion there is a sub-data-base (i.e. a subset thereof) for which the predicate is undefined.

The following describes the abstracted syntax of queries (before user-friendly "sugar"), yielding their assertional semantics. A query is expressed as a closed formula in an applied first order predicate calculus. For any virtual data base the formula is interpreted as *true, false* or *undefined.* The formula is composed of:

- constants, which are any objects of D, not necessarily in the virtual data base;
- quantified variables ranging over the set of objects which appear in the virtual data base;
- a unary predicate symbol interpreted as the equality of its argument to the object 'true';
- a predicate symbol interpreted as the belonging of a tuple of objects to a named relation in the virtual data base; (The objects are evaluated from terms. The relation-name is usually specified as a constant, but some rather "unreasonable" queries [see Theorem 4] may necessitate an evaluation of the name from a term.)
- operators: "and", etc; (In the principle variant of the language, tri-valued parallel logic is used.)
- function symbols expressing scalar mathematical operations over the domain of objects, including comparators (>,<, etc.) yielding Boolean values.

Two alternative variants of the language have been developed. The first one, focuses the assertional semantics on data base structure, while the scalar mathematical operations are expressed, for the sake of separation from information-manipulation, by an infinite set of function symbols syntaxed as recursive functional expressions having the least-fixed-point semantics. This extension of the set of functional symbols does not contribute to the expressive power of the language because every scalar function can be expressed by a logical assertion using only a fixed finite set of standard functions. In the other proposed variant ([Rishe-85]), only a finite set of "cataloged" function symbols is used, while the rest of computable scalar operations are generated from them exploiting the principal transformational-assertional semantics of the language. A very large class of transformations can be specified *without* function symbols at all, except the equality symbol "=", *inter alia* all those queries definable by: Codd's Algebra (without use of comparisons of objects; otherwise they are specifiable using one functional symbol ">"); Codd's Algebra extended by the fixed-point operator; Horn clauses; queries unexpressible by Horn clauses, e.g. Example 3 of the next section.

Sublanguages have been investigated where some function symbols are used, while other are prohibited in order to maintain data-independence. In a special case the domain of objects is split into concrete objects and abstract objects. Only "=" is defined on abstract objects, and a full function space is defined on the sub-domain of concrete objects.

The language is based on the abstracted syntax specified above and on syntactic "sugar" -- user friendly abbreviations of formal expressions. A complete "sugar" is specified in [Rishe-85]. Among these "sugar" abbreviations are: a full scope of logic operators; contextual defaults for quantifiers; abbreviations of sub-assertions expressing aggregative application of associative scalar functions, *e.g.*, summation, counting etc; substitution of variables by *examples* of objects (inspired by Zloof's *Query-By-Example*); representation of relationships by simple English phrases; distinct syntax variants for the Relational data base model and the Semantic Binary data base model. In the following section, some examples of queries with this "sugar" are given.

3. EXAMPLES OF QUERIES

The examples use the following semantic binary schema, specifying categories (unary relations) as squares and binary relations as arrows.

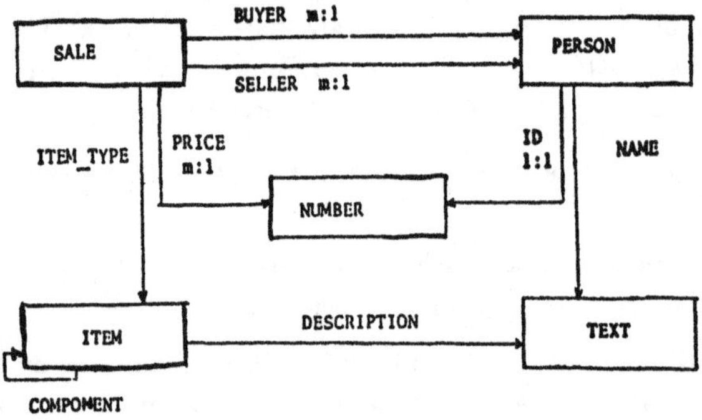

1) An example of using a transitive closure.

/* who bought a bolt directly or indirectly, *e.g.*, bought a lock, door, train car, train, etc.? */

∀b,s,c:
(if (b BUYER-*input* s) ∧ (b ITEM-TYPE-*input* c)
then (s GOT c)) ∧
∀s,c,d:
(if (s GOT c) ∧ ((c COMPONENT-*input* d))
then (s GOT d)) ∧

$\forall$ s,x,n:
(if ((x DESCRIPTION-*input* 'bolt') $\wedge$ (s NAME-*input* n))
$\wedge$ (s GOT x)
then ((x GOT-A-BOLT*result*)).

The same query using the standard sugar of the language:
if given:
somebody *is the* BUYER *of a* bargain,
car (*e.g.,*) is the ITEM-TYPE *of the* bargain
then somebody GOT a car *and*
if somebody GOT a car (*e.g.,*) *and*
given: door (*e.g.,*) *is a* COMPONENT *of* car
then somebody GOT a door *and*
if somebody GOT something *and*
given: the DESCRIPTION *of* something *is* 'bolt',
the NAME *of* somebody *is* smith (*e.g.,*)
then result: smith 'GOT A BOLT'

2) Table-oriented specification.
Table-oriented users would prefer a relational schema as follows:
relation PERSON [ID, NAME];
relation SALE [BUYER-ID, SELLER-ID, PRICE, ITEM_DESCR];
relation ITEM [DESCRIPTION];
relation COMPONENT [CONTAINING_DESCR, CONTAINED_DESCR]

The above query could be formulated by them as follows:

if given:
SALE [BUYER-ID: buyer, SELLER-ID: seller,
PRICE: price, ITEM-DESCR: item]
then GOT [OWNER: buyer, THING: thing] *and*
if GOT [OWNER: owner, THING: thing] *and*
given: COMPONENT [CONTAINING_DESCR: thing,
CONTAINED_DESCR: otherthing]
then GOT [OWNER: owner, THING: otherthing] *and*
if GOT [OWNER: owner_id, THING: bolt] *and*
given: PERSON [ID: owner_id, NAME: name]
then result THOSE_WHO_GOT_A_BOLT [NAME: name]

3) A query which cannot be specified by Horn clauses.

/* What items have no less components than the item described as 'car'? */

(This query does not use function symbols.)

given:
 'car' *is the* DESCRIPTION *of* c (*e.g.*),
 watch *is the* DESCRIPTION *of* w *and*
result:
 watch HAS-MANY-COMPONENTS *and*
if stone (*e.g.*) *is* PAIRED-TO wheel (*e.g.*) *and*
 then given:
  stone *is a* COMPONENT *of* watch,
  wheel *is a* COMPONENT *of* car *and*
if stone *is* PAIRED-TO wheel *and*
  stone *is* PAIRED-TO x
 then x=wheel *and*
if wheel *is a* COMPONENT *of* car
 then exists stone *s.t.*
  given:
   stone *is* PAIRED-TO wheel.

4) /* find every seller's total income */

if given: man *is a* PERSON, *the* NAME *of the* man *is* smith
 then exits income *s.t.*
  (income *is the sum*)[1] *of* PRICE *of*
   bargain *dependent on* man *s.t.* (man *is the* SELLER
   of the bargain)) and
  result: *the* INCOME *of* smith *is* income.

4. REVIEW OF MAIN THEOREMS ABOUT THE LANGUAGE

The following is a review of main results about the proposed language model. They are proven in [Rishe-85]. The proofs of the most important results are outlined in the appendices of this paper.

1) The language is **implementable**, i.e. it has an interpreter.

[1] This phrase, which might look aggregative and second order, is a syntactic sugar abbreviation for a longer *first-order non-aggregative* phrase using only one binary function symbol "+" which is applied to pairs of integers denoting prices.

2) The language is ***absolutely* complete,** i.e. for every partial computable function ϕ: $IDB \rightarrow IDB$ there exists a query $q \in L$ whose semantics is ϕ.

3) The sublanguage containing only **deterministic** queries is absolutely complete too. Thus, the non-determinism (being desirable for user-friendliness and implementation optimization) is not the reason for absolute completeness.

4) Every query whose whose result can be affected only by a finite set of relation-names, i.e. whose intrinsic meaning does not necessitate quantification over the set of names of relations (as can be for Data Base Administrator's queries) can be specified using only constants as names of relations. (*I.e.* the language can be seen syntacticly as ***first-order*** with relations as predicate symbols.)

5) A standard **finite set of function symbols** defined on the domain of objects is sufficient for absolute completeness of the language. The other functions on values can be represented by assertions, although such representations can be undesirable from a methodological point of view.

6) If the language is further restricted to any set of standard function symbols on values (in order to permit only meaningful operations on some domains, *e.g.* only equality-verification on abstract objects), then every query meaningful within this restrictions is expressible in the restricted language up to an isomorphism.

   More precisely: for every set Φ of functions over the domain of objects, for every computable (Φ, C)-preserving data base transformation ϕ, there exists a query q, using no other functions symbols or constants but Φ and C, whose semantics is ($\Phi \cup C$)-isomorphic to ϕ.

7) The language can be used to specify every **update** transaction.

8) The language can be used to specify every **integrity** and **inference** law in the data base.

9) There is a semantic extension of the language (without alteration of the syntax) to cover the behavior of queries and update transactions in the presence of integrity and inference laws.

5. FORMAL SEMANTICS

IDB ≡ *INSTANTANEOUS-DATA-BASES*[2]

***ASSERTION*:**

---

[2] For the relational model (having a denumerable domain D of objects),

$$IDB \equiv \text{POWERSET}(NAMES-OF\underset{\underset{D}{\cap}}{-}RELATIONS \times D^{*})$$

Using the binary model, $D \cup D \times D$ is sufficient instead of D^{*}

$[\mathit{THE\text{-}LANGUAGE} \rightarrow [\mathit{IDB} \rightarrow \mathit{BOOLEAN}_{\perp}]]$[3]

semantics-of-queries:

$[\mathit{THE\text{-}LANGUAGE} \rightarrow [\mathit{IDB} \rightarrow \mathit{OUTPUT}_{\perp}]]$

semantics-of-data-manipulation:

$[\mathit{DATA\text{-}SEMANTIC\text{-}FUNCTIONS} \rightarrow [\mathit{THE\text{-}LANGUAGE} \rightarrow [\mathit{IDB} \rightarrow \mathit{IDB}_{\perp} \times \mathit{OUTPUT}_{\perp}]]]$

DATA-SEMANTIC-FUNCTIONS=

$[\mathit{IDB} \rightarrow \mathit{IDB}_{\perp,\mathit{ERROR}}]$

semantics-of-laws:

$[\mathit{THE\text{-}LANGUAGE} \times \mathit{THE\text{-}LANGUAGE} \rightarrow \mathit{DATA\text{-}SEMANTIC\text{-}FUNCTIONS}]$

$$\textbf{semantics-of-queries}(\underset{\mathit{THE\text{-}LANGUAGE}}{\mathit{query} \in}, \underset{\mathit{INSTANTANEOUS\text{-}DATA\text{-}BASES}}{\mathit{idb} \in})=$$

let $\phi = \mathit{ASSERTION}(\mathit{query})$ **in**

$$\text{choose}_{\perp}\left(\left\{(\mathit{result},\mathit{temp}) \;\middle|\; \begin{array}{c} \phi(\mathit{idb} \dot{\cup} \mathit{result} \dot{\cup} \mathit{temp}) \wedge\ ^{4} \\ \forall \mathit{vdb}. \\ \textbf{if } \mathit{idb} \subseteq \mathit{vdb} \subset (\mathit{idb} \dot{\cup} \mathit{result} \dot{\cup} \mathit{temp}) \\ \textbf{then } \phi(\mathit{vdb}) \equiv \mathit{false} \end{array}\right\}\right)_{\text{project1 (take only } \mathit{result} \text{ component)}}$$

$$\mathbf{ASSERTION}_{\mathit{query}}(\underset{\mathit{INSTANTANEOUS\text{-}DATA\text{-}BASES}}{\mathit{idb} \in})=$$

case *query*:

$$\begin{bmatrix} \forall \mathit{variable}: q & \bigwedge_{x \text{ in } \mathit{idb}} \mathit{ASSERTION}_{q \mid^{x}_{\mathit{variable}}}(\mathit{idb}) \\ q_1 \supset q_2 & \mathit{ASSERTION}_{q_1}(\mathit{idb}) \supset \mathit{ASSERTION}_{q_2}(\mathit{idb})^{6} \\ \text{IsaRelationship}(\mathit{expression}_1,\ldots) & (\mathit{Evaluate}(\mathit{expression}_1),\ldots) \in \mathit{idb} \\ \text{IsTrue}(\mathit{expression}) & \mathit{Evaluate}(\mathit{expression}) \underset{\perp}{=} \underline{\mathit{true}} \end{bmatrix}$$

---

[3] $X_{\perp}$ is $X \cup \{\perp\}$; $\perp$ means *undefined*.

[4] $\dot{\cup}$ is a decomposable union: for $\alpha,\beta,\gamma,\delta \in \mathit{IDB}$, $\delta = (\alpha \dot{\cup} \beta \dot{\cup} \gamma)$ **iff** $(\alpha,\beta,\gamma) = \text{split}(\delta)$

[6] $\supset$ has a parallel logic tri-valued interpretation:
$(\mathit{false} \supset ?) \equiv (? \supset \mathit{true}) \equiv \mathit{true}$; $(\mathit{true} \supset \mathit{false}) \equiv \mathit{false}$. In the rest of the cases it is $\perp$ (The other operators, e.g. $\wedge, \vee$, and $\sim$, are syntactic abbreviations using $\supset$.)

ABSTRACTED SYNTAX

For any given decidable set D of all possible objects, for any given decidable set Φ of partial computable functions from D^* to D, $THE\text{-}LANGUAGE_{D,\Phi}$ is defined by:

$$assertion ::= \left[\begin{array}{c} \forall variable\ assertion \mid {}^{variable}_{constant} \\ assertion \supset assertion \\ \text{IsaRelationship}(expression^*)\text{[7]} \\ \text{IsTrue}(expression) \end{array}\right]$$

expression: $EXPRESSIONS_{D,\Phi} = D \cup \Phi \times EXPRESSIONS^*_{D,\Phi}$

variable: *VARIABLES* – a denumerable set

$\exists$, $\wedge$, $\vee$, $\neg$, TRUE, FALSE are standard abbreviations using $\forall$, $\supset$, IsTrue(*false*).

SPECIAL CASES

1) First Order: Relation Names May Not Be Quantified.

The head of any tuple in "IsaRelationship" is not quantified and stands for a name of a relation.

2) The *Uninterpreted Domain* case.

$$\Phi = \{=\}, \quad (= : D \times D \rightarrow \underset{\underset{D}{\cap}}{BOOLEAN})$$

$$assertion ::= \left[\begin{array}{c} \forall variable\ assertion \mid {}^{variable}_{constant} \\ assertion \supset assertion \\ \text{IsaRelationship}(constant^*) \\ constant = constant \end{array}\right]$$

constant: D

variable: *VARIABLES* – a denumerable set

---

[7] $expression^*$ is a tuple. Triples representing binary relationships are sufficient to consider since higher-order relations are derivable.

3) An *Uninterpreted Subdomain* and a *Fully Interpreted Subdomain*.

$D = U \cup I;$

$I = INTEGERS$

$\Phi = \{=\} \cup [I^{*} \underset{computable}{\overset{partial}{\longrightarrow}} I]$

APPENDICES

Appendix 1 - The Implementabilty Theorem

The proof of the implementability is *sketched* here by defining an implementation of a very high complexity. In practice a heuristic implementation is needed for the language or its sublanguages.

1. There is a procedure to implement the predicate

VERIFY (q, vdb, idb)

("does the virtual data base vdb satisfy the assertion q?").

The procedure acts as follows. First it checks whether idb is the given part of vdb. If not, it halts with false. Otherwise it continues. Quantifiers are resolved yielding a finite number n of atomic formulae connected by logical operators. n parallel processes are issued to evaluate the clauses. These processes are correlated so that a halting process will cause an abortion of those processes whose results will not influence the interpretation of the assertion (as defined by the tri-valued logic above).

2. An effective inclusion-preserving enumeration E of the set IDB of all instantaneous data bases is constructed.

3. The following is a procedure to evaluate a query. The inputs are: $q \in L$, $idb \in IDB$.

The procedure uses an unlimited quantity of parallel processes, but at every instant of time the number of processes is finite, and thus they can be implemented by one sequential process.

Let $vdb_1, vdb_2, \ldots, vdb_n, \ldots$ be the inclusion-preserving enumeration of IDB constructed in (2).

Let Q be a fixed quantity of time.

Let BUFFER be an unlimited, initially empty, interprocess storage (which will contain indices of virtual data base found as contradicting assertion q).

At the beginning, the first process PR_1 is invoked.

Every process PR_n acts as follows after its invocation:

A – Start computing VERIFY (q, vdb_n, idb) until "local" time Q elapsed.

B – Invoke the process PR_{n+1}.

C – Continue computing VERIFY (q, vdb_n, idb) until true of false is obtained or forever (unless externally aborted).

D – If *false* has been obtained then:

D1 – Insert the index n into BUFFER;

D2 – Loop forever (unless externally aborted).

E – If true has been obtained then:

E1 – If every proper subset of vdb_n is in BUFFER, then:

E2 – Output the "result part" of vdb_n;

E3 – Abort all the processes, including the current process.

else: repeat E1 (forever or until internally or externally aborted).

Appendix 2: Completeness Theorems.

A. Absolute completeness of the maximal language.

Theorem. The maximal language L defined above (were Φ contains every partial recursive function from D^* to D represented by a recursive expression) is absolutely complete, i.e., for every partial computable function ϕ: $IDB \rightarrow IDB$ there exists a query $q \in L$ whose semantics is ϕ.

The proof is preceded by its sketch.

A query q is constructed whose semantics is ϕ. The assertion of the query consists of three subassertions:

- an assertion implying existence of a special object in the virtual data base encoding the whole input data base,
- an assertion implying existence of an object encoding the resulting data base,
- and an assertion relating these two objects by a derivative of ϕ.

These assertions are constructed so that the following is insured:

- the query will be deterministic (to be used in the next theorem);

- the query is convertible for an appropriate query for the language L' not using variables or expressions as names of relations (to be used in "L' almost completeness" theorem);
- the conjunction of the assertions is undefined if and only if ϕ is undefined for the input data base, provided the evaluation is done by parallel communicating processes;
- the conjunction gives false for every subset of the desired virtual data base.

Proof:

Let ϕ: *IDB* $\rightarrow$ *IDB* be a partial computable function.

1) Encode *IDB* by D.

Let $*: D \times D \rightarrow D$, sc: THE-SET-OF-ALL-FINITE-SUBSETS-OF(D) $\rightarrow D$ be two two-way effective bijections (existence of which is well known). Let tr: *IDB* $\rightarrow D$ be the two-way effective bijection defined by:

$tr(db) = sc(\{r^*(\alpha^*\beta) \mid (\alpha\ r\ \beta) \in db\})$.

Let $f = tr \circ \phi \circ tr^{-1}$. By the Theory of Computability, f is a partial recursive function from D to D.

2) Define total recursive functions from D^2 to D simulating set operations:

$insert(s,d) = sc(sc^{-1}(s) \cup \{d\})$

$remove(s,d) = sc(sc^{-1}(s) - \{d\})$

$in(d,s) =$ if $d \in sc^{-1}(s)$ then *'true'* else *'false'*

3) Abbreviate:

∅–code — the constant representing $sc(\emptyset)$ (i.e. the constant encoding the empty set.)

f*, *in*, *insert*, *remove — recursive expressions representing the corresponding functions f, *in*, *insert*, and *remove*.

GIVEN (x, r, y) — IsaRelationship(x_1, r, y), where x_1 is an expression concatenating the string 'input' to the value of x (i.e. GIVEN is a predicate stating that a tuple belongs to the input part of the virtual data base).

RESULT (x, r, y) — analogously.

TEMP (x, r, y) — IsaRelationship(x, y, z) (to be used for tuples which are neither in the input part nor in the result part of the virtual data base.)

4) The query q.

The following sentence abbreviates the assertional syntax of the query and is composed of clauses (marked C_i), each of which is preceded by a comment (enclosed in /*...*/) outlining the subassertion expressed by the clause. The names of the unary relations (categories) of the virtual data base are given in enlarged italics.

/* C_0 and C_1: there is a temporary object encoding the whole input data base */

/* C_0: there is a temporary object encoding the empty set */

```
TEMP (∅–code 'encodes a subset of the input db') and
```

/* C_1: for every existing code of a subset and for every triple in the input db, there is a temporary object encoding that subset enriched with this triple */.

```
∀setcode, x,y,r
    if TEMP (setcode 'encodes a subset of the input db')
        and GIVEN (x,r,y) then
        TEMP (insert (setcode,(r * (s * y)))
           'encodes a subset of the input db') and
```

/* C_2: there is a temporary object which equals f(the encoding of the whole input data base); this object should encode the whole result */

```
∀inputdbcode
    if (∀x,r,y if GIVEN(x,r,y) then
                    IsTrue(in ((r * (x * y)), inputdbcode)))
      then TEMP (f (inputdbcode)
                 'encodes a subset of the result') and
```

/* C_3: the result is actually what is encoded by the above object */

```
∀setcode
    if TEMP (setcode 'encodes a subset of the result') then
```

/* $C_{3.1}$: the encoded set is either empty or contains a resulting triple */

```
((IsTrue (setcode = ∅–code ) or
  ∃x,r,y (RESULT (x r y) and
        IsTrue(in ((r * (x * y)), setcode)))) and
```

/* $C_{3.2}$: inductively, every triple contained in the set must be in the result; but using the above we invert this thus: */

```
∀x,r,y
  if RESULT (x r y) then
     TEMP (remove (setcode, r * (x * y))
          'encodes a subset of the result'))
```

5) Let $\overline{q}$ be the semantics of q. The following proves that $\overline{q} = \phi$.

Let $idb \in IDB$. Consider two cases:

(i) $\phi(idb)$ is undefined.
It has to be shown that $\overline{q}(idb)$ is also undefined. Assume the contrary. Then there exists $vdb \in IDB$ satisfying the assertion and containing idb. By definition of the "parallel and", all the four clauses are interpreted to *true* for vdb. $C_0 \wedge C_1$ imply inductively that there exists $inputdbcode = tr(idb)$ in vdb. This and C_2 imply that there is $f(inputdbcode)$ in vdb. Thus $f(tr(idb))$ is defined and so is $\phi(idb)$ in contradiction to the assumption. Thus $\overline{q}(idb)$ is undefined.

(ii) $\phi(idb)$ is well-defined (not $\perp$).
Let vdb be as follows: its input and result parts are idb and $\phi(idb)$ respectively, and its remainder consists of two instantaneous unary relations: '*encodes a subset of the input db*' is $\{tr(S) | S \subseteq idb\}$, '*encodes a subset of the result*' is $\{tr(S) | (S \subseteq \phi(idb)\}$.

vdb satisfies the assertion. It remains to show that every one of its proper subsets containing idb contradicts the assertion.

Assume the contrary. Let $idb \subseteq vdb' \subset vdb$ so that vdb' does not contradict the assertion. Then the interpretation of the assertion for vdb' is *true* or *undefined*.

Consider both cases:

(a) The interpretation is *true*. Then idb is the "input part" of vdb' and all the four clauses yield *true* for vdb'. $C_0 \wedge C_1$ imply that the instance of '*encodes a subset of the input db*' in vdb' includes $\{tr(S) \mid S \subseteq idb\}$. Thus, $tr(idb)$ is contained in this instance. Then, by C_2, $f(tr(idb))$ is in the instance of '*encodes a subset of the result*'. Then, by C_3, the result part includes $\phi(idb)$ and the instance of '*encodes a subset of the result*' includes $\{tr(S) | S \subseteq \phi(idb)\}$. Thus, $vdb \subseteq vdb'$, in contradiction.

(b) The interpretation is *undefined*. Then, by definition of "parallel and" at least one clause yields *undefined* for vdb' and no clause yields *false*. All the clauses, except C', involve only total functions. Thus, C_0, C_1 and C_3 yield *true* and C_2 yields *undefined*.

The "input part" of vdb' is idb (otherwise the assertion would yield *false*). This and $C_0 \wedge C_1$ imply that there is $tr(idb)$ in the instance of '*encodes a subset of the input db*'. But $f(tr(idb)) = tr^{-1}(\phi(idb))$ is defined. (Possibly there is another setcode in the above relation's instance such that $f(setcode)$ is *undefined* and setcode encodes a set containing all the triples of "the input part".) After the resolution of quantification, C_2 is a conjunction of many clauses, none of which yields *false* (otherwise C_2 would yield *false*). Thus, since

$f(tr(idb))$ is defined, the subclause for $tr(idb)$ must yield *true*. Thus, $f(tr(idb))$ is in the instance of *'encodes a subset of the result'*. Continuing the reasoning analogous to that of **(a)**, we get: $vdb \subseteq vdb'$, in analogous contradiction.

B. The completeness of deterministic queries.

Theorem. The sublanguage of L containing only deterministic queries is also absolutely complete.

Proof: Following the proof of the previous theorem, we find that if there is vdb' satisfying the assertion, then $vdb \subseteq vdb'$. Thus, no other but vdb can be chosen; so the query is deterministic.

C. Almost-completeness of The First-Order Sublanguage

I shall prove here that any query can be stated so that relations are named only by constants, unless the query must deal with infinitely many relevant relation-names (which usually would be meaningless in an end-user's query).

Definition. A set $S \subseteq D$ contains all relation names *relevant* for ϕ: $IDB \xrightarrow{P} IDB$ iff:

- $\{r \mid \exists idb \in dom(\phi), \exists x,y \in D: (x\ r\ y) \in \phi(idb)\} \subseteq S$, i.e., S contains every relation-name appearing in some output, and
- for every $idb \in IDB$

  $$\phi(idb) \equiv \phi(idb - D \times (D-S) \times D)$$

  ("$\equiv$" means that either both sides are undefined or they are equal).

Definition. A function ϕ: $IDB \xrightarrow{P} IDB$ has a *finite* set of relevant relation-names iff there is a finite set which contains all the relation-names relevant for ϕ.

Note: Transformations which do not have such a finite set intuitively do not represent specific needs on the application level but rather something on the DBMS level. For example, copy the whole data base, estimate its extent, list its relation-names.

Theorem. The language L' (i.e., those queries of L which use only constants as names of relation) generates all the partial computable functions from IDB to IDB having finite sets of relevant relation-names.

Proof: Let ϕ be a partial computable function from IDB to IDB having a finite set S of relevant relation-names. Denote the elements of S by $r_1, r_2, \ldots, r_n$. From the structure of the query q defined in the proof of the principal completeness theorem, obtain a query q_2 by resolving all the quantifications of the variable "r". Thus, "$\forall r\ \tau$" is transformed to "$\tau_1 \wedge \tau_2 \wedge \ldots \wedge \tau_n$" where τ_i is τ in which r is substituted for the constant representing r_i. (Respectively, "$\exists r\ \tau$" is transformed to "$\tau_1 \vee \ldots \vee \tau_n$".)

Let $\overline{q}_2$ be the semantics of q_2. I shall show that $\overline{q}' = \phi$.

Let $idb \in IDB$.

Consider the following cases:

1) All the relation-names appearing in idb belong to S. So do the relation-names of $\phi(idb)$, provided this exists. The assertions q and q_2 are interpreted equivalently, and thus the queries must yield the same results (or *undefined*).

2) There is a relation-name r_0 appearing in idb and not belonging to S. Following the proof of the principal completeness theorem, we find that $\overline{q}'(idb) \equiv \phi(idb - D \times (D-S) \times S)$ which in turn, by the condition of the theorem and the definitions above, is equivalent to $\phi(idb)$.

   Thus, in every case $\phi(idb) \equiv \overline{q}'(idb)$.

Appendix 3: Language Submodels with Restrictions of Value Calculation; Isomorphism of Queries.

The purpose of this appendix is to clarify the result 6 in section 4.

Finite set of basic functions without recursion can be sufficient to have the complete power of the language. (The rest of partial recursive functions ($[D^* \rightarrow D]$) can be expressed using the postconditional semantics of the query language). Unlike that "saving", in the following I wish to actually restrict the power of the language by removing from it the ability to specify computations which are extremely unnatural and should be forbidden in a user's system of concepts. The general case needed to be investigated is the one in which a user is provided with a family of functions on values considered legal for a given data base or a data base management system. This family does not necessarily contain a basic set sufficient to create all the computable functions over the domain of objects using the power of first-order predicate calculus. Usually no computation on abstract objects in the binary model of data bases may be regarded meaningful.

Families of special interest are those differentiating between *abstract objects* and *concrete values*. On the subdomain of the abstract objects there are only two meaningful functions: the characteristic function *is-abstract* giving *true* for abstract objects and *false* for concrete value, and the binary function *equality* giving *true* or *false* for pairs of objects. The rest of such a family is a basic set of functions on the subdomain of concrete values. Using this basic set and a program control power, every computable function on the subdomain of values can be expressed. (Instead of program control power, a first-order predicate calculus can be used.)

In the following, let Φ be a family of operations on the set of objects D, i.e. functions from D^* to $D \cup \{undefined\}$. (Φ is not necessarily a special case like described in the previous paragraph.) D is assumed to contain $\{error, true, false\}$.

$$D^* = D^0 \cup D \cup D^2 \cup D^3 \cdots$$

Though binary operations are sufficient to have the complete power of the language, I am aiming to restrict the power and to be able to model exactly any practical restriction. That's why I permit here n-ary operations – some of them cannot be generated from binary ones without choosing them strong enough to permit generation of functions which are beyond a desired restriction.

Let L_Φ be the language as defined above but using only function symbols from Φ (and no recursion.)

I claim, intuitively, that L_Φ has all the power reasonable within the restriction of Φ, including:

(a) the ability to generate every function computable using program control and the set of operations Φ;

(b) the ability to generate vertical functions, such as *sum* or *average* of values, i.e. to relate some objects to applications of functions (a) on sets of values;

(c) the ability to create new objects, including abstract objects:

(d) the ability to specify every data base transformation which does not involve computation of any values, but Φ-basable values, and does not condition data base structure on such values.

These claims and the following ones will be respecified rigorously after I define isomorphism of data base transformations.

In addition to Φ, queries of L_Φ may use constant symbols. But I claim (so far intuitively) that a query needs to use only those constants which are absolutely relevant to its purpose, i.e. any program would have to use these constants in addition to Φ.

The use of constants is not obsolete, i.e. the use of constants cannot be substituted by 0-ary functions from Φ, because:

1) The set Φ is fixed for the language L_Φ due to global restrictions which in a given data base or DBMS are desired to be imposed on all queries.

2) Not all permitted constants can be generated from Φ when it is intentionally more restricted. *E.g.,* when social security numbers are considered, only their comparison is permitted in Φ, but we would certainly wish to permit asking a query inquiring about any specific social security number, appearing as a constant in the query. Usually, the permitted constants are all nonabstract objects.

3) If instead of Φ we were fixing (globally for the language) a richer set containing (or able to generate) all the permitted constants, which is generally an infinite set, then every query would become undesirably less free and more deterministic due to fixed interpretation of constants which it does not need.

Now I shall formalize the discussion.

Definition

A bijection $\iota : D \rightarrow D$ is called a Φ - isomorphism iff

$$\forall (d_1, \ldots, d_n) \in D^* \quad \forall f \in \Phi \;\; f(\iota(d_1), \ldots, \iota(d_n)) \equiv \iota(f(d_1, \ldots, d_n))$$

(Note: the $\equiv$ symbol covers the case when both sides are undefined.)

Definition

For a given instantaneous data base *db*, a Φ-isomorphism ι is called *db-preserving* iff for every object *d* appearing in *db*,

$$\iota(d) \equiv d$$

Definition

A computable data base transformation ϕ: $IDB \xrightarrow{\prime} IDB$ is Φ-preserving if for every $db \in IDB$ and for every Φ-isomorphism ι, $\phi(\iota(db)) \equiv \iota(\phi(db)$.

Definition

Two data base transformations ϕ, ψ are called Φ-isomorphic iff for every instantaneous data base $db \in IDB$ there exists a *db*-preserving Φ-isomorphism ι such that $\phi(db) \equiv \iota(\psi(db))$.

Definition

Let C be a finite set of constants, a subset of D. Two data base transformations are called (Φ, C)-isomorphic iff they are ($\Phi \cup C'$)-isomorphic, where C' is the set of constant functions, equivalent to C. A Φ-isomorphism ι is called (Φ, C)-isomorphism if it is a $(\Phi \cup C')$-isomorphism.

Proposition

For every finite set of constants $C \subset D$, every computable (Φ, C)-preserving data base transformation is expressible up to a (Φ, C)-isomorphism in L_Φ with C, *i.e.*, for every such transformation ϕ there exists a query $q \in L_\Phi$ using no other constants but C, whose semantics ψ is (Φ, C)-isomorphic to ϕ.

Corollary

Every computable Φ-preserving data base transformation is expressible in L_Φ up to an isomorphism,

i.e., for every such transformation there exists a query $q \in L$ whose semantics ψ is Φ-isomorphic to ϕ, and the query q uses no constant symbols.

REFERENCES

[Abrial - 74] J.R. Abrial, "Data Semantics", in J.W. Klimbie and K.L. Koffeman (eds.), *Data Base Management,* North Holland, 1974.

[Aho and Ullman-79] A.V. Aho, J.D. Ullman, "Universality of Data Retrieval Languages", in *Proc. 6th ACM Symp. on Principles of Programming Languages,* 1979.

[Bancilhon - 78] F. Bancilhon "On the completeness of query languages for relational databases". Proc. Seventh Symp. on Mathematical Foundations of Computer Science. Springer-Verlag 1978.

[Codd - 72] E. F. Codd "Relational Completeness of Data Base Sublanguages" in *Data Base Systems* (ed. Rustin). Prentice-Hall, Englewood Cliff, N. J. 1972

[Codd - 70] E. F. Codd. "A Relational Model for Large Shared Data Banks." CACM . v. 13 n. 6. 1970.

[Chandra and Harel-80] A.K. Chandra and D. Harel, "Computable Queries for Relational Data Bases", J. of Computer and System Sciences, vol. 21, 1980.

[Chandra and Harel -82] A.K. Chandra and D. Harel, "Horn Clauses and the Fixpoint Query Hierarchy", Proceedings of the ACM Symposium on Principles of Database Systems. 1982.

[Gallaire-78] H. Gallaire and J. Minker, eds. *Logic and Data Bases.* Plenum Press, New York, 1978.

[Gallaire-81] H. Gallaire and J. Minker, eds. *Advances in Data Base Theory,* Plenum Press, New York, 198l.

[Li - 84] Deyi Li. *A Prolog Database System.* Research Studies Press Ltd, John Wiley & Sons Inc, Letchworth, Hertfordshire, England. 1984.

[Rishe-85] N. Rishe, *Semantics of Universal Languages and Informations Structures in Data Bases.* Technical report TRCS85-010, Computer Science Department, University of California, Santa Barbara, 1985.

WHAT IS A MODEL?
A CONSUMER'S PERSPECTIVE ON SEMANTIC THEORY

Jon Shultis
Department of Computer Science
University of Colorado
Boulder, Co 80309, USA

Introduction

By a "consumer" of semantic theory, I mean anyone who, like myself, is not primarily concerned with proving new results or otherwise contributing directly to the theory of semantics, but who finds (or could find) the concepts and methods of semantics useful for doing other work. Currently, consumers include programming language designers and, to some extent, language implementors. The results and methods of semantics could serve a much wider audience.

Insofar as everyday programming is a process of (language) specification and implementation, why should semantics seem so irrelevant to programmers? Whenever I treat semantic theory in my graduate programming languages class, the students listen patiently for about a week, and then begin asking: "What is this stuff good for?" I am getting better at finding answers to pacify my students, but the question nags at me more all the time. Take money, for example. How many cases can we point to where a result from semantic theory has saved someone a penny? Not one.

A thing is useful if it solves a problem that someone wants solved. So far, semantics has solved problems that are of interest mainly to semanticists: How can this kind of language be modelled? When are two programs equivalent? What do all models of this language have in common? When does a language have a relatively complete theory? And so forth. The answers that have been found for these and many other questions have unquestionably improved our understanding of the basic issues and methods of semantic theory.

Should I then tell my students that these concepts and techniques are good for doing more semantic theory? In other words, "this stuff is good for solving problems that most of you don't care about". If that's the best I can do, I shouldn't be teaching semantics to computer scientists.

Semantic theory can be far more relevant and useful to the practically-oriented computer scientist than it is at present. To see how, we need to take a careful look at the kinds of problems faced by consumers of semantics, and understand why the theory sometimes helps solve those problems, and sometimes doesn't.

1. Metalanguage Semantics and Constructivity

The controversy and confusion over how to interpret the definition of Algol 60 posed a problem that computer scientists wanted solved: some means had to be found of defining the meaning of a programming language in a precise and unambiguous way.

Strachey's solution [21] was to associate a mathematical denotation with each phrase of a language. In order to do this, he faced a subsidiary problem: how to write down the denotations, and how to write down the mapping from language structures to their denotations. He settled on Church's λ-notation for writing down the denotations, and syntax-directed translation for writing down the mapping. A third problem, noticed by Scott, is that the metalanguage used to specify the semantics also needs a semantic definition; reflexive domains provided the solution for λ-calculus.

The method of denotational semantics is now routinely used to define small languages and study their properties. Several examples of such applications are contained in these proceedings.

The similarity between the specification of a denotational semantics and a model has led to the identification of the two. Recall that, in mathematical logic, a domain together with a homomorphism from the syntax to that domain is called an *interpretation*. Given a notion of truth in the domain, an interpretation is a *model* of a logic (theory) if all of the axioms are true and all of the inference rules preserve truth. In the case of programming languages, we can think of a denotational semantics as giving a model of the language's Floyd-Hoare theory. In the case of λ-calculus models, we might use realizability as our notion of truth, in which case all that really needs to be checked is that the conversion rules are valid.

The identification of denotational semantics with models is unfortunate, however, because it misses a point of paramount importance to consumers. The success of denotational semantics is largely due to the fact that the λ-calculus semantics we use is constructive, in the sense that writing down the semantic equations for a language gives an effective way of computing the meaning of any phrase.

To illustrate the importance of this point, consider the denotational semantics for Communicating Sequential Processes given by Brookes et al. in [5]. The metalanguage used there is the language of classical first-order logic and set theory. Ignoring the philosophical issues, one thing is clear: whatever semantics we give to this metalanguage, it will not be effective. There is nothing "wrong" with this, unless we want to use the semantics as a basis for an implementation, or use some theorems about the semantics to manipulate actual programs. Because these are precisely the things that consumers want semantics for, however, a non-effective semantics is less useful to them than it might be.

Among other things, the non-effectiveness of the semantics causes trouble when operations for combining processes are defined. For example, Brookes *et al.*'s Theorem 2 asserts that the intersection of an arbitrary family of processes is a process. In order to understand why this is so from a computational standpoint, one needs a proof that yields a construction of the intersection, showing why the result is again a process. Unfortunately, the proof offered uses the method of contradiction, which is not effective. The burden of devising a constructive proof is therefore laid squarely on the shoulders of anyone who might wish to use the result as part of a computer program. Since there is no guarantee *a priori* that such a proof can be found, the "result" might just as well have been stated as a conjecture.

By contrast, consider the theorem that for every nondeterministic finite automaton there is an equivalent deterministic one. The usual proof of this gives a direct construction of the deterministic automaton from the nondeterministic one, and shows that the construction leaves invariant the language accepted. The theorem is useful to consumers of automata theory because its proof supplies an algorithm.

By analogy, denotations (for programming semantics, at least!) should be effective objects, effectively given, and effectively reasoned about. In short, a denotational semantics should provide an *effective* model, not just any model. For a discussion of effectiveness, see [24]. Adherence to this principle would go a long way toward making semantic theory more useful. But is it enough?

2. What is a Model?

Consider the category $\mathbf{N}_{\leq}$ having the natural numbers as objects, the arrows being given by the usual ordering. It is easy to model addition using $\mathbf{N}_{\leq}$ as the domain. Let the numeral n denote the corresponding arrow $\hat{n}:0 \leq \bar{n}$, where $\bar{n}$ is the (semantic) natural number corresponding to the (syntactic) numeral n. The semantics of addition is given by the following equation.

$$[\![n+m]\!] = [\![n]\!] \circ (trans([\![m]\!] , \overline{n}))$$

where

$$trans : (\overline{i} \leq \overline{j}, \overline{k}) \longmapsto (\overline{i+k}) \leq (\overline{j+k})$$

Imagine now that we have been given a machine (the **N≤** machine) with a screen that displays two numerals separated by the symbol "≤", and several buttons. There is a button for each digit, and buttons labelled "from", "to", and "compose". To operate the machine, we type in a sequence of digits, followed by "from", followed by a second sequence of digits, followed by "to". The digit sequences are displayed on either side of the "≤" on the screen. Next, we press "compose", then enter a second pair of digits. After the last digit has been entered and the "to" button pressed, one of two things happens. If the second sequence of digits of the first pair is the same as the first sequence of the second pair, then the first sequence of the first pair and the second sequence of the second pair are displayed on the screen. Otherwise, the screen displays the word "error".

The semantics given above tells how to model the language of addition expressions in **N≤**, but does this mean that we can use the **N≤** machine as an adding machine? Clearly not. The semantics is certainly effective, but it depends on a construction, viz. *trans*, that has no counterpart in **N≤** (and hence is not an operation of the machine).

The example of the **N≤** machine illustrates a common source of frustration with the methods of denotational semantics. Programmers constantly have to define the semantics of languages (i.e., software interfaces) in terms of (hardware and software) devices with limited capabilities, such as disk controllers, report generators, and so forth. For such purposes, the fact that the device is an effective model in some general sense of "effective" is not enough. The semantics has to be effective *with respect to the capabilities of the device.*

If we restrict ourselves to general-purpose programming languages, this problem is never apparent, as long as we use λ-calculus or some other constructive notation for our metalanguage. In many situations, however, it is important to recognize the problem and avoid it by adhering to the following principle: the semantics of a language should use constructions from the semantic domain(s) of the model, and nothing else. In the parlance of topos theory, the semantics should be defined entirely in terms of the internal structure of the domains.

Insofar as a model is supposed to capture the "meaning" of a language, shouldn't we always avoid shifting any of that meaning into a metalanguage the semantics of which is not explicitly represented in the model? Perhaps we should revise our definition of "model" to include the metalanguage somehow. In order to avoid confusion, however, we shall continue to use "model" in its conventional sense, and we shall refer to internally constructed models as "internal models".

To a large extent, interest in categories that admit universal objects [23] is motivated by the need to consider the semantics of the metalanguage when developing the semantics of a subject language. A universal domain, coupled with a language in which to express constructions in that domain (as in, e.g., ML [10]), allows one to focus on the details of a specific subject language (or, more generally, program). The problem of metalanguage semantics can be ignored because the metalanguage is fixed and predefined. Of course, this is exactly what we do when we use λ-notation and domain equations to give semantics to ordinary sequential programming languages.

Learning the structure of a universal domain such as Pω [22] requires a significant investment of time and effort. Unless the return on that investment is a great increase in practical problem-solving ability, consumers will not be motivated to make it. If the metalanguage is a powerful problem-solving tool, they are more likely simply to use it, and take the theory behind it for granted.

As with a first programming language, however, one's ability to conceive of alternative solutions to a problem may be limited by taking the universal domain for granted. This problem can become acute if the universal domain is inappropriate to a problem, e.g. $P\omega$ is inadequate for studying non-deterministic programs.

Suppose that, instead of a specific universal domain construction, the consumer were offered tools for effectively constructing (universal) domains, and shown some powerful applications of those tools. Such tools would make the study of domain constructions more appealing to consumers, because the results of such constructions would be perceived as having immediate practical application. We will return to this point in §4.

3. Cartesian Closure and λ-calculus Models

How does restricting attention to internal models affect the results of semantic investigations? To illustrate the difference between internal and external models, we reconsider Albert Meyer's question, "What is a Lambda-Calculus Model?" [19], taking the work of Berry [3] as a starting point.

Berry's thesis is that "*the cartesian closure is really the key property for semantic model constructions*" (Berry's emphasis). The main result supporting this claim is his theorem 5.2.9, which states that "Any categorical model defines a model of Λ." (We shall explain these terms presently.) To what extent is this thesis upheld when we replace "model" by "internal model"?

We begin by summarizing some definitions. (Caveat: we write both composition and application in diagrammatic order! So, for example, xf denotes f applied to x, which we prefer to enunciate as "x supplied to f". This perversity is the sorry result of having been brought up to read programs from left-to-right and top-to-bottom.)

Λ is the syntactic domain of λ-expressions. A *model of* Λ consists of the following data.

- Three domains D, V, Env, of denotations, values, and environments, respectively.
- A *semantic functor* $[\![\,]\!]:\Lambda \to D$
  $[\![\,]\!]$ must preserve (syntactic) α- and β-conversion,
  and semantic equivalence must imply syntactic substitutivity.
- An evaluation operator $eval: Env \times D \to V$
- An application operator $\bullet: V \times V \to V$

The environment domain is defined by the equation $Env = \prod_{\omega} V$. When no confusion is possible, we write ρd for $(\rho, d)eval$. These data must satisfy the following conditions.

$$(var) \qquad \rho[\![x]\!] = \rho\pi_x$$

$$(app) \qquad \rho[\![ee']\!] = (\rho[\![e]\!], \rho[\![e']\!])\bullet$$

$$(lambda) \qquad (\rho[\![\lambda x.e]\!], v)\bullet = (\rho[v/x])[\![e]\!]$$

$$(free) \qquad \rho|_{fv(e)} = \rho'|_{fv(e)} \Rightarrow \rho[\![e]\!] = \rho'[\![e]\!]$$

where $\rho|_{fv(e)}$ denotes the projection of ρ on the set of free variables of e.

A *categorical model* is given by the following data.

- A Cartesian-closed category **C** with terminal object $\top$ and evaluation arrow ev.
  $\hat{f}$ denotes the exponential adjoint of f.
- $V_{\mathbf{C}} \in Ob(\mathbf{C})$

- A retraction $\Theta: V_C^{V_C} \to V_C$ with Θ^{-1} the corresponding section
- $Env_C = \prod_{\omega} V_C$.

Updating in Env_C is accomplished by the collection of arrows $\{s_x: Env_C \times V_C \to Env_C \mid x \in \omega\}$, one for each "variable" x, defined by the equations $s_x \circ \pi_x = \pi_2$, and $s_x \circ \pi_y = \pi_1 \circ \pi_y$ for $x \neq y$.

We now attempt to prove that from every categorical model a model of Λ can be constructed *internally*. The problem is: internal to what? The statement that **C** is a Cartesian-closed category implies, for example, a bifunctor $\pi: \mathbf{C} \times \mathbf{C} \to \mathbf{C}$ which is a binary Cartesian product on **C**. Berry makes free use of π, which is external to **C**, but internal to the world in which **C** is defined.

Berry's thesis is ambiguous on this point; is the key property the property of *being* a Cartesian-closed category (with some additional structure), or is it the property of *containing* such a category? If we choose the second interpretation, then Berry's proof suffices. In that case, we interpret the theorem as saying that "any domain in which a categorical model can be defined is an internal model of Λ". If, on the other hand, we choose the first interpretation, then we need a new proof, and interpret the theorem as "every categorical model is an internal model of Λ".

Since there is nothing to do otherwise, we shall choose the first interpretation, and see how far we get. To start, we must choose objects of **C** for the domains. (For convenience, we shall henceforth drop the subscript C from the names of **C**-objects where no confusion is possible.) For denotations we take V^{Env}, for values we take V, and for environments we take Env.

For *eval* we take $ev: D \times Env \to V$. The restriction of ev to domain $D \times Env$ emphasizes that *eval* is a **C**-morphism, and so is internal to **C**; we do not at any time assume that the full unit of the exponential adjunction is available when constructing meanings. For $\bullet$ we take $(\Theta^{-1} \times 1) \circ eval$, also a **C**-morphism. It is vital that both of these be defined in advance as fixed **C**-morphisms, so that when they are used later in the semantic clauses no external constructions are inadvertently introduced.

The semantic clauses must associate with each syntactic phrase an element $\phi: \top \to V^{Env}$ of the semantic domain. ϕ must be specified either by a fixed **C**-morphism, or as a composition of such morphisms. The product and exponentiation functors are part of the external description (or specification) of **C** and so cannot be used except as a means of naming a particular **C**-morphism as in our definition of $\bullet$ above. We start with the semantics of variables.

$$[\![x]\!] = \hat{\pi}_x$$

Notice that the use of exponentiation is apparently allowed under the rules cited above, but we will find cause to object to it later. The "obvious" semantics of application is expressed as follows.

$$[\![ee']\!] = (\Delta_{Env} \circ (((!_D \circ [\![e']\!] \times 1_{Env}) \circ eval \circ \Theta^{-1}) \times ((!_D \circ [\![e]\!] \times 1_{Env}) \circ eval)) \circ eval)^{\wedge}$$

where $\Delta_{Env}: Env \to Env \times Env$ is the diagonal on Env, $!_D: D \to \top$ is the unique morphism, and 1_{Env} is the identity on Env, all of which are fixed **C**-morphisms. However, the clause makes explicit use of both exponentiation and product, which is disallowed. Though we have no formal proof to offer, we believe that they cannot be eliminated, in which case Berry's thesis is denied internally.

One could argue that the clause is merely a finite presentation of an indefinite sequence of associations of specific syntactic phrases to specific **C**-morphisms, and as such the use of the functors should be allowed. After all, isn't the use of external functors in this way implicit in the semantics of variables? It is; hence our objection to that clause. Berry considers the closure of **C** under ω-products a mere convenience, stating that "...it simply avoids counting variables...". If we wish to have effective models, we must interpret ω as representing the process of counting, not a completed whole. If we wish to have counting internally, we must have a natural numbers object in **C**. In short, counting variables is something we cannot really avoid!

We conclude that the second interpretation of Berry's theorem is the correct one, viz. that every domain in which a categorical model can be defined is an internal model of Λ. For the consumer, this means that if a device is capable of defining a categorical model, then it is capable of doing λ-calculus. A device which merely is a categorical model could be used by some more powerful device to represent the denotations of λ-expressions, but is not itself capable of being a λ-calculator.

Incidentally, the converse of Berry's theorem is also true; a categorical model can be defined in every internal model of Λ. The easiest way to prove this is to construct a categorical model using pure λ-calculus. The necessary λ-expressions for pairing, projection, exponentiation (Currying), evaluation, etc., can be found in any standard treatment of λ-calculus, e.g. [1].

4. Domains for Doing Semantics

Our program for making semantic theory more relevant to computing requires us, first, to make explicit the domain in which any construction is being carried out and, second, to ensure that all constructions (proofs) are effective. In this section we sketch a plan for effectively realizing these goals. In particular, we consider the design of a universal metalanguage within which to do semantic theory.

Semantics draws on many branches of mathematics: algebra, topology, set theory, logic, category theory, and so forth. Any language for doing semantics must therefore be capable of expressing concepts and results in all of these domains, as well as others that have not yet been invented. All of these areas share three things, however: the ability to define new structures, to quantify over those structures, and a set of basic rules for reasoning about them. Using these three tools - definition, quantification, and logic - all of modern mathematics is built up from some initial theory, e.g. set theory.

These three ingredients for the synthesis of mathematics therefore serve also as the basic ingredients of our language. Definition serves to specify new domains (externally), quantification serves to limit consideration to those domains (i.e., to their internal structure), and logic is the key to effectiveness.

Higher-order intuitionistic logic (or "intuitionistic type theory") provides all three ingredients. The use of intuitionistic logics for programming has been studied by several authors, notably [18], [20], [7]. Since we are concerned here primarily with semantic theory, and because categorial methods are becoming more popular in the semantics community, we are interested in finding a version of intuitionistic logic which can provide an effective basis for doing category theory in a straightforward way.

We therefore take as our basic system an axiomatization of the logic of partial elements, due to Fourman and Scott [8], which we will call **FS**. The syntax of the terms and formulae of **FS** is given by the following grammar.

$$\langle term \rangle ::= \langle var \rangle \mid \langle const \rangle \mid !\langle var \rangle \langle formula \rangle$$

$$\langle formula \rangle ::= \langle var \rangle \mid \mathbf{E}\langle \mathrm{term} \rangle \mid \langle \mathrm{term} \rangle \equiv \langle \mathrm{term} \rangle$$

$$\mid \langle term \rangle(\langle term \rangle, \cdots, \langle term \rangle) \mid \langle formula \rangle \wedge \langle formula \rangle$$

$$\mid \langle formula \rangle \rightarrow \langle formula \rangle \mid \forall \langle var \rangle \langle formula \rangle$$

The logic is couched in terms of schemata for the axioms and inference rules rather than actual formulae. A schema is just like a term or formula except that certain subterms and subformulae are replaced by metavariables standing for arbitrary terms or formulae.

As it happens, it is easier to give semantics to these schemata than it is to restrict ourselves to actual terms and formulae. In fact, instantiation of a schema has no effect on the "code" that realizes that schema, because the code given for the schema always works, for all instances; it is "universal".

Because we want proofs to be effective, we are primarily interested in ***realizability*** semantics [13] The important difference between our semantics and, for example, the **Ω-Set** semantics originally proposed by Fourman and Scott is that the latter lacks "computational content" (D. Scott, in response to my question posed at the conference). In other words, the **Ω-Set** semantics is precisely the kind of semantic theory which is of no use to consumers.

Here, the realization of a formula (schema) is (the program denoted by) some λ-expression. For concreteness, we take for our λ-calculus semantics Berry and Curien's sequential algorithms on concrete data structures [4]. An alternative would be to calculate a Gödel number from the λ-expressions, giving a more traditional realization, along the lines of Scott's recent work.

Certain formula schemata (the axioms) are given realizations *ab initio*. The inference rules transform formula schemata into new formula schemata, and their realizations into corresponding new realizations. The axiom schemata are listed below. The name of each schema is given first, followed by the formula, with the realization written on the following line.

4.1. Propositional Axioms

$K: \vdash \phi \rightarrow (\psi \rightarrow \phi)$

$\lambda x.\lambda y.x$

$S: \vdash (\phi \rightarrow (\psi \rightarrow \theta)) \rightarrow ((\phi \rightarrow \psi) \rightarrow (\phi \rightarrow \theta))$

$\lambda x.\lambda y.\lambda z.(x\ z)(y\ z)$

$\pi_1: \vdash (\phi \wedge \psi) \rightarrow \phi$

$\lambda(x,y).x$

$\pi_2: \vdash (\phi \wedge \psi) \rightarrow \phi$

$\lambda(x,y).y$

$pair: \vdash \phi \rightarrow (\psi \rightarrow (\phi \wedge \psi))$

$\lambda x.\lambda y.(x,y)$

The propositional axioms define a quasi-Cartesian-closed structure that is internal to the logic. **K** specifies the existence of all exponent objects, and **S** defines a kind of internal evaluation functor; the last three axioms specify the binary projections and pairing functor.

4.2. First-Order Axioms

Some preliminary remarks may help to clarify the semantics of the first-order axioms. Notice that all computation is essentially propositional. In particular, it is well-known that the combinators **S** and **K** are a sufficient basis for the partial recursive functions. First-order logic deals with the concept of *element*, thereby adding an infrastructure to the propositions. In terms of programs, first-order statements "merely" allow us to give more detailed interpretations to what are essentially propositional combinations.

In order to speak of elements, we must postulate for them a source, which we shall denote by "()" (or "*nil*"). () has the property that there is a unique arrow from any object to () (i.e., it is terminal). In the category of sets, for example, any singleton can be used as (). An *element* is defined as any arrow from () to any other object. Again, in the category of sets, we can identify the "elements" of any set S with the collection of functions $e:() \to S$. In keeping with categorial terminology, we shall refer to arrows with domain () as elements. The "value" of an element e, denoted by $e()$, will be called an *item*.

Conceptually, the formula $\tau \equiv \sigma$ represents an equivalence class of items. The realization of such an equivalence class will be a representative item. If $\vdash \sigma \equiv \tau$, then σ and τ denote indistinguishable items. We are now ready to present the first-order axioms.

substitutivity: $\vdash \phi[y/x] \wedge y \equiv z \to \phi[z/x]$

$\lambda(f,i).f$

Given that y and z are indistinguishable, a realization of $\phi[y/x]$ is equally satisfactory as a realization of $\phi[z/x]$.

extensionality: $\vdash \forall x(x \equiv y \leftrightarrow x \equiv z) \to y \equiv z$

$\lambda e.e()$

Given an element e, we can produce the corresponding item $e()$.

instantiation: $\vdash \forall x \phi \wedge \mathbf{E}\, x \to \phi$

$\lambda(f,x).(f\ x)$

This is just the law of functional application (essentially the evaluation functor), which asserts that a function can be applied to any existing element (of the appropriate sort - **FS** is a many-sorted logic, but the details of sorts are not needed for the current discussion. The interested reader is referred to [8].)

description: $\vdash \forall y(y \equiv !x\phi \leftrightarrow \forall x(\phi \leftrightarrow x \equiv y))$

$\lambda y.(\lambda e.\lambda x.e,\ \lambda x.x())$

This axiom asserts that we can convert freely between the equivalence class of an item specified uniquely by the formula ϕ and the corresponding element.

4.3. Higher-Order Axiom

comprehension: $\vdash \mathbf{E}!y\ \forall \overline{x}(\phi \leftrightarrow y(\overline{x}))$

$\lambda \overline{x}.()$

Higher-order logic deals with collections of elements, or "sets". The axiom of comprehension asserts that all specifiable collections exist or, more precisely, that all structures have characteristic terms (which can then be quantified over). The justification for this is that $\lambda \overline{x}.()$ exists. That is, we specify the unique map from any collection (including the empty collection) to (), the "terminal object"; everything else follows.

Incidentally, the original formulation of **FS** included an additional axioms of *predication*. Its effect is to give the logic strict semantics for predication. We do not include it here, however, because in order to realize it we would need to retain the entire history of a computation so that from any result we could recover the operator and operands which produced it. In practice, the absence of the axiom of predication is hardly noticed.

4.4. Inference Rules

There are four inference rules, each of which transforms formula schemata and their realizations into new formula schemata and realizations. In the rules, the realization of a formula is written beside it in set braces, "{ }".

4.4.1. Modus Ponens

$$\frac{\phi\ \{x\} \quad (\phi \rightarrow \psi)\ \{f\}}{\psi\ \{fx\}}$$

4.4.2. Curry (∀-introduction)

$$\frac{\psi \wedge \mathbf{E}x \rightarrow \phi\ \{f\}}{\psi \rightarrow \forall x\phi\ \{(\lambda x.\lambda y.f(x,y))\}}$$

(x not free in ψ)

4.4.3. Substitution

$$\frac{\phi\ \{f\}}{\phi[\tau/x]\ \{f\}}$$

(x a term variable)

4.4.4. Elaboration

$$\frac{\phi\ \{f\}}{\phi[\psi/x]\ \{f\}}$$

(x a formula variable)

Fourman shows how **FS** defines a free (elementary) topos $E()$. A topos is a Cartesian-closed category with a subobject classifier - an object Ω with the property that for every subobject $s{:}a \rightarrow b$ there is a unique morphism $\chi_a{:}b \rightarrow \Omega$ such that $\chi_a \circ s$ factors uniquely through $\top$ (i.e., *nil*). In terms of our semantics, the factorization is given by $\mathbf{true}\circ(\lambda\overline{x}.())$, where $\mathbf{true}$ is a distinguished element of Ω, the domain of "truth values".

Elementary topoi were discovered by Lawvere and Tierney in the late 60's (see [14] [15]). The early development of the theory, and its relationship to intuitionistic logic, is recorded in conference proceedings from the early 70's, especially [16], [17]. A good introduction to topos theory, which concentrates on the relation of topoi to logic, is Goldblatt [9]. A more technical treatment is given by Johnstone [11], but is less accessible to the non-specialist. MacLane has recently completed a book on the subject, as well, but I do not have an exact reference for it, nor have I seen it.

Elementary topoi are essentially versions of set theory. The fact that $E()$ is free in the "category" of elementary topoi means that there is a unique functor from $E()$ to any other topos; it is the least constrained set theory there is. Since the semantics of **FS** is effective, $E()$ is an effective domain. By building up mathematics, especially semantic theory, within $E()$, we can guarantee (Church-Turing) effectiveness. To do this, we can use the logic **FS** itself, or we may prefer a more purely categorial, but equivalent, notation.

An enhanced version of our **FS** realizability model is incorporated in a computer program called **Intuit**. **Intuit** supports natural deduction proofs, and actually works on a syntactic representation of the realization of a formula, which it optimizes extensively. A small library of theorems has been compiled, but so far no significant theories have been developed.

We must emphasize that a great deal of groundwork has to be done before we could hope even to start doing semantic theory with the **Intuit** system. An enormous body of mathematics has first to be reconstructed essentially "from scratch", a project of essentially the same scope and magnitude as Bourbaki, requiring contributions from many mathematicians over a period of decades. We envision a massive on-line library of definitions, theorems, and proofs, to be a repository of constructive mathematical knowledge in the public domain. Any qualified person could contribute to the library or draw from it for further work. If programming in this manner became sufficiently popular, one might even expect to see the formation of private libraries of proprietary theorems and proofs that can be used for a fee.

A major problem for such a project would be the organization of the library of definitions, theorems, and proofs into a coherent and easily-referenced whole. The PRL systems [2] support an organization based on simple lists of theorems, functions, definitions, and some primitive recursive utilities. This falls far short of their goal (inspired by Kenneth Wilson) of a "library of results organized into books, chapters, sections, and so on." We sketch one possible alternative organization in the following section.

5. Branches and Categories

Conventional libraries are surprisingly inefficient databases. They are highly redundant, badly cross-indexed, and do not support shared access to information. Much of the information is out-of-date, difficult to place in its proper context, and the relationships among data that are perceived by the expert in an area are nowhere apparent. Perhaps worst of all, knowledge is packaged by author, rather than by topic. We therefore reject the paradigm of a conventional library, and consider instead an organization of mathematical knowledge into branches, topics, results, and proofs (to which authorship may be appended as a footnote). At the highest level, all of the branches are organized under category theory, which captures knowledge about relationships among the various branches. (Books, written by various authors for a variety of approaches and styles, will of course continue to be useful as guides to using the library.)

As mentioned earlier, **FS** provides an effective language for doing "free set theory" (actually, topos theory). In order to work in other branches of mathematics, we need to introduce theories for them. Traditionally, a theory is defined by a set of sorts and constants, and a set of formulae (axioms). To prove a formula ϕ in a theory Γ is essentially the same as to prove the entailment $\Gamma \vdash \phi$ in the base logic. If Γ is defined as an extension to **FS** in this way and the proof uses **FS** freely, then we say that ϕ holds *externally to* Γ *within* **FS**.

We generalize this terminology in the obvious way. Given a theory Δ, a theory $\Gamma = \Delta \cup E$ is an *extension* of the *base theory* Δ. If $E \vdash \phi$ in Δ, then ϕ holds externally to E within Δ.

In order to support internal reasoning, we need to add a mechanism for encapsulating theories. To accomodate this new concept, we change the traditional definitions slightly. We define a *theory* to be any set Γ of definitions, formulae, and inference rules. A theory Δ is an *extension* of Γ if Δ includes Γ, and any new inference rules in Δ are derived from those in Γ together with the axioms of Δ. Δ is a *branch* of Γ if $\Delta \cup \Gamma$ is an extension of Γ. The important point here is that Δ may discard ("hide") parts of Γ. To continue with arboreal terminology, **FS** is the *root* theory; all other theories are either extensions or branches of **FS** (or its extensions and branches).

The concept of branch captures the notion of "internal theory"; a branch may be isolated from its base, though it may also inherit things from the base. Any formula proved in a branch, however, gives a construction that is completely internal to that branch. (Note that topoi are not the only structures having internal theories, though one might hesitate to call the internal theory of anything but a topos an internal *logic*.)

Branches enable us to define and work within various areas of mathematics, but they don't provide any means of relating one branch to another, except as base and extension. The goal of category theory, of course, is precisely to define and study relationships and transformations among the various branches of mathematics. Moreover, the search for universals is properly conducted within category theory. If category theory is simply added as another branch to the great tree of mathematics, however, it will be isolated from all of the other branches!

The resolution of this quandary is beyond the scope of the current work, but essentially involves the notion of *indexed categories* [12]. Briefly, the theory of indexed categories is a theory about the tree of mathematics. Its objects are "indexed categories" - families of morphisms "enumerated" by some object of a base topos. Instead of working directly with branches of **FS**, we can work with those branches as defined within the branch of indexed categories. (An alternative which will suggest itself readily to language designers would be to use multiple inheritance instead of the simple tree proposed here. We do not know how to introduce multiple inheritance in a clean way in this context, however.)

In order to avoid needless duplication, we propose to provide, as our universal domain for doing semantics, the branch of indexed category theory. In short, we propose to replace "set theory" by (indexed) category theory as the "initial object" from which all of mathematics would be derived. In this way, we can encourage all branches of mathematics to be developed in the appropriate categorial climate, so they can inherit categorial results directly instead of proving those results in each special case and later exhibiting them as "examples of the general concept".

At the outermost level, then, we would have a language for defining various categories and functors between them. Among those functors would be some basic ways of combining categories, along the lines of Clear [6]: extend, restrict, combine, etc. The categories, together with the base theory of indexed categories, would be the branches of mathematics. Knowledge within each branch would be catalogued according to topic, theorem, and proof. Beneath each branch that includes branch-growing functors would be sub-branches, with their own topics, theorems, proofs, and (possibly) sub-branches. The natural scope rules arising from this organization would effectively indicate the branch within which any construction is carried out.

References

1. H. P. Barendregt, *The Lambda-Calculus: Its Syntax and Semantics*, North-Holland, 1981.

2. J. L. Bates and R. L. Constable, Proofs as Programs, *ACM Trans. Prog. Lang. and Systems 7*, 1 (January 1985), 113-136.

3. G. Berry, Some Syntactic and Categorical Constructions of Lambda-Calculus Models, INRIA Rapport de Recherche No. 80, June 1981.

4. G. Berry and P. L. Curien, Sequential Algorithms on Concrete Data Structures, *Theoretical Computer Science*, , 1982.

5. S. D. Brookes, C. A. R. Hoare and A. W. Roscoe, A Theory of Communicating Sequential Processes, *J. ACM 31*, 3 (July 1984), 560-599.

6. R. M. Burstall and J. A. Goguen, Putting Theories Together To Make Specifications, *5th International Joint Conference on Artificial Intelligence*, , 1977, 1045-1058.

7. R. L. Constable and D. R. Zlatin, The Type Theory of PL/CV3, *ACM Trans. Prog. Lang. and Systems 6*, 1 (January 1984), 94-117.

8. M. P. Fourman, The Logic of Topoi, in *Handbook of Mathematical Logic*, J. Barwise (ed.), North-Holland, 1977, 1054-1090.

9. R. Goldblatt, *Topoi: the Categorial Analysis of Logic*, North-Holland, 1979.

10. M. J. Gordon, A. J. Milner and C. P. Wadsworth, Edinburgh LCF, in *Lecture Notes in Computer Science, Vol. 78*, Springer, Berlin, 1979.

11. P. T. Johnstone, *Topos Theory*, Academic Press, 1977.

12. P. T. Johnstone and R. Paré, eds., *Indexed Categories and Their Applications*, Springer Lecture Notes in Mathematics, 1978.

13. S. C. Kleene, On the Interpretation of Intuitionistic Number Theory, *J. Symbolic Logic 10*, (1945), 109-124.

14. F. W. Lawvere, Adjointness in Foundations, *Dialectica 23*, (1969), 281-296.

15. F. W. Lawvere, Quantifiers and Sheaves, in *Actes des Congrès International des Mathématiques, tome I*, 1970, 329-334.

16. F. W. Lawvere, ed., *Toposes, Algebraic Geometry, and Logic*, Springer Lecture Notes in Mathematics, 1972.

17. F. W. Lawvere, C. Maurer and G. C. Wraith, eds., *Model Theory and Topoi*, Springer Lecture Notes in Mathematics, 1975.

18. P. Martin-Löf, Constructive Mathematics and Computer Programming, *6th Int'l. Congress for Logic, Methodology, and Philosophy of Science*, Hannover, Aug. 1979.

19. A. R. Meyer, What is a Lambda-Calculus Model?, MIT LCS/TM-171, August 1980.

20. D. Scott, Constructive Validity, in *Proc. Symposium on Automatic Deduction, Lecture Notes in Mathematics 125*, Springer-Verlag, 1970, 237-275.

21. D. S. Scott and C. Strachey, Toward a Mathematical Semantics for Computer Languages, in *Proc. Symposium on Computers and Automata*, J. Fox (ed.), Polytechnic Institute of New York, New York, 1971, 19-46.

22. D. Scott, Data Types as Lattices, *SIAM J. Comput. 5*, 3 (Sept. 1976), 522-587.

23. M. B. Smyth and G. D. Plotkin, The Category-Theoretic Solution of Recursive Domain Equations, *Proc. 18th Symposium on Mathematical Foundations of Computer Science*, , 1977, 13-17.

24. M. B. Smyth, Effectively Given Domains, *Theoretical Computer Science 5*, (1978), .

MODAL THEORY, PARTIAL ORDERS, AND DIGITAL GEOMETRY

Jonathan D. H. Smith
Department of Mathematics
Iowa State University
Ames, Iowa 50011, U.S.A.

1. INTRODUCTION A long-standing problem in domain theory has been the search for algebra structures that ride naturally on the ordered sets involved. Indeed, the constructions in the theory of complete partial orders and continuous lattices, as applied to the recursive definition of a data structure, are usually independent of any algebra carried by the data structure, and do not mesh nicely with the algebra. The aim of the current paper is to provide an introduction to the kind of algebra that does guarantee a good mesh with partial orderings, and to present topological ideas and category-theoretical relationships showing how the algebra is automatically reproduced under order-theoretical constructions such as power domains. As a potential application of the algebra, a new direct approach to the programming of geometry and scientific models is proposed.

Giving a brief survey of an extensive theory, this paper is necessarily somewhat condensed. Fuller details of many of the topics treated here, as well as an introduction to the universal algebraic notations used, may be found in [6]. Note, too, that the whole theory as described here has so far only been worked out on the basis of finitary universal algebraic methods. There is great potential for future development of the theory using the monadic approach to algebra. Another aspect of the theory that has hardly been investigated at all is that of duality. Here, too, a great deal remains to be done.

2. MODES The basic algebraic concept is that of a mode. A mode is an algebra (A,Ω) satisfying the following conditions:

(2.1) The algebra is idempotent, i.e. each singleton subset $\{a\}$ of A is a subalgebra $(\{a\},\Omega)$ of (A,Ω); and

(2.2) the algebra is entropic, i.e. each operation ω in Ω (of arity $\omega\tau$), already a set mapping $\omega : A^{\omega\tau} \to A$; $(x_1,\ldots,x_{\omega\tau}) \mapsto x_1 \ldots x_{\omega\tau}\omega$, is also a homomorphism $\omega : (A^{\omega\tau},\Omega) \to (A,\Omega)$.

Some examples will serve to demonstrate the scope of this apparently restrictive definition, showing how various familiar mathematical concepts are brought into the purview of modal theory.

EXAMPLE 2.3. If Ω is empty, the conditions (2.1) and (2.2) are vacuously satisfied. Thus unstructured sets A are modes.

EXAMPLE 2.4. A semilattice $(L,\cdot)$ is a mode. Idempotence reduces to $x\cdot x = x$ for x in L, while the entropic law $(x\cdot y)\cdot(z\cdot t) = (x\cdot z)\cdot(y\cdot t)$ for the single infix binary operation $\cdot$ follows from the commutative and associative laws. The semilattice $(L,\cdot)$ has a partial order specified by

(2.5) $x \leq y$ if and only if $x\cdot y = x$.

With this order, $(L,\cdot)$ is called a meet semilattice. If a partial order $\leq$ is given on a set L, and this partial order is known to come from a meet semilattice structure on L (i.e. each pair of elements of L has a greatest lower bound), then (2.5) may be read backwards to specify the semilattice operation $\cdot$ on L. Sometimes the dual notion of join semilattice $(L,+)$ is used: $x \leq y$ if and only if $x + y = y$. Meet and join semilattices are the means by which order is dealt with in modal theory.

EXAMPLE 2.6. Let E be a vector space over a field R, or more generally a unital module over a commutative ring R with 1. For each r in R, define a binary operation $\underline{r}$ by

(2.7) $\underline{r} : E \times E \to E$; $(x,y) \mapsto x(1-r) + yr$.

Interpreting R as the set of these binary operations $\underline{r}$, the algebra (E,R) becomes a mode. Idempotence follows since $xx\underline{r} = x(1-r) + xr = x1 = x$, and a straightforward calculation establishes the entropic laws $xy\underline{r}zt\underline{rs} = xz\underline{s}yt\underline{sr}$. These algebras (E,R) serve to relate linear algebra to modal theory.

EXAMPLE 2.8. Let I° denote the open unit interval in the set $\mathbb{R}$ of real numbers. Given a real vector space E thought of as a mode $(E,\mathbb{R})$ according to Example 2.6, the reduct (E,I°), admitting just those operations $\underline{r}$ for which $0 < r < 1$, is also a mode. Subalgebras (S,I°) of this mode are then just convex subsets of E. In this way convexity becomes part of modal theory. An important application of these examples is to non-determinism. A convex subset S of E may represent (possibly) non-deterministic states of a machine. An extreme point x of E represents a deterministic state. Given two states x, y in S, and $0 < p < 1$, the state $xy\underline{p}$ represents a non-deterministic state obtained by choosing x with probability $1 - p$ and y with probability p.

EXAMPLE 2.9. Let T be the vertex set of a tree. Given three vertices x, y, z of T, let $xyzM$ denote the unique vertex that lies on each of the paths from x to y, from y to z, and from z to x. Note that if any two of x, y, z coincide to equal t, then $xyzM = t$. In particular $xxxM = x$, so the algebra (T,M) with the ternary operation M is idempotent. The entropic law

(2.10) $logMabeMpitMM = lapMobiMgetMM$

for (T,M) may also be verified (by a tedious case analysis). It is illustrated on the tree of Figure 1.

FIGURE 1

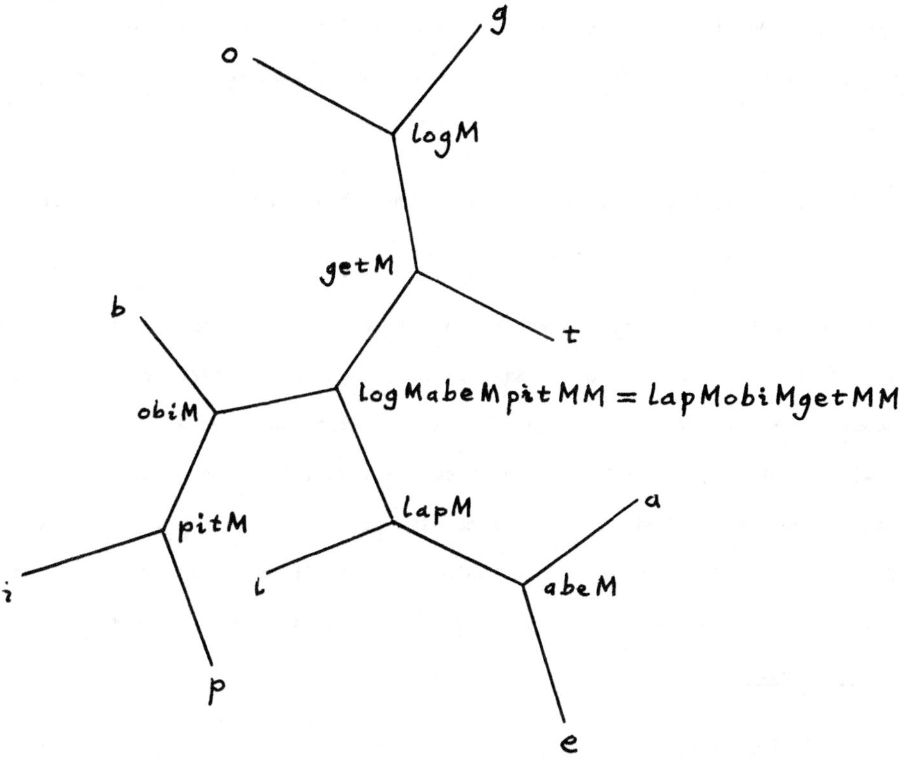

Given a tree, one thus obtains a mode (T,M), known as a <u>tree algebra</u> [3]. Conversely, conditions on a ternary algebra (T,M) ensuring that it comes from a tree T in this way have been given [3, 1.2-3]. Thus trees may be regarded as modes.

3. POWER DOMAINS Given a mode (A,Ω) , let AS denote the set of non-empty subalgebras of (A,Ω). For each ω in Ω (of arity $\omega\tau$), an operation known as <u>complex product</u> or <u>complex ω-product</u> may be defined on AS by

(3.1) $X_1 \dots X_{\omega\tau}\omega = \{x_1 \dots x_{\omega\tau}\omega \mid x_i \in X_i\}$.

That $X_1 \dots X_{\omega\tau}\omega$ is a subalgebra of (A,Ω) is a typical consequence of the entropic law. One then obtains the fundamental self-reproducing property of modes under this power domain construction that shows how well these concepts fit together.

PROPOSITION 3.2 [6, 146]. If (A,Ω) is a mode, then under the complex product operations of (3.1), (AS,Ω) is again a mode.

Let AP denote the set of <u>polytopes</u> or finitely generated non-empty subalgebras of (A,Ω). (If (A,Ω) is (E,I°) as in Example 2.8, then EP is precisely the set of polytopes of E in the geometric sense.) If non-empty subalgebras $S_1, \dots, S_{\omega\tau}$ of (A,Ω) are generated by sets $X_1, \dots, X_{\omega\tau}$ respectively, then an inductive proof [6, 147] shows that the complex product $S_1 \dots S_{\omega\tau}\omega$ is generated by $X_1 \dots X_{\omega\tau}\omega$. As a consequence of this, the set AP under the complex product operations forms a submode (AP,Ω) of (AS,Ω). Further, there is a homomorphic <u>canonical embedding</u>

(3.3) $\iota : (A,\Omega) \to (AP,\Omega); \ a \mapsto \{a\}$

of (A,Ω) into (AP,Ω), or indeed of (A,Ω) into (AS,Ω).

The sets AP and AS also carry additional structure, namely ordering by set inclusion. This order determines join semilattice structures $(AP,+)$ and $(AS,+)$, as discussed in Example 2.4. There is a special relationship between the Ω-algebra structures and the join semilattice structures on AP and AS, expressed by the following definition and proposition.

DEFINITION 3.4. An Ω-algebra structure (D,Ω) on a set D is said to <u>distribute</u> over a semilattice structure $(D,+)$ on D if, for each ω (of arity $\omega\tau$), and for each $1 \leq j \leq \omega\tau$ and $x_1, \dots, x_j, \dots, x_{\omega\tau}, x_j'$ in D,

$$x_1 \dots (x_j+x_j') \dots x_{\omega\tau}\omega = x_1 \dots x_j \dots x_{\omega\tau}\omega + x_1 \dots x_j' \dots x_{\omega\tau}\omega.$$

PROPOSITION 3.5. [6, 313]. For a mode (A,Ω), the complex product structure (AS,Ω) distributes over the semilattice $(AS,+)$.

This distributivity is surprising, as a priori there is no reason to expect any nice interaction between the two structures on AS and AP. It is further evidence of the good behaviour of mode algebra with respect to order. Some consequences of the distributivity are worked out in the next section. This section concludes with a simple example illustrating the power domain construction AP.

EXAMPLE 3.6. Let $(A,\cdot)$ denote the meet semilattice structure on $A = \{\bot\} \dot{\cup} \mathbf{N}$ (natural numbers with bottom element) in which $\mathbf{N}$ forms an antichain and $\bot$ is below each element of $\mathbf{N}$. The Hasse diagram of $(A,<)$, i.e. the directed graph of the relation "is covered by", is as follows:

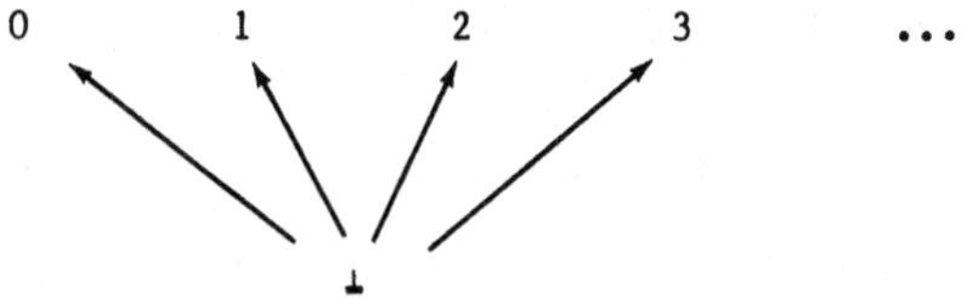

The power domain AP consists of all finite non-empty subsemilattices of $(A,\cdot)$. Aside from the singletons $\{n\}$ for n in $\mathbf{N}$, this comprises the unions of $\{\bot\}$ and finite subsets of $\mathbf{N}$. Now it follows from the stronger version of Proposition 3.2 given in [6, 146] (and requiring universal algebraic concepts for its formulation) that $(AP,\cdot)$ forms a (meet) semilattice under the complex product. Thus the power domain AP carries two semilattice structures, the meet semilattice $(AP,\cdot)$ and the join semilattice $(AP,+)$. In each of these, there is a copy of the lattice of finite subsets of $\mathbf{N}$, a finite subset F of $\mathbf{N}$ being represented by $F\dot{\cup}\{\bot\}$. In $(AP,\cdot)$, the singletons $\{n\}$ for n in $\mathbf{N}$ appear as maximal elements covering the corresponding $\{n,\bot\}$. In $(AP,+)$, these singletons $\{n\}$ appear as minimal elements covered by the corresponding $\{n,\bot\}$. Such algebras are investigated in detail in [5] and [6].

4. MODALS Let (A,Ω) be a mode, and let $(D,+,\Omega)$ denote either $(AP,+,\Omega)$ or $(AS,+,\Omega)$. Then the algebra $(D,+,\Omega)$ satisfies the following three conditions:

(4.1) (D,Ω) is a mode;

(4.2) $(D,+)$ is a join semilattice; and

(4.3) (D,Ω) distributes over $(D,+)$.

An algebra $(D,+,\Omega)$ satisfying these conditions (4.1) - (4.3) is said to be a modal. The name emphasizes the connection with modes, as well as being reminiscent of "modules", which are also algebras having a +-structure and operations distributing over it. Modal theory may be described as the study of modes, modals, and the relationships between them. Examples of modals beyond the $(AP,+,\Omega)$ and $(AS,+,\Omega)$ coming from a mode (A,Ω) are given below.

EXAMPLE 4.4. If Ω is empty, then a modal $(D,+,\Omega)$ is just a join semilattice. In particular, if A is a set considered as a mode $(A,\emptyset)$, then AP and AS are power sets of A considered as join semilattices (and without the empty set as bottom element).

EXAMPLE 4.5. Distributive lattices $(L,+,\cdot)$, for example the lattice reducts of Boolean algebras, are modals.

EXAMPLE 4.6. Let $(L,\cdot)$ be a semilattice. Then the stammered semilattice $(L,\cdot,\cdot)$, with the operation $\cdot$ taken twice, is a modal. Note that this method of considering semilattices as modals differs from the method of Example 4.4.

EXAMPLE 4.7 There is a common generalization of the distributive lattices of Example 4.5 and the stammered semilattices of Example 4.6. This is the concept of dissemilattice -- an algebra $(D,+,\cdot)$ in which $(D,+)$ and $(D,\cdot)$ are semilattices, and in which $(D,\cdot)$ distributes over $(D,+)$, i.e. the law $x\cdot(y+z) = x\cdot y + x\cdot z$ is satisfied. The power domain $(AP,+,\cdot)$ of Example 3.6 has such a structure. If lattices are regarded as generalizations of distributive lattices obtained by dropping the requirement of distributivity, then dissemilattices may be considered as parallel generalizations in which distributivity is retained but the absorption law is relaxed.

EXAMPLE 4.8. Let $\vee$ denote the binary operation of maximum on the set $\mathbf{R}$ of real numbers. Then $(\mathbf{R},\vee,I^{\circ})$, under this operation and the set I° of convex combinations as in Example 2.8, forms a modal.

EXAMPLE 4.9. Any space of functions mapping into the reals inherits the modal structure on the reals given in Example 4.8. For instance, if X is a topological space, the set $C(X)$ of continuous functions $f : X \to \mathbf{R}$ forms a modal $(C(X),\vee,I^{\circ})$.

The distributivity of (D,Ω) over $(D,+)$ in a modal $(D,+,\Omega)$ has a number of direct consequences for the way the mode structure (D,Ω) interacts with the join semilattice ordering $\leq$ on D. These are listed in the following lemmas. Note that a function $f : (A,\Omega) \to (D,+,\Omega)$ is said to be <u>convex</u> if $a_1 \ldots a_{\omega\tau}\omega f \leq a_1 f \ldots a_{\omega\tau} f\omega$ for each operation ω in Ω and $\omega\tau$-tuple $(a_1,\ldots,A_{\omega\tau})$ in $A^{\omega\tau}$. A function $f = (\mathbf{R},I^{\circ}) \to (\mathbf{R},\vee,I^{\circ})$ is convex in this sense if and only if it is convex in the classical sense as a function $f : \mathbf{R} \to \mathbf{R}$.

MONOTONICITY LEMMA 4.10 [6, 315]. Each operation ω on a modal $(D,+,\Omega)$ is monotone as a mapping $\omega : (D^{\omega\tau},\leq) \to (D,\leq)$, i.e. $a_1 \leq b_1, \ldots, a_{\omega\tau} \leq b_{\omega\tau}$ imply $a_1 \ldots a_{\omega\tau}\omega \leq b_1 \ldots b_{\omega\tau}\omega$.

CONVEXITY LEMMA 4.11 [6, 317]. For each positive integer r, the mapping

$$\sum_r : (D^r,\Omega) \to (D,+,\Omega) \; ; \; (a_1,\ldots,a_r) \to a_1 + \ldots + a_r$$

into a modal $(D,+,\Omega)$ is convex.

SUM-SUPERIORITY LEMMA 4.12 [6, 318]. For each operation ω on a modal $(D,+,\Omega)$, and for each $\omega\tau$-tuple $(a_1,\ldots,a_{\omega\tau})$,

$$a_1 \ldots a_{\omega\tau}\omega \leq a_1 + \ldots + a_{\omega\tau}.$$

In Section 3, the construction of the modal $(AP,+,\Omega)$ from a mode (A,Ω) was given. From the category theory standpoint, such constructions are indicative of a left adjoint functor. The adjointness present here, expressed by the theorem below, lies at the very heart of modal theory. The theorem may be interpreted as showing how functions are extended from the domain A to the power domain AP (cf. [2],[4],[5,Th. 3.1]).

THEOREM 4.12 [6, 351]. The construction of the modal $(AP,+,\Omega)$ from a mode (A,Ω) is left adjoint to the forgetful functor assigning the mode (D,Ω) to a modal $(D,+,\Omega)$. In other words, each mode homomorphism $f : (A,\Omega) \to (D,\Omega)$ may be extended to a unique modal homomorphism $\overline{f} : (AP,+,\Omega) \to (D,+,\Omega)$ whose composite $\iota\overline{f}$ with the canonical embedding ι of (3.3) is f.

For a subalgebra S of (A,Ω) finitely generated by a set X, the element $S\overline{f}$ of D is defined to be $\sum_{x \in X} xf$. That this is a good definition may be shown using the Sum-Superiority Lemma 4.12. Other details of the proof are given in [6].

5. APPROXIMATION Theorem 4.12 gives the abstract significance of the modal $(AP,+,\Omega)$ as the free modal over the mode (A,Ω). Questions then arise as to the abstract significance of the modal $(AS,+,\Omega)$, the abstract relationship between $(AP,+,\Omega)$ and $(AS,+,\Omega)$, and the possibility of extending functions from A through the power domain AP to the power domain AS. These questions are addressed by the concepts and results of this section, which build up to the equivalance of categories given in Theorem 5.8 below.

A join semilattice $(D,+)$ is said to be <u>complete</u> if arbitrary (non-empty) subsets of D have suprema. An Ω-algebra structure (D,Ω) on a set D is said to be completely distributive over a complete joint semilattice structure $(D,+)$ on D if for each ω in Ω, $1 \leq j \leq \omega\tau$, and subset

$\{x_1, \ldots, x_{j-1}, x_{j+1}, \ldots, x_{\omega\tau}\} \cup X$ of D $(X \neq \emptyset)$,

$$\sup \{x_1 \ldots x_{j-1} x x_{j+1} \ldots x_{\omega\tau}\omega \mid x \in X\}$$

$$= x_1 \ldots x_{j-1}(\sup X)\, x_{j+1} \ldots x_{\omega\tau}\omega.$$

A non-empty subset X of the complete join semilattice $(D,+)$ is said to cover an element d if $d \leq \sup X$. An element d of $(D,+)$ is called compact if each subset X of D covering d has a finite subset also covering d. The set of compact elements of the complete join semilattice $(D,+)$ will be denoted by DQ.

In analogy with [1, Defn. I. 4.6], the following definition is made.

DEFINITION 5.1. A modal $(D,+,\Omega)$ is said to be arithmetical if it satisfies the following conditions:

(i) $(D,+)$ is a complete join semilattice;

(ii) (D,Ω) is completely distributive over $(D,+)$;

(iii) each element of D is the supremum of the compact elements less than or equal to it;

(iv) DQ is a submode of (D,Ω).

A modal homomorphism $f : (D,+,\Omega) \to (E,+,\Omega)$ between arithmetical modals is said to be an arithmorphism if $DQf \subseteq EQ$.

For a mode (A,Ω), the modal $(AS,+,\Omega)$ of all non-empty submodes is arithmetical [6, 335]. The compact elements of AS are precisely the finitely generated non-empty submodes of (A,Ω), and each submode is the supremum (i.e. set-theoretical union) of the finitely generated submodes it contains. Indeed, each submode S of (A,Ω) can be expressed as $S = \sup \{\{x\} \mid x \in S\}$.

For a subset B of a partial order $(D,\leq)$, the <u>subordinate set</u> $\downarrow B$ is $\{d \in D | \exists b \in B.\ b \leq d\}$. For a modal $(D,+,\Omega)$, let DR denote the set of non-empty subsemilattices B of $(D,+)$ that are their own subordinate sets. By the Sum-superiority Lemma 4.12, such subsemilattices of $(D,+)$ are automatically submodes of (D,Ω). Given B, B' in DR, define $B + B'$ to be $\downarrow \{b+b' | b \in B, b' \in B'\}$. Under this operation, (DR,+) becomes a complete join semilattice. Given ω in Ω and elements $B_1, \dots, B_{\omega\tau}$ of DR, define a new element $(B_1,\dots,B_{\omega\tau})\omega$ of DR as the subordinate set of the complex ω-product $B_1 \dots B_{\omega\tau}\omega$ of the submodes $B_1, \dots, B_{\omega\tau}$ of (D,Ω). This gives a mode structure (DR,Ω) which is completely distributive over (DR,+), so that in particular $(DR,+,\Omega)$ is a modal [6, 332]. In fact, $(DR,+,\Omega)$ is an arithmetical modal [6, 341], having as its compact elements the elements $\downarrow\{d\}$ for d in D. Given a modal homomorphism $f = (D,+,\Omega) \to (E,+,\Omega)$ between two modals, the mapping

(5.2) $fR : DR \to ER;\ B \mapsto \sup\downarrow(Bf)$

becomes an arithmorphism $fR : (DR,+,\Omega) \to (ER,+,\Omega)$ [6, 343].

The relevance of the construction R for the power domains AP and AS of a mode (A,Ω) is described by the following result.

PROPOSITION 5.3. [6, 333]. For a mode (A,Ω), the arithmetical modals $(AS,+,\Omega)$ and $(APR,+,\Omega)$ are isomorphic via the arithmorphisms

(5.4) $\delta : AS \to APR;\ S \mapsto \{F \leq S | F \in AP\}$

and

(5.5) $\gamma : APR \to AS;\ B \mapsto \sup \{\{a\} | \exists F \in B.\ a \in F\}$.

If (A,Ω) is a convex subset (A,I°) of a real vector space E, as in Example 2.8, then Proposition 5.3 may be interpreted as showing how arbitrary convex subsets S of A are approximated by polytopes F contained within S.

Let $\mathfrak{D}$ be a variety of modals $(D,+,\Omega)$ in the sense of universal algebra -- the class of all modals satisfying some (possibly empty) set of identities in Ω. Consider $\mathfrak{D}$ as a category having modal homomorphisms as its morphisms. Let $\mathcal{E}$ be the subcategory of $\mathfrak{D}$ whose objects are the arithmetical modals in $\mathfrak{D}$ and whose morphisms are the arithmorphisms between them. Then the construction R gives a functor $R : \mathfrak{D} \to \mathcal{E}$. In the other direction, there is a functor $Q : \mathcal{E} \to \mathfrak{D}$ assigning the modal $(DQ,+,\Omega)$ of compact elements to each arithmetical modal $(D,+,\Omega)$ in $\mathcal{E}$. For an arithmorphism $f : (D,+,\Omega) \to (E,+,\Omega)$, the modal homomorphism $fQ : (DQ,+,\Omega) \to (EQ,+,\Omega)$ is just the restriction of f to the subset DQ of D. For each object D of $\mathfrak{D}$ there is a natural isomorphism

(5.6) $\eta_D : D \to DRQ;\ d \mapsto {\downarrow}\{d\}$.

For each object E of $\mathcal{E}$, there is a natural isomorphism

(5.7) $\varepsilon_E : EQR \to E;\ B \mapsto \sup B$ [6, 344].

THEOREM 5.8 [6, 345]. The categories $\mathfrak{D}$ and $\mathcal{E}$ are equivalent via the adjoint equivalence $(R,Q;\eta,\varepsilon)$.

Theorem 5.8 may be used to extend functions from the mode A through the power domain AP to the power domain AS.

THEOREM 5.9 [6, 356]. Let (A,Ω) be a mode, and $(D,+,\Omega)$ an arithmetical modal. Then each mode homomorphism $f : (A,\Omega) \to (DQ,\Omega)$ may be extended to a unique arithmorphism $f' : (AS,+,\Omega) \to (E,+,\Omega)$ such that the following diagram commutes:

$$\begin{array}{ccccc}
(A,\Omega) & \xrightarrow{\ \iota\ } & (AP,+,\Omega) & \hookrightarrow & (AS,+,\Omega) \\
\downarrow f & & \downarrow \overline{f} & & \downarrow f' \\
(DQ,\Omega) & \xrightarrow[1_{DQ}]{} & (DQ,+,\Omega) & \hookrightarrow & (E,+,\Omega).
\end{array}$$

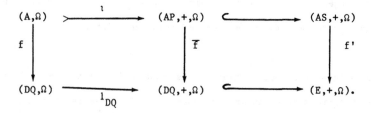

Here, $\overline{f}$ is given by Theorem 4.12, and ι is the canonical embedding (3.3). Then $f' : AS \to E$ is the composite

$$AS \xrightarrow{\ \delta\ } APR \xrightarrow{\ \overline{f}R\ } DQR \xrightarrow{\ \varepsilon_D\ } D$$

of the mappings δ of (5.4), $\overline{f}R$ of (5.2), and ε_D of (5.7).

6. DIGITAL GEOMETRY Present-day scientific computing is a long and roundabout exercise. To begin with, theoretical scientists create mathematical models reducing natural laws to differential equations relating real or complex-valued functions. These differential equations are then solved using programs developed by numerical analysts. The real and complex numbers involved are represented in the programs by floating-point numbers. When the programs are implemented and run on a machine, these floating-point numbers are converted into binary digits processed by the machine's circuitry. Each stage of this lengthy process introduces new potential errors that have to be kept under control. These errors may be conceptual in the theoretical stages or arithmetical in the computational stages. In the theoretical models, the real and complex numbers represent idealizations of the results of physical measurements. In the numerical analysis, the floating-point numbers used represent approximations to these real and complex numbers. In the machine implementation, the natural binary logic is contorted to deal with the decimal representations that are more appropriate to finger counting and other calculation methods used by human beings. A typical breakdown of this process occurs when one "proves" the convergence of an algorithm using real analysis, only to have the algorithm diverge in an implementaion because of an accumulation of rounding errors.

One of the main uses of modal theory is as a guide in the search for simpler and safer ways of performing scientific computation. The idea is to formulate new mathematical models that are directly computable, avoiding the roundabout route via real numbers and decimal or floating-point representations. From the computational side, the starting point is at those numbers directly representable in a binary machine, namely dyadic rational numbers $m \cdot 2^{-n}$ (m, n integral) or "finite binary decimals". The question raised is:

(6.1) What mathematical structures are carried naturally by finite binary strings?

The answers given to this question should suggest to theoretical scientists the mathematical language in which their theories ought to be formulated if they are to facilitate the practical computations that are the ultimate applications of the theories. Here, two typical answers to question (6.1) are given. A brief discussion then shows how modal theory might be used to apply these mathematical structures to the formulation of readily computable models.

To begin with, consider an infinite sequence of points equally spaced out along a line:

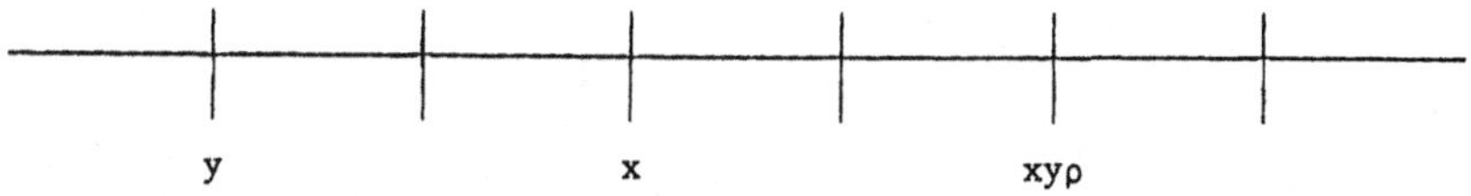

Given two points x, y, on the line, let $xy\rho$ denote the *reflexion* of y in x - the point that is as far behind x as y is in front. Starting with two adjacent points labelled 0 and 1, all the other points, labelled by the set $\mathbf{Z}$ of integers in the usual order, may be obtained by repeated reflexions of the points obtained from 0 and 1 by reflexion. Using binary notation for the integers, two or 10 is obtained by reflexion of 0 in 1, i.e. as 10ρ. Three or 11 is obtained as $10\rho 1\rho$, and four or 100 is obtained as $10\rho 0\rho$. On the negative side, -1 is obtained as 01ρ, -10 as $01\rho 0\rho$, -11 as $01\rho 1\rho$, -100 as $01\rho 0\rho 0\rho$, etc. A striking pattern begins to emerge, confirmed in Theorem 6.2 below. Define a *kei mode* to be a mode (A,ρ) with a single binary operation ρ satisfying the identity $xxy\rho\rho = y$. For a binary digit a, let a' denote the complementary digit, i. e. $0' = 1$ and $1' = 0$.

THEOREM 6.2 [6, 416]. The algebra $(\mathbb{Z},\rho)$ of reflexions on the integers is the free kei mode on the set $\{0,1\}$. A negative integer with binary representation

$-\sum_{i=0}^{r} a_i\, 2^{r-i}$ $(a_0 = 1)$ represents the word $01\rho a_1\rho \ldots a_r\rho$, while an integer

$n > 1$ for which $n - 1$ has the binary representation $\sum_{i=0}^{r} a_i\, 2^{r-i}$ $(a_0=1)$

represents the word $10\rho a_1'\rho \ldots a_r'\rho$.

The answer Theorem 6.2 gives to question (6.1) is that, if the binary strings represent integers, then the natural mathematical structure may be expressed geometrically as reflexion or algebraically as the free kei mode on 0 and 1.

Next, consider points x, y on a line. Let $xy\mu$ denote the *midpoint* of x and y.

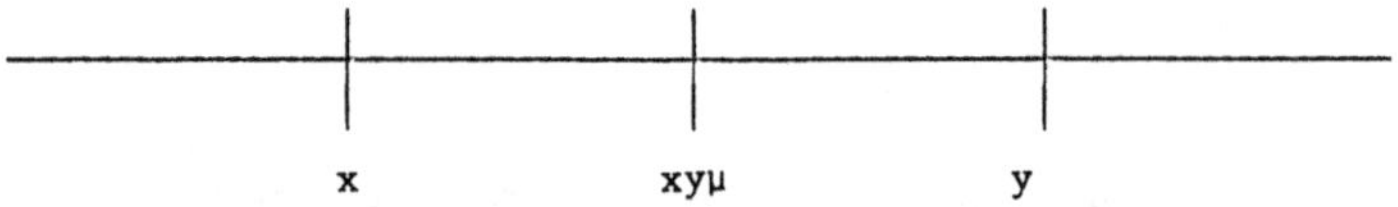

Starting with two points labelled 0 and 1, taking all the possible midpoints successively gives the intersection D_1 of the real unit interval $[0,1]$ with the set $D = \{m\cdot 2^{-n} \mid m,n \in \mathbb{Z}\}$ of dyadic rationals. The set D_1 is called the *dyadic unit interval*. Its elements are labelled by finite binary fractions. One-half or $\cdot 1$ is obtained as 10μ, three-quarters or $.11$ is obtained as $110\mu\mu$, three-eights or $\cdot 011$ is obtained as $0110\mu\mu\mu$, etc. Define a *commutative binary mode* to be a mode (A,μ) with a single binary operation μ satisfying the commutative law $xy\mu = yx\mu$. Then in analogy with Theorem 6.2, one has the following.

THEOREM 6.3 [6, 424]. The algebra (D_1,μ) of midpoints on the dyadic unit interval is the free commutative binary mode on the set $\{0,1\}$. A proper binary fraction

$$\sum_{i=0}^{r} a_i \, 2^{i-r-1} \quad (a_0=1) \text{ represents the word } a_r \ldots a_1 10\mu\mu \ldots \mu.$$

The answer Theorem 6.3 gives to question (6.1) is that, if the binary strings represent fractions, then the natural mathematical structure may be expressed geometrically as bisection or algebraically as the free commutative binary mode on 0 and 1.

Putting the structures of Theorems 6.2 and 6.3 together, one obtains the mode $(\mathbf{D},\mu,\rho)$, a commutative quasigroup on the set of dyadic rationals [6, 4.3], free on $\{0,1\}$. This structure often serves to replace the real numbers in the new formulations of scientific theories. For example, there are formulations of quantum mechanics based on convexity (mentioned and referenced in [6]). The reformulation designed for computing would then replace the convexity structure $(\mathbf{R},\underline{I}^{\circ})$ on the reals by the algebra $(\mathbf{D},\mu)$. Note that the modal $(\mathbf{R},\vee,0\cdot5)$ (notations of (2.7) and Example 4.8) reappears as a submodal of the modal $(\mathbf{DR},\vee,\mu)$ constructed as in Section 6. An interesting exercise in the application of the ideas discussed here would be to design a computer graphics package based on the modal structures on powers $\mathbf{D}^n$ of the dyadic rationals $\mathbf{D}$.

REFERENCES

[1] G. GIERZ et al., "A Compendium of Continuous Lattices," Springer-Verlag, Berlin 1980.

[2] M. G. MAIN, Free constructions of powerdomains, this volume.

[3] L. NEBESKÝ, "Algebraic Properties of Trees", Acta Universitatis Carolinae-Philogica Monographia XXV, Universita Karlova, Praha 1969.

[4] G. D. PLOTKIN, Computer science postgraduate course notes (unpublished), University of Edinburgh, Edinburgh 1980.

[5] A. B. ROMANOWSKA and J. D. H. SMITH, Bisemilattices of subsemilattices, J. Alg. 70 (1981), 78-88.

[6] A. B. ROMANOWSKA and J. D. H. SMITH, "Modal Theory", Heldermann-Verlag, Berlin 1985.

AN FP DOMAIN WITH INFINITE OBJECTS

Teresa A. Thomas
Donald F. Stanat

Department of Computer Science
University of North Carolina at Chapel Hill
Chapel Hill, NC 27514

0. Abstract

We describe a basis for extending Backus's FP languages to apply to infinite data objects, including streams, using data objects called prefixes, which can be viewed as approximations of either finite or infinite sequences. The resulting set of data objects, together with its limit points, admits not only an infinite number of entries in a sequence, but also infinitely nested expressions. Elements in this domain include arbitrarily good finite approximations to any of the infinite objects of the domain.

We also describe a mechanism for extending the primitive functions of an FP language over its domain to a corresponding stream FP language (or SFP language) capable of handling both finite and infinite elements over the extended domain. Extensions of the common functional forms are described. The algebra of FP programs is preserved nearly unchanged. Example programs are given.

I. Introduction

Backus's FP languages [Backus 1978] and the algebras associated with them promised to free the programmer from the word-at-a-time style of programming and give him powerful mathematical tools for reasoning about his programs. But in spite of the many attractive features of FP languages, it is not possible to use them in creating real programming environments, including history-sensitive systems, without substantial modification. The absence of infinite data objects is one of the deficiencies of these languages that prevents them from being widely used.

The work described here was motivated by the desire to extend Backus's FP languages to include infinite data objects without abandoning the style of programming advocated by Backus.

This work was supported in part by ARO grant number DAAG29-83-K-0090 and NSF grant number MCS- 8313312

We describe a semantic domain that includes all of the objects in Backus's domain plus infinite sequences (streams), infinitely nested objects, and partially computed objects (prefixes). The domain is shown to be a complete lattice, and we describe a mechanism for extending functions on Backus's domain to continuous functions on the extended domain. (Proofs for results can be found in a technical report [Thomas 1983].)

The work presented here satisfies the following desiderata:

- The domain for FP, given by Backus [Backus 1978], is "embedded" in the new domain.
- The new domain contains infinite objects, both those infinite in length and those infinitely nested.
- The new language is not substantially different in syntax from Backus's language.
- The primitive functions of an FP language extend in an intuitively satisfying way to continuous functions on the new domain. For example,

$$(distl : <4, <1, 2, 3, \ldots>>) = << 4, 1 >, < 4, 2 >, < 4, 3 >, \ldots >.$$

- The functional style of programming available with FP is preserved.

Seminal work in streams was done by Burge, Kahn, Kahn & McQueen, and Keller [Burge 1975, Kahn 1974, Kahn & McQueen 1977 and Keller 1978]. A number of workers have addressed the problem of extending functional languages, including Backus's FP and FFP languages, to streams. Broy [Broy 1982] describes a fixed point semantics for applicative languages based on the work of Scott [Scott 1982]. Feldman [Feldman 1982] used Backus's AST system to model a text editor. Earlier work by Keller [Keller 1977] describes a partially ordered set similar to that described herein, but that work focused on program graphs for data flow languages. Work more in the spirit of extending Backus's language includes that of Wadler [Wadler 1981], who described some list operators and transformations between different ways of processing lists. Ida and Tanaka [Tanaka & Ida 1981 and Ida & Tanaka 1983] describe an extension of FP and FFP languages that includes streams. The efforts that involve specific semantic domains are much more restricted than the one we propose. Dosch and Moller [Dosch & Moller 1982] consider evaluation strategies for FP languages whose domains are based on term algebra. Their domain is somewhat more restricted than the one we develop here. Halpern *et al.* [Halpern *et al.* 1985] developed a semantics for a specific FP language with streams; their domain is similar to ours except that they allow extension of a sequence by adding an element at any position, whereas we restrict extension to the right end of the sequence.

II. The Semantic Domain

We begin with a set of atoms **A** and construct an initial domain **B** similar to the one Backus chose for his FP languages, except that we add a greatest element, "top" ($\top$), which represents "error." "Bottom" ($\perp$) no longer represents "error." It is the least defined element; as such, it is used to denote a value about which we have no information, *e.g.*, a non-terminating computation. Sequences in this domain are $\top$-preserving, and if a sequence does not contain $\top$, then it is $\perp$-preserving. The domain **B** is flat; each element is related only to itself, bottom and top. We then construct an intermediate domain **C** that contains "partial" objects. These partial objects, called prefixes, are approximations to sequences (complete finite objects) or streams (complete infinite objects). The domain **D**, which is the domain of our new language, contains infinite objects and is constructed by forming the completion of the intermediate set **C** by adding limit points to it. Thus, for each object in **D**, the set **C** contains approximations arbitrarily close to that object.

There are two embedding maps, m_1 and m_2, connecting the three domains **B**, **C**, and **D**, where m_1 embeds **B** in **C** and m_2 embeds **C** in **D**. The choice of **C** as an extension of **B** and the specification of m_1 mapping **B** to **C** are novel and ensure the properties we seek; the completion of **C** to get **D** and the map m_2 are standard constructions. Specifically, **C** satisfies all the desiderata except that it does not have infinite objects, and its completion, **D**, satisfies all the desiderata.

In this section we describe the semantic domains **B**, **C**, and **D**. For each of these domains we define a partial order and show that it is a complete lattice. The definition of the semantic domain **D** is analogous to the definition of the real numbers by Cauchy sequences; a computational object in **D** is defined as an equivalence class of infinite sequences of finite objects.

The terms "atom," "object," "sequence," "stream," and "prefix" are used in this paper with specific meanings. An "atom" is a word used to represent an elementary datum; the set of atoms is nonempty and does not include the special characters $\perp$ (bottom) and $\top$ (top). The specific set chosen is unimportant; we will assume a set of atoms consisting of the integers, a set of alphabetic symbols, and the boolean constants *true* and *false*.

The term "object" denotes any element of our domain, including atoms and the nonelementary objects of sequences, streams and prefixes. "Sequences" and "streams" are objects comprised of a collection of objects (called "entries"), indexed by an initial segment of the natural numbers. A sequence has a finite number of entries, whereas the length of a stream is equal to the cardinality of the integers. We denote sequences and streams with angle brackets; e.g.,

$< 1,2,3 >$ and $< 1,2,3, \ldots >$

A "prefix" consists of a finite sequence of entries, but differs from a sequence in that it is not a "complete" datum. Intuitively, a prefix can be extended by adding another entry to its right end, giving a longer prefix. Prefixes serve the role of approximations; in particular, each prefix is an approximation to a class of sequences and streams. When a prefix is extended by adding an additional element to its right end, the corresponding set of sequences and streams for which the resulting prefix is an approximation is reduced. Prefixes are denoted similarly to sequences, except the right bracket is "$\not>$". The prefix

$< 1,2,3 \not>$

is an approximation to any sequence or stream whose first three entries are 1, 2, and 3, such as the sequences $< 1,2,3 >$, $< 1,2,3,4 >$ $< 1,2,3,4,5 >$ and $< 1,2,3,3,3 >$ and the stream $< 1,2,3, \ldots >$.

Finally, some notation employed here is new. Specifically,

$$\overset{n}{\underset{i=1}{<>}} \alpha_i = < \alpha_1, \ldots \alpha_n >,$$

$$\overset{n}{\underset{i=1}{<\not>}} \alpha_i = < \alpha_1, \ldots \alpha_n \not>$$

$$\overset{0}{\underset{i=1}{<>}} \alpha_i = <> \text{ (the empty sequence), and}$$

$$\overset{0}{\underset{i=1}{<\not>}} \alpha_i = <\not> \text{ (the empty prefix).}$$

A set of atoms **A** forms the basis for defining the domains **B**, **C**, and **D**.

Definition 1: Let **A** be a set of atoms (that is, **A** is a set that does not have $\perp$ and $\top$ as elements). The domain **B** based on **A** is defined by the following:

0) $\bot$, $\top$ are in **B**.

1) Any element of **A** is in **B**.

2) If $0 \leq n < \infty$ and $\alpha_i \in \mathbf{B}$ for $1 \leq i \leq n$, then $\overset{n}{\underset{i=1}{<>}} \alpha_i \in \mathbf{B}$. ($\overset{n}{\underset{i=1}{<>}} \alpha_i$ is a *sequence*.)

Any sequence containing $\top$ is equal to $\top$, and, if it does not contain $\top$, a sequence containing $\bot$ is equal to $\bot$.

3) **B** has no elements other than those implied by the above.

Upon the domain **B** a partial order $\sqsubseteq$ is imposed. The domain is flat and is similar to Backus's domain except for the extra element $\top$.

Definition 2: Let **B** be based on a set of atoms **A**. Then the relation $\sqsubseteq$ is defined on **B** as follows: For all $\alpha, \beta \in \mathbf{B}$, $\alpha \sqsubseteq \beta$ iff $\alpha = \beta$, $\alpha = \bot$, or $\beta = \top$. (This implies that $\bot \sqsubseteq \alpha$ and $\alpha \sqsubseteq \top$ for every $\alpha \in$ **B**.)

The proofs that $\sqsubseteq$ is a partial order on **B** and that $(\mathbf{B}, \sqsubseteq)$ is a complete lattice are trivial so we proceed with the definition of **C** and its partial order.

Definition 3: Let **A** be a set of atoms. The set of finite objects **C** based on **A** is defined by the following:

0) $\bot$, $\top$ are in **C**.

1) Any element of **A** is in **C**.

2) If $0 \leq n < \infty$ and $\alpha_i \in \mathbf{C}$ for $1 \leq i \leq n$, then

a) $\overset{n}{\underset{i=1}{<>}} \alpha_i \in \mathbf{C}$. ($\overset{n}{\underset{i=1}{<>}} \alpha_i$ is a *sequence*.)

b) $\overset{n}{\underset{i=1}{<\nrightarrow}} \alpha_i \in \mathbf{C}$. ($\overset{n}{\underset{i=1}{<\nrightarrow}} \alpha_i$ is a *prefix*.)

Furthermore, any sequence or prefix containing $\top$ is equal to $\top$.

(Thus, sequences and prefixes are "$\top$-preserving." Note, however, that sequences and prefixes are not $\bot$-preserving.)

3) **C** has no elements other than those implied by the above.

Examples of elements from **C** include -4, H, $<<\not> >, <\not>, <\perp \not>, <H, M \not>$, and $<<\not>, <\not>\not>$. Note that if **A** is a countable set, then so is **C**.

Upon this set of finite elements we impose a relation $\sqsubseteq$, which in fact is a partial order. The order can be thought of as "contains no more information than," or sometimes as "is a prefix of."

Definition 4: Let **C** be the set of finite objects based on **A**. Then $\sqsubseteq$ is defined on **C** by the following:

0) For every $\alpha \in \mathbf{C}$, $\perp \sqsubseteq \alpha$ and $\alpha \sqsubseteq \top$.

1) For every $\alpha \in \mathbf{A}$ and $\beta \in \mathbf{C}$, $\alpha \sqsubseteq \beta$ iff $\alpha = \beta$ or $\beta = \top$.

2) If $0 \leq n \leq m < \infty$, and $\alpha_i, \beta_i \in \mathbf{C}$ and $\alpha_i \sqsubseteq \beta_i$ for $1 \leq i \leq n$, then

   a) $\underset{i=1}{\overset{n}{<>}} \alpha_i \sqsubseteq \underset{i=1}{\overset{n}{<>}} \beta_i$

   b) $\underset{i=1}{\overset{n}{<\not>}} \alpha_i \sqsubseteq \underset{i=1}{\overset{m}{<>}} \beta_i$

   c) $\underset{i=1}{\overset{n}{<\not>}} \alpha_i \sqsubseteq \underset{i=1}{\overset{m}{<\not>}} \beta_i$

3) For all $\alpha, \beta \in \mathbf{C}$, $\alpha \sqsubseteq \beta$ only if it is implied by the above.

For example, part 2)a) of Definition 4 implies that $<1<2 \not>> \sqsubseteq <1<2, 3 \not>>$, part 2)b) implies that $<\perp, X \not> \sqsubseteq <\perp, X>$, and part 2)c) implies that $<1, 2 \not> \sqsubseteq <1, 2, 3 \not>$. If $\alpha \sqsubseteq \beta$, we will say α *precedes* β.

We next define what we mean by the *length* of an element of **C** and by its *nesting level*. In the following definitions, let $0 \leq n < \infty$ and $\alpha_i \in \mathbf{C}$ for $1 \leq i \leq n$.

Definition 5: The length of any element of **C** other than $\top$ is defined as follows:

0) The length of $\perp$ and all atoms is 0.

1) The length of $\underset{i=1}{\overset{n}{<>}} \alpha_i$ and $\underset{i=1}{\overset{n}{<\not>}} \alpha_i$ is n.

   The length of $\top$ is undefined.

Definition 6: The nesting level of any element of **C** other than $\top$ is defined as follows:

0) The nesting level of $\perp$ and atoms is 0.

1) The nesting level of $<>$ and $<\not>$ is 1.

2) For $n > 0$, the nesting level of $\overset{n}{\underset{i=1}{<>}} \alpha_i$ and $\overset{n}{\underset{i=1}{<\!\ddagger}} \alpha_i$ is $1 + \max_i$ {nesting level of α_i}.

The nesting level of $\top$ is undefined.

We now present without proof several propositions that describe some of the properties of the order $\sqsubseteq$ on **C**.

Proposition 7: Nothing precedes $\perp$ except itself. $\top$ precedes nothing except itself.

Proposition 8: An atom is related only to itself, $\perp$, and $\top$.

Proposition 9: If α is a sequence and $\alpha \sqsubseteq \beta$, then β is a sequence or $\top$. (Note, however, that α need not be equal to β; for example, $<<\!\ddagger> \sqsubseteq <<>>$.)

Proposition 10: If α and β are sequences or prefixes and $\alpha \sqsubseteq \beta$, then the length of α is less than or equal to the length of β.

Proposition 11: If α and β are sequences or prefixes and $\alpha \sqsubseteq \beta$, then the nesting level of α is less than or equal to the nesting level of β.

Proposition 12: If α is a prefix and $\alpha \sqsubseteq \beta$, then β is a prefix, a sequence, or $\top$.

Theorem 13: $\sqsubseteq$ is a partial order on C.

To establish that **C** is a complete lattice, it suffices to show that **C** has a lub (least upper bound) and that every nonempty subset of **C** has a glb (greatest lower bound) [Jacobson 1974]. The next series of lemmas and corollaries provides the basis for proving that **C** is a complete lattice.

Lemma 14: For every $\alpha, \beta \in$ **C**, $\alpha \sqcap \beta$ exists ($\alpha \sqcap \beta$ denotes the glb of α and β).

Corollary 15: Every non-empty finite set S $\subseteq$ **C** has a glb.

The next two lemmas exhibit properties of **C** that are used to establish that every nonempty subset of **C** has a glb.

Lemma 16: Any element of **C** not equal to $\top$ is preceded by only a finite number of elements of **C**.

Lemma 17: Let S be a non-empty subset of **C**. Then there exists a finite subset T of S such that the set of lower bounds of S is equal to the set of lower bounds of T.

Corollary 18: Every non-empty subset S of **C** has a glb.

Theorem 19: (C, $\sqsubseteq$) is a complete lattice.

Proof: Since we have shown that $\sqsubseteq$ is a partial order, it suffices to show that **C** has a lub and that every non-empty subset of **C** has a glb. $\top$ is clearly the lub of **C**, and Corollary 18 established that every non-empty subset of **C** has a glb. ∎

The next step in defining the set of objects is construction of the set of all chains of elements of **C**. This set, **D'**, is defined formally as:

$$\mathbf{D'} = \{\ \{\alpha_i\} \mid \text{for every } i,\ \alpha_i \in \mathbf{C} \text{ and } \alpha_i \sqsubseteq \alpha_{i+1}\}.$$

Each element of **D'** is called a *chain* (of elements of **C**). A chain is a sequence of approximations, where each approximation is at least as good as the preceding one. We will often use the expression $\{\alpha_i\}$ to denote a chain $\{\alpha_i | i \in \mathrm{N}\}$. Some examples of elements of **D'** are:

$\{\perp, \perp, \perp, \ldots\}$,

$\{<1 \not>, <1\ 2\ \not>, <1\ 2\ 3 \not>, \ldots\}$, and

$\{\perp, <1 \not>, <1>, <1>, <1>, \ldots\}$.

We associate with each chain the (unique) element that is approximated arbitrarily well by the infinite sequence of approximations. The set **D'** contains all of the kinds of objects we want, but the representations are not unique. For example, consider the following family of elements of **D'**:

$\{\perp, \mathbf{1}, \mathbf{1}, \mathbf{1}, \ldots\}$,

$\{\perp, \perp, \mathbf{1}, \mathbf{1}, \mathbf{1}, \ldots\}$,

$\{\perp, \perp, \perp, \mathbf{1}, \mathbf{1}, \mathbf{1}, \ldots\}$,

where the ellipses in each case denote an unending sequence of **1**'s. We wish to consider each of these to be an infinite representation of the finite object **1**. To eliminate the problem of non-unique representation, we define an equivalence relation that groups together elements of **D'** to reflect our intuitive notion of equality.

Definition 20: Let $\{\alpha_i\}$ and $\{\beta_i\}$ be elements of **D'**. Then $\{\alpha_i\} \sim \{\beta_i\}$ if for each $k \in$ N, there exists $n \in$ N such that $\alpha_k \sqsubseteq \beta_n$ and $\beta_k \sqsubseteq \alpha_n$.

Theorem 21: $\sim$ is an equivalence relation.

The quotient set $\mathbf{D} = \mathbf{D'}/\sim$ is the desired set of objects. The order $\sqsubseteq$ defined on **C** induces a relation $<$ on **D'** and a partial order $\sqsubseteq$ on **D**. The relation $<$ is a quasi-order (that is, reflexive and transitive but not anti-symmetric). In fact, the equivalence relation $\sim$ is the link between $<$ on **D'** and $\sqsubseteq$ on **D**, being the minimum equivalence relation that produces anti-symmetry.

Definition 22: Let $\{\alpha_i\}$ and $\{\beta_i\}$ be elements of **D'**. Then $\{\alpha_i\} < \{\beta_i\}$ if for each $k \in$ N, there exists n $\in$ N such that $\alpha_k \sqsubseteq \beta_n$.

Definition 23: Let Γ and Δ be elements of **D**, that is, they are equivalence classes in **D'**. Then $\Gamma \sqsubseteq \Delta$ if for every chain $\{\gamma_i\} \in \Gamma$ and for every chain $\{\delta_i\} \in \Delta$, $\{\gamma_i\} < \{\delta_i\}$.

The next result establishes that in order to show $\Gamma \sqsubseteq \Delta$, we need not compare all the chains of Γ with all those of Δ; it suffices to compare any pair of representatives from the equivalence classes.

Theorem 24: Let Γ, Δ be elements of D. Then $\Gamma \sqsubseteq \Delta$ iff there exist $\{\gamma_i\} \in \Gamma, \{\delta_i\} \in \Delta$ such that $\{\gamma_i\} < \{\delta_i\}$.

Theorem 25: The relation $\sqsubseteq$ on D is a partial order.

Theorem 26: If A is a countable set, then (D, $\sqsubseteq$) is a complete lattice.

Proof: It suffices to show that **D** has a glb and that any subset of **D** has a lub. Consider the equivalence class of the chain $\{\alpha_i \mid \alpha_i = \bot\}$. (In fact, this chain is the only element of its equivalence class.) Clearly this object precedes everything, and nothing else precedes this object, so this is the glb.

To show that any subset of **D** has a lub, let S be a subset of **D**. Choose one chain from each object in S. From these chains, we will construct a chain V whose equivalence class will be the lub of S. To show that the equivalence class of V is the lub of S, by Theorem 24 it will suffice to show that for each chosen chain $\{\alpha_i\}$, $\{\alpha_i\} <$ V, and that if for any other chain W such that $\{\alpha_i\} <$ W for all chosen chains $\{\alpha_i\}$, then V < W.

We will construct V by first constructing an infinite series of sets whose elements come from the chosen chains. Then we will form a chain of lub's of elements of these sets by diagonalization.

Let X_k be the set of kth elements of all of the chosen chains in **S**. Formally,

$$X_k = \{\alpha_k \mid \text{the chain } \{\alpha_i\} \text{ is one of the chosen chains}\}.$$

Each X_k is a subset of **C** and therefore is countable, since **A** is countable. Enumerate the X_k's:

$$X_1 = \{x_{11}, x_{12}, x_{13}, \ldots\}$$
$$X_2 = \{x_{21}, x_{22}, x_{23}, \ldots\}$$
$$\vdots$$

Construct the following sequence (to be shown a chain) V as a candidate for the lub of the chosen chains:

$$V = \{v_1, v_2, v_3, \ldots\}, \text{where}$$

$$v_1 = x_{11}$$
$$v_2 = x_{12} \sqcup x_{21} \sqcup v_1$$
$$v_3 = x_{13} \sqcup x_{22} \sqcup x_{31} \sqcup v_2$$
$$\vdots$$
$$v_n = x_{1n} \sqcup x_{2(n-1)} \sqcup \ldots \sqcup x_{n1} \sqcup v_{n-1}$$
$$\vdots$$

All of these lub's exist, since **C** is a lattice. V is a chain, since each element of V is the lub of the previous element and other elements, implying that the previous element certainly is a predecessor.

To show that V is the lub of the chosen chains, we can show that it is an upper bound and that it precedes all other upper bounds. V is an upper bound for the chosen chains if for all $\{\alpha_i\}$ where $\{\alpha_i\}$ is a chosen chain, $\{\alpha_i\} <$ V. $\{\alpha_i\} <$ V if for each α_k, there exists v_n such that $\alpha_k \sqsubseteq v_n$. Consider α_k. $\alpha_k \in X_k$. Therefore, $\alpha_k = x_{k(i)}$ for some i. Choose $n = k + i - 1$. Then $v_{(k+i-1)} = x_{1(k+i-1)} \sqcup x_{2(k+i-2)} \sqcup \ldots \sqcup x_{k(k+i-k)} \ldots \sqcup x_{(k+i-1)1} \sqcup v_{k+i-2}$. The kth element forming

$v_{(k+i-1)}$ is recognized as α_k. ($z_{k(k+i-k)} = z_{k(i)} = \alpha_k$.) Clearly, then, $\alpha_k \sqsubseteq v_{(k+i-1)}$. Hence, V is an upper bound.

Now suppose that $W = \{w_i\}$ is also an upper bound for the chosen chains, i.e., for every chosen chain $\{\alpha_i\}$, $\{\alpha_i\} < W$. We must show that $V < W$, which will be true if for each $k \in N$, there exists $n \in N$ such that $v_k \sqsubseteq w_n$. Observe that $v_k = z_{1k} \sqcup z_{2(k-1)} \sqcup \ldots \sqcup z_{k1} \sqcup v_{k-1}$. Each z_{ij} making up v_k comes from some chosen chain. Since W is an upper bound for the chosen chains, each $z_{ij}(i, j \leq k)$ precedes some element w_m in W. Choose the maximum one of these w_m's over the k z_{ij}'s. (The set of w_m's is totally ordered, since it is a subset of the chain W, and also is finite. Thus it has a maximum element.) Call it w_n. Since w_n is the maximum, each of the z_{ij}'s precedes it. Therefore, $v_k \sqsubseteq w_n$, since v_k is the lub of the z_{ij}'s. ∎

Thus we have established that the set **D** is a complete lattice, and this lattice will serve as the domain of a collection of continuous functions.

III. Functions on D

We wish to define functions on **D**, and in particular on streams, so that they will support a feasible computation mechanism. Although we want to be able to view a program mathematically as a process that maps one infinite object to another, from a computational view, the entire stream need not, indeed cannot, be known before the function begins to produce output; thus we want to be able to regard the same program computationally as a process that maps an approximation of the argument to an approximation of the result. It is therefore necessary that the functions be continuous over a suitable domain such as **D**.

In this section we describe a mechanism for producing useful continuous functions over **D**. We first show how to extend any monotonic function over an (altered) FP domain **B** to a monotonic function over **C**. We then invoke a standard procedure that extends any monotonic function over **C** to a continuous function over **D**.

We are abusing terminology by referring to f^* as an "extension" of f. The terminology is not misleading, however, in that the correspondence between objects in the domains **C** and **D** is maintained by corresponding functions f and f^*.

A function f from **C** to **C** is *monotonic* if for α, β elements of **C**, $\alpha \sqsubseteq \beta \rightarrow f(\alpha) \sqsubseteq f(\beta)$.

We will show how any monotonic function over **B** can be extended to a monotonic function over **C**. Because we are particularly interested in the primitives of Backus, we first show how any such function (which is monotonic over Backus's flat domain) can be used to define a corresponding monotonic function over the new domain **B**.

Definition 27: Let p be a Backus primitive. A new primitive $\hat{p}$ is defined on **B** as:

$\hat{p}$: x := $\bot$, if $x = \bot$

$\top$, if $x = \top$

$\top$, if p:x $= \bot$ and $x \neq \bot$

p:x otherwise.

Note that since each Backus primitive p is monotonic on the FP domain, the resulting function $\hat{p}$ on the flat lattice **B** is also monotonic.

We next show how to map a monotonic function on **B** to a monotonic extension on **C**.

Theorem 28: Let f be a monotonic function on **B**, and let f' be defined on **C** as:

$$f'(x) := \begin{cases} \bot, & \text{if } x = \bot \\ \text{glb}\{f(y) \mid x \sqsubseteq y \;\&\; y \in \mathbf{B}\}, & \text{otherwise.} \end{cases}$$

Then f' is a monotonic extension of f.

Proof: We first show that f' is an extension of f by showing that for $x \in \mathbf{B}$, $f(x) = f'(x)$. If $x = \bot$ or $x = \top$, then it is clear that $f(x) = f'(x)$. Otherwise, if $x \in \mathbf{B}$, then the only values of $y \in \mathbf{B}$ satisfying $x \sqsubseteq y$ are x and $\top$. Thus

$$f'(x) = \text{glb}\{f(x), f(\top)\}$$

and since f is monotonic, $f(x) \sqsubseteq f(\top)$, so

$$= \text{glb}\{f(x)\}$$

$$= f(x).$$

To show that f' is monotonic, suppose that $a, b \in \mathbf{C}$ such that $a \sqsubseteq b$. Then

$$\{f(y) \mid a \sqsubseteq y \;\&\; y \in \mathbf{B}\} \supseteq \{f(y) \mid b \sqsubseteq y \;\&\; y \in \mathbf{B}\}.$$

Therefore

$$\text{glb}\{f(y) \mid a \sqsubseteq y \;\&\; y \in \mathbf{B}\} \sqsubseteq \text{glb}\{f(y) \mid b \sqsubseteq y \;\&\; y \in \mathbf{B}\}.$$

Hence

$$f'(a) \sqsubseteq f'(b).$$

∎

We now use the fact that a monotonic function applied to a chain produces a chain to show that any monotonic function on **C** can be mapped to a continuous function on **D**.

Definition 29: Let f be monotonic on **C**. Then the function f^* from **D** to **D** is defined as follows: If $[\{\alpha_i\}]$ is the equivalence class of $\{\alpha_i\}$, and $[\{f(\alpha_i)\}]$ is the equivalence class of $\{f(\alpha_i)\}$, then $f^*([\{\alpha_i\}]) = [\{f(\alpha_i)\}]$.

Theorem 30: Let f be a monotonic function on **C**. Then f^* is well-defined on **D**.

Showing that a function is monotonic is usually easier than showing that it is continuous since continuity implies monotonicity. The following theorem establishes that if we show that f is monotonic on **C**, then f^* is continuous on the richer domain **D**.

Theorem 31: Let f be a monotonic function on **C**. Then f^* is continuous on **D**.

Proof: f^* is continuous on **D** if for every directed set $\mathbf{X} \subseteq \mathbf{D}$, $f^*(\text{lub } \mathbf{X}) = \text{lub } f^*(\mathbf{X})$. (A set **X** is *directed* if every finite subset of **X** has an upper bound in **X**.) The proof consists of establishing that $f^*(\text{lub } \mathbf{X}) \sqsubseteq \text{lub } f^*(\mathbf{X})$ and that $\text{lub } f^*(\mathbf{X}) \sqsubseteq f^*(\text{lub } \mathbf{X})$.

X and $f^*(\mathbf{X})$ are sets of equivalence classes of chains, and lub **X**, $f^*(\text{lub } \mathbf{X})$ and $\text{lub } f^*(\mathbf{X})$ are equivalence classes of chains. In view of the results of Theorem 24, we shall treat every equivalence class of chains as though it were a single (arbitrarily chosen) chain. Thus we shall treat **X** and $f^*(\mathbf{X})$ as though they were sets of chains and lub **X**, $f^*(\text{lub } \mathbf{X})$ and lub $f^*(\mathbf{X})$ as though they were simply chains. In the new denotations, the proof consists of showing that $f^*(\text{lub } \mathbf{X}) < \text{lub } f^*(\mathbf{X})$ and that $\text{lub } f^*(\mathbf{X}) < f^*(\text{lub } \mathbf{X})$.

It will be true that $f^*(\text{lub } X) < \text{lub } f^*(X)$ if for each point p on the chain $f^*(\text{lub } X)$ there is a point q on the chain $\text{lub } f^*(X)$ such that $p \sqsubseteq q$. If p is a point on $f^*(\text{lub } X)$, then there exists z on lub X such that $p = f(z)$. Since z is a point on the least upper bound of X, $z = \bigsqcup_{i=1}^{n} z_i$, where each z_i is a point on some chain in X. Let Z_i be the chain containing z_i. (In fact, there may be several containing z_i, but we choose the one which causes z_i to participate in the lub at this point.) Since X is directed, the set $\{Z_i | 1 \leq i \leq n\}$ has an upper bound in X, call it $\{a_i\}$. Since $\{a_i\}$ is an upper bound for $\{Z_i | 1 \leq i \leq n\}$, for each i, there exists $j \in \mathbf{N}$ such that $z_i \sqsubseteq a_j$. Let $m = \max\{j \in \mathbf{N} | z_i \sqsubseteq a_j\}$. For every $i, 1 \leq i \leq n, z_i \sqsubseteq a_m$. Therefore, $\bigsqcup_{i=1}^{n} z_i \sqsubseteq a_m$. Since f is monotonic, $f(\bigsqcup_{i=1}^{n} z_i) \sqsubseteq f(a_m)$, which implies that $f(z) \sqsubseteq f(a_m)$, which implies that $p \sqsubseteq f(a_m)$. $f(a_m)$ is a point on the chain $f(\{a_m\})$, which is a chain in $f^*(X)$. There is a q in the chain $\text{lub } f^*(X)$ such that $f(a_m) \sqsubseteq q$. This is the desired point, since $p \sqsubseteq f(a_m)$ and $f(a_m) \sqsubseteq q$ imply that $p \sqsubseteq q$.

It will be true that $\text{lub } f^*(X) < f(\text{lub } X)$ if for each point z on $\text{lub } f^*(X)$ there is a point $f(q)$ on $f(\text{lub } X)$ such that $z \sqsubseteq f(q)$. Since z is a point on a least upper bound, it can be written as $z = f(z_1) \sqcup f(z_2) \sqcup \ldots f(z_n)$. Each $f(z_i)$ is a point on some chain in $f^*(X)$, so each z_i is a point on some chain in X. Each z_i precedes some y_i where y_i is a point on lub X, since lub X is an upper bound for X. Choose the largest such y_i, call it q. Now $z_i \sqsubseteq q$ for every i, which implies that $\bigsqcup_{i=1}^{n} z_i \sqsubseteq q$. Because f is monotonic, we have that $f(\sqcup z_i) \sqsubseteq f(q)$. Therefore, $z \sqsubseteq f(q)$, and we have shown that $f(q)$ is the desired point. ∎

If a function f is not monotonic on **C**, the mechanism for mapping functions on **C** to functions on **D** fails to produce a function on **D** because the image of a chain under f might not be a chain. This is the case for each of the following:

a function that closes a prefix (converts a prefix into a sequence),

a function that measures the length of a prefix,

a function that tests whether an argument is a prefix,

a function that tests whether an argument is the null prefix.

Although **D** is the domain for our programs, it is often convenient to reason about programs using **C** as the domain. In particular, **D** can be viewed as **C** augmented by those infinite objects that are its limit points. Examples of these infinite objects include $< 1, 2, 3, 4, \ldots >$, $< 1, < 4, < 8, < 16, \ldots >>>>$ and $<<<< \ldots >>>>$. Because **D** contains all of **C** and its limit points, the behavior of continuous functions on points in **D** can usually be inferred from the behavior of the functions on points in **C**. Thus **C** is not merely an intermediate domain used in the construction of **D**; it also serves as an important guide to one's intuition, since reasoning about elements in **C** is generally easier than thinking about elements of **D**.

The nature of the final domain **D** is the basis for including $\top$ in these domains. Our goal is a computational system that includes nonterminating computations. For the system to have an attractive operational semantics, the functions of the system must be monotonic, and an implementation of the language must be able to produce a non-trivial approximation of the result from a sufficient approximation of the argument. If a computation has begun to produce output and then discovers that its input is "improper," the output must be altered in some way to reflect the error. Monotonicity requires that the alteration to the output must preserve the order of objects.

If the approximation to the inputs improves over time, then any output produced before an input becomes recognizably improper must precede (in the partial order) the error output produced from the improper input. There are various approaches to representing errors, such as using error-tagged objects at the "tops" of all branches in the partial order without $\top$. Another approach is to coalesce all of the errors into a single element, $\top$. For our work, the latter approach is more elegant mathematically, although the operational semantics of a practical system might well rely on the tagged-error approach.

IV. Functional Forms

In order to combine primitives into useful programs, we need a set of combining, or functional, forms. We restrict ourselves here to extensions of the functional forms found in the Turing Lecture [Backus 1978] to operate on functions on **D**. The definitions of some of those forms, such as *composition* and *construction*, hold in **D** without modification. Others, such as *insert* and *apply-to-all*, depend on the structure of the argument in their definition, and thus need to be modified to define their action on elements not in Backus's domain (prefixes, $\top$, and streams), but the new definitions are straightforward modifications.

The definition of the functional form *conditional* does not depend on the structure of the argument, but the definition must be modified, anyway, primarily because "error" has changed from $\perp$ to $\top$. The desired definition is the following:

$$
\begin{aligned}
p \rightarrow f; g : x \equiv\ & p : x = \text{true} \rightarrow f : x; \\
& p : x = \text{false} \rightarrow g : x; \\
& p : x = \perp \rightarrow \perp; \\
& \top
\end{aligned}
$$

Note that if p, f, and g are monotonic, then $p \rightarrow f; g$ is also monotonic.

The functional form *constant* must also be altered slightly to:

$$\bar{x} : y \equiv y = \top \rightarrow \top; x$$

V. Algebraic Laws

In his Turing Award Lecture [Backus 1978], Backus describes an algebra whose elements are the functions and whose operations are the functional forms of his language. In section 12.2, he gives a number of algebraic laws. With some uniform and straightforward modifications, these laws hold in our system.

Most of the laws, such as I.1 ($[f_1, \ldots, f_n] \circ g \equiv [f_1 \circ g, \ldots, f_n \circ g]$), remain true, although in some cases, the proofs must be changed slightly (for example, with I.10: $apndl \circ [f \circ g, \alpha f \circ h] \equiv \alpha f \circ apndl \circ [g, h]$). Laws containing an inequality, such as I.5 ($1 \circ [f_1, \ldots, f_n] \leq f_1$), are true if the direction of the inequality is reversed. Laws such as I.9 ($[\ldots,\overline{\bot},\ldots] \equiv \overline{\bot}$) that involve $\overline{\bot}$, will be true if they are modified by replacing $\overline{\bot}$ with $\overline{\top}$. Finally, some laws, such as I.6 ($defined \circ f_1 \rightarrow\!\rightarrow tail \circ [f_1] \equiv \overline{\phi}$), contain as part of a pre-condition a function named "*defined*" which is equivalent to $\overline{true}$. Although these laws hold in our system, it is perhaps misleading here to use the name "*defined*," since $\bot$ is the totally undefined element but $defined{:}\bot = true$. Perhaps a better name would be "*not.top*".

VI. Examples

In this section we give a number of simple examples illustrating the use of an FP language extended to the domain **D**. The primitive functions are all drawn from the Turing Award Lecture. These programs all use streams. They are, in general, simpler than their FP analogs because termination must be handled in FP, while these are all nonterminating.

Example 1: A program to generate an arithmetic progression:

$$< x, < x + k, < x + 2 * k, \ldots < x + n * k, \ldots > \ldots >>>$$

from an input argument of the form < *initial_value, increment* >. Note that the output is infinitely nested.

$$\text{arith.prog} := [\ \mathit{1},\ \text{arith.prog} \circ [+, \mathit{2}]\ ]$$

Thus arith.prog : < 5, 2 > = < 5, < 7, < 9, < ... >>>>.

Example 2: Streams are often defined to be pairs of the form < *first, rest* >, where *first* is the head of the stream and *rest* is a sequence that is the tail. There is an obvious correspondence between such a 'tree' representation of a stream and the 'flat', or sequence, representation. Either representation, however, can be used in the domain **D**. The following programs convert streams of the form < *first, rest* > to the 'flat' form and back again:

$$\text{flat} := \mathit{apndl} \circ [\ \mathit{1},\ \text{flat} \circ \mathit{2}\ ] \qquad \text{(tree to flat)}$$

$$\text{tree} := [\ \mathit{1},\ \text{tree} \circ \mathit{tail}\ ] \qquad \text{(flat to tree)}$$

Thus flat:< 1, < 2, < 3, ... >>> = < 1, 2, 3, ... >

tree:< 1, 2, 3, ... > = < 1, < 2, < 3, ... >>>

Example 3: *The Sieve of Eratosthenes.* This example uses the function *arith.prog* defined in Example 1 and the *flat* function defined in Example 2; the input to the program should be the pair <1,1>, which will cause *flat* ∘ *arith.prog* to produce the stream <1,2,3, ... >. Then primes:< 1, 1 > = *sieve* :< 2, 3, 4, ... >. The function sieve applied to a stream produces as an element of the result the first element of the stream and then filters (via the function "filter") all multiples of that first element from the remainder of the stream.

$$\text{primes} := \text{sieve} \circ \mathit{tail} \circ \text{flat} \circ \text{arith.prog}$$

$$\text{sieve} := \mathit{apndl} \circ [\ \mathit{1}, \text{sieve} \circ \text{filter}\ ]$$

$\text{filter} := eq0 \circ mod \circ [1, 2] \rightarrow \text{filter} \circ apndl \circ [1, tail \circ tail]; apndl \circ [2, \text{filter} \circ apndl \circ [1, tail \circ tail]]$

Example 4: **A 'history-sensitive' stream function. This approach is being developed as an alternative to schemes such as Backus's AST system. We describe a function that accepts an input of the form $< s_1, x_1, x_2, x_3, \ldots >$, where s_1 is an initial system state and the sequence $x_1, x_2, x_3, \ldots$ is a sequence of inputs to the system, and whose output is a sequence $< o_1, o_2, o_3, \ldots >$. Mathematically the function will map one infinite object to another, but it can be viewed as a system with functions that, for each i, use the current state s_i and the current input x_i to compute the next output o_i and the next state s_{i+1}.**

We define a functional form, denoted by braces, that requires two function arguments, a 'next state' function $S*$ and an 'output' function $O*$. The function $S*$ maps the domain $\mathbf{S} \times \mathbf{O}$ (where $\mathbf{S}$ is the set of states and $\mathbf{O}$ is the set of objects) into $\mathbf{S}$, and $O*$ maps the same domain into $\mathbf{O}$. (The set $\mathbf{S}$ can be chosen to be any subset of the set of objects $\mathbf{O}$.) The effect of applying a function constructed with this functional form applied to a stream argument can be described as follows:

$$(\{O*, S*\} :< s_1, x_1, x_2, x_3, \ldots >) = < o_1, o_2, o_3, \ldots >,$$

where $o_1 = O* :< s_1,\ x_1 >$, $o_2 = O* :< s_2,\ x_2 >$, $o_3 = O* :< s_3,\ x_3 >$, $\ldots$ and $s_2 = S* :< s_1,\ x_1 >$, $s_3 = S* :< s_2,\ x_2 >$, $\ldots$

Thus, the value of $S* :< s_i, x_i >$ is the next state s_{i+1} and the value of $O* :< s_i, x_i >$ is o_i, the result of processing input x_i when in state s_i. The definition of the functional form denoted by {} can be given entirely within SFP:

$\{f, g\} := apndl \circ [\ f \circ [\ 1, 2\ ], \{f, g\} \circ apndl \circ [\ g \circ [\ 1, 2\ ], tail \circ tail\ ]]$

There are other ways of describing similar functions based on extensions of FP functions; in particular, a functional form can be described such that the system state is an object parameter of the functional form rather than the first entry of a stream input. The function described above produces one entry o_i for each input entry x_i, but other functions can be defined that produce different or varying numbers of output entries for each single input entry x_i.

Example 5: **A program to generate the cartesian product of a pair of streams.**

$\text{cp} := \text{zip} \circ [\ f, g\ ]$

$f := distl \circ [\ 1 \circ 1, 2\ ]$

$g := \text{cp} \circ [\ tail \circ 1, 2\ ]$

$\text{zip} := apndl \circ [\ 1 \circ 1, apndl \circ [\ 1 \circ 2, \text{zip} \circ \alpha tail\ ]]$

Here the function f pairs the first element of the first stream with each element of the second stream. The function g finds the cartesian product of the tail of the first stream with the second stream. The function zip then interleaves these two streams into a single stream.

VII. Summary

We have described how an FP language can be extended to a domain with infinite objects, including streams, infinitely nested objects, and combinations of the two. The mechanisms we used for this extension ensure that any monotonic function, including the primitive functions of a Backus FP language, will be extended to continuous functions over the new domain. While no extension mechanism is given for functional forms, in all cases of which we know, definitions of functional forms over the extended domain are either unchanged from their original definition, or modified in a straightforward way.

Backus's FP languages are unique in that there exists a rich algebra of programs that can be applied to problems of program transformation as well as proofs of correctness. We considered the preservation of this algebra one of the most important criteria for judging the success of our efforts. The addition of a top element to the domain causes some changes in the algebra, but those changes are superfluous; the power of the algebra is intact.

Future work will concentrate on developing an operational semantics and exploring the application of program transformations to improve program efficiency.

Acknowledgments

The authors would like to acknowledge helpful discussions with David Plaisted, Bruce Smith, Barat Jayaraman, and Kent Dybvig, as well as Gyula Magó, Anne Presnell, and James Thatcher, who read various drafts of this paper. We are especially indebted to Dean Brock for his comments and suggestions. Finally, we wish to thank Leigh Pittman for her help with the formatting.

BIBLIOGRAPHY

[Backus 1978] Backus, J. Can programming be liberated from the vonNeumann style? A functional style and its algebra of programs. *Communications of the ACM*, **21**, No. 8, Aug 1978, pp. 613–641.

[Broy 1982] Broy, M. A fixed point approach to applicative multiprogramming, in *Theoretical Foundations of Programming Methodology*. D. Reidel, 1982. pp. 565–622. Ed. by M. Broy & G. Schmidt.

[Burge 1975] Burge, W.H. *Recursive programming techniques*. Reading, Mass: Addison-Wesley, 1975.

[Dosch & Moller 1982] Dosch, W. & Moller, B. Busy and lazy FP with infinite objects. In *Conference Record of the 1984 ACM Symposium on LISP and Functional Programming*, 1984. pp. 282–292.

[Feldman 1982] Feldman, G. Functional Specifications of a Text Editor. In *Conference Record of the 1982 ACM Symposium on LISP and Functional Programming*, 1982. pp. 37–46.

[Halpern *et al.* 1985] Halpern, J., J. Williams, E. Wimmers & T. Winkler. In *Conference Record of the Twelfth Annual ACM Symposium on Principles of Programming Languages*, 1985. pp. 108–120.

[Henderson 1982] Henderson, P. *Purely Functional Operating Systems in Functional Programming and its Applications*. Cambridge University Press, 1982. pp. 177–192.

[Ida & Tanaka 1983] Ida, T. & Tanaka, J. Functional programming with streams, in *Information Processing*. North-Holland, 1983. pp. 265–270.

[Jacobson 1974] Jacobson, N. *Basic Algebra I*. San Francisco: W.H.Freeman & Co., 1974.

[Kahn 1974] Kahn, G. The semantics of a simple language for parallel programming. In Proceedings, IFIP Congress 74, 1974 pp. 471–475.

[Kahn & Macqueen 1977] Kahn, G. & Macqueen, D.B. Coroutines and networks of parallel processes. In Proceedings, IFIP Congress 77, North-Holland, Jan 1977.

[Keller 1977] Keller, R.M. Semantics of parallel program graphs. Technical Report UUCS–77–110, University of Utah, July 22, 1977.

[Keller 1978] Keller, R.M. Denotational models for parallel programs with indeterminate operators, in *Formal Description of Programming Concepts*. North-Holland, 1978. pp. 337–366.

[Nakata & Sassa 1983] Nakata, I. & Sassa, M. Programming with streams. Technical Report RJ3751(43317). IBM. Jan 1983.

[Scott 1982] Scott, D.S. Lectures on a mathematical theory of computation, in *Theoretical Foundations of Programming Methodology*. D. Reidel, 1982. pp. 146–292. Ed. by M. Broy & G. Schmidt.

[Stoy 1982] Stoy, J.E. Some Mathematical Aspects of Functional Programming, in *Functional Programming and its Applications*. Cambridge University Press, 1982. pp. 217–252.

[Tanaka & Ida 1981] Tanaka, J. & Ida, T. Stream extension for fp-like language. 1981. (Unpublished paper.)

[Thomas 1983] Thomas, T.A. An fp domain with infinite objects. Technical Report TR 83-009. University of North Carolina at Chapel Hill. 1983.

[Turner 1982] Turner, D.A. Recursion Equations as a Programming Language, in *Functional Programming and its Applications*. Cambridge University Press, 1982. pp. 1–28.

[Wadler 1981] Wadler, P. Applicative style of programming, program transformation and list operators. In *ACM-MIT Proceedings of the 1981 Conference on Functional Programming Languages and Computer Architecture.*, Oct 1981. pp. 25–32.

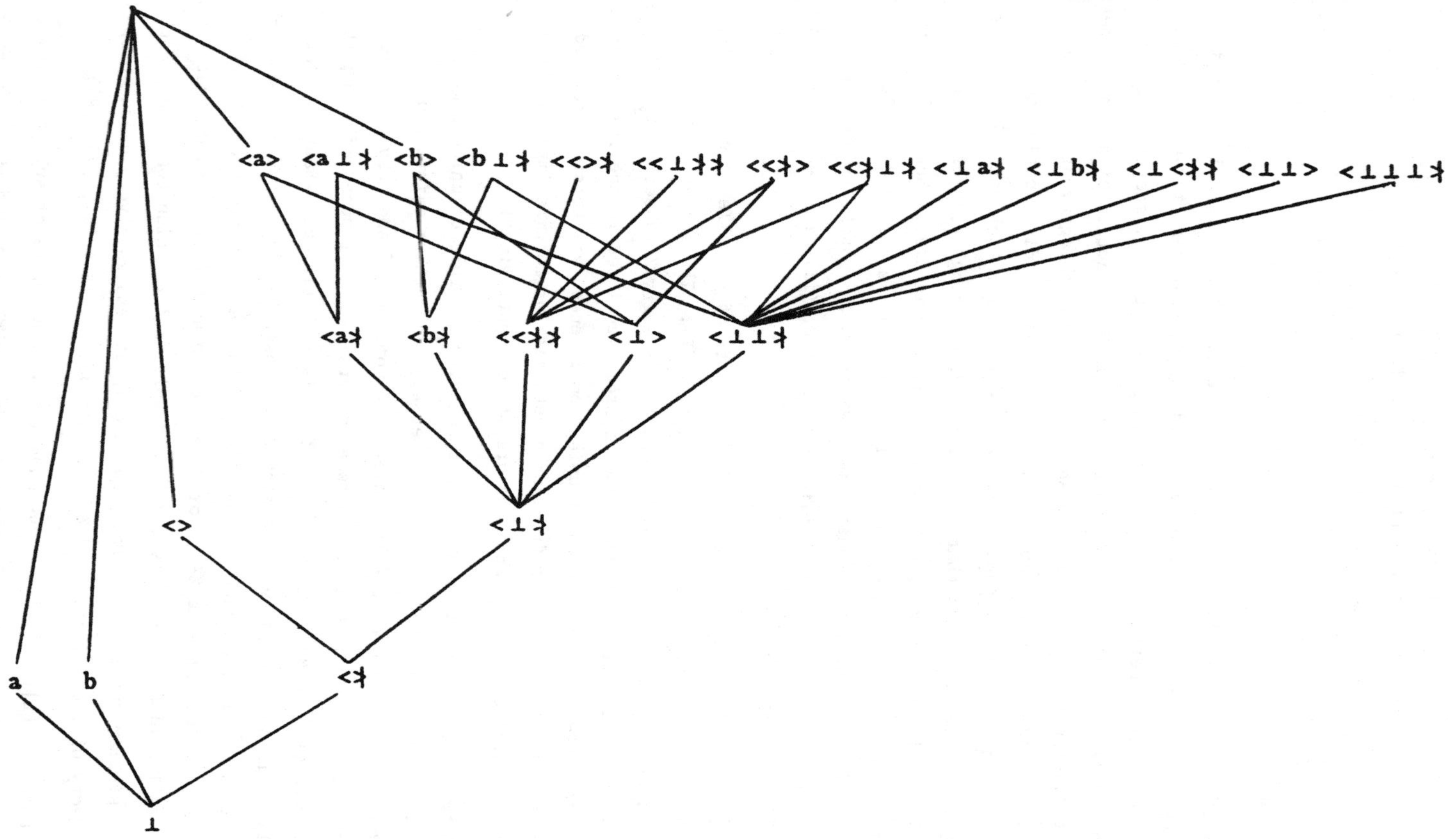

Part of the domain C based on a set with two atoms

UNION COMPLETE COUNTABLE SUBSET SYSTEMS

P. Venugopalan
University of Connecticut, Scofieldtown Road
Stamford, CT 06903

1. INTRODUCTION

The study of different kinds of completeness properties of partially ordered sets (posets) is an old theme in the theory of orderings; most familiar among these are the properties used to define semilattices, complete lattices, and chain complete posets. In [8], Wright, Wagner, and Thatcher generalized the notion of a completeness property by introducing the notion of a subset system on the category of posets and monotone maps and defining for each subset system Z a corresponding completeness property, Z-completeness. Each subset system Z determines for each poset P a family Z(P) of nonempty subsets of P such that (i) for all P, all singletons of P are in Z(P) and (ii) if f: $P \to Q$ is a monotone function and S is in Z(P), then f(S) is in Z(Q). Elements of Z(P) are called Z-subsets of P. A poset is called Z-complete if every Z-subset of P has a sup in P. Most common examples of subset systems are, under which Z(P) is the family of (i) finite subsets of P, (ii) directed subsets of P, and (iii) all nonempty subsets of P.

The family of all lower sets generated by Z-subsets of P (called the Z-ideals) is, under set inclusion, itself a poset, denoted by $I_Z(P)$. The subset system is called union complete if for every poset P the union of every Z-subset of $I_Z(P)$ is an element of $I_Z(P)$. Each of the three subset systems mentioned in the last paragraph is union complete. The condition of union completeness was first introduced in [8], where it was shown to be a sufficient hypothesis for certain important results but also declared to be "somewhat obscure if not mystifying".

Two more recently published papers help to clarify the role of union completeness. Meseguer [3] has shown that for any subset system Z, there exists a union complete subset system $\bar{Z}$ such that (i) a poset is Z-complete if and only if it is $\bar{Z}$-complete and (ii) a monotone function between posets is Z-continuous (meaning it preserves the sups of Z-subsets) if and only if it is $\bar{Z}$-continuous. Banaschewski and Nelson [1] defined for each subset system Z and poset P a (universal) Z-completion $\tilde{P}$. A desired property of such a completion is that each of the elements of $\tilde{P}$ is obtainable as the join of some Z-set of P, and these authors have shown that this property will hold for every poset P if and only if Z is union complete. See also [3] for a similar result. Moreover, union completeness is a very useful property in the theory of Z-continuous and Z-algebraic posets. (See [4], [7], [8])

Various authors ([1], [3], [8]) have made lists of examples of subset systems, most of which are union complete. To our knowledge, however, no systematic attempt has yet been made to survey the whole collection of union complete subset systems and to arrange its elements into an ordered structure. In this paper we begin that study giving primary attention to the subset systems Z for which in every poset P all Z subsets are countable. This seems a good way to start and these subset systems will probably be the ones of greatest importance in the theory of computation. However, several of the proofs for the countable case, can easily be converted into proofs that apply to the general case; we mention some of these in an appendix.

As a by product of our study we obtain two union complete subset systems that do not appear to have been previously noticed. Under one of these Z(P) is the collection of all connected subsets of P; under the other, Z(P) is the family of finitely bounded (see the definition below) subsets.

2. EQUIVALENCE CLASSES OF SUBSET SYSTEMS

In the study of Z-complete posets we can replace Z-sets by Z-ideals, since we are concerned only with the sups of Z-sets. Subset systems Z and Z' are called equivalent if, for all posets P, $I_Z(P) = I_{Z'}(P)$. This is clearly an equivalence relation. We denote the equivalence class containing Z by [Z]. If [Z] = [Z'], and if Z is union complete, then so is Z'. We call [Z] countable if there exists Z' such that [Z] = [Z'] and for all posets P, each set in Z'(P) is countable. Let $\mathcal{L} = \{[Z]$: [Z] is union complete and countable$\}$. We define a partial order on $\mathcal{L}$ by letting $[Z] \le [Z']$ if and only if for all posets P, $I_Z(P) \subseteq I_{Z'}(P)$. $\mathcal{L}$ is a complete lattice (see the discussion before Proposition 3.13 in [3]).

Our objective in this paper is to study the structure of $\mathcal{L}$. We show that $\mathcal{L}$ can be decomposed into intervals which themselves form a rather simple looking "three dimensional" distributive lattice (see Figure 1). Many of these intervals consist of just one equivalence class, but for others the interval structure is still an open question. Of these, some are known to contain at least two equivalence classes.

NOTATION: Let P be any poset and let $S \subseteq P$.

$\downarrow S = \{x\ P: x \le s$ for some s in $S\}$; $\downarrow x = \downarrow\{x\}$. For a family $\{Z_i : i \in I\}$ of subset systems we denote by $\bigcap_i Z_i$ the subset system Z such that for all posets P, Z(P) = $\bigcap_i Z_i(P)$. When I = {1,...,n}, we write $Z_1 \ldots Z_n$ for $Z_1 \cap \ldots \cap Z_n$. We use the following notations to denote different subset systems. Note that all these subset systems are union complete.

P(P) - All countable nonempty subsets of P.

K(P) - All countable connected subsets of P.
(A subset S of a poset P is called connected
if for every pair a, b in S there is a sequence

$x_1, x_2, \ldots x_n$ in S such that $x_1 = a$, $x_n = b$ and for $i = 2,\ldots,n-1$, x_i is comparable to both x_{i-1} and x_{i+1}.)

K'(P) - All countable connectible subsets of P.
(A subset S of a poset P is called connectible if there exists a connected subset T of P such that $S \subseteq T$.)

B(P) - All countable finitely bounded subsets of P
(A subset S of a poset P is finitely bounded if there exists a finite set F in P such that $S \subseteq \downarrow F$

F(P) - All finite subsets of P.

$C_i(P)$ - All countable i-compatible subsets of P.
(A subset S of P is i-compatible if for all $A \subseteq S$ such that $|A| \leq i$, there exists an x in P such that $A \subseteq \downarrow x$, $i = 2,\ldots$)

$C_\omega(P)$ - $\bigcap_i C_i(P)$; that is, all countable subsets S of P such that if A is any finite subset of S, then $A \subseteq \downarrow x$, for some x in P. If $S \in C_\omega(P)$, then S is called a compatible subset of P.

D(P) - All countable nonempty directed subsets of P.

U(P) - All countable subsets of P which have upper bounds in P.

$(P) - All singletons of P.

2.1 PROPOSITION: In $\mathcal{L}$ the following relations hold:

(1) $[\$] \leq [D] \leq [K] \leq [K'] \leq [P)$.

(2) $[\$] \leq [D] \leq [C_\omega] \leq [C_i] \leq [K'] \leq [P]$.

(3) $[\$] \leq [F] \leq [B] \leq [P]$.

(4) $[\$] \leq [U] \leq [B] \leq [P]$.

(5) $[\$[\leq [U] \leq [C_i] \leq [K'] \leq [P]$.

Here all the inequalities are strict.

The following lemma is due to Iwamura. See [2] for a sharpened version of this lemma.

2.2 LEMMA (IWAMURA): Any infinite directed subset S of a poset P can be expressed as the union of a nonempty chain of directed sets all of which have cardinalities less than that of S.

It is easy to see that $FU = FC_\omega$, and it follows from Iwamura's Lemma that $DB = DU$.

3. SUPS IN $\mathcal{L}$

3.1 PROPOSITION: $[D]V[F] = [P]$.

PROOF: Let $[Z] = [D]V[F]$. Clearly, $[Z] \leq [P]$. Let P be any poset and let $S \varepsilon P(P)$. Let T be the set of all finite subsets of S. Then T is directed and $\downarrow S = \bigcup_{F_i \varepsilon T} \downarrow F_i$. Now, by union completeness, it follows that $\downarrow S \varepsilon I_Z(P)$. Therefore $[P] \leq [Z]$.

3.2 COROLLARY: $[D]V[FK'] = [K']$

3.3 COROLLARY: $[DU]V[FU] = [U]$.

3.4 PROPOSITION: (i) $[FU]V[D] = [C_\omega]$.

(ii) $[FC_i]V[D] = [C_i]$.

PROOF: (i) Let $[Z] = [FU]V[D]$. Clearly $[Z] \leq [C_\omega]$. Let $S \varepsilon C_\omega(P)$ for some poset P. Let T be the set of all finite subsets of S. Then T is directed. Since $S \varepsilon C_\omega(P)$, every set E in T has an upper bound. Therefore $E \varepsilon I_Z(P)$ for all E in T. Therefore, by union completeness, $\downarrow S = \bigcup_{E \varepsilon T} \downarrow E$ is in $I_Z(P)$. Hence $[C_\omega] \leq [FU]V[D]$.

(ii) can be proved in a similar way.

3.5 PROPOSITION: $[D]V[FK] = [K]$.

PROOF: Let $[Z] = [D]V[FK]$. Clearly $[Z] \leq [K]$. Let S be any connected subset of P. Let T be the set of all finite connected subsets of S. Then T is directed and $\downarrow S = \bigcup_{F \varepsilon T} \downarrow F$. Then, by union completeness, we have $\downarrow S \varepsilon I_Z(P)$.

3.6 COROLLARY: $[D]V[FKU] = [KC_\omega]$.

3.7 COROLLARY: $[D]V[FKC_i] = [KC_i]$.

3.8 COROLLARY: $[DU]\ V[FKU] = [KU]$.

3.9 PROPOSITION: $[FU]V[FK] = [FK']$.

PROOF: Let $[Z] = [FU]V[FK]$. Clearly, $[Z] \leq [FK']$. We shall show that $[FK'] \leq [Z]$. Let P be any poset and let $I \varepsilon I_{FK'}(P)$. Write $I = I_1 U \ldots . UI_n$, where

$I_j \in I_K(P)$ for $j = 1,\dots,n$. If $a_j \in I_j$, for $j=1,..n$, then there exists a finite connected set $S \subseteq P$ containing all of the a_j's, since I is contained in a connected component of P. Then $I \cup {\downarrow} S$ is in $I_{FK}(P)$ and hence in $I_Z(P)$. Therefore the set $\{I_1,\dots I_n\}$ is in $FU(I_Z(P)) \subseteq Z(I_Z(P))$. Therefore $\bigcup_{i=1}^{n} I_i = I$ is in $I_Z(P)$. This completes the proof of the proposition.

3.10 PROPOSITION: $[DU]V[F] = [B]$.

PROOF: Let $[Z] = [DU]V[F]$. Clearly $[Z] \leq [B]$. Let P be any poset and let $I \in I_B(P)$. Then there exists a finite set S in P such that $I \subseteq {\downarrow} S$. Let $T = \{{\downarrow} R : R \subseteq I$ and R is finite$\}$. Then T is a directed subset of $I_Z(P)$ with an upper bound in $I_Z(P)$. Therefore, by hypothesis, $T \in Z(I_Z(P))$. Then, by union completeness, $\cup T = I$ is in $I_Z(P)$. This completes the proof of the proposition.

3.11 COROLLARY: $[DU]V[FK'] = [BK']$.

3.12 COROLLARY: $[DU]V[FK] = [BK]$.

4. PARTITION THEOREMS

In this section we define three different classes of basic intervals in $\mathcal{L}$. We show that each class forms a partition of $\mathcal{L}$.

The basic idea in the proofs of this section is that given a union complete subset system Z, a poset P, and a Z-ideal I in $I_Z(P)$, we can produce many other Z-ideals not only in P but also in all other posets.

4.1 LEMMA: Let $[Z] \in \mathcal{L}$. If there exists a poset P and a Z-ideal I of P such that I contains a countably infinite ascending chain C with no upper bound in I, then $[DU] \leq [Z]$. Moreover, if the Z-ideal I contains a countably infinite ascending chain which does not have an upper bound in P, then $[D] \leq [Z]$.

PROOF: Let C': $x_1 < x_2 < \dots$ be a cofinal infinite ascending subchain of C. Let $N^* = \{0, 1, 2, \dots \omega\}$. Define f: $P \to N$ as follow.

$$f(x) = \begin{cases} \omega, & \text{if } x \geq x_i \text{ for all } i; \\ n, & \text{if } x \geq x_n \text{ but } x \not\geq x_{n+1}; \\ 0, & \text{if } x \not\geq x_i \text{ for all } i. \end{cases}$$

Clearly, f is a monotone function. Therefore $f(I) = N^* - \{\omega\}$ is a Z-ideal of N^*.

Now let Q be any poset. Any countably infinite ascending chain with an upper bound in Q can be obtained as an image of $N^* - \{\omega\}$ under a monotone function from N^*.

Therefore for all posets every chain-ideal with an upper bound is a Z-ideal. Let $J \varepsilon I_{DU}(Q)$. Then, by Iwamura's Lemma, there is a chain T in Q such that $J = \bigcup_{x \varepsilon T} \downarrow x$. Since T is in Z(Q), by union completeness, it follows that J is in $I_Z(Q)$. Therefore $[DU] \leq [Z]$.

Now suppose C does not have an upper bound in P. Then the above argument shows that $N^* - \{\omega\}$ is a Z-ideal in itself and hence every chain ideal is in $I_Z(Q)$ for all posets Q; hence $I_D(Q) \subseteq I_Z(Q)$. Thus $[D] \leq [Z]$.

4.2 DEFINITION: Let L be the subset system defined as follows: For all posets P, $L(P) = \{S \subseteq P: S$ has a lower bound in $P\}$. Note that L is not union complete.

REMARK: Let $Q = \{a,b,o\}$ be the poset in which a and b are incomparable and 0 is the least element. It is easy to see that if Q is in $I_Z(Q)$, then $[FL] \leq [Z]$.

4.3 LEMMA: Let $[Z] \varepsilon \mathcal{L}$. If $[FL] \leq [Z]$, then $[FK] \leq [Z]$.

Let Q be any poset and let $I \varepsilon I_{FK}(P)$. Let S be the set of all maximal elements of I. We will prove that $I \varepsilon I_Z(P)$ by induction on the number of elements in S, denoted by $|S|$. If $|S| = 1$, then I is a principal ideal and hence is in $I_Z(P)$. Suppose the result is true for $|S| = n$. Let $S = \{a_o,\dots,a_n\}$. Since I is an FK-ideal there exists a sequence $\{b_o,b_1,\dots,b_m\}$ of elements of I such that b_i is comparable with both b_{i-1} and b_{i+1}, for $i = 1,\dots,m-1$, and such that the following three conditions are satisfied: (i) every element of S appears in this sequence at least once; (ii) $b_o = a_k$, for some k and $b_m = a_j$, for some j; (iii) a_j appears in this sequence exactly once. Now reorder the a_i's according to the order in which they appear in this sequence. Then $b_o = a_o$ and $b_m = a_n$. Then $J = \downarrow\{a_o,\dots,a_{n-1}\}$ is in $I_{FL}(P)$. Therefore, by induction hypothesis, J is in $I_{FK}(P)$. Also $\downarrow a_n$ is in $I_Z(P)$. Now there exists a b_i in the above sequence such that $b_i \leq a_n$ and also $b \leq a_t$ for some $t < n$. Let $Q = \{a,b,0\}$ be the poset in which a and b are incomparable and 0 is the least element. Define $f: Q \to I_Z(P)$ as follows: $f(a) = J$; $f(b) = \downarrow a_n$ and $f(0) = \downarrow b_i$. Then f is monotone and hence $\{J, \downarrow a_n, \downarrow b_i\}$ is a Z-set of $I_Z(P)$. Therefore, by union completeness, $J \cup \downarrow a_n \cup \downarrow b_i = I$ is in $I_Z(P)$. This completes the proof of the lemma.

4.4 COROLLARY: If $[FLU] \leq [Z]$, then $[FKU] \leq [Z]$.

NOTATION: Let $[Z_1], [Z_2] \varepsilon \mathcal{L}$. Then

$<[Z_1], [Z_2]> = \{[Z]: [Z_1] \leq [Z] \leq [Z_2]\}$.

4.5 DEFINITION: We define the following intervals in :

$A_1 = <[D],[P]>$; $A_2 = <[DU], [B]>$; $A_3 = <[\$],[F]>$;

$B_1 = <[F],[P]>$; $B_2 = <[FU],[K']>$; $B_3 = <[FKU],[K]>$;

$B_4 = <[\$],[D]>$; $L_1 = <[FK],[P]>$;

$L_i = <[FKC_i],[C_i]>$, $i = 2, 3, \ldots$;

$L_\omega = <[\$],[C_\omega]>$.

See Fig. 1.

4.6 PROPOSITION: For any $[Z]$ in $\mathcal{L}$, exactly one of the following is true:

(1) $[Z] \leq [F]$.

(2) $[DU] \leq [Z]$.

PROOF: Clearly both these cannot be true at the same time. Suppose $[Z] \not\leq [F]$. Then for some poset P, there exists an I in $I_Z(P)$ such that I is not in $I_F(P)$. Then either I has an infinite ascending chain with no upper bound in I, in which case, by 4.1, $[DU] \leq [Z]$. Otherwise $I = \downarrow S$ where $S = \{x_1, x_2, x_3 \ldots\}$ is the set of maximal elements of I. Define $f\colon P \to N^*$ as follows:

$$f(x) = \begin{cases} i, & \text{if } x = x_i; \\ \omega, & \text{if } x > x_j \text{ for some } j \\ 1, & \text{otherwise.} \end{cases}$$

Clearly, f is a monotone function and $f(I) = N$. Therefore N is a Z-ideal of N^* and hence by 4.1, $[DU] \leq [Z]$. This completes the proof of the proposition.

4.7 PROPOSITION: For any $[Z]$ in $\mathcal{L}$, exactly one of the following is true:

(1) $[Z] \leq [B]$.

(2) $[D] \leq [Z]$.

Again, it is clear that both these cannot be true. Suppose $[Z] \not\leq [B]$. Then for some poset P, there exists an I in $I_Z(P)$ such that I is not in $I_B(P)$. Let $S = \{x \in P\colon x \geq y \text{ for some } y \text{ in } I\}$. Let T be the set of all finite subsets of S. Then T is directed and by Iwamura's Lemma, $T = \downarrow_T C$ where C is a chain in T. Let $C'\colon F_1 \subseteq F_2 \subseteq \ldots\ldots$ be a cofinal chain in C. Define $f\colon P \to N$ as follows:

$$f(x) = \begin{cases} 1, & \text{if } x \in \downarrow F_1; \\ 2, & \text{if } x \in \downarrow F_2 \text{ and } x \notin \downarrow F_1 \\ \ldots\ldots\ldots\ldots & \\ n, & \text{if } x \in \downarrow F_n \text{ and } x \notin \downarrow F_{n-1} \\ \ldots\ldots\ldots\ldots & \\ 0, & \text{if } x \notin \downarrow (U_i F_i). \end{cases}$$

It can be easily checked that f is a monotone function. Since I is not in $I_B(P)$, f(I) = N and hence N is a Z-ideal of itself. Therefore, by 4.1, [D] $\leq$ [Z]. This completes the proof of the proposition.

4.8 PROPOSITION: For any [Z] in $\mathcal{L}$, exactly one of the following is true:

(1) [Z] $\leq$ [K'].

(2) [F] $\leq$ [Z].

PROOF: Clearly both these cannot be true. Suppose [Z] $\nleq$ [K']. Then for some poset P, there exists an I in $I_Z(P)$ such that I is not in $I_{K'}(P)$. Let a, b ε I such that a and b are in different connected components of P. Let Q = {a',b'} be a two element antichain. Define f: P $\rightarrow$ Q as follows:

$$f(x) = \begin{cases} a', & \text{if x and a are in the same connected component of I;} \\ b', & \text{otherwise.} \end{cases}$$

Then f is monotone and hence f(I) = Q is a Z-ideal of itself. Therefore, by union completeness of Z, [F] $\leq$ [Z].

4.9 PROPOSITION: For any [Z] in $\mathcal{L}$, exactly one of the following is true:

(1) [Z] $\leq$ [K].

(2) [FU] $\leq$ [Z].

PROOF: Clearly, both these cannot be true. Suppose [Z] $\nleq$ [K]. Then for some poset P, there is an I in $I_Z(P)$ such that I is not in $I_K(P)$. Let a, b ε P such that a and b are in different connected components of I. Let Q = {a',b',1} be a poset such that a' and b' are incomparable and 1 is the greatest element. Define f: P $\rightarrow$ Q as follows:

$$f(x) = \begin{cases} a', & \text{if x and a are in the same connected component of I;} \\ b', & \text{if } x \in I \text{ and x is not in the component of I to which a belongs;} \\ 1, & \text{otherwise.} \end{cases}$$

Clearly, f is monotone. Therefore f(I) = {a',b'} of a Z-ideal of Q. Then, by union completeness of Z, it follows that [FU] $\leq$ [Z].

4.10 PROPOSITION: For any [Z] in $\mathcal{L}$, exactly one of the following is true:

(1) [Z] $\leq$ [D].

(2) [FKU] $\leq$ [Z].

PROOF: Clearly, both these cannot be true. Suppose $[Z] \nleq [D]$. Then for some poset P there exists an I in $I_Z(P)$ such that I is not in $I_D(P)$. Then there exist a, b in I such that the set $\{a,b\}$ does not have an upper bound in I. Let Q = $\{a',b',0,1\}$ be a poset in which 1 is the greatest element, 0 is the least element and a' and b' are incomparable. Define f: P $\to$ Q as follows:

$$f(x) = \begin{cases} a', & \text{if } x \geq a \text{ and } x \ngeq b; \\ b', & \text{if } x \ngeq a \text{ and } x \geq b; \\ 1, & \text{if } x \geq a \text{ and } x \geq b \\ 0, & \text{otherwise} \end{cases}$$

Clearly, f is a monotone function. Therefore f(I) = $\{a',b',0\}$ is a Z-ideal of Q. Then, by 4.4, $[FKU] \leq [Z]$.

4.11 PROPOSITION: For any [Z] in $\mathcal{L}$, exactly one of the following is true:

(1) $[Z] \leq [C_2]$.

(2) $[FK] \leq [Z]$.

PROOF: Again, it is clear that both these cannot happen. Suppose $[Z] \nleq [C_2]$. Then for some poset P there exists an I in $I_Z(P)$ such that I is not in $I_{C_2}(P)$. Then there exist a, b $\in$ I such that the set $\{a,b\}$ does not have an upper bound in P. Let Q = $\{a',b',0\}$ be a poset such that a' and b' are incomparable and 0 is the least element of Q. Define

f: P $\to$ Q as follows:

$$f(x) = \begin{cases} a', & \text{if } x \geq a; \\ b', & \text{if } x \geq b; \\ 0, & \text{otherwise.} \end{cases}$$

Then f is monotone and hence $\downarrow f(I) = Q$ is a Z-ideal in itself. Then, by 4.3, $[FK] \leq [Z]$. This completes the proof of the proposition.

4.12 PROPOSITION: For any [Z] in $\mathcal{L}$, exactly one of the following is true:

(1) $[Z] \leq [C_{i+1}]$.

(2) $[FKC_i] \leq [Z]$.

PROOF: It is easy to see that both these cannot happen together. Suppose $[Z] \nleq [C_{i+1}]$. Then for some poset P there exists an I in $I_Z(P)$ such that I is not in $I_{C_{i+1}}(P)$. Then there exists a set $S \subseteq I$ such that $|S| = i+1$ and S does not have an upper bound in P. Let $S = \{x_1, x_2, \ldots, x_{i+1}\}$. Let S denote the poset of all subsets of the set $\{1, \ldots, i+1\}$ having less than i+1 elements. Define f: P $\to S_{i+1}$ as follows:

$$f(x) = \begin{cases} \{j\}, \text{ if } x = x_j; \\ \{j, \ldots, x_{j_r}\}, \text{ if } x \text{ is an upper bound of} \\ \quad \{x_{j_1}, \ldots, x_{j_r}\}, \text{ and } x \not\geq x_i \text{ for } i \neq j_1, \ldots j_r. \\ \phi, \text{ otherwise.} \end{cases}$$

Then f is a monotone function and therefore $f(I) = \{\{1\}, \ldots, \{i+1\}, \phi\}$ is a Z-ideal of S_{i+1}. Let $J \in I_{FLC_i}(Q)$ for some poset Q. We shall show that J is in $I_Z(Q)$ by induction on the number of maximal elements of J. If J has only one maximal element, clearly J is in $I_Z(Q)$. Suppose the result is true if the number of maximal elements is n-1. Let J have n maximal elements, namely $\{z_1, \ldots, z_n\}$. Let $R_j = \{z_1, \ldots, z_{n-i-1}\} \cup \{z_{n+j-i-1}\}$, $j = 1, \ldots, n$. Then the set containing all R_j's and the union of any i or less of them and principal ideal $\downarrow z_1$ is isomorphic to S_{i+1}. Therefore, by union completeness of Z, $\cup \downarrow R_j = J$ is in $I_Z(Q)$. Therefore $[FLC_i] \leq [Z]$. Then, by 4.3, $[FKC_i] \leq [Z]$.

4.13 PROPOSITION: For any [Z] in $\mathcal{L}$, exactly one of the following is true:

(1) $[Z] \leq [C_\omega]$.

(2) $[FKC_i] \leq [Z]$, for some i.

PROOF: Again, it is clear that both these cannot happen. Suppose $[Z] \not\leq [C_\omega]$. Then for some poset P, there exists an I in $I_Z(P)$ such that I is not in $I_{C_\omega}(P)$. Let S be a finite subset of I such that S does not have an upper bound in P. If $|S| = i+1$, i=1,2..., then, by 4.12, $[FKC_i] \leq [Z]$.

4.14 THEOREM: The intervals A_1, A_2, A_3 form a partition of $\mathcal{L}$. That is, $A_1 \cup A_2 \cup A_2 = \mathcal{L}$ and $A_i \cap A_j = \emptyset$, for $i \neq J$.

PROOF: If $[Z] \notin A_3$, then $[Z] \not\leq [F]$. Then by 4.6, $[DU] \leq [Z]$. Now either $[Z] \in A_2$ or $[Z] \not\leq [B[$. If $[Z] \not\leq [B]$, then by 4.7, $[D] \leq [Z]$. Therefore $[Z] \in A_1$. This proves that $L = A_1 \cup A_2 \cup A_3$. The fact that $A_i \cap A_j = \emptyset$ is immediate from 4.6 and 4.7.

4.15 THEOREM: The intervals B_1, B_2, B_3, B_4 form a partition of $\mathcal{L}$.

PROOF: This follows from Propositions 4.8, 4.9, and 4.10.

4.16 THEOREM: The intervals L_i, i = 1, 2, ... ω, form a partition of $\mathcal{L}$.

PROOF: This follows from Propositions 4.11, 4.12, and 4.13.

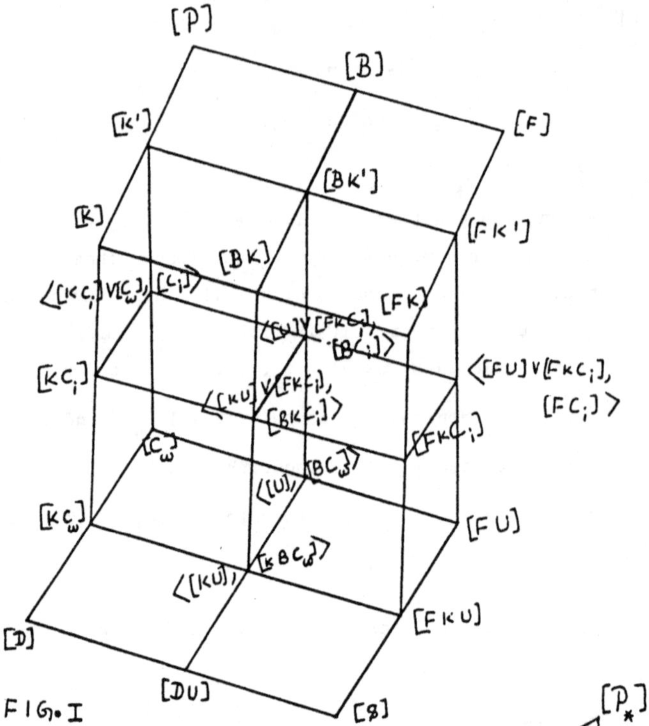

FIG. I

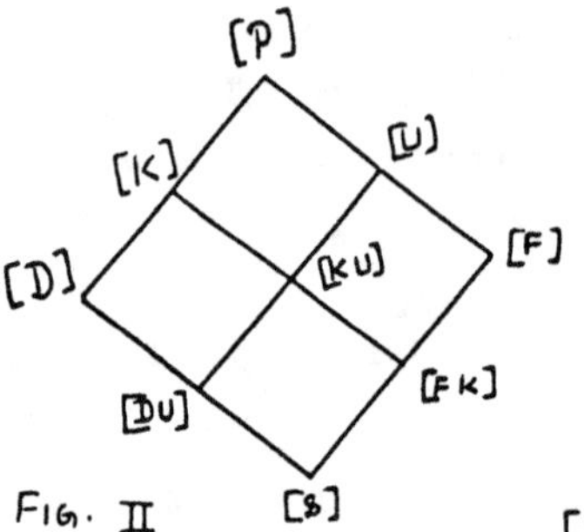

FIG. II

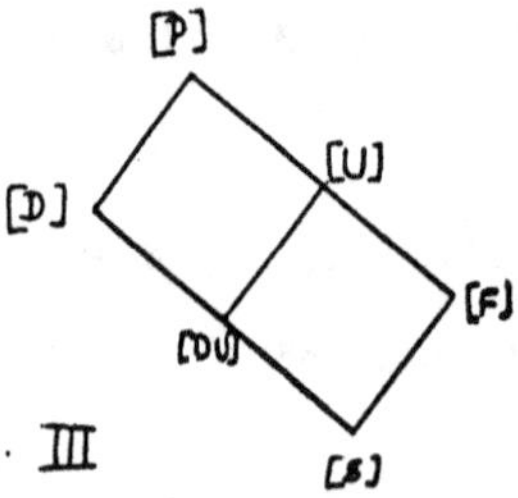

FIG. III

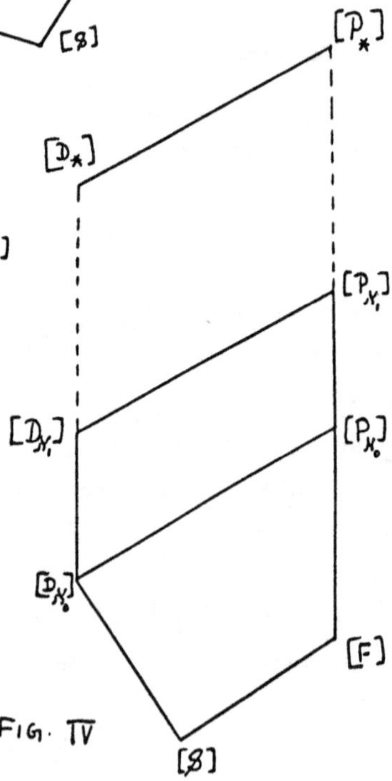

FIG. IV

This table describes the intersection of the intervals

A_i's, B_j's, and L_k's:

$A_1B_1L_1$	$[D] \vee [F] \vee [FK] \leq [Z] \leq [P] \wedge [P] \wedge [P]$	$[P]$
$A_1B_1L_i$	$[D] \vee [F] \vee [FKC_i] \leq [Z] \leq [P] \wedge [P] \wedge [C_i]$	$\emptyset$
$A_1B_1L_\omega$	$[D] \vee [F] \vee [\$] \leq [Z] \leq [P] \wedge [P] \wedge [C_\omega]$	$\emptyset$
$A_1B_2L_1$	$[D] \vee [FU] \vee [FK] \leq [Z] \leq [P] \wedge [K'] \wedge [P]$	$[K']$
$A_1B_2L_i$	$[D] \vee [FU] \vee [FKC_i] \leq [Z] \leq [P] \wedge [K'] \wedge [C_i]$	$\langle [KC_i] \vee [C_\omega], [C_i] \rangle$
$A_1B_2L_\omega$	$[D] \vee [FU] \vee [\$] \leq [Z] \leq [P] \wedge [K'] \wedge [C_\omega]$	$[C_\omega]$
$A_1B_3L_1$	$[D] \vee [FKU] \vee [FK] \leq [Z] \leq [P] \wedge [K] \wedge [P]$	$[K]$
$A_1B_3L_i$	$[D] \vee [FKU] \vee [FKC_i] \leq [Z] \leq [P] \wedge [K] \wedge [C_i]$	$[KC_i]$
$A_1B_3L_\omega$	$[D] \vee [FKU] \vee [\$] \leq [Z] \leq [P] \wedge [K] \wedge [C_\omega]$	$[KC_\omega]$
$A_1B_4L_1$	$[D] \vee [\$] \vee [FK] \leq [Z] \leq [P] \wedge [D] \wedge [P]$	$\emptyset$
$A_1B_4L_i$	$[D] \vee [\$] \vee [FKC_i] \leq [Z] \leq [P] \wedge [D] \wedge [C_i]$	$\emptyset$
$A_1B_4L_\omega$	$[D] \vee [\$] \vee [\$] \leq [Z] \leq [P] \wedge [D] \wedge [C_\omega]$	$[D]$
$A_2B_1L_1$	$[DU] \vee [F] \vee [FK] \leq [Z] \leq [B] \wedge [P] \wedge [P]$	$[B]$
$A_2B_1L_i$	$[DU] \vee [F] \vee [FKC_i] \leq [Z] \leq [B] \wedge [P] \wedge [P]$	$\emptyset$
$A_2B_1L_\omega$	$[DU] \vee [F] \vee [\$] \leq [Z] \leq [B] \wedge [P] \wedge [P]$	$\emptyset$
$A_2B_2L_i$	$[DU] \vee [FU] \vee [FK] \leq [Z] \leq [B] \wedge [P] \wedge [P]$	$[BK']$
$A_2B_2L_i$	$[DU] \vee [FU] \vee [FKC_i] \leq [Z] \leq [B] \wedge [P] \wedge [P]$	$\langle [U] \vee [FKC_i], [BC_i] \rangle$
$A_2B_2L_\omega$	$[DU] \vee [FU] \vee [\$] \leq [Z] \leq [B] \wedge [P] \wedge [P]$	$\langle [U], [BC_\omega] \rangle$
$A_2B_3L_1$	$[DU] \vee [FKU] \vee [FK] \leq [Z] \leq [B] \wedge [P] \wedge [P]$	$[BK]$
$A_2B_3L_i$	$[DU] \vee [FKU] \vee [FKC_i] \leq [Z] \leq [B] \wedge [P] \wedge [P]$	$\langle [KU \vee FKC_i], [BKC_i] \rangle$
$A_2B_3L_\omega$	$[DU] \vee [FKU] \vee [\$] \leq [Z] \leq [B] \wedge [P] \wedge [P]$	$\langle [KU], [KBC_\omega] \rangle$
$A_2B_4L_1$	$[DU] \vee [\$] \vee [FK] \leq [Z] \leq [B] \wedge [P] \wedge [P]$	$\emptyset$
$A_2B_4L_i$	$[DU] \vee [\$] \vee [FKC_i] \leq [Z] \leq [B] \wedge [P] \wedge [P]$	$\emptyset$
$A_2B_4L_\omega$	$[DU] \vee [\$] \vee [\$] \leq [Z] \leq [B] \wedge [P] \wedge [P]$	$[DU]$
$A_3B_1L_1$	$[\$] \vee [F] \vee [FK] \leq [Z] \leq [F] \wedge [P] \wedge [P]$	$[F]$
$A_3B_1L_i$	$[\$] \vee [F] \vee [FKC_i] \leq [Z] \leq [F] \wedge [P] \wedge [C_1]$	$\emptyset$
$A_3B_1L_\omega$	$[\$] \vee [F] \vee [\$] \leq [Z] \leq [F] \wedge [P] \wedge [C_\omega]$	$\emptyset$
$A_3B_2L_1$	$[\$] \vee [FU] \vee [FK] \leq [Z] \leq [F] \wedge [K'] \wedge [P]$	$[FK']$
$A_3B_2L_i$	$[\$] \vee [FU] \vee [FKC_i] \leq [Z] \leq [F] \wedge [K'] \wedge [C_i]$	$\langle [FU] \vee [FKC_i], [FC_i] \rangle$
$A_3B_2L_\omega$	$[\$] \vee [FU] \vee [S] \leq [Z] \leq [F] \wedge [K'] \wedge [C_\omega]$	$[FU]$
$A_3B_3L_1$	$[\$] \vee [FKU] \vee [FK] \leq [Z] \leq [F] \wedge [K] \wedge [P]$	$[FK]$
$A_3B_3L_i$	$[\$] \vee [FKU] \vee [FKC_i] \leq [Z] \leq [F] \wedge [K] \wedge [C_i]$	$[FKC_i]$
$A_3B_3L_\omega$	$[\$] \vee [FKU] \vee [\$] \leq [Z] \leq [F] \wedge [K] \wedge [C\ ]$	$[FKU]$
$A_3B_4L_1$	$[\$] \vee [\$] \vee [FK] \leq [Z] \leq [F] \wedge [D] \wedge [P]$	$\emptyset$
$A_3B_4L_i$	$[\$] \vee [\$] \vee [FKC_i] \leq [Z] \leq [F] \wedge [D] \wedge [C_i]$	$\emptyset$
$A_3B_4L_\omega$	$[\$] \vee [\$] \vee [\$] \leq [Z] \leq [F] \wedge [D] \wedge [C_\omega]$	$[\$]$

5. THE LATTICE $\mathcal{L}'$

Let $\mathcal{L}' = \{A_i \cap B_j \cap L_k \neq \emptyset$: $i = 1,2,3$; $j = 1,2,3,4$; $k = 1,\ldots,\omega\}$ We write $A_iB_jL_k$ for $A_i\ B_j\ L_k$. From Table 1, we know that all the elements of $\mathcal{L}'$ are intervals in $\mathcal{L}$. For $<[Z],[Z]>$, we write $[Z]$. We define $A_{i_1}B_{j_1}L_{k_1} \leq A_{i_2}B_{j_2}L_{k_2}$ if and only if $i_1 \geq i_2$, $j_1 \geq j_2$, and $k_1 \geq k_2$. This is a partial order on $\mathcal{L}'$.

Figure 1 is a pictorial representation of the poset $\mathcal{L}'$. Two elements are joined by an unbroken line when there is no element between them. For example there is no element between [F] and [B].

REMARK: For $<[Z_1],[Z_2]>$, $<[Z_1'],[Z_2']>$ in L', $<[Z_1],[Z_2]> \leq <[Z_1'],[Z_2']>$ if and only if $[Z_1] \leq [Z_1']$ and $[Z_2] \leq [Z_2']$.

5.1 THEOREM: $\mathcal{L}'$ is a complete homomorphic image of $\mathcal{L}$.

PROOF: Let $P = \{A_1, A_2, A_3, B_1, B_2, B_3, B_4, L_1, \ldots, L_\omega\}$ be the poset in which the only relations are the following:

$A_1 > A_2 > A_3$; $B_1 > B_2 > B_3 > B_4$; $L_1 > L_2 > \ldots > L_\omega$. Define h_A, h_B, h_L: $L \to P$ as follows:

$h_A([Z]) = A_i$, if $[Z]\varepsilon A_i$; $h_B([Z]) = B_j$, if $[Z]\varepsilon B_j$; $h_L([Z]) = L_k$, if $[Z]\varepsilon L_k$. Clearly these three maps are monotone and they preserve arbitrary infs and sups. Now define $h: \mathcal{L} \to \mathcal{L}'$ by $h([Z]) = h_A([Z])h_B([Z])h_L([Z])$. Clearly h is monotone. Now $h(\wedge_\alpha[Z_\alpha]) = h_A(\wedge_\alpha[Z_\alpha])h_B(\wedge_\alpha[Z_\alpha])h_L(\wedge_\alpha[Z_\alpha]) = \wedge_\alpha[(h_A([Z])h_B([Z])h_L([Z])] = \wedge_\alpha h([Z_\alpha])$. Thus h preserves arbitrary infs. Similarly it can be shown that h preserves arbitrary sups. This completes the proof of the theorem.

The following example shows that $[KU] < [KBC_\omega]$ and $[U] < [BC_\omega]$.

5.2 EXAMPLE: Let Q be the poset of all finite subsets of positive integers ordered by inclusion. Let $R = Q \cup \{x,y\}$ where elements of Q are ordered as before, x is greater than all singletons of Q containing odd integers, y is greater than all singletons of Q containing even integers, and x and y are incomparable with all other elements of R. Now it is easy to see that the lower set of R containing all singletons of Q is in $I_{BC_\omega}(R)$ but not in $I_U(R)$. Clearly for all posets P, $I_U(P) \subseteq I_{BC_\omega}(P)$. This shows that $[U] < [BC_\omega]$. By adding a bottom element to R, we also see that $[KU] < [KBC_\omega]$.

However, it is an open question whether the following inequalities in $\mathcal{L}$ are strict:

(1) $[KU] \vee [FKC_1] \leq [BKC_1]$.

(2) $[FU] \vee [FKC_i] \leq [FC_i]$.

(3) $[U] \vee [FKC_i] \leq [BC_i]$.

(4) $[KC_i \vee [C_\omega] \leq [C_i]$.

If one is interested only in a subclass of the class of all posets, then the number of non-equivalent union complete countable subset systems may be still smaller.

5.3 EXAMPLE: Suppose we are interested only in directed posets; that is, posets in which every finite set has an upper bound. Then there are only nine different equivalence classes. See Fig. 2.

If we consider only directed posets which have least elements, then there are only six different equivalence classes. See Fig. 3.

It is well known that a poset is P-complete if and only if it is F-complete and D-complete. Note that in the poset L, $[F] \vee [D] = [P]$. Similarly we can prove many results suggested by the poset L. For example,

(1) a poset is K'-complete if and only if it is FU-complete and K-complete;

(2) a poset is B-complete if and only if it is F-complete and DU-complete;

(3) a poset is K-complete if and only if it is D-complete and FK-complete.

We conclude with one more result in this direction. Recall that for x, y in a poset P, x is said to be Z-way-below y (written $x \underset{Z}{\ll} y$) if whenever $y \leq \sup_P S$ for some S in Z(P), there exists an s in S such that $x \leq s$. A poset is called Z-continuous if (i) it is Z-complete (meaning: for every S in Z(P), $\sup_P S$ exists), (ii) for every x in P, the set $\{y: y \underset{Z}{\ll} x\}$ is in $I_Z(P)$, and (iii) for every x in P, $x = \sup_P \{y: y \ll x\}$.

5.4 PROPOSITION: A poset is P-continuous if and only if it is F-complete and C_ω-continuous.

PROOF: Let P be an F-complete, C_ω-continuous poset. Then, clearly, P is P-complete. Since $[C_\omega] \leq [P]$, $x \underset{P}{\ll} y$ implies $x \underset{C_\omega}{\ll} y$. Now let $x \underset{C_\omega}{\ll} y$. Suppose $y \leq \sup_P S$ for some subset of P. Since $\sup_P S$ exists, $S \in C_\omega(P)$. Therefore, by the definition of the C_ω-way-below relation, there exists s in S such that $x \leq s$. This shows that $x \underset{P}{\ll} y$. Therefore, $\sup \{x: x \underset{P}{\ll} y\} = \sup \{x: x \underset{C_\omega}{\ll} y\} = y$. Thus P is P-continuous.

Now suppose that P is a P-continuous poset. Then it is P-complete and hence F-complete and C_ω-complete. Again, as shown in the last paragraph, $\sup_P \{x: x \underset{C_\omega}{\ll} y\} = \sup_P \{x: x \underset{P}{\ll} y\} = y$. Since every lower set which has an upper bound in P is in

$I_{C_\omega}(P)$, it follows that the set $\{x: x \ll_{C_\omega} y\}$ is in $I_{C_\omega}(P)$. This completes the proof of the proposition.

From Raney's classical theory of completely distributive complete lattices we know that a poset with a least element is a completely distributive complete lattice if and only if it is P-continuous. See [5]. Thus the above proposition gives a characterization of completely distributive complete lattices.

Appendix

As pointed out before several of the proofs in this paper can be easily modified to handle general (not necessarily countable) cases. For example, if D_* denotes the subset system of all directed subsets and P_* denotes the subset system of all subsets, then Proposition 3.1 can be generalized to $[D_*] \vee [F] = [P_*]$. More generally, if D_α denotes the subset system of all directed sets of cardinality less than or equal to α, and P_α denotes the subset system of all subsets of cardinality less than or equal to α, where α is any infinite cardinal, then $[D_\alpha] \vee [F] = [P_\alpha]$. We mention only one more result in this direction. Interested reader will have no difficulty finding other results.

Suppose one is interested only in posets which have greatest and least elements. Then the poset of equivalence classes of union complete subset systems (not just the countable ones!) can be pictorially represented as in figure 4.

REFERENCES

[1] B. Banaschewski, E. Nelson, Completions of partially ordered sets, SIAM J. Comput. 11(1982), 521-528.

[2] G. Markowsky, Chain-complete posets and directed sets with applications, Algebra Universalis, 6(1976), 138-147.

[3] J. Meseguer, Order completion monads, Algebra Universalis, 16(1983), 63-82.

[4] D. Novak, On a duality between the concepts of "finite" and "directed", Houston J. Math. 8(1982), 545-563.

[5] G.N. Raney, A subdirect-union representation for completely distributive lattices, Proc. Amer. Math. Soc. 4(1953), 518-522.

[6] D. Scott, Continuous lattices, Toposes, Algebraic Geometry and Logic, Lecture Notes in Math, Vol. 274, Springer-Verlag, New York, 1972, 97-136.

[7] P. Venugopalan, Z-continuous posets, Houston J. Math. (to appear).

[8] J.B. Wright, E.G. Wagner, and J.W. Thatcher, A uniform approach to inductive posets and inductive closure, Theor. Comp. Sci., 7(1978), 57-77.

On the Syntax and Semantics of Concurrent Computing

Maria Zamfir and David Martin
Computer Science Department
UCLA
Los Angeles
California 90024

0. Abstract.

A mathematical model is presented as a common framework within which to discuss and compare different models of concurrent computation. Central to the model is the concept of *flow net,* which is used to describe concurrent computation, just as a conventional flowchart is used to describe serial computation. A *flow-of-control algebra* of flow nets is presented by defining a minimal set of operations for composing flow nets, together with an equational system they satisfy. These operations suggest a corresponding minimal syntax - the flow-of-control algebra of *flow structures.* In this algebra, which is continuous, a flow net is represented by its unfoldment - a finite system of recursion equations. Deadlock and equivalence are examples of properties of concurrent computation formulated in the presented syntax.

1. Introduction

The current interest in concurrent computing systems derives mainly from technological and economic trends. A concurrent computing system seems to be the right structure for organizing the abundant hardware resources made available by the impressive advances in microelectronics. However, the declining cost of hardware only emphasizes the expense and difficulty of producing software. A concurrent computing system cannot be effectively utilized unless there is also available appropriate software to match the new hardware systems.

Many different theoretical models have been proposed to discuss and understand the behavior of concurrent computation. In this paper we attempt to provide a common framework within which to discuss and compare different models of concurrent computation, including the well known Petri nets [4] and Milner's behavioral algebra [3]. In addition, through the proposed model we present a minimal syntax of concurrent computation, which is sufficiently refined to permit simple formulations of fundamental properties of concurrent systems, such as equivalence and deadlock. Then, the syntactic formulations of these properties may be inferred in various existing models considered as semantic domains (via a unique homomorphism from the syntax).

Our approach can be outlined by analogy with the initial algebra semantics of serial computation. The work of ADJ [1], [6] from categories to many-sorted algebras and then to continuous algebraic theories is successfully used to define, explain, and unify those aspects most relevant to serial computation. In this way, many apparently divergent approaches to specify formal semantics of programming languages for serial computation are only applications of initial algebra semantics. The ADJ construction of initial continuous algebras permits a simple formulation of behaviors of conventional flowcharts. Conventional flowcharts enter into the formulation of models for serial computation, being an intermediary between programs and their semantics.

To return to our model, we think of a concurrent system as a compound computing agent constructed from smaller components which are themselves computing agents, using a minimal set of composition operations. The composition operations represent the possible interactions of computing agents, which communicate by message passing through distinct input and output ports. We consider parallelism and nondeterminism as the only primitive interactions of the computing agents activities, in order to achieve a mathematically tractable model. We represent compound computing agents by generalized flowcharts, called *flow nets,* together with a minimal set of operations to compose them, called *flow-of-control operations.* The algebraic framework that we need for discussing flow nets and their representation by unfoldments is provided by the extension of many sorted continuous algebras and algebraic theories to *many sorted continuous parallel-nondeterministic algebras,* and *algebraic theories,* respectively. In Section 2 we bring together what we need of this framework, but most of this paper (to a certain depth) can be understood without a detailed study of these algebraic results. A rigorous study of these concepts is provided in [8], and in a subsequent paper. As an example, we formulate the reader/writer problem as a composition of flow nets.

The present paper is a revision of the dissertation [8], which bears the same title. In this revision we have included a more careful intuitive description of our model and we have ensured compatibility with the subsequent paper.

2. Notation and Definitions

In this section we outline some notation and definitions that are useful for the development that follows. For detailed exposition of the algebraic background required here, see [1], [6], and [8].

Throughout this paper we use ω for the set of nonnegative integers, $[\omega]$ for $\{1,2,\ldots\}$, and $[n]$ for $\{1,2,\ldots,n\}$. For ordered pairs we write <a,b> with angle brackets. Let S be any set. Then S^n is the set of all strings over S of length n; $S^* = \bigcup_{n\geq 0} S^n$ is the set of all strings over S; λ is the empty string. We write $|w|$ for the length of the string w. Given the functions $f: A \to B$ and $g: B \to C$, we write their composite $fg: A \to C$, so $(a)fg = ((a)f)g$.

Let S be a set of symbols called *sorts*. An *S-sorted operator domain* (or *signature*) Σ is an $\langle S^* \times S\rangle$-indexed family of sets $\Sigma = \{\Sigma_{w,s} \mid w \in S^*,\ s \in S\}$. An element $\sigma \in \Sigma_{w,s}$ is an operator symbol of type $\langle w,s\rangle$, arity w, sort (or co-arity) s, and rank $|w|$. A *many S-sorted Σ-algebra A* consists of an S-indexed family of sets $\{A_s \mid s \in S\}$, where A_s is called the *carrier* of sort s, together with an indexed family of operations $\{\sigma_A : A^w \to A_s \mid \sigma \in \Sigma_{w,s}\}$, where $A^w = A_{s_1}\times\ldots\times A_{s_n}$ if $w = s_1\ldots s_n$. The operation σ_A is the operation of A named by σ. For $\sigma \in \Sigma_{\lambda,s}$, $\sigma_A \in A_s$ is a *constant* symbol. It is standard practice in universal algebra to let A ambiguously denote the S-sorted carrier of the Σ-algebra as well as the algebra itself.

Let A and B be S-sorted Σ-algebras. Then a Σ-homomorphism $h: A \to B$ is an S-indexed family of functions $h_s: A_s \to B_s$ such that for $\sigma \in \Sigma_{w,s}$ the following diagram "commutes":

$$\begin{array}{ccc} A^w & \xrightarrow{\sigma_A} & A_s \\ {\scriptstyle h_s}\downarrow & & \downarrow{\scriptstyle h_s} \\ B^w & \xrightarrow[\sigma_A]{} & B_s \end{array}$$

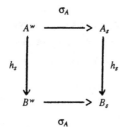

where $(a_1, \ldots, a_n) h_w = \langle (a_1) h_{s_1}, \ldots, (a_n) h_{s_n} \rangle$, $w = s_1 \ldots s_n$, and $\langle a_1, \ldots, a_n \rangle \in A^w$. Briefly, a Σ-homomorphism preserves all operations in Σ. A Σ-algebra T is said to be *initial* in the category of Σ-algebras iff for any other Σ-algebra A, there is a unique Σ-homomorphism h: T → A. The key property for the application of Σ-algebras to programming language semantics is given by the following

Proposition 2.1. For each operator domain Σ, there exists an initial Σ-algebra T_Σ. □

T_Σ is often called the Σ- *word algebra* and the carriers can be thought of as the sets of trees, or well formed expressions, built up in the usual way from the operator symbols of Σ. We illustrate below a typical tree,

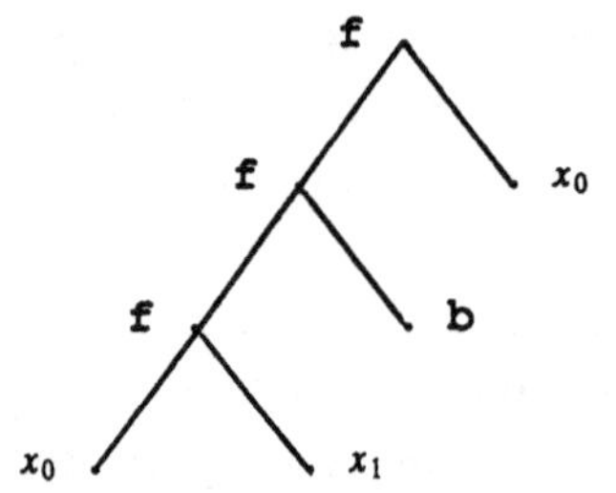

which represents the well-formed expression $(((x_0, x_1) f, b) f, x_0) f$, where $\Sigma_{\lambda,s} = \{b, x_0, x_1\}$, $\Sigma_{ss,s} = \{f\}$, for $S = \{s\}$.

Let X be an S-indexed family of disjoint sets of *variables*, $X = \{X_s \mid s \in S\}$, which is also disjoint from the set of operator symbols Σ. If Σ is an S-sorted operator domain, $T_\Sigma(X)$ denotes the Σ-algebra *freely generated by* X. $T_\Sigma(X)$ is used for presenting classes of algebras satisfying certain equational properties. A *Σ-equation of sort s* is just a pair of expressions $e = \langle e_1, e_2 \rangle$ from $T_\Sigma(X)_s$. An *equational system (over* $T_\Sigma(X)$) is a set E of Σ-equations. It is convenient to write $e_1 = e_2$ for $\langle e_1, e_2 \rangle \in E$. What makes these pairs "equations" is how they are interpreted. For any Σ-algebra A and S-indexed family of sets of variables X, an *interpretation* or *assignment* θ: X → A of values in A_s to variables X_s is an S-indexed family of functions $\theta = \{\theta_s : X_s \to A_s\}$ for all $s \in S$.

Proposition 2.2. Let I_X: X $\rightarrow$ T_Σ(X) be the (S-indexed family of) injection(s) of the generators X into the carriers of T_Σ(X). Then, for any Σ-algebra A and assignment θ: X $\rightarrow$ A, there exists a unique homomorphism $\bar{\theta}$: T_Σ(X) $\rightarrow$ A that extends θ in the sense that $I_X\bar{\theta} = \theta$.

Intuitively, θ gives values in A for the variables in t $\in T_\Sigma(X)_s$, and A, being a Σ-algebra, gives values for the operation symbols in t; $\bar{\theta}$ is the familiar process of *evaluating* an expression and nothing more. Given a term t $\in T_\Sigma(X)_s$ and varying the assignment θ: X $\rightarrow$ A, $t_A: A^w \rightarrow A$ where $(a_1,\ldots,a_n)t_A$ = (t)$\bar{\theta}^w$, $<a_1,\ldots,a_n> \in A^w$, $\bar{\theta}^w = \bar{\theta}_{s_1} \times\ldots\times\bar{\theta}_{s_n}$, $w = s_1\ldots s_n$, $(x_i)\theta_{s_i} = a_i$, i = 1,..,n, is a function called the *derived operation of* t in A.

For an equation e = $<e_1,e_2>$, let var(e) be the variables occuring in e. A Σ-algebra A *satisfies* e (or is a *model* for e) iff for every assignment θ : var(e) $\rightarrow$ A, $(e_1)\bar{\theta} = (e_2)\bar{\theta}$. For an equational system E, a Σ-algebra A *satisfies* E iff it satisfies every e $\in E$. A Σ-algebra A satisfying E is called a <Σ,E>-algebra. In the category of <Σ,E>-algebras there exists an initial <Σ,E>-algebra, which is the quotient of T_Σ by the congruence relation generated by substitution instances of E.

We present an S-sorted algebraic theory as a many <S* $\times$ S*>-sorted algebra. An S-sorted *algebraic theory* T consists of the following data:

i. a family of sets, T(u,v), indexed by pairs of strings u,v $\in$ S*; the elements of T(u,v) are called *morphisms from* u *to* v. We write α: u $\rightarrow$ v to mean $\alpha \in$ T(u,v);

ii. an associative *composition* operation o: T(u,v)$\times$T(v,w) defined for all u,v,w in S*. That composition operation has two-sided identities, 1_v: v $\rightarrow$ v, for all v $\in$ S*, such that for all α: u $\rightarrow$ v, $1_u o\alpha = \alpha = \alpha o 1_v$;

iii. a *distinguished morphism* or *injection* x_i^u: $u_i \rightarrow$ u, for each n $\in \omega$, u $\in S^n$ and i $\in$ [n];

iv. an operation < ,..., >: $\prod_{i\in[n]}$T(u_i,v) $\rightarrow$ T(u,v), for each n $\in \omega$, u $\in S^n$ and v $\in$ S*, which is called *source tupling;* The injections and source tupling operations are required to satisfy the following "coproduct conditions":

v. $x_i^u o<\beta_1,\ldots,\beta_n> = \beta_i$, for all n $\in \omega$, u $\in S^n$, v $\in$ S*, and all families {β_i: $u_i \rightarrow$ v | i $\in$ [n]};

vi. $<x_1^u o\beta,\ldots,x_n^u o\beta> = \beta$, for all n $\in \omega$, u $\in S^n$, v $\in$ S*, and β: u $\rightarrow$ v.

Now, if T_Σ is an initial S-sorted Σ-algebra, it generates an S-sorted theory Th_Σ in a natural way. The morphisms in $Th_\Sigma(u,v)$ are u-tuples of v-terms in T_Σ. Composition corresponds to substitution of terms, i.e., the composition of $\langle d_1, d_2, \ldots, d_n\rangle$ in $Th_\Sigma(u,v)$ with $\langle t_1, t_2, \ldots, t_m\rangle$ in $Th_\Sigma(v,w)$ simultaneously substitutes the term t_i for each occurrence of x_i (if any) in all d_j, i = 1,..,m, j = 1,..,n. The distinguished morphism $x_1^s: s \to v$ in Th_Σ is simply the one-tuple $\langle x_s\rangle$ and tupling is exactly that, tupling. An S-sorted Σ-algebra A generates an S-sorted theory Th(A) by considering Th(A)(u,v) as the set of all u-tuples of v-terms (in Th_Σ) as derived operations in A, composition as the ordinary functional composition, and identity functions as identities. Then, Proposition 2.2 applied to algebraic theories is the following

Proposition 2.3 Let I_Σ: $\Sigma \to Th_\Sigma$ be the (S*×S-indexed family of) injection(s) of the generators $\sigma \in \Sigma_{s_1..s_n s}$ to $\langle (x_{s_1..s_n})\sigma\rangle \in (Th_\Sigma)_s$. Then, for any S-sorted algebraic theory A and H: $\Sigma \to$ A, there exists a unique morphism of algebraic theories $\overline{H}$: $Th_\Sigma \to$ A that extends H in the sense that $I_\Sigma\overline{H} = H$. □

The discrete algebras introduced above can be generalized to ω-continuous algebras. ω-continuous algebras are rational, so we can talk about solving systems of rational equations, i.e., their least fixed-point solutions. It is assumed that the reader is familiar with the elementary theory of ω-complete partially ordered sets (ω-CPOs) and ω-continuous functions. We only consider strict CPOs, i.e., CPOs with a minimum element denoted $\perp$ ("bottom"). An *ω-continuous algebra* is an algebra whose carriers are strict ω-CPOs and whose operations are ω-continuous functions. The algebra of finite and infinite partial trees plays the role of the algebra of expressions for the continuous case. Finite and infinite partial trees are introduced as partial functions t: $\omega^* \multimap \Sigma\cup\{\perp\}$ for which the domain of definition has the tree domain property, and with $\perp$ called "totally undefined". Intuitively, a partial tree is a tree whose leaves can be labeled with $\perp$; then, the natural order relation $\le$ (called "less defined that") on partial trees is given by the following: a partial tree properly approximates another iff their corresponding nodes are identical except that the first contains $\perp$ in at least one position where the second contains a nontrivial subtree. An example of ω-chain follows:

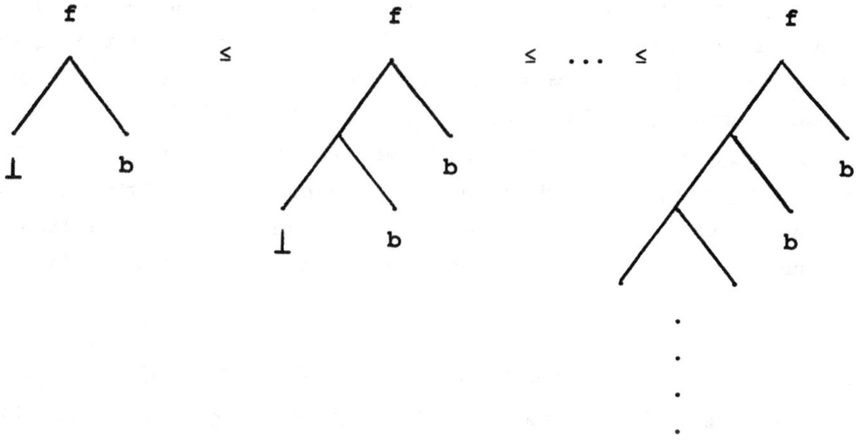

The second tree in the sequence is the partial function $t\colon \omega^* \multimap \{f,b\}$ with $\lambda, 0 \mapsto f$, $1, 01 \mapsto b$, and, undefined otherwise. The last tree is infinite, and it is the least upper bound of the chain.

The many sorted algebras defined above are not adequate for modeling concurrent systems. The need for an extra structure is necessary in order to capture "parallel" and "nondeterministic" activities of concurrent agents. We begin with the extension of sets to so called parallel-nondeterministic sets, whose role in modeling of concurrent computing agents is discussed in Section 3.

A *parallel-nondeterministic (par-nd) set* $\langle A, ||_A, @_A \rangle$ consists of a set A, an n-ary operation $||_A$, for each $n \in \omega$, which is called *pairing*, and a binary operation $@_A$, which is called *selection*, such that (*i*) $@_A$ is commutative and associative, and (*ii*) $||_A$ is distributive with respect to $@_A$.
The conditions (*i*) and (*ii*) determine in A an equational system, which is denoted EP_A. Throughout this paper we drop the subscripts of ||, @, and *EP*, which result from their context.

A function $f\colon \langle A, ||, @\rangle \to \langle B, ||, @\rangle$ is *linear (with respect to @)* iff it preserves the operation @, i.e., $(a_1 @ a_2)f = (a_1)f @ (a_2)f$, for $a_1, a_2 \in A$.

In some cases $\langle A, ||, @\rangle$ is used as a *parallel set* by "forgetting" the @ operation; in other cases $\langle A, ||, @\rangle$ is used as a *nondeterministic set* by forgetting the || operations.

An example of a par-nd set is the extension $\bar{S}$ of the set of sorts S of a many sorted algebra. $\bar{S}$ = <S*, ||, @> is obtained by defining on S* the operations $u_1||\ldots||u_n$ = $<u_1, \ldots, u_n>$ and $v_1@v_2$ = v_1 or v_2 (the choice being nondeterministic), for $u_i, v_j \in$ S*, i = 1,..,n, j = 1,2. We relate the pairing operation to the concatenation of strings by defining an operation *compact*, such that (<u,v>)compact = uv. The difference between the pairing and concatenation operations is that pairing provides a punctuation between component strings while concatenation does not.

Let X be an <S*×ω>-indexed family of variables X = $\{X_i^{u_i} \mid u_i \in$ S*, $i \in \omega\}$. We extend X to a par-nd set $\bar{X}$ by defining $x^u = x_1^{u_1}||\ldots||x_n^{u_n} = <x_1^{u_1}, \ldots, x_n^{u_n}>$, for u = $u_1||\ldots||u_n$ = $<u_1, \ldots, u_n>$, $u_i \in$ S*, and $x_i^{u_i} \in X_i^{u_i}$. We call $x_i^{u_i}$ a *component variable* of x^u.

For the purpose of this paper, we need to distinguish the input and output operator symbols of an operator domain Σ. (The operations of an algebra A named by input and output operator symbols are identity functions; their role is to transmit values without modifying them.) Let Γ = {α, β, γ,...} be a finite set of names and $\bar{\Gamma}$ = {$\bar{\alpha}$, $\bar{\beta}$, $\bar{\gamma}$,...} be a finite set of complementary names bijective with Γ such that $\gamma \in \Gamma$ implies $\bar{\gamma} \in \bar{\Gamma}$ and $\bar{\bar{\gamma}} = \gamma$. We call the names of Γ and $\bar{\Gamma}$ *input* and *output communication capabilities*, respectively; $\lambda = \bar{\lambda}$ is the *no communication capability* symbol. We have $\Gamma \cap \bar{\Gamma}$ = {λ}; let $\Gamma^+ = \Gamma - \{\lambda\}$ and $\bar{\Gamma}^+ = \bar{\Gamma} - \{\lambda\}$. An S-sorted *operator domain* Σ *with connection capabilities* Γ is an <S*×S*>-indexed operator domain Σ = $\{\Sigma_{u,v} \mid$ u, v $\in$ S*}, together with a labeling function from Σ onto $\Gamma \cup \bar{\Gamma}$. We call $\sigma^\alpha \in \Sigma^{\Gamma}$ an *input* operator symbol, $\sigma^{\bar{\beta}} \in \Sigma^{\bar{\Gamma}}$ an *exit* operator symbol, and $\sigma \in \Sigma^\lambda_{u,v}$ an *internal* operator symbol. We have $\Sigma^{\Gamma^+} = \bigcup_{\alpha \in \Gamma^+} \Sigma^\alpha_{u,u}$ and $\Sigma^{\bar{\Gamma}^+} = \bigcup_{\bar{\beta} \in \bar{\Gamma}^+} \Sigma^{\bar{\beta}}_{u,u}$; usually, we drop the subscripts u,u when we consider input and output operator symbols and the superscript λ when we consider internal operator symbols. (Notice that the arity and co-arity of input and output operator symbols are equal, condition imposed by the identity functions.)

A useful parallel structure is the extension $\bar{\Sigma}$ of the operator domain Σ with connection capabilities Γ. An $\bar{S}$-sorted *parallel operator domain* $\bar{\Sigma}$ *with connection capabilities* Γ is an $\bar{S}$-sorted operator domain Σ with connection capabilities Γ on which we define a pairing operation || for each $n \in \omega$, such that:

$\sigma_1 || \ldots || \sigma_n \in \Sigma^{\lambda}_{u,v}$ iff $\sigma_i \in \Sigma^{\lambda}_{u_i,v_i}$, $u = u_1 || \ldots || u_n$, $v_1 || \ldots || v_n$,
$u_i, v_i \in S^*$, $i = 1,..,n$, and
$\sigma_1 || \ldots || \sigma_n \in \Sigma^{\gamma}_{u,\mu}$ iff $\sigma_i \in \Sigma^{\gamma}_{u_i,\mu_i}$, $u = u_1 || \ldots || u_2$,
$u_i \in S^*$, $i = 1,..,n$, $\gamma \in \Gamma^+ \cup \bar{\Gamma}^+$.

The arity of $\sigma_1 || \ldots || \sigma_n$ is given by compact(u). An operator $\sigma \in \bar{\Sigma}_{u,v}$ for $u = u_1 @ u_2$, $|u_1| = |u_2|$, is an *overloaded* operator symbol; it has more than one arity with the same rank.

A many S-sorted *parallel-nondeterministic* $\bar{\Sigma}$-algebra $\bar{A}$ *with connection capabilities* Γ consists of an $\bar{S}$-indexed family of par-nd sets $\{\bar{A}^u \mid u \in \bar{S}\}$, an $<\bar{S}\times\bar{S}>$-indexed family of internal operations $\{\sigma_{\bar{A}}: \bar{A}^u \rightarrow \bar{A}^v \mid \sigma \in \bar{\Sigma}_{u,v}\}$, and a Γ-indexed family of input and exit operations $\{\sigma^{\gamma}_{\bar{A}}: \bar{A}^u \rightarrow \bar{A}^u \mid \sigma^{\gamma} \in \bar{\Sigma}^{\gamma}_{u,\mu}, \gamma \in \Gamma \cup \bar{\Gamma}\}$. The $||$ and @ operations defined on a par-nd set $\bar{A}^u$ are $a_1 || a_2 = <a_1, a_2>$ and $a_1 @ a_2 = a_1$ or a_2.

i. $A^u = A^{u_1} \times \ldots \times A^{u_n}$ for $u = u_1 || \ldots || u_n$, $u_i \in S^*$, $i = 1,..,n$;

ii. $A^u = A^{u_1} @ A^{u_2}$ for $u = u_1 @ u_2$, $|u_1| = |u_2|$, $u_i \in S^*$, $i = 1,2$,
($A^{u_1} @ A^{u_2}$ is interpreted as the nondeterministic choice of A^{u_1} or A^{u_2});

iii. $(A^{u_1} @ A^{u_2}) \times A^v = (A^{u_1} \times A^v) @ (A^{u_2} \times A^v)$, and
$A^u \times (A^{v_1} @ A^{v_2}) = (A^u \times A^{v_1}) @ (A^u \times A^{v_2})$,
for $u, v, u_i, v_i \in S^*$, $i = 1,2$;

iv. $\sigma^1_A || \ldots || \sigma^n_A: A^u \rightarrow A^v$ for $\sigma^i_A : A^{u_i} \rightarrow A^{v_i}$, u_i, $v_i \in S^*$, $i = 1,..,n$,
$u = u_1 || \ldots || u_n$, $v = v_1 || \ldots || v_n$;

v. linearity: $(a_1 @ a_2)\sigma_A = (a_1)\sigma_A @ (a_2)\sigma_A$ for $\sigma \in \Sigma_{u,v}$,
$u = u_1 @ u_2$, $|u_1| = |u_2|$, $u_i, v \in S^*$, $a_i \in A^u$, $i = 1,2$.

A many $\bar{S}$-sorted parallel-nondeterministic $\bar{\Sigma}$-algebra with connection capabilities Γ is called a par-nd $<\bar{\Sigma},\Gamma>$-algebra.

Let $\bar{A}$ and $\bar{B}$ be S-sorted par-nd $<\bar{\Sigma},\Gamma>$-algebras. Then a *par-nd* $<\bar{\Sigma},\Gamma>$*-homomorphism* $\bar{h}: \bar{A} \rightarrow \bar{B}$ is a Σ-homomorphism which is linear (with respect to @) and preserves the pairing, selection, input, and output operations.

Proposition 2.4. In the category of par-nd $<\bar{\Sigma},\Gamma>$-algebras there exists an initial par-nd $<\bar{\Sigma},\Gamma>$-algebra, $D_{\bar{\Sigma},\Gamma}$. □

We now turn to the definition of "diamonds", which provide the carriers of $D_{\bar{\Sigma},\Gamma}$.

A *directed graph* G = <E,V,s,t> consists of a set E of edges, a set V of vertices, and two functions s,t from the set of edges to the set of vertices; s(e) is the source vertex of e and t(e) is the target vertex of e.

An *AND/OR directed graph,* is a directed graph G together with a labeling function from V to {AND,OR}×{AND,OR}, such that: (*i*) if a node n has any outgoing edges, they are either all OR edges, in which case we say that n has the *Out-type OR,* or all AND edges, in which case we say that n has the *Out-type* AND; (*ii*) if a node n has any incoming edges, they are either all OR edges, in which case we say that n has the *In-type* OR, or all AND edges, in which case we say that n has the *In-type* AND. We represent these situations pictorially by

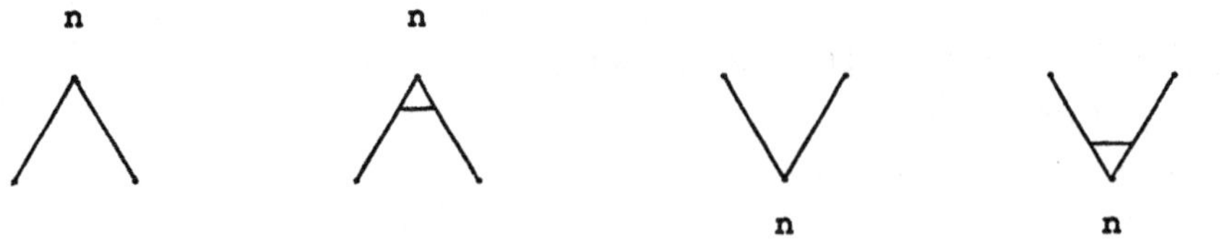

Out-type OR Out-type AND In-type OR In-type AND

A *diamond* is a kind of labeled AND/OR ordered directed acyclic graph, which we illustrate through the following example

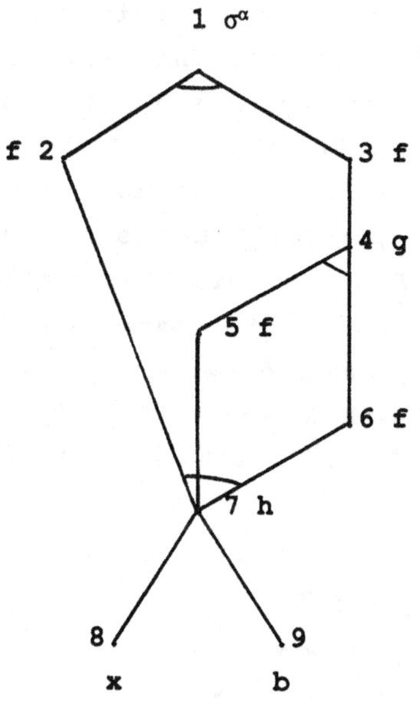

The diamond d_0

Intuitively, the nodes of Out-type and In-type AND of a diamond provide means by which a computation can "fork" by splitting into several parallel computations which can later "join" together again; the nodes of Out-type OR provide means by which a computation can split into several nondeterministic computations which never join together again. Section 3 contains a more detailed discussion of the types of nodes.

Diamonds are graphical representations of well-formed par-nd expressions of initial par-nd algebras, as trees are graphical representations of well-formed expressions of initial algebras. The diamond d_0 represents the following well-formed par-nd expression

$$(x@b)h(((f||f)gf)||f)\sigma^\alpha$$

where $\sigma^\alpha \in \Sigma^\alpha_{s||s,s||s}$, $g \in \Sigma^\lambda_{s||s,s}$, $h \in \Sigma^\lambda_{s@s,s||s||s}$, and $x,b \in \Sigma^\lambda_{\lambda,s}$, for $S = \{s\}$. The type of the operation at a node is consistent with the type of that node: $\sigma^\alpha \in \Sigma^\alpha_{s||s,s||s}$ is of arity s||s, which is consistent with the Out-type AND of node 1 with two descendants; $g \in \Sigma^\lambda_{s||s,s}$ is of arity s||s, which is consistent with the Out-type AND of node 4 with two descendants; $h \in \Sigma^\lambda_{s,s||s||s}$ is of co-arity s||s||s, which is consistent with the In-type AND of node 7 with three predecessors, and is of arity s@s, which is consistent with the Out-type OR of node 7 with two descendants.

Par-nd algebras are extended to ω-continuous par-nd algebras for solving systems of par-nd equations. An ω-continuous par-nd algebra is a par-nd algebra whose carriers are ω-CPOs, and operations are ω-continuous linear functions. The algebra of finite and infinite "partial diamonds" is initial in the category of ω-continuous par-nd algebras. Finite and infinite partial diamonds are introduced as partial functions d: $\langle\omega^*, ||\rangle$ -o→ $\bar{\Sigma}_{\cup\perp}$ for which the domain of definition has the tree domain property extended to elements of $\langle\omega^*, ||\rangle$. For example, the diamond d_0 is represented below as the partial function d: $\langle\omega^*, ||\rangle$ -o→ $\{\sigma^\alpha, f, g, h, x\}$ with $\lambda \mapsto \sigma^\alpha$, 0,1,100,101 $\mapsto$ f, 10 $\mapsto$ g, (0||100||101)0 $\mapsto$ h, (0||100||101)01 $\mapsto$ b, and undefined otherwise.

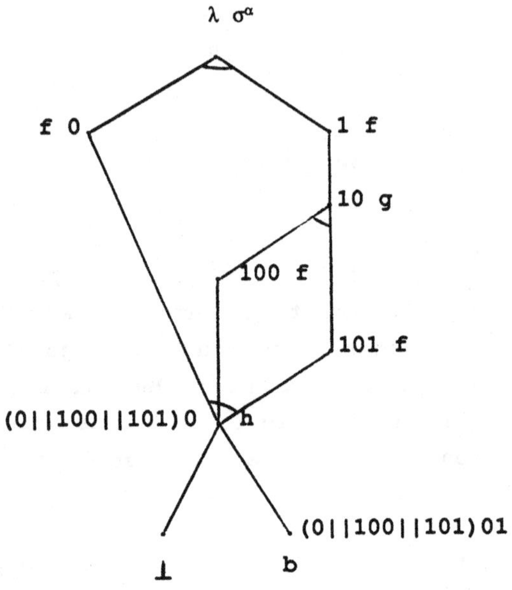

An ω-continuous par-nd algebra generates an ω-continuous par-nd algebraic theory in a natural way.

3. Flow Nets

We choose to represent a computing agent by a kind of graph, called *flow net*, which may be specified in terms of other flow nets and a set of operations. Like Milne and Milner in [3], Wirth [7], and Hoare [2], we consider rather separate the phase in which a composite flow net of activities is established and the phase in which the flow net is activated.

A flow net is an AND/OR graph whose nodes represent the activities that a computing agent is able to perform including the communications with its environment, and whose arcs represent communication channels among its activities. We label every node of a flow net by a pair consisting of a communication name from $\Gamma \cup \bar{\Gamma}$ and an operator symbol from $\bar{\Sigma}$. The communication name represents the communication capability of the computing agent at that node, and the operator symbol represents the operation the computing agent is able to perform at that node. The absence of a communication capability at a node is represented by λ (the no communication capability symbol). *Input nodes* are nodes labeled by names from Γ, *exit nodes* are nodes labeled by names from $\bar{\Gamma}$, and *inner nodes* are nodes labeled by λ. We will be concerned only with flow nets which have input and output nodes with distinct names; we call them *proper* flow nets. We allow nodes of complimentary names in the same flow net.

Intuitively, a node of Out-type AND and its descendants represent the splitting of a computation into several parallel computations; a node of Out-type OR and its descendants represent the splitting of a computation into several nondeterministic computations, i.e., a single computation, out of many possible ones, is chosen nondeterministically to be performed; a node of In-type AND and its predecessors represent parallel computations that join together again on a single task; a node of In-type OR and its predecessors represent several computations competing for exclusive access to a task. An example of a flow net with an input α and an output $\bar{\beta}$ is shown below. Our formal definition of a flow net is given in Appendix A.

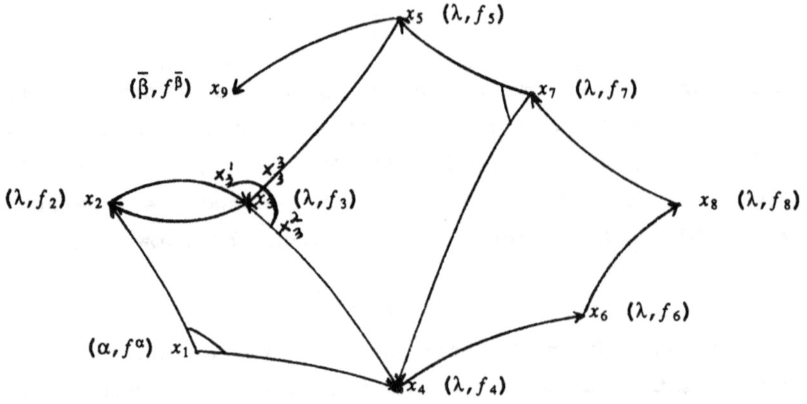

The flow net n_0

Although the nodes of a flow net are named by elements of N, we identify the nodes of the flow net illustrated above by variables x_i, whose role will be explained later. In n_0, the node x_4 is a node of In-type and Out-type OR, which has the label (λ, f_4), λ representing the absence of a communication capability of the flow net at that node with its exterior environment, and the operator symbol f_4 representing the operation that can take place at that node; the node x_1 is a node of In-type and Out-type AND, which has the label (α, f^{α}), α representing an input communication capability of the flow net at that node, and f^{α} representing an input operator symbol; the node x_9 is a node of In-type and Out-type AND, which has the label $(\bar{\beta}, f^{\bar{\beta}})$, $\bar{\beta}$ representing an output communication capability of the flow net at that node, and $f^{\bar{\beta}}$ representing an output operator symbol.

Let $FN(\mu, \bar{\nu})$ denote the family of flow nets with inputs $\mu \in (\Gamma^+)^*$ and outputs $\bar{\nu} \in (\bar{\Gamma}^+)^*$ (over a signature $\bar{\Sigma}$). The emphasis here is on the the input and output communication capabilities.
Then, $<\bar{\Sigma}, \Gamma>$-$FN = \bigcup_{\mu,\bar{\nu}} FN(\mu, \bar{\nu})$ denote the class of flow nets over $\bar{\Sigma}$ with communication capabilities from $\Gamma \cup \bar{\Gamma}$.

The passing of control in a flow net is similar to the execution of a Petri net by firing of transitions. (We assume a knowledge of the Petri net model.) The following figure shows the Petri net graph with a particular marking to which the flow net n_0 described above corresponds.

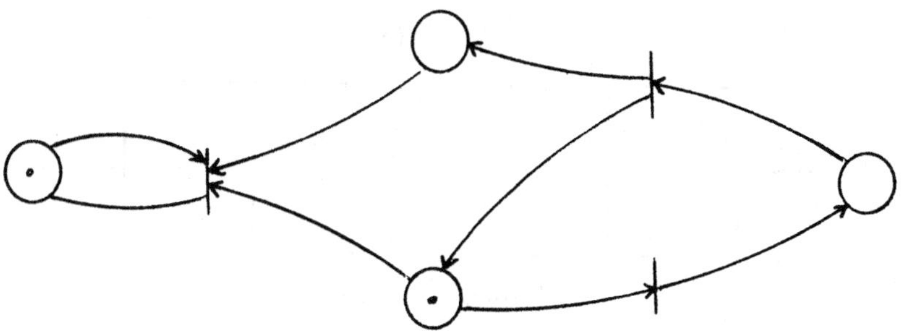

A Petri net graph

In general, any Petri net graph can be converted into a flow net. In a flow net, a place in a Petri net is represented by a node of In-type and Out-type OR; a transition in a Petri net is represented by a node of In-type and Out-type AND; the initial marking of places in a Petri net is given by an input node. Flow nets are more powerful than Petri nets, but a comparison between flow nets and Petri nets is beyond the scope of this paper.

4. An Algebra of Flow Nets

We now turn to the operations by which flow nets can be expressed in terms of other flow nets. We call these operations *flow-of-control operations.* They encapsulate all possible interactions of the activities of concurrent systems, i.e., parallelism, synchronization, nondeterminism, and mutual exclusion. The flow-of-control operations establish communication channels between flow nets by connecting nodes which the names associated to input and output nodes dictate. To help in the understanding of the flow-of-control operations, we will introduce them through examples. Our formal definitions of the flow-of-control operations can be found in Appendix A.

(i) Sequential communication of flow nets. Let $n_1 \in \mathbf{FN}(\alpha, \bar{\beta}_1\bar{\beta}_2)$ and $n_2 \in \mathbf{FN}(\beta_1\beta_2, \bar{\rho})$, which may be pictured thus:

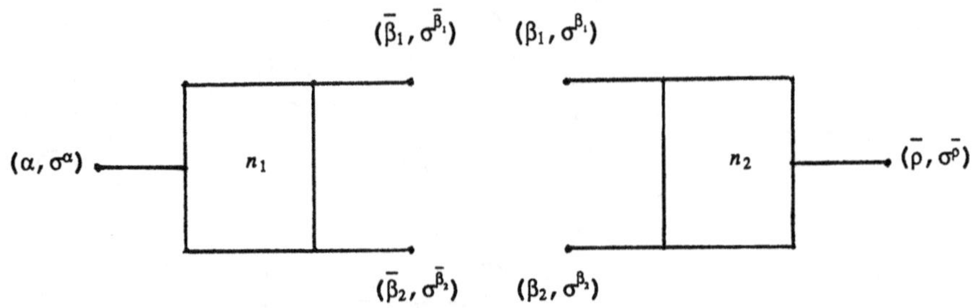

Their sequential communication, $n_1 \Rightarrow n_2 \in \mathbf{FN}(\alpha, \bar{\rho})$ may then be pictured as follow:

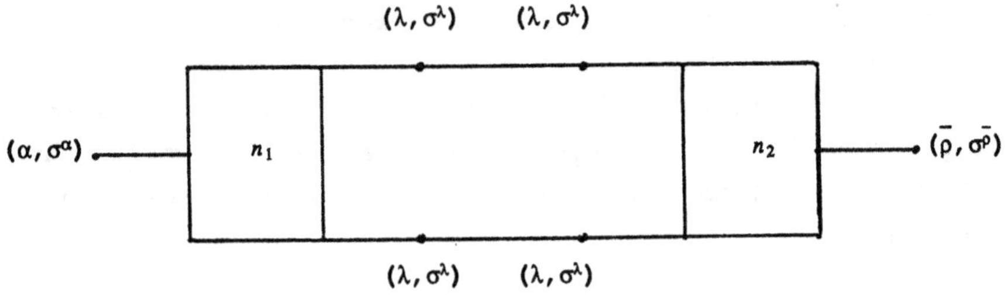

$n_1 \Rightarrow n_2$

That is, n_1 and n_2 are joint by connecting every exit node of n_1 with the input node of n_2 with a complementary name. The sequential communication is not defined if the flow nets have no exit and input nodes with complementary names.

Proposition 4.1. The class of flow nets $\langle\bar{\Sigma}, \Gamma\rangle$-FN is a category with strings over $\Gamma \cup \bar{\Gamma}$ as objects, the flow nets with inputs from Γ^+ and exits from $\bar{\Gamma}^+$ (over a signature $\bar{\Sigma}$) as morphisms, the sequential communication of flow nets as composition, and identity flow nets (defined below) as identities. □

For each $\mu \in (\Gamma^+)^*$ (and its complement $\bar{\mu} \in (\bar{\Gamma}^+)^*$) there is an *identity flow net* $1^{\mu} \in \mathbf{FN}(\mu, \bar{\mu})$, which has the input nodes connected directly to the exit nodes with complementary names.

(ii) Simultaneous input communication of flow nets. Let $n_3 \in \mathbf{FN}(\alpha\beta\delta_1, \bar{\varepsilon})$ and $n_4 \in \mathbf{FN}(\alpha\beta\delta_2, \bar{\rho})$, which may be pictured thus:

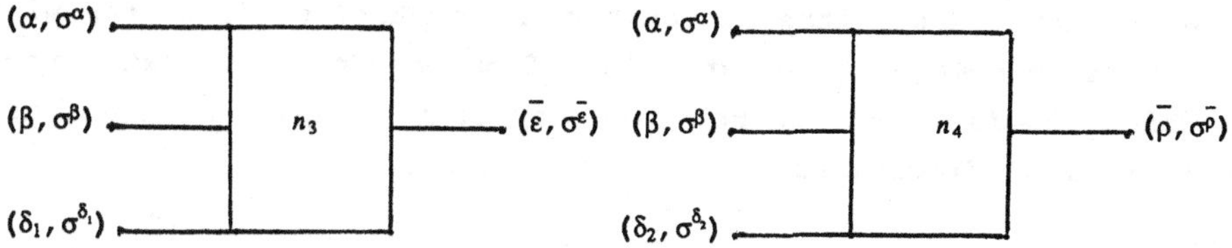

Their simultaneous input communication, $n_3||_I n_4 \in \mathbf{FN}(\alpha\beta\delta_1\delta_2, \overline{\varepsilon\rho})$ may then be pictured as follows:

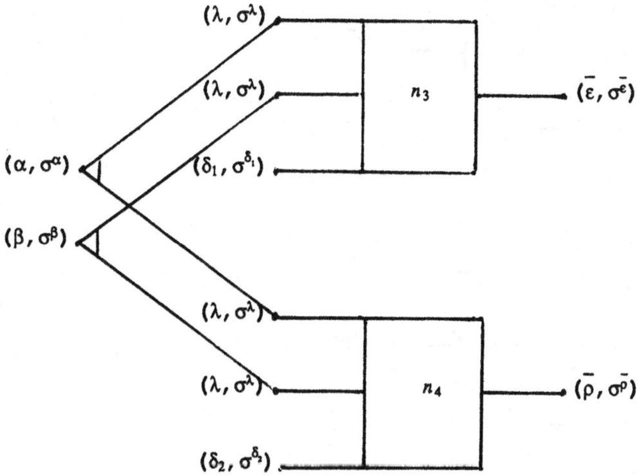

$n_3||_I n_4$

That is, n_3 and n_4 are joint by adding new input nodes of Out-type AND with the same names as the input nodes of n_3 and n_4, which have successors the input nodes of n_3 and n_4 with the corresponding names; the input nodes of n_3 and n_4 become internal nodes, i.e., they will get the same λ.

The simultaneous input communication of two flow nets without any input names in common is obtained by laying the two flow nets side-by-side, keeping their input and output nodes disjoint.

The simultaneous input communication operation of flow nets can be dualizat to obtain the *simultaneous exit communication of flow nets,* which is denoted $||_O$.

Note that the simultaneous exit communication of flow nets with input names in common is an extension of pairing of flowcharts; the case in which the flow nets do not have any common input names corresponds to summing of flowcharts.

(iii) Nondeterministic input communication of flow nets. The nondeterministic input communication of n_3 and n_4, as illustrated above, $n_3 @_I n_4 \in \mathrm{FN}(\alpha\beta\delta_1\delta_2, \overline{\varepsilon\rho})$, may then be pictured as follows:

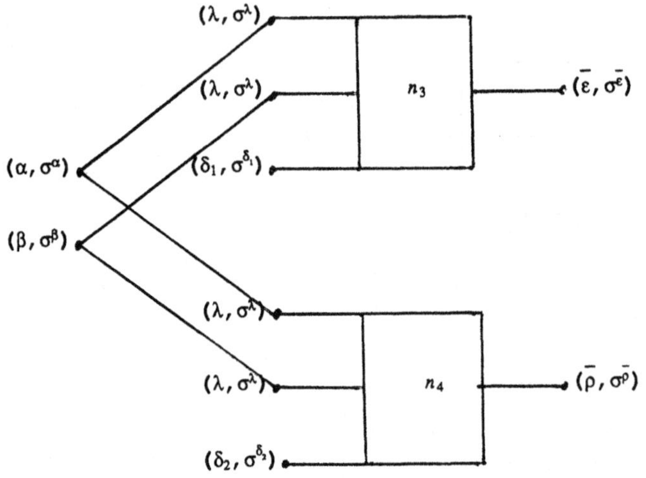

$n_3 @_I n_4$

That is, the flow nets n_3 and n_4 are joint by adding new input nodes of Out-type OR with the same names as the input nodes of n_3 and n_4, which have successors the input nodes of n_3 and n_4 with the corresponding names; the input nodes of n_3 and n_4 become internal nodes. This operation prohibits the flow nets n_3 and n_4 from having activities which may overlap in time. The nondeterministic input communication of two flow nets without any input names in common has as a result the nondeterministic selection of one flow net.

The nondeterministic input communication operation of flow nets can also be dualizat to obtain the *nondeterministic exit communication operation,* which is denoted $@_O$.

(iv) Relabeling of flow nets. All operations on flow nets establish communication channels which the names associated to input and output nodes dictate. Thus, some relabeling of nodes may be required "before" an operation is applied to flow nets, in order to allow or prevent certain connections. Relabeling of a flow net has the effect of changing the name of an input or output node; the resulting flow net has then different connection capabilities. We denote $n_1\rho/\alpha$ the result of relabeling by ρ of the input node of n_1 named α.

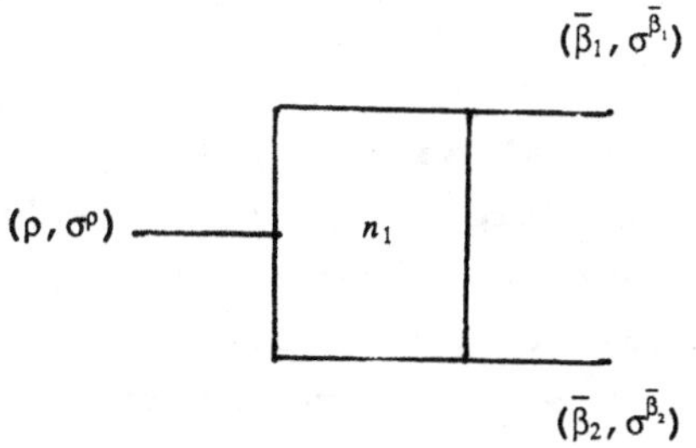

$n_1\gamma/\alpha$

(v) Iterate of flow nets. For any flow net $n \in FN(\alpha_1 \ldots \alpha_n, \bar{\alpha}_1 \ldots \bar{\alpha}_n \bar{\beta}_1 \ldots \bar{\beta}_p)$ the iterate n^* identifies the $\bar{\alpha}_i$ exit with α_i input, i = 1,..n, thus introducing loops.

Proposition 4.2. The following identities hold over flow nets, where we assume n_i are arbitrary flow nets, and α, α_i, β, β_i arbitrary names.

$n_1 \Rightarrow (n_2 \Rightarrow n_3) = (n_1 \Rightarrow n_2) \Rightarrow n_3;$
$n_1 @_i n_2 = n_2 @_i n_1$ for $i \in \{I,O\}$;
$n_1 ||_i (n_2 ||_i n_3) = (n_1 ||_i n_2) ||_i n_3$ for $i \in \{I,O\}$;
$n_1 @_i (n_2 @_i n_3) = (n_1 @_i n_2) @_i n_3$ for $i \in \{I,O\}$;
$n_1 ||_i (n_2 @_i n_3) = (n_1 ||_i n_2) @_i (n_1 ||_i n_3)$ for $i \in \{I,O\}$;
$(n_1 @_i n_2) ||_i n_3 = (n_1 ||_i n_3) @_i (n_2 ||_i n_3)$ for $i \in \{I,O\}$;
$(n\alpha_1/\alpha)\alpha_2/\alpha_1 = n\alpha_2/\alpha;$
$(n\bar{\beta}_1/\bar{\beta})\bar{\beta}_2/\bar{\beta}_1 = n\bar{\beta}_2/\beta$

These identities constitute an equational system *EF*, which is not hard to be verified from the formal definitions of flow nets and flow-of-control operations given in Appendix A. The system of equations *EF* is complete, i.e., any two flow net expressions which denote the same flow net can be proved equal by the identities.

Let Λ denote the signature induced by the flow-of-control operations defined above. The class of flow nets $\langle\bar{\Sigma},\Gamma\rangle$-FN together with the flow-of-control operations corresponding to Λ, which satisfies the system of equations *EF*, is called a *flow-of-control algebra*, and is denoted $\langle\bar{\Sigma},\Gamma\rangle\text{-}FN_{\Lambda,EF}$. This algebra is a suitable minimal language to describe concurrent computation, just as conventional flowcharts are suitable for describing sequential computation.

5. The Readers/Writers Problem

The readers/writers problem has several variants, but the basic structure is the same. Computing agents are of two types: *reader* computing agents and *writer* computing agents. All agents share a common file, variable, or data object. Reader computing agents when using the shared data never modify the object, while writer computing agents do modify it. Thus, writer computing agents must mutually exclude all other reader and writer computing agents when using the shared data, but several reader computing agents can access the shared data simultaneously. In our model this problem is solved for an unbounded number of readers in the following way: We denote by C the flow net representing the shared object, by R the flow net representing a reader, and by W the flow net representing a writer. Pictorially, we may have

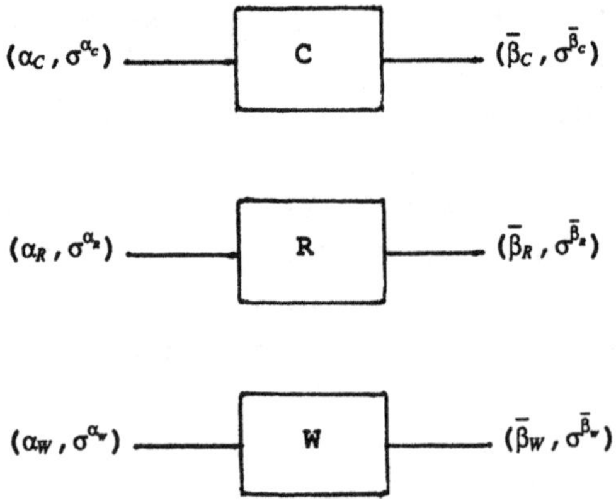

In C, the input node labeled α_C accepts a request to access the data for reading or writing the data; in R, the input node labeled α_R acknowledges the arrival of a new reader, and in W, α_W acknowledges the arrival of a writer; $\bar{\beta}_C$, $\bar{\beta}_R$, and $\bar{\beta}_W$ represent the outputs of C, R, and W, respectively.

First, let consider two readers R which access the shared data C simultaneously. The two flow nets R are joint together by the simultaneous exit communication operation, $||_O$. Then, the result is connected with the flow net C by the sequential communication operation =>, after an appropriate labeling (/ operation) takes place; $||_O$ is defined for flow nets with distinct inputs, and => requires the exit name of R to be complimentary with the input name of C. Thus, the expression $(R||_O R\alpha_R^1/\alpha_R)\bar{\alpha}_C/\bar{\beta}_R$ => C represents the given problem, which pictorially is

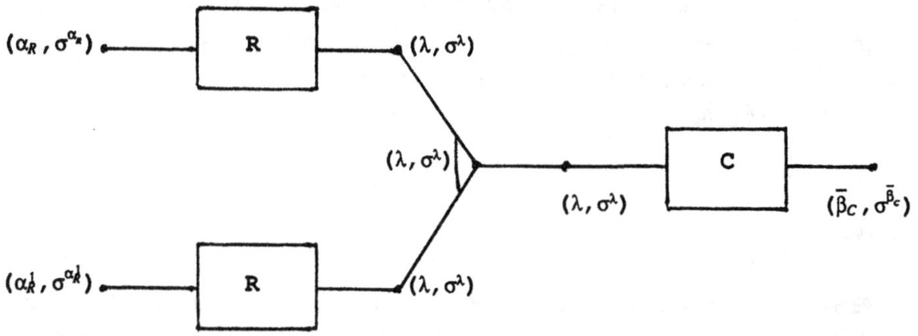

The problem with one writer and two readers which simultaneously access the shared object C is represented by the expression $(R^2 @_O W\bar{\beta}_R/\bar{\beta}_W)\bar{\beta}_C/\bar{\beta}_R$ => C, where $@_O$ is the nondeterministic exit communication operation, and $R^2 = (R||_O R\alpha_R^1/\alpha_R)\bar{\beta}_C/\bar{\beta}_R$. Pictorially, we have

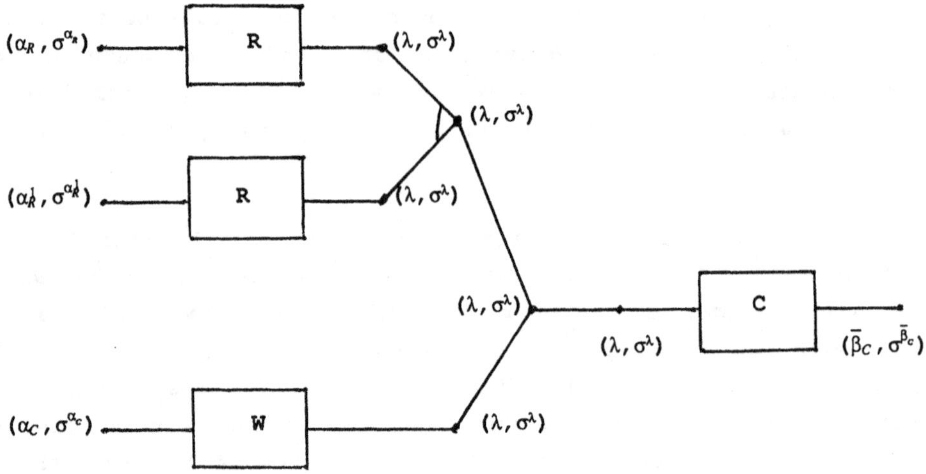

In words, either two simultaneous readers or a writer gets exclusive access to C. The exclusivity of the access is achieved by the $@_O$ operation. In general, for k $\in$ [ω] simultaneous readers and one writer we have the following flow net expression:

$$(R^k @_O W\bar{\beta}_R / \bar{\beta}_W)\, \bar{\beta}_C / \bar{\beta}_R \Rightarrow C\bar{\beta}_R / \bar{\beta}_C$$

6. Flow Structures

The flow-of-control algebra of flow nets introduced in the previous section is not free in the category of flow-of-control algebras. To find a suitable syntactic algebra for flow nets we follow the work of ADJ on the representation of recursive flowcharts by their unfoldments: every flowchart is represented by a finite system of equations in an initial ω-continuous algebra of infinite trees. Similarly, we represent a flow net by an equational system in an initial ω-continuous par-nd algebra of par-nd expressions (or diamonds). We appeal to *continuations* of C. Strachey and C.P. Wadsworth [5], and interpret as continuations the variables x_i that we used to identify the nodes of a flow net. Thus, an operation f_i associated with a node is function of the continuations associated with its successor nodes. For example, the system of equations *EN* given below represents the flow net n_0 illustrated in Section 2. Conversely, a flow net can be retrieved from a system of equations like *EN*.

$$x_1 = (x_2, x_4)f^{\alpha} \qquad x_4 = (x_3^2 @ x_6)f_4 \qquad x_7 = (x_4, x_5)f_7$$
$$x_2 = (x_3^1)f_2 \qquad x_5 = (x_3^3 @ x_9)f_5 \qquad x_8 = (x_7)f_8$$
$$x_3 = (x_2)f_3 \qquad x_6 = (x_8)f_6 \qquad x_9 = (x_9)f^{\beta},$$

where $x_3^1 || x_3^2 || x_3^3 = \langle x_3^1, x_3^2, x_3^3 \rangle = x_3$

We "unfold" the flow net n_0 by reducing $(x_2,x_4)f^{\alpha}$ using the system of equations *EN* as a reduction system and having in mind that all operations are linear (with respect to @). We have:

$$\begin{aligned}
&(x_2, x_4)f^{\alpha}\\
= \; &((x_3^1)f_2, (x_3^2 @ x_6)f_4)f^{\alpha}\\
= \; &((x_3^1)f_2, (x_3^2)f_4)f^{\alpha} \; @ \; ((x_3^1)f_2, (x_6)f_4)f^{\alpha}
\end{aligned}$$

further,

$$\begin{aligned}
&((x_3^1)f_2, (x_6)f_4)f^{\alpha}\\
= \; &((x_3^1)f_2, (x_8)f_6f_4)f^{\alpha}\\
= \; &((x_3^1)f_2, (x_7)f_8f_6f_4)f^{\alpha}\\
= \; &((x_3^1)f_2, (x_4, x_5)f_7f_8f_6f_4)f^{\alpha}\\
= \; &((x_3^1)f_2, ((x_3^2 @ x_6)f_4, (x_3^3 @ x_9)f_5)f_7f_8f_6f_4)f^{\alpha}\\
= \; &((x_3^1)f_2, ((x_3^2)f_4, (x_3^3)f_5)f_7f_8f_6f_4)f^{\alpha}\\
&@ \; ((x_3^1)f_2, ((x_6)f_4, (x_3^3)f_5)f_7f_8f_6f_4)f^{\alpha}\\
&@ \; ((x_3^1)f_2, ((x_3^2)f_4, (x_9)f_5)f_7f_8f_6f_4)f^{\alpha}\\
&@ \; ((x_3^1)f_2, ((x_6)f_4, (x_9)f_5)f_7f_8f_6f_4)f^{\alpha}
\end{aligned}$$

now,

$$\begin{aligned}
&((x_3^1)f_2, ((x_3^2)f_4, (x_3^3)f_5)f_7f_8f_6f_4)f^{\alpha}\\
= \; &((x_3^1)f_2, (x_3^2 || x_3^3)(f_4 || f_5)f_7f_8f_6f_4)f^{\alpha}\\
= \; &((x_3^1 || x_3^2 || x_3^3)(f_2 || ((f_4 || f_5)f_7f_8f_6f_4)))f^{\alpha}\\
= \; &(x_3)(f_2 || ((f_4 || f_5)f_7f_8f_6f_4))f^{\alpha}\\
= \; &(x_2)f_3(f_2 || ((f_4 || f_5)f_7f_8f_6f_4))f^{\alpha}\\
&\ldots\ldots\ldots\ldots
\end{aligned}$$

In an ω-continuous par-nd algebra a system of equations like *EN* has a solution, namely a least fixed-point solution. All this is perhaps clearer in the morphism of the par-nd algebraic theory of diamonds notation than in the par-nd expression notation. The morphism representation of the flow net n_0 is s_0, which is given below. The components of X, which identify the flow net nodes, are the algebraic theory variables which stand for the components of the morphism ξ; C is the connection labeling function that associates a connection name to every node, and thus, to every component of ξ. The morphism ξ is the theory notation of the equational system *EN;* for example, in s_0, the equations $x_1 = (x_2,x_4)f^{\alpha}$ and $x_5 = (x_3^3 @ x_9)f_5$ are represented by the first and fifth components of the morphism, respectively.

$$C: \langle \alpha, \lambda, \lambda, \lambda, \lambda, \lambda, \lambda, \lambda, \bar{\beta} \rangle$$

$$X: \langle x_1, x_2, x_3^1 || x_3^2 || x_3^3, x_4, x_5, x_6, x_7, x_8, x_9 \rangle$$

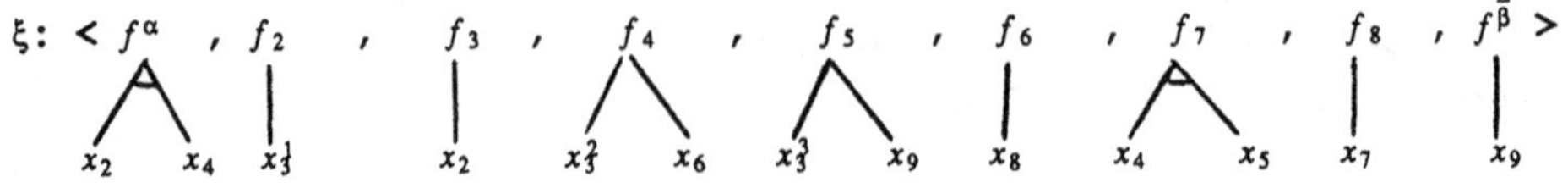

The primitive flow structure s_0

We call s_0 the *primitive flow structure* of n_0, which represents the flow net. In other words, a primitive flow structure of a flow net is a pair $\langle C, \xi \rangle$ where C is a connection function and ξ is the morphism (in the par-nd theory of diamonds) induced by the system of equations representing the flow net.

We "unfold" n_0 by composing (which corresponds to substitution of diamonds) the morphism component ξ of s_0 with itself. The picture below shows the morphism of the first unfolding of n_0, which is ξ composed with itself once.

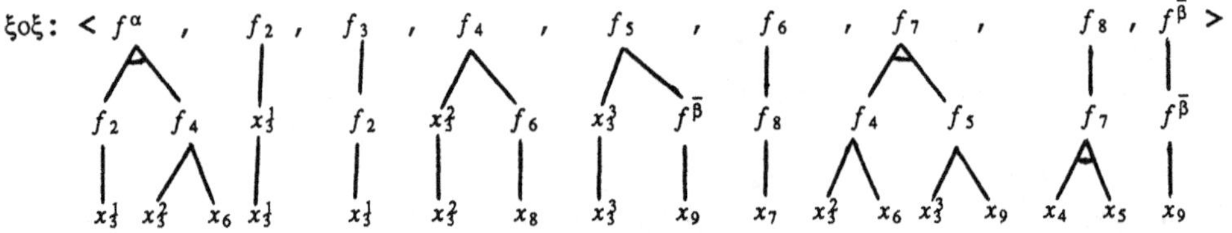

The feeling that we are unfolding a flow net is unmistakable. The nth unfolding corresponds very precisely to the intuitive idea of letting the computation proceed for n steps and then, ready or not, stopping.

In the ω-continuous par-nd algebraic theory of diamonds, which is rational, the unfoldings of a flow net reach the solution. Intuitively, as stated in Section 2, a finite partial diamond is a diamond whose leaves can be labeled with $\perp$; the natural order relation $\leq$ (called "less defined that") on partial diamonds is extended to morphisms of partial diamonds: a morphism properly approximates another iff their corresponding diamonds are identical except that the first contains $\perp$ in at least one position where the second contains a non-trivial diamond. Again consider the primitive flow structure s_0 of n_0. The diamonds of ξ are made partial by composing ξ with the least element $\perp = \langle \perp, \ldots, \perp \rangle$. In this way, a sequence of unfoldings of n_0 becomes a chain in the ω-continuous par-nd algebraic theory of diamonds, of which we show only the first components:

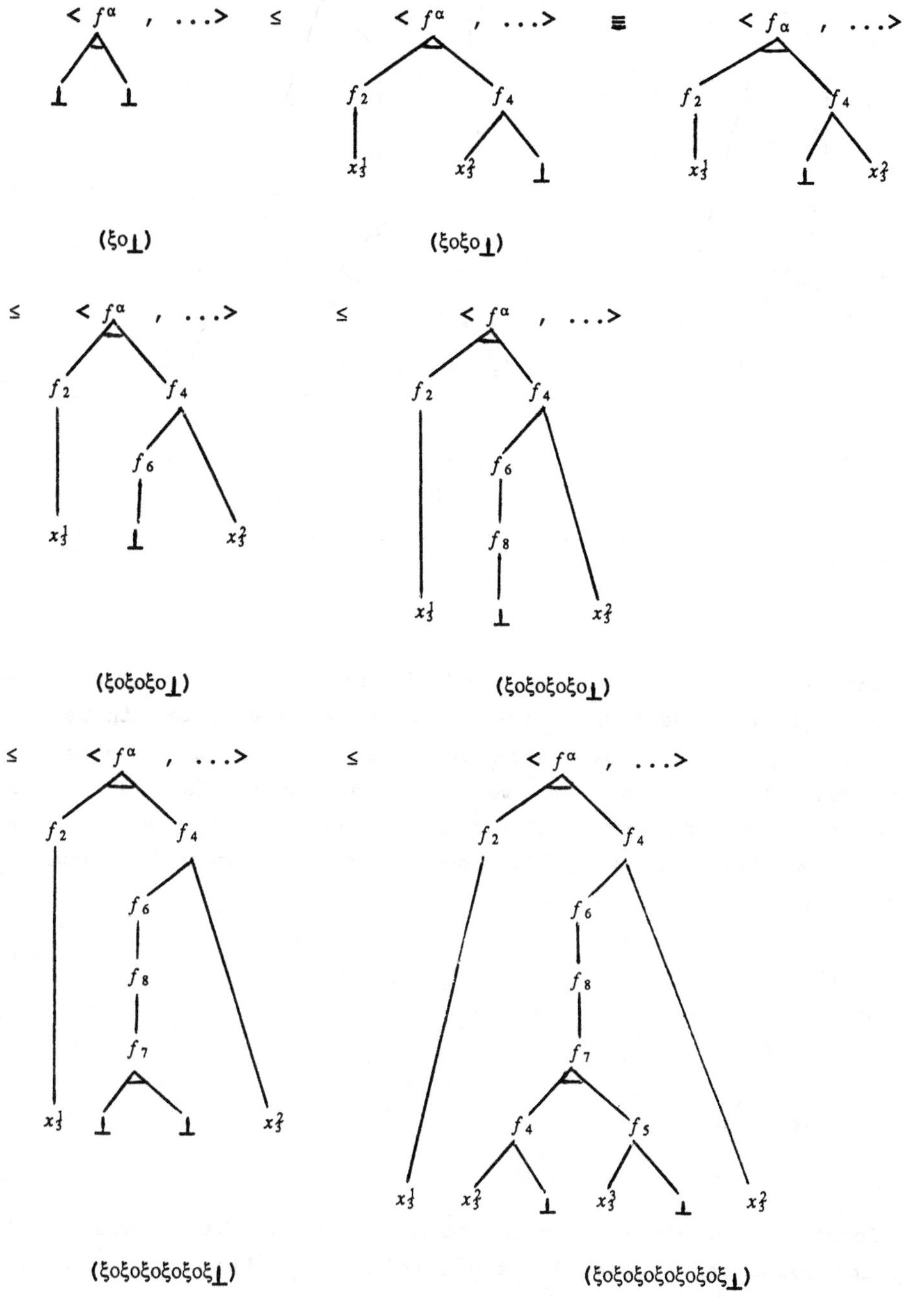

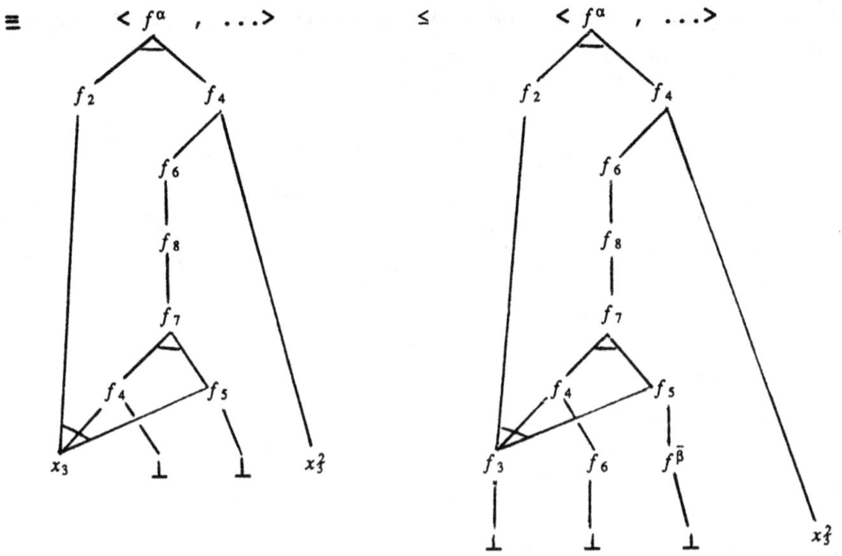

$(\xi\circ\xi\circ\xi\circ\xi\circ\xi\circ\xi\circ\xi\circ\xi_{\perp})$

. . . .

An equivalence relation ≡ on diamonds is generated by the equational system *EP* given in Section 2, the linearity of operations in par-nd algebras, and $x_3^1 || x_3^2 || x_3^3 = x_3$. This equivalence relation is extended to morphisms of diamonds: two morphisms are equivalent if their correspondent components are equivalent. As an example, consider the diamonds below. They are equivalent, because @ is a commutative operation: $(x_3^2 @ x_6)f_4 = (x_6 @ x_3^2)f_4$.

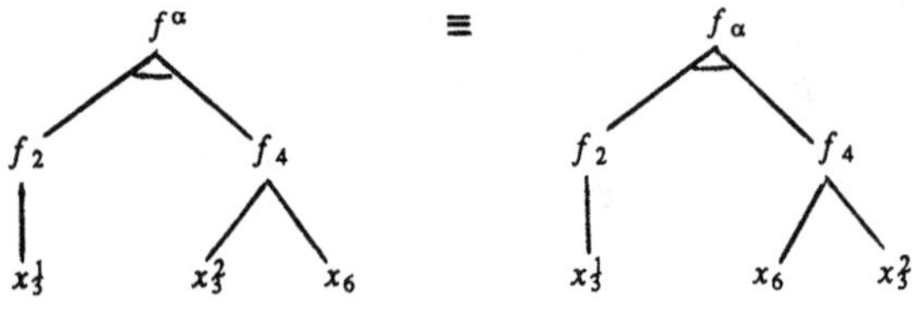

The least upper bound of the above chain is the unique least fixed-point solution representing the unfoldment of the flow net n_0.

We call a *flow structure* an unfolding of a flow net in the ω-continuous par-nd algebraic theory of diamonds. That is, a flow structure of a flow net is a pair <C,ζ>, where C is a connection function and ζ is a morphism (in the par-nd theory of diamonds) obtained by composing the morphism component of its primitive flow structure with itself. We write <C,ξ>* = <C,ζ> to mean that the unfoldment of <C,ξ> is <C,ζ>.

We now introduce for convenience another concept. The *frontier* of a diamond is the nondeterministic set of its leaves. It consists of @ (selection) of subsets, such that each subset contains the leaves of all paths in diamond connected by AND nodes and the leaf of only one path connected by OR nodes. For example, the above diamonds have the frontier set $\{\{x_3^1, x_3^2\}@\{x_3^1, x_6\}\}$. The frontier of a diamond is extended to the frontier of a flow structure <C,ζ>, by tupling the frontiers of all diamonds in ζ.

Our construction of flow structures captures the flow of control in flow nets. An interpretation of a flow structure <C,ζ> is introduced by considering an ω-continuous par-nd algebraic theory, Th, in which the operation symbols in ζ get values. A *flow action* is a pair <C,ζ> where C is a connection function and ζ is a morphism (in the par-nd theory T). It is not surprising that

Proposition 6.1 Flow structures and flow actions are flow-of-control algebras. □

The formal definitions of the flow-of-control operations of flow structures and flow actions can be found in Appendix B. Appendix B also contains a formal relation between flow nets and flow actions.

Let $<\bar{\Sigma},\Gamma>$-$FS_{\wedge,E}$ and $<\bar{\Sigma},\Gamma>$-$FA_{\wedge,E}$ denote the flow-of-control algebras of flow structures and flow actions, respectively, with inputs from Γ^+ and outputs from $\bar{\Gamma}^+$ (over $\bar{\Sigma}$). The following proposition proves that the flow-of-control algebra of flow structures is a suitable syntax for flow nets.

Proposition 6.2 The flow-of-control algebra of flow structures $<\bar{\Sigma},\Gamma>$-$FS_{\wedge,E}$ is free in the category of flow-of-control algebras over Γ and $\bar{\Sigma}$.

$$\begin{array}{ccc} <\bar{\Sigma},\Gamma> & \longrightarrow & <\bar{\Sigma},\Gamma>\text{-}FS_{\wedge,EF} \\ & \overset{H}{\searrow} & \big\downarrow \bar{H} \\ & & <\bar{\Sigma},\Gamma>\text{-}FA_{\wedge,EF} \end{array}$$

where $\overline{H}$ is a par-nd $<\overline{\Sigma},\Gamma>$-homomorphism which preserves the flow-of-control operations.

The proposition follows directly from Proposition 2.3 extended to ω-continuous par-nd algebraic theories, which guarantees the existence of a unique morphism of algebraic theories $\overline{H}$.

7. The Deadlock Problem

In this section we formulate the deadlock problem in terms of flow structures. A detailed analysis of various properties of concurrent systems and how they are inferred in other models considered as semantic domains for flow structures is subject of further investigation. In this paper we only attempt to give an intuitively acceptable definition of deadlock.

A system is *dead* when some of its computing agents are involved in a reciprocal waiting to establish new connections in order to proceed. Consider the flow net n_0 again. The flow of control in n_0 from the input f^α is given by the diamond below, which is the first component of the 8th unfolding of its primitive flow structure s_0.

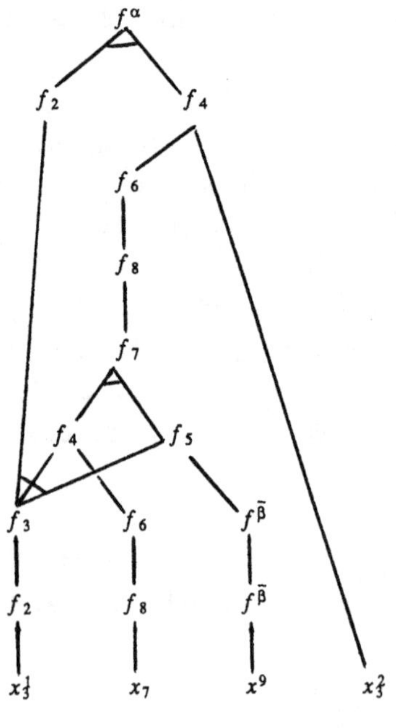

In this diamond f^α is executed first. Then, f_2 and f_4 are executed in parallel. After that, the sequence f_6, f_8, and f_7 is executed. f_3 is in a waiting state (interrupt); it cannot be executed before all its input components, which are represented by x_3^1, x_3^2, and x_3^3, are available (details of this unfolding are given in Section 6). It continues with the execution of f_4 and f_5 in parallel. The execution of f_4 and f_5 provides the remaining component variables x_3^2 and x_3^3, and f_3 can be executed. At this point there is a choice among f_3, f_6, and f_5; only one of them can be executed. If f_6 is executed, then f_8 is executed, and the computation proceed. If f_3 is executed, then f_2 is executed, after which n_0 enters a dead state. A step of computation is obtained by substituting all variables in diamond by their corresponding morphism components; nothing can be substituted for x_3^1, and the other components will be never available. The above discussion suggests the following definitions:

A flow structure $<C,\zeta>$ is *complete dead from the input* f^α if all subsets of the frontier of the diamond having the root f^α in $<C,\xi>^* = <C,\zeta>$ contain only component variables.

A flow structure $<C,\zeta>$ is *potentially dead from the input* f^α if in the frontier of the diamond having the root f^α in $<C,\xi>^* = <C,\zeta>$ there exist subsets containing some component variables.

The above diamond has the frontier $\{\{x_3^1\}@\{x_7\}@\{x_9\}@\{x_3^2\}\}$. The subsets $\{x_3^1\}$ and $\{x_3^2\}$ show that the flow structure containing the above diamond is potentially dead from f^α.

We also conclude that two flow structures are *equivalent* (have the same behavior) if their unfoldments are equal.

These definitions are inferred in a flow-of-control algebra of flow actions by the unique morphism $\overline{H}$ given in Proposition 6.2.

8. Conclusions and Directions for Further Study

We have developed a flow-of-control algebra of flow nets, a theory that may be useful in modeling of the behavior of concurrent systems. We believe that the proposed initial algebraic semantics applied to concurrency gives a firm basis for understanding and comparing a wide variety of existing features for communication, parallelism, and nondeterminism, including deadlock, termination, interrupts, and equivalence. The following problems are among those we have been considering.

(I) The study and comparison of different models of concurrent computation in a unified manner. According to the ADJ approach, the syntax should be an initial algebra, in some category in which the other algebras are candidates for the semantics (via a unique homomorphism from the syntax). We already know of the existence of models of concurrent systems that can be structured as flow-of control algebras; one of them is the Petri net theory, another is Milner's behavioral algebra [8]. Therefore, these models are semantic candidates for our syntax. In pictures,

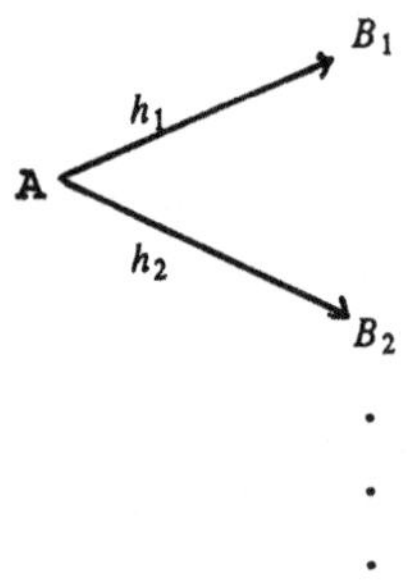

where A the flow-of-control algebra of flow structures, and B_i for i = 1,2,... is a model of concurrency structured as (or included in) a derived flow-of-control algebra. The model A is initial in the category of flow-of-control algebras, and B_i is a possible semantic domain of A; h_i is the uniquely determined homomorphism, assigning a meaning in B_i to each syntactic structure in A.

We must examine which features of various models of concurrent systems can be reformulated in our model (at the syntactic level), and thus, to determine whether they are preserved by the correspondent homomorphism h_i. We also need to know which properties of concurrency are modeled easier in one model than in another, and then, to transport them into the desired model via the syntax A.

(II) Least fixed-point semantics is successfully used to characterize sequential computation by considering finite representations of infinite computations. It is based on "finite approximation" techniques, which in sequential programming helps the study of correctness of programs and compilers with recursive definitions. Our model

creates the right framework for the least fixed-point semantics of parallel and nondeterministic computations. Future research may be done by applying it to the correctness of programs that exhibit the full power of concurrency.

(III) A difficult problem with the existing models of concurrency is their inability to handle error messages with precision. The initial algebra approach to the semantics of sequential computation made it possible to treat errors in a systematic manner [6]. We believe that our model is a proper framework for a reasonable treatment of errors in concurrent systems in an implementation independent manner.

(IV) We should explore the practical aspects of the work reported in this paper. Goguen and Tardo have implemented a programming and specification system, called OBJ, based on the ADJ work on the initial algebra semantics. Although categorical, our approach is constructive. We would like to consider it for the design and implementation of a specification programming language for concurrent systems.

Appendix A

An S-sorted Σ-*flow net* with inputs $\mu \in (\Gamma^+)^*$ and outputs $\bar{\nu} \in (\bar{\Gamma}^+)^*$ is n = <N,C,L,R,T,S>, which comprises the following:

1. A countable poset N of *nodes* partitioned into mutually disjoint sets of *input* nodes I, *internal* nodes P, and *output (exit)* nodes O; #P (the number of elements of P) is called the *weight of n;*

2. A *connection labeling* function C from N to $\Gamma \cup \bar{\Gamma}$, assigning an *input, internal* or *exit* name to each node in I, P, or O, respectively: $C|I: I \rightarrow \Gamma^+$, $C|P: P \rightarrow \{\lambda\}$, and $C|O: O \rightarrow \bar{\Gamma}^+$; $\mu = (i_1)C(i_2)C\ldots(i_m)C$ for $\{i_1, i_2, \ldots, i_m\} = I$; $\bar{\nu} = (o_1)C(o_2)C\ldots(o_n)C$ for $\{o_1, o_2, \ldots, o_n\} = O$;

3. An *operator labeling* function L from N to Σ, assigning an operator symbol $f \in \Sigma$ to each node $n \in N$ in the following way: $L|I: I \rightarrow \Sigma^{\Gamma}$ such that $(n)L = f^{\alpha}$ iff $(n)C = \alpha$, $n \in I$, $\alpha \in \Gamma^+$, $L|P: P \rightarrow \Sigma^{\lambda}$, and $L|O: O \rightarrow \Sigma^{\bar{\Gamma}}$ such that $(n)L = f^{\bar{\beta}}$ iff $(n)C = \bar{\beta}$, $n \in O$, $\bar{\beta} \in \bar{\Gamma}^+$;

4. A *type labeling* function T from N to the set {AND,OR}×{AND,OR}, assigning an *In-type* and *Out-type* to every node $n \in N$; we require that the type of the operator associated with a node be consistent with the type of that node;

5. A relation $R \subseteq N \times N$, the *set of directed arcs;* $r = <n,n'> \in R$ represents a directed arc from n to n'; for each $n \in N$ we define
$R_n = \{<n,n'> \mid <n,n'> \in R\}$ (the set of outgoing arcs of n) and
$R_{\bar{n}} = \{<n',n> \mid <n',n> \in R\}$ (the set of incoming arcs of n);
R_n and $R_{\bar{n}}$ are totally ordered sets;

6. A *sort labeling* function S from $\{R_n \mid n \in N\}$ to S*; we require that the sorts of the incoming and outgoing arcs of a node be consistent with the co-arity and arity of the operator at that node: if $(n)L = f \in \Sigma_{u,v}$ then $(R_n)S = v$ and $(R_{\bar{n}})S = u$.

We use $f|A' : A' \to B$ for the restriction of $f: A \to B$ to $A' \subseteq A$.

Note: The sort labeling function S will be omited in the sequel; the co-arity and arity of the operator at a node uniquely determine the sorts associated to arcs.

"Guards" may be introduced in flow nets by considering a second labeling of arcs; a guard represents the condition (boolean expression) under which a node is activated. We will discuss guarded flow nets in a different paper.

We now give the formal description of the flow net n_0 illustrated in Section 2, where

$S = \{s_1, s_2, s_3, s_4\}$,
$\Gamma = \{\lambda, \alpha, \beta\}$, $\bar{\Gamma} = \{\lambda, \bar{\alpha}, \bar{\beta}\}$,
$\Sigma = \{f^{\alpha}, f_2, f_3, f_4, f_5, f_6, f_7, f_8, f^{\bar{\beta}}\}$, where
$f^{\alpha} \in \Sigma_{s_1s_3,s_1s_3}$, $f_2 \in \Sigma_{s_1,s_1}$, $f_3 \in \Sigma_{s_1,s_1s_2s_3}$, $f_4 \in \Sigma_{s_3@s_3,s_3}$,
$f_5 \in \Sigma_{s_2,s_2}$, $f_6 \in \Sigma_{s_4,s_3}$, $f_7 \in \Sigma_{s_2s_3,s_4}$, $f_8 \in \Sigma_{s_4,s_4}$, $f^{\bar{\beta}} \in \Sigma_{s_2,s_2}$.

Then,

$N = \{1,2,3,4,5,6,7,8,9\}$,
$(1)C = \alpha$, $(9)C = \bar{\beta}$, $(2)C = \ldots (8)C = \{\lambda\}$,
$(1)L = f^{\alpha}$, $(9)L = f^{\bar{\beta}}$,
$(n)L = f_n$ for $n = 2,3,\ldots,8$,
(n)T = <AND,AND> for n = 1,2,3,6,7,8,9, and
(n)T = <AND,OR> for n = 4,5,
$R = \{<1,1>,<1,2>,<1,4>,<2,3>,<3,2>,<4,3>,<4,6>,<5,3>,$
$<5,9>,<6,8>,<7,4>,<7,5>,<8,7>,<9,9>\}$,
$(<1,1>)S = (<2,3>)S = (<3,2>)S = s_1$,
$(<5,3>)S = (<5,9>)S = (<7,5>)S = s_2$,
$(<4,3>)S = (<4,6>)S = (<7,4>)S = s_3$,

$(\langle 6,8\rangle)S = (\langle 8,7\rangle)S = s_4$.

An *identity* S-sorted Σ-*flow net* with inputs $\mu \in (\Gamma^+)^*$ and outputs $\bar{\mu} \in (\bar{\Gamma}^+)^*$ is $1_\mu = \langle N,C,L,R,T,S\rangle$, which comprises the following:

1. $N = I \cup O$;

2. for every $n \in I$ such that $(n)C = \alpha$, $\alpha \in \Gamma^+$, there exists $n' \in O$ such that $(n')C = \bar{\alpha}$, $\bar{\alpha} \in \bar{\Gamma}^+$; $\mu = (i_1)C(i_2)C\ldots(i_m)C$ for $\{i_1,i_2,\ldots,i_m\} = I$ and $\bar{\mu} = (o_1)C(o_2)C\ldots(o_m)C$ for $\{o_1,o_2,\ldots,o_m\} = O$;

3. $(n)L = f^\alpha$ and $(n')L = f^{\bar{\alpha}}$ for every $n \in I$ and $n' \in O$ with $(n)C = \alpha$ and $(n')C = \bar{\alpha}$; (f^α)arity $= (f^{\bar{\alpha}})$co-arity;

4. $T: N \rightarrow \{AND\}\times\{AND\}$;

5. $R = \{\langle n,n'\rangle \mid n \in I,\ n' \in O,\ (n)C = \alpha,\ (n')C = \bar{\alpha},\ \alpha \in \Gamma^+,\ \bar{\alpha} \in \bar{\Gamma}^+\}$.

We now turn to the operations defined on flow nets. Consider two S-sorted Σ-flow nets $n_1 = \langle N_1,C_1,L_1,R_1,T_1,S_1\rangle \in \mathbf{FN}(\mu_1,\bar{v}_1)$ and $n_2 = \langle N_2,C_2,L_2,R_2,T_2,S_2\rangle \in \mathbf{FN}(\mu_2,\bar{v}_2)$.

The *sequential communication* operation $n_1 \Rightarrow n_2 = \langle N,C,L,R,T,S\rangle \in \mathbf{FN}(\mu_1,\bar{v}_2)$ of n_1 and n_2, is defined when $\bar{v}_1 = \bar{\mu}_2$, and comprises the following:

1. $N = N_1 \cup N_2$;

2. $C = C_1 | (I_1 \cup P_1) \cup C_2 | (P_2 \cup O_2) \cup C'$ where $C': O_1 \cup I_2 \rightarrow \{\lambda\}$, i.e., $(n)C' = \lambda$ for $n \in O_1 \cup I_2$;

3. $L = L_1 | (I_1 \cup P_1) \cup L_2 | (P_2 \cup O_2) \cup L'$ where $L': O_1 \cup I_2 \rightarrow \Sigma^\lambda$, such that $(n)L' = f^\lambda \in \Sigma^\lambda_{u\mu}$ if $(n)L_1 = f^{\bar{\beta}} \in \Sigma^{\bar{\Gamma}^+}_{u\mu}$, $n \in O_1$, and $(n)L_2 = f^\alpha \in \Sigma^{\Gamma^+}_{u\mu}$, $n \in I_2$;

4. $T = T_1 \cup T_2$;

5. $R = R_1 \cup R_2 \cup R'$ where $R' = \{\langle n_1,n_2\rangle \mid n_1 \in O_1,\ n_2 \in I_2\}$, such that $(n_1)C_1 = (n_2)\bar{C}_2$.

The *simultaneous input communication* operation $n_1 \ ||_I\ n_2 = \langle N,C,L,R,T,S\rangle \in \mathbf{FN}(\mu_1,\bar{v}_1\bar{v}_2)$ of n_1 and n_2, when $\mu_1 = \mu_2$, comprises the following:

1. $N = N_1 \cup N_2 \cup I'$ where $N_1 \cap N_2 \cap I' = \Phi$, and $\#I' = \#I_1 = \#I_2$;

2. $C = C_1|(P_1 \cup O_1) \cup C_2|(P_2 \cup O_2) \cup C'$ where
$C': I_1 \cup I_2 \cup I' \rightarrow \Gamma$, such that $(n)C' = (n_1)C_1 = (n_2)C_2$, and
$(n_1)C' = (n_2)C' = \lambda$ for $n \in I'$, $n_1 \in I_1$, $n_2 \in I_2$;

3. $L = L_1|(P_1 \cup O_1) \cup L_2|(P_2 \cup O_2) \cup L'$ where
$L': I_1 \cup I_2 \cup I' \rightarrow \Sigma^{\Gamma}$, such that $(n)L' = (n_1)L_1 = (n_2)L_2$, and
$(n_1)L' = (n_2)L' = f^{\lambda} \in \Sigma^{\lambda}_{u,\mu}$ if $(n_1)L_1, (n_2)L_2 \in \Sigma^{\Gamma_*}_{u,\mu}$, $n_1 \in I_1$, $n_2 \in I_2$;

4. $T = T_1 \cup T_2 \cup T'$, where $T': I' \rightarrow \{AND\}\times\{AND\}$;

5. $R = R_1 \cup R_2 \cup R'$ where
$R' = \{\langle n,n_1\rangle, \langle n,n_2\rangle \mid n \in I', n_1 \in I_1, n_2 \in I_2\}$, such that
$(n)C' = (n_1)C_1 = (n_2)C_2$.

The simultaneous input communication operation $n_1 \ ||_I \ n_2 = \langle N,C,L,R,T,S\rangle \in FN(\mu_1\mu_2, \bar{\nu}_1\bar{\nu}_2)$ of n_1 and n_2, which do not have any input names in common, has as components the union of corresponding components of n_1 and n_2.

The *nondeterministic input communication* operation $n_1 \ @_I \ n_2 = \langle N,C,L,R,T,S\rangle \in FN(\mu_1, \bar{\nu}_1\bar{\nu}_2)$ of n_1 and n_2, when $\mu_1 = \mu_2$, comprises the following:

1. $N = N_1 \cup N_2 \cup I'$ where $N_1 \cap N_2 \cap I' = \Phi$, and $\#I' = \#I_1 = \#I_2$;

2. $C = C_1|(P_1 \cup O_1) \cup C_2|(P_2 \cup O_2) \cup C'$ where
$C': I_1 \cup I_2 \cup I' \rightarrow \Gamma$, such that $(n)C' = (n_1)C_1 = (n_2)C_2$, and
$(n_1)C' = (n_2)C' = \lambda$ for $n \in I'$, $n_1 \in I_1$, $n_2 \in I_2$;

3. $L = L_1|(P_1 \cup O_1) \cup L_2|(P_2 \cup O_2) \cup L'$ where
$L': I_1 \cup I_2 \cup I' \rightarrow \Sigma^{\Gamma}$, such that $(n)L' = (n_1)L_1 = (n_2)L_2$, and
$(n_1)L' = (n_2)L' = f^{\lambda} \in \Sigma^{\lambda}_{u,\mu}$ if $(n_1)L_1, (n_2)L_2 \in \Sigma^{\Gamma_*}_{u,\mu}$, $n_1 \in I_1$, $n_2 \in I_2$;

4. $T = T_1 \cup T_2 \cup T'$, where $T': I' \rightarrow \{OR\}\times\{OR\}$;

5. $R = R_1 \cup R_2 \cup R'$ where
$R' = \{\langle n,n_1\rangle, \langle n,n_2\rangle \mid n \in I', n_1 \in I_1, n_2 \in I_2\}$, such that
$(n)C' = (n_1)C_1 = (n_2)C_2$.

The *relabeling* by ρ of the input node of $n = \langle N,C,L,R,T,S\rangle$ named α is $n\rho/\alpha = \langle N',C',L',R',T',S'\rangle$, such that:

1. $N' = N$;

2. $C' = C|(N-\{n\}) \cup C''$ where

C": $\{n\} \to \Gamma^{+}$ is $(n)C'' = \rho$ for $(n)C = \alpha$;

3. $L' = L|(N-\{n\}) \cup L''$ where
   L": $\{n\} \to \Sigma^{\Gamma^{*}}$ is $(n)L'' = f^{\rho}$ for $(n)L = f^{\alpha}$;

4. $T' = T$;

5. $R' = R$;

Consider the flow net $n = \langle N,C,L,R,T,S\rangle \in FN(\alpha_1\ldots\alpha_n, \bar{\alpha}_1\ldots\bar{\alpha}_n\bar{\beta}_1\ldots\bar{\beta}_p)$, and let $O_{\bar{\alpha}}$ be the set $O = \{o_1,\ldots,o_n\}$ such that $(o_j)C = \bar{\alpha}_j$, $j = 1,..,n$.

The *k^{th} iterate* of n is $n^k = \langle N^k, C^k, L^k, R^k, T^k, S^k\rangle$ defined recursively in the following way:

1. $n^0 = n$;

2. $N^k = N^{k-1} \cup N$;

3. $C^k = C^{k-1} \cup C \cup C'$ where $C' : O_{\bar{\alpha}}^{k-1} \cup I \to \{\lambda\}$;

4. $L^k = L^{k-1} \cup L \cup L'$ where $L' : O_{\bar{\alpha}}^{k-1} \cup I \to \Sigma^{\lambda}$;

5. $T^k = T^{k-1} \cup T$;

6. $R^k = R^{k-1} \cup R \cup R'$ where $R' = \{\langle n, n_1\rangle \mid n \in O_{\bar{\alpha}},\ n_1 \in I\}$ such that $(n)\bar{C} = (n_1)C$

In the dual category of flow nets the simultaneous input communication, the nondeterministic input communication, and relabeling of input nodes determine the simultaneous exit communication, the nondeterministic exit communication, and relabeling of output nodes operations.

Appendix B

Let $CDh_{\bar{\Sigma},\Gamma}$ be the ω-continuous par-nd algebraic theory of diamonds generated by the par-nd algebra of diamonds $D_{\bar{\Sigma},\Gamma}$ generalized to an ω-continuous par-nd algebra. The variables that are used to identify the nodes of a flow net are variables in $CDh_{\bar{\Sigma},\Gamma}$; let them be $x_1^{w_1},\ldots,x_n^{w_n}$, $x_{n+1}^{w||u_1},\ldots,x_{n+r}^{w||u_r}, x_{n+r+1}^{w||u||v_1},\ldots,x_{n+r+p}^{w||u||v_p}$; $w_1,\ldots,w_n$ represent the co-arities of the input operations $f^{\alpha_1},\ldots,f^{\alpha_n}$ at the input nodes, $u_1,\ldots,u_r$ represent the co-arities of the internal operations at the internal nodes, and

$v_1, \ldots, v_p$ represent the co-arities of the exit operations $f^{\bar\beta_1}, \ldots, f^{\bar\beta_p}$ at the exit nodes; $w = w_1 || \ldots || w_n$, $u = u_1 || \ldots || u_r$, and $v = v_1 || \ldots || v_p$, $w_i, u_j, v_k \in \bar{S}$, $i = 1,..,n$, $j = 1,..,r$, $k = 1,..,p$.

A *primitive flow structure* (of a flow net) with n *inputs* $\mu = <\alpha_1, \ldots, \alpha_n>$, $\alpha_i \in \Gamma^+$, $i = 1,..,n$, and p *outputs* $\bar\nu = <\bar\beta_1, \ldots, \bar\beta_p>$, $\bar\beta_k \in \bar\Gamma^+$, $k = 1,..,p$, of *weight* r, over an S-sorted par-nd algebraic theory $CDh_{\bar\Sigma,\Gamma}$, is a pair $<B,\xi>$, where $\xi = <\xi^\mu, \xi^\lambda, \xi^{\bar\nu}>$ is a morphism in $CDh_{\bar\Sigma,\Gamma}$, such that:
the *input* is $\xi^\mu = <(w_1)f^{\alpha_1}, \ldots, (w_n)f^{\alpha_n}>$, $f^{\alpha_i}: w_i \to w_i$, $i = 1,..,n$,
the *body* is $\xi^\lambda = <(u_1)f_1, \ldots, (u_r)f_r>$, $f_i: u_j \to u_j$, $j = 1,..,r$,
the *exit* is $\xi^\nu = <(v_1)f^{\bar\beta_1}, \ldots, (v_p)f^{\bar\beta_p}>$, $f^{\bar\beta_k}: v_k \to v_k$, $k = 1,..,p$;
the *connection function* is $B: CDh_{\bar\Sigma,\Gamma} \to \Gamma \cup \bar\Gamma$, such that
$(<\xi^\mu, \xi^\lambda, \xi^{\bar\nu}>)B = <\mu, \lambda_r, \bar\nu>$ for $\lambda_r = <\lambda, \ldots, \lambda>$.

A *flow structure* of a primitive flow structure $<B,\xi>$ with n inputs $\mu = <\alpha_1, \ldots, \alpha_n>$, $\alpha_i \in \Gamma^+$, $i = 1,..,n$, p outputs $\bar\nu = <\bar\beta_1, \ldots, \bar\beta_p>$, $\bar\beta_k \in \bar\Gamma^+$, $k = 1,..,p$, and of weight r, is a pair $<B,\zeta>$, such that $\zeta = \xi^k$, where ξ^k is the kth iterate of a morphism in $CDh_{\bar\Sigma,\Gamma}$. It results that a flow structure has also n inputs $\mu = <\alpha_1, \ldots, \alpha_n>$, $\alpha_i \in \Gamma^+$, $i = 1,..,n$, p outputs $\bar\nu = <\bar\beta_1, \ldots, \bar\beta_p>$, $\bar\beta_k \in \bar\Gamma^+$, $k = 1,..,p$, and is of weight r.

An *identity* flow structure with inputs μ and outputs $\bar\mu$ of weight s, is $1^\mu = <B,\zeta>$, where $\zeta = <f^\mu, 0_s, f^{\bar\mu}>$, and $(<f^\mu, 0_s, f^{\bar\mu}>)B = <\mu, \lambda_s, \bar\mu>$.

Consider two flow structures $s_i = <B,\zeta_i>$, with n_i inputs μ_i, p_i outputs $\bar\nu_i$, of weight r_i, where $\zeta_i = <\zeta_i^{\mu_i}, \zeta_i^\lambda, \zeta_i^{\bar\nu_i}>$, $i = 1,2$. Flow-of-control operations are defined on flow structures in the following way:

The *sequential communication* operation $s_1 \Rightarrow s_2$ of s_1 and s_2 is defined when $\bar\nu_1 = \bar\mu_2$, and it is $<B,\zeta>$, where
$\zeta = <\zeta_1^{\mu_1}, \zeta_1^\lambda, \zeta_1^{\bar\nu_1}, \zeta_2^{\mu_2}, \zeta_2^\lambda, \zeta_2^{\bar\nu_2}> \circ <x_1^{\mu_1}, x_1^\lambda, x_1^{\bar\nu_1}, x_2^{\mu_2}, x_2^\lambda, x_2^{\bar\nu_2}>$, and
$(<\zeta_1^{\mu_1}, \zeta_1^\lambda, \zeta_1^{\bar\nu_1}, \zeta_2^{\mu_2}, \zeta_2^\lambda, \zeta_2^{\bar\nu_2}>)B = <\mu_1, \lambda_{r_1+p_1+n_2+r_2}, \bar\nu_2>$.

The *simultaneous input communication* operation $s_1 ||_I s_2$ of s_1 and s_2, when $\mu_1 = \mu_2$, is $<B,\zeta>$, where $\zeta = <\zeta^\mu, \zeta_1^{\mu_1}, \zeta_1^\lambda, \zeta_1^{\bar\nu_1}, \zeta_2^{\mu_2}, \zeta_2^\lambda, \zeta_2^{\bar\nu_2}>$, $\zeta^\mu = <f_1^{\alpha_1}, \ldots, f_n^{\alpha_n}>$, $\mu = \mu_1 = \mu_2 = <\alpha_1, \ldots, \alpha_n>$, and $f^{\alpha_i}: w_1 || w_2 \to w_1 || w_2$, $i = 1,..,n$;
$(<\zeta^\mu, \zeta_1^{\mu_1}, \zeta_1^\lambda, \zeta_1^{\bar\nu_1}, \zeta_2^{\mu_2}, \zeta_2^\lambda, \zeta_2^{\bar\nu_2}>)B = <\mu_1, \lambda_{n_1+r_1}, \bar\nu_1, \lambda_{n_2+r_2}, \bar\nu_2>$.

The *nondeterministic input communication* operation $s_1 \,||_I\, s_2$ of s_1 and s_2, when $\mu_1 = \mu_2$, is $<B, \zeta>$, where $\zeta = <\zeta^{\mu}, \zeta_1^{\mu_1}, \zeta_1^{\lambda}, \zeta_1^{\bar{\nu}_1}, \zeta_2^{\mu_2}, \zeta_2^{\lambda}, \zeta_2^{\bar{\nu}_2}>$, $\zeta^{\mu} = <f_1^{\alpha_1}, \ldots, f_n^{\alpha_n}>$, $\mu = \mu_1 = \mu_2 = <\alpha_1, \ldots, \alpha_n>$, and $f^{\alpha_i}: w_1 @ w_2 \rightarrow w_1 @ w_2$, $i = 1, .., n$; $(<\zeta^{\mu}, \zeta_1^{\mu_1}, \zeta_1^{\lambda}, \zeta_1^{\bar{\nu}_1}, \zeta_2^{\mu_2}, \zeta_2^{\lambda}, \zeta_2^{\bar{\nu}_2}>)B = <\mu_1, \lambda_{n_1+r_1}, \bar{\nu}_1, \lambda_{n_2+r_2}, \bar{\nu}_2>$.

The *relabeling* by ρ of the input node of $s = <B, \zeta>$ named α_1, is $s\rho/\alpha_1 = <B, \zeta'>$, where $\zeta' = <\zeta^{\mu'}, \zeta^{\lambda}, \zeta^{\bar{\nu}}>$, $\zeta^{\mu'} = <f_1^{\rho}, \ldots, f_n^{\alpha_n}>$, $\mu = \mu_1 = \mu_2 = <\rho, \ldots, \alpha_n>$.

The kth *iterate* of $s = <B, \zeta>$ for $\zeta = <\zeta^{\mu}, \zeta^{\lambda}, \zeta^{\bar{\mu}}, \zeta^{\bar{\nu}}>$ is $s^k = <B, \zeta^k>$, where ζ^k is the kth iterate of a morphism in $CDh_{\bar{\Sigma},\Gamma}$. $<B, \zeta>^*$ is the iterate of or minimum solution for $<B, \zeta>$, which exists in $CDh_{\bar{\Sigma},\Gamma}$.

It is not hard to verify that the operations on flow structures defined above satisfy the system of equations *EF*. We conclude that the class of flow structures is a flow-of-control algebra.

Proposition. Let H be any interpretation of the S-sorted parallel signature $\bar{\Sigma} \cup \{\_\}$ with connection capabilities Γ into an S'-sorted ω-continuous theory Th over $\bar{\Sigma}' \cup \{\_\}$, i.e., H is an indexed family of linear functions $<H^{u,v}: \bar{\Sigma}_{u,v} \rightarrow Th(f(u), f(v))>$ that preserves the input and output operations, as well as the operations || and @, and $f: <S^*, ||, @> \rightarrow <S'^*, ||, @>$ is a linear function that preserves the operations || and @.
We define $\bar{H}: <\bar{\Sigma}, \Gamma>\text{-FN} \rightarrow <\bar{\Sigma}, \Gamma>\text{-FA}$ by $(<N, C, L, R, T, S>)\bar{H} = <B, \zeta>$, where $\zeta = <\xi^{\mu}, \xi^{\lambda}, \xi^{\bar{\nu}}>$, $x_n^{(R_n)S)f} \circ \zeta = ((n)L)H \circ <((n_1')L)H, \ldots, ((n_p')L)H>$ for $n, n_i' \in N$, $<n, n_i'> \in R_n$, $i = 1, .., p$, such that $(((n)L)H)\text{type} = (n)T$, and $x_n^{(\bar{R}_n)S)f} \circ (\zeta)B = (n)C$. Then $\bar{H}$ is a functor which preserves the flow-of-control operations. □

Aknowledgments

Aside from the obvious technical debt to the entire ADJ group, we would like to thank Dr. Joseph Goguen for his valuable suggestions and encouragement to write this paper. We are grateful to Dr. Sheila Greibach for her persuasion to publish this work. We would also like to show our appreciation to Drs. Milne and Milner, whose work was an inspiration for us.

References

[1] Goguen, J.A., Thatcher, J.W., Wagner, E.G., and Wright, J.B.
Initial Algebra Semantics and Continuous Algebras.
Jour. ACM 24(1): 68-95, 1977.

[2] Hoare, C.A.R.
Communicating Sequential Processes.
Comm. ACM 21(8): 666-677, Aug. 1978.

[3] Milne, G., and Milner, R.
Concurrent Processes and their Syntax.
Jour. ACM 26(2): 302-321, April, 1979.

[4] Peterson, J.L.
Petri Net Theory and the Modelling of Systems.
Prentice-Hall, 1981.

[5] Strachey, C., and Wadworth, C.P.
Continuations - A Mathematical Semantic Model for Handling Full Jumps.
Technical Monograph PRG-11, Programming Research Group, Oxford University, Computing Laboratory, 1974.

[6] Thatcher, J.W., Wagner, E.G., and Wright, J.B.
Notes on Algebraic Fundamentals for Theoretical Computer Science.
In J.B. De Bakker (editor), Foundations of Computer Science, Part 2: Languages, Logic, Semantics. Addison-Wesley, Amsterdam, 19

[7] Wirth, N.
MODULA: A language for modular multiprogramming.
Res. Rep. 18, Inst. fur Informatik, Zurich, Switzerland, 1975.

[8] Zamfir, M.
On the Syntax and Semantics of Concurrent Computing.
PhD Thesis, UCLA-CSD-820819, 1982.

PARTICIPANTS

D.B. Benson
D. Bodle
N. Boonyavatana
S.D. Brookes
J. Campbell
J. Carlson
G. Castellini
C. Castro
M. Clark
C. Chen
H. Chua
R. Courtney
B. Coxe
K.L Davis
G. Dietrich
D. Eaton
W. Erickson
K.M. George
P.C. Gilmore
Wm. Golson
R.J. Greechie
C.A. Gunter
D.A. Gustafson
Wm. J. Hankley
I.D. Harden
G.E. Hedrick
H. Herrlich
T. Hines
H. Ho
R. Hochberg
J. Holt
Y. Hsia
S. Hsieh
G. Jason
T. Kamimura
F. Kazemian
R.F. Keller
M. Kim
J. Koslowski
M. Lanchbury
D. Land
D. Lass
J.D. Lawson
D. Leasure
F. Lin
S. Lindley
M. Lovegreen
M.G. Main
E.G. Manes
S.W. Margolis
R.A. McBride
B. McDaniel
A. Melton
C. Michelson
Wm. Miller
M. Mislove
J. Morrell
D. Moyer
S. Moukaddan
R.W. Neufeld
N. Nikravan
J. Nino
D.G.P. Palenz
A. Pasztor
D. Pivonka
S. Powell
M. Rice
N. Rishe
M. Roesner
M. Saaltink
D.A. Schmidt
D.S. Scott
T. Scott
A. Shoenberger
J. Shultis
G. Smith
J.D.M. Smith
B. Snyder
J. Sossville
D.E. Stevenson
G.E. Strecker
E. Schweppe
A. Tang
T.A. Thomas
N. Tavakoli
B. Treece
S. Tseng
E. Tu
R. Tucker
A. Ukena
E.A. Unger
N. Veeder
P. Venugopalan
V.E. Wallentine
R.C. Wherritt
G. White
L. Wilson
M. Wilson
D.S. Wise
M. Zamfir

Vol. 192: Automata on Infinite Words. Proceedings, 1984. Edited by M. Nivat and D. Perrin. V, 216 pages.1985.

Vol. 193: Logics of Programs. Proceedings, 1985. Edited by R. Parikh. VI, 424 pages. 1985.

Vol. 194: Automata, Languages and Programming. Proceedings, 1985. Edited by W. Brauer. IX, 520 pages. 1985.

Vol. 195: H. J. Stüttgen, A Hierarchical Associative Processing System. XII, 273 pages. 1985.

Vol. 196: Advances in Cryptology. Proceedings of CRYPTO '84. Edited by G. R. Blakley and D. Chaum. IX, 491 pages. 1985.

Vol. 197: Seminar on Concurrency. Proceedings, 1984. Edited by S. D. Brookes, A. W. Roscoe and G. Winskel. X, 523 pages. 1985.

Vol. 198: A. Businger, PORTAL Language Description. VIII, 186 pages. 1985.

Vol. 199: Fundamentals of Computation Theory. Proceedings, 1985. Edited by L. Budach. XII, 533 pages. 1985.

Vol. 200: J. L. A. van de Snepscheut, Trace Theory and VLSI Design. VI, 0–140 pages. 1985.

Vol. 201: Functional Programming Languages and Computer Architecture. Proceedings, 1985. Edited by J.-P. Jouannaud. VI, 413 pages. 1985.

Vol. 202: Rewriting Techniques and Applications. Edited by J.-P. Jouannaud. VI, 441 pages. 1985.

Vol. 203: EUROCAL '85. Proceedings Vol. 1, 1985. Edited by B. Buchberger. V, 233 pages. 1985.

Vol. 204: EUROCAL '85. Proceedings Vol. 2, 1985. Edited by B. F. Caviness. XVI, 650 pages. 1985.

Vol. 205: P. Klint, A Study in String Processing Languages. VIII, 165 pages. 1985.

Vol. 206: Foundations of Software Technology and Theoretical Computer Science. Proceedings, 1985. Edited by S. N. Maheshwari. IX, 522 pages. 1985.

Vol. 207: The Analysis of Concurrent Systems. Proceedings, 1983. Edited by B. T. Denvir, W. T. Harwood, M. I. Jackson and M. J. Wray. VII, 398 pages. 1985.

Vol. 208: Computation Theory. Proceedings, 1984. Edited by A. Skowron. VII, 397 pages. 1985.

Vol. 209: Advances in Cryptology. Proceedings of EUROCRYPT '84. Edited by T. Beth, N. Cot and I. Ingemarsson. VII, 491 pages. 1985.

Vol. 210: STACS 86. Proceedings, 1986. Edited by B. Monien and G. Vidal-Naquet. IX, 368 pages. 1986.

Vol. 211: U. Schöning, Complexity and Structure. V, 99 pages. 1986.

Vol. 212: Interval Mathematics 1985. Proceedings, 1985. Edited by K. Nickel. VI, 227 pages. 1986.

Vol. 213: ESOP 86. Proceedings, 1986. Edited by B. Robinet and R. Wilhelm. VI, 374 pages. 1986.

Vol. 214: CAAP '86. 11th Colloquium on Trees in Algebra and Programming. Proceedings, 1986. Edited by P. Franchi-Zannettacci. VI, 306 pages. 1986.

Vol. 215: Mathematical Methods of Specification and Synthesis of Software Systems '85. Proceedings, 1985. Edited by W. Bibel and K. P. Jantke. 245 pages. 1986.

Vol. 216: Ch. Fernstrom, I. Kruzela, B. Svensson, LUCAS Associative Array Processor: Design, Programming and Application Studies. XII, 323 pages. 1986.

Vol. 217: Programs as Data Objects. Proceedings, 1985. Edited by H. Ganzinger and N. D. Jones. X, 324 pages. 1986.

Vol. 218: Advances in Cryptology – CRYPTO '85. Proceedings, 1985. Edited by H. C. Williams. X, 548 pages. 1986.

Vol. 219: Advances in Cryptology – EUROCRYPT '85. Proceedings, 1985. Edited by F. Pichler. IX, 281 pages. 1986.

Vol. 220: RIMS Symposia on Software Science and Engineering II. Proceedings, 1983 and 1984. Edited by E. Goto, K. Araki and T. Yuasa. XI, 323 pages. 1986.

Vol. 221: Logic Programming '85. Proceedings, 1985. Edited by E. Wada. IX, 311 pages. 1986.

Vol. 222: Advances in Petri Nets 1985. Edited by G. Rozenberg. VI, 498 pages. 1986.

Vol. 223: Structure in Complexity Theory. Proceedings, 1986. Edited by A. L. Selman. VI, 401 pages. 1986.

Vol. 224: Current Trends in Concurrency. Overviews and Tutorials. Edited by J. W. de Bakker, W.-P. de Roever and G. Rozenberg. XII, 716 pages. 1986.

Vol. 225: Third International Conference on Logic Programming. Proceedings, 1986. Edited by E. Shapiro. IX, 720 pages. 1986.

Vol. 226: Automata, Languages and Programming. Proceedings, 1986. Edited by L. Kott. IX, 474 pages. 1986.

Vol. 227: VLSI Algorithms and Architectures – AWOC 86. Proceedings, 1986. Edited by F. Makedon, K. Mehlhorn, T. Papatheodorou and P. Spirakis. VIII, 328 pages. 1986.

Vol. 228: Applied Algebra, Algorithmics and Error-Correcting Codes. AAECC-2. Proceedings, 1984. Edited by A. Poli. VI, 265 pages. 1986.

Vol. 229: Algebraic Algorithms and Error-Correcting Codes. AAECC-3. Proceedings, 1985. Edited by J. Calmet. VII, 416 pages. 1986.

Vol. 230: 8th International Conference on Automated Deduction. Proceedings, 1986. Edited by J. H. Siekmann. X, 708 pages. 1986.

Vol. 231: R. Hausser, NEWCAT: Parsing Natural Language Using Left-Associative Grammar. II, 540 pages. 1986.

Vol. 232: Fundamentals of Artificial Intelligence. Edited by W. Bibel and Ph. Jorrand. VII, 313 pages. 1986.

Vol. 233: Mathematical Foundations of Computer Science 1986. Proceedings, 1986. Edited by J. Gruska, B. Rovan and J. Wiedermann. IX, 650 pages. 1986.

Vol. 234: Concepts in User Interfaces: A Reference Model for Command and Response Languages. By Members of IFIP Working Group 2.7. Edited by D. Beech. X, 116 pages. 1986.

Vol. 235: Accurate Scientific Computations. Proceedings, 1985. Edited by W. L. Miranker and R. A. Toupin. XIII, 205 pages. 1986.

Vol. 236: TEX for Scientific Documentation. Proceedings, 1986. Edited by J. Désarménien. VI, 204 pages. 1986.

Vol. 237: CONPAR 86. Proceedings, 1986. Edited by W. Händler, D. Haupt, R. Jeltsch, W. Juling and O. Lange. X, 418 pages. 1986.

Vol. 238: L. Naish, Negation and Control in Prolog. IX, 119 pages. 1986.

Vol. 239: Mathematical Foundations of Programming Semantics. Proceedings, 1985. Edited by A. Melton. VI, 395 pages. 1986.